Econometric Society Monographs No. 10

Longitudinal analysis of labor market data

Sponsored by the Social Science Research Council

Econometric Society Monographs

Editors:
Jean-Michel Grandmont *Centre d'Études Prospectives d'Économie Mathématique Appliquées à la Planification, Paris*
Charles F. Manski *University of Wisconsin, Madison*

The Econometric Society is an international society for the advancement of economic theory in relation to statistics and mathematics. The Econometric Society Monograph Series is designed to promote the publication of original research contributions of high quality in mathematical economics and theoretical and applied econometrics.

Other titles in the series:

Werner Hildenbrand, Editor *Advances in economic theory*
Werner Hildenbrand, Editor *Advances in econometrics*
G. S. Maddala *Limited-dependent and qualitative variables in econometrics*
Gerard Debreu *Mathematical economics: twenty papers by Gerard Debreu*
Jean-Michel Grandmont *Money and value: a reconsideration of classical and neoclassical monetary economics*
Franklin M. Fisher *Disequilibrium foundations of equilibrium economics*
Bezalel Peleg *Game theoretic analysis of voting in committees*
Roger J. Bowden and Darrell A. Turkington *Instrumental variables*
Andreu Mas-Colell *The theory of general economic equilibrium: a differentiable approach*

Longitudinal analysis of labor market data

Edited by

JAMES J. HECKMAN and BURTON SINGER
University of Chicago *Yale University*

The right of the University of Cambridge to print and sell all manner of books was granted by Henry VIII in 1534. The University has printed and published continuously since 1584.

CAMBRIDGE UNIVERSITY PRESS

Cambridge
London New York New Rochelle
Melbourne Sydney

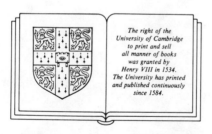

Published by the Press Syndicate of the University of Cambridge
The Pitt Building, Trumpington Street, Cambridge CB2 1RP
32 East 57th Street, New York, NY 10022, USA
10 Stamford Road, Oakleigh, Melbourne 3166, Australia

First published 1985

Printed in the United States of America

Library of Congress Cataloging in Publication Data

Main entry under title:

Longitudinal analysis of labor market data.

"Sponsored by the Social Science Research Council" – Verso t.p.

1. Labor supply – Longitudinal studies – Addresses, essays, lectures. 2. Labor supply – Statistical methods – Addresses, essays, lectures. I. Heckman, James J. (James Joseph) II. Singer, Burton. III. Social Science Research Council (U.S.)
HD5706.L66 1985 331.12′01′5195 84–23253
ISBN 0 521 30453 9

To
Lynne Carol Pettler
and
Eugenia McGinniss

Contents

Contributors

Per Kragh Andersen
Statistical Research Unit
Danish Medical and Social Science Research Councils
Universitetsparken 5
DK–2100
Copenhagen, Denmark

Gary Chamberlain
Department of Economics
University of Wisconsin
Madison, Wisc. 53705

Halina Frydman
Department of Statistics, Operations Research, and Actuarial Science
College of Business and Public Administration
New York University
New York, N.Y. 10003

James J. Heckman
Department of Economics
University of Chicago
1126 E. 59th St.
Chicago, Il. 60637

Jan. M. Hoem
Department of Statistics
University of Stockholm
P. O. Box 6701
S-113 85
Stockholm, Sweden

Thomas E. MaCurdy
Department of Economics
Stanford University
Stanford, Calif. 94305

Robert D. Mare
Department of Sociology
University of Wisconsin
Madison, Wisc. 53705

Richard Robb, Jr.
Department of Economics
University of Chicago
1126 E. 59th St.
Chicago, Il. 60637

Burton Singer
Epidemiology and Public Health
School of Medicine
Yale University
New Haven, Conn. 06510

Nancy Brandon Tuma
Department of Sociology
Stanford University
Stanford, Calif. 94305

Christopher Winship
Department of Sociology
Northwestern University
Evanston, Il. 60201

Introduction and overview

Longitudinal data are widely and uncritically regarded as a panacea. Given the substantial cost of collecting such data, it is surprising that so little attention has been devoted to justifying the expense. The conventional wisdom in social science equates "longitudinal" with "good," and discussion of the issue rarely rises above this level.

The essays presented in this volume assess the benefits, if any, of having access to longitudinal data in order to investigate a variety of labor market phenomena. It is natural that current research focuses on longitudinal labor market questions because most recently available longitudinal data are for labor market activity. However, the methodological message of most of the chapters is much more general and applies to all types of longitudinal data collected for whatever purpose.

Several themes recur throughout this book. The chapters by Chamberlain, by MaCurdy, and by Heckman and Robb demonstrate how access to longitudinal data sometimes enables analysts to determine parameters that cannot be identified in cross-section or repeated cross-section data or that can only be identified by making stronger or at least different assumptions. These chapters consider the tradeoffs in assumptions that are possible when analysts have access to longitudinal data. Longitudinal data can be used to test maintained cross-sectional assumptions (Chamberlain) or can be used to relax such assumptions, but usually at the cost of invoking different assumptions (Heckman and Robb).

The chapters by Heckman and Singer, by Heckman and Robb, by Hoem, and by Andersen consider the problems that arise in using longitudinal data. Problems of measurement error become exaggerated when using longitudinal data. Length-biased sampling rules, truncation bias, and choice-based sampling plague many available data sets. Certain cross-section data problems are accentuated in longitudinal data and new problems arise.

The essays by Frydman and Singer, by Heckman and Singer, by Heckman and Robb, and by Andersen examine the robustness issue. Many longitudinal and cross-sectional estimators proposed in the literature make special assumptions about the true model generating the data (e.g., membership in the exponential family of distributions). At issue is the robustness of estimators to departures from such assumptions, the benefit of longitudinal data in testing and relaxing such assumptions, and the exploration of nonparametric and partially nonparametric alternatives.

Another related topic addressed in these essays is the investigation of minimal assumption sets required to secure behaviorally interpretable models. The chapters by MaCurdy, by Heckman and Robb, and by Heckman and Singer consider assumptions required to identify the parameters of dynamic models produced from optimizing theory.

The chapters by MaCurdy and by Tuma present empirical examples of longitudinal analyses. MaCurdy's chapter is particularly valuable in comparing estimates obtained from repeated cross-section data with estimates obtained from longitudinal data. Mare and Winship offer an empirical example of the limits of cross-section data.

We now describe the contents of each chapter.

Gary Chamberlain's chapter, "Heterogeneity, omitted variable bias, and duration dependence," presents a clear discussion of the problem of heterogeneity bias and offers a novel framework for estimating a class of discrete time and continuous time duration models free of such bias. Versions of this essay have circulated since 1978 and have had an important impact. Chamberlain presents a test for heterogeneity bias and discusses conditional maximum likelihood estimators that can solve the problems raised by the presence of omitted time-invariant variables and initial conditions, provided that conditional duration models are members of the exponential family.

James Heckman and Burton Singer in "Social science duration analysis" consider the unique aspects of duration analysis that are not addressed in the existing statistics literature on continuous time duration models. Four distinctive features of social science duration analysis are emphasized: (1) Because of the limited size of samples available in economics and because of the abundance of candidate-observed and -unobserved variables, standard nonparametric procedures used in biostatistics are of limited value in social science. Failure to control for observed and unobserved variables leads to biased inference. Controlling for such variables creates new problems that are the focus of much current research. (2) Time inhomogeneity in the environment leads to substantial bias in econometric duration analysis if it is ignored in securing estimates. Ad hoc methods for controlling for time inhomogeneity produce badly biased estimates. (3) Length-biased sampling characterizes many available longitudinal samples. The authors present new results on length-biased sampling in time-inhomogeneous environments for models with unobservables and relate the length-biased sampling problem to the choice-based sampling problem in econometrics. (4) The authors demonstrate how estimation of structural duration models derived from explicit optimization problems raises many new issues not addressed in the existing literature.

Thomas MaCurdy in "Interpreting empirical models of labor supply in an intertemporal framework with uncertainty" presents an innovative model of life cycle labor supply in an uncertain environment and considers estimation of this model using longitudinal data. Using the life cycle framework developed in his chapter, MaCurdy interprets previous cross-section work on labor supply and accounts, in part, for the wide diversity of cross-section labor supply estimates found in the published literature. He also uses his framework to interpret macro time series labor supply functions.

An empirically tractable model of life cycle labor supply is formulated and estimated using longitudinal data on working hours and wages. The estimates secured from panel data are compared to estimates from other models estimated on cross-section and repeated cross-section data. MaCurdy's chapter presents a valuable synthesis of economic theory and empirical work. It demonstrates the benefits from access to longitudinal data in testing and estimating dynamic models of labor supply.

James Heckman and Richard Robb in "Alternative methods for evaluating the impact of interventions" consider the potential benefits from longitudinal data in estimating the impact of interventions when the assignment of persons to "treatments" is the outcome of a selection process. They focus on the estimation of the impact of training on earnings. The analysis of this problem serves as a prototype for the analysis of such closely related problems as securing a selection-bias-free estimate of the impact of schooling, unionism, job turnover, and migration on earnings.

Heckman and Robb present several models of the enrollment decision and consider the assumptions required to estimate a selection-bias-free training effect from cross-section data, repeated cross-section data (of unrelated persons) and longitudinal data that are characterized by measurement error in training status and choice-based sampling. A major focus in this essay is an investigation of the tradeoff in the assumptions required to identify the training impact using the three sources of data. New estimators are presented and the plausibility of a variety of estimators in light of the implications of various selection rules is discussed. A major conclusion of the essay is that the benefits of longitudinal data have been overstated in the recent literature because assumptions conventionally adopted in cross-section analysis are not required. Another major conclusion is that many estimators thought to be longitudinal in nature can be implemented using repeated cross-section data.

The chapter by Jan Hoem, "Weighting, misclassification, and other issues in the analysis of survey samples of life histories," discusses a variety of important practical problems that arise in using longitudinal surveys. Special attention is devoted to the problem of informative sampling and its impact on estimates of the parameters of continuous time Markov chain models that ignore the informative nature of the sampling plan. Many available longitudinal samples are collected conditional on a respondent having experienced some event. Hoem discusses the statistical implications of such sampling plans and links his discussion of this topic to the problem of choice-based sampling in discrete choice theory.

In addition, Hoem discusses the problem of measurement error and nonresponse bias in a discrete state–continuous time Markov model. Contrasts with conventional analyses of measurement error in regression models are presented and methods for solving the measurement error problem are discussed. Hoem also considers the topic of optimal weighting of the data collected under various sampling plans.

Per Kragh Andersen's chapter, "Statistical models for longitudinal labor market data based on counting processes," discusses how to use longitudinal labor market data to estimate multivariate counting processes. Andersen surveys recent work on the nonparametric estimation of counting process models developed in the Scandinavian statistics literature and presents new models for multivariate counting processes with both observed and unobserved variables in time-homogeneous and time-inhomogeneous economic environments.

The chapter "Assessing qualitative features of longitudinal data" by Halina Frydman and Burton Singer considers robust inference in structural duration models. The authors analyze both discrete time and continuous time models produced from economic theory. They present a simple strategy for rejecting broad classes of models using the concepts of exchangeability, partial exchangeability, and sign regularity. Test statistics are presented for a variety of hypotheses about underlying economic models for both time-homogeneous and time-inhomogeneous environments. The procedures developed in this chapter permit testing of the assumptions underlying many plausible economic models with unobservables in time homogeneous environments without adopting strong parametric functional forms.

Nancy Tuma's chapter, "Effects of labor market structure on job shift patterns," demonstrates how a continuous time Markov model can be used to estimate alternative models of job mobility.

The chapter "School enrollment, military enlistment, and the transition to work: implications for the age pattern of employment" by Robert Mare and Chris Winship considers various cross-section approaches to this problem and explicitly discusses the limitations of synthetic cohort methods and the benefits of access to longitudinal data.

The editors wish to acknowledge the work of the Committee on the Methodology of Longitudinal Research of the Social Science Research Council. From 1976 to 1980 this committee[1] sponsored a series of workshops and conferences that addressed a range of methodological issues in the use of longitudinal data. The committee meetings focused on the application of innovative techniques to the dynamic analysis of labor market data. Stimulated by these early discussions we commissioned a set of essays that elaborate the developing techniques and provide sound examples of their application. This volume reflects the maturation of ideas and methods that were only beginning to be articulated by researchers in the late 1970s and should be a most valuable resource for social scientists who wish to understand the benefits and limitations of longitudinal data.

Last, but by no means least, we wish to acknowledge the excellent editorial assistance of Vicky Longawa in the preparation of this manuscript.

James J. Heckman

Burton Singer

[1] SSRC Committee on the Methodology of Longitudinal Research (1976–1980) members: Burton H. Singer, Yale University, Chairman; Gary Chamberlain, University of Wisconsin; James S. Coleman, University of Chicago; James J. Heckman, University of Chicago; Douglas A. Hibbs, Jr., Harvard University; Paul Holland, Educational Testing Service (Princeton, N.J.); Gregory Markus, University of Michigan; John R. Nesselroade, Pennsylvania State University; Seymour Spilerman, Columbia University; Nancy Brandon Tuma, Stanford University; Peter B. Read, Staff, Social Science Research Council.

PART I

Econometric studies

CHAPTER 1

Heterogeneity, omitted variable bias, and duration dependence

Gary Chamberlain

This chapter will discuss models for longitudinal data in which a sample of individuals or firms is followed over time. A primary advantage of such data is that they allow us to test and relax assumptions that are implicit in a cross-sectional analysis. Section 1 considers the main issue in the context of the familiar linear model. Here a basic specification test is a comparison of a regression based on changes with a cross-sectional regression. This test is put in a general framework that relates it to tests for strict exogeneity in time series analysis. We show that the failure of strict exogeneity may be due to heterogeneity, which suggests a reformulation in which there is a mixture of strictly exogenous processes. The assumption of strict exogeneity in a mixture model is itself testable, and such tests should be routine whenever the standard analysis-of-covariance estimator is used.

The treatment of heterogeneity leads to the statistical problem of incidental parameters. Since the typical panel has a large number of individuals observed over a short time period, the relevant limiting distributions have the number of individuals increasing but not the time dimension. If we allow for individual specific parameters, then maximizing the joint likelihood function does not in general provide a consistent estimator of the parameters common to all individuals. We discuss procedures that are valid in general, based on conditional, marginal, and posterior likelihood functions.

Section 2 of the chapter discusses models for discrete data in discrete time. A multivariate probit model for binary sequences has the appealing property that the normal-theory linear model for continuous data translates directly into that framework. In particular, our discussion of specification tests and heterogeneity carries over directly. New issues do arise, however, with autoregressive models. We discuss the distinction between serial correlation and state dependence and argue that it cannot be made just on the basis of the multinomial distribution of the binary sequence.

Some distinctions are possible if we consider the distribution of the binary sequence conditional on observed variables.

These discrete time models are appropriate if the time interval has some natural significance. In many problems, however, the basic datum is the amount of time spent in a state. In studying labor force participation, a complete description of the process is the duration of the first spell of participation and the date it began, the duration of the following spell of nonparticipation, and so on. This complete history will generate a binary sequence when it is cut up into fixed-length periods, but these periods may have little to do with the underlying process.

In particular, the measurement of serial correlation depends on the interval between observations. As this interval becomes shorter, the probability that a person who participated last period will participate this period approaches 1. So a more fruitful question is whether an individual's history helps to predict his future given his current state. A stationary version of this Markov property implies that the durations of the spells are independently distributed with exponential distributions. With heterogeneity, each individual has his own exponential rate parameters. Departures from this model constitute duration dependence. We show that the binary sequences generated by various sampling schemes do allow us to test for duration dependence in the continuous time model. A particularly interesting and relevant case is the sampling procedure that asks whether the individual was ever in a particular state (participation, for example) during the previous period.

Section 3 develops methods for using the underlying data on duration when it is available. We model the distribution of duration conditional on other variables, allowing for duration dependence. Using models with log-linear hazard functions, we discuss the restrictive features of Cox's conditional likelihood analysis, including the role of strict exogeneity and the sense in which age and time are not strictly exogenous. The restrictive features are relaxed in a posterior likelihood analysis. We also consider marginal and conditional likelihood methods in models based on the Weibull, gamma, and lognormal distributions for duration.

1 Linear models in discrete time

1.1 *Specification tests, strict exogeneity, and analysis of covariance*

The linear case will illustrate the issues that arise in more complex models. We shall discuss a class of specification tests for panel data and the relationship of these tests to heterogeneity and omitted variable bias. A primary value of panel data is in testing assumptions that are implicit in a cross-sectional analysis. An important example of such a test is a comparison of regressions based on levels and changes. Consider the following cross-sectional regression in period t:

$$E(y_t|\mathbf{x}_t) = \boldsymbol{\beta}'\mathbf{x}_t$$

It can be estimated by the least squares regression of y_{it} on $\mathbf{x}_{it}$, where we have a sample of ($i = 1, \ldots, N$) individuals in period t. The substantive interpretation of this regression may imply the following prediction:

$$E(y_t - y_{t-1}|\mathbf{x}_t - \mathbf{x}_{t-1}) = \boldsymbol{\beta}'(\mathbf{x}_t - \mathbf{x}_{t-1})$$

This test is worth developing in some detail.

A general starting point is the multivariate regression of each y_t on all past, current, and future $\mathbf{x}$:

$$E(\mathbf{y}|\mathbf{x}) = \boldsymbol{\Pi}\mathbf{x}$$

where $\mathbf{y}' = (y_1, \ldots, y_T)$ and $\mathbf{x}' = (\mathbf{x}'_1, \ldots, \mathbf{x}'_T)$; there are T periods and K variables in $\mathbf{x}_t$, so that $\boldsymbol{\Pi}$ has dimensions $T \times TK$. Then a general specification test is

$$\boldsymbol{\Pi} = \mathbf{I}_T \otimes \boldsymbol{\beta}'$$

The test is straightforward to implement, given a sample of N individuals followed for T periods. We assume that the values of $\mathbf{y}$ for distinct individuals are uncorrelated, conditional on $\mathbf{x}$; $V(\mathbf{y}|\mathbf{x}) = \boldsymbol{\Sigma}$ can be left unconstrained.

If the cross-sectional sample did not include information on previous periods, then a failure of the test may simply indicate that a distributed lag is needed. If, however, the cross-sectional sample did have sufficient retrospective information (so that $\mathbf{x}_t$ includes lagged values), then a failure of the test is due to the significance of future values of the $\mathbf{x}$ variables.

This test is motivated by tests for strict exogeneity in time series analysis.[1] We begin with $E(\mathbf{y}_t|\mathbf{x}_t) = \boldsymbol{\beta}'\mathbf{x}_t$; this defines $\boldsymbol{\beta}$. The assumption of linear expectation can be dropped by reinterpreting the expectation operator as a linear minimum mean square error projection. The test is whether

$$E(y_t|\mathbf{x}_1, \ldots, \mathbf{x}_T) = E(y_t|\mathbf{x}_t)$$

The appropriateness of this test depends very much on the particular model. In the next section, we shall present a production function example in which it is appropriate. For an example where it is not appropriate, say that x_{it} is individual i's expectation of y_{it} based on information available in period $t - 1$. Then $E(y_t|x_t) = \beta x_t$ has a behavioral interpretation, and yet $E(y_t|x_t, x_{t+1}) \neq E(y_t|x_t)$, since x_{t+1} will in part be based on y_t.[2] We shall not attempt to give a general statement of when it is appropriate to test for strict exogeneity; rather we shall focus on relating such tests to the widely used analysis-of-covariance model.

One response to a failure of strict exogeneity is to ask whether the data can be interpreted as a mixture of processes for which strict exogeneity holds. In particular,

$$E(y_t | \mathbf{x}_t, \alpha) = \boldsymbol{\beta}'\mathbf{x}_t + \alpha$$

where α is a random variable that varies across individuals but not over time. It captures omitted variables that are not changing over the period of the sample, such as characteristics of the individual that are not included in $\mathbf{x}$. We specify

$$E(\alpha | \mathbf{x}_1, \ldots, \mathbf{x}_T) = \boldsymbol{\delta}'_1\mathbf{x}_1 + \cdots + \boldsymbol{\delta}'_T\mathbf{x}_T = \boldsymbol{\delta}'\mathbf{x}$$

Then strict exogeneity conditional on α (i.e., at the individual level) is the assumption that

$$E(y_t | \mathbf{x}_1, \ldots, \mathbf{x}_T, \alpha) = E(y_t | \mathbf{x}_t, \alpha), \qquad t = 1, \ldots, T$$

This assumption is testable, since marginal on α we have the following implication:

$$E(y_t | \mathbf{x}_1, \ldots, \mathbf{x}_T) = \boldsymbol{\beta}'\mathbf{x}_t + \boldsymbol{\delta}'\mathbf{x}$$

so that

$$\boldsymbol{\Pi} = \mathbf{I} \otimes \boldsymbol{\beta}' + \mathbf{l}\boldsymbol{\delta}'$$

where $\mathbf{l}$ is a $T \times 1$ vector of ones. So the suggestion is to test whether strict exogeneity can be maintained in an analysis-of-covariance model. This test should be routine whenever the standard analysis-of-covariance estimator of $\boldsymbol{\beta}$ is used with short time series, since we shall see that strict exogeneity is necessary in order for that estimator to be consistent as $N \to \infty$ for fixed T.

Note that the assumption of stationarity is not needed. We can have

$$E(y_t | \mathbf{x}_t) = \boldsymbol{\beta}'_t\mathbf{x}_t$$

Then strict exogeneity implies that

$$\boldsymbol{\Pi} = \text{diag}\{\boldsymbol{\beta}'_1, \ldots, \boldsymbol{\beta}'_T\}$$

The mixture model is

$$E(y_t | \mathbf{x}_t, \alpha) = \boldsymbol{\beta}'_t\mathbf{x}_t + \lambda_t\alpha$$

so that strict exogeneity conditional on α implies that

$$\boldsymbol{\Pi} = \text{diag}\{\boldsymbol{\beta}'_1, \ldots, \boldsymbol{\beta}'_T\} + \boldsymbol{\lambda}\boldsymbol{\delta}'$$

where $\boldsymbol{\lambda}' = (\lambda_1, \ldots, \lambda_T)$. This is testable if $T \geq 3$.

If strict exogeneity fails to hold in the mixture model, then a variety of alternatives may be fruitful. We shall briefly discuss one of them, an errors-in-variables model. Say that $K = 1$ and

$$E(y_t | x_1^*, \ldots, x_T^*, \alpha) = \beta x_t^* + \alpha$$

but that x^* is not observed. The proxy variable x satisfies

$$E(x_t | x_1^*, \ldots, x_T^*) = x_t^*$$

Then if $E(x_t^* | x_1, \ldots, x_T)$ is linear, or reinterpreting the expectation as a linear projection, we have

$$\mathbf{\Pi} = \beta V(\mathbf{x}^*)V^{-1}(\mathbf{x}) + \mathbf{l}\delta'$$

This cannot, in general, be represented as $\gamma\mathbf{I} + \mathbf{ld}'$. Hence a strictly exogenous mixture model can be ruled out – past and future values of x will enter the regression even after allowing for heterogeneity.

A special case in which this is not true is $V(\mathbf{x}) = \tau(\mathbf{I} + \rho\mathbf{ll}')$, $V(\mathbf{x}|\mathbf{x}^*) = \sigma^2\mathbf{I}$; for then we have

$$\mathbf{\Pi} = \beta\left(1 - \frac{\sigma^2}{\tau}\right)\mathbf{I} + \mathbf{ld}', \qquad \text{where } \mathbf{d} = \delta + \frac{\beta\sigma^2\rho}{\tau(1 + \rho T)} l$$

In this case we cannot distinguish between an errors-in-variables model and a mixture model; the result continues to hold if the error covariance matrix also has a variance components structure $V(\mathbf{x}|\mathbf{x}^*) = \sigma^2(\mathbf{I} + \psi\mathbf{ll}')$. This special case is very relevant for sibling data, where i indexes families and t indexes siblings within the family. With time series on individuals, we do expect departures from the variance components structure. Note, however, that if we allow for nonstationarity, then the special case is $V(\mathbf{x}) = \mathbf{D} + \mathbf{cc}'$, where $\mathbf{D}$ is a diagonal matrix. With short time series, this one-factor model may provide quite a good approximation to $V(\mathbf{x})$.

1.2 *A production function example*

We shall illustrate this approach with a production function example that leads to a linear regression model.[3] Say that a farmer is producing a product under the following Cobb–Douglas technology: $Y = L^\beta Q^\gamma e^\varepsilon$, where Y is output, L is a variable factor (labor), Q is a fixed factor (soil quality), ε is stochastic (rainfall), and $0 < \beta < 1$. Assume that ε is distributed independently of Q; persistent differences in average rainfall can be incorporated into Q. We assume that the farmer knows the product price (P) and the factor price (W), which do not depend upon his decisions, and that he knows Q; the factor input decision, however, is made before knowing ε, and we assume that L is chosen to maximize expected profit: $E(PY - WL | P, W, Q)$.

There are observations on N farms in each of T periods. Assume that Q is constant over the period of the sample and that the distribution of ε conditional on Q, W, and P has ε_{it} independent and identically distributed (i.i.d.) $N(0, \sigma^2)$. Then we have the following production and factor demand functions:

$$y_{it} = \beta x_{it} + \alpha_i + \varepsilon_{it}$$

$$x_{it} = \mu + \frac{1}{1-\beta}(z_{it} + \alpha_i) + v_{it}, \qquad i = 1, \ldots, N, \qquad t = 1, \ldots, T$$

where $y = \ln Y$, $x = \ln L$, $\alpha = \ln Q$, $\mu = (\ln \beta + \frac{1}{2}\sigma^2)/(1-\beta)$, $z = \ln(P/W)$, and v is a random term, reflecting optimization and other errors, which is independent of α and ε. Although Q is known to the farmer and reflects his factor demand decisions, we assume that it is not observed by the econometrician; α is included in order to capture this omitted variable. The example is useful in showing explicitly how a correlation between x and α might arise.

In this model the strict exogeneity assumption that $E(y_t|x_1, \ldots, x_T) = E(y_t|x_t)$ does not hold, but we do have strict exogeneity in the mixture model. Let $w_{it} = z_{it}/(1-\beta) + v_{it}$, and assume that $\mathbf{w}$ is uncorrelated with α; then we have

$$\mathbf{\Pi} = \beta \mathbf{I} + \mathbf{l}\boldsymbol{\delta}'$$

where

$$\boldsymbol{\delta} = \frac{\sigma_\alpha^2}{1-\beta}\left[\frac{\sigma_\alpha^2}{(1-\beta)^2}\mathbf{l}\mathbf{l}' + V(\mathbf{w})\right]^{-1}\mathbf{l}$$

Strict exogeneity in the mixture model can fail for a variety of reasons. We have already discussed the case of measurement error in x. In this particular model, a likely reason is that ε is partly anticipated by the farmer, so that it affects the factor demand decisions. We can decompose $\varepsilon = \varepsilon_1 + \varepsilon_2$, with $x = \mu + (z + \alpha + \varepsilon_1)/(1-\beta) + v$. Then we have

$$\mathbf{\Pi} = \beta \mathbf{I} + \mathbf{l}\boldsymbol{\delta}' + \frac{1}{1-\beta}V(\boldsymbol{\varepsilon}_1)V^{-1}(\mathbf{x})$$

In general we can distinguish this from the case of strict exogeneity in the mixture model. A special case when we cannot is $V(\mathbf{x}) = \tau(\mathbf{I} + \rho\mathbf{l}\mathbf{l}')$, $V(\boldsymbol{\varepsilon}_1) = \sigma^2(\mathbf{I} + \psi\mathbf{l}\mathbf{l}')$. Then we have

$$\mathbf{\Pi} = \left[\beta + \frac{\sigma^2}{\tau(1-\beta)}\right]\mathbf{I} + \mathbf{l}\mathbf{d}'$$

where **d** is a linear combination of $\boldsymbol{\delta}$ and **l**. Hence a mixture model would fit $\boldsymbol{\Pi}$, but it would not identify β in the underlying structural model.

1.3 *Incidental parameters*

Consider the problem of estimating $\boldsymbol{\beta}$ in the following model:

$$y_{it} = \boldsymbol{\beta}'\mathbf{x}_{it} + \alpha_i + \varepsilon_{it}, \qquad i = 1, \ldots, N, \qquad t = 1, \ldots, T$$

where, conditional on $(\mathbf{x}_1, \ldots, \mathbf{x}_T)$, ε_{it} is i.i.d. $N(0, \sigma^2)$. We shall deal with the case in which T is small, so that asymptotic arguments will be based on $N \to \infty$ for fixed T. Large N and small T characterize many of the currently available panel data sets.

If there is sufficient variation in $\mathbf{x}_{it}$ to obtain a consistent estimator of $\boldsymbol{\Pi} = \mathbf{I} \otimes \boldsymbol{\beta}' + \mathbf{l}\boldsymbol{\delta}'$, then a consistent estimator of $\boldsymbol{\beta}$ can be obtained from $\boldsymbol{\Pi}$. This corresponds to a random effects model, in which we base the likelihood function on the density of **y** marginal on α, obtained as the mixture of the density conditional on α:

$$f(\mathbf{y}\,|\,\mathbf{x}) = \int \prod_{t=1}^{T} f(y_t\,|\,x_t, \alpha) f(\alpha\,|\,\mathbf{x})\, d\alpha$$

We shall call this a posterior likelihood function.[4] The important point here is that the distribution of α conditional on **x** is needed, and in general this should be allowed to depend upon **x**. If there was omitted variable bias before introducing α, and if α is incorrectly assumed to be independent of **x**, then the random effects estimator will also be biased.

There are other approaches that will be pursued in more complex models, and it is useful to illustrate them in this simple case. They are based on conditional and marginal likelihood functions. These are "fixed effects" approaches in that they only use the distribution of **y** conditional on α; hence they have the advantage of not requiring a specification for the distribution of α conditional on **x**.

First consider using $f(\mathbf{y}\,|\,\mathbf{x}, \alpha)$ to form a joint likelihood function which is then maximized over $\boldsymbol{\beta}$, σ, and $\alpha_1, \ldots, \alpha_N$. In general this estimator is inconsistent, since the number of parameters is increasing with the number of observations.[5] In the special case of the linear model, however, we know that it gives

$$\hat{\boldsymbol{\beta}} = \left[\sum_{i,t} (\mathbf{x}_{it} - \bar{\mathbf{x}}_i)(\mathbf{x}_{it} - \bar{\mathbf{x}}_i)'\right]^{-1} \sum_{i,t} (\mathbf{x}_{it} - \bar{\mathbf{x}}_i)(y_{it} - \bar{y}_i)$$

where $\bar{\mathbf{x}}_i = (1/T)\sum_t \mathbf{x}_{it}$ and $\bar{y}_i = (1/T)\sum_t y_{it}$. This does converge to $\boldsymbol{\beta}$ as $N \to \infty$ provided that there is sufficient variation in $\mathbf{x}_{it} - \bar{\mathbf{x}}_i$.

Note that our specification for ε implies that $E(y_t\,|\,\mathbf{x}_1, \ldots, \mathbf{x}_T, \alpha) = E(y_t\,|\,\mathbf{x}_t, \alpha)$; that is, we have strict exogeneity conditional on α. We cannot do without some assumption of this sort if we are to have plim $\hat{\beta} = \beta$ as $N \to \infty$.[6] For example, say that

$$y_{it} = \beta y_{i,t-1} + \alpha_i + \varepsilon_{it}, \qquad \varepsilon_{it} \text{ i.i.d. } N(0, \sigma^2)$$

Then clearly the analysis of covariance estimator is not consistent for fixed T. If $T = 2$ and we condition on y_{i0}, then the maximum likelihood (ML) estimator can be obtained from a least squares regression of $y_{i2} - y_{i1}$ on $y_{i1} - y_{i0}$. The inconsistency follows immediately since

$$y_{i2} - y_{i1} = \beta(y_{i1} - y_{i0}) + \varepsilon_{i2} - \varepsilon_{i1}$$

and ε_1 is correlated with y_1. If the joint distribution of (y_0, y_1, y_2) is stationary, then the estimator converges to $(\beta - 1)/2$ as $N \to \infty$. There is a similar result for the example in which x_{it} is individual i's expectation of y_{it} based on the information available in period $t - 1$.

The conditional likelihood function is based on the distribution of $\mathbf{y}$ conditional on a sufficient statistic for α.[7] In the model where $\mathbf{x}$ is strictly exogenous, the minimum sufficient statistic for α is $\sum_t y_t$. The conditional likelihood function depends only upon $\boldsymbol{\beta}$ and σ. The marginal likelihood function is based on the one-to-one transformation of $y_1, \ldots, y_T$ to $\sum_t y_t$, $y_2 - (1/T)\sum_t y_t, \ldots, y_T - (1/T)\sum_t y_t$, from which we obtain the marginal distribution of $y_2 - (1/T)\sum_t y_t, \ldots, y_T - (1/T)\sum_t y_t$.[8] This distribution does not depend on α and so the marginal likelihood function depends only on $\boldsymbol{\beta}$, σ. The standard asymptotic distribution theory applies to ML estimators based on the conditional or the marginal likelihood functions, since the incidental parameters have been eliminated. There are, of course, the usual regularity conditions which must be satisfied.

The linear model is special in that both the conditional ML estimator and the marginal ML estimator coincide with the joint ML estimator. This provides one interpretation of why the joint ML estimator is consistent in spite of the incidental parameter problem. Consider the following decomposition of the joint likelihood function:

$$f(y_1, \ldots, y_T | \mathbf{x}, \alpha) = f\left(y_1, \ldots, y_T \middle| \mathbf{x}, \sum_t y_t\right) f\left(\sum_t y_t \middle| \mathbf{x}, \alpha\right)$$

Note that $\boldsymbol{\beta}$ and α enter the distribution of $\sum_t y_t$ only through the term $(\beta' \sum_t \mathbf{x}_t + T\alpha)$. For any β, we can choose α so that this term takes on any desired value; hence the $\boldsymbol{\beta}$ that maximizes the conditional likelihood function also maximizes the joint likelihood function. For marginal likelihood, let $\Delta_j = y_j - (1/T)\sum_t y_t$; then we have

$$f(y_1, \ldots, y_T | \mathbf{x}, \alpha) = f(\Delta_2, \ldots, \Delta_T | \mathbf{x}) f\left(\sum_t y_t \middle| \mathbf{x}, \alpha\right)$$

since Δ_j is independent of $\sum_t y_t$ ($j = 2, \ldots, T$). Hence the marginal likelihood function coincides with the conditional likelihood function.

Our final result is that a prior for α can be chosen so that the posterior ML estimator also coincides with the three fixed effects ML estimators. We have

$$\int f(y_1, \ldots, y_T | \mathbf{x}, \alpha) f(\alpha | \mathbf{x})\, d\alpha$$

$$= f\left(y_1, \ldots, y_T | \mathbf{x}, \sum_t y_t\right) \int f\left(\sum_t y_t | \mathbf{x}, \alpha\right) f(\alpha | \mathbf{x})\, d\alpha$$

If $\alpha_i = \boldsymbol{\delta}'\mathbf{x}_i + v_i$, where v_i is i.i.d. $N(0, \sigma_v^2)$, then $\boldsymbol{\beta}$ and $\boldsymbol{\delta}$ enter the integrand only through the term $(\boldsymbol{\beta}'\sum_t \mathbf{x}_t + T\boldsymbol{\delta}'\mathbf{x})$. If $\boldsymbol{\delta}$ is unconstrained, then for any $\boldsymbol{\beta}$ we can choose $\boldsymbol{\delta}$ to maintain this term at the value that maximizes the integral in the posterior likelihood; hence the $\boldsymbol{\beta}$ that maximizes the conditional likelihood function also maximizes the posterior likelihood function.

Note that we still obtain this result if $\boldsymbol{\delta}$ is constrained to $\boldsymbol{\delta} = \mathbf{l} \otimes \boldsymbol{\psi}$, where $\mathbf{l}$ is a $T \times 1$ vector of ones.[9] This follows since $\boldsymbol{\beta}'\sum_t \mathbf{x}_t + T\boldsymbol{\delta}'\mathbf{x} = (\boldsymbol{\beta} + T\boldsymbol{\psi})'\sum_t \mathbf{x}_t$, which is functionally independent of $\boldsymbol{\beta}$ if $\boldsymbol{\psi}$ is unconstrained. This is a case in which certain misspecifications of the prior are innocuous. Note that the prior is not dominated by the sample as $N \to \infty$ for fixed T. Constraining $\boldsymbol{\delta} = \mathbf{0}$ will in general result in an inconsistent estimator of $\boldsymbol{\beta}$. But even if $\boldsymbol{\delta}$ does not have the form $\mathbf{l} \otimes \boldsymbol{\psi}$, the ML estimator based on this incorrect assumption is identical to the one obtained for an unconstrained $\boldsymbol{\delta}$.

In the next section we shall begin by discussing a multivariate probit model for binary data. Part of its appeal is that the familiar normal-theory linear model for continuous data translates directly into that framework. In particular, our discussion of specification tests and heterogeneity carries over directly.

2 Models for discrete data in discrete time

2.1 *Multivariate probit models; specification tests, strict exogeneity, and analysis of covariance*

An appealing approach is to model discrete variables in terms of continuous, possibly latent variables crossing thresholds.[10] The appeal is that much of the normal-theory linear modeling carries over directly. Let y_{it} equal 0 or 1 with

$$y_{it} = \begin{cases} 1 & \text{if } y_{it}^* \geq 0 \\ 0 & \text{otherwise} \end{cases}$$

where the latent variables $\mathbf{y}'^* = (y_1^*, \ldots, y_T^*)$ are modeled as

$$\mathbf{y}_i^* = \mathbf{\Pi x}_i + \mathbf{u}_i, \mathbf{u}_i \quad \text{i.i.d.} \quad N(\mathbf{0}, \mathbf{\Sigma}), \qquad i = 1, \ldots, N$$

The strict exogeneity assumption is $f(y_t | \mathbf{x}_1, \ldots, \mathbf{x}_T) = f(y_t | \mathbf{x}_t)$, which implies that

$$\mathbf{\Pi} = \mathbf{I}_T \otimes \boldsymbol{\beta}'$$

Strict exogeneity in the mixture model is $f(y_t | \mathbf{x}_1, \ldots, \mathbf{x}_T, \alpha) = f(y_t | \mathbf{x}_t, \alpha)$. We can specify

$$y_{it}^* = \boldsymbol{\beta}'\mathbf{x}_{it} + \alpha_i + \varepsilon_{it}, \qquad \boldsymbol{\varepsilon}_i \quad \text{i.i.d.} \quad N(\mathbf{0}, \mathbf{\Omega})$$

but we need auxiliary assumptions to estimate this model, due to the incidental parameter problem. A convenient assumption is that

$$\alpha_i = \boldsymbol{\delta}'\mathbf{x}_i + v_i, \qquad v_i \quad \text{i.i.d.} \quad N(0, \sigma_v^2)$$

Then strict exogeneity conditional on α implies that

$$\mathbf{\Pi} = \mathbf{I} \otimes \boldsymbol{\beta}' + \mathbf{l}\boldsymbol{\delta}'$$

Hence given a consistent (as $N \to \infty$) estimator of $\mathbf{\Pi}$, we can obtain a consistent estimator of $\boldsymbol{\beta}$. Furthermore, the model generates constraints on $\mathbf{\Pi}$, which allow us to test whether strict exogeneity holds in the mixture model.

We should stress that the auxiliary assumption of a specific distribution for α is not innocuous, unlike the linear model. In particular, we cannot reinterpret $E(\alpha | \mathbf{x}) = \boldsymbol{\delta}'\mathbf{x}$ as a linear minimum mean square error predictor; if the regression function is not linear, then our estimator of $\boldsymbol{\beta}$ will be inconsistent.

2.2 *Serial correlation or state dependence?*

The above discussion was a straightforward translation of results for the linear model. New issues do arise, however, with autoregressive models. For consider the following:

1. $y_t^* = \alpha + \gamma y_{t-1} + \varepsilon_t$
2. $y_t^* = \alpha + u_t, \qquad u_t = \rho u_{t-1} + \varepsilon_t$

where in both cases ε is i.i.d. $N(0, 1)$. It is intriguing that in general we can distinguish between these two models.[11] A possible terminology for the distinction is to refer to γ as state dependence and to refer to ρ as serial correlation. The intuitive notion is that if occupancy of a state affects an individual's preferences or opportunities, then there is state dependence. The notion of serial correlation is simply that random shocks persist, so that the individual's current state helps to predict his future state, even though the individual is not affected by the state he is in.

In the first model,

$$\begin{aligned}\text{Prob}(y_t = 1 \mid \alpha, y_{t-1}, y_{t-2}, \ldots) &= \text{Prob}(y_t = 1 \mid \alpha, y_{t-1}) \\ &= \Phi(\alpha + \gamma y_{t-1})\end{aligned}$$

where Φ is the standard normal distribution function. In the second model, however, $\text{Prob}(y_t = 1 \mid \alpha, y_{t-1}, y_{t-2}, \ldots)$ depends on the entire history of the process. If we observed u_{t-1}, then previous outcomes would be irrelevant. In fact, we only observe whether $u_{t-1} \geq -\alpha$; hence conditioning in addition on whether $u_{t-2} \geq -\alpha$ affects the distributions of u_{t-1} and y_t. So the lagged y implies a first-order Markov chain, whereas the first-order Markov process for the probit residual does not imply a first-order Markov chain for the discrete sequence that it generates.

There is a close analogy with the following linear models:

1. $y_t = \alpha + \gamma y_{t-1} + \varepsilon_t$
2. $y_t = \alpha + u_t, \qquad u_t = \varepsilon_t + \rho \varepsilon_{t-1}$

where ε is i.i.d. $N(0, \sigma^2)$. We know that if $u_t = \rho u_{t-1} + \varepsilon_t$, then no distinction would be possible, without introducing more structure, since both models would imply a first-order Markov process.[12] With the moving average residual, however, the serial correlation model implies that the entire past history is relevant for predicting y. So the distinction rests on the order of the dependence on previous realizations.

More generally, consider

$$y_t^* = \alpha + u_t, \; \mathbf{u} \quad \text{i.i.d.} \quad N(\mathbf{0}, \mathbf{\Sigma})$$

with $\mathbf{\Sigma}$ unrestricted except for the normalization $V(u_1) = 1$. This model has $T(T+1)/2$ free parameters; hence if $T \geq 3$, it implies restrictions on the $2^T - 1$ parameters of the multinomial distribution of the $\mathbf{y}$ sequence. In particular, this multivariate probit model with an arbitrary serial correlation structure cannot generate a first-order Markov chain; hence we can introduce a y_{t-1} term and identify γ.

Basing the distinction between state dependence and serial correlation on the order of the serial dependence is not, however, very appealing. It makes the distinction an artifact of the probit specification, unless the distinction can be made directly in terms of the underlying multinomial probabilities. I do not think that this is feasible without introducing more structure.

In particular, a key distinction is whether or not there is a dynamic response to an observed variable. Say that we have

$$\begin{aligned}&\text{Prob}(y_t = 1 \mid \alpha, x_t, x_{t-1}, \ldots, y_{t-1}, y_{t-2}, \ldots)\\ &\quad \neq \text{Prob}(y_t = 1 \mid \alpha, x_t, x_{t-1}, \ldots)\\ &\text{Prob}(y_t = 1 \mid \alpha, x_t, x_{t-1}, \ldots) = \text{Prob}(y_t = 1 \mid \alpha, x_t)\end{aligned}$$

Then there is serial correlation conditional on α and x, but there is no state dependence; for if x is increased in period $t - 1$ and then returned to its former level, there is no effect on $\text{Prob}(y_t = 1)$. The increased probability of occupying the state last period (if $\beta > 0$) does not result in an increased probability of occupying the state this period. A test, which should not be very sensitive to functional form, is to simply include lagged x terms without lagged y, allowing for heterogeneity.

Note that the force of this distinction is somewhat asymmetric. If the response to a change in x is not dynamic, then there is no state dependence; but a distributed lag response could arise for other reasons, such as expectations. In order to make the distinction operational, there must be at least one variable which would not have a distributed lag response in the absence of state dependence.

In the next section we shall reconsider these issues in a continuous time model. This leads us to reformulate the interesting questions, since serial independence in continuous time is implausible.

2.3 *Serial correlation reinterpreted*

These models for discrete panel data are appropriate when the observational period has some natural significance. If an individual votes for either a Republican or a Democrat at each election, then the sequence of binary decisions provides a complete description of the process. In many problems, however, the basic data consist of the amount of time spent in a state. For example, in studying labor force participation, a complete description of the process is the duration of the first spell of participation and the date it began, the duration of the following spell of nonparticipation, and so on. This complete history will generate a binary sequence when it is cut up into fixed-length periods, but these periods may have little to do with the underlying process.[13]

In particular, the measurement of serial correlation depends on the period of observation. As the period becomes shorter, the probability that a person who participated last period will participate this period approaches 1. So finding significant serial correlation may say very little about the underlying process. Or consider a spell that begins near the end of a period (perhaps a calendar year); then it is likely to overlap into the next period, so that previous participation raises the probability of current participation.

Consider the underlying process of time spent in one state followed by time spent in the other state. If an individual's history does not help to predict his future given his current state, then this is a Markov process. Whereas serial independence in continuous time has the absurd implication that mean duration of a spell is zero, the Markov property does provide a fruitful starting point, from which we can build more complex models. It has two implications: The individual's history prior to the current spell should not affect the distribution of the length of the current spell, and the amount of time spent in the current state should not affect the distribution of remaining time in that state.

So the first requirement of the Markov property is that durations of the spells be independent of each other. Assuming stationarity, this implies an alternating renewal process. The second requirement is that the distribution of duration be exponential, so that we have an alternating Poisson process. Then allowing for heterogeneity, each individual is characterized by his own two exponential rate parameters. Departures from this model constitute duration dependence at the individual level.

The nature of the test for duration dependence in a binary sequence depends upon the sort of sampling scheme being used. The simplest case is point sampling, where each period we determine the individual's state at a particular point in time. Then if an individual is following an alternating Poisson process, his history prior to that point is irrelevant in predicting his state at the next interview. So if there is no duration dependence, then the binary sequence generated by point sampling should be a first-order Markov chain. The statistical problem in formulating a test is to allow each individual to have his own first-order Markov chain and to test for second- (or higher-) order dependence.

Using a logistic formulation gives the following model:

$$\begin{aligned}\text{Prob}(y_{it} = 1 \mid y_{i,t-1}, y_{i,t-2}) \\ = \frac{\exp(\alpha_i + \gamma_{i1} y_{i,t-1} + \gamma_2 y_{i,t-2})}{1 + \exp(\alpha_i + \gamma_{i1} y_{i,t-1} + \gamma_2 y_{i,t-2})}\end{aligned}$$

The parameters α_i and γ_{i1} allow each individual to have a separate first-order Markov chain. Hence if $\gamma_2 = 0$, the logistic formulation imposes no restrictions and provides a general framework for testing if $\gamma_2 = 0$. The importance and significance of duration dependence is measured by an estimate of γ_2 with a confidence interval.

We have the following probability for the binary sequence (dropping i subscripts):

$\text{Prob}(y_1, \ldots, y_T)$

$$= \frac{\text{Prob}(y_1, y_2) \exp\left(\alpha \sum_{t=3}^{T} y_t + \gamma_1 \sum_{t=3}^{T} y_t y_{t-1} + \gamma_2 \sum_{t=3}^{T} y_t y_{t-2}\right)}{(1+e^{\alpha})^{m_1}[1+\exp(\alpha+\gamma_1)]^{m_2}[1+\exp(\alpha+\gamma_2)]^{m_3}[1+\exp(\alpha+\gamma_1+\gamma_2)]^{m_4}}$$

where

$$m_4 = \sum_{t=2}^{T} y_t y_{t-1} - y_{T-1} y_T; \qquad m_3 = \sum_{t=1}^{T} y_t - y_{T-1} - y_T - m_4$$

$$m_2 = \sum_{t=1}^{T} y_t - y_1 - y_T - m_4; \qquad m_1 = T - 2 - m_2 - m_3 - m_4$$

We see that m_4 is the number of elements preceded by (1, 1); m_3 is the number preceded by (1, 0); m_2 is the number preceded by (0, 1); and m_1 is the number preceded by (0, 0). So sufficient statistics for α and γ_1 are provided by $y_1, y_2, s = \sum_{t=1}^{T} y_t, s_{11} = \sum_{t=2}^{T} y_t y_{t-1}, y_{T-1}, y_T$. Conditioning on y_1 and y_2 also deals with the problem of initial conditions.[14]

Then we have the following conditional probability:

$$\text{Prob}(y_1, \ldots, y_T | y_1, y_2, s, s_{11}, y_{T-1}, y_T) = \frac{\exp\left(\gamma_2 \sum_{t=3}^{T} y_t y_{t-2}\right)}{\sum_{\mathbf{d} \in B} \exp\left(\gamma_2 \sum_{t=3}^{T} d_t d_{t-2}\right)}$$

where

$$B = \left\{ \mathbf{d} = (d_1, \ldots, d_T) | d_t = 0 \text{ or } 1 \right.$$

$$d_1 = y_1$$

$$d_2 = y_2$$

$$\sum_t d_t = \sum_t y_t$$

$$\sum_t d_t d_{t-1} = \sum_t y_t y_{t-1}$$

$$d_{T-1} = y_{T-1}$$

$$\left. d_T = y_T \right\}$$

The conditional log-likelihood function is

$$L = \sum_{i=1}^{N} \ln \left[\frac{\exp\left(\gamma_2 \sum_{t=3}^{T} y_{it} y_{i,t-2}\right)}{\sum_{\mathbf{d} \in B_i} \exp\left(\gamma_2 \sum_{t=3}^{T} d_t d_{t-2}\right)} \right]$$

For example, consider the following probabilities:

1. $\text{Prob}[(1,0,1,0,0,0) \mid y_1 = 1, y_2 = 0, s = 2, s_{11} = 0, y_5 = y_6 = 0]$

$$= \text{Prob}[(1,0,1,0,0,0) \mid (1,0,1,0,0,0) \text{ or } (1,0,0,1,0,0)] = \frac{\exp(\gamma_2)}{1 + \exp(\gamma_2)}$$

2. $\text{Prob}[(0,1,0,1,1,1) \mid y_1 = 0, y_2 = 1, s = 4, s_{11} = 2, y_5 = y_6 = 1]$

$$= \text{Prob}[(0,1,0,1,1,1) \mid (0,1,0,1,1,1) \text{ or } (0,1,1,0,1,1)] = \frac{\exp(\gamma_2)}{1 + \exp(\gamma_2)}$$

With $T = 6$ there are two other pairs of sequences giving conditional probabilities that depend upon γ_2.

An alternative to point sampling is some sort of interval sampling, such as asking whether an individual was ever in one of the states during the previous year. For example, in the Michigan Panel Study of Income Dynamics, female labor force participation sequences can be generated by the question, "Did your wife do any work for money last year?"[15] This leads to a more complex analysis, since even if the individual is following an alternating Poisson process, the binary sequence generated by this sort of sampling does not have the first-order Markov property. For say that $y_{t-1} = 1$, so that we know that the individual was in state 1 at some point during the previous period. What is relevant, however, is the individual's state at the end of last period, and y_{t-2} will affect the probability that the spell in state 1 occurred early in period $t - 1$ instead of late in the period.

Nevertheless, it is possible to test whether the underlying process is alternating Poisson. The reason is that if $y_{t-1} = 0$, we know that the individual was never in state 1 during the previous period, and so we know the state at the end of that period; hence $y_{t-2}, y_{t-3}, \ldots$ are irrelevant. So we have

$$\begin{aligned} \text{Prob}(y_t = 1 \mid y_{t-1}, y_{t-2}, \ldots) &= \text{Prob}(y_t = 1 \mid y_{t-1} = \ldots \\ &= y_{t-J} = 1, y_{t-J-1} = 0) \\ &= \text{Prob}(y_t = 1 \mid J) \end{aligned}$$

where J is the number of consecutive preceding periods that the individual was in state 1.

A logistic parameterization of this dependence is

$$\text{Prob}(y_{it} = 1 \mid y_{i,t-1}, y_{i,t-2}, \ldots) = \frac{\exp(A_i)}{1 + \exp(A_i)}$$

where

$$A_i = \alpha_i + \sum_{k=1}^{\infty} \psi_{ik} \prod_{j=1}^{k} y_{i,t-j}$$

Note that no constraints have been imposed on the conditional probabilities, since each individual has his own set of parameters α_i, ψ_{ik}. Then a test for duration dependence in the underlying process can be based on a simple extension of this model, such as

$$\text{Prob}(y_{it} = 1 \mid y_{i,t-1}, y_{i,t-2}, \ldots) = \frac{\exp(A_i + \gamma_2 y_{i,t-2})}{1 + \exp(A_i + \gamma_2 y_{i,t-2})}$$

The test is based on the magnitude and significance of $\hat{\gamma}_2$.

Sufficient statistics for α_i and the ψ_{ik} are $s_{i01}, s_{i011}, \ldots$, where, for example, s_{i0111} is the number of times in the sequence that 1 is preceded by (0, 1, 1). In addition, we must condition on y_{i1}, on $y_{i,T-1}$, and on the number of consecutive ones at the end of the sequence (n_{iT}). We deal with initial conditions by conditioning on the number of consecutive ones at the beginning of the sequence (n_{i1}), which implies y_{i1}, and on y_{i2}. Let the alternative set be

$$B_i = \{\mathbf{d} = (d_1, \ldots, d_T) \mid d_t = 0 \text{ or } 1, n_{d1} = n_{i1}, n_{dT} = n_{iT}, d_2 = y_{i2}, \\ d_{T-1} = y_{i,T-1}, s_{d01} = s_{i01}, s_{d011} = s_{i011}, \ldots\}$$

Then the conditional log-likelihood function is

$$L = \sum_{i=1}^{N} \ln \frac{\exp\left(\gamma_2 \sum_{t=n_{i1}+2}^{T} y_{it} y_{i,t-2}\right)}{\sum_{\mathbf{d} \in B_i} \exp\left(\gamma_2 \sum_{t=n_{d1}+2}^{T} d_t d_{t-2}\right)}$$

For example, the first pair of sequences considered under point sampling remains relevant:

$$\text{Prob}[(1,0,1,0,0,0) \mid n_1 = 1, n_6 = 0, y_5 = 0, s_{01} = 1, s_{011} = \cdots = 0] \\ = \text{Prob}[(1,0,1,0,0,0) \mid (1,0,1,0,0,0) \text{ or } (1,0,0,1,0,0)] \\ = \frac{\exp(\gamma_2)}{1 + \exp(\gamma_2)}$$

The two sequences in the second pair, however, no longer belong to the same alternative set.

A test based on a confidence interval for γ_2 has the advantage that the size of the confidence interval gives a direct indication of the power of the test. Also γ_2 is a readily interpretable parameter that allows us to assess the substantive as well as the statistical significance of the departure from $\gamma_2 = 0$. For N sufficiently large, trivial departures will be significant at conventional levels. There are, however, additional tests based on certain sequences being equally likely under the null hypothesis of $\gamma_2 = 0$.

Under point sampling with $\gamma_2 = 0$, sufficient statistics for α and γ_1 are $\sum_t y_t$, $\sum_t y_t y_{t-1}$, and y_T. In addition, we must condition on y_1 in order to deal with initial conditions. An equivalent set of sufficient statistics is s_{00}, s_{01}, s_{10}, s_{11}, where s_{pq} is the number of times that p is followed by q; that is, sufficient statistics for a first-order Markov chain are the transition counts. Then sequences with the same transition counts are equally likely.

In the case of interval sampling with $y_t = 1$ if the individual was ever in state 1 during period t, sufficient statistics if $\gamma_2 = 0$ are $s_{01}, s_{011}, \ldots,$ as well as the number of consecutive ones at the beginning (n_1) and at the end (n_T) of the sequence. For example, with $n_1 = 0$, $n_5 = 0$, $s_{01} = 1$, $s_{011} = 1$, $s_{0111} = \cdots = 0$, we have

$$\begin{aligned}\text{Prob}(0,1,1,0,0) &= \text{Prob}(y_1 = 0)\text{Prob}(1\,|\,0)\text{Prob}(1\,|\,01) \\ &\quad \cdot \text{Prob}(0\,|\,011)\text{Prob}(0\,|\,0) \\ &= \text{Prob}(0,0,1,1,0) \\ &= \text{Prob}(y_1 = 0)\text{Prob}(0\,|\,0)\text{Prob}(1\,|\,0)\text{Prob}(1\,|\,01) \\ &\quad \cdot \text{Prob}(0\,|\,011)\end{aligned}$$

These tests can determine whether an individual's past has predictive power, given the current state and allowing for heterogeneity. If it does, then there is duration dependence, which may reflect state dependence. For example, say that the distribution of time spent in state 1 depends on the amount of time spent in that state during previous spells. This could reflect an effect on the individual of occupying the state, or it could be that unobserved variables that affected duration of previous spells are serially correlated and affect the duration of the current spell. In order to make this distinction, there must be observed variables (x) that affect duration. Say that x is constant during a spell but varies from spell to spell. Consider two individuals who differ in their histories of previous x values but have the same current x. If they have the same distribution for duration of the current spell, not conditioning on previous durations, then there is no state dependence; for state dependence should induce a distributed lag response, so that the history of previous levels of x will affect current duration.

In the next section we begin a discussion of models that use the underlying data on duration of the spells. We model the distribution of duration conditional on other variables in the simple case of a single-state, renewal-type process; it allows for duration dependence within a spell but maintains independence from spell to spell. A primary focus is on allowing for heterogeneity in these models.

3 Heterogeneity models for duration

This section will develop methods to control for unobserved heterogeneity in panel data models for duration. For example, consider a sample of individuals with data on segments of their job histories, giving the durations of each of the jobs during some period. The heterogeneity is in individual specific differences in separation rates; we may have various proxies for such differences, but they may not provide adequate controls in assessing the effects of other variables.

Let Y denote duration and let $G(y) = \text{Prob}(Y \geq y)$ be the survivor function. An equivalent description of the distribution is provided by the hazard function:

$$\lambda(y) = \frac{\lim\limits_{\Delta \to 0+} \text{Prob}(y < Y \leq y + \Delta \mid Y > y)}{\Delta}$$

$$= \frac{-G'(y)}{G(y)}$$

In our example, this is the separation rate as a function of tenure on the job. The survivor function can be recovered from

$$G(y) = \exp\left[-\int_0^y \lambda(s)\,ds\right]$$

The density function is

$$f(y) = -G'(y) = \lambda(y) \exp\left[-\int_0^y \lambda(s)\,d(s)\right]$$

A model with a constant hazard function corresponds to an exponential distribution for duration and a Poisson process for the number of events (separations) in some interval. It provided the null model of the previous section, where λ was constant for an individual but was allowed to vary across individuals. We shall extend that model by allowing the hazard function to depend on duration and by introducing observed variables into a conditional distribution of duration.

Given that λ is nonnegative, a promising specification is

$$\ln \lambda_{ij}(y) = \boldsymbol{\beta}'\mathbf{x}_{ij}(y) + (\gamma - 1)h(y) + \alpha_i, \qquad i = 1, \ldots, N$$

where $\mathbf{x}_{ij}(y)$ is the value of a vector of explanatory variables in the jth spell of the ith individual when the duration of that spell equals y. We specify $h(y)$ as a function of duration such as $h(y) = y$ or $\ln y$. The $\ln y$ specification corresponds to the Weibull distribution commonly used in reliability analysis.[16] We could also allow h to depend upon unknown parameters: $h(y) = y + \tau y^2$, for example.

The α_i parameters are included to capture individual specific differences in separation rates that are not adequately measured by the variables in $\mathbf{x}$. If such unmeasured heterogeneity is important, then constraining the model to $\alpha_i = \alpha$ will give a seriously downward-biased estimate of the duration dependence parameter γ. Separation rates will spuriously appear to decline with tenure since the individuals with high tenure will systematically be the low-α individuals. If the unmeasured heterogeneity is correlated with $\mathbf{x}$, then we also expect that constraining $\alpha_i = \alpha$ will result in biased estimates of $\boldsymbol{\beta}$.

We shall begin by discussing a conditional likelihood approach to the estimation of this model. It has the disadvantage of not providing an estimate of γ. We then discuss models based on the Weibull, gamma, and lognormal distributions; a marginal likelihood approach is used to obtain estimators of $\boldsymbol{\beta}$ and a duration dependence parameter.

Both the conditional and the marginal likelihood approaches are limited by the necessity of conditioning on $\mathbf{x}$ within each spell; this excludes the use of age or a time trend. They are also limited by the requirement that the number of spells observed for an individual be independent of the duration of the spells. These limitations are removed in a conditional likelihood analysis of a model based on the gamma distribution, but that model has its own restrictive features. Our final topic is posterior likelihoods for random effects specifications. The restrictive features of the other approaches are removed at the cost of a parametric specification for the conditional distribution of α given $\mathbf{x}$. The fixed effects approaches, when applicable, have the advantage of allowing for a very general relationship between α and $\mathbf{x}$.

3.1 *A conditional likelihood for log-linear hazard functions*

A conditional likelihood approach to the estimation of this model is due to Cox (1972a,b; 1975). Consider an individual on whom we have observed three completed spells with durations y_1, y_2, y_3. Order the spells by their length: $y_{(1)} < y_{(2)} < y_{(3)}$. The random variable (1) indicates which of the three spells is shortest. Assume that the spells are independent of each other and consider the distribution of (1) conditional on the length of the shortest spell.

For example, the conditional probability that the third spell is shortest, conditional on the duration of the shortest spell, is given by

$$\begin{aligned}&\text{Prob}[(1)=3 \mid Y_{(1)} = y_3, \mathbf{x}_1, \mathbf{x}_2, \mathbf{x}_3, \alpha]\\&= \frac{G_1(y_3)G_2(y_3)f_3(y_3)}{f_1(y_3)G_2(y_3)G_3(y_3) + G_1(y_3)f_2(y_3)G_3(y_3) + G_1(y_3)G_2(y_3)f_3(y_3)}\\&= \frac{\lambda_3(y_3)}{\sum_{j=1}^{3} \lambda_j(y_3)} = \frac{\exp[\boldsymbol{\beta}'\mathbf{x}_3(y_3)]}{\sum_{j=1}^{3} \exp[\boldsymbol{\beta}'\mathbf{x}_j(y_3)]}\end{aligned}$$

where G_j and f_j are the survivor function and the density function of the jth spell: $f_j(y) = \lambda_j(y)G_j(y)$; we have suppressed the i subscript. This conditional probability does not depend upon α_i; hence mild regularity conditions will insure that an ML estimator based on it will converge to $\boldsymbol{\beta}$ as $N \to \infty$, provided that there is sufficient variation in $\mathbf{x}_{ij} - \mathbf{x}_{i1}$, $j = 2, 3$.

Furthermore, this conditional probability does not depend upon $h(y)$. So we can respecify the model as

$$\ln \lambda_{ij}(y) = \boldsymbol{\beta}'\mathbf{x}_{ij}(y) + m_i(y)$$

where we can have, for example, $m_i(y) = \gamma_i y + \alpha_i$ or $\gamma_i \ln y + \alpha_i$. We can obtain a consistent (as $N \to \infty$) estimator for $\boldsymbol{\beta}$ allowing for arbitrary heterogeneity in the shape of the hazard function. This is very powerful indeed.

There is additional information in the distribution of the second shortest spell. We condition on the duration of the second shortest spell and on the number and duration of the shortest spell. For example, consider the conditional probability that the first spell is the second shortest, given that the duration of the second shortest spell is y_1 and given that the third spell was the shortest with duration y_3; this is

$$\begin{aligned}&\text{Prob}[(2) = 1 \mid Y_{(2)} = y_1, Y_{(1)} = y_3, (1) = 3, \mathbf{x}_1, \mathbf{x}_2, \mathbf{x}_3, m]\\&= \frac{f_1(y_1)G_2(y_1)f_3(y_3)}{f_1(y_1)G_2(y_1)f_3(y_3) + G_1(y_1)f_2(y_1)f_3(y_3)}\\&= \frac{\lambda_1(y_1)}{\lambda_1(y_1) + \lambda_2(y_1)} = \frac{\exp[\boldsymbol{\beta}'\mathbf{x}_1(y_1)]}{\exp[\boldsymbol{\beta}'\mathbf{x}_1(y_1)] + \exp[\boldsymbol{\beta}'\mathbf{x}_2(y_1)]}\end{aligned}$$

Once again we have a conditional probability that does not depend upon $m_i(y)$.

This conditional probability conditions on the shortest spell; hence the corresponding ML estimator is asymptotically independent of the previous estimator, which was based on the distribution of the shortest spell. The two estimators can be pooled using their precision matrices. It is more convenient, however, to do the pooling by multiplying the two conditional likelihood functions and maximizing their product. Note that this product of conditional likelihood functions does not correspond to a conditional probability, since the first conditional likelihood function does not condition on $Y_{(2)}$; were it to do so, the simple form of the conditional probability, and in particular its independence from $m_i(y)$, would be lost. Cox (1975) terms this product of conditional likelihood functions a *partial likelihood*. He shows that the ML estimator based on it converges to $\boldsymbol{\beta}$, and that its distribution can be approximated in the usual way by a normal distribution with precision matrix equal to minus the Hessian of the log of the partial likelihood function.

We assume that n completed spells are available for each individual. For example, a retrospective survey might ask for the durations of the n most recent jobs held by the individual. An alternative sampling plan is to choose a sampling interval $[a, b]$ and to obtain for each individual the times at which events (separations) occurred during that interval. Then the number of events experienced during the interval will vary for different individuals. If we let the number of spells vary in the conditional likelihood formula, then we are implicitly conditioning on n; but that affects the simple form of the conditional probabilities. For example,

$$\text{Prob}[(1) = 2 \,|\, Y_{(1)} = y_2, n = 2] = \frac{\lambda_2(y_2)P_2}{\lambda_1(y_2)P_1 + \lambda_2(y_2)P_2}$$

where

$$P_1 = \text{Prob}(n = 2 \,|\, Y_1 = y_2, Y_2 > y_2)$$

$$P_2 = \text{Prob}(n = 2 \,|\, Y_1 > y_2, Y_2 = y_2)$$

This equals $\lambda_2(y_2)/[\lambda_1(y_2) + \lambda_2(y_2)]$ only if $P_1 = P_2$; but in general $P_1 \neq P_2$ unless Y_1 and Y_2 have the same distribution.

Note that it is valid to select the first two spells for everyone, provided that the sampling interval is long enough so that (essentially) everyone has two completed spells. A systematic bias would be introduced if a nonnegligible fraction of the sample were discarded for having fewer than two completed spells.

The partial log-likelihood function is

$$L = \sum_{i=1}^{N} \sum_{j=1}^{n-1} \ln\left(\frac{\exp\{\boldsymbol{\beta}'\mathbf{x}_{i(y)}[y_{i(j)}]\}}{\sum_{k=j}^{n} \exp\{\boldsymbol{\beta}'\mathbf{x}_{i(k)}[y_{i(j)}]\}} \right)$$

This is the form of a conditional logit log-likelihood function and can be maximized by standard programs.[17] The alternative set corresponding to the jth shortest job held by an individual consists of all jobs held by that individual that were longer. The explanatory variables for the jobs in the alternative set are evaluated at duration equal to the completed duration of the jth shortest job.

This conditioning argument was originally used by Cox (1972a) in the context of a life table, where there are N individuals followed until death or the end of the sample period. The model is

$$\ln \lambda_i(y) = \boldsymbol{\beta}'\mathbf{x}_i(y) + m(y), \qquad i = 1, \ldots, N$$

The power of the conditional likelihood approach is that $m(y)$ does not have to be specified in order to estimate $\boldsymbol{\beta}$ consistently. There is only one spell (life) per individual. If, however, we translate the assumption of independent spells across individuals into independence of the spells over time, then the approach is relevant for regression analysis in a renewal process. The case of many spells for a single individual is developed in Cox (1972b), where the asymptotic arguments are based on the number of spells for that individual approaching infinity. The application we are proposing is to the case of a few spells for many individuals with the same function m for each of an individual's spells, but with m varying arbitrarily across individuals.

A limitation of this approach is that it does not provide an estimate of duration dependence. We shall consider in the next section some special cases in which the dependence of separation rates on tenure can be estimated within a fixed effects model. We apply marginal likelihood analysis to models based on the Weibull, gamma, and lognormal distributions.

A second limitation, which also applies to the marginal likelihood analysis, is the restriction to conditioning on $\mathbf{x}$ within each of the spells. This precludes using a variable like age, since we would have to condition on the individual's age at the beginning of each of the spells. If an individual is always employed, then his change in age between the beginnings of two consecutive jobs is the duration of the first job. The problem is that the strict exogeneity assumption

$$f(y_j \mid x_1, \ldots, x_n, \alpha) = f(y_j \mid x_j, \alpha)$$

is not appropriate in this case, since $x_{j+1}(0) - x_j(0) = y_j$. When age is treated as a spell specific variable, it is not strictly exogenous. An identical problem arises in using a time trend or aggregate time series variables.

In Section 3.3 we shall consider a conditional likelihood analysis of a model based on the gamma distribution. In that model, we condition on the time path of the explanatory variables, and so a proper specification for age or a time trend is possible. In addition, the model does not suffer from a third limitation of Cox's model (which is shared by the marginal likelihood approaches), in that the number of spells need not be independent of their durations. The limitation of the conditional gamma model is that it does not allow for conditioning on explanatory variables during particular spells; for example, the model cannot incorporate job-specific variables like the union status of the job. The final section develops a random effects specification that allows us to relax these various restrictive features.

3.2 *Marginal likelihood for the Weibull, gamma, and lognormal distributions*

3.2.1. The Weibull distribution. We set $h(y) = \ln(y)$ and consider the special case in which $\mathbf{x}_{ij}(y) = \mathbf{x}_{ij}$, so that $\mathbf{x}$ does not vary within a spell. The hazard function is

$$\ln \lambda_{ij}(y) = \boldsymbol{\beta}'\mathbf{x}_{ij} + \alpha_i + (\gamma - 1)\ln y$$

We assume that n completed spells are available for each individual. This puts the same limitations on the sampling scheme that were required in the previous section. We assume that the spells are independent of each other and that $\mathbf{x}$ is strictly exogenous in the following sense:

$$f(y_1, \ldots, y_n | \mathbf{x}_1, \ldots, \mathbf{x}_n, \alpha) = \prod_{j=1}^{n} f(y_j | \mathbf{x}_j, \alpha)$$

We transform to Y_1, $Y_2/Y_1, \ldots, Y_n/Y_1$, and base our inferences on the marginal distribution of $Y_2/Y_1, \ldots, Y_n/Y_1$. This gives the following marginal log-likelihood function: $L = \sum_i L_i$, where

$$L_i = (n-1)\ln\gamma + \frac{\boldsymbol{\beta}'}{\gamma}\sum_{j=2}^{n}(\mathbf{x}_{ij} - \mathbf{x}_{i1}) + (\gamma - 1)\sum_{j=2}^{n}\ln\left(\frac{y_{ij}}{y_{i1}}\right)$$
$$- n\ln\left\{1 + \sum_{j=2}^{n}\left(\frac{y_{ij}}{y_{i1}}\right)^{\gamma}\exp\left[\frac{\boldsymbol{\beta}'(\mathbf{x}_{ij} - \mathbf{x}_{i1})}{\gamma}\right]\right\}, \qquad i = 1, \ldots, N$$

This marginal likelihood function does not depend upon α_i, and so standard asymptotic ($N \to \infty$) theory applies to the ML estimator based on it.

If $\mathbf{x}_{ij}$ does not vary in j, then $\boldsymbol{\beta}$ is not estimable but γ is. We illustrate with $n = 2$; it is convenient to consider the density of $R = Y_1/(Y_1 + Y_2)$:

$$f(r) = \frac{\gamma[r(1-r)]^{\gamma-1}}{[r^\gamma + (1-r)^\gamma]^2}, \qquad 0 \leq r \leq 1$$

In the exponential case, $\gamma = 1$ and we have a uniform distribution on $[0, 1]$. If the hazard function is decreasing, so that separation rates decline with tenure, then the density is U-shaped; it is symmetric about its minimum at $r = \frac{1}{2}$ and has singularities at 0 and 1.

3.2.2. The gamma distribution. An alternative model that allows a similar elimination of the incidental parameters is based on the gamma distribution:

$$f(y) = \frac{\rho^\gamma y^{\gamma-1} e^{-\rho y}}{\Gamma(\gamma)}, \qquad \gamma \geq 0, \qquad \rho > 0$$

It includes the exponential distribution as a special case ($\gamma = 1$). The hazard function declines monotonically if $\gamma < 1$ and increases monotonically if $\gamma > 1$. The main difference from the Weibull case is that the Weibull hazard function approaches zero as $y \to \infty$ if $\gamma < 1$, whereas the gamma hazard function approaches an asymptote equal to ρ.

We shall again consider the special case in which $\mathbf{x}_{ij}(y) = \mathbf{x}_{ij}$, so that $\mathbf{x}$ is constant during a spell. We specify

$$\ln \rho_{ij} = \boldsymbol{\beta}'\mathbf{x}_{ij} + \alpha_i$$

and assume that $\mathbf{x}$ is strictly exogenous conditional on α. The spells are assumed to be independent of each other.

As in the Weibull case, we base the likelihood function on the marginal distribution of $Y_2/Y_1, \ldots, Y_n/Y_1$. This gives $L = \sum_i L_i$, where

$$\begin{aligned} L_i = {} & \ln \Gamma(n\gamma) - n \ln \Gamma(\gamma) + \gamma\boldsymbol{\beta}' \sum_{j=2}^{n} (\mathbf{x}_{ij} - \mathbf{x}_{i1}) \\ & + (\gamma - 1) \sum_{j=2}^{n} \ln\left(\frac{y_{ij}}{y_{i1}}\right) \\ & - \gamma n \ln\left\{1 + \sum_{j=2}^{n} \frac{y_{ij}}{y_{i1}} \exp[\boldsymbol{\beta}'(\mathbf{x}_{ij} - \mathbf{x}_{i1})]\right\}, \qquad i = 1, \ldots, N \end{aligned}$$

it has the form of an inverted Dirichlet density. Again we see that α_i does not appear in the marginal likelihood function, and so standard asymptotic theory can be applied.

Note that $\mathbf{x}$ enters only in differenced form. Hence we cannot estimate $\boldsymbol{\beta}$ if $\mathbf{x}$ varies only across individuals and not across the spells of a given individual. We can, however, estimate γ. We shall illustrate for $n = 2$ by considering the marginal density of $R = Y_1/(Y_1 + Y_2)$:

$$f(r) = \frac{\Gamma(2\gamma)}{\Gamma^2(\gamma)} [r(1 - r)]^{\gamma - 1}, \qquad 0 \leq r \leq 1$$

This is a beta density. In the exponential case it is uniform. If $\gamma < 1$, it is U-shaped, symmetric about its minimum at $r = \frac{1}{2}$, and has singularities at $r = 0$ and $r = 1$.

3.2.3. The lognormal distribution. For the case in which $\mathbf{x}$ is constant during a spell, another useful distribution for duration is the lognormal. We specify

$$\ln y_{ij} = \boldsymbol{\beta}'\mathbf{x}_{ij} + \alpha_i + u_{ij}$$

where, conditional on $\mathbf{x}$, u_{ij} is i.i.d. $N[0, \ln(1 + \gamma^{-2})]$. The hazard function of this distribution increases to a maximum and then decreases to an asymptote of zero. So we do not have the sharp contrast between a rising and a falling hazard function corresponding to $\gamma > 1$ and $\gamma < 1$ in the Weibull and gamma cases. Nevertheless, γ continues to play a similar role since it is the inverse of the coefficient of variation. A distribution with a monotone hazard function has a coefficient of variation greater (less) than 1 if and only if the hazard function decreases (increases) with duration.[18]

There is a related result for the relationship between complete and incomplete spells. Consider the spell that includes the beginning of the sample period. The forward recurrence time is the remaining tenure on that job; the backward recurrence time is the tenure on that job at the beginning of the sample period. If the spells have a common distribution ($\boldsymbol{\beta} = \mathbf{0}$), then after the process has been running for a long time, the probability density of both the forward and the backward recurrence times is $G(y)/\mu$, where μ is the mean of the G distribution $[\mu = \int_0^\infty yf(y)\,dy]$.[19] Hence the means of these incomplete spells are both given by

$$\tilde{\mu} = \frac{1}{\mu} \int_0^\infty yG(y)\,dy = \frac{1}{2\mu} \int_0^\infty y^2 f(y)\,dy = \frac{\mu(\sigma^2/\mu^2 + 1)}{2}$$

So the incomplete spell covering a preassigned point has mean greater than μ if and only if the coefficient of variation exceeds 1. In our notation, $\gamma < 1$ is the appropriate condition for $\tilde{\mu} > \mu$ for the Weibull, gamma, and lognormal distributions.

The treatment of incidental parameters in the lognormal case is straightforward, since the standard results on analysis of covariance in linear models apply. There are n completed spells for each individual with durations $y_1, \ldots, y_n$. We set $z = \ln y$ and use

$$\hat{\boldsymbol{\beta}} = \left[\sum_{i,j} (\mathbf{x}_{ij} - \bar{\mathbf{x}}_i)(\mathbf{x}_{ij} - \bar{\mathbf{x}}_i')\right]^{-1} \left[\sum_{i,j} (\mathbf{x}_{ij} - \bar{\mathbf{x}}_i)(z_{ij} - \bar{z}_i)\right]$$

$$\hat{\tau}^2 = \frac{1}{N(n-1)} \sum_{i,j} [(z_{ij} - \bar{z}_i) - \hat{\boldsymbol{\beta}}'(\mathbf{x}_{ij} - \bar{\mathbf{x}}_i)]^2$$

$$\hat{\gamma}^2 = [\exp(\hat{\tau}^2) - 1]^{-1}, \qquad i = 1, \ldots, N, \qquad j = 1, \ldots, n$$

We should stress that the validity of this procedure hinges on the strict exogeneity assumption that

$$E(\ln y_{ij} \mid \mathbf{x}_{i1}, \ldots, \mathbf{x}_{in}, \alpha_i) = E(\ln y_{ij} \mid \mathbf{x}_{ij}, \alpha_i) = \boldsymbol{\beta}'\mathbf{x}_{ij} + \alpha_i$$

For consider the case $n = 2$. Then our estimator is a least squares regression based on the following equation:

$$\ln y_{i2} - \ln y_{i1} = \boldsymbol{\beta}'(\mathbf{x}_{i2} - \mathbf{x}_{i1}) + u_{i2} - u_{i1}$$

Failure of strict exogeneity implies that u_1 is correlated with $\mathbf{x}_2$ or u_2 is correlated with $\mathbf{x}_1$. Hence the least squares regression of $y_2 - y_1$ on $\mathbf{x}_2 - \mathbf{x}_1$ will not in general converge to $\boldsymbol{\beta}$. For example, if x_j is age at the beginning of the jth job, then $x_2 - x_1$ is y_1, and there is a clear downward bias. Here it is plausible that α is not correlated with x, and so a regression of y_1 on x_1 or of y_2 on x_2 would be consistent, whereas the difference regression clearly is not. This example clarifies the need for strict exogeneity in Cox's conditional likelihood analysis.

Assuming strict exogeneity, the analysis-of-covariance estimator can be obtained as a conditional ML estimator, conditioning on $\sum_j \ln y_{ij}, j = 1, \ldots, n; i = 1, \ldots, N$; or as a marginal ML estimator, using the marginal distribution of $Y_2/Y_1, \ldots, Y_n/Y_1$. It can also be obtained as a posterior ML estimator, by specifying that the conditional distribution of α given $\mathbf{x}' = (\mathbf{x}_1', \ldots, \mathbf{x}_n')$ is given by

$$\alpha_i = \boldsymbol{\delta}'\mathbf{x}_i + v_i, \qquad v_i \text{ i.i.d. } N(0, \sigma_v^2)$$

Then we can base the likelihood function on the distribution of y marginal on α, obtained as the mixture of the conditional distributions of y given α.

3.3 *A conditional likelihood for the gamma distribution*

We shall consider conditioning on the time path over a sample period of a set of explanatory variables, instead of conditioning on them as a function of duration during each of the separate spells. We denote these variables by $\mathbf{z}_i(t)$ for t in the sample interval $[a, b]$. Examples include time trends, aggregate time series variables, and individual specific variables based on age.

We obtain for each individual the times at which events (separations) occurred during the sampling interval $[a, b]$: $t_0, t_1, \ldots, t_n$. Then $y_1 = t_1 - t_0, \ldots, y_n = t_n - t_{n-1}$ are the completed spell durations. We shall carry along the job tenure example, maintaining a single state process by assuming that the individual always has a job.

The amount of time that the individual remained on the job held at the beginning of the sampling period is $y_0 = t_0 - a$. In some cases, information will be available on the date when that job began, so that we know y_0^*, the complete duration of the job. Great care is needed in using such information, however, since that spell was chosen to include a preassigned date; a longer spell is more likely to be chosen and so the distribution is not given by G.

In the exponential case with $\boldsymbol{\beta} = 0$, the distribution of y_0 is given by G and the mean of y_0^* is 2μ, where μ is the mean of the G distribution $[\mu = \int_0^\infty yf(y)\,dy]$. In general, if the process has been running long enough to achieve its limiting distribution, then the density function for Y_0^* is $y_0 f(y_0)/\mu$ and the density for Y_0 is $G(y_0)/\mu$.[20] We could use these results to include y_0^* or y_0 in the likelihood function if the stationarity assumption were plausible; but typically it will not be, especially given our objective of including conditioning variables $\mathbf{x}$, some of which will be nonstationary.

We specify

$$f(y_{ij} \mid t_{i,j-1}, \mathbf{z}_i, \alpha_i)$$

$$= \rho_i(t_{ij}) \left[\int_{t_{i,j-1}}^{t_{ij}} \rho(u)\,du \right]^{\gamma - 1} \frac{\exp\left[-\int_{t_{i,j-1}}^{t_{ij}} \rho(u)\,du \right]}{\Gamma(\gamma)}$$

where

$$\ln \rho_i(t) = \boldsymbol{\psi}'\mathbf{z}_i(t) + \alpha_i \quad \text{and} \quad t_{ij} = t_{i,j-1} + y_{ij}$$

This amounts to assuming that the process is homogeneous on the transformed time scale

$$w(t) = \int_0^t \rho(u)\,du$$

so that the distribution of $W = w(Y)$ is gamma with unit scale parameter and with γ for the shape parameter.

We can no longer maintain independence of the spells, since we must specify the time when the spell begins in order to condition on the relevant segment of $\mathbf{z}(t)$. Hence we must condition on $t_{j-1} = a + y_0 \cdots + y_{j-1}$.

The joint distribution is

$$f(y_0, \ldots, y_n, n | C) = f(y_0 | C) f(y_1 | t_0, C) \cdots f(y_n | t_{n-1}, C) Q$$

$$= f(y_0 | C) \prod_{j=1}^{n} \left\{ \rho(t_j) \left[\int_{t_{j-1}}^{t_j} \rho(u)\, du \right]^{\gamma - 1} \right\} \frac{\exp\left[-\int_{t_0}^{t} \rho(u)\, du \right] Q}{\Gamma^n(\gamma)}$$

where $C = \{\mathbf{z}, \alpha\}$ and $Q = \text{Prob}\{\text{no events in } [t_n, b] | t_n\}$.

We shall eliminate α_i by using a conditional likelihood function that conditions on n and on the total duration of the complete spells: $y_1 + \cdots + y_n = t_n - t_0$. We also condition on y_0 in order to specify when the first complete spell begins. On the transformed time scale, $y_1 + \cdots + y_n$ is the sum of n independent random variables with a common gamma distribution, and so the distribution of the sum is gamma with unit scale parameter and with $n\gamma$ for the shape parameter. Therefore,

$$f(y_0, n, t_n - t_0 | C) = f(y_0 | C) f(t_n - t_0 | y_0, C) Q$$

$$= f(y_0 | C) \rho(t_n) \left[\int_{t_0}^{t_n} \rho(u)\, du \right]^{n\gamma - 1} \frac{\exp\left[-\int_{t_0}^{t_n} \rho(u)\, du \right] Q}{\Gamma(n\gamma)}$$

The conditional log-likelihood function is $L = \sum_i L_i$, where

$$L_i = \ln \Gamma(n_i \gamma) - n_i \ln \Gamma(\gamma) + \psi' \sum_{j=1}^{n_i - 1} \mathbf{z}_i(t_j)$$

$$+ (\gamma - 1) \sum_{j=1}^{n_i} \ln \int_{t_{j-1}}^{t_j} \exp[\psi' \mathbf{z}_i(u)]\, du$$

$$- (n_i \gamma - 1) \ln \int_{t_0}^{t_n} \exp[\psi' \mathbf{z}_i(u)]\, \mathrm{du}$$

$$(i = 1, \ldots, n)$$[21]

The α_i do not enter, and so standard asymptotic results can be applied. Since we are explicitly conditioning on n, it has been straightforward to allow for different individuals completing different numbers of spells within the sampling period. If $\psi = \mathbf{0}$, then the conditional likelihood function for γ can be obtained as a marginal likelihood function, since $Y_2/Y_1, \ldots, Y_n/Y_1$ are independent of $Y_1 + \cdots + Y_n$.

In the next section we shall consider a random effects specification for models with log-linear hazard functions. This will allow us to incorporate both types of explanatory variables, so that we can condition on the path of an explanatory variable either during a particular spell or as a function of time. In addition, we shall be able to use sampling schemes in which the number of spells observed for an individual is not independent of the durations of the spells.

3.4 *Random effects models*

We shall consider models with log-linear hazard functions:

$$\ln \lambda_{ij}(y,t) = \boldsymbol{\beta}'\mathbf{x}_{ij}(y) + \boldsymbol{\psi}'\mathbf{z}_i(t) + (\gamma - 1)h(y) + \alpha_i,$$
$$i = 1,\ldots,N, \qquad j = 1,2,\ldots, \qquad t \in [a,b]$$

$\mathbf{x}_{ij}(y)$ is the value of $\mathbf{x}$ for the ith individual at duration y of his jth spell; we shall condition separately on $\mathbf{x}_1, \mathbf{x}_2, \ldots$. We use $\mathbf{z}$ to distinguish a second set of explanatory variables for which we condition on the time path over the sample period $[a,b]$ without reference to a particular spell. Our specification of the hazard function involves two sorts of strict exogeneity assumptions: that only $\mathbf{x}_j(y)$ is relevant during the jth spell and that only $\mathbf{z}(t)$ is relevant at time t (conditional on α). In the turnover example, these assumptions would not be appropriate if age were included in $\mathbf{x}$ or if the union status of the job were included in $\mathbf{z}$.

We have a sampling interval $[a,b]$, and (dropping the i subscripts) we observe events at $t_0, t_1, \ldots, t_n$; hence the durations are $y_0 = t_0 - a$, $y_1 = t_1 - t_0, \ldots, y_n = t_n - t_{n-1}$. We assume that the distribution of y_j is independent of the previous spells, conditional on the time at which the jth spell began. Hence the density is

$$f(y_0,\ldots,y_n,n \mid C,\alpha)$$
$$= f(y_0 \mid C,\alpha) f(y_1 \mid t_0, C, \alpha) \cdots f(y_n \mid t_{n-1}, C, \alpha) Q$$

where $Q = \text{Prob}\{\text{no events in } [t_n, b] \mid t_n, C, \alpha\}$ and $C = \{\mathbf{x}_0, \mathbf{x}_1, \ldots, \mathbf{z}\}$. Given the difficulty of specifying $f(y_0 \mid C, \alpha)$, we shall condition on y_0:

$$f(y_1,\ldots,y_n,n \mid y_0, C, \alpha)$$
$$= \left\{\prod_{j=1}^{n} \lambda(y_j, t_{j-1} + y_j)\right\} \exp\left[-\sum_{j=1}^{n+1} \int_0^{y_j} \lambda(s, t_{j-1} + s)\, ds\right]$$

where $y_{n+1} = b - t_n$.

We shall specify a gamma prior distribution for $\tau = e^{\alpha}$:

$$f(\tau \mid y_0, C, \rho, \kappa) = \rho^{\kappa}\tau^{\kappa-1} \frac{e^{-\rho\tau}}{\Gamma(\kappa)}$$

where ρ and κ will be specified as functions of y_0, $\mathbf{x}$, and $\mathbf{z}$.[22] Then we have

$$f(y_1,\ldots,y_n,n \mid y_0, C, \rho, \kappa)$$
$$= \int f(y_1,\ldots,y_n,n \mid y_0, C, \tau) f(\tau \mid y_0, C, \rho, \kappa)\, d\tau$$
$$= \frac{\Gamma(n+\kappa)}{\Gamma(\kappa)} \rho^{-n} A \left[1 + \frac{B}{\rho}\right]^{-(n+\kappa)}$$

where

$$A = \exp\left[\sum_{j=1}^{n} \boldsymbol{\beta}'\mathbf{x}_j(y_j) + \boldsymbol{\psi}'\mathbf{z}(t_{j-1} + y_j) + (\gamma - 1)h(y_j)\right]$$

$$B = \sum_{j=1}^{n+1} \int_0^{y_j} \exp[\boldsymbol{\beta}'\mathbf{x}_j(s) + \boldsymbol{\psi}'\mathbf{z}(t_{j-1} + s) + (\gamma - 1)h(s)]\, ds$$

Note that when we form the posterior likelihood function based on this density, n will vary across the individuals in the sample. This has been allowed for, since n is included explicitly in the likelihood function.

In order to obtain some guidance on the specification of ρ and κ, consider the following case: $\boldsymbol{\psi} = 0$ and there is only a single variable in $\mathbf{x}$, which is constant during a spell: $\mathbf{x}_{ij}(y) = x_{ij}$. Since $\boldsymbol{\psi} = 0$, we can use the marginal distribution of $y_1, \ldots, y_n, n$, without conditioning on y_0. Then we have

$$\int f(x_0, \ldots, x_{n+1}, y_1, \ldots, y_n, n \mid \alpha) f(\alpha)\, d\alpha$$

$$= \int f(y_1, \ldots, y_n, n \mid x_0, \ldots, x_{n+1}, \alpha) f(x_0, \ldots, x_{n+1} \mid \alpha) f(\alpha)\, d\alpha$$

$$= k(\mathbf{x}) \int f(y_1, \ldots, y_n, n \mid x_0, \ldots, x_{n+1}, \alpha) f(\alpha \mid x_0, \ldots, x_{n+1})\, d\alpha$$

Assume that the distribution of $\mathbf{x}$ conditional on α is given by

$$x_{ij} = \zeta_1 + \zeta_2 \alpha_i + e_{ij}, \qquad j = 0, \ldots, n + 1$$

where $\mathbf{e}_i$ is i.i.d. $N(\mathbf{0}, \boldsymbol{\Sigma})$. If the marginal distribution of α is $N(0, \sigma_\alpha^2)$, then the conditional distribution of α given $\mathbf{x}' = (x_0, \ldots, x_{n+1})$ is $N(\zeta + \boldsymbol{\delta}_n'\mathbf{x}, \sigma_v^2)$, where

$$\boldsymbol{\delta}_n = \zeta_2 \sigma_\alpha^2 (\zeta_2^2 \sigma_\alpha^2 \mathbf{l}\mathbf{l}' + \boldsymbol{\Sigma})^{-1} \mathbf{l}$$

and $\mathbf{l}' = (1, \ldots, 1)$. In the special case $\boldsymbol{\Sigma} = \sigma^2(\mathbf{I} + a\mathbf{l}\mathbf{l}')$, we have

$$\boldsymbol{\delta}_n = \frac{\delta_1}{1 + (n + 2)\delta_2} \mathbf{l}$$

We could also consider other cases, such as low-order autoregressive-moving average models for $\boldsymbol{\Sigma}$, which would impose restrictions on $\boldsymbol{\delta}_n$. Note that if $\boldsymbol{\Sigma}$ is unrestricted, then there are no restrictions across the $\boldsymbol{\delta}_n$ terms for different values of n.

The normal posterior distribution for α implies a lognormal distribution for $\tau = e^\alpha$. We shall approximate it with a gamma distribution by equating the means and variances; this gives

$$\rho_i = \eta \exp(-\boldsymbol{\delta}_n'\mathbf{x}_i)$$
$$\kappa = (e^{\sigma_v^2} - 1)^{-1}$$

Under this specification, β appears in the likelihood function only in the form $(\beta x_{ij} + \boldsymbol{\delta}_n'\mathbf{x}_i)$. As a result, if $x_{ij} = x_i$, so that x does not vary across the spells, then we can only estimate $\beta + \mathbf{l}'\boldsymbol{\delta}_n$. So β is not estimable if $\boldsymbol{\delta}_n$ is unrestricted. In fact, in this case we would have $x_i = \zeta_1 + \zeta_2\alpha_i + e_i$, so that $\rho_i = \eta e^{-\delta x_i}$, where $\delta = \zeta_2\sigma_\alpha^2/(\zeta_2^2\sigma_\alpha^2 + \sigma_e^2)$ is unconstrained. Only $\beta + \delta$ would be estimable. If we are to allow the conditional distribution of α given x to depend fairly freely upon x, then it is plausible that β should not be estimable if x varies only across individuals.

If $\boldsymbol{\psi} \neq \mathbf{0}$, then we have to consider whether the conditional distribution of α should be allowed to depend upon $\mathbf{z}$. For aggregate time series variables and for age-related variables, it may be plausible that there is no dependence.

In order to obtain some guidance on how the conditional distribution of α depends on y_0, consider the case $\boldsymbol{\beta} = \boldsymbol{\psi} = \mathbf{0}$, $h(y) = \ln y$. Assume that the process has been running long enough so that the limiting distribution is relevant. Then the density function for the distribution of y_0 is G/μ and

$$f(y_0|\tau) = \Gamma^{-1}\left(1 + \frac{1}{\gamma}\right)\left(\frac{\tau}{\gamma}\right)^{1/\gamma} \exp\left(\frac{-\tau y_0^\gamma}{\gamma}\right)$$

We specify that the prior distribution for $\tau = e^\alpha$ is gamma with scale and shape parameters equal to ρ^* and κ^*. Then the conditional distribution for τ given y_0 is gamma with

$$\rho_i = \frac{1}{\gamma} y_{i0}^\gamma + \rho^*$$

$$\kappa = \frac{1}{\gamma} + \kappa^*$$

This suggests that in general we might adopt the specification

$$\rho_i = \eta \exp(-\boldsymbol{\delta}_n'\mathbf{x}_i + \zeta \ln y_{i0})$$

with a constant shape parameter (κ). We can consider restrictions such as $\boldsymbol{\delta}_n = \{\delta_1/[1 + (n+2)\delta_2]\}\mathbf{l}$. Other specifications are plausible; clearly some sensitivity analysis is called for.

These models for duration have assumed independence of the spells, conditional on explanatory variables and person effects. An important extension will be to develop models that relax this assumption. Then if there are several states, we shall have to consider how the duration distribution depends on previous durations in each of the states, as well as modeling the transition probabilities. Also there are many interesting questions in specifying and estimating joint distributions for systems of variables followed through time.

4 Conclusion

We have seen that longitudinal data allow us to test and relax some of the assumptions implicit in a cross-sectional analysis. The basic notion of comparing a cross-sectional regression with one based on changes has been related to tests for strict exogeneity in time series analysis. The failure of strict exogeneity may be due to individual specific omitted variables that are correlated with the included explanatory variables. This leads to a reformulation in which we test for strict exogeneity in a mixture model. This strict exogeneity property is required in order for the standard linear analysis-of-covariance estimator to be consistent as the number of individuals increases.

The discussion of linear models carried over directly to multivariate probit models for binary sequences. We also considered distinctions between serial correlation and state dependence, and argued that it is difficult to make a useful distinction just on the basis of the multinomial distribution of the binary sequence. A more important point is that the extent of serial correlation depends on the sampling interval between observations. Surely there is serial correlation in continuous time.

So a more fruitful starting point is to ask whether the individual's previous history is informative given the current state. Departures from this Markov property constitute duration dependence. It is possible to test for duration dependence using binary sequences generated by various sampling schemes. We expect to see serial correlation in the binary sequences, even after controlling for heterogeneity; only certain forms of serial correlation indicate duration dependence.

This question can be addressed more directly if we have the underlying data on durations in the states. We have developed models for measuring duration dependence and the effects of observed explanatory variables. The emphasis has been on eliminating omitted variable bias due to unmeasured heterogeneity. Unlike the linear case, the different techniques for dealing with incidental parameters do lead to different estimators.

The advantage of "fixed effects" techniques based on conditional or marginal likelihood functions is that they do not require specific parametric assumptions about the conditional distribution of heterogeneity given the explanatory variables. There is, of course, an efficiency loss if there is a parametric family of distributions that can confidently be imposed. A disadvantage of the fixed effects approaches is that they are only available for certain distributions. The random effects approach can always be used. We have seen, however, that there is considerable latitude in specifying how the heterogeneity distribution should be allowed to depend on the explanatory variables (and on the initial conditions). A sensitivity analysis over a variety of specifications is called for. In all of our approaches, strict exogeneity in the mixture model is necessary in order for the estimators to be consistent as the number of individuals increases.

ACKNOWLEDGMENT

This chapter originally appeared as Harvard Institute of Economic Research Discussion Paper Number 691, March 1979. The material in the first two sections has been extended, with empirical applications, in my paper "Panel Data" forthcoming in the *Handbook of Econometrics* edited by Z. Griliches and M. Intriligator. Financial support was provided by the National Science Foundation.

NOTES

1 See Sims (1972, 1977).

2 A more sophisticated version of this example is the following: $y_t = \beta x_t^* + \varepsilon_t$, where y_t is the firm's output and x_t^* is expected price, based on information available in period $t-1$: $x_t^* = E(P_t|B_{t-1})$. Using actual price would result in an errors-in-variables bias: $y_t = \beta P_t + [\varepsilon_t - \beta(P_t - x_t^*)]$; but following Muth (1962), we note that if $\mathbf{z}_{t-1}$ is a set of variables known in period $t-1$ (i.e., $\mathbf{z}_{t-1} \in B_{t-1}$), then $E(P_t - x_t^*|\mathbf{z}_{t-1}) = 0$. Hence $\mathbf{z}_{t-1}$ can be used to form an instrumental variable for P_t, provided that $\text{cov}(\varepsilon_t, \mathbf{z}_{t-1}) = 0$. So we can obtain a consistent estimator of the supply elasticity (as $T \to \infty$), even though we have only an incomplete specification of the firm's information set; for example, we can set $\mathbf{z}_{t-1} = P_{t-1}$. Then a two-stage least squares procedure corresponds to forming $x_t = E(P_t|\mathbf{z}_{t-1})$ and setting $y_t = \beta x_t + [\varepsilon_t + \beta(x_t^* - x_t)]$. Since the second-stage regression of y_t on x_t gives a consistent estimator of β, it must be that $\text{cov}(x_t, x_t^* - x_t) = 0$. This follows from $E(x_t^*|x_t) = E[E(P_t|B_{t-1})|x_t] = E(P_t|x_t) = x_t$ (Shiller, 1972).

Our expectation proxy (x) is not strictly exogenous if $x \neq x^*$, since $E(x_t^*|x_t, x_{t+1}) \neq x_t$ (Sims, 1974). Nevertheless, there can be serial correlation in ε without affecting the consistency of least squares. If $\mathbf{z}$ does not include enough lagged prices, then $x^* - x$ will be serially correlated, again without affecting the consistency of least squares. So even though x is only predetermined, we can allow the residuals to be serially correlated; the failure of strict exogeneity does not imply that a fully recursive model is necessary to justify least squares estimation of behavioral parameters.

3 This example is discussed in Mundlak (1961, 1963).

4 See Kiefer and Wolfowitz (1956). The posterior likelihood terminology is used by Cox and Hinkley (1974, p. 401). Kalbfleisch and Sprott (1970) refer to this as an integrated likelihood function.

5 See Neyman and Scott (1948).

6 We clearly cannot allow an arbitrary covariance between $\mathbf{x}_t$ and ε_s, $t \neq s$. There are special cases, however, which appear to be uninteresting. For example, with $T = 2$, it is sufficient that $\text{cov}(\mathbf{x}_2, \varepsilon_1) = -\text{cov}(\mathbf{x}_1, \varepsilon_2)$ if we assume that $\text{cov}(\mathbf{x}_1, \varepsilon_1) = \text{cov}(\mathbf{x}_2, \varepsilon_2) = 0$.

7 The use of conditional likelihood functions for incidental parameter problems is discussed in Andersen (1970, 1973), Kalbfleisch and Sprott (1970), and Barndorff-Nielsen (1978).

8 The use of marginal likelihood functions for incidental parameters is discussed in Kalbfleisch and Sprott (1970) and Barndorff-Nielsen (1978).
9 This result is discussed in Mundlak (1978).
10 This approach has been pursued in the recent work of Heckman (1978a, b). For an application of the multivariate probit model in a different context, see Hausman and Wise (1978).
11 See Heckman (1978b).
12 This point has arisen in previous work on distinguishing between serial correlation and partial adjustment; see Griliches (1967).
13 Spilerman (1972), Bartholomew (1973), Singer and Spilerman (1974, 1976), and Tuma, Hannan, and Groeneveld (1979) work with continuous time models for discrete data.
14 A conditional likelihood analysis of autoregressive logistic models is presented in Cox (1958); there the emphasis is on eliminating nuisance parameters in order to obtain a test statistic that depends on a single unknown parameter.
15 See Heckman and Willis (1977) and Heckman (1978b).
16 Some of the commonly used distributions and their hazard functions are discussed in Cox (1962).
17 The conditional logit model is developed in McFadden (1974).
18 See Watson and Wells (1961) and Barlow, Marshall, and Proschan (1963).
19 See Feller (1971, p. 370).
20 See Feller (1971, pp. 370, 371).
21 This generalizes the conditional likelihood analysis of the inhomogeneous Poisson model presented in Cox and Lewis (1966, p. 45) and Cox (1972b). There it is only necessary to condition on *n*.
22 The gamma distribution has been used to model heterogeneity by Spilerman (1972) and Singer and Spilerman (1974, 1976).

REFERENCES

Andersen, E. B. (1970). "Asymptotic Properties of Conditional Maximum Likelihood Estimators." *Journal of the Royal Statistical Society*, Series B, 32:283–301.

(1973). *Conditional Inference and Models for Measuring*. Copenhagen: Mentalhygiejnisk Forlag.

Barlow, R. E., A. W. Marshall, and F. Proschan (1963). "Properties of Probability Distributions with Monotone Hazard Rate." *Annals of Mathematical Statistics*, 34:375–89.

Barndorff-Nielsen, O. (1978). *Information and Exponential Families in Statistical Theory*. New York: Wiley.

Bartholomew, D. J. (1973). *Stochastic Models for Social Processes*. New York: Wiley.

Cox, D. R. (1958). "The Regression Analysis of Binary Sequences." *Journal of the Royal Statistical Society*, Series B, 20:215–32.

(1962). *Renewal Theory*. London: Methuen.

(1972a). "Regression Models and Life Tables." *Journal of the Royal Statistical Society*, Series B, 34:187–202.

(1972b). "The Statistical Analysis of Dependencies in Point Processes." In *Stochastic Point Processes: Statistical Analysis, Theory, and Applications*, edited by P. A. W. Lewis, pp. 56–66. New York: Wiley.

(1975). "Partial Likelihood." *Biometrika*, 62:269–76.

Cox, D. R., and D. V. Hinkley (1974). *Theoretical Statistics.* London: Chapman and Hall.
Cox, D. R., and P. A. W. Lewis (1966). *The Statistical Analysis of Series of Events.* London: Methuen.
Feller, W. (1971). *An Introduction to Probability Theory and Its Applications,* Vol. II. New York: Wiley.
Griliches, Z. (1967). "Distributed Lags: A Survey." *Econometrica,* 35:16–49.
Hausman, J. A., and D. A. Wise (1978). "A Conditional Probit Model for Qualitative Choice: Discrete Decisions Recognizing Interdependence and Heterogeneous Preferences." *Econometrica,* 46:403–26.
Heckman, J. J. (1978a). "Dummy Endogenous Variables in a Simultaneous Equation System." *Econometrica,* 46:931–59.
(1978b). "Simple Statistical Models for Discrete Panel Data Developed and Applied to Test the Hypothesis of True State Dependence against the Hypothesis of Spurious State Dependence." *Annales de l'INSEE,* 30–31:227–69.
Heckman, J. J., and R. J. Willis (1977). "A Beta-Logistic Model for the Analysis of Sequential Labor Force Participation by Married Women." *Journal of Political Economy,* 85:27–58.
Kalbfleisch, J. D., and D. A. Sprott (1970). "Application of Likelihood Methods to Models Involving Large Numbers of Parameters." *Journal of the Royal Statistical Society,* Series B, 32:175–208.
Kiefer, J., and J. Wolfowitz (1956). "Consistency of the Maximum Likelihood Estimator in the Presence of Infinitely Many Incidental Parameters." *Annals of Mathematical Statistics,* 27:887–906.
McFadden, D. (1974). "Conditional Logit Analysis of Qualitative Choice Behavior." In *Frontiers in Econometrics,* edited by P. Zarembka, pp. 105–42. New York: Academic Press.
Mundlak, Y. (1961). "Empirical Production Function Free of Management Bias." *Journal of Farm Economics,* 43:44–56.
(1963). "Estimation of Production and Behavioral Functions from a Combination of Cross-Section and Time-Series Data." In *Measurement in Economics,* edited by C. Christ et al. Stanford, Calif.: Stanford University Press.
(1978). "On the Pooling of Time Series and Cross-Section Data." *Econometrica,* 46:69–85.
Muth, J. F. (1962). "Distributed Leads" (abstract). *Econometrica,* 30:585.
Neyman, J., and E. L. Scott (1948). "Consistent Estimates Based on Partially Consistent Observations." *Econometrica,* 16:1–32.
Shiller, R. (1972). "Rational Expectations and the Structure of Interest Rates." Ph.D. dissertation, Dept. of Economics, Massachusetts Institute of Technology.
Sims, C. A. (1972). "Money, Income, and Causality." *American Economic Review,* 62:540–52.
(1974). "Distributed Lags." In *Frontiers of Quantitative Economics,* Vol. II, edited by M. D. Intriligator and D. A. Kendrick, pp. 289–332. Amsterdam: North-Holland.
(1977). "Exogeneity and Causal Ordering in Macroeconomic Models." In *New Methods in Business Cycle Research,* edited by C. A. Sims, pp. 23–43. Minneapolis: Federal Reserve Bank.
Singer, B., and S. Spilerman (1974). "Social Mobility Models for Heterogeneous Populations." In *Sociological Methodology 1973–1974,* edited by H. L. Costner, pp. 356–401. San Francisco: Jossey-Bass.

(1976). "Some Methodological Issues in the Analysis of Longitudinal Surveys." *Annals of Economic and Social Measurement*, 5:447–74.

Spilerman, S. (1972). "Extensions of the Mover Stayer Model." *American Journal of Sociology*, 78:599–627.

Tuma, N. B., M. T. Hannan, and L. P. Groeneveld (1979). "Dynamic Analysis of Event Histories." *American Journal of Sociology*, 84:820–54.

Watson, G. S., and W. T., Wells (1961). "On the Possibility of Improving the Mean Useful Life of Items by Eliminating Those with Short Lives." *Technometrics*, 3:281–98.

CHAPTER 2

Social science duration analysis

James J. Heckman and Burton Singer

Introduction

In analyzing discrete choices made over time, two arguments favor the use of continuous time models: (1) In most economic models there is no natural time unit within which agents make their decisions and take their actions. Often it is more natural and analytically convenient to characterize the agent's decision and action processes as operating in continuous time. (2) Even if there were natural decision periods, there is no reason to suspect that they correspond to the annual or quarterly data that are typically available to empirical analysts, or that the discrete periods are synchronized across individuals. Inference about an underlying stochastic process that is based on interval or point sampled data may be very misleading, especially if one falsely assumes that the process being investigated operates in discrete time. Conventional discrete choice models such as logit and probit when defined for one time interval are of a different functional form when applied to another time unit, if they are defined at all. Continuous time models are invariant to the time unit used to record the available data. A common set of parameters can be used to generate probabilities of events occurring in intervals of different length. For these reasons the use of continuous time duration models is becoming widespread in economics.

This chapter considers the formulation and estimation of continuous time econometric duration models. Research on this topic is relatively new, and much of the available literature has borrowed freely and often uncritically from reliability theory and biostatistics. As a result, most papers in econometric duration analysis present statistical models only loosely motivated by economic theory and assume access to experimental data that are ideal in comparison to the data actually available to social scientists.

This chapter is in two parts. Part I – which is by far the largest – considers single-spell duration models which are the building blocks for the more elaborate multiple-spell models considered in Part II. Many issues that arise in multiple-spell models are more easily discussed in a single-spell setting, and in fact many of the available duration data sets only record single spells.

Our discussion of single-spell duration models is in six sections. In Section 1 we present some useful definitions and statistical concepts. In Section 2 we present a short catalog of continuous time duration models that arise from choice theoretic economic models. In Section 3 we consider conventional methods for introducing observed and unobserved variables into reduced form versions of duration models. We discuss the sensitivity of estimates obtained from single-spell duration models to inherently ad hoc methods for controlling for observed and unobserved variables.

The extreme sensitivity to ad hoc parameterizations of duration models that is exhibited in this section leads us to ask the question "What features of duration models can be identified nonparametrically?" Our answer is the topic of Section 4. There we present nonparametric procedures for assessing qualitative features of conditional duration distributions in the presence of observed and unobserved variables. We discuss nonparametric identification criteria for a class of duration models (proportional hazard models) and discuss tradeoffs among criteria required to secure nonparametric identification. We also discuss these questions for a more general class of duration models. The final topic considered in this section is nonparametric estimation of duration models.

In Section 5 we discuss the neglected problem of initial conditions. There are few duration data sets for which the beginning of the sample observation period coincides with the start of a spell. More commonly, the available data for single-spell models consist of interrupted spells or portions of spells observed after the sample observation period begins. The problem raised by this sort of sampling frame and its solution are well known for duration models with no unobservables in time-homogeneous environments. We present these solutions and then discuss this problem for the more difficult but empirically relevant case of models with unobservable variables in time-inhomogeneous environments. In Section 6 we return to the structural duration models discussed in Section 2 and consider new econometric issues that arise in attempting to recover explicit economic parameters.

Part II on multiple spells is divided into two sections. The first (Section 7) presents a general framework that contains many interesting multiple-spell models as a special case. The second (Section 8) presents a multiple-spell event history model and considers conditions under which access to multiple-spell data aids in securing model identification. The chapter concludes with a brief summary.

I Single-spell models

1 Statistical preliminaries

There are now a variety of excellent textbooks on duration analysis that discuss the formulation of duration models, and so a lengthy introduction to standard survival models is unnecessary.[1] In an effort to make this chapter self-contained, however, this section sets out the essential ideas that we need from this literature in the rest of the chapter.

A nonnegative random variable T with absolutely continuous distribution function $G(t)$ and density $g(t)$ may be uniquely characterized by its hazard function. The hazard for T is the conditional density of T given $T > t \geq 0$; that is,

$$h(t) = f(t \mid T > t) = \frac{g(t)}{1 - G(t)} \geq 0 \tag{1.1}$$

Knowledge of G determines h.

Conversely, knowledge of h determines G because, by integration of (1.1),

$$\int_0^t h(u)\,du = -\ln[1 - G(x)]\Big|_0^t + c$$

$$G(t) = 1 - \exp\left[-\int_0^t h(u)\,du\right] \tag{1.2}$$

and $c = 0$ since $G(0) = 0$. The density of T is

$$g(t) = h(t)\exp\left[-\int_0^t h(u)\,du\right] \tag{1.3}$$

For the rest of this chapter we assume that the distribution of T is absolutely continuous, and we associate T with spell duration.[2] In this case it is also natural to interpret $h(t)$ as an *exit rate* or *escape rate* from the state because it is the limit (as $\Delta \to 0$) of the probability that a spell terminates in interval $(t, t + \Delta)$ given that the spell has lasted t periods; that is,

$$\begin{aligned} h(t) &= \lim_{\Delta \to 0} \Pr(t < T < t + \Delta \mid T > t)/\Delta \\ &= \lim_{\Delta \to 0} \left[\frac{G(t + \Delta) - G(t)}{\Delta}\right] \frac{1}{1 - G(t)} \\ &= \frac{g(t)}{1 - G(t)} \end{aligned} \tag{1.4}$$

Equation (1.4) constitutes an alternative definition of the hazard that links the models discussed in Part I to the more general multistate models discussed in Part II.

The survivor function is the probability that a duration exceeds t. Thus

$$S(t) = \Pr(T > t) = 1 - G(t) = \exp\left[-\int_0^t h(u)\,du\right] \tag{1.5}$$

In terms of the survivor function we may write the density $g(t)$ as

$$g(t) = h(t)S(t)$$

Note that there is no requirement that

$$\lim_{t\to\infty} \int_0^t h(u)\,du \to \infty \tag{1.6}$$

or equivalently that

$$S(\infty) = 0$$

If (1.6) is satisfied, the duration distribution is termed *nondefective*. Otherwise, it is termed *defective*.

The technical language here creates the possibility of confusion. There is nothing wrong with defective distributions. In fact, they emerge naturally from many optimizing models. For example, Jovanovic (1979) derives an infinite horizon worker–firm matching model with a defective job tenure distribution. Condition (1.6) is violated in his model, and so $S(\infty) > 0$ because some proportion of workers find that their current match is so successful that they never wish to leave their jobs.

Duration dependence is said to exist if

$$\frac{dh(t)}{dt} \neq 0$$

The only density with no duration dependence almost everywhere is the exponential distribution. For in this case $h(t) \equiv h$, a constant, and hence from (1.2) T is an exponential random variable. Obviously, if G is exponential, $h(t) \equiv h$.

If $dh(t)/dt > 0$, at $t = t_0$, there is said to be *positive duration dependence at* t_0. If $dh(t)/dt < 0$, at $t = t_0$, there is said to be *negative duration dependence* at t_0. In job search models of unemployment, positive duration dependence arises in the case of a "declining reservation wage" (see, e.g., Lippman and McCall, 1976). In this case the exit rate from unemployment is monotonically increasing in t. In job turnover models negative duration dependence (at least asymptotically) is associated with worker–firm matching models (see, e.g., Jovanovic, 1979).

For many econometric duration models it is natural to analyze conditional duration distributions where the conditioning is with respect to observed $\mathbf{x}(t)$ and unobserved $\boldsymbol{\theta}(t)$ variables. Indeed, by analogy with conventional regression analysis, much of the attention in many duration analyses focuses on the effect of regressors $\mathbf{x}(t)$ on durations.

We define the conditional hazard as

$$h(t\,|\,\mathbf{x}(t), \boldsymbol{\theta}(t)) = \lim_{\Delta \to 0} \frac{\Pr[t < T < t + \Delta\,|\,T > t, \mathbf{x}(t), \boldsymbol{\theta}(t)]}{\Delta} \tag{1.7}$$

The dating on regressor vector $\mathbf{x}(t)$ is an innocuous convention. Variable $\mathbf{x}(t)$ may include functions of the entire past or future or the entire paths of some variables; for example,

$$x_1(t) = \int_t^{\infty} k_1(z_1(u))\,du$$

$$x_2(t) = \int_{-\infty}^{t} k_2(z_2(u))\,du$$

$$x_3(t) = \int_{-\infty}^{\infty} k_3(z_3(u), t)\,du$$

where the $z_i(u)$ are underlying time-dated regressor variables.

We make the following assumptions about these conditioning variables:

(A.1) $\boldsymbol{\theta}(t)$ is distributed independently of $x(t')$ for all t, t'. The distribution of $\boldsymbol{\theta}$ is $\mu(\boldsymbol{\theta})$. The distribution of $\mathbf{x}$ is $D(\mathbf{x})$.

(A.2) There are no functional restrictions connecting the conditional distribution of T given $\boldsymbol{\theta}$ and $\mathbf{x}$ and the marginal distributions of $\boldsymbol{\theta}$ and $\mathbf{x}$.

Speaking very loosely, $\mathbf{x}$ is assumed to be "weakly exogenous" with respect to the duration process. More precisely, $\mathbf{x}$ is ancillary for T.[3]

By analogy with the definitions presented for the raw duration models, we may integrate (1.7) to produce the conditional duration distribution

$$G(t\,|\,\boldsymbol{\theta}, \mathbf{x}) = 1 - \exp\left[-\int_0^t h(u\,|\,\mathbf{x}(u), \boldsymbol{\theta}(u))\,du\right] \tag{1.8}$$

the conditional survivor function

$$S(t\,|\,\boldsymbol{\theta}, \mathbf{x}) = P(T > t\,|\,\boldsymbol{\theta}, \mathbf{x})$$

$$= \exp\left[-\int_0^t h(u\,|\,\mathbf{x}(u), \boldsymbol{\theta}(u))\,du\right] \tag{1.9}$$

and the conditional density

$$g(t\,|\,\boldsymbol{\theta}, \mathbf{x}) = h(t\,|\,\mathbf{x}(t), \boldsymbol{\theta}(t))S(t\,|\,\boldsymbol{\theta}, \mathbf{x}) \tag{1.10}$$

One specification of conditional hazard (1.7) that has received much attention in the literature is the *proportional hazard specification* (see Cox, 1972)

$$h(t\,|\,\mathbf{x}(t), \boldsymbol{\theta}(t)) = \psi(t)\phi(\mathbf{x}(t))\eta(\boldsymbol{\theta}(t)) \tag{1.11}$$

which postulates that the log of the conditional hazard is linear in functions of t, $\mathbf{x}$ and $\boldsymbol{\theta}$ and that

$$\psi(t) \geq 0, \qquad \eta(\boldsymbol{\theta}(t)) > 0, \qquad \phi(\mathbf{x}(t)) \geq 0 \quad \text{for all} \quad t$$

We assume that η is continuous and monotone increasing in $\boldsymbol{\theta}$. There is no duration dependence if $\psi(t)$ is constant for all t.

2 Examples of duration models produced by economic theory

In this section of the chapter, we present three examples of duration models produced by economic choice models. These examples are (A) a continuous time model of labor supply, (B) a continuous time search unemployment model, and (C) a continuous time consumer purchase model that generalizes conventional discrete choice models in a straightforward way.

Examples A and B contain most of the essential ideas. We demonstrate how a continuous time formulation avoids the need to specify arbitrary decision periods as is required in conventional discrete time models (see, e.g., Heckman, 1981a). We also discuss a certain identification problem that arises in single-spell models that is "solved" by assumption in conventional discrete time formulations.

2.1 *Example A: a dynamic model of labor force participation*

The one-period version of this model is the workhorse of labor economics. Consumers at age a are assumed to possess a concave twice-differentiable one-period utility function defined over goods $X(a)$ and leisure $L(a)$. Denote this utility function by $U(X(a), L(a))$. Define leisure hours so that $0 \leq L(a) \leq 1$. The consumer is free to choose his hours of work at parametric wage $W(a)$. There are no fixed costs of work, and for convenience taxes are ignored. At each age the consumer receives unearned income $Y(a)$. There is no saving or borrowing. Decisions are assumed to be made under perfect certainty.

The consumer works at age a if the marginal rate of substitution between goods and leisure evaluated at the no-work position (also known as the nonmarket wage)

$$M(Y(a)) = \frac{U_2(Y(a), 1)}{U_1(Y(a), 1)} \tag{2.1}$$

is less than the market wage $W(a)$. For if this is so, his utility is higher in the market than at home. The subscripts on U denote partial derivatives with respect to the appropriate argument. It is convenient to define an index function $I(a)$ written as

$$I(a) = W(a) - M(Y(a))$$

If $I(a) \geq 0$, the consumer works at age a, and we record this event by setting $d(a) = 1$. If $I(a) < 0$, $d(a) = 0$.

In a discrete time model, a spell of employment begins at a_1 and ends at $a_2 + 1$ provided that $I(a_1 - 1) < 0$, $I(a_1 + j) \geq 0$, $j = 0, \ldots, a_2 - a_1$, $I(a_2 + 1) < 0$. Reversing the direction of the inequalities generates a characterization of a nonwork spell that begins at a_1 and ends at a_2.

To complete the econometric specification, error term $\varepsilon(a)$ is introduced. Under an assumption of perfect certainty, the error term arises from variables observed by the consumer but not observed by the econometrician. In the current context, $\varepsilon(a)$ can be interpreted as a shifter of household technology and tastes. For each person successive values of $\varepsilon(a)$ may be correlated, but it is assumed that $\varepsilon(a)$ is independent of $Y(a)$ and $W(a)$. We define the index function inclusive of $\varepsilon(a)$ as

$$I^*(a) = W(a) - M(Y(a)) + \varepsilon(a) \tag{2.2}$$

If $I^*(a) \geq 0$, the consumer works at age a.

The distribution of $I^*(a)$ induces a distribution on employment spells. To demonstrate this point in a simple way we assume that (i) the $\varepsilon(a)$ are serially independent, (ii) the environment is time-homogeneous and so $W(a)$ and $Y(a)$ remain constant over time for the individual, (iii) the probability that a new value of ε is received in an interval is P, and (iv) that the arrival times of new values of $\varepsilon(a)$ are independent of W, Y, and other arrival times. We denote the cumulative distribution function (cdf) of ε by F. By virtue of the perfect certainty assumption, the individual knows when new values of ε will arrive and what they will be. The econometrician, however, does not have this information at his disposal. He never directly observes $\varepsilon(a)$ and only knows that a new value of nonmarket time has arrived if the consumer actually changes state.

The probability that an employed person does not leave the employed state is

$$1 - F(\psi) \tag{2.3}$$

where $\psi = M(Y) - W$. The probability of receiving j new values of ε in interval t_e is

$$P_j = \binom{t_e}{j} P^j(1 - P)^{t_e - j}$$

The probability that a spell is longer than t_e is the sum over j of the products of the probability of receiving j innovations in $t_e(P_j)$ and the probability that the person does not leave the employed state on each of the j occasions $[1 - F(\psi)]^j$. Thus

$$\begin{aligned} P(T_e > t_e) &= \sum_{j=0}^{t_e} \binom{t_e}{j} P^j(1 - P)^{t_e - j}[1 - F(\psi)]^j \\ &= [1 - P(F(\psi))]^{t_e} \end{aligned} \tag{2.4}$$

Thus the probability that an employment spell terminates *at* t_e is

$$\begin{aligned} P(T_e = t_e) &= P(T_e > t_e - 1) - P(T_e > t_e) \\ &= [1 - P(F(\psi))]^{t_e - 1}[P(F(\psi))] \end{aligned} \tag{2.5}$$

By similar reasoning it can be shown that the probability that a nonemployment spell terminates in t_n periods is

$$P(T_n = t_n) = [(1 - P(1 - F(\psi))]^{t_n - 1} P(1 - F(\psi)) \tag{2.6}$$

In conventional models of discrete choice over time (see, e.g., Heckman, 1981a) P is implicitly set to 1. Thus in these models it is assumed that the consumer receives a new draw of ε each period. The model just presented generalizes these models to allow for the possibility that ε may remain constant over several periods of time. Such a generalization creates an identification problem because from a single-employment or nonemployment spell it is only possible to estimate $PF(\psi)$ or $P(1 - F(\psi))$, respectively. This implies that any single-spell model of the duration of employment or unemployment is consistent with the model of equation (2.2) with $P = 1$ or with another model in which (2.2) does not characterize behavior but in which the economic variables determine the arrival time of new values of ε. However, access to both employment and nonemployment spells solves this problem because $P = PF(\psi) + P(1 - F(\psi))$, and hence $F(\psi)$ and P are separately identified.

The preceding model assumes that there are natural periods of time within which innovations in ε may occur. For certain organized markets there may be well-defined trading intervals, but for the consumer's problem considered here no such natural time periods exist. This suggests the following continuous time reformulation.

In place of the Bernoulli assumption for the arrival of fresh values of ε, suppose instead that a Poisson process governs the arrival of shocks. As is well known (see, e.g., Feller, 1970) the Poisson distribution is the limit of a Bernoulli trial process in which the probability of success in each interval $\eta = \Delta/n$, P_η, goes to zero in such a way that $\lim_{n\to 0} nP_\eta \to \lambda \neq 0$. Thus in the reformulated continuous time model it is assumed that an infinitely large number of very-low-probability Bernoulli trials occur within a specified interval of time.

For a time-homogeneous environment the probability of receiving j offers in time period t_e is

$$P(j|t_e) = \exp(-\lambda t_e)\frac{(\lambda t_e)^j}{j!} \tag{2.7}$$

Thus for the continuous time model the probability that a person who begins employment at $a = a_1$ will stay in the employment state at least t_e periods is, by reasoning analogous to that used to derive (2.6),

$$\begin{aligned}\Pr(T_e > t_e) &= \sum_{j=0}^{\infty} \exp(-\lambda t_e)\frac{(\lambda t_e)^j}{j!}[1 - F(\psi)]^j \\ &= \exp[-\lambda F(\psi)t_e] \end{aligned} \tag{2.8}$$

so the density of spell lengths is

$$g(t_e) = \lambda F(\psi)\exp[-\lambda F(\psi)t_e]$$

A more direct way to derive (2.8) notes that from the definition of a Poisson process, the probability of receiving a new value of ε in interval $(a, a + \Delta)$ is

$$p = \lambda\Delta + o(\Delta)$$

where $\lim_{\Delta\to 0}[o(\Delta)/\Delta] \to 0$, and the probability of exiting the employment state conditional on an arrival of ε is $F(\psi)$. Hence the exit rate or hazard rate from the employment state is

$$\begin{aligned} h_e &= \lim_{\Delta\to 0}\frac{\lambda\Delta F(\psi)}{\Delta} + o(\Delta) \\ &= \lambda F(\psi) \end{aligned}$$

Using (1.4) relating the hazard function and the survivor function, we conclude that

$$\Pr(T_e > t_e) = \exp\left[-\int_0^{t_e} h_e(u)\,du\right] = \exp[-\lambda F(\psi)t_e]$$

By similar reasoning, the probability that a person starting in the nonemployed state will stay on in that state for at least duration t_n is

$$\Pr(T_n > t_n | \lambda) = \exp[-\lambda(1 - F(\psi))t_n]$$

Analogous to the identification result already presented for the discrete time model, it is impossible using single-spell employment or nonemployment data to separate λ from $F(\psi)$ or $1 - F(\psi)$, respectively. However, access to data on both employment and nonemployment spells makes it possible to identify both λ and $F(\psi)$.

The assumption of time homogeneity of the environment is made only to simplify the argument. Suppose that nonmarket time arrives via a nonhomogeneous Poisson process so that the probability of receiving one nonmarket draw in interval $(a, a + \Delta)$ is

$$p(a) = \lambda(a)\Delta + o(\Delta) \tag{2.9}$$

Assuming that W and Y remain constant, the hazard rate for exit from employment at time period a for a spell that begins at a_1 is

$$h_e(a | a_1) = \lambda(a)F(\psi) \tag{2.10}$$

so that the survivor function for the spell is[4]

$$P(T_e > t_e | a_1) = \exp\left[-F(\psi)\int_{a_1}^{a_1+t_e} \lambda(u)\, du\right] \tag{2.11}$$

By similar reasoning,

$$P(T_n > t_n | a_1) = \exp\left[-(1 - F(\psi))\int_{a_1}^{a_1+t_n} \lambda(u)\, du\right]$$

2.2 *Example B: a one-state model of search unemployment*

The one-state model of search unemployment is well exposited in Lippman and McCall (1976). The environment is assumed to be time-homogeneous. Agents are assumed to be income maximizers. If an instantaneous cost c is incurred, job offers arrive from a Poisson process with parameter λ independent of the level of c (>0). The probability of receiving a wage offer in time interval Δt is $\lambda\,\Delta t + o(\Delta t)$.[5] Thus the probability of two or more job offers in interval Δt is negligible.[6]

Successive wage offers are independent realizations from a known absolutely continuous wage distribution $F(w)$ with finite mean that is assumed to be common to all agents. Once refused, wage offers are no longer available. Jobs last forever, there is no on-the-job search, and workers live forever. The instantaneous rate of interest is $r\,(>0)$.

Define V as the value of search. Using Bellman's optimality principle for dynamic programming (see, e.g., Ross, 1970), V may be decomposed into three components plus a negligible component [of order $o(\Delta t)$]:

$$V = -\frac{c\Delta t}{1 + r\,\Delta t} + \frac{(1 - \lambda\,\Delta t)}{1 + r\,\Delta t} V + \frac{\lambda\,\Delta t}{1 + r\,\Delta t} E \max\left[\frac{w}{r}; V\right] + o(\Delta t) \quad \text{for} \quad V > 0$$
$$= 0 \qquad \text{otherwise} \tag{2.12}$$

The first term on the right of (2.12) is the discounted cost of search in interval Δt. The second term is the probability of not receiving an offer, $(1 - \lambda\,\Delta t)$, times the discounted value of search at the end of interval Δt. The third term is the probability of receiving a wage offer $(\lambda\,\Delta t)$ times the discounted value of the expectation [computed with respect to $F(w)$] of the maximum of the two options confronting the agent who receives a wage offer: to take the offer (with present value w/r) or to continue searching (with present value V). Note that equation (2.12) is defined only for $V > 0$. If $V = 0$, we may define the agent as out of the labor force (see Lippman and McCall, 1976). As a consequence of the time homogeneity of the environment, once out the agent is always out. Sufficient to ensure the existence of an optimal reservation wage policy in this model is $E(|W|) < \infty$ (Robbins, 1970).

Collecting terms in (2.12) and passing to the limit, we reach the familiar formula (Lippman and McCall, 1976)

$$c + rV = \frac{\lambda}{r} \int_{rV}^{\infty} (w - rV)\, dF(w) \quad \text{for} \quad V > 0, \tag{2.13}$$

where rV is the reservation wage, which is implicitly determined from (2.13). For any offered wage $w \geqq rV$, the agent accepts the offer. The probability that an offer is unacceptable is $F(rV)$.

To calculate the probability that an unemployment spell T_u exceeds t_u, we may proceed as in the preceding discussion of labor supply models and note that the probability of receiving an offer in time interval $(a, a + \Delta)$ is

$$p = \lambda\Delta + o(\Delta) \tag{2.14}$$

and further note that the probability that an offer is accepted is $1 - F(rV)$, and so

$$h_u = \lambda(1 - F(rV)) \tag{2.15}$$

and

$$P(T_u > t_u) = \exp[-\lambda(1 - F(rV))t_u] \tag{2.16}$$

For discussion of the economic content of this model, see, for example, Lippman and McCall (1976) or Flinn and Heckman (1982a).

Accepted wages are truncated random variables with rV as the lower point of truncation. The density of accepted wages is

$$g(w \mid w > rV) = \frac{f(w)}{1 - F(rV)}, \qquad w \geqq rV \tag{2.17}$$

Thus the one-spell search model has the same statistical structure for accepted wages as other models of self-selection in labor economics (Lewis, 1974; Heckman, 1974; and the references in Amemiya, 1984).

From the assumption that wages are distributed independently of wage arrival times, the joint density of duration times t_u and accepted wages (w) is the product of the density of each random variable,

$$\begin{aligned} m(t_u, w) &= \{\lambda(1 - F(rV)) \exp[-\lambda(1 - F(rV))t_u]\} \frac{f(w)}{1 - F(rV)} \\ &= \{\lambda \exp[-\lambda(1 - F(rV))t_u]\} f(w), \qquad w \geqq rV \end{aligned} \tag{2.18}$$

Time homogeneity of the environment is a strong assumption to invoke, especially for the analysis of data on unemployment spells. Even if the external environment were time-homogeneous, finiteness of life induces time inhomogeneity in the decision process of the agent. We present a model for a time-inhomogeneous environment.

For simplicity we assume that a reservation wage property characterizes the optimal policy, noting that for general time-inhomogeneous models it need not.[7] We denote the reservation wage at time τ as $rV(\tau)$.

The probability that an individual receives a wage offer in time period $(\tau, \tau + \Delta)$ is

$$p(\tau) = \lambda(\tau)\Delta + o(\Delta) \tag{2.19}$$

The probability that it is accepted is $1 - F(rV(\tau))$. Thus the hazard rate at time τ for exit from an unemployment spell is

$$h(\tau) = \lambda(\tau)(1 - F(rV(\tau)) \tag{2.20}$$

so that the probability that a spell that began at τ_1 lasts at least t_u is

$$P(T_u > t_u \mid \tau_1) = \exp\left[-\int_{\tau_1}^{\tau_1 + t_u} \lambda(z)(1 - F(rV(z)) \, dz \right] \tag{2.21}$$

The associated density is[8]

$$\begin{aligned} g(t_u \mid \tau_1) = {} & \lambda(\tau_1 + t_u)[1 - F(rV(\tau_1 + t_u))] \\ & \times \exp\left[-\int_{\tau_1}^{\tau_1 + t_u} \lambda(z)(1 - F(rV(z)) \, dz \right] \end{aligned}$$

2.3 *Example C: a dynamic McFadden model*

As in the marketing literature (see, e.g., Hauser and Wisniewski, 1982a,b; and its nonstationary extension in Singer, 1982), we imagine consumer choice as a sequential affair. An individual goes to a grocery store at randomly selected times. Let $\lambda(\tau)$ be the hazard function associated with the density generating the probability of the event that the consumer goes to the store at time τ. We assume that the probability of two or more visits to the store in interval Δ is $o(\Delta)$. Conditional on arrival at the store, he may purchase one of J items. Denote the purchase probability by $P_j(\tau)$. Choices made at different times are assumed to be independent, and they are also independent of arrival times. Then the probability that the consumer purchases good j at time τ is

$$h(j|\tau) = \lambda(\tau)P_j(\tau) \tag{2.22}$$

so that the probability that the next purchase is item j at a time $t = \tau + \tau_1$ or later is

$$P(t, j|\tau_1) = \exp\left[-\int_{\tau_1}^{\tau_1+t} \lambda(u)P_j(u)\,du\right] \tag{2.23}$$

The P_j may be specified using one of the many discrete choice models discussed in Amemiya's survey (1981). For the McFadden random utility model with Weibull errors (1974), the P_j are multinomial logit. For the Domencich–McFadden (1975) random coefficients preference model with normal coefficients the P_j are specified by multivariate probit.

In the dynamic McFadden model few new issues of estimation and specification arise that have not already been discussed above or in Amemiya (1984). For concreteness, we consider the most elementary version of this model.

Following McFadden (1974), the utility associated with each of J possible choices at time τ is written as

$$U_j(\tau) = V(s, \mathbf{x}_j(\tau)) + \varepsilon(s, \mathbf{x}_j(\tau)), \qquad j = 1, \ldots, J$$

where s denotes vectors of measured attributes of individuals, $\mathbf{x}_j(\tau)$ represents vectors of attributes of choices, V is a nonstochastic function and $\varepsilon(s, \mathbf{x}_j(\tau))$ are independent, identically distributed (i.i.d.) Weibull variables; that is,

$$P(\varepsilon(s, \mathbf{x}_j(\tau)) \le \phi) = \exp[-\exp(-\phi)]$$

Then as demonstrated by McFadden (p. 110),

$$P_j(s, \mathbf{x}_j(\tau)) = \frac{\exp[V(s, \mathbf{x}_j(\tau))]}{\sum_{l=1}^{J} \exp[V(s, \mathbf{x}_l(\tau))]}$$

Adopting a linear specification for V, we write

$$V(s, \mathbf{x}_j(\tau)) = \mathbf{x}_j'(\tau)\boldsymbol{\beta}(s)$$

so that

$$P_j(s, \mathbf{x}_j(\tau)) = \frac{\exp[\mathbf{x}_j'(\tau)\boldsymbol{\beta}(s)]}{\sum_{l=1}^{J} \exp[\mathbf{x}_l'(\tau)\boldsymbol{\beta}(s)]}$$

In a model without unobservable variables, the methods required to estimate this model are conventional.

The parameter $\boldsymbol{\beta}(s)$ can be estimated by standard logit analysis using data on purchases made at purchase times. The estimation of the times between visits to stores can be conducted using the conventional duration models described in Section 3. More general forms of Markovian dependence across successive purchases can be incorporated (see Singer, 1982, for further details).

3 Conventional reduced form models

The most direct approach to estimating the economic duration models presented in Section 2 is to specify functional forms for the economic parameters and their dependence on observed and unobserved variables. This approach is both costly and controversial. It is controversial because economic theory usually does not produce these functional forms – at best it specifies potential lists of regressor variables some portion of which may be unobserved in any data set. Moreover, in many areas of research, such as in the study of unemployment durations, there is no widespread agreement in the research community about the correct theory. The approach is costly because it requires nonlinear optimization of criterion functions that often can be determined only as implicit functions. We discuss this point further in Section 6.

Because of these considerations and because of a widespread belief that it is useful to get a "feel for the data" before more elaborate statistical models are fit, reduced form approaches are common in the duration analysis literature. Such an approach to the data is inherently ad hoc because the true functional form of the duration model is unknown. At issue is the robustness of the qualitative inferences obtained from these models with regard to alternative ad hoc specifications. In this section of the chapter we review conventional approaches and reveal their lack of robustness. Section 4 presents our response to this lack of robustness.

The problem of nonrobustness arises solely because regressors and unobservables are introduced into the duration model. If unobservables were ignored and the available data were sufficiently rich, it would be possible to estimate a duration model by a nonparametric Kaplan–Meier procedure (see, e.g., Lawless, 1982, or Kalbfleisch and Prentice, 1980). Such a general nonparametric approach is unlikely to prove successful in econometrics because (a) the available samples are small, especially after cross-classification by regressor variables, and (b) empirical modesty leads most analysts to admit that some determinants of any duration decision may be omitted from the data sets at their disposal.

Failure to control for unobserved components leads to a well-known bias toward negative duration dependence. This is the content of the following proposition:

Proposition 1. *Uncontrolled unobservables bias estimated hazards toward negative duration dependence.*

The proof is a straightforward application of the Cauchy–Schwartz theorem. Let $h(t \mid \mathbf{x}, \boldsymbol{\theta})$ be the hazard conditional on $\mathbf{x}$, $\boldsymbol{\theta}$ and $h(t \mid \mathbf{x})$ be the hazard conditional only on $\mathbf{x}$. These hazards are associated respectively with conditional distributions $G(t \mid \mathbf{x}, \boldsymbol{\theta})$ and $G(t \mid \mathbf{x})$.

From the definition,

$$h(t \mid \mathbf{x}) = \frac{\int_{\underline{\theta}} g(t \mid \mathbf{x}, \boldsymbol{\theta})\, d\mu(\boldsymbol{\theta})}{\int_{\underline{\theta}} [1 - G(t \mid \mathbf{x}, \boldsymbol{\theta})]\, d\mu(\boldsymbol{\theta})}$$

Thus[9]

$$\frac{\partial h(t \mid \mathbf{x})}{\partial t} = \frac{\int_{\underline{\theta}} [1 - G(t \mid \mathbf{x}, \boldsymbol{\theta})] \dfrac{\partial h(t \mid \mathbf{x}, \boldsymbol{\theta})}{\partial t}\, d\mu(\boldsymbol{\theta})}{\int_{\underline{\theta}} [1 - G(t \mid \mathbf{x}, \boldsymbol{\theta})]\, d\mu(\boldsymbol{\theta})}$$
$$+ \frac{\left[\int_{\underline{\theta}} g(t \mid \mathbf{x}, \boldsymbol{\theta})\, d\mu(\boldsymbol{\theta})\right]^2 - \int_{\underline{\theta}} \dfrac{g^2(t \mid \mathbf{x}, \boldsymbol{\theta})}{1 - G(t \mid \mathbf{x}, \boldsymbol{\theta})}\, d\mu(\boldsymbol{\theta}) \int_{\underline{\theta}} [1 - G(t \mid \mathbf{x}, \boldsymbol{\theta})]\, d\mu(\boldsymbol{\theta})}{\left[\int_{\underline{\theta}} [1 - G(t \mid \mathbf{x}, \boldsymbol{\theta})]\, d\mu(\boldsymbol{\theta})\right]^2} \tag{3.1}$$

The second term on the right-hand side is always nonpositive as a consequence of the Cauchy–Schwartz theorem. □

Intuitively, more mobility-prone persons are the first to leave the population leaving the less mobile behind and hence creating the illusion of stronger negative duration dependence than actually exists.

To ignore unobservables is to bias estimated hazard functions in a known direction. Ignoring observables has the same effect. So in response to the limited size of our samples and in recognition of the myriad of plausible explanatory variables that often do not appear in the available data, it is unwise to ignore observed or unobserved variables. The problem is how to control for these variables.

There are many possible conditional hazard functions (see, e.g., Lawless, 1982). One class of proportional hazard models that nests many previous models as a special case and therefore might be termed "flexible" is the Box–Cox conditional hazard

$$h(t|\mathbf{x}, \boldsymbol{\theta}) = \exp\left[\mathbf{x}'(t)\boldsymbol{\beta} + \left(\frac{t^{\lambda_1} - 1}{\lambda_1}\right)\gamma_1 + \left(\frac{t^{\lambda_2} - 1}{\lambda_2}\right)\gamma_2 + \boldsymbol{\theta}(t)\right] \tag{3.2}$$

where $\lambda_1 \neq \lambda_2$, $\mathbf{x}(t)$ is a $1 \times k$ vector of regressors and β is a $k \times 1$ vector of parameters, and $\boldsymbol{\theta}$ is assumed to be scalar. (See Flinn and Heckman, 1982b.) Exponentiating ensures that the hazard is nonnegative, as is required for a conditional density.

Setting $\gamma_2 = 0$ and $\lambda_1 = 0$ produces a Weibull hazard; setting $\gamma_2 = 0$ and $\lambda_1 = 1$ produces a Gompertz hazard. Setting $\gamma_1 = \gamma_2 = 0$ produces an exponential model. Conditions under which this model is identified for the case $\gamma_2 = 0$ are presented in Section 4.

The conventional approach to single-spell econometric duration analysis assumes a specific functional form known up to a finite set of parameters for the conditional hazard and a specific functional form known up to a finite set of parameters for the distribution of unobservables. Usually $\boldsymbol{\theta}(t)$ is assumed to be a time-invariant scalar random variable θ. An implicit assumption in most of this literature is that the origin date of the sample is also the start date of the spells being analyzed, so that initial conditions or left-censoring problems are ignored. We question this assumption in Section 5.

The conventional approach does, however, allow for right-censored spells assuming independent censoring mechanisms. We consider two such schemes.

Let $V(t)$ be the probability that a spell is censored at duration t or later. If

$$\begin{aligned} V(t) &= 0, \qquad t < L \\ V(t) &= 1, \qquad t \geq L \end{aligned} \tag{3.3}$$

there is censoring at fixed duration L. This type of censoring is common in many economic data sets. More generally, for continuous censoring times let $v(t)$ be the density associated with $V(t)$. In an independent censoring scheme, the censoring time is assumed to be independent of the survival time, and the censoring distribution is assumed to be functionally independent of the survival distribution and does not depend on θ.

Let $d = 1$ if a spell is not right-censored and $d = 0$ if it is. Let t denote an observed spell length. Then the joint frequency of (t, d) conditional on

x for the case of absolutely continuous distribution $V(t)$ is

$$f(t, d \mid \mathbf{x}) = v(t)^{1-d} \int_{\underline{\theta}} [h(t \mid \mathbf{x}(t), \theta) V(t)]^d S(t \mid \mathbf{x}(t), \theta)\, d\mu(\theta)$$

$$= \{v(t)^{1-d} V(t)^d\} \int_{\underline{\theta}} [h(t \mid \mathbf{x}(t), \theta)]^d S(t \mid \mathbf{x}(t), \theta)\, d\mu(\theta) \tag{3.4}$$

By the assumption of functional independence between $V(t)$ and $G(t \mid \mathbf{x})$, we may ignore the V and v functions in estimating $\mu(\theta)$ and $h(t \mid \mathbf{x}(t), \theta)$ via maximum likelihood.

For the Dirac censoring distribution (3.3), the density of observed durations is

$$f(t, d \mid \mathbf{x}) = \int_{\underline{\theta}} [h(t \mid \mathbf{x}(t), \theta)]^d S(t \mid \mathbf{x}(t), \theta)\, d\mu(\theta) \tag{3.5}$$

It is apparent from (3.4) or (3.5) that without further restrictions, a variety of $h(t \mid \mathbf{x}, \boldsymbol{\theta})$ and $\mu(\theta)$ pairs will be consistent with any $f(t, d \mid \mathbf{x})$.[10] Conditions under which a unique pair is determined are presented in Section 4. It is also apparent from (3.4) or (3.5) that given the functional form of either $h(t \mid \mathbf{x}, \theta)$ or $\mu(\theta)$ and the data $[f(t, d \mid \mathbf{x})]$ it is possible, at least in principle, to appeal to the theory of integral equations and solve for either $\mu(\theta)$ or $h(t \mid \mathbf{x}, \theta)$. Current practice thus *overparameterizes* the duration model by specifying the functional form of both $h(t \mid \mathbf{x}, \theta)$ and $\mu(\theta)$. In Section 4, we discuss methods for estimating $\mu(\theta)$ nonparametrically given that the functional form of $h(t \mid \mathbf{x}, \theta)$ is specified up to a finite number of parameters. In the rest of this section we demonstrate consequences of incorrectly specifying either $h(t \mid \mathbf{x}, \theta)$ or $\mu(\theta)$.

First consider the impact of incorrect treatment of time-varying regressor variables. Many conventional econometric duration analyses are cavalier about such variables because introducing them into the analysis raises computational problems. Except for special time paths of variables, the term

$$\int_0^t h(u \mid \mathbf{x}(u), \theta)\, du$$

which appears in survivor function (1.8) does not have a closed form expression. To evaluate it requires numerical integration.

To circumvent this difficulty, one of two expedients is often adopted (see, e.g., Lundberg, 1981; Cox and Lewis, 1966):

(i) Replacing time-trended variables with their within-spell average

$$\bar{\mathbf{x}}(t) = \frac{1}{t} \int_0^t \mathbf{x}(u)\, du, \qquad t > 0$$

(ii) Using beginning-of-spell values

$$\mathbf{x}(0)$$

Table 1. *Weibull model: employment-to-nonemployment transitions (absolute value of normal statistics in parentheses)*

	Regressors fixed at average value over the spell [expedient (i)]	Regressors fixed at value as of start of spell [expedient (ii)]	Regressors vary freely
Intercept	.971 (1.535)	−3.743 (12.074)	−3.078 (8.670)
ln Duration (γ_1)	−.137 (1.571)	−.230 (2.888)	−.341 (3.941)
Married with spouse present? (=1 if yes; =0 otherwise)	−1.093 (2.679)	−.921 (2.310)	−.610 (1.971)
National unemployment rate	−1.800 (6.286)	.569 (3.951)	.209 (1.194)

Source: Flinn and Heckman (1982b, p. 69).

Expedient (i) has the undesirable effect of building spurious dependence between duration time t and the manufactured regressor variable. To see this most clearly, suppose that $\mathbf{x}$ is a scalar and $\mathbf{x}(u) = a + bu$. Then clearly

$$\bar{x}(t) = a + \frac{b}{2}t$$

and t and $\bar{x}(t)$ are linearly dependent. Expedient (ii) ignores the time inhomogeneity in the environment.[11]

To illustrate the potential danger from adopting these expedients consider the numbers presented in Table 1. These record Weibull hazards [(3.2) with $\gamma_2 = 0$ and $\lambda_1 = 0$] estimated on data for employment-to-nonemployment transitions using the CTM program described by Hotz (1983). In these calculations, unobservables are ignored.

A job turnover model estimated using expedient (i) indicates weak negative duration dependence (column 1, row 2) and a strong *negative* effect of high national unemployment rates on the rate of exiting jobs. The same model estimated using expedient (ii) now indicates (see column 2) strong negative duration dependence and a strong *positive* effect of high national unemployment rates on the rate of exiting employment. Allowing regressors to vary freely reveals that the strong negative duration dependence effect remains, but now the effect of the national unemployment rate on exit rates from employment is weak and statistically insignificant.

These empirical results are typical. Introducing time-varying variables into single-spell duration models is inherently dangerous, and ad hoc methods for doing so can produce wildly misleading results. More basically, separating the effect of time-varying variables from duration depen-

Table 2. *Sensitivity to misspecification of the mixing distribution $\mu(\theta)$ (standard errors in parentheses)*

	Normal heterogeneity	Lognormal heterogeneity	Gamma heterogeneity
Intercept	−3.92	−13.2	5.90
	(2.8)	(4.7)	(3.4)
ln Duration (γ)	−.066	−.708	−.576
	(.15)	(.17)	(.17)
Age	.0036	−.106	−.202
	(.048)	(.03)	(.06)
Education	.0679	−.322	−.981
	(.233)	(.145)	(.301)
Tenure on previous job	−.0512	.00419	−.034
	(.0149)	(.023)	(.016)
Unemployment benefits	−.0172	.0061	−.003
	(.0036)	(.0051)	(.004)
Married (=1)	.833	.159	−.607
	(.362)	(.30)	(.496)
Unemployment rate	−26.12	25.8	−17.9
	(9.5)	(10.3)	(11.2)
Education × Age	−.00272	.00621	.0152
	(.0044)	(.034)	(.0053)

Note: Sample size is 456.
Source: Heckman and Singer (1982).

dence is only possible if there is "sufficient" independent variation in $\mathbf{x}(t)$. To see this, consider hazard (3.2) with $\gamma_2 = 0$ and $\mathbf{x}(t)$ scalar. Taking logs, we reach

$$\ln[h(t\,|\,x, \theta)] = x(t)\beta + \left(\frac{t^{\lambda_1} - 1}{\lambda_1}\right)\gamma_1 + \theta(t)$$

If

$$x(t) = \frac{t^{\lambda_1} - 1}{\lambda_1}$$

it is obviously impossible to separately estimate β and γ_1. There is a classical multicollinearity problem. For a single-spell model in a time-inhomogeneous environment with general specifications for duration dependence, the analyst is at the mercy of the data to avoid such linear dependence problems. Failure to control for time-varying regressor variables may mislead, but introducing such variables may create an identification problem.

Next we consider the consequence of misspecifying the distribution of unobservables. Table 2 records estimates of a Weibull duration model with three different specifications for $\mu(\theta)$, as indicated in the column headings. The estimates and inference vary greatly depending on the functional form selected for the mixing distribution. Trussell and Richards (1983) report similar results and exhibit similar sensitivity to the choice of the functional form of the conditional hazard $h(t|\mathbf{x},\theta)$ for a fixed $\mu(\theta)$.

4 Identification and estimation strategies

In our experience the rather vivid examples of the sensitivity of estimates of duration models to changes in specification presented in the previous section are the rule rather than the exception. This experience leads us to address the following three questions in this section:

1. What features, if any, of $h(t|\mathbf{x},\theta)$ and/or $\mu(\theta)$ can be identified from the "raw data," that is, $G(t|\mathbf{x})$?
2. Under what conditions are $h(t|\mathbf{x},\theta)$ and $\mu(\theta)$ identified? That is, how much a priori information has to be imposed on the model before these functions are identified?
3. What empirical strategies exist for estimating $h(t|\mathbf{x},\theta)$ and/or $\mu(\theta)$ nonparametrically, and what is their performance?

We assume a time-homogeneous environment throughout. Little is known about the procedure proposed below for general time-inhomogeneous environments.

4.1 *Nonparametric procedures to assess the structural hazard $h(t|\mathbf{x},\theta)$*

This subsection presents criteria that can be used to test the null hypothesis of no structural duration dependence and that can be used to assess the degree of model complexity that is required to adequately model the duration data at hand. The criteria to be set forth here can be viewed in two ways: as identification theorems and as empirical procedures to use with data.

We consider the following problem: $G(t|\mathbf{x})$ is estimated. We would like to infer properties of $G(t|\mathbf{x},\theta)$ without adopting any parametric specification for $\mu(\theta)$ or $h(t|\mathbf{x},\theta)$. We ignore any initial conditions problems. We further assume that $\mathbf{x}(t)$ is time-invariant.[12]

As a consequence of Proposition 1 proved in the preceding section, if $G(t|\mathbf{x})$ exhibits positive duration dependence for some intervals of t values, $h(t|\mathbf{x},\theta)$ must exhibit positive duration dependence for some interval of θ values in those intervals of t. As noted in Section 3, this is so because the effect of scalar heterogeneity is to make the observed conditional duration distribution exhibit more negative duration dependence (more precisely, never less negative duration dependence) than does the structural hazard $h(t|\mathbf{x}, \theta)$.

In order to test whether or not an empirical $G(t|\mathbf{x})$ exhibits positive duration dependence, it is possible to use the *total time on test statistic* (Barlow et al., 1972, p. 267). This statistic is briefly described here. For each set of $\mathbf{x}$ values, constituting a sample of $I_{\mathbf{x}}$ durations, order the first k durations starting with the smallest

$$t_1 \leq t_2 \leq \cdots \leq t_k, \qquad 1 \leq k \leq I_{\mathbf{x}}$$

Let $D_{i:I_{\mathbf{x}}} = [I_{\mathbf{x}} - (i+1)](t_i - t_{i-1})$, where $t_0 \equiv 0$. Define

$$V_k = k^{-1} \frac{\sum_{i=1}^{k-1} \left[\sum_{j=1}^{i} D_{j:I_{\mathbf{x}}} \right]}{k^{-1} \sum_{i=1}^{k} D_{i:I_{\mathbf{x}}}}$$

Now V_k is called the cumulative total time on test statistic. If the observations are from a distribution with an increasing hazard rate, V_k tends to be large. Intuitively, if $G(t|\mathbf{x})$ is a distribution that exhibits positive duration dependence, $D_{1:I_{\mathbf{x}}}$ stochastically dominates $D_{2:I_{\mathbf{x}}}$, $D_{2:I_{\mathbf{x}}}$ stochastically dominates $D_{3:I_{\mathbf{x}}}$, and so forth. Critical values for testing the null hypothesis of no duration dependence have been presented by Barlow and associates (1972, p. 269). This test can be modified to deal with censored data (Barlow et al., 1972, p. 302). The test is valuable because it enables the econometrician to test for positive duration dependence without imposing any arbitrary parametric structure on the data.

Negative duration dependence is more frequently observed in economic data. That this should be so is obvious from equation (3.1) in the proof of Proposition 1. Even when the structural hazard has a positive derivative $[\partial h(t|\mathbf{x}, \theta)/\partial t > 0]$, it often occurs that the second term on the right-hand side of (3.1) outweighs the first term. It is widely believed that it is impossible to distinguish structural negative duration dependence from a pure heterogeneity explanation of observed negative duration dependence when the analyst has access only to single-spell data. To investigate duration distributions exhibiting negative duration dependence, it is helpful to distinguish two families of distributions.

Let $\mathscr{G}_1 = \{G\colon -\ln[1 - G(t|\mathbf{x})]$ is concave in t holding $\mathbf{x}$ fixed$\}$. Membership in this class can be determined from the total time on test statistic. If $\mathscr{G}_1$ is log concave, the $D_{i:I_{\mathbf{x}}}$ defined earlier are stochastically increasing in i for fixed $I_{\mathbf{x}}$ and $\mathbf{x}$. Ordering the observations from the largest to the smallest and changing the subscripts appropriately, we can use V_k to test for log concavity.

Next let $\mathscr{G}_2 = \{G\colon G(t|\mathbf{x}) = \int_0^\infty (1 - \exp[-t\phi(\mathbf{x})\eta(\theta)])\, d\mu(\theta)$ for some probability measure μ on $[0, \infty]\}$. It is often erroneously suggested that $\mathscr{G}_1 = \mathscr{G}_2$, that is, that negative duration dependence by a homogeneous population ($G \in \mathscr{G}_1$) cannot be distinguished from a pure heterogeneity explanation ($G \in G_2$).

In fact, by virtue of Bernstein's theorem (see, e.g., Feller, 1971, pp. 439–40) if $G \in \mathscr{G}_2$, it is completely monotone, that is,

$$(-1)^n \frac{\partial^n}{\partial t^n}[1 - G(t|\mathbf{x})] \geq 0 \quad \text{for} \quad n \geq 1 \quad \text{and all} \quad t \geq 0 \tag{4.1}$$

and if $G(t|\mathbf{x})$ satisfies (4.1), $G(t|\mathbf{x}) \in \mathscr{G}_2$.

Setting $n = 3$, (4.1) is violated if

$$(-1)^3 \frac{\partial^3}{\partial t^3}[1 - G(t|\mathbf{x})] < 0$$

that is, if for some $t = t_0$,

$$\left[-\frac{\partial^2 h(t|\mathbf{x})}{\partial t^2} + 3h(t|\mathbf{x})\frac{\partial h(t|\mathbf{x})}{\partial t} - h^3(t|\mathbf{x})\right]_{t=t_0} > 0$$

(see Heckman and Singer, 1982; Lancaster and Nickell, 1980).

Formal verification of (4.1) requires uncensored data sufficiently rich to support numerical differentiation twice. Note that if the data are right-censored at $t = t^*$, we may apply (4.1) over the interval $0 < t \leq t^*$ provided that we define

$$1 - G^*(t|\mathbf{x}) = \frac{\int_0^\infty \{1 - \exp[-t\phi(\mathbf{x})\eta(\theta)]\}\, d\mu(\theta)}{\int_0^\infty \{1 - \exp[-t^*\phi(\mathbf{x})\eta(\theta)]\}\, d\mu(\theta)}$$

and test whether

$$(-1)^n \frac{\partial^n}{\partial t^n}(1 - G^*(t|\mathbf{x})) \geq 0 \quad \text{for} \quad n \geq 1 \quad \text{and} \quad 0 < t \leq t^* \tag{4.2}$$

Satisfaction of (4.2) for all $0 < t < t^*$ is only a necessary condition. It is sufficient only if $t^* \to \infty$.

Chamberlain (1980) has produced an alternative test of the *necessary* conditions that must be satisfied for a distribution to belong to $\mathscr{G}_2$ that does not require numerical differentiation of empirical distribution functions and that can be applied to censored data.

The key insight in his test is as follows. For $G \in \mathscr{G}_2$, the probability that $T > k$ is the survivor function

$$S(k|\mathbf{x}) = \int_0^\infty [\exp - k\phi(\mathbf{x})\eta(\theta)]\, d\mu(\theta) \tag{4.3}$$

By a transformation of variables $z = \exp[-\phi(\mathbf{x})\eta(\theta)]$, we may transform (4.3) for fixed $\mathbf{x}$ to

$$S(k \mid \mathbf{x}) = \int_0^1 z^k \, d\mu^*(z) \tag{4.4}$$

that is, as the kth moment of a random variable defined on the unit interval.

From the solution to the classical Hausdorff moment problem (see, e.g., Shohat and Tamarkin, 1943, p. 9) it is known that there exists a $\mu^*(z)$ that satisfies (4.4) if

$$\Delta^k S(l \mid \mathbf{x}) \geq 0, \qquad k, l = 0, 1, \ldots, \infty \tag{4.5}$$

where

$$\Delta^0 S(l \mid \mathbf{x}) = S(l \mid \mathbf{x})$$

$$\Delta^1 S(l \mid \mathbf{x}) = S(l \mid \mathbf{x}) - S(l + 1 \mid \mathbf{x})$$

$$\Delta^k S(l \mid \mathbf{x}) = S(l \mid \mathbf{x}) - \binom{k}{1} S(l \mid \mathbf{x}) + \binom{k}{2} S(l + 2 \mid \mathbf{x}) + \cdots + (-1)^k S(l + k \mid \mathbf{x})$$

Choosing equispaced intervals $(0, 1, \ldots, [t^*])$ where $[t^*]$ is the nearest whole integer less than t^*, form the $S(l \mid \mathbf{x})$ functions $l = 0, \ldots, [t^*]$. Compute the survivor functions so defined and test a subset of the necessary conditions $(l = 1, \ldots, k)$. The estimated survivor functions are asymptotically normally distributed as the number of independent observations becomes large, and thus the asymptotic distribution of the subset of survivor functions is straightforward to compute. Failure of these necessary conditions implies that (4.4) and hence (4.3) cannot represent the underlying duration distribution. Thus it is possible to reject $G \in G_2$ if some subset of conditions (4.5) is not satisfied. Note that if x are i.i.d., the same test procedure can be applied to the full sample based on the unconditional survivor functions $S(l)$, $l = 1, \ldots, [t^*]$. In an important paper Robb (1984) extends this analysis by presenting a larger set of necessary conditions and by producing finite sample test statistics for the strengthened conditions.

It is important to note that (4.5) or (4.1) are rejection criteria. There are other models that may satisfy (4.1). For example,

$$S(t) = \int_0^\infty [\exp(-t^\alpha \theta)] \, d\mu(\theta) \tag{4.6}$$

for $\alpha < 1$ is completely monotone. By Bernstein's theorem this distribution has one representation in G_2.

4.2 *Nonparametric procedures to assess the mixing distribution*

In this subsection we consider some procedures that enable us to assess the modality of the mixing distribution. For expositional simplicity we suppress the dependence on **x**. Let $G_3 = \{G\colon G(t) = \int_0^t g(u)\,du,\ g(t) = \int g(t|\theta)m(\theta)\,d\theta$ for some probability density $m(\theta)$ and $g(t|\theta) = k(t|\theta)v(t)$, where $k(t|\theta)$ is sign-regular of order 2 $(SR_2)\}$.

Sign regularity means that if $t_1 < t_2$ and $\theta_1 < \theta_2$, then

$$\varepsilon_2 \det \begin{bmatrix} k(t_1|\theta_1) & k(t_1|\theta_2) \\ k(t_2|\theta_1) & k(t_2|\theta_2) \end{bmatrix} \geq 0$$

where ε_2 is either $+1$ or -1. If $\varepsilon_2 = +1$, then $k(t|\theta)$ is called totally positive of order 2, abbreviated TP_2. From the point of view of inferring properties about the density of a mixing density from properties of g, models with SR_2 conditional densities allow us to obtain lower bounds on the number of modes in $m(\theta)$ from knowledge of the number of modes in $g(v)$. Models for which $k(t|\theta) = g(t|\theta)/v(t)$ satisfies SR_2 include all members of the exponential family. In fact, for the exponential family, $k(t|\theta)$ is TP_2. Thus an assessment of modality of an estimated density, using, for example, the procedure of Larkin (1979), is an important guide to specifying the characteristics of the density of Θ.

Sign-regular (particularly totally positive) kernels include many examples that are central to model specification in economics. In particular, if $dv(t)$ is any measure on $[0, +\infty)$ such that $\int_0^\infty [\exp(t\theta)]\,dv(t) < +\infty$ for $\theta \in \underline{\theta}$ (an ordered set), let

$$\beta(\theta) = \frac{1}{\int_0^\infty [\exp(t\theta)]\,dv(t)}$$

and, in what follows, set $dv(t) = v(t)\,dt$ and $g(t|\theta) = \beta(\theta)[\exp t\theta]v(t)$. Then the density $g(t) = \int \beta(\theta)\exp(t\theta)v(t)m(\theta)\,d\theta$ governs the observable durations of spells, $g(t|\theta)$ is a member of the exponential family, and $k(t|\theta) = \beta(\theta)\exp(t\theta)$ is TP_2 (Karlin, 1968). The essential point in isolating this class of duration densities is that knowledge of the number and character of the modes of g/v implies that the density m of the mixing measure must have at least as many modes. In particular, if g/v is unimodal, m cannot be monotonic; it must have at least one mode. More generally, if

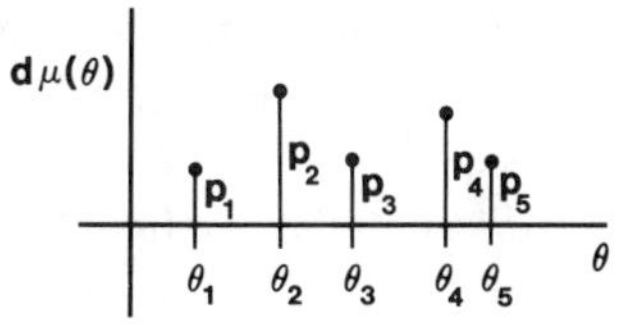

Figure 1

c is an arbitrary positive level and $g(t)/v(t) - c$ changes sign k times as t increases from 0 to $+\infty$, then $m(\theta) - c$ must change sign at least k times as θ traverses the parameter set $\underline{\theta}$ from left to right (Karlin, 1968, p. 21).

The importance of this variation-diminishing character of the transformation $\int k(t|\theta)m(\theta)\,d\theta$ for modeling purposes is that if we assess the modality of g using, for example, the method of Larkin (1979), then because v is given a priori, we know the modality of g/v, which in turn, implies restrictions on m in fitting mixing densities to data. In terms of a strategy of fitting finite mixtures, a bimodal g/v suggests fitting a measure with support at, say, five points to the data, but subject to the constraints that $p_1 < p_2$, $p_2 > p_3$, $p_3 < p_4$, and $p_4 > p_5$, as shown in Figure 1.

Subsequent specification of a mixing density $m(\theta)$ to describe the same data could proceed by fitting spline polynomials with knots at $\theta_1, \ldots, \theta_5$ to the estimated discrete mixing distribution.

4.3 *Identifiability*

In the preceding subsection, nonparametric procedures were proposed to assess qualitative features of conditional hazards and mixing distributions. These procedures aid in model selection but provide only qualitative guidelines to aid in model specification. In this subsection we consider conditions under which the conditional hazards and mixing distributions are identified. Virtually all that is known about this topic is for proportional hazard models (1.10) with scalar time-invariant heterogeneity $[\boldsymbol{\theta}(t) = \theta]$ and time-invariant regressors $[\mathbf{x}(t) = \mathbf{x}]$. Thus identification conditions are presented for the model

$$h(t|\mathbf{x}, \theta) = \psi(t)\phi(\mathbf{x})\theta \tag{4.7}$$

Before stating identifiability conditions, it is useful to define

$$Z(t) = \int_0^t \psi(u)\,du$$

Then for the proportional hazard model (4.7) we have the following proposition due to Elbers and Ridder (1982).

Proposition 2. *If (i)* $E(\Theta) = 1$, *(ii)* $Z(t)$ *defined on* $[0, \infty)$ *can be written as the integral of a nonnegative integrable function* $\psi(t)$ *defined on* $[0, \infty)$, $Z(t) = \int_0^t \psi(u)\,du$, *and (iii) the set* $\mathbf{S}, \mathbf{x} \in \mathbf{S}$, *is an open set in* R^k *and the function* ϕ *is defined on* $\mathbf{S}$ *and is nonnegative, differentiable, and nonconstant on* $\mathbf{S}$, *then* Z, ϕ, *and* $\mu(\theta)$ *are identified.*

The important point to note about Proposition 2 is that the identification analysis is completely nonparametric. No restrictions are imposed on ψ, ϕ, or $\mu(\theta)$ except for those stated in the proposition. Condition (iii) requires the existence of at least one continuous-valued regressor variable defined on an interval. In the appendix to their paper, Elbers and Ridder modify their proof to establish identifiability in models with only discrete-valued regressor variables. However, the existence of at least one regressor variable in the model is essential in securing identification. Condition (i) requires the existence of a mean for the distribution of θ. This assumption excludes many plausible fat-tailed mixing distributions. Defining η by $\theta = e^{\eta}$, condition (i) is not satisfied for distributions of η which do not possess a moment-generating function. For example, Pareto Θ with finite mean, Cauchy-distributed η, and certain members of the gamma family fail condition (i).[13]

The requirement that $E(\Theta) < \infty$ is essential to the Elbers–Ridder proof. If this condition is not satisfied and if no further restrictions are placed on $\mu(\theta)$, the duration model is not identified.

As an example of this point, suppose that the true model is Weibull with $Z_0(t) = t^{\alpha_0}$, $\phi_0(\mathbf{x}) = e^{\mathbf{x}'\boldsymbol{\beta}_0}$, and μ_0 such that $E(\Theta) < \infty$. The survivor function for this model is

$$S_0(t|\mathbf{x}) = 1 - G_0(t|\mathbf{x}) = \int_0^\infty \{\exp[-t^{\alpha_0} \exp(\mathbf{x}'\boldsymbol{\beta}_0)]\}\, d\mu_0(\theta)$$

Define $\omega = t^{\alpha} \exp(\mathbf{x}'\boldsymbol{\beta})$. Then

$$S_0(\omega) = \int_0^\infty [\exp(-\omega\theta)]\, d\mu_0(\theta) = L_0(\omega)$$

is the Laplace transform (L) of random variable Ω.

We have already noted in the discussion surrounding (4.6) that by virtue of Bernstein's theorem, if $0 < c < 1$,

$$L_1(\omega^c) = \int_0^\infty [\exp(-\omega^c\theta^*)]\, d\mu_1(\theta^*)$$

is completely monotone and is the Laplace transform of some random variable Θ^*, where $E(\Theta^*) = \infty$. Thus

$$1 - G_1(t|\mathbf{x}) = L_1(\omega^c) = L_0(\omega) = 1 - G_0(t|\mathbf{x})$$

and so a model with

$$Z_1(t) = t^{\alpha_0 c}, \qquad \phi_1(\mathbf{x}) = \exp(c\mathbf{x}'\boldsymbol{\beta}_0), \quad \text{and} \quad \mu_1 \quad \text{such that} \quad E(\Theta^*) = \infty$$

explains the data as well as the original model [$\alpha = \alpha_0$, $\boldsymbol{\beta} = \boldsymbol{\beta}_0$, and $\mu = \mu_0$ with $E(\Theta) < \infty$].

The requirement that $E(\Theta) < \infty$ is overly strong. Heckman and Singer (1984a) establish identifiability when $E(\Theta) = \infty$ by restricting the tail behavior of the admissible mixing distribution. Their results are recorded in the following proposition.

Proposition 3. *If*

(i) *The random variable Θ is nonnegative with a nondefective distribution μ. For absolutely continuous μ, the density $m(\theta)$ is restricted so that*

$$m(\theta) \sim \frac{c}{(\ln \theta)^{\gamma}\theta^{(1+\varepsilon)}L(\theta)} \tag{4.8}$$

as $\theta \to \infty$, where $c > 0$, $0 < \varepsilon < 1$, and $\gamma \geq 0$, where $L(\theta)$ is slowly varying in the sense of Karamata.[14] *Here ε is assumed known.*

(ii) *$\mathscr{Z} \in \mathbf{Z} = \{Z(t), t \geq 0; Z(t)$ is a nonnegative increasing function with $Z(0) = 0$ and $\exists c > 0$ and t_+ not depending on the function $Z(t)$ such that $Z(t_+) = c$ where c is a known constant$\}$.*

(iii) *$\phi \in \boldsymbol{\Phi} = \{\phi(\mathbf{x}), \mathbf{x} \in \mathbf{S}$: ϕ is nonconstant on $\mathbf{S}$, $\exists$ at least one coordinate x_i defined on $(-\infty, \infty)$ such that $\phi(0, 0, \ldots, x_i, 0, \ldots)$ traverses $(0, \infty)$ as x_i traverses $(-\infty, \infty)$, $\mathbf{0} \in \mathbf{S}$, and $\phi(\mathbf{0}) = 1\}$.*

Then Z, ϕ, and μ are identified. (*For proof, see Heckman and Singer 1984a.*)

Condition (i) is weaker than the Elbers and Ridder condition (i). Here $\boldsymbol{\Theta}$ need not possess moments of any order nor need the distribution function μ have a density. However, in order to satisfy (i) the tails of the true distribution are assumed to die off at a fast enough rate and the rate is assumed known. The condition that $Z(t_+) = c$ for some $c > 0$ and $t_+ > 0$ for all admissible Z plays an important role. This condition is satisfied, for example, by a Weibull-integrated hazard since for all α, $Z(1) = 1$. The strengthened condition (ii) substitutes for the weakened (i) in our analysis. Condition (iii) has identical content in both analyses. The essential idea in both is that ϕ varies continuously over an interval. In the absence of a finiteness of first-moment assumption, Proposition 3 gives a conditional identification result. Given ε, it is possible to estimate ψ, μ, ϕ provided crossover condition (ii) is met.

A key assumption in the Heckman–Singer proof and in the main proof of Elbers and Ridder is the presence in the model of at least one exogenous variable that takes values in an interval of the real line. In duration models with no regressors or with only categorical regressors both proofs of identifiability break down. This is so because both proofs require exogenous variables that trace out the Laplace transform of Θ over some interval in order to uniquely identify the functions of interest.[15]

The requirement that a model possess at least one regressor is troublesome. It explicitly rules out an interaction detection strategy that cross-classifies the data on the basis of exogenous variables and estimates separate $Z(t)$ and $\mu(\theta)$ functions for different demographic groups. It rules out interactions between $\mathbf{x}$ and θ and between $\mathbf{x}$ and Z.

In fact, some widely used parametric hazard models can be identified together with the mixing distribution $\mu(\theta)$ even when no regressors appear in the model. Identification is secured under these conditions by specifying the functional form of the hazard function up to a finite number of unknown parameters and placing some restrictions on the moments of admissible μ distributions.

A general strategy of proof for this case is as follows (for details see Heckman and Singer, 1984a). Assume that $Z'_{\boldsymbol{\alpha}}(t)$ is a member of a parametric family of nonnegative functions and that the pair $(\boldsymbol{\alpha}, \mu)$ is not identified. Assuming that $Z'_{\boldsymbol{\alpha}}$ is differentiable to order j, nonidentifiability implies that the identities

$$1 = \frac{g_1(t)}{g_0(t)} = \frac{Z'_{\boldsymbol{\alpha}_1}(t) \int_0^\infty \theta\{\exp[-Z_{\boldsymbol{\alpha}_1}(t)\theta]\}\, d\mu_1(\theta)}{Z'_{\boldsymbol{\alpha}_0}(t) \int_0^\infty \theta\{\exp[-Z_{\boldsymbol{\alpha}_0}(t)]\}\, d\mu_0(\theta)}$$

$$\cdots$$

$$1 = \frac{g_1^{(j)}(t)}{g_0^{(j)}(t)}$$

for all $t \geq 0$ must hold for at least two distinct pairs $(\boldsymbol{\alpha}_0, \mu_0)$, $(\boldsymbol{\alpha}_1, \mu_1)$. We then derive contradictions. We demonstrate under certain stated conditions that these identities cannot hold unless $\boldsymbol{\alpha}_1 = \boldsymbol{\alpha}_0$. Then μ is identified by the uniqueness theorem for Laplace transforms.

To illustrate this strategy consider identifiability for the class of Box–Cox hazards [see equation (3.2) with $\gamma_2 = 0$]:

$$Z'_{\boldsymbol{\alpha}} = \exp\left[\gamma\left(\frac{t^\lambda - 1}{\lambda}\right)\right]$$

For this class of hazard models there is an interesting tradeoff between the interval of admissible λ and the number of bounded moments that is assumed to restrict the admissible $\mu(\theta)$. More precisely, the following propositions are proved in our joint work.

Proposition 4. *For the true value of* λ, λ_0, *defined so that* $\lambda_0 \leq 0$, *if* $E(\Theta) < \infty$ *for all admissible* μ, *and for all bounded* γ, *then the triple* $(\gamma_0, \lambda_0, \mu_0)$ *is uniquely identified. (For proof, see Heckman and Singer, 1984a.)*

Proposition 5. *For the true value of* λ, λ_0, *such that* $0 < \lambda_0 < 1$, *if all admissible* μ *are restricted to have a common finite mean that is assumed to be known a priori* $[E(\Theta) = m_1]$ *and a bounded (but not necessarily common) second moment* $E(\Theta^2) < \infty$, *and all admissible* γ *are bounded, then the triple* $(\gamma_0, \lambda_0, \mu_0)$ *is uniquely identified. (For proof, see Heckman and Singer, 1984a.)*

Proposition 6. *For the true value of* λ, λ_0, *restricted so that* $0 < \lambda_0 < j$, j *a positive integer, if all admissible* μ *are restricted to have a common finite mean that is assumed to be known a priori* $[E(\Theta) = m_1]$ *and a bounded (but not necessarily common)* $(j + 1)$*st moment* $[E(\Theta^{j+1}) < \infty]$, *and all admissible* γ *are bounded, then the triple* $(\gamma_0, \lambda_0, \mu_0)$ *is uniquely identified. (For proof, see Heckman and Singer, 1984a.)*

It is interesting that each integer increase in the value of $\lambda_0 > 0$ requires an integer increase in the highest moment that must be assumed finite for all admissible μ.

The general strategy of specifying a flexible functional form for the hazard and placing moment restrictions on the admissible μ works in other models besides the Box–Cox class of hazards. For example, consider a nonmonotonic log-logistic model used by Trussell and Richards (1985):

$$Z'(t) = \frac{(\lambda\alpha)(\lambda t)^{\alpha-1}}{1 + (\lambda t)^{\alpha}}, \qquad \infty > \lambda, \alpha > 0 \tag{4.9}$$

Proposition 7. *For hazard model (4.9),* the triple $(\lambda_0, \alpha_0, \mu_0)$ *is identified provided that the admissible* μ *are restricted to have a common finite mean* $E(\Theta) = m_1 < \infty$. *(For proof, see Heckman and Singer, 1984a.)*

An interesting and more direct strategy of proof of identifiability which works for some of the hazard model specifications given above is due to Arnold and Brockett (1983). To illustrate their argument, consider the Weibull hazard

$$h(t \mid \theta) = \alpha t^{\alpha-1}\theta$$

and mixing distributions restricted to those having a finite mean. Then a routine calculation shows that α may be calculated directly in terms of the observed survivor function via the recipe

$$\alpha = \lim_{t \to 0} \frac{\ln[tS'(t)/S(t)]}{\ln t}$$

The mixing distribution is then identified using the uniqueness theorem for Laplace transforms. Their proof of identifiability is constructive in that it also provides a direct procedure for estimation of $\mu(\theta)$ and α that is distinct from the procedure discussed below.

Provided that one adopts a parametric position on $h(t|\theta)$, these propositions show that it is possible to completely dispense with regressors. Another way to interpret these results is to note that since for each value of $\mathbf{x}$ we may estimate Z_α and $\mu(\theta)$, it is not necessary to adopt proportional hazards specification (4.7) in order to secure model identification. All that is required is a conditional (on $\mathbf{x}$) proportional hazards specification. Now Z and μ may be arbitrary functions of $\mathbf{x}$.

Although we have no theorems yet to report, it is obvious that it should be possible to reverse the roles of $\mu(\theta)$ and $h(t|\theta)$; that is, if $\mu(\theta)$ is parameterized, it should be possible to specify conditions under which $h(t|\theta)$ is identified nonparametrically.

The identification results reported here are quite limited in scope. First, as previously noted in Section 3, the restriction that the regressors are time-invariant is crucial. If the regressors contain a common (to all observations) time-trended variable, ϕ can be identified from ψ only if strong functional form assumptions are maintained so that $\ln \psi$ and $\ln \phi$ are linearly independent. Since one cannot control the external environment, it is always possible to produce a ψ function that fails this linear independence test. Moreover, even when $\mathbf{x}(t)$ follows a separate path for each person, so that there is independent variation between $\ln \psi(t)$ and $\ln \phi(t)$, at least for some observations, a different line of proof is required than has been produced in the literature.

Second, and more important, the proportional hazard model is not derived from an economic model. It is a statistically convenient model. As is implicit from the models presented in Section 2 and as will be made explicit in Section 6, duration models motivated by economic theory cannot in general be cast into a proportional hazards mold. Accordingly, the identification criteria discussed in this section are of limited use in estimating explicitly formulated economic models. In general, the hazard functions produced by economic theory are not separable as is assumed in (4.7).

Research is underway on identifiability conditions for nonseparable hazards. As a prototype we present the following identification theorem for a specific nonseparable hazard.

Proposition 8. *Nonseparable model with (i)* $Z_\alpha(t) = t^{(\alpha x)^2+\theta}$, *(ii) density* $w_\beta(x|\theta) = (\theta + \beta)\exp[-(\theta + \beta)x]$, *and (iii)* $\int \theta \, d\mu(\theta) < \infty$ *is identified. (For proof, see Heckman and Singer, 1983.)*

Note that not only is the hazard nonseparable in $\mathbf{x}$ and θ, but the density of $\mathbf{x}$ depends on θ so that $\mathbf{x}$ is not weakly exogenous with respect to θ.

Before concluding this discussion of identification, it is important to note that the concept of identifiability employed in this chapter and elsewhere is the requirement that the mapping from a space of (conditional hazards) × (a restricted class of probability distributions) to (a class of joint frequency functions for durations and covariates) be one-to-one and onto. This formulation of identifiability is standard. In this literature there is no requirement of a metric on the spaces or of completeness. Such requirements are essential if consistency of an estimator is desired. In this connection, Kiefer and Wolfowitz (1956) propose a definition of identifiability in a metric space whereby the above-mentioned mapping is one-to-one on the completion (with respect to a given metric) of the original spaces. Without some care in defining the original space, undesirable distributions can appear in the completion.

As an example, consider a Weibull hazard model with conditional survivor function given an observed k-dimensional covariate $\mathbf{x}$ defined as

$$1 - G(t, \mathbf{x}, \boldsymbol{\beta}) = S(t|\mathbf{x}) = \int_0^\infty \exp[-t^\alpha(\exp \mathbf{x}'\boldsymbol{\beta}_0)v] \, dF_0(v)$$

where $0 < \alpha \leq A < +\infty$, $\boldsymbol{\beta} \in$ compact subset of k-dimensional Euclidean space, and F_0 is restricted to be a probability distribution on $[0, +\infty)$ with $\int_0^\infty v \, dF_0(v) = 1$. As a specialization of Elbers and Ridder's (1982) general proof, α_0, $\boldsymbol{\beta}_0$, and F_0 are identified. Now consider the completion with respect to the Kiefer–Wolfowitz (1956) metric of the Cartesian product of the parameter space of allowed α and $\boldsymbol{\beta}$ values and the probability distributions on $[0, +\infty)$ satisfying $\int_0^\infty v \, dF_0(v) = 1$. The completion contains distributions F_1 on $[0, +\infty)$ satisfying $\int_0^\infty v \, dF_1(v) = \infty$. Now observe that if $S(t|\mathbf{x})$ has a representation as defined above for some $\alpha \in (0, 1)$ and F_0 with mean 1, then it is also a completely monotone function of t. Thus we also have the representation

$$S(t|\mathbf{x}) = \int_0^\infty \{\exp[-t(\exp(\mathbf{x}'\boldsymbol{\beta}_1))v]\} \, dF_1(v)$$

but now F_1 must have an infinite mean. This implies that $(\alpha_0, \boldsymbol{\beta}_0, F_0)$ and $(1, \boldsymbol{\beta}_1, F_1)$ represent the same survivor function. Hence the model is not identifiable on the completion of a space where probability distributions are restricted to have a finite mean.

This difficulty can be eliminated by further restricting F_0 to belong to a uniformly integrable family of distribution functions. Then all elements in the completion with respect to the Kiefer–Wolfowitz and a variety of other metrics will also have a finite mean and identifiability is again ensured. The comparable requirement for the case when $E_0(V) = \infty$ is that (4.8) converge uniformly to its limit.

The a priori restriction of identifiability considerations to complete metric spaces is not only central to establishing consistency of estimation methods but also provides a link between the concept of identifiability as it has developed in econometrics and notions of identifiability which are directly linked to consistency as in the engineering literature on control theory.

4.4 *Nonparametric estimation*

Securing identifiability of a nonparametric model is only the first step toward estimating the model. At the time of this writing, no nonparametric estimator has been devised that consistently estimates the general proportional hazard model (4.7).

In Heckman and Singer (1984b) we consider consistent estimation of the proportional hazard model when $\psi(t)$ and $\phi(\mathbf{x})$ are specified up to a finite number of parameters but $\mu(\theta)$ is unrestricted except that it must have either a finite mean and belong to a uniformly integrable family or satisfy a tail condition (4.8) with uniform convergence. We verify sufficiency conditions due to Kiefer and Wolfowitz (1956) which, when satisfied, guarantee the existence of a consistent nonparametric maximum likelihood estimator. We analyze a Weibull model for censored and uncensored data and demonstrate how to verify the sufficiency conditions for more general models. The analysis only ensures the existence of a consistent estimator. The asymptotic distribution of the estimator is unknown.

Drawing on results due to Laird (1978) and Lindsey (1983a,b) we characterize the computational form of the nonparametric maximum likelihood estimator.[16] To state these results most succinctly, we define

$$t^* = \phi(\mathbf{x}) \int_0^t \psi(u)\, du = \phi(\mathbf{x}) Z(t)$$

For any fixed value of the parameters determining $\phi(\mathbf{x})$ and $Z(t)$ in (4.7), t^* conditional on θ is an exponential random variable; that is,

$$f(t^* \mid \theta) = \theta \exp(-t^*\theta), \qquad \theta \geq 0 \tag{4.10}$$

For this model, the following propositions can be established for the nonparametric maximum likelihood estimator (NPMLE).

Proposition 9. *Let I^* be the number of distinct t^* values in the sample of $I(\geq I^*)$ observations. Then the NPMLE of $\mu(\theta)$ is a finite mixture with at most I^* points of increase; that is, for censored and uncensored data (with $d = 1$ for uncensored observations)*

$$f(t^*) = \sum_{i=1}^{I^*} \theta_i^d \exp(-t^*\theta_i)P_i$$

where $P_i \geq 0$, $\sum_{i=1}^{I^*} P_i = 1$.

Thus the NPMLE is a finite mixture, but in contrast to the usual finite mixture model, I^* is estimated along with the P_i and θ_i. Other properties of the NPMLE are as follows.

Proposition 10. *Assuming that no points of support $\{\theta_i\}$ come from the boundary of $\boldsymbol{\theta}$ the NPMLE is unique. (See Heckman and Singer, 1984b.)*

Proposition 11. *For uncensored data, $\hat{\theta}_{\min} = 1/t^*_{\max}$ and $\hat{\theta}_{\max} = 1/t^*_{\min}$ where the "hat" (^) denotes the NPMLE estimate, and $t^*_{\max}$ and $t^*_{\min}$ are, respectively, the sample maximum and minimum values for t^*. For censored data, $\hat{\theta}_{\min} = 0$ and $\hat{\theta}_{\max} = 1/t^*_{\min}$. (See Heckman and Singer, 1984b.)*

These propositions show that the NPMLE for $\mu(\theta)$ in the proportional hazard model is in general unique and the estimated points of support lie in a region with known bounds (given t^*). In computing estimates one can confine attention to this region. Further characterization of the NPMLE is given in Heckman and Singer (1984b).

It is important to note that all of these results are for a given $t^* = Z(t)\phi(\mathbf{x})$. The computational strategy we use fixes the parameters determining $Z(t)$ and $\phi(\mathbf{x})$ and estimates $\mu(\theta)$. For each estimate of $\mu(\theta)$ so achieved, $Z(t)$ and $\phi(\mathbf{x})$ are estimated by traditional parametric maximum likelihood methods. Then fresh t^* are generated and a new $\mu(\theta)$ is estimated until convergence occurs. There is no assurance that this procedure converges to a global optimum.

In a series of Monte Carlo runs reported in Heckman and Singer (1984b) the following results emerge:

(i) The NPMLE recovers the parameters governing $Z(t)$ and $\phi(\mathbf{x})$ rather well.
(ii) The NPMLE does not produce reliable estimates of the underlying mixing distribution.
(iii) The estimated cdf for duration times $G(t|\mathbf{x})$ produced via the NPMLE predicts the sample cdf of durations quite well even in fresh samples of data with different distributions for the $\mathbf{x}$ variables.

Table 3. *Results from a typical estimation*
$d\mu(\theta) = [\exp(\Delta\theta)] \exp - (e^{\theta}/\beta)\, d\theta$ with $\Delta = \frac{1}{2}$, $\beta = 1$

True model:	$\alpha_1 = 1$	$\alpha_2 = 1$
Estimated model:	.9852	.9846
	(.0738)[a]	(.1022)[a]

where $Z(t) = t^{\alpha_1}$ and $\alpha(\mathbf{x}) = \exp(\alpha_2 \mathbf{x})$

Sample size:	L = 500
Log likelihood:	−1886.47

Estimated mixing distribution

Estimated θ_i	Estimated P_i	Estimated cdf	True cdf	Observed cdf
−12.9031	.008109	.008109	.001780	.0020
−7.0938	.06524	.07335	.03250	.0400
−4.0107	.1887	.2621	.1510	.1620
−1.7898	.3681	.6302	.4366	.4280
−0.0338	.3698	1.000	.8356	.8320

Estimated cumulative distribution of duration vs. actual $[\hat{G}(t)$ *vs.* $G(t)]$

Value of t	Estimated t cdf	Observed cdf
.25	.1237	.102
.50	.2005	.186
1.00	.3005	.296
3.00	.4830	.484
5.00	.5661	.556
10.00	.6675	.660
20.00	.7512	.754
40.00	.8169	.818
99.00	.8800	.880

[a] Standard error from the estimated information matrix for $(\boldsymbol{\alpha}, \mathbf{P}, \boldsymbol{\theta})$ given I^*. As noted in the text, these have no rigorous justification.

A typical run is reported in Table 3. The structural parameters (α_1, α_2) are estimated rather well. The mixing distribution is poorly estimated but the within-sample agreement between the estimated cdf of T and the observed cdf is good. Table 4 records the results of perturbing a model by changing the mean of the regressors from 0 to 10. There is still close agreement between the estimated model [with parameters estimated on a sample where $X \sim N(0, 1)$] and the observed durations [where $X \sim N(10, 1)$].

The NPMLE can be used to check the plausibility of any particular parametric specification of the distribution of unobserved variables. If the

Table 4. *Predictions on a fresh sample,* $X \sim N(10, 1)$

Estimated cumulative distribution of duration vs. actual $\hat{G}(t)$ vs. $G(t)$		
Value of t ($\times 10^5$)	Estimated t cdf	Observed cdf
1.0	.1118	.1000
4.0	.2799	.2800
8.0	.3924	.3920
10.0	.4300	.4360
25.0	.5802	.5740
100.0	.7607	.7640
300.0	.8543	.8620
5000.0	.9615	.9660

Note: The model used to fit the parameters is $X \sim N(0, 1)$.

estimated parameters of a structural model achieved from a parametric specification of the distribution of unobservables are not "too far" from the estimates of the same parameters achieved from the NPMLE, the econometrician would have much more confidence in adopting a particular specification of the mixing distribution. Development of a formal test statistic to determine how far is "too far" is a topic for the future. However, because of the consistency of the nonparametric maximum likelihood estimator, a test based on the difference between the parameters of $Z(t)$ and $\phi(\mathbf{x})$ estimated via the NPMLE and the same parameters estimated under a particular assumption about the functional form of the mixing distribution would be consistent.

The fact that we produce a good estimator of the structural parameters while producing a poor estimator for μ suggests that it might be possible to protect against the consequences of misspecification of the mixing distribution by fitting duration models with mixing distributions from parametric families, such as members of the Pearson system, with more than the usual two parameters. Thus the failure of the NPMLE to estimate more than four or five points of increase for μ can be cast in a somewhat more positive light. A finite mixture model with five points of increase is, after all, a nine (independent) parameter model for the mixing distribution. Imposing a false, but very flexible, mixing distribution may not cause bias in estimates of the structural coefficients. Moreover, for small I^*, computational costs are *lower* for the NPMLE than they are for traditional parametric maximum likelihood estimators of $\mu(\theta)$. The computational costs of precise evaluation of $\mu(\theta)$ over "small enough" intervals of θ are avoided by estimating a finite mixtures model.

We conclude this section noting that the Arnold and Brockett (1983) estimator for α discussed in Section 4.3 circumvents the need to estimate $d\mu(\theta)$ and so in this regard is more attractive than the estimator discussed in this subsection. Exploiting the fact that t^* is independent of $\mathbf{x}$, it is possible to extend their estimator to accommodate models with regressors. (The independence conditions provide orthogonality restrictions from which it is possible to identify $\boldsymbol{\beta}$.) However, it is not obvious how to extend their estimator to deal with censored data. Our estimator can be used without modification on censored data.

5 Sampling plans and initial conditions problems

There are few duration data sets for which the start date of the sample coincides with the origin date of all sampled spells. Quite commonly the available data are random samples of interrupted spells or are spells that begin after the start date of the sample. For interrupted spells one of the following duration times may be observed: (1) time in the state up to the sampling date (T_b), (2) time in the state after the sampling date (T_a), or (3) total time in a completed spell observed at the origin of the sample ($T_c = T_a + T_b$). Durations of spells that begin after the origin date of the sample are denoted T_d.

In this section we derive the density of each of these durations for time-homogeneous and time-inhomogeneous environments and for models with and without observed and unobserved explanatory variables. The main message of this section is that in general the distributions of each of the random variables T_a, T_b, T_c, and T_d differ from the population duration distribution $G(t)$. Estimators based on the wrong duration distribution in general produce invalid estimates of the parameters of $G(t)$ and will lead to incorrect inference about the population duration distribution.

5.1 *Time-homogeneous environments and models without observed and unobserved explanatory variables*

We first consider the analytically tractable case of a single-spell duration model without regressors and unobservables in a time-homogeneous environment.[17] To simplify notation we assume that the sample at our disposal begins at calendar time 0. Looking backward, a spell of length t_b interrupted at 0 began t_b periods ago. Looking forward, the spell lasts t_a periods after the sampling date. The completed spell is $t_c = t_b + t_a$ in length. We ignore right censoring and assume that the underlying distribution is nondefective. (These assumptions are relaxed in Section 5.2.)

Let $k(-t_b)$ be the intake rate; that is, t_b periods before the sample begins, $k(-t_b)$ is the proportion of the population that enters the state of interest at time $\tau = -t_b$. The time homogeneity assumption implies that

$$k(-t_b) = k \quad \text{for all} \quad t_b \tag{5.1}$$

Let $g(t) = h(t)\exp[-\int_0^t h(u)\,du]$ be the density of completed durations *in the population.* The associated survivor function is

$$S(t) = 1 - G(t) = \exp\left[-\int_0^t h(u)\,du\right]$$

The proportion of the population experiencing a spell at calendar time $\tau = 0$, P_0, is obtained by integrating over the survivors from each cohort, that is,

$$\begin{aligned} P_0 &= \int_0^\infty k(-t_b)[1 - G(t_b)]\,dt_b \\ &= \int_0^\infty k(-t_b)\exp\left[-\int_0^{t_b} h(u)\,du\right]dt_b \end{aligned}$$

Thus the density of an interrupted spell of length t_b is the ratio of the proportion surviving from those who entered t_b periods ago to the total stock

$$f(t_b) = \frac{k(-t_b)[1 - G(t_b)]}{P_0} = \frac{k(-t_b)\exp\left[-\int_0^{t_b} h(u)\,du\right]}{P_0} \tag{5.2}$$

Assuming $m = \int_0^\infty xg(x)\,dx < \infty$ (and so ruling out defective distributions) and integrating the denominator of the preceding expression by parts, we reach the familiar expression (see, e.g., Cox and Lewis, 1966)

$$f(t_b) = \frac{1 - G(t_b)}{m} = \frac{S(t_b)}{m} = \frac{1}{m}\exp\left[-\int_0^{t_b} h(u)\,du\right] \tag{5.3}$$

The density of sampled interrupted spells is *not* the same as the population density of completed spells.

The density of sampled completed spells is obtained by the following straightforward argument. In the population, the conditional density of t_c given $0 < t_b < t_c$ is

$$g(t_c \mid t_b) = \frac{g(t_c)}{1 - G(t_b)} = h(t_c)\exp\left[-\int_{t_b}^{t_c} h(u)\,du\right], \qquad t_c > t_b \tag{5.4}$$

Using (5.3), the marginal density of t_c in the sample is

$$f(t_c) = \int_0^{t_c} g(t_c \mid t_b) f(t_b)\,dt_b = \int_0^{t_c} \frac{g(t_c)}{m}\,dt_b \tag{5.5}$$

and so

$$f(t_c) = \frac{t_c g(t_c)}{m}$$

The density of the forward time t_a can be derived from (5.4). Substitute for t_c using $t_c = t_a + t_b$ and integrate out t_b using density (5.3). Thus

$$f(t_a) = \int_0^\infty g(t_a + t_b | t_b) f(t_b)\, dt_b = \int_0^\infty \frac{g(t_a + t_b)}{m}\, dt_b$$

$$= \frac{1}{m}\int_{t_a}^\infty g(z)\, dz = \frac{1 - G(t_a)}{m}$$

$$= \frac{S(t_a)}{m} = \frac{\exp\left[-\int_0^{t_a} h(u)\, du\right]}{m} \tag{5.6}$$

So in a time-homogeneous environment the functional form of $f(t_a)$ is identical to $f(t_b)$.

The following results are well known about the distributions of the random variables T_a, T_b, and T_c.

(i) If $g(t)$ is exponential with parameter θ [i.e., $g(t) = \theta \exp(-t\theta)$], then so are $f(t_a)$ and $f(t_b)$. The proof is immediate.
(ii) $E(T_a) = (m/2)(1 + \sigma^2/m^2)$,[18] where $\sigma^2 = E(T - m)^2 = \int_0^\infty (t - m)^2 g(t)\, dt$.
(iii) $E(T_b) = (m/2)(1 + \sigma^2/m^2)$ (since T_a and T_b have the same density).
(iv) $E(T_c) = m(1 + \sigma^2/m^2)$,[19] and so $E(T_c) = 2E(T_a) = 2E(T_b)$ and $E(T_c) > m$ unless $\sigma^2 = 0$.
(v) If $-\ln[1 - G(t)]/t \uparrow$ in t, $\sigma^2/m^2 > 1$. (This condition is implied if $h(t) = g(t)/[1 - G(t)]$ is increasing in t, i.e., $h'(t) > 0$.) In this case, $E(T_a) = E(T_b) > m$. (See Barlow and Proschan, 1975, for proof.)
(vi) If $-\ln[1 - G(t)]/t \downarrow$ in t, $\sigma^2/m^2 < 1$. [This condition is implied if $h'(t) < 0$.] In this case $E(T_a) = E(T_b) < m$. (See Barlow and Proschan, 1975, for proof.)

Result (i) restates the classical result (see Feller, 1970) that if the population distribution of durations is exponential, so are the sample distributions of T_a and T_b. Result (iii) coupled with result (v) indicates that if the population distribution of durations exhibits positive duration dependence, the mean of interrupted spells (T_b) *exceeds* the population mean duration. Result (iii) coupled with (vi) reverses this ordering for duration distributions with negative duration dependence. Result (iv) indicates that sampled completed spells have a mean in excess of the population mean unless $\sigma^2 = 0$ (hence the term *length-biased sampling*) and that completed spells have a mean twice that of interrupted (T_b) or partially completed forward spells (T_a).

We next present the distribution of T_d, the duration time for spells that begin after the origin date of the sample. Let $\mathscr{T}$ denote the time a spell begins. The density of $\mathscr{T}$ is $k(\tau)$. Assuming that $\mathscr{T}$ and T_d are independent, the joint probability that a spell begins at $\mathscr{T} = \tau$ and lasts less than t_d periods is

$$\Pr\{\mathscr{T} = \tau \text{ and } T_d < t_d\} = k(\tau)G(t_d)$$

Thus the density of T_d in a time-homogeneous environment is

$$f(t_d) = g(t_d) \tag{5.7}$$

The distributions of T_a, T_b, and T_c are of a different functional form than the distribution of T. The only exception is the case in which T is an exponential random variable with parameter λ; in this case T_a and T_b are also exponential with parameter λ. The distribution of T_d has the same functional form as the distribution of T.

Thus in a typical longitudinal sample in which data are available for the completed portions of durations of spells in progress (T_a) and on durations initiated after the origin date of the sample (T_d), two different distributions are required to analyze the data.

It is common to "solve" the left-censoring problem by assuming that $G(t)$ is exponential. The bias that results from invoking this assumption when it is false can be severe. As an example, suppose that the population distribution of t is Weibull, so that

$$g(t) = \alpha\phi t^{\alpha-1}\exp(-\phi t^{\alpha}), \qquad \phi > 0, \qquad \alpha > 0 \tag{5.8}$$

Suppose that the sample data are on the completed portions of interrupted spells and that there is no right censoring, so that, using formula (5.6),

$$f(t_a) = \frac{\exp(-t^{\alpha}\phi)}{\dfrac{\Gamma(1/\alpha + 1)}{\phi^{1/\alpha+1}}}$$

If it is falsely assumed that $g^*(t) = \lambda e^{-t\lambda}$, the maximum likelihood estimator of λ for a random sample of durations is

$$\hat{\lambda} = \left(\frac{\sum t_i}{I}\right)^{-1}$$

which has probability limit

$$\operatorname{plim} \hat{\lambda} = \phi^{1/\alpha}\frac{\Gamma(1/\alpha)}{\Gamma(2/\alpha)}$$

For $\alpha = 2$,

$$\text{plim } \hat{\lambda} = (\phi)^{1/2}\Gamma(\tfrac{1}{2})$$

As another example, suppose the sample being analyzed consists of complete spells sampled at time zero (i.e., T_c) generated by an underlying population exponential density

$$g(t) = \lambda \exp(-t\lambda)$$

Then, from (5.5),

$$f(t_c) = \lambda^2 t_c \exp(-\lambda t_c)$$

If it is falsely assumed that $g(t)$ characterizes the duration data and λ is estimated by maximum likelihood

$$\text{plim } \hat{\lambda} = 2\lambda$$

This is an immediate consequence of results (i) and (iv) previously stated.

Continuing this example, suppose instead that a Weibull model is falsely assumed, that is,

$$g^*(t) = \alpha t^{\alpha-1}\phi \exp(-t^{\alpha}\phi)$$

and the parameters α and ϕ are estimated by maximum likelihood. The maximum likelihood estimator solves the following equations:

$$\frac{1}{\hat{\phi}} = \frac{\sum_{i=1}^{I} t_i^{\hat{\alpha}}}{I}$$

$$\frac{1}{\hat{\alpha}} + \frac{\sum_{i=1}^{I} \ln t_i}{I} = \frac{\hat{\phi} \sum_{i=1}^{I} (\ln t_i) t_i^{\hat{\alpha}}}{I}$$

so that

$$\frac{1}{\hat{\alpha}} + \frac{\sum_{i=1}^{I} \ln t_i}{I} = \frac{\sum_{i=1}^{I} t_i^{\hat{\alpha}} \ln t_i}{\sum_{i=1}^{I} t_i^{\hat{\alpha}}} \tag{5.9}$$

Using the easily verified result that

$$\int_0^{\infty} t^{P-1}(\ln t)\exp(-t\lambda)\,dt = \lambda^{-P}\left[\frac{\partial\Gamma(P)}{\partial P} - \ln \lambda\Gamma(P)\right]$$

and the fact that in large samples plim $\hat{\alpha} = \alpha^*$ is the value of α^* that solves (5.9), α^* is the solution to

$$\frac{1}{\alpha^*} + E(\ln t) = \frac{E(t^{\alpha^*} \ln t)}{E(t^{\alpha^*})}$$

and we obtain the equation

$$\frac{1}{\alpha^*} + \left(\frac{\partial \Gamma(P)}{\partial P}\bigg|_{P=2} - \ln \lambda \right) = \left(\frac{\partial \ln \Gamma(P)}{\partial P}\bigg|_{P=\alpha^*+2} - \ln \lambda \right) \tag{5.10}$$

Using the fact that

$$\frac{\Gamma'(P+1)}{\Gamma(P+1)} = \frac{1}{P} + \frac{\Gamma'(P)}{\Gamma(P)}$$

and collecting terms, we may rewrite (5.10) as

$$\frac{1}{\alpha^*(\alpha^*+1)} + \frac{\partial \Gamma(P)}{\partial P}\bigg|_{P=2} = \frac{1}{\Gamma(P)} \frac{\partial \Gamma(P)}{\partial P}\bigg|_{P=\alpha^*+1} \tag{5.11}$$

Since $\Gamma(2) = 1$, it is clear that $\alpha^* = 1$ is never a solution of this equation. In fact, since the left-hand side is monotone decreasing in α^* and the right-hand side is monotone increasing in α^*, and since at $\alpha^* = 1$, the left-hand side exceeds the right-hand side, the value of α^* that solves (5.11) exceeds unity. Thus if a Weibull model is fit by maximum likelihood to length-biased completed spells generated by an exponential population model, in large samples positive duration dependence will always be found; that is, $\alpha^* > 1$.

It can also be shown that

$$\text{plim } \hat{\phi} = \frac{\lambda^{\alpha^*-1}}{\Gamma(\alpha^*+2)}$$

If the Weibull is fit to data on T_a and T_b generated from an exponential population, $\alpha^* = 1$.

These examples dramatically illustrate the importance of recognizing the impact of the sampling plan on the distribution of observed durations. As a general proposition, only the distribution of T_d (the length of spells initiated after the origin date of the sample) is invariant to the sampling plan. As a shortcut, one can obtain inefficient but consistent estimates of $G(t)$ by confining an empirical analysis to such spells.

However, in the presence of unobserved variables this strategy will in general produce inconsistent parameter estimates. We turn next to consider initial conditions problems in models with observed and unobserved explanatory variables.

5.2 The densities of T_a, T_b, T_c, and T_d in time-inhomogeneous environments for models with observed and unobserved explanatory variables

We define $k(\tau|\mathbf{x}(\tau),\theta)$ to be the intake rate into a given state at calendar time τ. We assume that θ is a scalar heterogeneity component and $\mathbf{x}(\tau)$ is a vector of explanatory variables. It is convenient and correct to think of $k(\tau|\mathbf{x}(\tau),\theta)$ as the density associated with the random variable $\mathcal{T}$ for a person with characteristics $[\mathbf{x}(\tau),\theta]$. We continue the useful convention that spells are sampled at $\mathcal{T}=0$. The densities of T_a, T_b, T_c, and T_d are derived for two cases: (a) conditional on a sample path $\{\mathbf{x}(u)\}_{-\infty}^{t}$ and (b) marginally on the sample path $\{\mathbf{x}(u)\}_{-\infty}^{t}$ (i.e., integrating it out). We denote the distribution of $\{\mathbf{x}(u)\}_{-\infty}^{t}$ as $D(\mathbf{x})$ with associated density $dD(\mathbf{x})$.

The derivation of the density of T_b conditional on $\{\mathbf{x}(u)\}_{-\infty}^{0}$ is as follows. The proportion of the population in the state at time $\tau=0$ is obtained by integrating over the survivors of each cohort of entrants. Thus

$$P_0(\mathbf{x})=\int_0^\infty\int_{\underline{\theta}} k(-t_b|\mathbf{x}(-t_b),\theta) \times\exp\left[-\int_0^{t_b} h(u|\mathbf{x}(u-t_b),\theta)\,du\right]d\mu(\theta)\,dt_b \tag{5.12}$$

Note that, unlike the case in the models analyzed in Section 5.1, this integral may exist even if the underlying distribution is defective provided that the $k(\cdot)$ factor damps the survivor function. (We require

$$\lim_{\substack{\text{sup}\\ \tau\to-\infty}} |\tau|^{1+\varepsilon}k(\tau)S(\tau)=0$$

for $\varepsilon>0$.) The proportion of people in the state with sample path $\{\mathbf{x}(u)\}_{-\infty}^{0}$ whose spells are exactly of length t_b is the set of survivors from a spell that initiated at $\tau=-t_b$ or

$$\int_{\underline{\theta}} k(-t_b|\mathbf{x}(-t_b),\theta)\exp\left[-\int_0^{t_b} h(u|\mathbf{x}(u-t_b),\theta)\,du\right]d\mu(\theta)$$

Thus the density of T_b conditional on $\{\mathbf{x}(u)\}_{-\infty}^{0}$ is

$$f(t_b|\{x(u)_{-\infty}^{0}\})=\frac{\int_{\underline{\theta}} k(-t_b|\mathbf{x}(-t_b),\theta)\exp\left[-\int_0^{t_b} h(u|\mathbf{x}(u-t_b),\theta)\,du\right]d\mu(\theta)}{P_0(\mathbf{x})} \tag{5.13}$$

The marginal density of T_b (integrating out $\mathbf{x}$) is obtained by an analogous argument: Divide the marginal flow rate as of time $\mathcal{T}=-t_b$ (the integrated flow rate) by the marginal (integrated) proportion of the population in the state at $\tau = 0$.

Thus defining

$$P_0 = \int_{\mathbf{X}} P_0(\mathbf{x})\, dD(\mathbf{x})$$

where $\mathbf{X}$ is the domain of integration for $\mathbf{x}$, we write

$$f(t_b) = \frac{\int_{\mathbf{X}} \int_{\underline{\theta}} k(-t_b | \mathbf{x}(-t_b), \theta) \exp\left[-\int_0^{t_b} h(u | \mathbf{x}(u - t_b), \theta)\, du \right] d\mu(\theta)\, dD(\mathbf{x})}{P_0} \tag{5.14}$$

Note that we use a function space integral to integrate out $\{\mathbf{x}(u)\}_{-\infty}^{0}$. (See Kac, 1959, for a discussion of such integrals.) Note further that one obtains an incorrect expression for the marginal density of T_b if one integrates (5.13) against the population density of $\mathbf{x}\,[dD(\mathbf{x})]$. The error in this procedure is that the appropriate density for $\mathbf{x}$ against which (5.13) should be integrated is a density of $\mathbf{x}$ conditional on the event that an observation is in the sample at $\tau = 0$. By Bayes' theorem this density is

$$f(\mathbf{x} | T_b > 0) = \left[\int_0^{\infty} f(t_b | \{\mathbf{x}(u)\}_{-\infty}^{0})\, dD(\mathbf{x})\, dt_b \right] \frac{P_0(\mathbf{x})}{P_0}$$

which is not in general the same as the density $dD(\mathbf{x})$. For proper distributions for T_b,

$$f(\mathbf{x} | T_b > 0) = dD(\mathbf{x}) \frac{P_0(\mathbf{x})}{P_0}$$

The derivation of the density of T_c, the completed length of a spell sampled at $\mathscr{T} = 0$, is equally straightforward. For simplicity we ignore right-censoring problems so that we assume that the sampling frame is of sufficient length that all spells are not censored and further assume that the underlying duration distribution is not defective. (But see the remarks at the conclusion of this section.) Conditional on $\{\mathbf{x}(u)\}_{-\infty}^{\tau}$ and θ, the probability that the spell began at τ is

$$k(\tau | \mathbf{x}(\tau), \theta)$$

The conditional density of a completed spell of length t that begins at τ is

$$h(t | \mathbf{x}(\tau + t), \theta) \exp\left[-\int_0^{t} h(u | \mathbf{x}(\tau + u), \theta)\, du \right]$$

For any fixed $\tau \le 0$, t_c by definition exceeds $-\tau$. Conditional on $\mathbf{x}$, the probability that T_c exceeds τ is $P_0(\mathbf{x})$. Thus, integrating out τ, respecting the fact that $t_c > -\tau$,

$$f(t_c|\{\mathbf{x}(u)\}_{-\infty}^{t_c}) = \int_{-t_c} \int_{\underline{\theta}} k(\tau|\mathbf{x}(\tau),\theta)h(t|\mathbf{x}(\tau+t_c),\theta) \times \exp\left[-\int_0^{t_c} h(u|\mathbf{x}(\tau+u),\theta)\,du\right] d\mu(\theta)\,d\tau \bigg/ P_0(\mathbf{x}) \tag{5.15}$$

The marginal density of T_c is

$$f(t_c) = \int_{-t_c}^{0} \int_{\mathbf{X}} \int_{\underline{\theta}} k(\tau|\mathbf{x}(\tau),\theta)h(t_c|\mathbf{x}(\tau+t),\theta) \times \exp\left[-\int_0^{t_c} h(u|\mathbf{x}(\tau+u),\theta)\,du\right] d\mu(\theta)\,dD(\mathbf{x})\,d\tau \bigg/ P_0 \tag{5.16}$$

Ignoring right censoring, the derivation of the density of T_a proceeds by recognizing that T_a conditional on $\mathscr{T} \le 0$ is the right tail portion of random variable $-\mathscr{T} + T_a$, the duration of a completed spell that begins at $\mathscr{T} = \tau$. The probability that the spell is sampled is $P_0(\mathbf{x})$. Thus the conditional density of $T_a = t_a$ given $\{\mathbf{x}(u)\}_{-\infty}^{t_a}$ is obtained by integrating out τ and correctly conditioning on the event that the spell is sampled, that is,

$$f(t_a|\{\mathbf{x}(u)\}_{-\infty}^{t_a}) = \int_{-\infty}^{0} \int_{\underline{\theta}} k(\tau|\mathbf{x}(\tau),\theta)h(t_a-\tau|\mathbf{x}(t_a),\theta) \times \exp\left[-\int_0^{t_a-\tau} h(u|\mathbf{x}(u+\tau),\theta)\,du\right] d\mu(\theta)\,d\tau \bigg/ P_0(\mathbf{x}) \tag{5.17}$$

and the corresponding marginal density is

$$f(t_a) = \int_{-\infty}^{0} \int_{\mathbf{X}} \int_{\underline{\theta}} k(\tau|\mathbf{x}(\tau),\theta)h(t_a-\tau|\mathbf{x}(t_a),\theta) \times \exp\left[-\int_0^{t_a-\tau} h(u|\mathbf{x}(u+\tau),\theta)\,du\right] d\mu(\theta)\,dD(\mathbf{x})d\tau \bigg/ P_0 \tag{5.18}$$

Of special interest is the case $k(\tau|\mathbf{x},\theta) = k(\mathbf{x})$ in which the intake rate does not depend on unobservables and is constant for all τ given $\mathbf{x}$, and in which $\mathbf{x}$ is time-invariant. Then (5.13) specializes to

$$f(t_b|\mathbf{x}) = \frac{1}{m(\mathbf{x})} \int_{\underline{\theta}} \exp\left[-\int_0^{t_b} h(u|\mathbf{x},\theta)\,du\right] d\mu(\theta) \tag{5.13$'$}$$

where

$$m(\mathbf{x}) = \int_0^\infty \int_{\underline{\theta}} \exp\left[-\int_0^z h(u|\mathbf{x},\theta)\,du \right] d\mu(\theta)\,dz$$

This density is very similar to (5.3). Under the same restrictions on k and $\mathbf{x}$, (5.15) and (5.17) specialize respectively to

$$f(t_c|\mathbf{x}) = \frac{t_c \int_{\underline{\theta}} h(t_c|\mathbf{x},\theta) \exp\left[-\int_0^{t_c} h(u|\mathbf{x},\theta)\,du \right] d\mu(\theta)}{m(\mathbf{x})} \tag{5.15'}$$

which is to be compared to (5.5), and

$$f(t_a|\mathbf{x}) = \frac{\int_{\underline{\theta}} \exp\left[-\int_0^{t_a} h(u|\mathbf{x},\theta)\,du \right] d\mu(\theta)}{m(\mathbf{x})} \tag{5.17'}$$

which is to be compared to (5.6). For this special case all of the results (i)–(vi) stated in Section 5.1 go through with obvious redefinition of the densities to account for observed and unobserved variables.

It is only for the special case of $k(\tau|\mathbf{x},\theta) = k(\tau|\mathbf{x})$ *with time-invariant regressors that the densities of* T_a, T_b, *and* T_c *do not depend on the parameters of* k.

In order to estimate the parameters of $h(t|\mathbf{x},\theta)$ from data on T_a, T_b, or T_c gathered in a time-inhomogeneous environment for a model with unobservables, knowledge of k is required. As long as θ appears in the conditional hazard and k depends on θ *or* τ *or* if $\mathbf{x}$ is not time-invariant, k must be specified along with $\mu(\theta)$ and $h(t|\mathbf{x},\theta)$.

The common expedient for "solving" the initial conditions problem for the density of T_a – assuming that $G(t|\mathbf{x},\theta)$ is exponential – does not avoid the dependence of the density of T_a on k even if k does not depend on θ as long as it depends on τ or $\mathbf{x}(\tau)$, where $\mathbf{x}(\tau)$ is not time-invariant. Thus in the exponential case in which $h(u|\mathbf{x}(u+\tau),\theta) = h(\mathbf{x}(u+\tau),\theta)$, we may write (5.17) for the case $k = k(\tau|\mathbf{x}(\tau))$ as

$$f(t_a|\{\mathbf{x}(u)\}_{-\infty}^{t_a}) = \frac{\begin{aligned}&\int_{-\infty}^0 \int_{\underline{\theta}} k(\tau|\mathbf{x}(\tau)) \exp\left[-\int_0^{-\tau} h(\mathbf{x}(u+\tau),\theta)\,du \right] \\ &\quad \times h(\mathbf{x}(t_a),\theta) \exp\left[-\int_0^{t_a} h(\mathbf{x}(u),\theta)\,du \right] d\mu(\theta)\,d\tau\end{aligned}}{\int_{-\infty}^0 \int_{\underline{\theta}} k(\tau|\mathbf{x}(\tau)) \exp\left[-\int_0^{-\tau} h(\mathbf{x}(u+\tau),\theta)\,du \right] d\mu(\theta)\,d\tau}$$

Only if $h(\mathbf{x}(u+\tau),\theta) = h(\mathbf{x}(u+\tau))$, so that unobservables do not enter the model (or equivalently that the distribution of Θ is degenerate), does k

cancel in the expression. In that case the numerator factors into two components, one of which is the denominator of the density. Now k also disappears if it is a time-invariant constant that is functionally independent of θ.[20]

At issue is the plausibility of alternative specifications of k. Although nothing can be said about this matter in a general way, for a variety of economic models it is plausible that k depends on θ, τ, and $\mathbf{x}(\tau)$ and that the $\mathbf{x}$ are not time-invariant. For example, in a study of unemployment spells over the business cycle, the onset of a spell of unemployment is the result of prior job termination or entry into the workforce. So k is the density of the length of a spell resulting from a prior economic decision. The same unobservables that determine unemployment are likely to determine such spells as well. In addition, it is odd to assume a time-invariant general economic and person-specific environment in an analysis of unemployment spells: Aggregate economic conditions change, and person-specific variables like age, health, education, and wage rates change over time. Similar arguments can be made on behalf of a more general specification of k for most economic models.

The initial conditions problem for the general model has two distinct components:

(i) The functional form of $k(\tau|\mathbf{x}(\tau),\theta)$ is not in general known. This includes as a special case the possibility that for some unknown $\tau^* < 0$, $k(\tau|\mathbf{x}(\tau),\theta) \equiv 0$ for $\tau < \tau^*$. In addition, the value of τ^* may vary among individuals, so that if it is unknown, it must be treated as another unobservable.

(ii) If $\mathbf{x}(\tau)$ is not time-invariant, its value may not be known for $\tau < 0$, so that even if the functional form of k is known, the correct conditional duration densities cannot be constructed.

These problems exacerbate the problem of securing model identification. Assumptions made about the functional form of k and the presample values of $\mathbf{x}(\tau)$ inject a further source of arbitrariness into single-spell model specification. Even if $\mathbf{x}(\tau)$ is known for $\tau \leq 0$, k, μ, and h cannot all be identified nonparametrically.

The initial conditions problem stated in its most general form is intractable. However, various special cases of it can be solved. For example, suppose that the functional form of k is known up to some finite number of parameters, but presample values of $\mathbf{x}(\tau)$ are not. If the distribution of these presample values is known or can be estimated, one method of solution to the initial conditions problem is to define duration distributions conditional on past sample values of $\mathbf{x}(\tau)$ but marginal on presample values, that is, to integrate out presample $\mathbf{x}(\tau)$ from the model using the distribution of their values. This suggests using (5.14) rather than (5.13) for the density of T_b. In place of either (5.15) or (5.16) for the density of T_c, this approach suggests using

$$f(t_c|\{\mathbf{x}(u)\}_0^{t_c}) = \int_{-t_c}^{0} \int_{\underline{\theta}} \int_{\{\mathbf{x}(\tau):\tau<0\}} k(\tau|\mathbf{x}(\tau),\theta)h(t_c|\mathbf{x}(t_c+\tau),\theta) \times \exp\left[-\int_0^{t_c} h(u|\mathbf{x}(\tau+u),\theta)\,du\right] dD(\mathbf{x})\,d\mu(\theta)\,d\tau \bigg/ P_0 \tag{5.19}$$

with a similar modification in the density of T_a.

This procedure requires either that the distribution of presample $\mathbf{x}(\tau)$ be known or that it be estimated along with the other functions in the model. The latter suggestion further complicates the identification problem. The former suggestion requires either access to another sample from which it is possible to estimate the distribution of presample values of $\mathbf{x}$ or that it be possible to use within sample data on $\mathbf{x}$ to estimate the distribution of the presample data, as would be possible, for example, if presample and within sample data distributions differed only by a finite-order polynomial time trend.

Recall, however, that the distribution of $\mathbf{x}$ within the sample is *not* the distribution of $\mathbf{x}$ in the population, $D(\mathbf{x})$. This is a consequence of the impact of the sample selection rule on the joint distribution of $\mathbf{x}$ and T.[21] The distribution of the $\mathbf{x}$ within the sample depends on the distribution of θ and on the parameters of $h(t|\mathbf{x},\theta)$ and the presample distribution of $\mathbf{x}$. Thus, for example, the joint density of T_a and $\mathbf{x}$ for $\tau > 0$ is

$$f(t_a, \mathbf{x}(\tau)|\tau \geq 0) = \int_{-t_a} \int_{\underline{\theta}} \int_{\{\mathbf{x}:\tau<0\}} k(\tau|\mathbf{x}(\tau),\theta)h(t_a-\tau|\mathbf{x}(t_a),\theta) \times \exp\left[-\int_0^{t_a-\tau} h(u|\mathbf{x}(u+\tau),\theta)\,du\right] dD(x)\,d\mu(\theta)\,d\tau \bigg/ P_0 \tag{5.20}$$

and so the density of within sample $\mathbf{x}(\tau)$ is

$$\begin{aligned} f(\mathbf{x}(\tau)|\tau \geq 0) &= \int_0^\infty f(t_a, \mathbf{x}(\tau))\,dt_a \\ &= \frac{dD(\mathbf{x})}{P_0} \int_0^\infty \int_{-t_a}^{0} \int_{\underline{\theta}} \int_{\{\mathbf{x}:\tau<0\}} k(\tau|\mathbf{x}(\tau),\theta)h(t_a-\tau|\mathbf{x}(t_a),\theta) \\ &\quad \times \exp\left[-\int_0^{t_a-\tau} h(u|\mathbf{x}(u+\tau),\theta)\,du\right] dD(\mathbf{x})\,d\mu(\theta)\,d\tau\,dt_a \end{aligned}$$

It is *this* density and not $dD(\mathbf{x})$ that is estimated using within sample data on $\mathbf{x}$.

This insight suggests two further points: (1) By direct analogy with results already rigorously established in the choice-based sampling literature (see, e.g., Manski and Lerman, 1977; Manski and McFadden, 1981; Cosslett, 1981) more efficient estimates of the parameters of $h(t|\mathbf{x},\theta)$ and $\mu(\theta)$ can be secured using the joint densities of T_a and $\mathbf{x}$ since the density of within sample data depends on the structural parameters of the model as a consequence of the sample selection rule. (2) Access to other sources of data on the $\mathbf{x}$ will be essential in order to "integrate out" presample $\mathbf{x}$ via formulas like (5.19).

A partial avenue of escape from the initial conditions problem exploits T_d, that is, durations for spells initiated after the origin date of the sample. The density of T_d conditional on $\{\mathbf{x}(u)\}_0^{t_d+\tau_d}$, where $\tau_d > 0$ is the start date of the spell, is

$$f(t_d|\{\mathbf{x}(u)\}_0^{t_d+\tau_d}) = \frac{\begin{array}{c}\int_0^\infty \int_{\underline{\theta}} k(\tau|\mathbf{x}(\tau),\theta)h(t_d|\mathbf{x}(\tau+t_d),\theta) \\ \times \exp\left[-\int_0^{t_d} h(u|\mathbf{x}(\tau+u),\theta)\,du\right] d\mu(\theta)\,d\tau\end{array}}{\int_0^\infty \int_{\underline{\theta}} k(\tau|\mathbf{x}(\tau),\theta)\,d\mu(\theta)\,d\tau} \tag{5.21}$$

The denominator is the probability that $\mathscr{T} \geq 0$. Only if k does not depend on θ will the density of T_d not depend on the parameters of k. More efficient inference is based on the joint density of $\mathscr{T}$ and t_d:

$$f(t_d,\tau|\{\mathbf{x}(u)\}_0^{t_d+\tau_d}) = \frac{\begin{array}{c}\int_{\underline{\theta}} k(\tau|\mathbf{x}(\tau),\theta)h(t_d|\mathbf{x}(\tau+t_d),\theta) \\ \exp\left[-\int_0^{t_d} h(u|\mathbf{x}(\tau+u),\theta)\,du\right] d\mu(\theta)\,d\tau\end{array}}{\int_0^\infty \int_{\underline{\theta}} k(\tau|\mathbf{x}(\tau),\theta)\,d\mu(\theta)\,d\tau} \tag{5.22}$$

Inference based on (5.21) or (5.22) requires *fewer* a priori assumptions than are required to use data on T_a, T_b, or T_c. Unless $\mathbf{x}$ is specified to depend on lagged values of explanatory variables, presample values of $\mathbf{x}$ are not required. Since the start dates of spells are known, it is now in principle possible to estimate k nonparametrically. Thus in samples with spells that originate after the origin date of the sample, inference is more robust.

As previously noted, the densities of the durations of T_a, T_b, T_c, and T_d are in general different. However, they depend on a common set of parameters. In samples with spells that originate after the start date of the sample, these cross-density restrictions aid in solving the initial conditions problem because the parameters estimated from the relatively more informative density of T_d can be exploited to estimate parameters from the other types of duration densities.

Before concluding this section, it is important to recall that we have abstracted from the problems raised by a finite-length sample frame and the problems of right censoring. If the sampling frame is such that $\tau^* > \mathscr{T} > 0$, for example, the formulas for the durations of T_a, T_c, and T_d presented above must be modified to account for this data generation process.

For example, the density of measured completed spells that begin after the start date of the sample incorporates the facts that $0 \leq \mathscr{T} \leq \tau^*$ and $T_d \leq \tau^* - \mathscr{T}$, that is, that the onset of the spell occurs after $\tau = 0$ and that all completed spells must be of length $\tau^* - \mathscr{T}$ or less. Thus in place of (5.21) we write (recalling that τ_d is the start date of the spell)

$$f(t_d | \{\mathbf{x}(u)\}_0^{t_d+\tau_d}, T_d \leq \tau^* - \mathscr{T}, \mathscr{T} \geq 0)$$

$$= \frac{\left(\displaystyle\int_0^{\tau^*-t_d} \int_{\underline{\theta}} k(\tau | \mathbf{x}(\tau), \theta) h(t_d | \mathbf{x}(\tau + t_d), \theta) \times \exp\left[-\int_0^{t_d} h(u | \mathbf{x}(\tau + u), \theta)\, du \right] d\mu(\theta)\, d\tau \right)}{\left(\displaystyle\int_0^{\tau^*} \int_0^{\tau^*-t_d} \int_{\underline{\theta}} k(\tau | \mathbf{x}(\tau), \theta) h(t_d | \mathbf{x}(\tau + t_d), \theta) \times \exp\left[-\int_0^{t_d} h(u | \mathbf{x}(\tau + u), \theta)\, du \right] d\mu(\theta)\, d\tau\, dt_d \right)}$$

The denominator is the joint probability of the events $0 < \mathscr{T} < \tau^* - T_d$ and $0 < T_d < \tau^*$, which must occur if we are to observe a completed spell that begins during the sampling frame $0 < \mathscr{T} < \tau^*$. As $\tau^* \to \infty$, this expression is equivalent to the density in (5.21).

The density of right-censored spells that begin after the start date of the sample is simply the joint probability of the events $0 < \mathscr{T} < \tau^*$ and $T_d > \tau^* - \mathscr{T}$, that is,

$$P(0 < \mathscr{T} < \tau^* \wedge T_d > \tau^* - \mathscr{T} | \{\mathbf{x}(u)\}_0^{\tau^*})$$

$$= \int_0^{\tau^*} \int_{\tau^*-\tau}^{\infty} \int_{\underline{\theta}} k(\tau | \mathbf{x}(\tau), \theta) \times \exp\left[-\int_0^{\tau^*-t_d} h(u | \mathbf{x}(\tau + u), \theta)\, du \right] d\mu(\theta)\, dt_d\, d\tau$$

The modifications required in the other formulas presented in this subsection to account for the finiteness of the sampling plan are equally straightforward . For spells sampled at $\tau = 0$ for which we observe presample values of the duration and postsample *completed* durations (T_c), it must be the case that (a) $\mathscr{T} \le 0$ and (b) $\tau^* - \mathscr{T} \ge T_c \ge -\mathscr{T}$, where $\tau^* > 0$ is the length of the sampling plan. Thus in place of (5.15) we write

$$f(t_c | \{\mathbf{x}(u)\}_{-\infty}^{t_c}, -\mathscr{T} \le T_c \le \tau^* - \mathscr{T}, \mathscr{T} \le 0)$$

$$= \frac{\left(\begin{array}{l} \displaystyle\int_{-t_c}^{\tau^* - t_c} \int_{\underline{\theta}} k(\tau | \mathbf{x}(\tau), \theta) h(t_c | \mathbf{x}(\tau + t_c), \theta) \\ \qquad \times \exp\left[-\displaystyle\int_0^{t_c} h(u | \mathbf{x}(\tau + u), \theta)\, du \right] d\mu(\theta)\, d\tau \end{array} \right)}{\left(\begin{array}{l} \displaystyle\int_{-\infty}^{0} \int_{-\tau}^{\tau^* - \tau} \int_{\underline{\theta}} k(\tau | \mathbf{x}(\tau), \theta) h(t_c | \mathbf{x}(\tau + t_c) \theta) \\ \qquad \times \exp\left[-\displaystyle\int_0^{t_c} h(u | \mathbf{x}(\tau + u), \theta)\, du \right] d\mu(\theta)\, dt_c\, d\tau \end{array} \right)}$$

The denominator of this expression is the joint probability of the events that $-\mathscr{T} < T_c < \tau^* - \mathscr{T}$ and $\mathscr{T} \le 0$. For spells sampled at $\tau = 0$ for which we observe presample values of the duration and postsample *right-censored durations,* it must be the case that (a) $\mathscr{T} < 0$ and (b) $T_c \ge \tau^* - \mathscr{T}$, and so the density for such spells is

$$f(t_c | \{\mathbf{x}(u)\}_{-\infty}^{t_c}, T_c \ge \tau^* - \mathscr{T}, \mathscr{T} \le 0)$$

$$= \int_{-\infty}^{0} \int_{\tau^* - \tau}^{\infty} \int_{\underline{\theta}} k(\tau | \mathbf{x}(\tau), \theta) h(t_c | \mathbf{x}(\tau + t_c), \theta) \times \exp\left[-\int_0^{t_c} h(u | \mathbf{x}(\tau + u), \theta)\, du \right] d\mu(\theta)\, dt_c\, d\tau$$

The derivation of the density for T_a in the presence of a finite-length sample frame is straightforward and for the sake of brevity is omitted. It is noted in Sheps–Menken (1973) (for models without regressors) and Flinn–Heckman (1982b) (for models with regressors) that failure to account for the sampling frame produces the wrong densities and that inference based on such densities may be seriously misleading.

6 New issues that arise in formulating and estimating choice theoretic duration models

In this section we briefly consider new issues that arise in the estimation of choice theoretic duration models. For specificity, we focus on the model of search unemployment in a time-homogeneous environment that is presented in Section 2.2. Our analysis of this model serves as a prototype for a broad class of microeconomic duration models produced from optimizing theory.

We make the following points about this model, assuming that the analyst has access to longitudinal data on I independent spells of unemployment.

A. Without data on accepted wages, the model of equations (2.12)–(2.21) is hopelessly underidentified even if there are no regressors or unobservables in the model.

B. Even with data on accepted wages, the model is not identified unless the distribution of wage offers satisfies a recoverability condition to be defined below.

C. For models without unobserved variables, the asymptotic theory required to analyze the properties of the maximum likelihood estimator of the model is nonstandard.

D. Allowing for individuals to differ in observed and unobserved variables injects an element of arbitrariness into model specification, creates new identification and computational problems, and virtually guarantees that the hazard is not of the proportional hazards functional form.

E. A new feature of duration models with unobservables produced by optimizing theory is that the support of Θ now depends on parameters of the model.

We consider each of these points in turn.

6.1 *Point A*

From a random sample of durations of unemployment spells in a model without observed or unobserved explanatory variables, it is possible to estimate h_u [in equation (2.15)] via maximum likelihood or Kaplan–Meier procedures (see, e.g., Kalbfleisch and Prentice, 1980, pp. 10–16). It is obviously not possible using such data alone to separate λ from $1 - F(rV)$ much less to estimate the reservation wage rV.

6.2 *Point B*

Given access to data on accepted wage offers, it is possible to estimate the reservation wage rV. A consistent estimator of rV is the minimum of the accepted wages observed in the sample

$$\widehat{rV} = \min\{W_i\}_{i=1}^{I} \tag{6.1}$$

For proof, see Flinn and Heckman (1982a).

Access to accepted wages does not secure identification of F. Only the truncated wage offer distribution can be estimated:

$$F(w \mid W \geq rV) = \frac{F(w) - F(rV)}{1 - F(rV)}, \qquad w \geq rV$$

To recover an untruncated distribution from a truncated distribution with a known point of truncation requires further conditions. If F is normal, such recovery is possible. If it is Pareto, it is not.[22] A sufficient condition that ensures recoverability is that $F(w)$ be real analytic over the support of W so that by an analytic continuation argument, $F(w)$ can be continued outside of the region of truncation.[23] In the Pareto example, the support of W is unknown.

If the recoverability condition is not satisfied, it is not possible to determine F even if rV can be consistently estimated. Hence it is not possible to decompose h_u in (2.15) into its constituent components.

If the recoverability condition is satisfied, it is possible to estimate F, λ, and rV. From (2.13), it is possible to estimate a linear relationship between r and c. The model is identified only by restricting r or c in some fashion. The most commonly used assumption fixes r at a prespecified value.

6.3 *Point C*

Using density (2.18) in a maximum likelihood procedure creates a nonstandard statistical problem. The range of random variable W depends on a parameter of the model ($W \geq rV$). For a model without observed or unobserved explanatory variables, the maximum likelihood estimator of rV is in fact the order statistic estimator (6.1). The likelihood based on (2.18) is monotonically increasing in $\widehat{rV}$, so that imposing the restriction that $W \geq rV$ is essential in securing maximum likelihood estimates of the model. Assuming that the density of W is such that $f(rV) \neq 0$, the consistent maximum likelihood estimator of the remaining parameters of the model can be obtained by inserting $\widehat{rV}$ in place of rV everywhere in (2.18) and the *sampling distribution of this estimator is the same whether or not rV is known a priori or estimated.* For proof, see Flinn and Heckman (1982a). In a model with observed explanatory variables but without unobserved explanatory variables, a similar phenomenon occurs. However, at the time of this writing, a rigorous asymptotic distribution theory is available only for models with discrete-valued regressor variables which assume a finite number of values.

6.4 *Point D*

Introducing observed and unobserved explanatory variables into a structural duration model raises the same sort of issues about ad hoc model specifications already discussed in the analysis of reduced form models in Section 3. However, there is the additional complication that structural restriction (2.13) produced by economic theory must be satisfied. One is not free to arbitrarily specify the parameters of the model.

It is plausible that c, r, λ, and F in (2.13) all depend on observed and unobserved explanatory variables. Introducing such variables into the econometric search model raises three new problems:

(i) Economic theory provides no guidance on the functional form of the c, r, λ, and F functions [other than the restriction given by (2.13)].[24] Estimates secured from these models are very sensitive to the choice of these functional forms. Model identification is difficult to check and is very functional-form-dependent.

(ii) In order to impose the restrictions produced by economic theory to secure estimates, it is necessary to solve nonlinear equation (2.13). Of special importance is the requirement that $V > 0$. If this restriction is not satisfied, the model cannot explain the data. If $V < 0$, an unemployed individual will not search. Closed form solutions exist only for special cases and, in general, numerical algorithms must be developed to impose or test these restrictions. Such numerical analysis procedures are costly even for a simple one-spell search model and for models with more economic content often become computationally intractable. (One exception is a dynamic McFadden model with no restrictions between the choice and interarrival time distributions.)

(iii) Because of restrictions like (2.13), proportional hazard specifications (1.10) are rarely produced by economic models.

6.5 *Point E*

In the search model without unobserved variables, the restriction that $W \geq rV$ is an essential piece of identifying information. In a model with unobservable Θ introduced in c, r, λ, or F, $rV = rV(\theta)$ as a consequence of functional restriction (2.13). In this model, the restriction that $W \geq rV$ is replaced with an implicit equation restriction on the support of Θ; that is, for an observation with accepted wage W and reservation wage $rV(\theta)$, the admissible support set for Θ is

$$\{\theta : 0 \leq rV(\theta) \leq W\}$$

This set is not necessarily connected.

The left-hand side of the inequality states the requirement that must be satisfied if search is undertaken ($rV > 0$ for $r > 0$). The right-hand side of the inequality states the requirement that accepted wages must exceed reservation wages. Unless this restriction is imposed on the support of Θ, the structural search model is not identified. (See Flinn and Heckman, 1982a.)[25]

Thus in a duration model produced from economic theory not only is the conditional hazard $h(t|\mathbf{x}(t), \theta)$ unlikely to be of the proportional hazard functional form, but the support of Θ will depend on parameters of the model. The mixing distribution representations presented in Sections 2.1.3 and 2.1.4 are unlikely to characterize structural duration models. Accordingly, the nonparametric identification and estimation strategies presented in Section 4 require modification before they can be applied to explicit economic models.

II Multiple-spell models

The single-spell duration models discussed in Part I are the principal building blocks for the richer, more behaviorally interesting models presented in this part of the chapter. Sequences of birth intervals, work histories involving movements among employment states, the successive issuing of patents to firms, and individual criminal victimization histories are examples of multiple-spell processes which require a more elaborate statistical framework than the one presented in Part I.

In this part we confine our attention to new issues that arise in the analysis of multiple-spell data. Issues such as the sensitivity of empirical estimates to ad hoc specifications of mixing distributions and initial conditions problems which also arise in multiple-spell models are not discussed except in cases where access to multiple-spell data aids in their resolution.

This part is in two sections. In Section 7 we present a unified statistical framework within which a rich variety of discrete state continuous time processes can be formulated and analyzed. We indicate by example how specializations of this framework yield a variety of models, some of which already appear in the literature. We do not present a complete analysis of multiple-spell processes including their estimation and testing on data generated by various sampling processes because at the time of this writing too little is known about this topic.

Section 8 considers in somewhat greater detail a class of multiple-spell duration models that have been developed for the analysis of event history data. In this section we also consider some alternative approaches to initial conditions problems and some alternative approaches to controlling for unobserved variables that are possible if the analyst has access to multiple-spell data.

7 A unified framework

7.1 *A general construction*

To focus on main issues, in this section we ignore models with unobserved variables. We retain the convention that the sample at our disposal starts at calendar time $\tau = 0$.

Let $\{Y(\tau), \tau > 0\}$, $Y(\tau) \in \bar{N}$, where $\bar{N} = \{1, \ldots, C\}$, $C < \infty$, be a finite state continuous time stochastic process. We define random variable $R(j)$, $j \in \{1, \ldots, \infty\}$ as the value assumed by Y at the jth transition time. Here $Y(\tau)$ or $R(j)$ is generated by the following sequence.

(i) An individual begins his evolution in a state $Y(0) = R(0) = r(0)$ and waits there for a random length of time T_1 governed by a conditional survivor function

$$\Pr(T_1 > t_1 | r(0)) = \exp\left[-\int_0^{t_1} h(u | \mathbf{x}(u), r(0))\, du \right]$$

As before, $h(u | \mathbf{x}(u), r(0))$ is a calendar-time-dependent (or age-dependent) function, and we now make explicit the origin state of the process.

(ii) At time $\mathscr{T}(1) = \tau(1)$, the individual moves to a new state $R(1) = r(1)$ governed by a conditional probability law

$$\Pr(R(1) = r(1) | \tau(1), r(0))$$

which may also be age-dependent.

(iii) The individual waits in state $R(1)$ for a random length of time T_2 governed by

$$\Pr(T_2 > t_2 | \tau(1), r(1), r(0)) = \exp\left[-\int_0^{t_2} h(u | \mathbf{x}(u + \tau(1)), r(1), r(0))\, du \right]$$

Note that one coordinate of $\mathbf{x}(u)$ may be $u + \tau(1)$ and that $\mathscr{T}(2) - \mathscr{T}(1) = T_2$. At the transition time $\mathscr{T}(2) = \tau(2)$ he switches to a new state $R(2) = r(2)$, where the transition probability

$$\Pr(R(2) = r(2) | \tau(1), \tau(2), r(1), r(0))$$

may be calendar-time-dependent.

Continuing this sequence of waiting times and moves to new states gives rise to a sequence of random variables

$$R(0) = r(0), \quad \mathscr{T}(1) = \tau(1), \quad R(1) = r(1), \quad \mathscr{T}(2) = \tau(2),$$
$$R(2) = r(2), \ldots$$

and suggests the definitions

$$Y(\tau) = R(k) \quad \text{for} \quad \tau(k) \le \tau < \tau(k+1)$$

where $R(k)$, $k = 0, 1, 2, \ldots$ is a discrete-time stochastic process governed by the conditional probabilities

$$\Pr(R(k) = r(k) \mid \mathbf{t}_k, \mathbf{r}_{k-1})$$

where

$$\mathbf{t}_k = (t_1, \ldots, t_k) \quad \text{and} \quad \mathbf{r}_{k-1} = (r(0), \ldots, r(k-1))$$

Now $T_k = \mathscr{T}(k) - \mathscr{T}(k-1)$ is governed by the conditional survivor function

$$\Pr(T_k \ge t_k \mid \mathbf{t}_{k-1}, \mathbf{r}_{k-1}) = \exp\left[-\int_0^{t_k} h(u \mid \mathbf{x}(u + \tau(k-1)), \mathbf{t}_{k-1}, \mathbf{r}_{k-1})\, du \right]$$

7.2 *Specializations of interest*

We now present a variety of special cases to emphasize the diversity of models encompassed by the preceding construction.

7.2.1. Repeated events of the same kind. This is a one-state process – for example, births in a fertility history. Now $R(\cdot)$ is a degenerate process, and attention focuses on the sequence of waiting times $T_1, T_2, \ldots$.

One example of such a process writes

$$\Pr(T_k > t_k \mid \mathbf{t}_{k-1}) = \exp\left[-\int_0^{t_k} h_k(u \mid \mathbf{x}(u + \tau(k-1)))\, du \right]$$

The hazard for the kth interval depends on the number of previous spells. This special form of dependence is referred to as *occurrence dependence.* In a study of fertility, $k-1$ corresponds to birth parity for a woman at risk. Heckman and Borjas (1980) consider such models for the analysis of unemployment.

Another variant writes the hazard of a current spell as a function of the mean duration of previous spells; that is, for spell $j > 1$,

$$h(u \mid \mathbf{x}(u + \tau(j-1)), \mathbf{t}_{j-1}) = h\left(u \,\middle|\, \frac{1}{j-1} \sum_{i=1}^{j-1} t_i, \tau(j-1) + u \right)$$

(See, e.g., Braun and Hoem, 1979.)

Yet another version of the general model writes for the jth spell

$$h(u \mid \mathbf{x}(u + \tau(j-1)), \mathbf{t}_{j-1}) = h_j(u \mid \mathbf{x}, t_1, t_2, \ldots, t_{j-1})$$

This is a model with both occurrence dependence and lagged duration dependence, where the latter is defined as dependence on lengths of preceding spells.

A final specification writes

$$h(u|\mathbf{x}(u+\tau(j-1)),\mathbf{t}_{j-1}) = h(\mathbf{x}(u+\tau(j-1)))$$

For spell j this is a model for independent nonidentically distributed durations; and $Y(\tau)$ is a nonstationary renewal process.

7.2.2. Multistate processes. Let

$$\Pr(R(k)=r(k)|\mathbf{t}_k,\mathbf{r}_{k-1}) = m_{r(k-1),r(k)}$$

where

$$\|m_{ij}\| = M$$

is a finite stochastic matrix

$$\Pr(T_k > t_k|\mathbf{t}_{k-1},\mathbf{r}_{k-1}) = \exp(-\lambda_{r(k-1)}t_k)$$

where the elements of $\{\lambda_i\}$ are positive constants. Then $Y(\tau)$ is a time-homogeneous Markov chain with constant intensity matrix

$$Q = \Lambda(M-I)$$

where

$$\Lambda = \begin{pmatrix} \lambda_1 & & \mathbf{0} \\ & \ddots & \\ \mathbf{0} & & \lambda_C \end{pmatrix}$$

and C is the number of states in the chain.[26]

In the dynamic McFadden model for a stationary environment presented in Part I, Section 2.3, M has the special structure $m_{ij} = m_{lj} = P_j$ for all i and l; that is, the origin state is irrelevant in determining the destination state. This restricted model can be tested against a more general specification.[27]

A time-inhomogeneous semi-Markov process emerges as a special case of the general model if we let

$$\Pr(R(k)=r(k)|\mathbf{t}_k,\mathbf{r}_{k-1},\tau(k-1)) = \pi_{r(k-1),r(k)}(\tau(k),t_k)$$

where

$$\|\pi_{ij}(\tau,u)\| = \mathbf{\Pi}(\tau,u)$$

is a two-parameter family of time (τ) and duration (u) dependent stochastic matrices with each element a function τ and u and

$$m_{ii} = 0$$

We further define

$$\Pr(T_k > t_k | \mathbf{t}_{k-1}, \mathbf{r}_{k-1}, \tau(k-1)) = \exp\left[-\int_0^{t_k} h(u | r_{(k-1)}, \tau(k-1))\, du \right]$$

With this restricted form of dependence, $Y(\tau)$ is a time-inhomogeneous semi-Markov process. (Hoem, 1972, provides a nice expository discussion of such processes.)

Moore and Pyke (1968) consider the problem of estimating a time-inhomogeneous semi-Markov model without observed or unobserved explanatory variables. The natural estimator for a model without restrictions connecting the parameters of $\Pr(R(k) = r(k) | \mathbf{t}_k, r_{k-1}, \tau(k-1))$ and $\Pr(T_k > t_k | \mathbf{t}_{k-1}, r_{k-1}, \tau(k-1))$ breaks the estimation into two components:

(i) Estimate $\mathbf{\Pi}$ by using data on transitions from i to j for observations with transitions having identical (calendar time τ, duration u) pairs. A special case of this procedure for a model with no duration dependence in a time-homogeneous environment pools i to j transitions for all spells to estimate the components of M (see also Billingsley, 1961). Another special case for a model with duration dependence in a time-homogeneous environment pools i *to* j transitions for all spells of a given duration.
(ii) Estimate $\Pr(T_k > t_k | \mathbf{t}_{k-1}, r_{k-1}, \tau(k-1))$ using standard survival methods (as described in Section 3 or in Lawless, 1982) on times between transitions.

These two estimators are consistent, asymptotically normal, and efficient and are *independent* of each other as the number of persons sampled becomes large. There is no efficiency gain from joint estimation. The same results carry over if $\mathbf{\Pi}$ and $\Pr(T_k > t_k | \mathbf{t}_{k-1}, r_{k-1}, \tau(k-1))$ are parameterized [e.g., elements of $\mathbf{\Pi}$ as a logit, $\Pr(T_k > t_k | \cdot)$ as a general duration model] provided, for example, the regressors are bounded i.i.d. random variables. The two-component procedure is efficient. However, if there are parameter restrictions connecting $\mathbf{\Pi}$ and the conditional survivor functions, the two-component estimation procedure produces inefficient estimators. If $\mathbf{\Pi}$ and the conditional survivor functions depend on a common unobservable, a joint estimation procedure is required to secure a consistent random effect estimator.

8 General duration models for the analysis of event history data

In this section we present a multistate duration model for event history data, that is, data that give information on times at which people change state and on their transitions. We leave for another occasion the analysis of multistate models designed for data collected by other sampling plans. This is a major area of current research.

An equivalent way to derive the densities of duration times and transitions for the multistate processes described in Section 7 that facilitates the derivation of the likelihoods presented below is based on the exit rate concept introduced in Part I. An individual event history is assumed to evolve according to the following steps.

(i) At time $\tau = 0$, an individual is in state $\mathbf{r}_{(0)} = (i)$, $i = 1, \ldots, C$. Given occupancy of state i, there are $N_i \leq C - 1$ possible destinations.[28] The limit (as $\Delta t \to 0$) of the probability that a person who starts in i at calendar time $\tau = 0$ leaves the state in interval $(t_1, t_1 + \Delta t)$ given regressor path $\{\mathbf{x}(u)\}_0^{t_1+\Delta t}$ and unobservable θ is the conditional hazard or escape rate

$$\lim_{\Delta t \to 0} \frac{\Pr(t_1 < T_1 < t_1 + \Delta t \,|\, \mathbf{r}_{(0)} = (\mathrm{i}), \mathscr{T}(0) = 0, \mathbf{x}(t_1), \theta, T_1 > t_1)}{\Delta t}$$
$$= h(t_1 \,|\, \mathbf{r}_{(0)} = (i), \mathscr{T}(0) = 0, \mathbf{x}(t_1), \theta) \tag{8.1}$$

This limit is assumed to exist.

The limit (as $\Delta t \to 0$) of the probability that a person starting in $\mathbf{r}_{(0)} = (i)$ at time $\tau(0)$ leaves to go to $j \neq i$, $j \in N_i$ in interval $(t_1, t_1 + \Delta t)$ given regressor path $\{\mathbf{x}(u)\}_0^{t_1+\Delta t}$ and θ is

$$\lim_{\Delta t \to 0} \frac{\Pr(t_1 < T_1 < t_1 + \Delta t, R(1) = j \,|\, \mathbf{r}_{(0)} = (\mathrm{i}), \mathscr{T}(0) = 0, \mathbf{x}(t_1), \theta, T_1 \geq t_1)}{\Delta t}$$
$$= h(t_1, j \,|\, \mathbf{r}_{(0)} = (i), \mathscr{T}(0) = 0, \mathbf{x}(t_1), \theta) \tag{8.2}$$

From the laws of conditional probability,

$$\sum_{j=1}^{N_i} h(t_1, j \,|\, \mathbf{r}_{(0)} = (i), \mathscr{T}(0) = 0, \mathbf{x}(t_1), \theta)$$
$$= h(t_1 \,|\, \mathbf{r}_{(0)} = (i), \mathscr{T}(0) = 0, \mathbf{x}(t_1), \theta)$$

(ii) The probability that a person starting in state i at calendar time $\tau = 0$ survives to $T_1 = t_1$ is [from the definition of the survivor function in (1.8) and from hazard (8.1)]

$$\Pr(T_1 > t_1 \mid \mathbf{r}_{(0)} = (i), \mathcal{T}(0) = 0, \{\mathbf{x}(u)\}_0^{t_1}, \theta)$$
$$= \exp\left[-\int_0^{t_1} h(u \mid \mathbf{r}_{(0)} = (i), \mathcal{T}(0) = 0, \mathbf{x}(u), \theta)\, du \right]$$

Thus the density of T_1 is

$$f(t_1 \mid \mathbf{r}_{(0)} = (i), \mathcal{T}(0) = 0, \{\mathbf{x}(u)\}_0^{t_1}, \theta)$$
$$= -\frac{\partial \Pr(T_1 > t_1 \mid \mathbf{r}_{(0)} = (i), \mathcal{T}(0) = 0, \{\mathbf{x}(u)\}_0^{t_1}, \theta)}{\partial t_1}$$
$$= h(t_1 \mid \mathbf{r}_{(0)} = i, \mathcal{T}(0) = 0, x(t_1), \theta)$$
$$\times \Pr(T_1 > t_1 \mid \mathbf{r}_{(0)} = (i), \mathcal{T}(0) = 0, \{\mathbf{x}(u)\}_0^{t_1}, \theta)$$

The density of the joint event $R(1) = j$ and $T_1 = t_1$ is

$$f(t_1, j \mid \mathbf{r}_{(0)} = (i), \mathcal{T}(0) = 0, \{\mathbf{x}(u)\}_0^{t_1}, \theta)$$
$$= h(t_1, j \mid \mathbf{r}_{(0)} = (i), \mathcal{T}(0) = 0, \mathbf{x}(t_1), \theta)$$
$$\times \Pr(T_1 > t_1 \mid \mathbf{r}_{(0)} = (i), \mathcal{T}(0) = 0, \{\mathbf{x}(u)\}_0^{t_1}, \theta)$$

This density is sometimes called a subdensity. Note that

$$\sum_{j=1}^{N_i} f(t_1, j \mid \mathbf{r}_{(0)} = (i), \mathcal{T}(0) = 0, \{\mathbf{x}(u)\}_0^{t_1}, \theta)$$
$$= f(t_1 \mid \mathbf{r}_{(0)} = (i), \mathcal{T}(0) = 0, \{\mathbf{x}(u)\}_0^{t_1}, \theta)$$

Proceeding in this fashion, one can define densities corresponding to each duration in the individual's event history. Thus, for an individual who starts in state $\mathbf{r}_{(m)}$ after his mth transition, the subdensity for $T_{m+1} = t_{m+1}$ and $R(m+1) = j, j = 1, \ldots, N_m$ is

$$f(t_{m+1}, j \mid \mathbf{r}_{(m)}, \mathcal{T}(m) = \tau(m), \{\mathbf{x}(u)\}_0^{\tau(m+1)}, \theta)$$

where

$$\tau(m+1) = \sum_{n=1}^{m+1} t_n \tag{8.3}$$

As in Part I, we assume an independent censoring mechanism. The most commonly encountered form of such a mechanism is upper limit truncation on the final spell. As noted in Part I, in forming the likelihood we can ignore the censoring densities.

The conditional density of completed spells $T_1, \ldots, T_k$ and right-censored spell T_{k+1} given $\{\mathrm{x}(u)\}_0^{\tau(k)+t_{k+1}}$ assuming that $\mathcal{T}(0) = 0$ is the exogenous start date of the event history (and so corresponds to the origin date of the sample) is, allowing for more general forms of dependence,

$$g(t_1, r(1), t_2, r(2), \ldots, t_k, r(k), t_{k+1} \,|\, \{x(u)\}_0^{\tau(k)+t_{k+1}})$$
$$= \int_{\underline{\theta}} \left[\prod_{i=1}^{k} f(t_i, r(i) \,|\, \mathbf{r}_{(i-1)}, \mathbf{t}_{(i-1)}, \tau(i-1), \{\mathbf{x}(u)\}_{\tau(i-1)}^{\tau(i)}, \theta) \right]$$
$$\times [\Pr(T_{k+1} > t_{k+1} \,|\, \mathbf{r}_{(k)}, \mathbf{t}_k, \tau(k), \{\mathbf{x}(u)\}_{\tau(k)}^{\tau(k)+t_k}, \theta)] \, d\mu(\theta) \qquad (8.4)$$

As noted in Section 5, it is unlikely that the origin date of the sample coincides with the start date of the event history. Let

$$\phi(r(0), \mathscr{T}(0) = 0, r(1), t_{1a}, \{\mathbf{x}(u)\}_{-\infty}^{\tau(1)}, \theta)$$

be the probability density for the random variables describing the events that a person is in state $R(0) = r(0)$ at time $\mathscr{T}(0) = 0$ with a spell of length t_{1a} (measured after the start of the sample) that ends with an exit to state $R(1) = r(1)$ given $\{\mathbf{x}(u)\}_0^{\tau(1)}$ and θ. The derivation of this density in terms of the intake density k appears in Section 5 (see the derivation of the density of T_a). The only new point to notice is that the h in Section 5 should be replaced with the appropriate h as defined in (8.2). The joint density of $[r(0), t_{1c}, r(1)]$, the *completed spell* density sampled at $\mathscr{T}(0) = 0$ terminating in state $r(1)$, is defined analogously. For such spells we write the density as

$$\phi(r(0), \mathscr{T}(0) = 0, t_{1c}, r(1), \{\mathbf{x}(u)\}_{-\infty}^{\tau(1)}, \theta)$$

In a multiple-spell model setting in which it is plausible that the process has been in operation prior to the origin date of the sample, intake rate k introduced in Section 5 is the density of the random variable $\mathscr{T}$ describing the event "entered the state $r(0)$ at time $\mathscr{T} = \tau \le 0$ and did not leave the state until $\mathscr{T} > 0$." The expression for k in terms of exit rate (8.2) depends on (i) presample values of $\mathbf{x}$ and (ii) the date at which the process began. Thus in principle, given (i) and (ii), it is possible to determine the functional form of k. In this context it is plausible that k depends on θ.

The joint likelihood for $r(0)$, t_{1l} $(l = a, c)$, $r(1)$, $t_2, \ldots, r(k)$, t_{k+1} conditional on θ and $\{\mathbf{x}(u)\}_{-\infty}^{\tau(k)+t_{k+1}}$ for a right-censored $(k+1)$st spell is

$$g(r(0), t_{1l}, r(1), t_2, r(2), \ldots, t_k, r(k), t_{k+1} \,|\, \{\mathbf{x}(u)\}_{-\infty}^{\tau(k)+t_{k+1}}, \theta)$$
$$= \phi(r(0), \mathscr{T}(0) = 0, t_{1l}, r(1) | \{\mathbf{x}(u)\}_{-\infty}^{\tau(1)}, \theta)$$
$$\times \left[\prod_{i=2}^{k} f(t_i, r(i) \,|\, \mathbf{r}_{(i-1)}, \mathbf{t}_{(i-1)}, \tau(i-1), \{\mathbf{x}(u)\}_{\tau(i-1)}^{\tau(i)}, \theta) \right]$$
$$\times \Pr(T_{k+1} > t_{k+1} \,|\, \mathbf{r}_k, \mathbf{t}_{(k)}, \tau(k-1), \{\mathbf{x}(u)\}_{\tau(k-1)}^{\tau(k)+t_{k+1}}, \theta) \qquad (8.5)$$

The marginal likelihood obtained by integrating out θ is

$$g(r(0), t_{1l}, r(1), t_2, \ldots, t_k, r(k), t_{k+1} \,|\, \{\mathbf{x}(u)\}_{-\infty}^{\tau(k)+t_{k+1}})$$
$$= \int_{\underline{\theta}} g(r(0), t_{1l}, r(1), t_2, \ldots, t_k, r(k), t_{k+1} \,|\, \{\mathbf{x}(u)\}_{-\infty}^{\tau(k)+t_{k+1}}, \theta)\, d\mu(\theta) \qquad (8.6)$$

Equation (8.5) makes explicit that the date of onset of spell $m + 1$ ($\mathcal{T}(m + 1)$) depends on the durations of the preceding spells. Accordingly, in a model in which the exit rates (8.2) depend on θ, the distribution of time-varying $\mathbf{x}$ variables (including date of onset of the spell) *sampled at the start of each spell* depends on θ. Such variables are not (weakly) exogenous or ancillary in duration regression equations, and least squares estimators of models that include such variables are, in general, inconsistent. (See Flinn and Heckman, 1982b.) Provided that in the population $\mathbf{X}$ is distributed independently of Θ, time-varying variables create no econometric problem for maximum likelihood estimators based on density (8.6), which accounts for the entire history of the process. However, a maximum likelihood estimator based on a density of the *last* $n < k + 1$ spells that conditions on $\tau(k + 1 - n)$ or $\{\mathbf{x}(u)\}_{-\infty}^{\tau(k+1-n)}$ assuming they are independent of Θ is inconsistent.

Using (8.5) and conditioning on $T_{1l} = t_{1l}$ produces conditional likelihood

$$g(r(0), t_{1l}, r(1), t_2, \ldots, t_k, r(k), t_{k+1} \,|\, \{\mathbf{x}(u)\}_{-\infty}^{\tau(k)+t_{k+1}}, \theta, T_{1l} = t_{1l})$$
$$= \prod_{i=2}^{k} f(t_i, r(i) \,|\, \mathbf{r}_{(i-1)}, \mathbf{t}_{(i-1)}, \tau(i-1), \{x(u)\}_{\tau(i-1)}^{\tau(i)}, \theta)$$
$$\times \Pr(T_{k+1} > t_{k+1} \,|\, \mathbf{r}_k, \mathbf{t}_k, \tau(k), \{x(u)\}_{\tau(k)}^{\tau(k)+t_{k+1}}, \theta) \qquad (8.7)$$

For three reasons, inference based on conditional likelihood (8.7) appears to be attractive (see Heckman, 1981b): (1) With this likelihood it is not necessary to specify or estimate the distribution $\mu(\theta)$. It thus appears possible to avoid one element of arbitrariness in model specification. (2) With this likelihood we avoid the initial conditions problem because ϕ and $\{\mathbf{x}(u)\}_{-\infty}^{\tau(1)}$ do not appear in density (8.7). (3) Treating θ as a parameter allows for arbitrary dependence between θ and $\mathbf{x}$. These three reasons demonstrate the potential gains that arise from having multiple-spell data.[29]

However, for general duration distributions, inference based on (8.7) fit on panel data produces inconsistent estimators. This is so because the conditional likelihood function depends on person-specific component θ. Estimating θ as a parameter for each person along with the other parameters of the model produces inconsistent estimators of all parameters if $k < \infty$ in the available panel data because the likelihood equations are not in general separable in θ (see Neyman and Scott, 1948). In most panel data sets, k is likely to be small.

No Monte Carlo study of the performance of the inconsistent estimator has been performed. By analogy with the limited Monte Carlo evidence reported in Heckman (1981b) for a fixed effect discrete choice model, if $\mathbf{x}$ does not contain lagged values of the dependent variable, the inconsistency is likely to be negligible even if the likelihood is fit on short panels. The inconsistency issue may be a matter of only theoretical concern.

Chamberlain (Chapter 1, this volume), drawing on results due to Andersen (1973, 1980), presents a class of multiple-spell duration models for which it is possible to find sufficient or ancillary statistics for θ. Estimation within this class of models avoids the inconsistency problem that arises in likelihoods based on (8.7). The class of exponential family distributions for which the Andersen–Chamberlain procedures are valid is very special and does not provide arbitrarily close approximations to a general duration density. Most economically motivated duration models are not likely to be members of the exponential family. With these procedures it is not possible to estimate duration dependence parameters. These procedures avoid the need to specify or estimate $\mu(\theta)$ and solve the problem of initial conditions by making very strong and nonrobust assumptions about the functional form of the conditional hazard $h(t|\mathbf{x},\theta)$.

The random effect maximum likelihood estimator based on density (8.6) is the estimator that is likely to see the greatest use in multispell models that control for unobservables. Flinn and Heckman (1982b) and Hotz (1983) have developed a general computational algorithm called CTM for a likelihood based on (8.6) that has the following features:

(i) It allows for a flexible Box–Cox hazard for (8.2) with scalar heterogeneity.

$$h(t|\mathbf{x},\theta) = \exp\left(\mathbf{x}(t)\boldsymbol{\beta} + \left(\frac{t^{\lambda_1}-1}{\lambda_1}\right)\gamma_1 + \left(\frac{t^{\lambda_2}-1}{\lambda_2}\right)\gamma_2 + c\theta\right), \quad \lambda_1 < \lambda_2 \qquad (3.2)'$$

where $\boldsymbol{\beta}$, γ_1, γ_2, λ_1, λ_2, and c are permitted to depend on the origin state, the destination state, and the serial order of the spell. Lagged durations may be included among the $\mathbf{x}$. Using maximum likelihood procedures, it is possible to estimate all of these parameters except for one normalization of c.

(ii) It allows for general time-varying variables and right censoring. The regressors may include lagged durations.[30]

(iii) $\mu(\theta)$ can be specified as either normal, lognormal, or gamma, or the NPMLE procedure discussed in Section 4.1 can be used.[31]

(iv) It addresses the left-censoring or initial conditions problem by assuming that the functional form of the initial duration distribution for each origin state is different from that of the other spells.[32]

The burden of computing likelihoods based on (8.6) is lessened by the following recursive estimation strategy. (1) Integrate out $T_2, \ldots, T_{k+1}$ from (8.6) and estimate the parameters of the reduced likelihood. (2) Then integrate out $T_3, \ldots, T_{k+1}$ from (8.6) and estimate the parameters of the reduced likelihood fixing the parameters estimated from stage 1. (3) Proceed in this fashion until all parameters are estimated. One Newton step from these parameter values produces efficient maximum likelihood estimators.

For more details on the CTM program see Hotz (1983). For further details on the CTM likelihood function and its derivatives, see Flinn and Heckman (1983).[33] For examples of structural multispell duration models see Coleman (1983) and Flinn and Heckman (1982a).

9 Summary

This chapter considers the formulation and estimation of continuous time social science duration models. The focus is on new issues that arise in applying statistical models developed in biostatistics to analyze economic data and formulate economic models. Both single-spell and multiple-spell models are discussed. In addition, we present a general time-inhomogeneous multiple-spell model which contains a variety of useful models as special cases.

Four distinctive features of social science duration analysis are emphasized:

1. Because of the limited size of samples available in economics and because of an abundance of candidate observed explanatory variables and plausible omitted explanatory variables, standard nonparametric procedures used in biostatistics are of limited value in econometric duration analysis. It is necessary to control for observed and unobserved explanatory variables to avoid biasing inference about underlying duration distributions. Controlling for such variables raises many new problems not discussed in the available literature.
2. The environments in which economic agents operate are not the time-homogeneous laboratory environments assumed in biostatistics and reliability theory. Ad hoc methods for controlling for time inhomogeneity produce badly biased estimates.
3. Because the data available to economists are not obtained from the controlled experimental settings available to biologists, doing econometric duration analysis requires accounting for the effect of sampling plans on the distributions of sampled spells.

4. Econometric duration models that incorporate the restrictions produced by economic theory only rarely can be represented by the models used by biostatisticians. The estimation of structural econometric duration models raises new statistical and computational issues.

Because of point 1 it is necessary to parameterize econometric duration models to control for both observed and unobserved explanatory variables. Economic theory only provides qualitative guidance on the matter of selecting a functional form for a conditional hazard, and it offers no guidance at all on the matter of choosing a distribution of unobservables. This is unfortunate because empirical estimates obtained from econometric duration models are very sensitive to assumptions made about the functional forms of these model ingredients.

In response to this sensitivity we present criteria for inferring qualitative properties of conditional hazards and distributions of unobservables from raw duration data sampled in time-homogeneous environments, that is, from unconditional duration distributions. No parametric structure need be assumed to implement these procedures.

We also note that current econometric practice *overparameterizes* duration models. Given a functional form for a conditional hazard determined up to a finite number of parameters, it is possible to consistently estimate the distribution of unobservables nonparametrically. We report on the performance of such an estimator and show that it helps to solve the sensitivity problem.

We demonstrate that in principle it is possible to identify both the conditional hazard and the distribution of unobservables without assuming parametric functional forms for either. Tradeoffs in assumptions required to secure such model identification are discussed. Although under certain conditions a fully nonparametric model can be identified, the development of a consistent fully nonparametric estimator remains to be done.

We also discuss conditions under which access to multiple-spell data aids in solving the sensitivity problem. A superficially attractive conditional likelihood approach produces inconsistent estimators, but the practical significance of this inconsistency is not yet known. Conditional inference schemes for eliminating unobservables from multiple-spell duration models that are based on sufficient or ancillary statistics require unacceptably strong assumptions about the functional forms of conditional hazards and so are not robust. Contrary to recent claims, they offer no general solution to the model sensitivity problem.

The problem of controlling for time-inhomogeneous environments (point 2) remains to be solved. Failure to control for time inhomogeneity produces serious biases in estimated duration models. Controlling for time inhomogeneity creates a potential identification problem.

For single-spell data it is impossible to separate the effect of duration dependence from the effect of time inhomogeneity by a fully nonparametric procedure. Although it is intuitively obvious that access to multiple-spell data aids in the solution of this identification problem, the development of precise conditions under which this is possible is a topic left for future research.

We demonstrate how sampling schemes distort the functional forms of sample duration distributions away from the population duration distributions that are the usual object of econometric interest (point 3). Inference based on misspecified duration distributions is in general biased. New formulas for the densities of commonly used duration measures are produced for duration models with unobservables in time-inhomogeneous environments. We show how access to spells that begin after the origin date of a sample aids in solving econometric problems created by the sampling schemes that are used to generate economic duration data.

We also discuss new issues that arise in estimating duration models explicitly derived from economic theory (point 4). For a prototypical search unemployment model we discuss and resolve new identification problems that arise in attempting to recover structural economic parameters. We also consider nonstandard statistical problems that arise in estimating structural models that are not treated in the literature. Imposing or testing the restrictions implied by economic theory requires duration models that do not appear in the received literature and often requires numerical solution of implicit equations derived from optimizing theory.

ACKNOWLEDGMENTS

This research was supported by NSF Grant SES-8107963 and NIH Grant NIH-1-R01-HD16846-01 to the Economics Research Center, NORC, 6030 S. Ellis, Chicago, Illinois 60637. We thank Takeshi Amemiya and Aaron Han for helpful comments.

NOTES

1 See especially Kalbfleisch and Prentice (1980), Lawless (1982), and Cox and Oakes (1984).

2 For a treatment of duration distributions that are not absolutely continuous see, e.g., Lawless (1982).

3 See, e.g., Cox and Hinkley (1974) for a discussion of ancillarity.

4 As first noted by Lundberg (1903), it is possible to transform this model to a time-homogeneous Poisson model if we redefine duration time to be

$$\Omega^*(t_e, a_1) = \int_{a_1}^{a_1 + t_e} \lambda(u)\, du$$

Allowing for time inhomogeneity in $Y(a)$ and $W(a)$ raises a messy but not especially deep problem. It is possible that the values of these variables would change at a point in time in between the arrival of ε values and that such changes would result in a reversal of the sign of $I^*(a)$ so that the consumer would cease working at points in time when ε did not change. Conditioning on the paths of $Y(a)$ and $W(a)$ formally eliminates the problem.

5 $o(\Delta t)$ is defined as a term such that $\lim_{\Delta t \to 0} o(\Delta t)/\Delta t \to 0$.

6 For one justification of the Poisson wage arrival assumption, see, e.g., Burdett and Mortensen (1978).

7 For time inhomogeneity induced solely by the finiteness of life, the reservation wage property characterizes an optimal policy (see, e.g., DeGroot, 1970).

8 Note that in this model it is trivial to introduce time-varying forcing variables because by assumption the agent cannot accept a job in between arrival of job offers. Compare with the discussion in note 4.

9 We use the fact that

$$\frac{\partial h(t|\mathbf{x},\boldsymbol{\theta})}{\partial t} = \frac{\dfrac{\partial g(t|\mathbf{x},\boldsymbol{\theta})}{\partial t}}{1 - G(t|\mathbf{x},\boldsymbol{\theta})} + \left[\frac{g(t|\mathbf{x},\boldsymbol{\theta})}{1 - G(t|\mathbf{x},\boldsymbol{\theta})}\right]^2$$

10 Heckman and Singer (1982) present some examples. They are not hard to generate for anyone with access to tables of integral transforms.

11 Moreover, in the multistate models with heterogeneity that are presented in Part II of this chapter, treating $\mathbf{x}(0)$ as exogenous is incorrect because the value of $\mathbf{x}(0)$ at the start of the current spell depends on the lengths of outcomes of preceding spells. See the discussion in Section 9. This problem is also discussed in Flinn and Heckman (1982b, p. 62).

12 If $\mathbf{x}(t)$ is not time-invariant, additional identification problems arise. In particular, nonparametric estimation of $G(t|\mathbf{x}(t))$ becomes much more difficult.

13 For

$$f(\eta) = [\exp(-\lambda\eta)]\frac{(\lambda\eta)^{r-1}}{\Gamma(r)} \quad \text{and} \quad \lambda < 1,\ E(\exp \eta) = \infty$$

14 Heckman and Singer also present conditions for $\mu(\theta)$ that are not absolutely continuous. For a discussion of slowly varying functions see Feller (1971, p. 275).

15 As previously noted, in their appendix Elbers and Ridder (1982) generalize their proofs to a case in which all of the regressors are discrete valued. However, a regressor is required in order to secure identification.

16 In computing the estimator it is necessary to impose all of the identifiability conditions in order to secure consistent estimators. For example, in a Weibull model with $E(\Theta) < \infty$, it is important to impose this requirement in securing estimates. As our example in the preceding subsection indicated, there are other models with $E(\Theta) = \infty$ that will explain the data equally well. In large samples, this condition is imposed, for example, by picking estimates of $\mu(\theta)$ such that $|\int [1 - \hat{\mu}(\theta)]\, d\theta| < \infty$ or equivalently $|\int [1 - \hat{\mu}(\theta)]\, d\theta|^{-1} > 0$. Similarly, if identification is secured by tail condition (4.8), this must be imposed in selecting a unique estimator. See also the discussion at the end of Section 4.3.

17 See Cox (1962), Cox and Lewis (1966), Sheps and Menken (1973), Salant (1977),

and Baker and Trevedi (1982) for useful presentations of time-homogeneous models.

18 *Proof:* $E(T_a) = (1/m) \int_0^\infty t_a(1 - G(t_a))\, dt_a$. Integrating by parts assuming that $E(T^2) = \int_0^\infty t^2 g(t)\, dt < \infty$, we obtain

$$E(T_a) = \frac{1}{m} \int_0^\infty \frac{t_a^2}{2} g(t_a)\, dt_a + \frac{1}{m}[1 - G(t_a)] \frac{t_a^2}{2}\bigg|_0^\infty$$

$$= \frac{1}{m} \frac{\sigma^2 + m^2}{2} = \frac{m}{2}\left(1 + \frac{\sigma^2}{m^2}\right)$$

19 $E(T_c) = \dfrac{1}{m} \int_0^\infty x^2 g(x)\, dx = \dfrac{\sigma^2 + m^2}{m} = m\left(1 + \dfrac{\sigma^2}{m^2}\right)$

20 We note that one "shortcut" procedure frequently used does not avoid these problems. The argument correctly notes that conditional on θ and the start date of the sample,

$$f(t_a | \{\mathbf{x}(u)\}_0^{t_a}, \theta) = h(\mathbf{x}(t_a), \theta) \exp\left[- \int_0^{t_a} h(\mathbf{x}(u), \theta)\, du \right] \qquad (*)$$

This expression obviously does not depend on k. The argument runs astray by integrating this expression against $d\mu(\theta)$ to get a marginal (with respect to θ) density. The correct density of θ is not $d\mu(\theta)$ and depends on k by virtue of the fact that sample values of θ are generated by the selection mechanism that an observation must be in the sample at $\tau = 0$. Precisely the same issue arises with regard to the distribution of $\mathbf{x}$ in passing from (5.13) to (5.14). However, density $(*)$ can be made the basis of a simpler estimation procedure in a multiple-spell setting, as we note in Section 8.

21 Precisely the same phenomenon appears in the choice-based sampling literature (see, e.g., Manski and Lerman, 1977; Manski and McFadden, 1981; Cosslett, 1981). In fact the suggestion of integrating out the missing data is analogous to the suggestions offered in Section 1.7 of the Manski and McFadden paper.

22 Thus if $F(w) = \phi w^\beta$, $c_2 \le w \le \infty$, $\beta \le -2$, where $\phi = -(\beta + 1)/(c_2)^{\beta+1}$, $F(w | W \ge rV) = -(\beta + 1)w^\beta/(rV)^{\beta+1}$, and so ϕ (or c_2) does not appear in the conditional distribution.

23 For a good discussion of real analytic functions, see Rudin (1974). If a function is real analytic, knowledge of the function over an interval is sufficient to determine the function over its entire domain of definition.

24 As discussed in Flinn and Heckman (1982a), some equilibrium search models place restrictions on the functional form of F.

25 Kiefer and Neumann (1981) fail to impose this requirement in their discrete time structural model, and so their proposed estimator is inconsistent. See Flinn and Heckman (1982c).

26 Note that without further restrictions on the elements of M, it is not possible to separate λ_i from $(m_{ii} - 1)$, so that one might as well normalize $m_{ii} = 0$.

27 Note that in the McFadden model it is not necessary to normalize $m_{ii} = 0$ to identify λ_i because of the cross-row restrictions on M.

28 If some transitions are prohibited, then $N_i < C - 1$.

29 The conditional likelihood cannot be used to analyze single-spell data. Estimating θ as a person-specific parameter would explain each single-spell

observation perfectly and no structural parameters of the model would be identified.

30 The random effect maximum likelihood estimator based on (8.6) can be shown to be consistent in the presence of θ with lagged durations included in $\mathbf{x}$.

31 The NPMLE procedure of Heckman and Singer (1984b) can be shown to be consistent for multiple-spell data.

32 This procedure is identical to the procedure discussed in Section 5.2, using spells that originate after the origin of the sample.

33 In Flinn and Heckman (1983), the likelihood is derived using a "competing risks" framework. (See, e.g., Kalbfleisch and Prentice, 1980, for a discussion of competing risks models.) This framework is in fact inessential to their approach. A more direct approach starts with hazards (8.1) and (8.2) that are not based on "latent failure times." This direct approach, given hazard specification (3.2′), produces exactly the same estimating equations as are given in their paper.

REFERENCES

Amemiya, T. 1981. "Qualitative Response Models: A Survey." *Journal of Economic Literature*, Vol. 19, pp. 1483–1536.

1984. "Tobit Models: A Survey." *Journal of Econometrics*, Vol. 24, pp. 1–63.

Andersen, E. B. 1973. *Conditional Inference and Models for Measuring.* Copenhagen: Mentalhygiejnisk Forlag.

1980. *Discrete Statistical Models with Social Science Applications.* Amsterdam: North-Holland.

Arnold, Barry, and P. Brockett. 1983. "Identifiability for Dependent Multiple Decrement/Competing Risks Models." *Scandinavian Actuarial Journal*, Vol. 10, pp. 117–127.

Baker, G., and P. Trevedi. 1982. "Methods for Estimating the Duration of Periods of Unemployment." Australian National University Working Paper.

Barlow, R. E., D. J. Bartholomew, J. M. Bremner, and H. D. Brunk. 1972. *Statistical Inference under Order Restrictions.* London: Wiley.

Barlow, R. E., and F. Proschan. 1975. *Statistical Theory of Reliability and Life Testing.* New York: Holt, Rinehart and Winston.

Billingsley, P. 1961. *Statistical Inference for Markov Processes.* Chicago: University of Chicago Press.

Braun, H., and J. Hoem. 1979. "Modelling Cohabitational Birth Intervals in the Current Danish Population: A Progress Report." Copenhagen University, Laboratory of Actuarial Mathematics, Working Paper #24.

Burdett, K., and D. Mortensen. 1978. "Labor Supply under Uncertainty." In R. Ehrenberg, ed., *Research in Labor Economics*, Vol. 2. Greenwich, Conn.: JAI Press.

Chamberlain, G. 1980. "Comment on Lancaster and Nickell." *Journal of Royal Statistical Society*, Series A, Vol. 144, p. 160.

Coleman, T. 1983. "A Dynamic Model of Labor Supply under Uncertainty." Typescript, University of Chicago, presented at 1983 Summer Meetings of the Econometric Society, Evanston, Ill.

Cosslett, S. 1981. "Efficient Estimation of Discrete Choice Models." In C. Manski and D. McFadden, eds., *Structural Analysis of Discrete Data with Econometric Applications.* Cambridge: MIT Press.

Cox, D. R. 1962. *Renewal Theory*. London: Methuen.
1972. "Regression Models and Lifetables." *Journal of the Royal Statistical Society*, Series B, Vol. 34, pp. 187–220.
Cox, D. R., and D. Hinkley. 1974. *Theoretical Statistics*. London: Chapman and Hall.
Cox, D. R., and P. A. W. Lewis. 1966. *The Statistical Analysis of a Series of Events*. London: Chapman and Hall.
Cox, D. R., and D. O. Oakes. 1984. *Analysis of Survival Data*. London: Chapman and Hall.
DeGroot, M. 1970. *Optimal Statistical Decisions*. New York: McGraw-Hill.
Domencich, T., and D. McFadden. 1975. *Urban Travel Demand*. Amsterdam: North-Holland.
Elbers, C., and G. Ridder. 1982. "True and Spurious Duration Dependence: The Identifiability of the Proportional Hazard Model." *Review of Economic Studies*, Vol. 49, pp. 403–410.
Feller, W. 1970. *An Introduction to Probability Theory and Its Applications*, Vol. I, 3rd ed. New York: Wiley.
1971. *An Introduction to Probability Theory and Its Applications*, Vol. II, 3rd ed. New York: Wiley.
Flinn, C., and J. Heckman. 1982a. "New Methods for Analyzing Structural Models of Labor Force Dynamics." *Journal of Econometrics*, Vol. 18, pp. 115–168.
1982b. "Models for the Analysis of Labor Force Dynamics." In R. Bassmann and G. Rhodes, eds., *Advances in Econometrics*, Vol. 1. Greenwich, Conn.: JAI Press.
1982c. "Comment on 'Individual Effects in a Nonlinear Model: Explicit Treatment of Heterogeneity in the Empirical Job Search Literature.'" Typescript, University of Chicago.
1983. "The Likelihood Function for the Multistate–Multiepisode Model in 'Models for the Analysis of Labor Force Dynamics.'" In R. Bassmann and G. Rhodes, eds., *Advances in Econometrics*, Vol. 3. Greenwich, Conn.: JAI Press.
Hauser, J. R., and K. Wisniewski. 1982a. "Dynamic Analysis of Consumer Response to Marketing Strategies." *Management Science*, Vol. 28, pp. 455–486.
1982b. "Application, Predictive Test, and Strategy Implications for a Dynamic Model of Consumer Response." *Marketing Science*, Vol. 1, pp. 143–179.
Heckman, J. 1974. "Shadow Prices, Market Wages, and Labor Supply." *Econometrica*, Vol. 42, No. 4, pp. 679–694.
1981a. "Statistical Models for Discrete Panel Data." In C. Manski and D. McFadden, eds., *Structural Analysis of Discrete Data with Econometric Applications*. Cambridge: MIT Press.
1981b. "The Incidental Parameters Problem and the Problem of Initial Conditions in Estimating a Discrete Time–Discrete Data Stochastic Process." In C. Manski and D. McFadden, eds., *Structural Analysis of Discrete Data with Econometric Applications*. Cambridge: MIT Press.
Heckman, J., and G. Borjas. 1980. "Does Unemployment Cause Future Unemployment? Definitions, Questions, and Answers from a Continuous Time Model of Heterogeneity and State Dependence." *Economica*, Vol. 47, pp. 247–283.
Heckman, J., and B. Singer. 1982. "The Identification Problem in Econometric Models for Duration Data." In W. Hildenbrand, ed., *Advances in Econo-*

metrics. Proceedings of World Meetings of the Econometric Society, 1980 Cambridge: Cambridge University Press.

1983. "The Identifiability of Nonproportional Hazard Models." Typescript, University of Chicago.

1984a. "The Identifiability of the Proportional Hazard Model." *Review of Economic Studies*, Vol. 60, No. 2, pp. 231–243.

1984b. "A Method for Minimizing the Impact of Distributional Assumptions in Econometric Models for Duration Data." *Econometrica*, Vol. 52, pp. 271–320.

Hoem, J. 1972. "Inhomogeneous Semi Markov Processes, Select Actuarial Tables, and Duration Dependence in Demography." In T. Greville, ed., *Population Dynamics*. New York: Academic Press.

Hotz, J. 1983. "Continuous Time Models (CTM): A Manual." ERC/NORC, Chicago, Illinois.

Jovanovic, B. 1979. "Job Matching and the Theory of Turnover." *Journal of Political Economy*, Vol. 87 (October), pp. 972–990.

Kac, M. 1959. *Probability and Related Topics in the Physical Sciences*. New York: Wiley.

Kalbfleisch, J., and R. Prentice. 1980. *The Statistical Analysis of Failure Time Data*. New York: Wiley.

Karlin, S. 1968. *Total Positivity*. Stanford, Calif.: Stanford University Press.

Kiefer, J., and J. Wolfowitz. 1956. "Consistency of the Maximum Likelihood Estimator in the Presence of Infinitely Many Incidental Parameters." *Annals of Mathematical Statistics*, Vol. 27, pp. 887–906.

Kiefer, N., and G. Neumann. 1981. "Individual Effects in a Nonlinear Model." *Econometrica*, Vol. 49, No. 4 (July), pp. 965–980.

Laird, N. 1978. "Nonparametric Maximum Likelihood Estimation of a Mixing Distribution." *Journal of the American Statistical Association*, Vol. 73 (December), pp. 805–811.

Lancaster, T., and S. Nickell. 1980. "The Analysis of Reemployment Probabilities for the Unemployed." *Journal of the Royal Statistical Society*, Series A, Vol. 143, pp. 141–165.

Larkin, R. 1979. "An Algorithm for Assessing Bimodality vs. Unimodality in a Univariate Distribution." Typescript Rockefeller University.

Lawless, J. F. 1982. *Statistical Models and Methods for Lifetime Data*. New York: Wiley.

Lewis, H. G. 1974. "Comments on Selectivity Biases in Wage Comparisons." *Journal of Political Economy*, Vol. 82, No. 6 (November), pp. 1145–1156.

Lindsey, B. 1983a. "The Geometry of Mixture Likelihoods, Part I." *Annals of Statistics*, Vol. 11, No. 3, pp. 86–94.

1983b. "The Geometry of Mixture Likelihoods, Part II." *Annals of Statistics*, Vol. 11, No. 3, pp. 783–792.

Lippman, S., and J. McCall. 1976. "The Economics of Job Search: A Survey." *Economic Inquiry*, Vol. 14 (September), pp. 113–126.

Lundberg, F. 1903. Vol. I: *Approximerad Framställning af Sannolikhetsfunktionen*; Vol. II: *Aterforsakring af Kollektivrisker*. Uppsala: Almquist und Wicksell.

Lundberg, S. 1981. "The Added Worker: A Reappraisal." National Bureau of Economic Research Working Paper #706, Cambridge, Mass.

Manski, C., and S. Lerman. 1977. "The Estimation of Choice Probabilities from Choice Based Samples." *Econometrica*. Vol. 45, pp. 1977–1988.

Manski, C., and D. McFadden. 1981. "Alternative Estimators and Sample Designs for Discrete Choice Analysis." In C. Manski and D. McFadden, *Structural Analysis of Discrete Data with Econometric Applications.* Cambridge: MIT Press.

McFadden, D. 1974. "Conditional Logit Analysis of Qualitative Choice Behavior." In P. Zarembka, ed., *Frontiers in Econometrics.* New York: Academic Press.

Moore, E., and R. Pyke. 1968. "Estimation of the Transition Distributions of a Markov Renewal Process." *Annals of the Institute of Statistical Mathematics* (Tokyo), Vol. 20, No. 3, pp. 411–424.

Neyman, J., and E. Scott. 1948. "Consistent Estimates Based on Partially Consistent Observations." *Econometrica.* Vol. 16, pp. 1–32.

Robb, R. 1984. "Three Essays on the Identification of Economic Models." Ph.D. Thesis, University of Chicago.

Robbins, H. 1970. "Optimal Stopping." *American Mathematical Monthly.* Vol. 77, pp. 333–343.

Ross, S. M. 1970. *Applied Probability Models with Optimization Applications.* San Francisco: Holden-Day.

Rudin, W. 1974. *Real and Complex Analysis.* New York: McGraw-Hill.

Salant, S. 1977. "Search Theory and Duration Data: A Theory of Sorts." *Quarterly Journal of Economics*, Vol. 91 (February), pp. 39–57.

Sheps, M., and J. Menken. 1973. *Mathematical Models of Conception and Birth.* Chicago: University of Chicago Press.

Shohat, J., and J. Tamarkin. 1943. *The Problem of Moments.* New York: American Mathematical Society.

Singer, B. 1982. "Aspects of Nonstationarity." *Journal of Econometrics*, Vol. 18, No. 1, pp. 169–190.

Trussell, J., and T. Richards. 1985. "Correcting for Unobserved Heterogeneity in Hazard Models: An Application of the Heckman–Singer Procedure to Demographic Data." in N. Tuma, ed., *Sociological Methodology, 1985*, Jossey—Bass, San Francisco.

CHAPTER 3

Interpreting empirical models of labor supply in an intertemporal framework with uncertainty

Thomas E. MaCurdy

Introduction

Much of the empirical work on labor supply ignores life cycle theory, and practically none of it admits the possibility that consumers are uncertain about future events. A natural question that arises concerns the implications of these factors when evaluating and interpreting estimates of wage and income effects found in the existing literature. This study provides an answer to this question. While the discussion here concentrates on hours of work behavior, it fully applies to the analysis of consumption behavior as well.

The chapter begins with the development of an economic model of consumption and labor supply behavior in an intertemporal environment in which the consumer is uncertain about his future income, the future relative prices of consumption and leisure, and variables influencing his future preferences. A consumer making decisions in this model reacts differently to changes in variables than he would in a deterministic setting. In response to a change in the current wage rate, for example, the adjustment the consumer makes in his consumption and in hours of work depends on how much of this change was anticipated and how it alters expectations concerning future wages. Because the economic model considered here explicitly addresses such issues, it provides some direction on how to account for the various aspects of uncertainty when specifying empirical relations.

Using this economic model as a guide, this study formulates a tractable empirical model of labor supply that recognizes decision making in a multiperiod setting where the future is uncertain. The economic model implies functions for consumption and hours of work that decompose current decisions at any point in time into one argument or component that summarizes the consumer's history and expectations and a second set of arguments consisting of only variables actually observed in the current period. An empirical model based on the function associated with hours of work offers a simple framework for estimating parameters related to intertemporal and uncompensated substitution effects. These parameters determine the response of labor supply to life cycle wage growth and shifts in the anticipated lifetime wage path. A main consequence of admitting uncertainty into the analysis concerns the way in which randomness enters the empirical model. In a model formulated in a deterministic setting, the main sources of sample variation are population heterogeneity in unobserved characteristics and measurement error. In the model with uncertainty, uncertainty about the future and the discrepancy between anticipated future values of random variables and their realizations becomes another source of sample variation. The economic model provides strong implications on how this new source of sample variation affects the analysis of the life cycle relationships. In particular, holding a consumer's wages and characteristics fixed, it implies that hours of work and consumption follow a nonstationary stochastic process over the lifetime.

The empirical model developed here provides a natural framework for interpreting estimates found in both the cross section and the macro time series literature on labor supply. It indicates how cross-section specifications can be modified with the introduction of control variables so that wage coefficients have behavioral interpretations in a life cycle context. The model also provides an interpretation of work based on synthetic cohort data of the sort considered by Ghez and Becker (1975) and Smith (1977). Furthermore, it provides insights into the appropriate behavioral interpretation of substitution elasticities estimated in macro time series studies, including the work of Lucas and Rapping (1969).

Section 1 outlines a theoretical model of life cycle behavior under uncertainty, and Section 2 uses this theoretical apparatus to formulate an empirical model of labor supply. Sections 3–5 interpret various empirical specifications for hours of work found elsewhere in the literature. Finally, Section 6 surveys estimates of substitution effects.

1 A life cycle model of consumption and labor supply under uncertainty

This section presents a simple theoretical characterization of consumption and hours-of-work behavior which provides the basis for the empirical specifications developed in subsequent sections. In the multiperiod model of lifetime consumption and hours of work outlined below, there are three sources of uncertainty in future periods: real rates of interest, wages, and preferences. A consumer, then, is uncertain about his future income, tastes, and the relative future prices of both consumption and leisure. In each period the consumer is viewed as choosing consumption, hours of work, and savings to maximize expected utility subject to asset accumulation constraints.

Developing a description of consumption and labor supply behavior requires specifications for preferences and asset accumulation constraints. The lifetime preference function of a consumer is assumed to be strongly separable over time with utility in period t given by the function $U(C(t), L(t), \mathbf{Z}(t))$, where $C(t)$ is a Hicks's composite commodity of all market goods, $L(t)$ is the number of hours spent in nonmarket activities, and $\mathbf{Z}(t)$ is a vector of "taste shifter" variables at age t. The vector $\mathbf{Z}(t)$ may include observed variables such as the number of children or unobserved variables such as taste for work. A lifetime is assumed to consist of at most T periods with $\bar{L}$ being the total number of hours in each period. When discounting the value of future utility, the consumer uses a rate of time preference equal to ρ. It is assumed that a consumer can hold any combination of g different assets. The variables $A_j(t)$ and $A_j^*(t)$ denote the real value of asset j owned by the consumer at the beginning and the end of period t, respectively. Thus, $\Omega(t) \equiv \sum_{j=1}^{g} A_j(t)$ equals the real value of a consumer's nonhuman wealth at the start of period t; $\Omega^*(t) \equiv \sum_{j=1}^{g} A_j^*(t)$ is real wealth at the end of the period; the quantity $A_j^*(t) - A_j(t)$ represents the consumer's savings in asset j in period t; and $S(t) = \Omega^*(t) - \Omega(t)$ is total savings in the period. Assuming each real dollar of asset j held at the end of period t earns a rate of interest equal to $r_j(t+1)$ at the beginning of period $t+1$, property income earned on asset j equals $Y_j(t+1) = r_j(t+1)A_j^*(t)$, and total property income in period $t+1$ is $Y(t+1) = \sum_{j=1}^{g} Y_j(t+1)$. At each age t the consumer faces a real wage rate equal to $W(t)$, and this wage rate is assumed to be unaffected by the consumer's behavior.

The vectors $\mathbf{e}(t')$ defined by $\mathbf{e}(t') = [Z(t'), W(t'), r_1(t'), \ldots, r_g(t')]$, $t' \geq t$, contain all the variables that are uncertain prior to period t. The random vector $\mathbf{e}(t)$ is realized at the beginning of period t and is unknown prior to this time. The unknown future $\mathbf{e}(t')$ terms constitute the source of uncertainty in this model, and so future tastes, wages, and interest rates are uncertain. Except for moments, which are assumed to exist in the subsequent analysis, this discussion assumes nothing about the form of the distribution generating these random vectors. Taste shifter variables, wages, and rates of interest may be contemporaneously or serially correlated in any fashion.

Formally, at each age t the consumer's problem is to choose policies for $C(k)$, $L(k)$, and assets $A_1^*(k), \ldots, A_g^*(k)$ for $k \geq t$, to maximize the expected value of the time-preference-discounted sum of total utility

$$E_t\left\{\sum_{k=t}^{T}\frac{1}{(1+\rho)^{k-t}}U(C(k),L(k),\mathbf{Z}(k))\right\}$$
$$= U(C(t),L(t),\mathbf{Z}(t))$$
$$+\frac{1}{1+\rho}E_t\left\{\sum_{k=t+1}^{T}\frac{1}{(1+\rho)^{k-t-1}}U(C(k),L(k),\mathbf{Z}(k))\right\} \quad (1)$$

subject to the budget constraint

$$S(k) = \Omega^*(k) - \Omega(k) = W(k)N(k) - C(k), \qquad k = t, \ldots, T \quad (2)$$

and the asset accumulation constraints

$$A_j(k+1) = A_j^*(k)(1 + r_j(k+1)), \qquad j = 1, \ldots, g, \qquad k = t, \ldots, T \quad (3)$$

where $N(k) \equiv \bar{L} - L(k)$ is hours of work, the asset levels $A_1(t), \ldots, A_g(t)$ are predetermined variables, and the "t" subscript associated with the expectation operator E_t indicates that the consumer accounts for all information available in period t when calculating expected values. Expectations are calculated over the random vectors $\mathbf{e}(t+1), \ldots, \mathbf{e}(T)$. Equation (2) represents the consumer's period k budget constraint; savings $S(k)$ must equal labor earnings $W(k)N(k)$ minus expenditure on goods consumption $C(k)$. Equation (3) indicates that the endowment of tangible wealth in asset j at the beginning of period $k+1$, $A_j(k+1)$, equals the wealth held at the end of period k, $A_j^*(k)$, plus property income earned at the beginning of period $k+1$, $A_j^*(k) \cdot r_j(k+1)$. For a complete formulation of the consumer's lifetime optimization problem, one must introduce a terminal condition on wealth in the form of either an inequality constraint on wealth at the end of life [e.g., $\Omega^*(T) \geq 0$] or a bequest function; most of the subsequent analysis applies in either case.

A dynamic programming or functional equation formulation of this optimization problem provides a convenient framework for characterizing period t consumption and labor supply decisions. Define the value function corresponding to period $t+1$ by

$$V(t+1) \equiv V(\Omega(t+1), t+1)$$
$$= \max\left[E_{t+1}\left\{\sum_{k=t+1}^{T}\frac{1}{(1+\rho)^{k-t-1}}U(C(k),L(k),\mathbf{Z}(k))\right\}\right]$$

where the maximization is carried out satisfying the appropriate budget and asset accumulation constraints. Given initial wealth $\Omega(t+1)$, $V(t+1)$ shows the maximum expected lifetime utility a consumer can attain in period $t+1$ and is analogous to an indirect utility function. Because $V(\cdot)$ depends on the realized value of $\mathbf{e}(t+1)$, it is uncertain in period t.

Formally, $V(\cdot)$ is a function of many other variables such as the parameters of the distribution generating future $\mathbf{e}(k)$ terms, but they are suppressed as arguments for simplicity. As an alternative to the above formulation of the lifetime optimization problem, one can view the consumer as acting to maximize

$$U(C(t), L(t), \mathbf{Z}(t)) + \frac{1}{1+\rho} E_t\{V(\Omega(t+1), t+1)\} \tag{4}$$

instead of (1).

For decision variables $C(t)$, $L(t)$, and $A_1^*(t), \ldots, A_g^*(t)$, optimization of (4) subject to equations (2) and (3) for period $k = t$ implies the following first-order conditions:

$$U_C(C(t), L(t), \mathbf{Z}(t)) = \lambda(t) \tag{5}$$

$$U_L(C(t), L(t), \mathbf{Z}(t)) \geq \lambda(t)W(t) \tag{6}$$

$$\lambda(t) = \frac{1}{1+\rho} E_t\{\lambda(t+1)(1 + r_j(t+1))\}, \qquad j = 1, \ldots, g \tag{7}$$

where $\lambda(k)$ is the Lagrangian multiplier associated with the period k budget constraint [i.e., condition (2)], and the subscripts on U denote partial derivatives. The derivation of (7) uses the result

$$\lambda(t) = \frac{\partial V(t)}{\partial \Omega(t)}$$

which follows from a straightforward application of the envelope theorem. The quantity $\lambda(t)$, then, represents the marginal utility of wealth in period t. Relation (6) determines the choice of leisure; the consumer chooses not to work when this relation becomes a strict inequality for all feasible values of leisure. The equations given by (7) determine the consumer's savings allocation rule and dictate how resources are allocated over time. According to these equations, the consumer chooses a portfolio to equate the marginal utility of the last dollar invested in each asset. Assuming there exists an asset f available to the consumer that earns a riskless real rate of interest equal to $r_f(t+1)$ at the beginning of period $t+1$ [i.e., $r_f(t+1)$ is nonstochastic], condition (7) implies the relation[1]

$$\lambda(t) = \frac{1 + r_f(t+1)}{1+\rho} E_t\{\lambda(t+1)\} \tag{8}$$

This condition indicates that the consumer chooses his savings so that the marginal utility of wealth in period t equals the discounted expected value of next period's marginal utility of wealth, where the rate of discount is 1 plus the riskless rate of interest over 1 plus the rate of time preference.

1.1 *Functions determining consumption and hours of work*

First-order conditions (5) and (6) imply that $C(t)$ and $N(t) \equiv \bar{L} - L(t)$ are determined by functions of the form

$$C(t) = C(\lambda(t), W(t), \mathbf{Z}(t)) \tag{9}$$

$$N(t) = N(\lambda(t), W(t), \mathbf{Z}(t)) \tag{10}$$

which this analysis hereafter refers to as the marginal utility of wealth constant (MUWC) functions for consumption and labor supply.[2] The functional form of $C(\cdot)$ and $N(\cdot)$ depends only on the specification of the period-specific utility function $U(\cdot)$ and on whether corner solutions are optimal for hours of work at age t.[3] These functions decompose consumption and labor supply decisions at a point in time into a "life cycle" component $\lambda(t)$ that summarizes all historic and future information relevant to the consumer's current choices and a second set of components, $W(t)$ and $\mathbf{Z}(t)$, that represent variables actually observed in the decision period. Consumption and labor supply decisions in any period t, then, are related to variables outside the decision period only through $\lambda(t)$. Changes in such variables as wealth, expected future wages, expected future rates of interest, or uncertainty about future resources affect consumption and labor supply only by changing the value of $\lambda(t)$. For example, if wealth increases, $\lambda(t)$ decreases assuming concave preferences; and given this decline in $\lambda(t)$, consumption increases and labor supply decreases according to their respective functions. The increase in wealth influences consumption and labor supply through no other mechanism. After computing $\lambda(t)$, the consumer need only examine the value of the current wage rate and current taste shifter variables to determine his optimal consumption and labor supply. The MUWC functions, then, extend Friedman's (1957) permanent income theory to a situation in which the relative prices of consumption and leisure vary over the life cycle and the future is uncertain. The life cycle component λ is like permanent income in the theory of the consumption function. At each point in time it is a sufficient statistic for all retrospective and prospective information about lifetime wages and property income pertinent to the consumer when selecting current consumption and hours of work.

1.2 *Determination of λ*

The value of the life cycle component $\lambda(t)$ varies over the consumer's lifetime; in fact, $\lambda(t)$ is a random variable which is not realized until the beginning of period t. If this variation were not systematic, then the MUWC functions would be of little value in understanding a consumer's life cycle behavior. The value of $\lambda(t)$, however, is determined by optimizing behavior, and this leads to variation in $\lambda(t)$ that has a behavioral interpretation.

The savings allocation rule given by (8) determines the stochastic properties of the marginal utility of wealth over time. According to this condition, the consumer sets his savings policy so that the marginal utility of wealth follows a martingale; that is, $E_t\{\lambda(t+1)\}$ depends only on $\lambda(t)$. The consumer controls the time path of $\lambda(t)$ through his accumulation of financial wealth. Because the consumer cannot perfectly control the level of his wealth due to random interest rates, and because the consumer's environment changes as he acquires more information as he ages, $\lambda(t)$ is stochastic. Condition (8) dictates how the consumer allocates his resources to account for any unanticipated shocks. He sets his savings policy so that the expectation of next period's marginal utility of wealth is revised by the full amount of the unanticipated elements; in other words, the consumer revises the means of all future values of λ to account for all forecasting errors when they are realized.

The martingale property of λ implies that certain transformations of consumption and leisure also follow a martingale process. Inspection of conditions (5) and (6) reveals that the marginal utility of consumption [i.e., $U_C(t)$] and the marginal utility of leisure divided by the real wage rate [i.e., $U_L(t)/W(t)$] both equal the marginal utility of wealth, assuming interior solutions. Since $\lambda(t)$ obeys a martingale, $U_C(t)$ and $U_L(t)/W(t)$ also follow a martingale as the result of rational economic behavior.[4]

There is an alternative way to characterize the stochastic process generating the marginal utility of wealth which the next section uses in the development of empirical specifications. Write $\lambda(t)$ as $\lambda(t) = \exp[\ln \lambda(t)]$. One can always relate the actual value of $\ln \lambda(t)$ to its expected value in period $t-1$ by the equation $\ln \lambda(t) = E_{t-1}\{\ln \lambda(t)\} + \varepsilon^*(t)$, where $\varepsilon^*(t)$ represents a one-period forecast error which arises from unanticipated realizations of wages, income, and variables influencing tastes in period t. Since

$$E_{t-1}\{\lambda(t)\} = \exp[E_{t-1}\{\ln \lambda(t)\}]E_{t-1}\{\exp[\varepsilon^*(t)]\}$$

it follows that one may write $\lambda(t)$ as

$$\lambda(t) = [E_{t-1}\{\exp[\varepsilon^*(t)]\}]^{-1}E_{t-1}\{\lambda(t)\}\exp[\varepsilon^*(t)]$$

Substituting the expression for $E_{t-1}\{\lambda(t)\}$ implied by condition (8) into this relation for $\lambda(t)$ yields

$$\lambda(t) = [E_{t-1}\{\exp[\varepsilon^*(t)]\}]^{-1}\frac{1+\rho}{1+r_f(t)}\lambda(t-1)\exp[\varepsilon^*(t)]$$

Taking natural logs gives

$$\ln \lambda(t) = b_t^* + \ln \lambda(t-1) + \varepsilon^*(t) \tag{11}$$

where

$$b_t^* \equiv \ln\left(\frac{1+\rho}{1+r_f(t)}\right) - \ln(E_{t-1}\{\exp[\varepsilon^*(t)]\})$$

and repeated substitution implies

$$\ln \lambda(t) = \sum_{j=0}^{t} b_j^* + \ln \lambda(0) + \sum_{j=1}^{t} \varepsilon^*(j) \tag{12}$$

These latter equations indicate that the latent variable $\ln \lambda(t)$ follows a stochastic process resembling a random walk with drift.[5] This process is a consequence of rational economic behavior which requires the consumer to revise the value of his marginal utility of wealth fully each period to account for new information contained in the realization of unanticipated elements. In a deterministic world, notice that $\varepsilon^*(j) = 0$ and $b_j^* = \ln(1+\rho) - \ln[1 + r_f(j)]$ for all j.

The consumption and labor supply functions given by (9) and (10) and the equations governing the motion of λ given by (8) and (11) suggest a simple view of behavior in a life cycle setting where the future is uncertain. At the start of the lifetime the consumer sets the initial value of his life cycle component $\lambda(0)$ so that it incorporates all the information he has available at that time concerning his expectations of future wages, income, and factors affecting tastes. As he ages the consumer acquires additional information about his current and future prospects, and he responds to this new information by adjusting the value of his life cycle component $\lambda(t)$ according to equations (8) or (12). At each age the consumer only has to keep track of his updated life cycle component and the variables he actually observes during the period to determine his optimal consumption and labor supply. As a consequence of this simple decision process, both consumption and hours of work follow a nonstationary stochastic process over the life cycle.

1.3 *Extensions*

The above economic model of life cycle consumption and labor supply behavior is more general than it may first appear.[6] All of the above characterizations, for example, are applicable without any modification if one introduces human capital accumulation. In addition, there is no gain in generality if one incorporates employment constraints in the above model. The above characterizations allow corner solutions for hours of work, and they assume nothing about the distribution generating wages; so it is always possible for the wage rate in any period or set of periods to be sufficiently low so that the consumer chooses not to work. Finally, with random components in each period's utility function, the above model already allows for the possibility of an uncertain length of life.

There are also some obvious extensions of the above economic model of life cycle behavior that are simple to implement. The model, for example, can be extended to allow for the presence of more than one form of market goods consumption or type of leisure. This extension is particularly useful if one is interested in modeling the consumption and labor supply behavior of a two-person household. In the context of the framework presented above, a natural way to model this behavior is to write utility at age t as a function of three forms of consumption: market goods, leisure of the husband, and leisure of the wife. The household can then be viewed as acting to maximize a lifetime preference function [similar to the one given by (1)] subject to wealth accumulation constraints, where budget constraints in those periods of marriage include both the husband's and the wife's earnings. This economic model clearly implies the existence of MUWC functions for household consumption and the labor supply of both spouses with the same features as those described above. A significant point here is that the life cycle component $\lambda(t)$ appears in the labor supply and the participation functions of both spouses as well as the consumption function. The martingale and random walk properties of $\lambda(t)$ given by (8) and (12) are also applicable without modification. If one combines this extension of the model with the simple consumer specifications presented above, it is possible to incorporate uncertainty with regard to future marital status; one of the random elements of each period's utility function can be a dummy variable indicating whether the consumer is married or not.[7]

2 An empirical specification for hours of work

This section formulates an empirical model of labor supply which is based on the economic model described above with a major emphasis on predicting the effect of wage changes on the choice of hours of work over the lifetime. Although the analysis focuses on the effects of wages, it also provides a simple framework for analyzing the response of hours of work to changes in other variables such as financial wealth or demographic characteristics. Furthermore, it is directly applicable to the analysis of consumption behavior as well.

According to the economic model of life cycle behavior under uncertainty outlined in the previous section, the labor supply function at each point in time has two sets of arguments: a life cycle component and current variables. This decomposition of behavior suggests that the formulation of an empirical model naturally divides into two parts: The first is the construction of an estimable specification for a MUWC hours-of-work function, and the second is the formulation of an empirical specification for the life cycle component. The discussion below pursues this two-part formulation, closely following the development of an empirical model found in the work of MaCurdy (1981a) with the aim of reinterpreting this work to account for uncertainty.

2.1 *An empirical specification for the MUWC hours-of-work function*

Assume that consumer i at age t has utility given by

$$U_i(t) = G(C_i(t), \mathbf{Z}_i(t)) - \Upsilon_i(t)(N_i(t))^{\sigma}, \qquad t = 0, \ldots, T \tag{13}$$

where $G(\cdot)$ is a monotonically increasing function in $C_i(t)$, $\sigma > 1$ is a time-invariant parameter common across consumers, and $\Upsilon_i(t) > 0$ is a function of a consumer's characteristics $\mathbf{Z}_i(t)$ which plausibly affect his preference at age t. The following analysis assumes that $\Upsilon_i(t)$ is related to a consumer's characteristics by the function $\Upsilon_i(t) = \exp\{-\mathbf{X}_i(t)\psi^* - v_i^*(t)\}$, where $\mathbf{X}_i(t)$ represents measured characteristics, ψ^* is a vector of parameters, and $v_i^*(t)$ reflects the contribution of unmeasured characteristics.

Assuming an interior optimum, the implied MUWC hours-of-work function is

$$\ln N_i(t) = F_i(t) + \delta \ln W_i(t) + \mathbf{X}_i(t)\psi + v_i(t) \tag{14}$$

where $\delta \equiv 1/(\sigma - 1)$, $F_i(t) \equiv \delta(\ln \lambda_i(t) - \ln \sigma)$, $\psi \equiv \delta\psi^*$, and $v_i(t) \equiv \delta v_i^*(t)$ If one is willing to assume that the drift terms b_t^* appearing in the random-walk-type specification for $\lambda(t)$ given by (12) are constant across both consumers and time,[8] then substituting (12) into (14) yields

$$\ln N_i(t) = F_i(0) + bt + \delta \ln W_i(t) + \mathbf{X}_i(t)\psi + \eta_i(t) \tag{15}$$

where $\eta_i(t) \equiv v_i(t) + \sum_{j=1}^{t} \varepsilon_i(j)$, $\varepsilon_i(j) \equiv \delta\varepsilon_i^*(j)$, and $b \equiv \delta b_t^*$. Thus, the natural log of hours of work at age t is a simple linear function of an individual specific intercept $F_i(0)$, a linear trend, the wages in period t, measured characteristics, and a disturbance term which is the sum of an unobserved component representing omitted variables and the accumulation of all past forecast errors. There is an alternative representation of labor supply at age t which will prove useful in later analysis. First differencing (15) yields

$$D \ln N_i(t) = b + \delta\, D \ln W_i(t) + D\mathbf{X}_i(t)\psi + Dv_i(t) + \varepsilon_i(t) \tag{16}$$

where D denotes the difference operator [i.e., $D\mathbf{X}_i(t) = \mathbf{X}_i(t) - \mathbf{X}_i(t-1)$].

2.2 *A specification for individual effects*

Estimating the MUWC hours-of-work function provides only part of the information needed to predict the effect of wages on lifetime labor supply; formulating and estimating an explicit specification for the life cycle component $\lambda_i(t)$ is also needed. A specification for this component is needed for two reasons. First, according to equation (15), the level of a consumer's hours of work depends on the value of his individual effect, and this in turn depends on the value of his life cycle component. According to the economic model outlined above, $\lambda_i(t)$ is a function of variables such as the parameters of the distribution generating lifetime wages; so a shift in anticipated future wages generally causes the consumer to set a new value for $\lambda_i(t)$. The parameters of the function for $\lambda_i(t)$, then, are needed to predict the hours-of-work response to parametric wage changes, and this information is needed to explain how labor supply varies across consumers.

The second reason for formulating an empirical specification for the life cycle component concerns the influence of uncertainty. As the consumer acquires information in the form of unanticipated shocks, he revises his current and planned future hours of work. The precise form of this updating depends on the explicit functional relationship between the life cycle component and the distribution of wages, income, and characteristics in and after period t. An estimated specification for $\lambda_i(t)$, then, provides the information one requires to predict the effect of unanticipated parametric wealth and wage changes.

The analysis of the previous section indicates that $\lambda_i(t)$ is a function of literally every conceivable variable relevant to decision making in a lifetime context; it depends on assets, wages, and characteristics observed in period t and all the parameters of the distribution generating future wages, interest rates, and variables affecting tastes. Only rarely is it possible to obtain an analytical solution for $\lambda_i(t)$ in terms of these variables.

To formulate an empirical model capable of predicting the variation in hours of work across consumers, one requires an empirical specification for the life cycle component evaluated at some base age 0. For this empirical specification, assume that one can approximate $\ln \lambda_i(0)$ by the equation

$$\ln \lambda_i(0) = \mathbf{M}_{0i}\boldsymbol{\phi}_0^* + \sum_{j=0}^{\tau} \gamma_0^*(j)E_0\{\ln W_i(j)\} + \theta_0^*\Omega_i(0) + a_i^*(0)$$

where $\mathbf{M}_{0i}$ is a vector of demographic characteristics either observed at age 0 or anticipated in future periods which influence lifetime preferences, $a_i^*(0)$ is an error term representing the contribution of unmeasured variables, and $\boldsymbol{\phi}_0^*$, $\gamma_0^*(j)$, and θ_0^* are parameters. Given the definition of the individual intercept $F_i(0)$, this specification for $\lambda_i(0)$ implies

$$F_i(0) = \mathbf{M}_{0i}\boldsymbol{\phi}_0 + \sum_{j=0}^{\tau} \gamma_0(j)E_0\{\ln W_i(j)\} + \theta_0\Omega_i(0) + a_i(0) \tag{17}$$

where $\boldsymbol{\phi}_0$, $\gamma_0(j)$, θ_0, and $a_i(0)$ equal their superscript "*" counterparts multiplied by δ, and with the intercept defined to include the term $-\delta \ln \sigma$. This empirical approximation imposes very strong simplifying restrictions. It assumes that the consumer knows he is going to work τ periods.[9] The effects of interest rates and time preference are assumed to be absorbed into the intercept and the other parameters.[10] In addition to the possibility that one should include interactions between the variables appearing in (17), $\ln \lambda_i(t)$ also depends on other variables not included in (17) at all. One such set of variables would measure uncertainty associated with future events such as the variance of future wages or rates of interest.[11]

The use of equation (17) in an empirical analysis requires an assumption concerning the formulation of expectations for future wages. One needs only to generate unbiased predictions of these expectations to produce a specification whose parameters can be consistently estimated. Assume that the lifetime wage path anticipated in period 0 is

$$E_0\{\ln W_i(t)\} = \pi_{0i} + \pi_{1i}t + \pi_{2i}t^2 + v_i(t), \qquad t = 0, \ldots, \tau \tag{18}$$

where π_{0i}, π_{1i}, and π_{2i} are deterministic functions of time-invariant characteristics of consumer i, and $v_i(t)$ is a disturbance representing the contribution of unobserved variables. It is assumed that one may treat the error $v_i(t)$ as randomly distributed across consumers with zero mean in the sample period and as uncorrelated with the demographic characteristics and age-invariant variables included in $\mathbf{M}_{0i}$ and used to predict wages and wealth. This path assumes that wages follow a quadratic equation in age with an intercept and slope coefficients that depend on measured variables.

Obtaining an estimate for the wealth effect θ is complicated by the fact that most data sets do not contain measures of a consumer's initial assets, $\Omega_i(0)$. Some measure of a consumer's property or nonwage income during the sample period is usually available, and this can be used to predict $\Omega_i(0)$. Property income in period t for consumer i is defined by $Y_i(t) = \Omega_i^*(t-1)\bar{r}_i(t)$, where $\Omega_i^*(t-1)$ is consumer i's assets held at the end of period $t-1$, and $\bar{r}_i(t)$ is a weighted average of period t interest rates. Suppose that the lifetime path for property income expected at age 0 is approximated by the equation

$$Y_i(t) = \alpha_{0i} + \alpha_{1i}t + \alpha_{2i}t^2 + v_i(t) \tag{19}$$

where α_{0i}, α_{1i}, and α_{2i} are estimable functions of consumer i's age-invariant characteristics, and $\upsilon_i(t)$ is an error term with the same properties specified above for $v_i(t)$. The asset accumulation constraints given by (3) imply the relation

$$\Omega_i(0) = \frac{1 + \bar{r}_i(0)}{\bar{r}_i(0)} Y_i(0)$$

so the quantity

$$\frac{1 + \bar{r}_i(0)}{\bar{r}_i(0)} \alpha_{0i}$$

predicts initial wealth $\Omega_i(0)$. The following analysis assumes that one may treat the interest rate factors

$$\frac{1 + \bar{r}_i(0)}{\bar{r}_i(0)}$$

as randomly distributed across individuals with a mean equal to $(1 + \bar{r})/\bar{r}$ and uncorrelated with measured characteristics used to predict expected wages, income, or factors affecting preferences.

Combining the anticipated paths for wages and income with equation (17) creates an estimable equation for $F_i(0)$. Substituting the expected wage equation given by (18) into equation (17) and using $[(1 + \bar{r})/\bar{r}]\alpha_{0i}$ as a predictor for $\Omega_i(0)$ yields

$$F_i(0) = \mathbf{M}_{0i}\boldsymbol{\phi}_0 + \pi_{0i}\bar{\gamma}_0 + \pi_{1i}\bar{\gamma}_1 + \pi_{2i}\bar{\gamma}_2 + \alpha_{0i}\bar{\theta} + \bar{a}_i \tag{20}$$

where

$$\bar{\gamma}_k = \sum_{j=0}^{\tau} j^k \gamma_0(j) \quad \text{for} \quad k = 0, 1, 2, \qquad \bar{\theta} = \frac{\theta_0(1 + \bar{r})}{\bar{r}}$$

and $\bar{a}_i$ is an error term. This equation relates a consumer's individual effect to the parameters of his wage and income profiles. The parameter $\bar{\gamma}_0$ determines the response of $F_i(0)$ to a constant percentage change in wages over the entire lifetime; $\bar{\gamma}_1$ and $\bar{\gamma}_2$ determine the effect of a change in the slope of the anticipated lifetime wage path on $F_i(0)$; and $\bar{\theta}$ determines the response of a consumer's labor supply profile to changes in a measure of his initial "permanent income."

2.3 *Predicting responses to adjustments in expectations*

Empirical specifications (17) and (20) only partially satisfy the two reasons for introducing parametric expressions for individual effects noted at the beginning of this section. These specifications are adequate for the purpose of predicting how labor supply varies *across consumers*, but each fails to introduce sufficient structure for the purpose of updating hours of work to account for unanticipated elements *for a given consumer*. To provide a framework for analyzing how a consumer adjusts hours of work to account for revisions of expectations, one essentially requires a specification for the values of the life cycle components at each age. Analogous to the specification for $F_i(0)$ given by (17), suppose one can write each individual effect as

$$F_i(t) = \mathbf{M}_{ti}\boldsymbol{\phi}_t + \sum_{j=t}^{\tau} \gamma_t(j)E_t\{\ln W_i(j)\} + \theta_t\Omega_i(t) + a_i(t) \tag{21}$$

where the vector $\mathbf{M}_{ti}$ includes measured characteristics associated with period t and subsequent periods that affect preferences, $a_i(t)$ represents a disturbance, and $\boldsymbol{\phi}_t$, $\gamma_t(j)$, and θ_t denote parameters. Given these specifications, the implied forecast error for period t which represents the update component for $F_i(t)$ is defined by

$$\begin{aligned} \varepsilon_i(t) = {} & [\mathbf{M}_{it} - E_{t-1}\{\mathbf{M}_{it}\}]\boldsymbol{\phi}_t \\ & + \sum_{j=t}^{\tau} \gamma_t(j)\,[E_t\{\ln W_i(j)\} - E_{t-1}\{\ln W_i(j)\}] \\ & + [\Omega_i(t) - E_{t-1}\{\Omega_i(t)\}]\theta_t + [a_i(t) - E_{t-1}\{a_i(t)\}] \end{aligned} \tag{22}$$

It is important to recognize that expectations in (22) refer to those actually used by the consumer. In contrast to the estimation of the response of individual effects to shifts in wealth and the anticipated lifetime wage path considered above, unbiased predictions of expectations are insufficient to calculate $\varepsilon_i(t)$.

One never has sufficient information actually to compute $\varepsilon_i(t)$ or its various components. Besides the impossible task of formulating the consumer's exact expectations, one must obtain estimates for the coefficients associated with individual effects equations for each age. As revealed in the above analysis, one cannot hope to identify and estimate all the parameters of equation (21) for even a single age unless one introduces more a priori information; most expectation schemes assumed for wages and income will allow one to identify only linear combinations of parameters (such as the $\bar{\gamma}_j$ terms in the above analysis). A factor complicating matters further concerns the relationships between the parameters for the different individual effects equations. As discussed more fully in the next section, the parameters $\boldsymbol{\phi}_t$, $\gamma_t(j)$, and θ_t associated with the different ages t are distinct and are not easily related to one another; in fact, very stringent conditions are needed even to assume that the $F_i(t)$ terms each have an approximate representation given by (21). It is, then, a very demanding task to formulate an empirical specification for $\varepsilon_i(t)$ or to predict this forecast error. Constructing such predictions, at the very least, requires estimates for linear combinations of the parameters associated with equations determining the $F_i(t)$ for each age.

3 Relating different measures of substitution effects

This and the next two sections relate the empirical model developed above to empirical specifications of labor supply commonly found in the literature. The essential question answered here concerns the appropriate interpretation of the substitution effect estimated in each specification. To clarify issues, the following analysis begins with a discussion of the MUWC hours-of-work function and what one can learn from estimating such a function. It next considers other representations of the labor supply function that often serve as the basis for an empirical analysis of hours-of-work behavior in a multiperiod setting. The subsequent sections concentrate on interpreting empirical specifications for labor supply found in three types of work: cross-section, synthetic cohort, and macro time series analyses.

In investigating the effect of wages on labor supply, it is important to distinguish between two types of wage changes: One type is called evolutionary and the other is called parametric. An evolutionary wage change arises from movement along a *given* lifetime wage path, while a parametric wage change arises from *shifts* in a lifetime wage path. In an environment of perfect certainty a consumer only experiences evolutionary wage changes, but in an uncertain environment a consumer experiences both evolutionary and parametric wage changes. In an uncertain environment, there is anticipated wage growth which influences the timing of hours of work over the life cycle; and as a consumer ages, he acquires new information concerning his future prospects which causes him to adjust his forecasts of wage profiles. It is important to identify the type of wage variation under consideration in an empirical analysis because the substitution effect needed to compute the hours-of-work response depends on the source of the wage change and whether it constitutes an evolutionary or parametric change. The analysis below sharply distinguishes between these different substitution effects.

3.1 *Uses of the MUWC labor supply function*

Estimating the parameters of equation (15), which constitutes an empirical specification for the MUWC hours-of-work function, provides all the information required to predict the effect of an evolutionary wage change on labor supply. For a given consumer in a deterministic setting, all wage changes are of an evolutionary type. In such a setting there are, of course, no forecast errors; so $\varepsilon_i(j) = 0$ for all j. In this case, since $F_i(0)$ is a constant over time, it is evident from equation (15) that the parameter δ determines the response of labor supply to changes in the wage rate over time. Hereafter, I will refer to δ as the intertemporal substitution elasticity.[12] The theoretical prediction of a positive sign for δ reflects the consumer's desire to supply more hours in those periods with highest wages. The intertemporal substitution elasticity is the principal determinant of the effect of life cycle wage growth on the timing of hours of work over the life cycle and would be the elasticity relevant for predicting how a consumer's labor supply responds to changes in wages arising from movement over a perfectly foreseen business cycle.

Besides explaining the variation in a given consumer's hours of work over time, another potential use of the MUWC labor supply function relates to testing the implications of optimizing behavior in the presence of uncertainty. According to specifications (15) and (16), log hours of work follows a random-walk-type process with drift after adjustment for wage differentials, shifts in preferences, and any measurement error. Thus, neglecting errors in measurement and the influences of changes in wages and tastes, labor supply at age $t - 1$ summarizes all past information that is relevant to the choice of labor supply at age t.[13] Testing this random walk property of labor supply obviously requires one to hold the effects of measurement error, wages, and tastes constant. Holding wages and measured taste shifter variables constant is feasible, but the presence of measurement error and the error $v_i(t)$ reflecting the contribution of unmeasured taste shifter variables creates serious problems. Unfortunately, because one has little information regarding the stochastic process generating measurement error or $v_i(t)$, optimizing behavior imposes few restrictions on the distribution of the composite error terms of the labor supply equation, $\eta_i(t)$, except that one would expect them to be serially correlated and nonstationary.[14]

3.2 *Conventional specifications for lifetime hours of work*

There are two theoretical characterizations for life cycle labor supply behavior that underlie many empirical studies. Substituting the expression for the individual effect $F_i(t)$ given by (21) into (14) yields

$$\ln N_i(t) = \mathbf{S}_{ti}(t)\mathbf{g}_t + [\delta + \gamma_t(t)] \ln W_i(t) + \sum_{j=t+1}^{\tau} \gamma_t(j) E_t\{\ln W_i(j)\}$$
$$+ \theta_t \Omega_i(t) + u_{ti} \tag{23}$$

where $\mathbf{S}_{ti}(t)\mathbf{g}_t \equiv \mathbf{M}_{ti}\boldsymbol{\phi}_t + \mathbf{X}_i(t)\boldsymbol{\psi}$, and $u_{ti} \equiv a_i(t) + v_i(t)$. Alternatively, replacing $F_i(0)$ in (15) by the expression given in (17) implies a relation which one may write as

$$\ln N_i(t) = \mathbf{S}_{0i}(t)\mathbf{g}_0 + bt + [\delta + \gamma_0(t)] \ln W_i(t) + \sum_{\substack{j=0 \\ j \neq t}}^{\tau} \gamma_0(j) E_0\{\ln W_i(j)\} + \theta_0 \Omega_i(0) + \mu_{ti}^* \tag{24}$$

where $\mathbf{S}_{0i}(t)\mathbf{g}_0 \equiv \mathbf{M}_{0i}\boldsymbol{\phi}_0 + \mathbf{X}_i(t)\boldsymbol{\psi}$, and $\mu_{ti}^* \equiv a_i(0) + \eta_i(t) - \gamma_0(t)(\ln W_i(t) - E_0\{\ln W_i(t)\})$. These equations, of course, represent familiar forms for the lifetime labor supply function. According to (23), current hours of work depend on current wealth and on current and anticipated future wage rates; and according to (24), hours of work at any age depend on the consumer's initial wealth, his lifetime wage path anticipated at age 0, and a sum of forecast errors reflecting revisions of expectations.

Specification (23) suggests the following parameter interpretations: $\gamma_t(t) + \delta$ represents an own uncompensated substitution elasticity that determines the impact of a change in the period t wage rate on hours of work in period t; $\gamma_t(j)$, $j > t$, corresponds to a cross-uncompensated substitution elasticity that determines the effect of a change in the wage rate expected in period j on period t's hours of work; and θ_t determines the effect of a change in current assets on current hours of work.[15] Turning to the specification for hours of work given by (24), one sees that the parameters $\gamma_0(t) + \delta$ and $\gamma_0(j)$, $j > t$, are also related to own and cross-uncompensated substitution elasticities; and like θ_t, the coefficient θ_0 determines the effect of wealth on hours of work at age t. Whereas the parameters $\gamma_0(t) + \delta$, $\gamma_0(j)$, and θ_0 provide measures of substitution and wealth effects that hold *initial* wealth and the *entire* ex ante wage path constant, the parameters $\gamma_t(t) + \delta$, $\gamma_t(j)$, and θ_t constitute measures of these effects when one holds wealth *at age t* and expected wages only *after age t* − 1 constant. It is possible to show in a deterministic framework that $\theta_t < \theta_0$ and $\gamma_t(j) < \gamma_0(j)$ for all j,[16] which indicates that the own and cross-substitution elasticities and the wealth effect associated with specification (23) are algebraically smaller than their counterparts in the alternative specification for labor supply given by (24). This result reflects the fact that the total wealth effect arising from a parametric change in a wage rate at any future age is spread over fewer periods for a consumer at age t versus a consumer at age 0; so there is a larger wealth effect in each period. Consequently, uncompensated substitution and wealth coefficients fall monotonically as one advances the lifetime optimization problem to a later age.

These specifications for labor supply, then, are designed to estimate the response of hours of work to parametric wage changes in the form of shifts of the anticipated lifetime wage path. Such wage changes are the sort usually contemplated in comparative static exercises and constitute a major source of wage variation when considering different consumers. Thus, in constrast to the reasons for estimating the MUWC labor supply function, one estimates equations like (23) or (24) to obtain information needed to explain differences in labor supply across consumers or to predict how any particular consumer will adjust his hours of work in response to a change in wealth or in expectations regarding future wages. Notice that in order to use a specification like (23) in an empirical analysis, one must introduce rigorous assumptions describing exactly how the parameters $\mathbf{g}_t$, $\gamma_t(j)$, and θ_t decline with age (i.e., with t) which makes use of this specification unattractive relative to using (24).

4 Interpreting cross-section specifications in a life cycle context

Most cross-section work on labor supply in the literature to date ignores life cycle theory. Typically, annual hours of work are regressed on the current hourly wage rate and some measures of property income. The estimated wage and income coefficients from such a regression are interpreted as measuring uncompensated substitution and income effects.

Recognition of life cycle considerations suggests two questions: (1) What behavioral parameters are actually being estimated in the typical cross-section model of labor supply? (2) Is it possible to modify cross-section models so that they account for life cycle factors? The following analysis answers these two questions.

The specification of labor supply commonly found in the cross-section literature is an equation of the form

$$\ln N_i(t) = \beta_1 + \beta_2 \ln \hat{W}_i(t) + \beta_3 \hat{Y}_i(t) + \mathbf{Q}_i \boldsymbol{\beta}_4 + e_i \qquad (25)$$

where $\ln \hat{W}_i(t)$ and $\hat{Y}_i(t)$ are the predicted values of the log of the consumer's current wage rate and of property income, $\mathbf{Q}_i$ is a vector of exogenous variables that control for demographic characteristics, the β terms are parameters, and e_i is an error term. Equation (25) assumes estimation using simultaneous equation techniques. Such techniques recognize that a consumer's wage rate and property income are likely to be endogenous variables due to such problems as reporting error, the presence of "transitory" components in wages and income,[17] and mutual dependence induced by past investment decisions.[18]

Equation (25) provides a useful framework for restating the two questions posed above. In the typical cross-section analysis, a researcher either excludes all control variables $\mathbf{Q}_i$ (i.e., he sets $\beta_4 = 0$) or includes variables $\mathbf{Q}_i$ without any explicit justification. Our first question amounts to asking whether the parameters β_2 and β_3 have a behavioral interpretation when one sets $\beta_4 = 0$. The second question asks whether one can introduce a set of control variables $\mathbf{Q}_i$ so that β_2 and β_3 represent parameters relevant for describing lifetime labor supply behavior.

To answer these questions one requires a cross-section specification that is consistent with life cycle theory. Substituting the expression for the individual effect $F_i(0)$ given by (20) into the MUWC labor supply function given by (15), and using the prediction equation for wages given by (18), one obtains

$$\ln N_i(t) = \mathbf{S}_{0i}(t)\mathbf{g}_0 + \pi_{0i}\bar{\gamma}_0 + \pi_{1i}\bar{\gamma}_1 + \pi_{2i}\bar{\gamma}_2 + \alpha_{0i}\bar{\theta} + bt + \delta \ln \hat{W}_i(t) + f_i \tag{26}$$

where

$$\ln \hat{W}_i(t) = \pi_{0i} + \pi_{1i}t + \pi_{2i}t^2$$

$\mathbf{S}_{0i}(t)\mathbf{g}_0 = \mathbf{M}_{0i}\boldsymbol{\phi}_0 + \mathbf{X}_i(t)\boldsymbol{\psi}$, and f_i is an error term. If one assumes that each of the quantities $\mathbf{S}_{0i}\mathbf{g}_0$, π_{0i}, π_{1i}, π_{2i}, and α_{0i} is a linear function of the variables contained in a vector $\mathbf{K}_i$, then one may rewrite (26) as

$$\ln N_i(t) = \mathbf{K}_i\mathbf{q} + bt + \delta \ln \hat{W}_i(t) + f_i \tag{27}$$

where $\mathbf{q}$ denotes a vector of coefficients.

While it is reasonably straightforward to obtain estimates for the parameters $\mathbf{g}_0$, $\bar{\gamma}_0$, $\bar{\gamma}_1$, $\bar{\gamma}_2$, $\bar{\theta}$, b, and δ using data from a single cross section by jointly estimating equations (26), (18), and (19) with nonlinear constraints imposed across equations, it is enlightening to introduce assumptions to simplify this equation. In particular, if one assumes that $\mathbf{S}_{0i}(t)$ includes only an intercept and that the coefficients on age and age-squared for the lifetime wage and income paths (i.e., π_1, π_2, α_1, and α_2) are constant across consumers, then (26) can be rewritten as

$$\ln N_i(t) = d_1 + (\delta + \bar{\gamma}_0) \ln \hat{W}_i(t) + \bar{\theta}\hat{Y}_i(t) + d_4 t + d_5 t^2 + f_i \tag{28}$$

where $d_1 = g_0 + \pi_1\bar{\gamma}_1 + \pi_2\bar{\gamma}_2$, $d_4 = b - \bar{\gamma}_0\pi_1 - \bar{\theta}\alpha_1$, and $d_5 = -\bar{\gamma}_0\pi_2 - \bar{\theta}\alpha_2$. The derivation of (28), then, assumes that the predicted values for wages and income are $\ln \hat{W}_i(t) = \mathbf{K}_i\pi_0 + \pi_1 t + \pi_2 t^2$ and $\bar{Y}_i(t) = \mathbf{K}_i\alpha_0 + \alpha_1 t + \alpha_2 t^2$, where $\boldsymbol{\pi}_0$ and $\boldsymbol{\alpha}_0$ are parameter vectors, and the vector $\mathbf{K}_i$ contains such variables as education and family background variables. Prediction equations such as these are often found in cross-section analysis.

Let us start by answering our second question first. According to equation (27), if a researcher excludes property income from the cross-section specification given by (25) (i.e., sets $\beta_3 = 0$) and chooses age and all the age-invariant characteristics determining either the lifetime wages path or initial permanent income as control variables (i.e., includes t and all the elements of $\mathbf{K}_i$ in $\mathbf{Q}_i$), then the coefficient on the current wage rate is the intertemporal substitution elasticity (i.e., $\beta_2 = \delta$). Intuitively, this set of control variables accounts for differences in the value of $F_i(0)$ across consumers and only age variables identify the wage coefficients.

If, on the other hand, a researcher chooses age and age-squared as control variables in equation (25), inspection of equation (28) reveals that the wage coefficient measures the response of labor supply to a parallel shift in the wage profile (i.e., $\beta_2 = \bar{\gamma}_0 + \delta$), and the income coefficient measures the response of labor supply to changes in initial permanent income (i.e., $\beta_3 = \bar{\theta}$).[19] Intuitively, this set of control variables adjusts for age effects and the only remaining difference in wages and income across consumers is due to profile shifts.[20]

Using different sets of control variables, then, allows one to estimate different behavioral parameters. If the rate of time preference equals the rate of interest (i.e., $b = 0$), including education and background variables in a cross-section specification of labor supply yields an estimate of the hours-of-work response to an evolutionary wage change. If, instead, one includes polynomials in age, the estimated wage coefficient measures the response of labor supply to a change in the lifetime average wage rate.

To answer our first question concerning the interpretation of parameters in the usual cross-section models of labor supply, consider equation (28). This equation relates hours of work to measures of average lifetime wages and income, which is the interpretation that most analysts would give to cross-section models of labor supply. Typically, however, these cross-section specifications fail to include age and age-squared as explanatory variables; they assume that the parameters d_4 and d_5 in equation (28) are zero. Hence, the usual cross-section analysis suffers from omitted variable problems. As a result, wage and income coefficients are inconsistently estimated to the extent that the predicted values of wages and income are correlated with age. This bias of these estimates may be either positive or negative. The degree of bias depends on the age distribution of the population. Changing this age distribution in general will change the estimated values of the wage and income coefficients. This is certainly a disturbing feature of typical cross-section estimates.

Excluding all control variables from a cross-section analysis of labor supply, then, generally estimates wage and income coefficients that do not have an economic interpretation. Because this analysis fails to include age variables as controls, estimates confuse shifts of profiles with movements along profiles for both wages and income. The resulting wage and income coefficients are, in general, complicated functions of wage effects, income effects, and the distribution of consumer characteristics. Additional sources of bias are introduced if the slopes of the lifetime paths for wages and income are allowed to depend on a consumer's characteristics. Not only will estimates in this case confuse profile shifts from movements along profiles, they will also confuse tilts in profiles from parallel shifts. It is difficult to see why anyone would be interested in estimates produced by such an analysis, especially if their ultimate interest is policy recommendations.

4.1 *Synthetic cohort specifications*

Two of the best-known empirical studies of life cycle labor supply are by Becker in Ghez and Becker (1975) and by Smith (1977). These studies use cross-section data to estimate the effect of life cycle wage growth on the timing of hours of work. Although Becker and Smith do not interpret their parameter estimates as those of a MUWC labor supply function, they are in fact estimating such a relationship. Since they analyze only the effects of evolutionary wage change and do not analyze parametric wage change, the parameters of the MUWC hours-of-work function completely characterize the behavior of interest to Becker and Smith.

Estimating equation (15) using cross-section data is complicated by the presence of individual effects $F_i(0)$. Economic theory implies that $F_i(0)$ is correlated with a consumer's wages and all of his other characteristics. Therefore, it is not reasonable to assume that $F_i(0)$ is a "random factor" uncorrelated with explanatory variables. One, then, cannot directly use observations on individuals from a cross section to estimate the parameters of (15) even if one uses simultaneous equation estimation procedures. Such procedures implicitly treat individual effects as random variables, and this leads to inconsistent parameter estimates.

The synthetic cohort approach, implemented by Becker and Smith, provides a simple way to estimate the MUWC hours-of-work function using cross-section data. A synthetic cohort is constructed by computing geometric means of wage rates and hours worked for each age group, and it is assumed to represent the life cycle of a typical individual. The data for the synthetic cohort are then used to estimate equation (15). Averaging observations over individuals in the same age group, equation (15) becomes

$$\overline{\ln N(t)} = \overline{F(0)} + bt + \delta\,\overline{\ln W(t)} + \overline{\mathbf{X}(t)}\psi + \overline{\eta(t)}, \qquad t = 0, \ldots, \tau \tag{29}$$

where the bars denote means and t designates the age group. This equation closely resembles the one actually estimated by Becker using least squares. The crucial assumption underlying this approach is that the value of $\overline{F(0)}$ is the same for all age groups. Averaging observations for each age group produces a consistent estimate of the group intercept $\overline{F(0)}$. In contrast to using observations on individuals, least squares estimation of equation (29) produces consistent parameter estimates using the averaged or the synthetic cohort data if there are no cohort effects. One eliminates endogeneity of wages by using group means as instruments. The issue of treating $\overline{F(0)}$ as a random variable does not arise since it is assumed to be the same for all age groups.

Instead of the single-worker model of labor supply assumed throughout this chapter and by Becker, Smith estimates MUWC hours-of-work functions that are consistent with households in which both the husband and the wife work. As noted in Section 1, one can easily extend the economic model to allow for a two-worker household. To analyze the husband's hours of work, Smith estimates an equation like (29), except the natural log of the wife's wage enters as well.[21]

To allow for smooth vintage effects, both Becker and Smith treat $\overline{F(0)}$ as a linear function of age, average property income, and average family size.[22] A measure of the permanent wage rate is the obvious variable missing from this relationship. If one cannot delete this variable, however, it is impossible to identify the intertemporal substitution effect using the synthetic cohort approach. After controlling for age, income, and family size, this approach requires all vintage effects to be uncorrelated with wages. This seems to be a strong and implausible assumption which suggests that cohort effects may contaminate estimates produced by the synthetic cohort method.

There has been some confusion in the literature concerning the interpretation of the wage coefficient estimated in the synthetic cohort analysis.[23] As emphasized several times, this coefficient is an intertemporal substitution elasticity, and while it constitutes an upper bound for compensated and uncompensated elasticities, it is not one of the familiar elasticities associated with parametric wage changes. Thus, the estimated wage coefficients cannot be used for policy analysis of the sort encountered in predicting labor supply responses to negative income tax experiments or other proposed changes in tax policies. Without imposing nontrivial restrictions on preferences, estimating the parameters of only the MUWC labor supply functions for the household does not provide the information one requires to construct the quantities necessary for predicting responses to parametric wage variations of the sort normally considered in policy analysis.

5 Interpreting macro time series specifications in a life cycle context

The following discussion argues that it is straightforward to use macro time series data on hours of work, wages, and income to estimate intertemporal substitution elasticities. It is not, however, possible to estimate elasticities associated with parametric wage changes without introducing strong and arbitrary assumptions concerning uncertainty about future wages and cohort effects.

Estimating the parameters of the MUWC hours-of-work function using macro data does not in principle involve any significant difficulties. If one averages observations over individuals in a given period j, equation (15) becomes

$$\overline{\ln N(t_j)} = \bar{F} + b\bar{t}_j + \delta\,\overline{\ln W(t_j)} + \overline{\mathbf{X}(t_j)}\psi + \overline{\eta(t_j)} \tag{30}$$

where bars denote simple means and the notation t_j denotes a consumer's age in period j (so $\bar{t}_j$ is the average age of the working population in period j).[24] This equation expresses the MUWC labor supply function in terms of macro variables; it relates the log of the geometric mean of hours of work to the average age and the log of the geometric mean of wage rates, where all means are computed in period j.[25] Assuming there are no cohort effects implies that $\bar{F}$ is constant over time, in which case it can be treated as an intercept in the estimation of the parameters of equation (30) using simultaneous equation procedures. Using such a procedure, it is clear that one can estimate the intertemporal substitution elasticity using macro data.

Let us now turn to the topic of estimating the substitution elasticities needed to predict responses to parametric wage changes using macro data. One of the best-known empirical studies in this area is the work of Lucas and Rapping (1969). The analysis below considers a simple version of the model of labor supply used by Lucas–Rapping in their empirical analysis. While Lucas–Rapping allow for the price of market goods or, equivalently, the real rate of interest to vary over the lifetime, the following discussion assumes that the real rate of interest is constant to simplify the exposition.

Lucas–Rapping formulate their empirical specification for hours of work along traditional lines. They write log hours of work as a log-linear function of the current real wage rate, the anticipated future real wage rate, and the level of wealth. This formulation is a restricted version of the specification given by (23). They write this specification as

$$\begin{aligned}\ln N(t) = g &+ \delta(\ln W(t) - E_t\{\overline{\ln W}\}) \\ &+ (\delta + \bar{\gamma})E_t\{\overline{\ln W}\} + \theta\Omega(t) + u(t)\end{aligned} \tag{31}$$

where cross-uncompensated elasticities and wealth coefficients are assumed to be constant for all ages and equal to γ and θ, respectively, $\bar{\gamma} = (\tau - t)\gamma$, and $\overline{\ln W}$ is the average future wage rate defined by

$$\frac{1}{\tau - t}\sum_{j=t+1}^{\tau} \ln W(j)$$

Lucas–Rapping call $\overline{\ln W}$ the permanent or normal real wage rate, and they refer to its coefficient, $\delta + \bar{\gamma}$, as the long-run wage elasticity. Indeed, given their assumptions, $\delta + \bar{\gamma}$ is similar to the coefficient $\delta + \bar{\gamma}_0$ defined above which determines the response of labor supply to a parallel shift in the wage profile. The coefficient on the deviation of the current wage rate from the anticipated permanent wage is the intertemporal wage elasticity. Lucas–Rapping call this the short-run elasticity.

Lucas–Rapping estimate the parameters of their model using average U.S. time series data covering the years 1930–65. Converting most of their variables to per household terms and assuming these data refer to a representative household, they report a long-run wage elasticity equal to .03, or essentially zero, and a short-run elasticity equal to 1.4.[26] Wealth is not found to be an important factor in explaining variations in labor supply.

There is, however, a serious difficulty with this interpretation of the parameter estimates of equation (31). How is one able to estimate labor supply responses to parametric wage changes, such as the long-run wage elasticity? To appreciate the difficulties involved here, consider a world in which there is perfect certainty and no cohort effects. In such a world there are no parametric wage changes as one advances the economy over time. All wage changes arise from movements along lifetime wage paths; there are no shifts in wage profiles. In such a world, then, it is not possible to identify labor supply responses to parametric wage changes using macro data; and so one cannot estimate an empirical specification like (31). All one can hope to isolate is responses to evolutionary wage changes.

The MUWC labor supply function, like the one given by (30) with the averages $\bar{t}_j$ and $\overline{\mathbf{X}(t_j)}$ assumed constant over time, offers a more reasonable description of the empirical relation actually estimated by Lucas–Rapping. It is this specification of the hours-of-work function that explicitly recognizes that the value of the life cycle component λ fully summarizes the effects of the permanent wage rate and wealth and that λ is naturally absorbed into the constant term of the labor supply equation. Since the constant term summarizes all information on wealth and future wages relevant to the current labor supply decision, measures of either the permanent wage rate or wealth should not directly enter the labor supply equation. In the light of this argument, it is not surprising that Lucas–Rapping find a long-run elasticity near zero in value and no effect of wealth on hours of work.

5.1 *Estimating responses to parametric wage changes arising from uncertainty*

In contrast to the world of perfect certainty assumed in the above argument, Lucas–Rapping consider an uncertain environment in which it is theoretically possible to estimate the effects of parametric wage and income changes on hours of work. Their model explicitly recognizes that consumers are uncertain about future wages and prices and that these individuals experience and respond to shifts in expected lifetime wage and income paths as a consequence. To estimate the responses of labor supply to these revisions in expectations is, however, a truly demanding task.

One encounters two fundamental problems requiring solution in any attempt to exploit the presence of uncertainty as a source for estimating responses in hours of work to parametric changes in wage rates and/or in wealth. The first problem involves the development of an empirical specification for the forecast error $\varepsilon(t)$, which is an essential item needed to estimate the responses of interest; while the second problem concerns the availability of variables that can serve as instruments to estimate the desired effects. The specification for $\varepsilon(t)$ obviously plays a key role in estimation, since all the effects of uncertainty operate solely through their impact on this forecast error. Relation (22) provides an expression for $\varepsilon(t)$ that is consistent with the model developed in this chapter. As the discussion following (22) emphasizes, it is a formidable task to develop an estimable variant of this specification. Accomplishing this task requires the introduction of two distinct sets of assumptions: One set is needed to provide for a precise characterization for all types of uncertainty, including explicit expressions for wage uncertainty [i.e., for the terms $E_t\{\ln W(j)\} - E_{t-1}\{\ln W(j)\}$ in (22)], for income uncertainty [i.e., for $\Omega(t) - E_{t-1}\{\Omega(t)\}$ in (22)], and for uncertainty about factors influencing preferences [i.e., for the terms $\mathbf{M}_t - E_{t-1}\{\mathbf{M}_t\}$ and $a(t) - E_{t-1}\{a(t)\}$]; and a second set of assumptions is needed to ensure the parametric identification of equation (22), which requires either the introduction of parameter restrictions or a reparameterization of the equation. Not surprisingly, the particular sets of assumptions introduced determine which variables can properly serve as valid instruments in estimation.

To obtain a clearer understanding of these problems, it is useful to consider the implications of a very restrictive collection of assumptions which yields a simple variant of the empirical model developed in Section 2. In particular, assume the following: (i) The wage rate (for any representative individual i) is determined by the stochastic process $\ln W(t) = \ln W(t-1) + \xi(t) + \omega(t)$, where $\xi(t)$ represents a disturbance fully known to consumers prior to period t (but unknown to the econometrician) and $\omega(t)$ denotes an error distributed independently of all $\xi(t)$ terms and over time which reflects the nonforecastable component of the wage rate unknown to a consumer until period t;[27] (ii) the parameter restrictions and definitions implicitly assumed in deriving the Lucas–Rapping specification given by (30) apply here as well;[28] and (iii) consumers have perfect foresight regarding future asset income and factors affecting preferences [so the $\omega(t)$ terms constitute the only source of uncertainty]. According to (i), wages follow a random-walk-type process if the $\xi(t)$ terms are independently and identically distributed or have a degenerate distribution. Given these three assumptions, inspection of (22) reveals that the forecast error $\varepsilon(t)$, representing a consumer's adjustment of planned life cycle profiles to account for the information conveyed by the realization of unanticipated wage shocks, takes the simple form $\varepsilon(t) = \bar{\gamma}\omega(t)$.

With this simplification, the specification of the MUWC labor supply function given by (16) – which can be aggregated to obtain a first-differenced variant of the macro specification given by (30) – may be written as

$$D \ln N(t) = \delta D \ln W(t) + \bar{\gamma}\omega(t) + Dv(t) \qquad (32)$$

where the effects of measured characteristics and the intercept are assumed to be absent for expositional convenience. Alternatively, using the stochastic process for wages assumed by (i), one may rewrite (32) as

$$D \ln N(t) = (\delta + \bar{\gamma})D \ln W(t) - \bar{\gamma}\xi(t) + Dv(t) \qquad (33)$$

Empirical relations such as these, rather than the sort of relation for labor supply considered by Lucas–Rapping [e.g., equation (31)], provide the specifications best suited for analyzing hours-of-work behavior using time series data. As argued above, these relations clearly illustrate that in the absence of wage uncertainty [i.e., with $\omega(t) = 0$], one cannot estimate certain key parameters – in this case $\bar{\gamma}$ – which are necessary to predict responses to parametric wage changes.

In contrast, when part of the change in wage rates is unanticipated by consumers, it is evident from these relations that one can in principle estimate the combination of parameters $\delta + \bar{\gamma}$ using macro time series data which enable one to predict responses in hours of work to a particular type of parametric wage change (namely, to a proportionate shift in expected future wages). Equation (33) offers the most convenient empirical specification for this purpose. It is, however, important to recognize that one must maintain very stringent assumptions to estimate the parameters of this equation consistently. In particular, estimation of this equation requires the availability of instruments for the differenced wage variable $D \ln W(t)$ that are uncorrelated with both the errors $\xi(t)$ and $Dv(t)$ which reflect the contribution of characteristics unmeasured by the econometrician that determine current changes in wage rates and in factors influencing preferences for hours of work. To estimate the coefficient $\delta + \bar{\gamma}$, then, one must have available an instrument for the *unanticipated* component of the change in the wage rate that is uncorrelated with any unmeasured variation in wages and preferences. Such instruments are hard to find in any analysis. This is not to say, of course, that one cannot think of a set of assumptions implying the existence of appropriate instruments. One obvious choice, for example, is to assume that $\xi(t) = 0$ – which implies the consumer has no better information to forecast his wage rate than the econometrician – and that the growth in wage rates is unrelated to unmeasured shifts in factors affecting preferences [i.e., $D \ln W(t)$ is uncorrelated with $Dv(t)$]. Given these assumptions, least squares applied to (33) yields consistent estimates.

Relaxing any of the three simplifying assumptions maintained in the above discussion significantly complicates the task of estimating responses to parametric wage changes arising from uncertainty and renders this task intractable in many cases. With regard to assumption (i), if one admits the possibility that the uncertainty component of the wage change $\omega(t)$ is autocorrelated rather than being serially independent as this assumption maintains, then the wage uncertainty terms $E_t\{\ln W(j)\} - E_{t-1}\{\ln W(j-1)\}$ appearing in specification (22) no longer simply equal $\omega(t)$ as in the above discussion; instead, each term depends on a unique and often complicated weighted average of current and past $\omega(t)$ values. To analyze this case, then, one not only has to distinguish between the parts of the wage change representing the realization of uncertainty from those due to the presence of pure measurement error or of variables omitted by the econometrician, but also isolate the autocorrelation structures associated with these different sources of error. Clearly, the imposition of arbitrary and untestable assumptions provides the only route for achieving this end. Considering the relaxation of assumption (ii), its replacement with a more plausible set of parameter restrictions leads in most cases to significant complications in formulating an estimable specification for the forecast error $\varepsilon(t)$.

Recognizing that consumers are uncertain about future asset income or taste shifter variables, which is ruled out by assumption (iii), or acknowledging that wage rates may be inaccurately measured has the consequence of adding a new disturbance to the specifications for changes in hours of work given by (32) and (33). This disturbance includes all the components of the forecast error $\varepsilon(t)$ attributable to the realizations of unanticipated shocks in wealth and in factors influencing preferences and also includes any measurement error components. The presence of this new disturbance further limits the variables that can properly serve as instruments to estimate responses to parametric wage changes arising from adjustments in expectations. In the case of specification (33), for example, estimation of the relevant coefficients requires instruments for the *unanticipated* components of the current wage that are uncorrelated with unanticipated changes in interest rates, asset income, and tastes, with any measurement error in wages, and with any source of change in the wage rate anticipated by the consumer but unknown to the econometrician. Finding variables that satisfy these criteria and can be used as valid instruments is a demanding task indeed. It is difficult to argue that Lucas–Rapping identify responses to unanticipated changes in wages. In their application of two-stage least squares they predict wages using predetermined variables, real GNP, and the GNP deflator as instruments. Given any sort of rational expectations scheme, predetermined variables will not be correlated with unanticipated components in wages. Real GNP and the GNP deflator are likely to be correlated with unanticipated changes in asset income and interest rates. Thus, none of these variables constitutes an appropriate instrument. Even in this uncertainty environment, then, it is difficult to see how Lucas–Rapping are able to estimate the impact of a permanent wage change.

5.2 *Other methods for estimating responses to parametric wage changes*

Besides uncertainty, differences in lifetime wages and income across cohorts offer another source of parametric wage change in macro data that, in principle, can be used to identify and estimate hours of work responses to shifts in wage profiles. In terms of the macro version of the MUWC specification given by (30), such cohort differences imply that the intercept, or the average of the individual effects, $\bar{F}$, varies over time as a function of the wage profiles and the initial wealth of the working cohorts. If one can explicitly model this functional relationship for the intercept as an empirical specification like the one given by (20), then it is possible to estimate parameters relevant for predicting hours-of-work responses to parametric wage changes using macro data.

Jointly estimating specifications for the MUWC labor supply and consumption functions offers yet another way of using macro data to identify and estimate the parameters required to calculate the effects of parametric wage and income changes on hours of work and consumption. Estimation of these functions yields an entire set of parameter estimates for period specific functions. Using these estimates to formulate a lifetime preference function and introducing assumptions regarding the constraints faced by consumers over their life cycle, it is possible to perform a simulation analysis and directly calculate consumers' responses to any sort of parametric changes in lifetime constraints.

6 A comparison of empirical results

The following discussion compares estimates of intertemporal and uncompensated substitution elasticities for prime-age males obtained using four distinct sources of data: synthetic cohorts, macro data, longitudinal data, and cross-section data on individuals. This discussion is not meant to constitute a comprehensive survey of results, but instead provides only an indication of the degree to which various estimates agree.

6.1 *Estimates of the intertemporal substitution elasticity*

As shown in the previous analysis, it is possible to estimate the MUWC labor supply function and the substitution effect δ using any one of the four data sources. For estimates of δ derived by using synthetic cohort data, this discussion presents results reported in the work of Ghez and Becker (1975) and Smith (1977). Both of these studies estimate a variant of equation (29). Ghez–Becker form synthetic cohorts using the 1960 U.S. Census; and Smith uses data from the 1967 Survey of Economic Opportunity (SEO). For estimates based on macro time series data, this discussion takes results from the study of Lucas and Rapping (1969), interpreting their work as estimating equation (30). Lucas–Rapping use aggregate U.S. time series data covering the years 1930–65 in their empirical work. For results computed using longitudinal data, the following analysis reports estimates taken from the work of MaCurdy (1981a), who applies simultaneous equation procedures to estimate equation (16) using the Michigan Panel Study of Income Dynamics for the years 1967–76. Finally, the cross-section estimates for δ presented here come from Appendix A of this chapter. While it would be desirable to use estimates from the existing cross-section literature on labor supply in the following comparisons, I am aware of no study in this literature that performs the empirical analysis needed to interpret their results within the framework presented in Section 4; these studies either fail to include the appropriate control variables in specifications or do not compute estimates using instrumental variable procedures as assumed in the above discussion of cross-section results. For this reason and to make results more comparable with those calculated using other data sources, Appendix A computes cross-section estimates for δ by two-stage least squares estimation of equation (27) using data on individuals from the Michigan Panel Study of Income Dynamics (PSID), with each of the years 1967–75 treated as a separate cross section.[29] Rather than presenting the estimation results for all nine cross sections which are described in Appendix A, the following discussion only reports a simple average and range for the estimates.

While many of the studies from which these various estimates of δ are taken ignore uncertainty in their theoretical frameworks, it is possible to interpret their empirical results in an uncertainty setting. The presence of uncertainty implies that the structural error terms of the hours-of-work equation [i.e., see equation (15) or (16)] contain forecast errors as one of their components. This formulation has three implications for empirical analysis: (1) Because wages are uncertain, the current wage rate contains unanticipated components; so, ln $W_i(t)$ is correlated with current and past values of $\varepsilon_i(j)$. Thus, in addition to the usual reasons for treating wages as endogenous variables in an empirical analysis,[30] uncertainty about future wages provides one more reason for such a treatment. (2) Similarly, if measured taste shifter variables $\mathbf{X}_i(t)$ are uncertain and not realized until period t, then $\mathbf{X}_i(t)$ must also be treated as endogenous variables. Therefore, in addition to assuming that $\mathbf{X}_i(t)$ is uncorrelated with unobserved taste factors $v_i(t)$, one must also assume that $\mathbf{X}_i(t)$ is known to the consumer prior to period 1 if the elements of $\mathbf{X}_i(t)$ are to be treated as predetermined variables in specification (15); in specification (14), on the other hand, one must assume that $\mathbf{X}_i(t)$ is known prior to period t.[31] (3) Finally, variables used to predict either ln $W_i(t)$ or the elements of $\mathbf{X}_i(t)$ must also be uncorrelated with unanticipated elements if they are to be valid instruments. To account, then, for the presence of uncertainty in an empirical analysis, one must recognize a wider variety of reasons why variables may not be predetermined or exogenous. The studies whose results are reported here use instrumental-variable-type techniques to compute estimates and pick as instruments variables that one can argue are not necessarily rendered endogenous as a consequence of admitting uncertainty into the analysis.

Of the four types of data, longitudinal data offer the source best suited for estimating the intertemporal substitution elasticity. The availability of this type of data allows one to compute estimates for δ that are free of cohort bias and do not rely on any assumptions regarding the formulation of expectations. When using longitudinal data to estimate the specification of the MUWC hours of work function given by (15), one may treat the individual specific quantities $F_i(0)$ as fixed effects unique to each consumer and estimate them as parameters in a simultaneous equation analysis. This procedure avoids the need to introduce any assumptions concerning how the $F_i(0)$ terms vary across consumers or cohorts or how they are related to measured characteristics. Alternatively, one may use longitudinal data to estimate the first-differenced specification of the MUWC function given by (16) in which the $F_i(0)$ terms do not even appear.[32] With the inclusion of year dummies in either specification, one does not require the assumption that interest rates are constant over time. As noted in the previous section, one can admit the existence of vintage effects when using synthetic cohort data to estimate the MUWC functions, but to avoid contaminating the estimates of δ, these effects must be completely uncorrelated with the wage rate after controlling for other measured variables. One requires a similar assumption when using cross-section data on individuals and specifications (26) or (28) to estimate δ. When analyzing macro data, one must essentially assume the complete absence of cohort effects and ignore aggregation issues.

Table 1. *Estimates of the intertemporal substitution elasticity*

Data source	Sample composition	Estimates
Synthetic cohort[a]	1960 Census–white males, ages 22–65	.58 (−.07, .74)
	1967 SEO–white males, ages 22–64	.33 (.02, .4)
Macro time series[b]	U.S. aggregate data in per household units	1.4 (.78, 3.93)
Longitudinal[c]	PSID–white males, ages 25–56	.24 (.1, .5)
Cross section[d]	PSID–white males, ages 25–56	.15 (−.07, .28)

[a] Estimates taken from Ghez and Becker (1975, p. 116) and Smith (1977, p. 244). For both these studies, the representative estimate reported in column 3 is a simple average of the estimates for δ computed using the sample with all education levels included.
[b] Estimates taken from Lucas and Rapping (1969, p. 745 and appendix). The representative estimate is the estimate preferred by Lucas and Rapping.
[c] Estimates taken from Table 1 in MaCurdy (1981a). The representative estimate is a simple average of the results presented in this table.
[d] Estimates taken from Table 3 of this chapter. The representative estimate is a simple average of the estimates obtained for the different cross sections.

Table 1 presents a summary of the estimates for δ obtained from the sources listed above. Rather than giving a single estimate, each of these sources reports a variety of estimates for δ computed for various subsamples of their data and/or for alternative empirical specifications of the MUWC labor supply function. The third column of Table 1 summarizes the estimates obtained in these studies with two sets of numbers. One may view the upper number as a "representative" estimate. This number is formed either by computing a simple average of the estimates reported in the study under consideration or by taking the estimate for δ obtained in the study that is most comparable with the other results summarized in the table.[33] The lower numbers in each row give the range of estimates presented in each study. If one ignores the macro results for the moment, the representative estimates for δ associated with the various data sources lie in the range .15–.6. While one may be tempted to draw conclusions from differences in these representative estimates, one should note that the range of estimates reported for δ obtained using any particular data source is approximately as wide as the range formed by the representative estimates associated with the different data sources. In other words, the variability of estimates across studies is comparable to the variability found within studies. If one compares the ranges of estimates obtained using synthetic cohort, longitudinal, and cross-section data, one finds extensive overlap, with all ranges covering the interval .1–.3. Consequently, on the basis of the results in Table 1, there is no evidence supporting the hypothesis that synthetic cohort and cross-section analyses are subject to cohort bias. The estimates based on macro data clearly lie well outside the range implied by other estimates. While this phenomenon may in part be due to the impact of vintage effects and the aggregation that occurs in the macro data, the more likely explanation for the larger size of the macro estimate relates to the fact that the aggregate data include demographic groups other than prime-age males who make up the sample analyzed in the other studies. These other demographic groups, such as women, teenagers, and older workers, are likely to possess higher intertemporal substitution responses, with movement in and out of the labor force a principal component of this response – a factor ignored in macro analysis and in this discussion.

6.2 *Estimates of uncompensated substitution elasticities*

The previous discussion argues that synthetic cohort and macro data are not well suited for estimating coefficients determining the response of labor supply to parametric wage changes; so the following analysis only considers estimates derived using longitudinal and cross-section data. The quantities of interest in this discussion are the parameters $\bar{\gamma}_0$ and $\bar{\gamma}_0 + \delta$ which determine the average values of the own and cross-uncompensated substitution elasticities. For the estimates of these parameters computed using longitudinal data, this discussion takes results from the work of MaCurdy (1981a), which estimates an empirical specification for individual effects like the one given by (20) using two-stage least squares procedures; while this earlier paper assumes a deterministic setting, its estimation is fully consistent with the uncertainty environment considered in this chapter. In the empirical analysis, the coefficients of the lifetime wage and income paths (i.e., the π_{ji} terms and the α_{ji} terms for $j = 0, 1, 2$) are assumed to be linear equations in education and family background variables. For estimates derived from cross-section data, this analysis uses results reported in Appendix A. These estimates are obtained from two-stage least squares estimation of equation (28), whose derivation assumes that the slopes of the lifetime wage and income paths depend only on a consumer's age and not other measured characteristics (i.e., it assumes that the coefficients π_{1i}, π_{2i}, α_{1i}, and α_{2i} are constant across consumers).

Table 2 presents the estimates for $\bar{\gamma}_0$ and $\bar{\gamma}_0 + \delta$ computed using these different data sources. As in the previous presentation of empirical results, this table reports both representative estimates and the range of estimates

Table 2. *Estimates of parameters determining uncompensated substitution elasticities*

Data source	$\bar{\gamma}_0$	$\bar{\gamma}_0 + \delta$
Longitudinal[a]	$-.07$	.08
	$(-.1, -.05)$	(.05, .1)
Cross section[b]	$-.07$	.08
	$(-.21, .09)$	$(-.06, .24)$

[a] Estimates for $\bar{\gamma}_0$ taken from table 2 in MaCurdy (1981a). The representative estimate for $\bar{\gamma}_0$ is a simple average of the results presented in this table. The range and the representative estimate for $\bar{\gamma}_0 + \delta$ are computed by adding the estimate $\hat{\delta} = 1.5$ to the estimates of $\bar{\gamma}_0$ given in column 2. This particular estimate for δ is used in the computations to make the results consistent with MaCurdy (1981a, table 2, row 2).

[b] Estimates for $\bar{\gamma}_0 + \delta$ taken from Table 3 of this chapter. The representative estimate for $\bar{\gamma}_0 + \delta$ is a simple average of the results presented in this table. The range and the representative estimate for $\bar{\gamma}_0$ are computed by subtracting the estimate $\hat{\delta} = .15$ from the estimates of $\bar{\gamma}_0 + \delta$ given in column 3.

obtained in the various studies. The results derived for the two types of data are almost identical. This similarity of results may not be all that surprising given the similarity of the data sets used to carry out these two analyses and the fact that the use of longitudinal data to estimate parameters of the individual effects equation offers no obvious advantages over the use of cross-section data in terms of avoiding biases due to cohort effects. Dividing the estimates of $\bar{\gamma}_0$ by the length of the working life produces an estimate of the average cross-uncompensated substitution elasticity. Assuming a working life of 40 years implies an estimate for this elasticity equal to $-.0018$. Adding an estimate of δ to this average cross-elasticity creates an estimate for the average own uncompensated elasticity. Using the estimate .15 reported for δ in Table 1, one finds that the average own elasticity is approximately .15. These estimates for the average own and cross elasticities, then, indicate that a 10 percent wage rate increase expected in period 0 to take place in period t leads to an average increase of 1.5 percent in a consumer's hours of work in period t and essentially no change in his hours of work in other periods. The estimate of $\bar{\gamma}_0 + \delta$ provides the information needed to predict a consumer's labor supply response to a proportional shift in his anticipated wage profile. Thus, in response to a uniform 10 percent increase in expected wages at all ages, the results of Table 2 suggest that the consumer will adjust his planned hours of work by an amount equal to 1 percent at all ages. These results, then, are generally consistent with the popular notion that the labor supply of prime-age males is not very responsive to permanent changes in the wage rate.

These estimates provide some information on the importance of a consumer's adjustments in hours of work to unanticipated changes in wages. In particular, inspection of the formula for forecast errors given by relation (22) reveals that the cross-uncompensated substitution elasticities determine the consumer's adjustment to revisions in expected future wages. The results of Table 2 imply small values for these cross-elasticities, which suggests that adjustments for unanticipated wage changes are not very important except when big shocks occur. This finding implies that it is the value of the intertemporal substitution elasticity that constitutes the primary determinant of the movement in hours of work over the business cycle even in an uncertainty environment where cyclical variations in wages are unanticipated.

When using estimates of the parameters associated with the individual effects equation, it is important to recognize that their interpretations rely on numerous assumptions.[34] Besides all the obvious functional form assumptions, these estimates neglect the presence of taxes, they presume the existence of perfect capital markets, and they assume that equations (18) and (19) generate unbiased expectations for wages and income. In contrast to estimating the MUWC labor supply equation, the use of longitudinal data to estimate the individual effects equation does not avoid cohort effects.[35] Finally, it is difficult to justify using any of the consumer's characteristics as instruments to predict lifetime wages and income. Formally, the life cycle component is a function of all characteristics over the entire lifetime, so there are no exclusion restrictions. Also, the use of measured characteristics requires the assumption that they are uncorrelated with all the consumer's unmeasured characteristics and all unanticipated elements, which seems unlikely.

6.3 *Conclusion*

While the presence of uncertainty introduces several new elements into an empirical model of lifetime consumption and hours of work, this study shows that much of the empirical analysis based on deterministic life cycle theory carries over with full force to the uncertainty framework. In the case of the model considered here, adding uncertainty about the future results in two important changes in empirical specifications. The first relates to the way randomness enters the model and the structure of disturbances. When a consumer is uncertain about future variables, one component of the disturbances consists of forecast errors representing the consumer's adjustments for unanticipated elements. Consequently, one must recognize another reason why variables may not be predetermined or exogenous in a statistical analysis. The second change in specifications concerns the way in which future variables affect current decisions. In an uncertainty setting, it is predictions of future variables rather than the actual values of these variables that determine current behavior. Given empirical specifications derived from a deterministic model of life cycle behavior, one can in general account for the implications and the presence of uncertainty in estimation by utilizing simultaneous equation techniques, picking as instruments variables that are not rendered endogenous as a consequence of being dependent on unanticipated components which are correlated with forecast errors.

This chapter interprets empirical specifications of labor supply found in cross-section, synthetic cohort, and macro time series analyses in the context of a life cycle model. The central question answered in this work concerns the appropriate interpretation of the substitution effect that is estimated in each specification. It is shown that the wage coefficient in the typical cross-section specification represents either an intertemporal or an uncompensated substitution elasticity depending on the particular set of control variables one includes in the labor supply equation. If one includes education and family background variables as controls, then the wage coefficient is the intertemporal elasticity. If, on the other hand, one includes polynomials in age, then this coefficient is the uncompensated elasticity associated with a uniform change in the lifetime average wage rate. For specifications of labor supply found in either synthetic cohort or macro time series analysis, the wage coefficient represents an intertemporal substitution elasticity; thus, studies like Ghez and Becker (1975) and Lucas and Rapping (1969) estimate the same structural wage elasticity which measures the effect of an evolutionary wage change on hours of work.

The analysis discusses how one can use various sources of data to estimate intertemporal and uncompensated substitution elasticities. While one may use either longitudinal, macro time series, cross-section, or synthetic cohort data to estimate the parameters needed to predict the response of labor supply to anticipated changes in the wage rate over time, only the use of longitudinal data allows one to obtain estimates of these parameters that are free of cohort bias. Estimating the parameters needed to predict hours-of-work response to permanent wage changes or shifts in anticipated wage paths is a far more complicated problem. One can estimate such parameters directly using either longitudinal or cross-section data, but it is not possible to do so using either macro time series or synthetic cohort data without strong assumptions and a significant modeling effort.

The last section of the chapter surveys estimates of substitution effects computed using the different sources of data. There is an extensive overlap in the results based on longitudinal, cross-section, and synthetic cohort data, which suggests that cohort effects are not an important factor in cross-section and synthetic cohort analyses of the labor supply behavior of prime-age males. These results suggest a range of .1–.3 for men's intertemporal substitution elasticity and imply an estimate equal to .08 for the uncompensated substitution elasticity associated with a uniform percentage increase in the wage rate over the lifetime. The results further suggest that a consumer's adjustments for anticipated wage changes are small.

APPENDIX A

This appendix reports estimates for intertemporal and uncompensated substitution elasticities based on the cross-section specifications for labor supply described in Section 4. The sample employed here is from the Michigan Panel Study of Income Dynamics. It consists of observations on 561 prime-age white married males for the years 1967–75. To be included in the sample, these males had to be continuously married to the same spouse during the period 1968–76 and they had to be between the ages of 25 and 48 in 1967 (or 33–56 in 1975). This analysis treats data from each year as a separate cross section; so there are nine cross sections in total, each of which contains the same individuals with only their ages different. The labor supply variable used in the empirical analysis is annual hours of work. The wage variable is average hourly earnings deflated by the Consumer Price Index. Appendix B contains summary statistics for these variables and a more complete description of the data set.

This discussion presents estimates for only three of the cross-section specifications outlined in Section 4; it ignores the most general specification given by (26), which requires joint estimation and the imposition of nonlinear constraints across equations. The three models considered here include equations (25), (27), and (28), which can be estimated by conventional two-stage least squares procedures. Because the derivation of equation (28) assumes that the slopes of lifetime wage and income paths depend only on a consumer's age, the following analysis imposes this restriction by using reduced form equations for log wages and income that include education, education-squared, age, age-squared, and family background variables as explanatory variables.

As a point of reference, the first row of Table 3 presents estimates for wage coefficients obtained by instrumental variable estimation of equation

Table 3. *Cross-section estimation (absolute value of t statistics in parentheses)*

Specification estimated	Coefficient on ln W										Variables included in addition to intercept[b]
	67	68	69	70	71	72	73	74	75	Average[a]	
Equation (25)	.04	.05	.07	.12	.32	.11	.11	.23	.12	.13	Predicted income
	(.89)	(1.07)	(1.66)	(2.01)	(1.65)	(1.58)	(1.42)	(2.13)	(1.55)		
Equation (27)	.13	.25	.27	.24	.20	.07	−.05	.28	−.07	.15	Background variables, education, and age
	(.5)	(.6)	(.9)	(.6)	(.7)	(.3)	(.3)	(.6)	(.3)		
Equation (28)	.005	−.06	−.03	.05	.24	.07	.09	.18	.18	.08	Predicted income, age, and age-squared
	(.07)	(.51)	(.35)	(.8)	(1.32)	(1.14)	(1.3)	(1.8)	(1.9)		

[a] Simple average of coefficient estimates for all years.

[b] Reduced form equations for log wages and earnings include education, education-squared, age, age-squared, and family background variables, where background variables include the consumer's father's education, his mother's education, and a dummy variable representing the income level of his parents.

(25) with $\beta_4 = 0$, which represents an empirical specification for labor supply commonly found in cross-section analyses. According to this equation, hours of work are regressed on predicted wages and income. As noted in Section 3, the wage coefficient associated with this specification confuses wage effects, income effects, and properties of the population age distribution and consequently does not have a behavioral interpretation. The estimates of this coefficient are always positive. The estimates of the income coefficients, which are not presented, were all negative. This analysis yields wage and income coefficients with signs that are opposite to those typically found in cross-section empirical work on male labor supply because both wages and income are treated as endogenous variables in this analysis.

The second row of Table 3 reports estimates for equation (27). Theoretically, the wage coefficient in this specification represents the intertemporal substitution effect δ. The estimates of δ for the years 1967–72 and 1974 range between .07 and .28 and are generally consistent with the estimates for δ reported in Section 4. Estimates for the years 1973 and 1975 are negative. When considering these results, it is important to recognize that all wage coefficients in this row are imprecisely estimated, reflecting the fact that only the age-squared variable identifies the variation in predicted wages.

The last row of Table 3 presents estimates for equation (28). If wage and income profiles have slopes that are the same across consumers of a given age, the wage coefficient in this specification theoretically determines the response of labor supply to a uniform 100 percent increase in wages over the entire lifetime. While the estimates for this wage coefficient are generally small with most near zero, there is a fair amount of variation in estimates from one year to the next, so much so that for two of the years (1974 and 1975) one would reject the hypothesis that the coefficients are zero using conventional levels of significance.

APPENDIX B

This appendix reports the exclusion criteria used to generate the samples used in the empirical analysis of Appendix A. The primary sample is the Michigan Panel Study of Income Dynamics for 1976.

The following criteria were used in order to construct the sample of nine years of data on 561 white males who were between the ages 25 and 48 in 1967 (or 33–56 in 1976). Households included in the sample had to satisfy the following criteria: (1) A stable family composition prevailed over the period in the sense that the husband and wife remained together. (2) A worker must be classified as employed or unemployed (i.e., permanently disabled and retired were deleted). (3) Wage and labor supply data must be available for all years; a worker's years of schooling must also be available. (4) A worker must report less than 4680 hours worked per year. The absolute value of the difference in his real average hourly earnings in adjacent years cannot exceed \$16 or a change of 200 percent. The absolute value of the difference in the number of hours he works in adjacent years cannot exceed 2900 hours or a change of 190 percent. The purpose of this last criterion is to minimize difficulties arising from the presence of outliers. (Twenty-four workers were deleted by this outlier criterion.)

Table 4 presents summary statistics for annual hours of work and real average hourly earnings.

ACKNOWLEDGMENTS

This research originates from the author's dissertation and was supported by grants from the NSF SOC77-27136, the Social Security Administration 10-P-90748/9-02, and from the National Institute for Child Health and Human Development. The final revision of this paper was completed in July, 1982. The author is grateful for comments from James Heckman, John Pencavel, Mark Gritz and Frank Howland.

NOTES

1 Assuming the existence of a riskless, real interest rate is not needed to derive a relation like (8). See MaCurdy (1978, 1981b) for further discussion.

2 Heckman and MaCurdy (1980) and MaCurdy (1978, 1981a) call (9) and (10) the "λ constant" functions for consumption and labor supply. This different terminology is used to emphasize that $\lambda(t)$ represents the marginal utility of wealth for only one particular transformation of the lifetime preference function given by (1); since expected utility functions are unique up to linear transformations, $\lambda(t)$ need only be proportional to the marginal utility of wealth in period t. Hopefully, the terminology used in this chapter will not cause the reader any confusion. These MUWC functions have been used extensively in the analysis of life cycle theory, with Heckman (1974) representing the first application of these functions of which I am aware.

3 In particular, let the functions $C^*(\cdot)$ and $N^*(\cdot)$ denote the solutions to equations (5) and (6) with (6) holding as an equality. If, when evaluated at the relevant arguments, $N^*(\cdot) > 0$, then $C(\cdot) = C^*(\cdot)$ and $N(\cdot) = N^*(\cdot)$. If, on the other hand, $N^*(\cdot) \leq 0$, then $N(\cdot) = 0$, and $C(\cdot)$ is the solution to the equation $U_L(C(t), \bar{L}, \mathbf{Z}(t)) = \lambda(t)$. In either case, $C(\cdot)$ and $N(\cdot)$ contain only the variables $\lambda(t)$, $W(t)$, and $Z(t)$ as arguments, and their functional form depends only on the form of $U(\cdot)$. See Heckman and MaCurdy (1980) for details.

4 This result is a generalization of one reported by Hall (1978). In Hall's model there is only consumption of market goods and a riskless asset (i.e., hours of work is not a choice variable), and the only source of randomness is future income.

Table 4. *Sample summary statistics*

Variable definitions	Variable	Mean	Standard deviation	Minimum value	Maximum value	Skewness	Kurtosis
$W(t)$ = average hourly earnings in year t	W67	4.08	2.16	.75	25.76	2.82	19.42
	W68	4.26	2.18	.41	21.57	2.04	8.94
	W69	4.48	2.37	.22	20.87	2.11	8.45
	W70	4.53	2.40	.34	21.49	1.94	7.04
	W71	4.60	2.61	.52	21.49	2.68	13.81
	W72	4.80	2.56	.68	26.17	1.80	5.71
	W73	4.96	2.83	.68	19.24	2.52	10.55
	W74	4.94	2.90	.71	24.61	2.48	10.08
	W75	4.82	2.92	.31	25.42	2.91	15.22
$DW(t) = W(t) - W(t-1)$	DW68	.18	1.20	−5.09	9.12	1.66	13.50
	DW69	.22	1.12	−6.24	8.20	.80	11.07
	DW70	.04	1.27	−10.24	10.34	−.61	20.52
	DW71	.07	1.45	−7.05	15.54	3.43	41.03
	DW72	.19	1.34	−14.06	5.33	−2.57	28.89
	DW73	.15	1.41	−7.56	11.21	1.23	14.18
	DW74	−.01	1.60	−7.67	10.52	1.50	12.26
	DW75	−.12	1.48	−11.08	5.78	−2.04	13.49
$N(t)$ = annual hours worked in year t	N67	2392.33	568.16	920.00	4368.00	.97	1.56
	N68	2402.14	544.46	1031.99	4560.00	1.03	1.43
	N69	2363.22	543.38	400.00	4639.99	.93	2.23
	N70	2315.52	522.58	520.00	4339.99	.78	1.67
	N71	2324.89	546.10	552.00	4455.00	.79	1.48

	N72	2351.55	523.09	800.00	4310.00	.80	1.41
	N73	2340.83	520.65	600.00	4420.00	1.06	2.14
	N74	2289.95	529.57	400.00	4215.00	.63	1.28
	N75	2268.25	506.19	879.99	4160.00	.61	1.03
$DN(t) = N(t) - N(t-1)$	DN68	9.81	447.82	−2397.99	1920.00	−.10	3.83
	DN69	−38.91	421.21	−2382.00	2186.00	−.15	4.54
	DN70	−47.69	431.45	−2366.99	1520.00	−.41	4.59
	DN71	9.36	418.12	−1937.99	2660.00	.62	5.72
	DN72	26.66	451.03	−2030.00	2136.99	.23	3.89
	DN73	−10.72	447.57	−1740.00	2150.00	.11	3.79
	DN74	−50.88	431.80	−2508.00	1617.00	−.51	4.32
	DN75	−21.70	393.13	−2324.99	1324.00	−.52	3.96

5 There is no guarantee that this process is an exact random walk since the error terms $\varepsilon^*(t)$ may not be identically distributed or even homoscedastic over time. In a more general context, there is no guarantee that either $\lambda(t)$ or $\ln \lambda(t)$ follow even a Markov process. See MaCurdy (1978, 1981b) for details.

6 See MaCurdy (1978, 1981b) for further discussion of these general features.

7 The marriage dummy variable in this model is not viewed as a choice variable; it is determined outside the model. It, however, can be correlated with other random variables such as wages of the two spouses. See MaCurdy (1981b) for further discussion.

8 To treat b_t^* as a constant across consumers and over time, the riskless rate of interest must be constant, and the distribution generating forecast errors must be one such that $E_{t-1}\{\exp[\varepsilon^*(t)]\}$ does not vary with a change in consumer characteristics. Since $E_{t-1}\{\exp[\varepsilon^*(t)]\}$ represents a moment-generating function evaluated at "1," a sufficient condition for this moment to be constant is that the $\varepsilon^*(t)$ terms are identically distributed across consumers and time. Assumptions of this nature are unlikely to be satisfied and are not needed to carry out some of the analysis, but they are maintained throughout this discussion to simplify the exposition.

9 This specification, then, neglects the possibility that the consumer may not work in some period or that he could die prior to period τ as the result of unforeseen events.

10 If one has measures of the interest rate, they obviously could be included in (17).

11 It is possible to modify the above specification and the following analysis to account for such effects; to account for the uncertainty of future wages, for example, one could include terms like $E_0\{\ln W_i(k) \cdot \ln W_i(l)\}$ where $k, l > 0$, which incorporate measures of dispersion.

12 Notice that δ is not a compensated substitution elasticity. A compensated elasticity determines the labor supply response to a parametric wage change which holds utility constant and not to an evolutionary wage change. See MaCurdy (1981a) for further discussion.

13 For this statement to be valid, one also must rule out the possibility that the variance and the higher-order moments of the forecast errors $\varepsilon_i(j)$ depend on hours of work prior to age $t-1$.

14 Most empirical work that attempts to test the implications of optimizing behavior uses the MUWC function for consumption rather than for labor supply to perform these tests (e.g., Hall, 1978). All the discussion here, of course, applies regardless of whether one uses consumption or hours of work data.

15 These are, of course, loose interpretations of these parameters. Formally, uncompensated substitution and wealth elasticities hold the actual values of future wages constant. Here, only the expected values of future wages are being held constant. In the case of a more general empirical specification for the life cycle component, it is the distribution of future wages that is held constant rather than the actual values.

16 In particular, with $M(t) \equiv \partial\Omega(t)/\partial\Omega(0)$ and $R(t) \equiv [1 + r_f(1)] \cdots [1 + r_f(t)]$, one can show that the life cycle model of Section 1 with no uncertainty implies

$$\frac{\partial \ln \lambda(0)}{\partial\Omega(0)} = \frac{\partial \ln \lambda(t)}{\partial\Omega(t)} M(t)$$

and, for $k \geq t$,

$$\frac{\partial \ln \lambda(0)}{\partial \ln W(k)} = \frac{\partial \ln \lambda(t)}{\partial \ln W(k)} \cdot \frac{M(t)}{R(t)}$$

Interpreting parameters as derivatives, it follows that $\theta_t = \theta_0/M(t)$ and $\gamma_t(j) = \gamma_0(j) \cdot R(t)/M(t)$. The inequality result proposed in the text follows since $0 < M(t) < 1$ and $R(t)/M(t) > 1$.

17 The implicit interpretation of cross-section estimates held by most researchers relates to some sort of "lifetime average" relationship between hours, wages, and income. To estimate such a relationship, observations of $\ln W_i(t)$ and $Y_i(t)$ must be purged of their transitory components so that they measure their lifetime average. Predicting $\ln W_i(t)$ and $Y_i(t)$ is one way of accomplishing this task.

18 Accounting for the endogeneity of $\ln W_i(t)$ and $Y_i(t)$ has been shown to have a significant effect on cross-section estimates. See DaVanzo, De Tray, and Greenberg (1976).

19 There have been several cross-section studies that have used age variables to control for "life cycle factors" (e.g., Heckman, 1971; Ashenfelter and Heckman, 1973; and DaVanzo, De Tray, and Greenberg, 1976), although these studies are not specific about how these age variables control for such effects.

20 Notice that this latter choice of control variables crucially depends on the assumption that the lifetime wage and income path coefficients on age and age-squared are not functions of a consumer's characteristics. Violation of this assumption implies that age-invariant characteristics as well as interactions between these characteristics and t and t^2 must also be included as control variables in equation (28). Inclusion of such variables requires one to estimate equations (26), (18), and (19) jointly with nonlinear methods.

21 The coefficient on the wife's wage is known in the literature on consumer demand as the cross-specific substitution elasticity. It determines the effect of an evolutionary change in the wife's wage rate on the husband's hours of work. Notice that this coefficient is zero when utility in each period is additive in the husband's and the wife's leisure.

22 Some of these variables may, of course, enter equation (29) directly as components of the taste shifter vector $\mathbf{X}(t)$.

23 See, for example, Smith (1975) who uses these estimated coefficients to predict the effect of income maintenance programs on hours of work.

24 In constructing this equation, one has an obvious problem in mixing participation and labor supply functions when changes in the wage rate result in a different working population. To obtain (30) one must assume that the working population is fixed.

25 Notice that the derivation of (30) assumes constancy of the riskless real rate of interest over time. Relaxing this assumption requires one to replace the term $b\bar{t}_j$ in (30) by a complicated average of trends.

26 See Lucas and Rapping (1969, p. 745).

27 Adding a deterministic component to this specification for the wage rate does not alter any of the subsequent discussion. For most of this analysis, one may think of $\xi(t)$ as incorporating all deterministic components.

28. Formally, this discussion assumes that the parameter $\bar{\gamma} = \sum_{j=t+1}^{\tau} \gamma_t(j)$ is constant for all t.

29 The data set used in this cross-section analysis is almost identical to the one used by MaCurdy (1981a) in his longitudinal work. For a more complete description of this data set, see Appendix B of this chapter.

30 Some of the usual reasons are the presence of measurement error, transitory components, or common individual components in hours of work and wage equations.

31 Thus, in specification (16), even if a variable that affects tastes, such as education, is uncertain early in a consumer's life, it is possible to treat education as a predetermined variable (at least with respect to the forecast error components of the structural disturbance).

32 There is one reason why a researcher might prefer the first-differenced over the level specification in an empirical analysis. Because differencing removes all forecast errors except the current period's, there may be more predetermined variables that can serve as instruments in an estimation procedure. As noted previously, variables that are uncertain at the beginning of life but realized prior to the current period can serve as instruments in equation (16) if they are uncorrelated with the taste components $v_i(t)$ and $v_i(t-1)$.

33 For more information concerning these numbers, see the footnotes of Table 1.

34 Some of these assumptions are, of course, also required to interpret the estimates of the MUWC labor supply equation discussed above.

35 Consider, for example, the anticipated lifetime wage path. Even if it is a quadratic equation in age, the coefficients of this equation may vary across cohorts. Since most longitudinal data sources offer only a short time series, in the estimation process one is normally forced to assume that these coefficients are constant across cohorts. This leads to a contamination of the estimates of the individual effects equation if cohort effects are present.

REFERENCES

Ashenfelter, O., and Heckman, J. 1973. "Estimating Labor Supply Functions." In G. Cain and H. Watts (eds.), *Income Maintenance and Labor Supply*. Chicago: Markham.

DaVanzo, J., De Tray, D., and Greenberg, D. 1976. "The Sensitivity of Male Labor Supply Estimates to the Choice of Assumptions." *Review of Economics and Statistics* 58:313.

Friedman, M. 1957. *A Theory of the Consumption Function*. New York: National Bureau of Economic Research.

Ghez, G., and Becker, G. 1975. *The Allocation of Time and Goods over the Life Cycle*. New York: National Bureau of Economic Research.

Hall, R. 1978. "Stochastic Implications of the Life Cycle–Permanent Income Hypothesis: Theory and Evidence." *Journal of Political Economy* (December):971–88.

Heckman, J. J. 1971. "Three Essays on the Supply of Labor and the Demand for Goods." Ph.D. thesis, Princeton University.

1974. "Life Cycle Consumption and Labor Supply: An Explanation of the Relationship between Income and Consumption over the Life Cycle." *American Economic Review* (March):188–94.

Heckman, J. J., and MaCurdy, T. 1980. "A Life Cycle Model of Female Labor Supply." *Review of Economic Studies* 46:47–74.

Lucas, R. E., and Rapping, L. 1969. "Real Wages, Employment, and Inflation." *Journal of Political Economy* 77, no. 5:721–54.

MaCurdy, T. 1978. "Two Essays on the Life Cycle." Ph.D. thesis, University of Chicago.

1981a. "An Empirical Model of Labor Supply in a Life Cycle Setting." *Journal of Political Economy* 89, no. 6:1059–85.

1981b. "An Intertemporal Model of Portfolio Choice and Human Capital Accumulation under Uncertainty with Extensions Incorporating Taxes, Consumer Durables, Imperfection in Capital Markets, and Nonseparable Preferences." Working Paper No. E-80-4, Domestic Studies Program, Hoover Institute, Stanford University.

Smith, J. 1975, "On the Labor Supply Effects of Age-Related Income Maintenance Programs." *Journal of Human Resources* (Winter): 25–43.

1977. "Family Labor Supply over the Life Cycle." *Explorations in Economic Research* 4, no. 2:205–76.

CHAPTER 4

Alternative methods for evaluating the impact of interventions

James J. Heckman and Richard Robb, Jr.

1 The problem and an overview of solutions to it

This chapter considers the problem of estimating the impact of interventions in the presence of selection decisions by agents. For specificity we focus on the problem of estimating the impact of training on earnings when the enrollment of persons into training is the outcome of a selection process. The analysis of training presented here serves as a prototype for the analysis of the closely related problems of deriving selection-bias-free estimates of the impacts of unionism, migration, job turnover, unemployment, and affirmative action programs on earnings.

This chapter investigates the prior restrictions needed to secure consistent estimators of the selection-bias-free impact of training on earnings. We examine their plausibility in the light of economic theory.

We present assumptions required to use three types of widely available data to solve the problem of estimating the impact of training on earnings free of selection bias: (1) a single cross section of posttraining earnings, (2) a temporal sequence of cross sections of unrelated people (repeated cross-section data), and (3) longitudinal data in which the same individuals are followed over time. These three types of data are listed in the order of their availability and in inverse order of their cost of acquisition.[1] Assuming random sampling techniques are applied to collect all three types of data, the three sources form a hierarchy: Longitudinal data can be used to generate a single cross section or a set of temporal cross sections in which the identities of individuals are ignored, and repeated cross sections can be used as single cross sections.

Longitudinal data are widely regarded as a panacea for selection and simultaneity problems. Yet to date there has been no systematic statement of conditions under which longitudinal data are required to isolate estimates of the impact of training on earnings free of selection bias. This chapter presents such conditions. En route to deriving these conditions we investigate the assumptions required to use less costly cross-section and repeated cross-section data to estimate the impact of training on earnings. Once this is done, it is possible to state what assumptions can be relaxed or tested if the analyst has access to longitudinal data.

Our conclusions are rather startling. Provided that conventional fixed effect specifications of earnings functions are adopted, there is no need to use longitudinal data to identify the impact of training on earnings. Estimators based on repeated cross-section data for unrelated persons identify the same parameter. However, we question the plausibility of conventional specifications. They are not motivated by economic theory, and when examined in that light they seem implausible. We propose richer longitudinal specifications of the earnings process and enrollment decision derived from economic theory. In addition, we propose a variety of new estimators. Some of these require longitudinal data, but for others longitudinal data are still not required. A major conclusion of our chapter is that the relative benefits of longitudinal data have been overstated, because the potential benefits of cross-section and repeated cross-section data have been understated.

We also question recent claims that cross-section approaches to estimating the impact of training on earnings are strongly dependent on arbitrary assumptions about distributions of unobservables. While some widely used cross-section estimators suffer from this defect, such assumptions are not an essential feature of the cross-section approach. However, we demonstrate that unless explicit distributional assumptions are invoked, all cross-section estimators require the presence of at least one regressor variable in the decision rule determining training. This requirement may seem innocuous, but it rules out a completely nonparametric cross-section approach. Without prior restrictions, it is not possible to cross-classify observations on the basis of values assumed by explanatory variables in the earnings function and the enrollment rules and do a "regressor-free" estimation of the impact of training on earnings that is free of selection bias. A regressor is required in the enrollment rule, and for most cross-section estimators this requires specification of the functional form of the decision rule. Longitudinal and repeated cross-section estimators do not require this condition.

In analyzing the assumptions required to use various data sources to consistently estimate the impact of training on earnings free of selection bias we discuss the following topics:

1. How much prior information about the earnings function must be assumed?

2. How much prior information about the decision rule governing participation must be assumed?
3. How robust are the proposed methods to the following commonly encountered features of data on training?
   a. Nonrandomness of available samples and especially oversampling of trainees (the choice-based sample problem).
   b. Time inhomogeneity in the environment ("nonstationarity").
   c. The absence of a control group of nontrainees or the contamination of the control group so that the training status is not known for a random sample of the population

Notably absent from this list of questions is any mention of the relative efficiency of estimators for cross-section, repeated cross-section, and longitudinal data. A discussion of efficiency makes sense only within the context of a fully specified model. The focus in this chapter is on the tradeoffs in assumptions that must be imposed in order to estimate a common coefficient when the analyst has access to different types of data. Since different assumptions about the underlying model are invoked in order to justify the validity of different estimators, an efficiency comparison is often meaningless. Under the assumptions about an underlying model that justify one estimator, another estimator may not be applicable. Only by postulating a common assumption set that is unnecessarily large for any single estimator is it possible to compare the efficiency of alternative estimators. For the topic of this chapter – model identification – the efficiency issue is a red herring.

This chapter is divided into six sections. Section 1 presents a formal statement of the problem considered in this chapter and an intuitive statement of our principal results. Section 2 presents a set of prototypical decision rules that are assumed to characterize a person's decision to enroll in training. One contribution of this chapter to the literature on training is to make explicit the econometric implications of various decision processes that confront agents contemplating enrollment in training. The validity of many estimators hinges on the specification of decision rules. Previous work is statistical in nature and advocates various estimators on the basis of implicit enrollment rules that are never fully articulated. For this reason there has been little use of economic theory in previous work to guide the choice of appropriate estimators.

Section 3 examines cross-section estimators. Section 4 presents repeated cross-section estimators when the training status of persons is unknown, and Section 5 considers longitudinal estimators and other repeated cross-section estimators when the training status of persons is known. The chapter concludes with a summary and comparison of procedures and a brief discussion of the efficiency of alternative methods when that concept is well defined.

1.1 *The problem and some notation*

In seeking to determine the impact of training on earnings in the presence of nonrandom assignment of persons to training, it is useful to distinguish two questions that are frequently confused in the literature:

Question 1:
What would be the impact of training on earnings if people were randomly assigned to training?

Question 2:
How do the postprogram earnings of the trained compare to what they would have been in the absence of training?

The second question makes a hypothetical contrast between the post-program earnings of the people who would be selected as trainees in the presence and in the absence of training programs. This hypothetical contrast eliminates factors that would make the earnings of trainees different from those of nontrainees even in the absence of any training program. The two questions have the same answer only when training has the same impact on earnings for everyone or when assignment to training is random.

In the presence of nonrandom assignment and variation in the impact of training among persons, the two questions have different answers. Question 2 is the appropriate one to ask if interest centers on forecasting the increment in the posttraining earnings of trainees when the same selection rule characterizes past and future trainees. Question 1 is intrinsically more difficult to answer because it asks to forecast the increment in the earnings of trainees over their pretraining earnings when no selection bias characterizes enrollment while selection bias characterizes the available data. It is really a special case of the more general question:

Question 3:
What would be the effect of training on the earnings of the trained if the future selection rule for trainees differs from the past selection rule?

It is important to note that the answer to the more modest question 2 is all that is required to estimate the future program impact if future selection criteria are like past criteria.

To focus on essential aspects of the problem, we initially assume that training has the same effect on everyone (so the three questions have the same answers). We further assume that training is offered only once (in period k) in a person's life cycle. If the training option is pursued, it takes one period to complete. During a period of training, trainees receive no employment income.

The earnings of individual i in period t (Y_{it}) are assumed to depend on characteristics ($\mathbf{X}_{it}$). Postprogram earnings depend on a dummy variable (d_i) that equals 1 if a person participated in training and is 0 otherwise. To account for unobserved characteristics, a mean zero disturbance (U_{it}) is assumed. A linear version of this specification may be written as

$$\begin{aligned} Y_{it} &= \mathbf{X}_{it}\boldsymbol{\beta} + d_i\alpha + U_{it}, \qquad t > k \\ Y_{it} &= \mathbf{X}_{it}\boldsymbol{\beta} \qquad\quad + U_{it}, \qquad t \leq k \end{aligned} \tag{1.1}$$

where $E(U_{it}) = 0$. U_{it} is assumed to be independently distributed across persons.

Boldfaced variables, denoted by Roman letters, are understood to be row vectors. Boldfaced parameters, denoted by Greek letters, are understood to be column vectors. We adopt this convention throughout this chapter.

For the moment we assume that α is the same for everyone. Later we alter (1.1) and substitute α_i for α to obtain a random coefficient model. In that case the three questions have different answers. We also abstract from likely depreciation or growth effects of training that would suggest writing α_t in place of α in (1.1). We indicate below how the analysis can be modified to account for temporal variation in program impact.

The decision to participate in training may be determined by a trainee, a program administrator, or both. Whatever the specific content of the rule, it can be described in terms of an index function framework. Let IN_i be an index of benefits (to the appropriate decision makers) of taking training. It is a function of observed ($\mathbf{Z}_i$) and unobserved (v_i) variables. Thus,

$$IN_i = \mathbf{Z}_i\gamma + V_i \tag{1.2}$$

In terms of this function

$$\begin{aligned} d_i &= 1 \qquad \text{iff} \quad IN_i > 0 \\ d_i &= 0 \qquad \text{otherwise} \end{aligned}$$

We normalize V_i so that $E(V_i) = 0$ and $\text{Var}(V_i) = 1$. The distribution function of V_i [$\Pr(V_i \leq v_i)$] is denoted as $F(v_i)$. V_i is assumed to be independently and identically distributed across persons.

At this point, nothing has been stated about the nature of the stochastic dependence among $\mathbf{X}_{it}$, d_i, U_{it}, V_i, and $\mathbf{Z}_i$. Our vagueness is deliberate. This chapter explores a variety of assumptions about stochastic dependence relations among these variables. Below we are very precise about our stochastic dependence assumptions.

The central problem considered in this chapter arises when the decision to take training is not random with respect to the disturbance term in earnings function (1.1). More precisely, the problem of selection bias arises when

(A-1) $E(U_{it}d_i) \neq 0$

This may occur because of stochastic dependence between U_{it} and the unobservable V_i in (1.2) (selection on the unobservables) or because of stochastic dependence between U_{it} and $\mathbf{Z}_i$ in (1.2) (selection on the observables). When condition (A-1) occurs a standard least squares assumption is violated and α is not identified without invoking additional assumptions.

This is not the only potential source of nonidentifiability of α. For example, even if $E(U_{it}d_i) = 0$, α is not identified without further assumptions when $E(\mathbf{X}_{it}U_{it}) \neq 0$ unless $\mathbf{X}_{it}$ is orthogonal to d_i. This source of nonidentifiability for α is entirely conventional, and we have little to say about it here. Throughout most of this chapter we focus on models in which (A-1) characterizes the data and is the sole source of nonidentifiability of α. When $\mathbf{X}_{it}$ contains lagged values of Y_{it}, we assume that (1.1) can be solved for a reduced form expression of exogenous variables and we use that expression in place of (1.1).

An extreme form of model (1.1) that focuses on (A-1) as the principal source of nonidentifiability is one with no regressors other than the program dummy so that

$$\begin{aligned} Y_{it} &= \beta_t + d_i\alpha + U_{it}, \qquad t > k \\ Y_{it} &= \beta_t \qquad\qquad\; + U_{it}, \qquad t \leq k \end{aligned} \tag{1.3}$$

If $\mathbf{X}_{it}$ assumes a finite number of possible values, this model is actually more general than (1.1) in that it can arise by stratifying (1.1) on the basis of values of the $\mathbf{X}_{it}$ regressors allowing β_t to differ across strata. In the remainder of this section, we adopt earnings specification (1.3) and decision rule (1.2). Although there is no regressor in the earnings equation, regressors may appear in enrollment equation (1.2).

1.2 *Estimators for models without selection bias*

To fix ideas it is useful to begin by considering estimation of the training effect in a model without selection bias so that $E(U_{it}d_i) = 0$ for all t, except possibly for $t = k$. We consider cross-section, repeated cross-section, and longitudinal estimators of α. We assume access to random samples of I_t individuals for each period t, and we assume that we know an individual's training status and age without error. We confine our attention to data on a single cohort.

One cross-section estimator for α is the difference between the earnings of participants and nonparticipants in a postprogram period ($t > k$). Define the mean earnings of trainees and nontrainees in period t as $\bar{Y}_t^{(1)}$ and $\bar{Y}_t^{(0)}$, respectively, so that

$$\bar{Y}_t^{(1)} = \frac{\sum Y_{it} d_i}{\sum d_i} \quad \text{and} \quad \bar{Y}_t^{(0)} = \frac{\sum Y_{it}(1 - d_i)}{\sum (1 - d_i)}$$

for $0 < \sum d_i < I_t$. The cross-section estimator of α is

$$\hat{\alpha}_C = \bar{Y}_t^{(1)} - \bar{Y}_t^{(0)} \quad \text{for} \quad t > k \tag{1.4}$$

Because $E(U_{it} | d_i) = 0$, we have

$$\text{plim}(\hat{\alpha}_C) = \alpha \quad \text{if} \quad 0 < \Pr(d_i = 1) < 1$$

Note that this estimator is robust to violations of the random sampling assumption provided that $E(U_{it} | d_i) = 0$.

One possible repeated cross-section estimator is $\hat{\alpha}_C$ applied to each cross section. Under the current assumptions, access to repeated cross sections only improves the capacity to estimate a separate α ($= \alpha_t$) for each period or if $\alpha_t = \alpha$ improves the efficiency of the estimator of α.

If the training status of persons is unknown, $\hat{\alpha}_C$ is useless. If, however, the analyst has access to the sample means of the earnings of cohorts in different years, it is sometimes possible to recover α without knowledge of an individual's training status. For a given cohort assume access to at least one postprogram and one preprogram mean of earnings, say $\bar{Y}_t$ and $\bar{Y}_{t'}$, where $t > k > t'$. In each cross section the individual identities of trainees or nontrainees need not be known. Assume that the postprogram population proportion that has taken training (p_t) is known or can be consistently estimated. Let $\hat{\alpha}_{RC}$ denote the repeated cross-section estimator defined as

$$\hat{\alpha}_{RC} = \bar{Y}_t - \bar{Y}_{t'} \quad \text{for} \quad t > k > t'$$

$$E(\hat{\alpha}_{RC}) = \beta_t - \beta_{t'} + p_t \alpha \tag{1.5}$$

If the environment is time-homogeneous (so that $\beta_t = \beta_{t'}$) and p_t is known or can be consistently estimated, then α can be estimated (without bias or consistently, respectively) by dividing $\hat{\alpha}_{RC}$ by p_t.

Unlike the cross-section estimator, the repeated cross-section estimator does not require that the identities of trainees be known in each cross section (provided that p_t is known). In this sense it is more robust. However, it is not robust to departures from the time homogeneity assumption, whereas the cross-section estimator is.

If the environment is sufficiently smooth, it is still possible to use $\hat{\alpha}_{RC}$ to consistently estimate α in a time-inhomogeneous environment. To do so requires that β_t expressed as a function of t be described by at least one fewer parameter than the number of available cross sections. For example, from the mean earnings of three temporally distinct cross sections, if $\beta_t = \beta^0 + \beta_t^1$, then β^0, β^1, and α can be consistently estimated provided that (a) $p_t > 0$, (b) p_t can be consistently estimated, and (c) data for at least one year of postprogram earnings and one year of preprogram earnings are available.

If year effects are identical across cohorts, access to multiple-cohort data can aid in identifying α in a time-inhomogeneous environment. To see why this is so, suppose that three adjacent cohorts denoted A, B, C are followed. A is the oldest and C is the youngest. The mean of C's earnings in the period preceding their enrollment is an unbiased estimator of β_t—the period effect component of the mean earnings of A in their first post-program year. Given p_t for cohort A, it is possible to consistently estimate α by subtracting the mean earnings of C from the mean earnings of A and dividing by p_t. Note further that with different (known or consistently estimable) proportions of trainees in posttraining cross sections t, t'' it follows that

$$\begin{aligned} \text{plim } \hat{\alpha}_{RC} &= \text{plim}(\bar{Y}_t - \bar{Y}_{t''}), \qquad t, t'' > k \\ &= \alpha(p_t - p_{t''}) \end{aligned}$$

so that α is consistently estimable solely from postprogram cross sections by dividing $\bar{Y}_t - \bar{Y}_{t''}$ by a consistent estimator of $p_t - p_{t''}$.

If the identity of trainees and nontrainees is known in each cross section, it is possible to estimate α consistently (using $\hat{\alpha}_C$) and hence β_t without any smoothness assumptions.

Abstracting from potential gains in devising more efficient estimators, longitudinal data provide no additional information beyond their use as cross-section or repeated cross-section data in models without selection bias.

1.3 *Models with selection bias*

All of the assumptions of Section 1.1 are retained except that we no longer assume that $E(U_{it}d_i) = 0$. We continue to assume that a random sampling scheme generates the data.

1.3.1. Cross-section estimators. The cross-section estimator $\hat{\alpha}_C$ is always biased for α. For each observation

$$\begin{aligned} E(Y_{it} | d_i = 1) &= \beta_t + \alpha + E(U_{it} | d_i = 1) \\ E(Y_{it} | d_i = 0) &= \beta_t + E(U_{it} | d_i = 0) \end{aligned}$$

Assuming that the data are generated by a random sampling scheme, we have

$$\operatorname{plim} \hat{\alpha}_C = \alpha + [E(U_{it}|d_i = 1) - E(U_{it}|d_i = 0)]$$

Since $E(U_{it}) = 0$ for all i, the expectation of each term inside the square brackets is nonzero and of opposite sign if $E(U_{it}d_i) \neq 0$, and so the expectation of the entire term is nonzero.

If there are no regressors in decision rule (1.2), so that $\Pr(d_i = 1) = p$ is the same constant for each observation and the U_{it} are i.i.d. (independent and identically distributed), then

$$E(U_{it}|d_i = 1) = \phi \quad \text{so} \quad E(U_{it}|d_i = 0) = -\frac{p}{1-p}\phi$$

and so then

$$\operatorname{plim} \hat{\alpha}_C = \alpha + \frac{\phi}{1-p}$$

Even if p is known, using $\hat{\alpha}_C$, α cannot be separated from ϕ when data on means and variances are used.[2]

Another way to state this nonidentification result is to write the regression function

$$E(Y_{it}|d_i) = [\beta_t + E(U_{it}|d_i = 0)] \\ + d_i(\alpha + E(U_{it}|d_i = 1) - E(U_{it}|d_i = 0)) \tag{1.6}$$

If

$$E(U_{it}|d_i = 1) = \phi \quad \text{and} \quad \Pr(d_i = 1) = p$$

then

$$E(Y_{it}|d_i) = \left(\beta_t - \frac{p}{1-p}\phi\right) + d_i\left(\alpha + \frac{\phi}{1-p}\right)$$

Unless $\beta_t = 0$ or other prior information is assumed, α is not identified.

If $E(U_{it}|d_i = 1, \mathbf{Z}_i)$ is a nonconstant function of $\mathbf{Z}_i$, it is possible (with additional assumptions) to solve this identification problem. Securing identification in this fashion explicitly precludes a fully nonparametric strategy in which both the earnings function (1.1) and decision rule (1.2) are estimated in each $(\mathbf{X}_{it}, \mathbf{Z}_i)$ stratum. For within each stratum, $E(U_{it}|d_i = 1, \mathbf{Z}_i)$ is not a constant function of $\mathbf{Z}_i$ and α is not identified from cross-section data.

If $E(U_{it}|d_i = 1, \mathbf{Z}_i)$ is a nonconstant function of $\mathbf{Z}_i$, it is possible to exploit this information in a variety of ways depending on what else is assumed about the model. Here we simply sketch the alternative strategies. In Section 3 we present a systematic discussion of each approach.

(i) Suppose $\mathbf{Z}_i$ or a subset of $\mathbf{Z}_i$ is exogenous with respect to U_{it}. Under conditions specified more fully in Section 3, the exogenous subset may be used to construct an instrumental variable for d_i in equation (1.3), and α can be consistently estimated by instrumental variables methods. No distributional assumptions are required (Heckman, 1978).

(ii) Suppose that $\mathbf{Z}_i$ is distributed independently of V_i and the functional form of the distribution of V_i is known. Under standard conditions, γ in (1.2) can be consistently estimated using conventional methods in discrete choice analysis (Amemiya, 1981). If $\mathbf{Z}_i$ is distributed independently of U_{it}, $F(-\mathbf{Z}_i\hat{\gamma})$ can be used as an instrument for d_i in equation (1.2) (Heckman, 1978).

(iii) Under the same conditions as specified in (ii),

$$E(Y_{it}|\mathbf{Z}_i) = \beta_t + \alpha(1 - F(-\mathbf{Z}_i\gamma)) \tag{1.7}$$

β_t and α can be consistently estimated using $F(-\mathbf{Z}_i\hat{\gamma})$ in place of $F(-\mathbf{Z}_i\gamma)$ in equation (1.7) (Heckman, 1976, 1978) or else the equation can be fit by nonlinear least squares estimating β_t, α, and γ jointly (given the functional form of F) (Barnow, Cain, and Goldberger, 1980).

(iv) If the functional forms of $E(U_{it}|d_i = 1, \mathbf{Z}_i)$ and $E(U_{it}|d_i = 0, \mathbf{Z}_i)$ as functions of $\mathbf{Z}_i$ are known up to a finite set of parameters, it is sometimes possible to consistently estimate β_t, α and the parameters of the conditional means from the (nonlinear) regression function

$$\begin{aligned} E(Y_{it}|d_i, \mathbf{Z}_i) = \beta_t + d_i\alpha + d_i E(U_{it}|d_i = 1, \mathbf{Z}_i) \\ + (1 - d_i)E(U_{it}|d_i = 0, \mathbf{Z}_i) \end{aligned} \tag{1.8}$$

One way to acquire information about the functional form of $E(U_{it}|d_i = 1, \mathbf{Z}_i)$ is to assume knowledge of the functional form of the joint distribution of (U_{it}, V_i) (e.g., that it is bivariate normal) but this is not required in principle. Note further that this procedure does not require that $\mathbf{Z}_i$ be distributed independently of V_i in (1.2) (Barnow, Cain, and Goldberger, 1980).

(v) Instead of (iv), it is possible to do a two-stage estimation procedure if the joint density of (U_{it}, V_i) is asssumed to be known up to a finite set of parameters. In stage 1, $E(U_{it}|d_i = 1, \mathbf{Z}_i)$ and $E(U_{it}|d_i = 0, \mathbf{Z}_i)$ are determined up to some unknown parameters ψ by conventional discrete choice analysis. Then regression (1.8) is run using the estimated E in place of E on the right-hand side of the equation (Heckman, 1978, 1979).

(vi) Under the assumptions of (v), use maximum likelihood to consistently estimate α (Heckman, 1978).

Conventional selection bias approaches (iv)–(vi) rely on strong distributional assumptions, but in fact these are not required. Given that a regressor appears in decision rule (1.2), if it is exogenous with respect to

U_{it}, the regressor is an instrumental variable for d_i. It is not necessary to invoke strong distributional assumptions, but if they are invoked, Z_i need not be exogenous with respect to U_{it}. In practice, however, it is usually assumed to be so.

A regressor is not required in the decision rule if some other identifying information is invoked. For example, assuming joint normality of (U_{it}, V_i), Heckman (1978) establishes that α is identified in the absence of any regressor in selection rule (1.2). In Section 3, we demonstrate that if the marginal distribution of U_{it} satisfies some moment restrictions [e.g., $E(U_{it}^3) = 0$ and $E(U_{it}^5) = 0$ or other such conditions], α is identified from cross-section data without any regressor in (1.2) and without specifying the full joint distribution of (U_{it}, V_i).

1.3.2. Repeated cross-section estimators. Assuming a time-homogeneous environment and random sampling, the repeated cross-section estimator identifies α (a) without any regressor in decision rule (1.2), (b) without need to specify the joint distribution of U_{it} and V_i, and (c) without any need to identify the training status of individuals in the cross sections (but the proportion of trainees must be known or consistently estimable).

To understand why this claim is true, it is useful to distinguish two different sampling schemes. Above we defined d_i as a random variable that equals 1 if a member of the population has received training and is 0 otherwise. When random sampling is assumed, the probability of sampling a trainee is $\Pr(d_i = 1)$. When some other sampling rule is assumed, the probability of sampling a trainee is not $\Pr(d_i = 1)$. In year t, let this probability be $\Pr_t(d_i = 1) = p_t^*$. If $p_t^* = \Pr_t(d_i = 1) = \Pr(d_i = 1)$ and if the sampling is only on the basis of training status, then the available data are a random sample of the population.[3]

With this notation and assuming that (A-1) characterizes the data so that there is selection into training and that successive observations are independently and identically distributed across individuals, we get

$$E(\hat{\alpha}_{RC}) = \beta_t - \beta_{t'} + p_t^*\alpha + [p_t^*E(U_{it}|d_i = 1) + (1 - p_t^*)E(U_{it}|d_i = 0)]$$
$$- [p_{t'}^*E(U_{it'}|d_i = 1) + (1 - p_{t'}^*)E(U_{it'}|d_i = 0)] \quad \text{for} \quad t > k > t'$$

In data from a random sample, the terms in square brackets are zero. As a consequence of time homogeneity, $\beta_t = \beta_{t'}$. Thus

$$\text{plim } \hat{\alpha}_{RC} = p_t^*\alpha = p_t\alpha$$

and if p_t^* is known or consistently estimable, α is identified by dividing $\hat{\alpha}_{RC}$ by p_t^* assuming $p_t^* \neq 0$.

Thus under the stated conditions, $\hat{\alpha}_{RC}$ can be used to identify α while $\hat{\alpha}_C$ is inconsistent for α. If the environment is time-inhomogeneous, $\hat{\alpha}_{RC}$

does not identify α, for reasons already presented in Section 1.1. It is necessary to invoke a smoothness assumption in order to use $\hat{\alpha}_{RC}$ to identify α. Unlike the case considered in Section 1.1, access to the trainee identity of individuals does not break the identification problem raised by time inhomogeneity.

The random sampling requirement is overly strong. Abstracting from time inhomogeneity, all that is required for $\hat{\alpha}_{RC}$ to identify α given knowledge of p_t^* is that

$$\text{(A-2)} \quad p_t^* E(U_{it} | d_i = 1) + (1 - p_t^*) E(U_{it} | d_i = 0) = p_{t'}^* E(U_{it'} | d_i = 1) + (1 - p_{t'}^*) E(U_{it'} | d_i = 0)$$

that is, that the expectations of the mean disturbances be equal in t and t', not that they both equal zero. In principle, it is possible for $\Pr_t(d_i = 1) \neq \Pr(d_i = 1)$ and condition (A-2) to be satisfied. Further, if (A-2) is satisfied and $p_t^* \neq p_{t'}^*$, then it is possible to use two postprogram cross sections to identify α.[4] While it is possible that (A-2) is satisfied in nonrandom samples, there is little evidence that suggests that available samples are collected so that they satisfy (A-2).

The random sampling requirement or the weaker condition (A-2) is the Achilles' heel of the repeated cross-section estimator $\hat{\alpha}_{RC}$. If (A-2) is violated, the repeated cross-section estimator does not identify α.

Provided that the training status of persons is known in each cross section and specific assumptions are made about the time series process generating U_{it} and its stochastic dependence on V_i, it is possible to construct other repeated cross-section estimators that are robust to general forms of time inhomogeneity in the environment. The proposed estimators do not require that the data be generated by a random sampling scheme or even that the same sampling rules be used in any two cross sections. Knowledge of the proportion of the population taking training is not required.

To exhibit one such estimator, suppose that decision rule (1.2) contains no regressor ($\mathbf{Z}_i = 1$) so that in principle α cannot be identified using the cross-section methods previously discussed. Assume further that for each t the pair (U_{it}, V_i) is independently and identically distributed across persons. Suppose further that the following additional information is available:

$$\text{(A-3)} \quad E(U_{it} | d_i = 1) = E(U_{it'} | d_i = 1), \qquad t > k > t'$$

and hence

$$E(U_{it} | d_i = 0) = E(U_{it'} | d_i = 0), \qquad t > k > t'$$

Then α is identified in a general time-inhomogeneous environment.

The proposed repeated cross-section estimator subtracts the mean of trainee earnings in t from the mean of earnings in t' of those who will subsequently be trained. This identifies $\beta_t - \beta_{t'} + \alpha$. Subtracting the mean of nontrainee earnings in t from the mean of nontrainee earnings in t' identifies $\beta_t - \beta_{t'}$. Hence α can be identified by subtracting the second difference from the first.

Define $\hat{\alpha}^*_{RC}$ as the proposed estimator

$$\hat{\alpha}^*_{RC} = (\bar{Y}_t^{(1)} - \bar{Y}_{t'}^{(1)}) - (\bar{Y}_t^{(0)} - \bar{Y}_{t'}^{(0)}), \qquad t > k > t'$$

As a consequence of (A-3),

$$\begin{aligned} \text{plim } \hat{\alpha}^*_{RC} &= (\beta_t - \beta_{t'} + \alpha) - (\beta_t - \beta_{t'}) \\ &= \alpha \end{aligned}$$

Note that longitudinal data are not required to implement the estimator although if they are available and if (A-3) is satisfied, they can be used to form $\hat{\alpha}^*_{RC}$. All that is required are data on the means of period t and period t' earnings for trainees and nontrainees.

One way that (A-3) can arise is if (a) the disturbance in the earnings equation (1.3) of person i is of the permanent–transitory form

$$U_{it} = \phi_i + \varepsilon_{it} \tag{1.9}$$

where ϕ_i is a mean zero i.i.d. random variable across i and ε_{it} is a mean zero i.i.d. random variable for all i and t and is distributed independently of ϕ_i; and (b) $\mathbf{Z}_i\gamma + V_i$ in decision rule (1.2) is distributed independently of ε_{it}. To justify (A-3) in the general case requires adopting a specification of the time series process generating the unobservables in person i's earnings equation and its time series relationship to the unobservable in decision rule (1.2). Longitudinal data can be used to test the validity of the assumed time series process for earnings even though they are not required to estimate the model if (A-3) is true. Other assumptions produce (A-3). Examples are given in Section 5.

In one respect this example is contrived. It assumes that in preprogram cross section t' ($<k$) we know the identity of future trainees. Such data might exist (e.g., individuals in training period k might be asked about their pre-period-k earnings to see if they qualify for admission), but this seems unlikely. One advantage of longitudinal data for estimating α in the model of this example is that if the survey extends before k, the identity of prospective trainees is known.

The need for preprogram earnings to identify α is, however, only an artifact of assumption (A-3) or the permanent–transitory error structure (1.9). Suppose instead that U_{it} follows a first-order autoregressive process so that

$$U_{it} = \rho U_{it-1} + \varepsilon_{it}, \qquad \rho \neq 1 \tag{1.10}$$

where ε_{it} is an i.i.d. mean zero disturbance. For $t > k$ suppose that

$$\text{(A-4)} \quad E(\varepsilon_{it} \mid d_i) = 0, \qquad t > k$$

[In Section 2 we justify (A-4) for a broad class of models.] With three successive postprogram cross sections in which the identity of trainees is known, it is possible to identify α.

To establish this result let the three postprogram periods be t, $t + 1$, and $t + 2$. Assuming, as before, that (U_{it}, V_i) is i.i.d. across i and that no regressor appears in (1.2),

$$\text{plim } \bar{Y}_j^{(1)} = \beta_j + \alpha + E(U_j^{(1)})$$
$$\text{plim } \bar{Y}_j^{(0)} = \beta_j \qquad + E(U_j^{(0)}), \qquad j = t, t+1, t+2$$

where $E(U_j^{(1)})$ is shorthand notation for $E(U_{ij} \mid d_i = 1)$ and $E(U_j^{(0)}) = E(U_{ij} \mid d_i = 0)$. Assuming that (A-4) is true,

$$E(U_{t+1}^{(1)}) = \rho E(U_t^{(1)})$$
$$E(U_{t+1}^{(0)}) = \rho E(U_t^{(0)})$$
$$E(U_{t+2}^{(1)}) = \rho^2 E(U_t^{(1)})$$
$$E(U_{t+2}^{(0)}) = \rho^2 E(U_t^{(0)})$$

With these formulas, it is straightforward to verify that $\hat{\rho}$ defined by

$$\hat{\rho} = \frac{(\bar{Y}_{t+2}^{(1)} - \bar{Y}_{t+2}^{(0)}) - (\bar{Y}_{t+1}^{(1)} - \bar{Y}_{t+1}^{(0)})}{(\bar{Y}_{t+1}^{(1)} - \bar{Y}_{t+1}^{(0)}) - (\bar{Y}_t^{(1)} - \bar{Y}_t^{(0)})}$$

is consistent for ρ (plim $\hat{\rho} = \rho$) and that $\hat{\alpha}$ defined by

$$\hat{\alpha} = \frac{(\bar{Y}_{t+2}^{(1)} - \bar{Y}_{t+2}^{(0)}) - \hat{\rho}(\bar{Y}_{t+1}^{(1)} - \bar{Y}_{t+1}^{(0)})}{1 - \hat{\rho}}$$

is consistent for α (plim $\hat{\alpha} = \alpha$).

Thus, with autoregressive error structure (1.10) and assumption (A-4), it is possible to consistently estimate α in a general time-inhomogeneous environment using only three cross sections of postprogram data if the training status of individuals is known. Longitudinal data can also be used for this purpose, but they are not required. They are not even required to test assumption (1.10) if four or more cross sections are available.

For this model, the advantage of longitudinal data is clear. Only two time periods of longitudinal data are required to identify α, but three periods of repeated cross-section data are required to recover the same parameter.[5]

To establish why two periods of posttraining longitudinal data suffice to identify α, use (1.10) to write

$$\begin{aligned} Y_{i,t+1} &= \beta_{t+1} + d_i\alpha + U_{i,t+1} \\ &= \beta_{t+1} + d_i\alpha + \rho U_{it} + \varepsilon_{i,t+1} \end{aligned}$$

and substitute for U_{it} from (1.3) and collect terms to reach

$$Y_{i,t+1} = \beta_{t+1} - \rho\beta_t + d_i\alpha(1-\rho) + \rho Y_{it} + \varepsilon_{i,t+1} \tag{1.11}$$

As a consequence of (A-4) and the serial independence of ε_{it}, regression estimators of (1.11) are consistent for ρ and $\alpha(1-\rho)$ so that α can be consistently estimated. Heckman and Wolpin (1976) invoke (A-4) and estimate a multivariate version of (1.11) in their study of the impact of affirmative action programs.

Note, however, that the repeated cross-section estimator based on sample means is robust to mean zero measurement error in income. The regression estimator of equation (1.11) is not. An instrument is required for Y_{it}. One natural candidate is $Y_{i,t-1}$ if the additional assumption is made that the measurement error is independently distributed across t. But if this instrument is used, three periods of panel data are required to consistently estimate α. Thus in the presence of measurement error in income, the clear advantage of longitudinal data disappears. The main point, however, is that cross-section and repeated cross-section estimators based on means are robust to mean zero measurement error whereas regression estimators are not.

1.3.3. Longitudinal estimators.

Many longitudinal data estimators considered in this chapter use an individual's earnings path (future or retrospective) to construct a control function which, when inserted into earnings function (1.1) or (1.3), purges the equation of covariance between d_i and U_{it}. We define a control function for the more general equation (1.1) so that the concept will not have to be defined twice.

(D-1) K_{it} is a control function for (1.1) if it depends on variables, ... $Y_{i,t+1}, Y_{it}, Y_{i,t-1}, \ldots, \mathbf{X}_{i,t+1}, \mathbf{X}_{it}, \mathbf{X}_{i,t-1}, \ldots, d_i$ and parameters ψ and if
(a) $E(U_{it} - K_{it})d_i = 0$,
(b) $E(U_{it} - K_{it})\mathbf{X}_{it} = 0$,
(c) $E(U_{it} - K_{it})K_{it} = 0$, and
(d) ψ is identified.

For many models discussed below it is sometimes possible to use a weaker form of conditions (a)–(c) that requires that

$$\operatorname*{plim}_{I_t \to \infty} \frac{\sum (U_{it} - K_{it})M_i}{I_t} = 0$$

for M_i equal to d_i, $\mathbf{X}_{it}$, and K_{it}. We use the stronger form of the conditions because it facilitates the exposition.

The basic idea underlying the control function is that when it is inserted into (1.1) and therefore implicitly subtracted from U_{it}, the purged disturbance $\{U_{it} - K_{it}\}$ is orthogonal, at least in large samples, to all of the right-hand-side variables in the new equation

$$Y_{it} = \mathbf{X}_{it}\boldsymbol{\beta} + d_i\alpha + K_{it} + \{U_{it} - K_{it}\} \tag{1.12}$$

Requirement (d) is simply that ψ can be identified from (nonlinear) regression estimation of (1.12).

We have already encountered a control function. For the model satisfying (A-4) and (1.10),

$$K_{it} = \rho(Y_{it-1} - \beta_{t-1} - d_i\alpha), \qquad t > k + 1$$

so $\psi = (\rho, \beta_{t-1}, \alpha)$. Other examples of control functions will be given in Sections 3 and 5.

1.4 *Random coefficient specifications*

We now consider a random coefficient version of (1.3) in which α varies in the population. The motivation for this model is that the impact of training may differ across persons and may even be negative for some people. To capture this idea we write in place of (1.3)

$$Y_{it} = \beta_t + d_i\alpha_i + U_{it} \quad \text{for} \quad t > k$$

We define $E(\alpha_i) = \bar{\alpha} < \infty$ and $\varepsilon_i = \alpha_i - \bar{\alpha}$. $E(\varepsilon_i) = 0$ and $\text{Var}(\varepsilon_i) < \infty$. With this notation we can rewrite the preceding equation as

$$Y_{it} = \beta_t + d_i\bar{\alpha} + \{U_{it} + d_i\varepsilon_i\} \tag{1.13}$$

An alternative way to express this equation is as a two-sector switching regression model following Roy (1951), Heckman and Neumann (1977), and Lee (1978). Let

$$Y_{1it} = \beta_{1t} + U_{1it}$$

be the wage of individual i in sector 1 in period t. Let

$$Y_{0it} = \beta_{0t} + U_{0it}$$

be the wage of individual i in sector 0. Letting $d_i = 1$ if a person is in sector 1 and letting $d_i = 0$ otherwise, we may write the observed wage as

$$\begin{aligned} Y_i &= d_i Y_{1it} + (1 - d_i) Y_{0it} \\ &= \beta_{0t} + (\beta_{1t} - \beta_{0t})d_i + U_{0it} + (U_{1it} - U_{0it})d_i \end{aligned}$$

Letting $\bar{\alpha} = \beta_{1t} - \beta_{0t}$, $\varepsilon_i = (U_{1it} - U_{0it})$, $\beta_{0t} = \beta_t$, and $U_{0it} = U_{it}$ produces equation (1.13). The difference between fixed coefficient and random coefficient specifications has not been appreciated in studies of unionism by Chamberlain (1984) and Lewis (1982), among others. (See note 24.) Björklund and Moffitt (1983) consider random coefficient models of training.

In this model there is a fundamental nonidentification result when no regressors appear in decision rule (1.2). Without a regressor in (1.2) and in the absence of any further distributional assumptions it is not possible to identify $\bar{\alpha}$ unless $E(\varepsilon_i | d_i = 1, \mathbf{Z}_i) = 0$ or some other known constant.

To see this note that

$$E(Y_{it} | d_i = 1, \mathbf{Z}_i) = \beta_t + \bar{\alpha} + E(\varepsilon_i | d_i = 1, \mathbf{Z}_i) + E(U_{it} | d_i = 1, \mathbf{Z}_i)$$

and

$$E(Y_{it} | d_i = 0, \mathbf{Z}_i) = \beta_t \qquad\qquad + E(U_{it} | d_i = 0, \mathbf{Z}_i)$$

Unless $E(\varepsilon_i | d_i = 1, \mathbf{Z}_i)$ is known, it is impossible without invoking distributional assumptions to decompose $\alpha + E(\varepsilon_i | d_i = 1, \mathbf{Z}_i)$ into its constituent components unless there is independent variation in $E(\varepsilon_i | d_i = 1, \mathbf{Z}_i)$ across observations [i.e., a regressor appears in (1.2)]. Without a regressor, $E(\varepsilon_i | d_i = 1, \mathbf{Z}_i)$ is a constant that is indistinguishable from $\bar{\alpha}$.

This means that in models without regressors in the decision rule we might as well work with the redefined model

$$Y_{it} = \beta_t + d_i\alpha^* + \{U_{it} + d_i(\varepsilon_i - E(\varepsilon_i | d_i = 1))\} \tag{1.14}$$

where

$$\alpha^* = \bar{\alpha} + E(\varepsilon_i | d_i = 1)$$

and content ourselves with the estimation of α^*. If everywhere in Sections 1.1 and 1.2 we replace α with α^*, the preceding analysis goes through as before.

The parameter α^* answers question 2 of Section 1. It addresses the question of determining the effect of training on the people selected as trainees. This parameter is useful in making forecasts only when the same selection rule operates in the future as has operated in the past. It may not answer question 1 or 3. Indeed, without regressors in decision rule (1.2), these questions cannot be answered unless specific distributional assumptions are invoked.

A major conclusion of this subsection is that structural question 1 or 3 cannot be answered in a fully nonparametric random coefficient model without invoking distributional assumptions. A shifter or regressor in the decision rule is required.

However, it is not obvious that $E(\varepsilon_i | d_i = 1) \neq 0$. In Section 2 we present a model in which enrollment decisions are made in the presence of uncertainty about ε_i (i.e., a person may not know his or her value of ε_i at the time decisions to enroll are made). In this case it is possible that $\alpha^* = \bar{\alpha}$, and if everywhere in Sections 1.2 and 1.3 we replace α with $\bar{\alpha}$, the preceding analysis goes through as before.

With a regressor in the decision rule, and under further conditions presented in Section 3 below, it is possible to estimate α even if $E(\varepsilon_i | d_i = 1) \neq 0$. To do so requires more a priori structure than is required in the fixed coefficient model for α. All of the known consistent estimators of $\bar{\alpha}$ work in a single cross section, but not all of the cross-section estimators listed in Section 1.3.1 will identify $\bar{\alpha}$.[6] For this reason, we do not discuss random coefficient models in Sections 4 and 5.

1.5 *Robustness to nonrandom sampling schemes and contamination bias*

This section discusses the problems of choice-based sampling and contamination bias and indicates their relevance to the problem of estimating the impact of training on the earnings of trainees. It is more productive to defer a detailed discussion of these problems to later sections of the chapter after specific estimators have been presented. Here these concepts are introduced for the fixed coefficient earnings function (1.3) and general approaches to solving these problems are presented.

1.5.1. Choice-based sampling plans. The data available for analyzing the impact of training on earnings are often nonrandom samples. More often they consist of pooled data from two sources: (a) a sample of trainees selected from program records and (b) a sample of nontrainees selected from some national sample. The sampling rule used to generate the nontrainee data is often (simple) random sampling. Typically, trainees are overrepresented in such samples relative to their proportion in the population. This creates the problem of choice-based sampling analyzed by Manski and Lerman (1977) and Manski and McFadden (1981).

The problem of choice-based sampling occurs if in the available data the probability of sampling a trainee is not the population probability that an individual is a trainee. In the population let the joint frequency of $(d, \mathbf{Z})$ be $f(d, \mathbf{Z})$. Let $f(d)$ and $f(\mathbf{Z})$ be the population marginal frequencies of d and $\mathbf{Z}$, respectively, and $f(d|\mathbf{Z})$ be the conditional frequency of d given $\mathbf{Z}$.

In a choice-based sample, the rule generating the available sample selects proportion $\phi(d) \neq f(d)$ (see Manski and McFadden, 1981) and selection depends only on training status. Thus as the sample becomes large so that sampling fluctuations can be ignored, the frequency of the data is

$$h(\mathbf{Z}) = \sum_{d=0,1} f(\mathbf{Z}|d)\phi(d)$$

In a large sample the conditional probability of d given $\mathbf{Z}$ is

$$k(d|\mathbf{Z}) = \frac{f(\mathbf{Z}|d)\phi(d)}{h(\mathbf{Z})}$$

Using Bayes's rule we reach

$$k(d|\mathbf{Z}) = f(d|\mathbf{Z})\frac{\phi(d)}{f(d)} \frac{1}{\sum_{j=0,1} f(j|\mathbf{Z})\frac{\phi(j)}{f(j)}}$$

The sample regression function relating Y_{it} to d_i (sampled in year t) may be written as

$$E(Y_{it}|d_i) = \beta_t + d_i\alpha + \{d_iE(U_{it}|d_i = 1) + (1 - d_i)E(U_{it}|d_i = 0)\} \tag{1.15}$$

In the absence of random sampling, the term in braces does not have mean zero, because the sample proportion of d_i does not converge to $\Pr(d_i = 1)$. Estimators such as the instrumental variable estimator (i) in Section 1.3 for cross-section data that exploit the fact that this term has zero mean will be biased and inconsistent for α if they are mechanically applied to choice-based samples.

The repeated cross-section estimator $\hat{\alpha}_{RC}$ that exploits condition (A-2) is inconsistent when applied to choice-based samples if in different samples the means of the term in braces in (1.15) differ. In this case, (A-2) is not satisfied and $\hat{\alpha}_{RC}$ is inconsistent for α even in a time-homogeneous environment. It is necessary to know the identity of trainees in order to weight the sample back to a sample with proportions of trainees that would be produced by a random sample in order to obtain consistent estimators. Hence one of the advantages of $\hat{\alpha}_{RC}$ is lost if the data are generated by a choice-based sample.

Some of the cross-sectional and longitudinal estimators that are control function estimators are robust to choice-based sampling. Instead of (D-1) we define a subset of control functions such that K_{it} is in the subset if

(D-2) (a) $E(U_{it} - K_{it}|d_i, \mathbf{X}_{it}, K_{it}) = 0$,
(b) ψ is identified.

If (D-2) holds, then by construction the error term in braces in (1.12) has mean zero in any choice-based sample because it has mean zero for each subsample of d_i values, and the error term in any choice-based sample is orthogonal to all the right-hand-side variables in the equation because it is orthogonal to the regressors in each subsample of d_i values. More precisely, using (1.12),

$$\begin{aligned} E(Y_{it}|\mathbf{X}_{it}, d_i, K_{it}) = {} & \mathbf{X}_{it}\boldsymbol{\beta} + d_i\alpha + K_{it} \\ & + d_i E(U_{it} - K_{it}|d_i = 1, \mathbf{X}_{it}, K_{it}) \\ & + (1 - d_i)E(U_{it} - K_{it}|d_i = 0, \mathbf{X}_{it}, K_{it}) \end{aligned}$$

Using (D-2), condition (a),

$$E(Y_{it}|\mathbf{X}_{it}, d_i, K_{it}) = \mathbf{X}_{it}\boldsymbol{\beta} + d_i\alpha + K_{it}$$

Thus α can be consistently estimated under general conditions specified in Section 3. Models that satisfy (A-3) and those that satisfy (A-4) and (1.10) produce K functions satisfying (D-2), and so both repeated cross-section and longitudinal estimators proposed for those models may be applied without modification to data generated from choice-based samples. The robustness of the K function estimators to choice-based sampling plans is a very attractive feature of this class of estimators since most of the available data are choice-based samples.

1.5.2. Contamination bias. The problem of contamination bias arises when the training status of certain individuals is recorded with error. Many control samples such as the Current Population Survey (CPS) or Social Security Work History File do not reveal whether or not persons have received training.

The contamination bias problem is one of measurement error in d_i in equation (1.1) or (1.3). In the analysis of training programs, the population proportion of trainees is known or can be consistently estimated (Barnow, 1983). With this information in hand, consistent estimators for α can be constructed using methods developed by Cochran (1968), Aigner (1973), and the authors in Section 3.8 of this chapter.

2 Prototypical enrollment rules

2.1 *Introduction*

The nature of the stochastic dependence relationships among the regressors and unobservables in (1.1) and (1.2) is critical in designing consistent estimators for α. Of the estimators considered thus far, only $\hat{\alpha}_{RC}$ can produce a consistent estimator for α under any specification of stochastic dependence among the variables in earnings and enrollment equations (1.1) and (1.2) (provided that the environment is time-homogeneous or sufficiently regular in a sense to be made precise in Section 4.1).

Previous work on evaluating the impact of training on earnings has not specified explicit choice rules that govern program participation. For this reason it is difficult to evaluate the plausibility of proposed estimation procedures when measured against economically appealing models of the life cycle evolution of earnings and of the decision to enroll in training.

This section of the chapter presents several prototypical decision rules that are motivated by economic theory and that are analytically and empirically tractable. The models presented here serve as a framework within which it is possible to evaluate the economic plausibility of the estimators proposed in the remaining sections of this chapter. We consider models in certain and uncertain environments with α both fixed and random.

2.2 *A perfect-foresight model*

A natural starting point is a model of trainee self-selection based on a comparison of the present value of earnings with and without training in an environment of perfect foresight. The earnings function is assumed to be (1.1). For simplicity we assume that training programs accept all applicants. This assumption is relaxed in Section 2.5.

The prospective trainee is assumed to discount all earnings streams by a common discount factor $1/(1 + r)$. From (1.1) training raises trainee earnings by α per period. While in training, individual i receives subsidy S_i, which may be negative (so there may be costs of program participation.) Income in training period k is forgone for trainees. To simplify the expressions we assume that people live forever.

As of period k, the present value of earnings for an individual who does not receive training is

$$PV_i(0) = \sum_{j=0}^{\infty} \left(\frac{1}{1+r}\right)^j Y_{i,k+j}$$

(Recall that training is an option available only in period k.) The present value of earnings for a trainee is

$$PV_i(1) = S_i + \sum_{j=1}^{\infty} \left(\frac{1}{1+r}\right)^j Y_{i,k+j} + \sum_{j=1}^{\infty} \frac{\alpha}{(1+r)^j}$$

The perfect-foresight present value maximizing decision rule is to enroll in the program if $PV_i(1) > PV_i(0)$ or, letting IN_i denote the index function in decision rule (1.2),

$$IN_i = PV_i(1) - PV_i(0) = S_i - Y_{ik} + \frac{\alpha}{r} \tag{2.1}$$

Thus

$$\begin{aligned} d_i &= 1 \quad \text{iff} \quad S_i - Y_{ik} + \frac{\alpha}{r} > 0 \\ d_i &= 0 \quad \text{otherwise} \end{aligned} \tag{2.2}$$

Recall that Y_{ik} is not observed for trainees. To make (2.2) empirically operational, substitute for Y_{ik} in (2.2) from (1.1) and write

$$S_i = \mathbf{W}_i\boldsymbol{\phi} + \tau_i \tag{2.3}$$

where $\mathbf{W}_i$ is observed by the econometrician and τ_i is not. Collecting terms, we reach

$$\begin{aligned} d_i &= 1 \quad \text{iff} \quad \mathbf{W}_i\boldsymbol{\phi} + \frac{\alpha}{r} - \mathbf{X}_{ik}\boldsymbol{\beta} + \tau_i - U_{ik} > 0 \\ d_i &= 0 \quad \text{otherwise} \end{aligned} \tag{2.4}$$

Now $(\tau_i - U_{ik}) = V_i$ in (1.2), and $(\mathbf{W}_i, \mathbf{X}_{ik})$ corresponds to $\mathbf{Z}_i$ in (1.2). Assuming that $(\mathbf{W}_i, \mathbf{X}_{ik})$ is distributed independently of V_i makes (2.4) a standard discrete choice model.

Maintaining the assumption that $E(\mathbf{X}'_{it}U_{it}) = 0$, if

$$E(U_{it}d_i) = 0 \tag{2.5}$$

under general conditions (see White, 1980, or Section 3) least squares consistently estimates $\boldsymbol{\beta}$ and α in (1.1).

If the costs of program participation are independent of U_{it} for all t (so both $\mathbf{W}_i$ and τ_i are independent of U_{it}), (2.5) is satisfied only if the unobservables in period t are (mean) independent of the unobservables in period k so that

$$E(U_{it} | U_{ik}) = 0 \quad \text{for} \quad t > k$$

Whether (2.5) is satisfied hinges on the serial correlation properties of U_{it}. If U_{it} is a moving average of order m, and so

$$U_{it} = \sum_{j=1}^{m} a_j \varepsilon_{i,t-j}$$

where the $\varepsilon_{i,t-j}$ are i.i.d., then for $t - k > m$, (2.5) is satisfied. On the other hand, if U_{it} obeys a first-order autoregressive scheme, (2.5) is not satisfied.

2.3 *A perfect-foresight random coefficients model*

The assignment rule for the case of a perfect-foresight random coefficients model is the same as (2.4) except that α varies in the population. Recalling that $E(\alpha_i) = \bar{\alpha}$ and that $\varepsilon_i = \alpha_i - \bar{\alpha}$, we write

$$d_i = 1 \quad \text{iff} \quad \mathbf{W}_i\boldsymbol{\phi} - \mathbf{X}_{ik}\boldsymbol{\beta} + \frac{\bar{\alpha}}{r} + \tau_i - U_{ik} + \frac{\varepsilon_i}{r} > 0$$

$$d_i = 0 \quad \text{otherwise} \tag{2.6}$$

Even if U_{it} is (mean) independent of U_{ik} and τ_i, so that

$$E(U_{it} | U_{ik}, \tau_i) = 0, \qquad t > k$$

the composite error term in (2.6) is not mean independent of the error term in earnings function (1.14) because of their common dependence on ε_i for $t > k$.

If there are no regressor variables in the enrollment equation (2.6) (so $\boldsymbol{\phi}$ and $\boldsymbol{\beta}$ are zero), $E(\varepsilon_i | d_i = 1, \mathbf{X}_{it})$ is constant and $\bar{\alpha}$ cannot be identified but α^* in (1.14) might be identified. If there are regressor variables in $\mathbf{W}_i$ or $\mathbf{X}_{ik}$, $\bar{\alpha}$ might be identified as noted in Section 1.

The random coefficients model captures the key idea in Roy's model of self-selection (1951) that has been revived in recent work by Lee (1978) and Willis and Rosen (1979). In the Roy model it is solely the population variation in X_{ik}, α_i, and U_{ik} that sorts people into training status [so $\tau_i = 0$ and $\mathbf{0} = \mathbf{W}_i$ in (2.6)].

2.4 *Introducing uncertainty*

It is unlikely that prospective trainees know all components of future earnings and the costs and benefits of program participation at the time they make enrollment decisions. More likely the enrollment decision is made in an environment of uncertainty. When risk aversion is ignored the natural generalization of decision rules (2.2) and (2.6) assumes that a prospective trainee compares the expectation of $PV_i(0)$ evaluated at date $k - 1$ with the expectation of $PV_i(1)$ evaluated at the same date.

We are thus led to write

$$d_i = 1 \quad \text{iff} \quad E_{k-1}\left[S_i - Y_{ik} + \frac{\alpha_i}{r}\right] > 0$$

$$d_i = 0 \quad \text{otherwise} \tag{2.7}$$

where E_{k-1} denotes the expectation of the argument in brackets conditional on the information available in period $k-1$, and α_i is set to α for the fixed coefficient model.

Introducing uncertainty can sometimes simplify the econometrics of a problem (see, e.g., Zellner et al., 1966). For example, in the random coefficients model suppose that at time $k-1$ individuals do not know the value of α_i they will draw upon completion of training but they know the population distribution of α_i. Suppose further that their best estimate of training impact is the population mean $\bar{\alpha}$. Then in equation (1.14),

$$E(\varepsilon_i | d_i = 1) = 0$$

and so

$$E(\varepsilon_i d_i) = 0$$

and the error component $\varepsilon_i d_i$ creates no new econometric problem that does not appear in the fixed coefficient model.[7] If the only source of uncertainty is in α_i, decision rule (2.2) is identical to decision rule (2.7) provided that all agents have the same estimate of α_i.[8]

In the general case in which future earnings are not known, the optimal forecast rule for Y_{ik} depends on the time series process that generates U_{it}. For example, suppose that

$$U_{it} = \theta_i + v_{it} \tag{2.8}$$

where

$$v_{it} = \rho v_{i,t-1} + \xi_{it}$$

and where

$$E(\theta_i) = E(\xi_{it}) = 0, \qquad |\rho| < 1$$
$$\mathrm{Var}(\theta_i) < \infty, \qquad \mathrm{Var}(\xi_{it}) < \infty$$
$$E(\xi_{it}\theta_i) = 0 \quad \text{for all} \quad t$$

Suppose that in period $k-1$ agents know current earnings, θ_i, α_i, and all future values of $\mathbf{X}_{it}$, $t \geq k$, but they do not know future values of ξ_{it}. By an application of the standard Wiener–Kolmogorov prediction formula (see, e.g., Sargent, 1979),

$$\begin{aligned} E_{k-1}(Y_{ik}) &= \mathbf{X}_{ik}\boldsymbol{\beta} + \theta_i + \rho(Y_{i,k-1} - \mathbf{X}_{i,k-1}\boldsymbol{\beta} - \theta_i) \\ &= (\mathbf{X}_{ik} - \rho\mathbf{X}_{i,k-1})\boldsymbol{\beta} + \theta_i(1-\rho) + \rho Y_{i,k-1} \end{aligned}$$

If it is further assumed that S_i is known with certainty by the prospective trainee and the specification of S_i is given by (2.3), assignment rule

(2.7) may be written as

$$d_i = 1 \quad \text{iff} \quad \mathbf{W}_i\boldsymbol{\phi} - (\mathbf{X}_{ik} - \rho\mathbf{X}_{i,k-1})\boldsymbol{\beta} + \frac{\bar{\alpha}}{r} - \rho Y_{i,k-1} + \left[\tau_i + \frac{\varepsilon_i}{r} - (1-\rho)\theta_i\right] > 0$$

$$d_i = 0 \quad \text{otherwise} \tag{2.9}$$

In this case, the assignment rule contains $Y_{i,k-1}$ among the $\mathbf{Z}_i$ in (1.2) and $\mathbf{Z}_i$ is not independent of

$$V_i = \tau_i + \frac{\varepsilon_i}{r} - (1-\rho)\theta_i$$

unless $\rho = 1$ or $\theta_i = 0$ and τ_i is distributed independently of $U_{i,k-1}$. Hence cross-section method (ii) listed in Section 1.3 cannot be applied directly without invoking very strong and implausible assumptions.

Note that one implication of decision rule (2.9) is that if τ_i is distributed independently of v_{it}, transitory dips in preprogram earnings make participation in the training program more likely. This specification is thus consistent with the empirical evidence on program enrollment presented by Ashenfelter (1978).

In the absence of uncertainty regarding earnings in period k and with α a fixed known constant, inequality (2.4) characterizes the enrollment decision (setting $U_{ik} = \theta_i + v_{ik}$). In a world of perfect certainty $\mathbf{X}_{i,k-1}$ is not an argument of the decision rule.[9] A general feature of an uncertainty model is that it expands the candidate instrumental variable set [the $\mathbf{Z}_i$ in (1.2)] and so in this sense aids in identification.

With longitudinal earnings data of sufficient length it is possible to test for any assumed time series error structure for U_{it} (see, e.g., MaCurdy, 1982). However, such tests cannot reveal which components of U_{ik} are known to the agent and which are not, nor can they reveal the nature of the dependence between τ_i and U_{it}. Extending assignment rule (2.4) to account for uncertainty requires additional assumptions about forecasting rules used by prospective trainees and the information sets available to them. Knowledge of the time series process generating the unobservables in earnings data does not shed light on the information set confronting an agent. This injects an extra element of arbitrariness into the analysis that is not present in a certainty setting.

The analysis presented for error structure (2.8) carries over to more general models. In general, the error structure of V_i [in (1.2)] is induced in part by the expectations mechanism assumed to be used by the agent. In the example just presented V_i is correlated with future U_{it} via their common dependence on θ_i and $v_{i,k-1}$. The covariance structure of V_i induced by the assumed estimators is presented below in Section 5.

2.5 *Multiple selection rules*

For convenience we have assumed that only one assignment rule governs program participation; any individual who desires to enroll in training is free to do so. In fact, satisfaction of inequality (2.1) may be a necessary but not sufficient condition for program participation; a candidate trainee may also have to be selected by a program administrator.

In principle all of our analysis carries over to a more general case in which multiple selection governs program participation. Let

$$\{IN_l\}_{l=1}^{L}$$

be a set of L index functions all of which must be positive for a person to be enrolled in training. For example, IN_1 may be $PV(1) - PV(0)$, IN_2 may be the index function for a program administrator.

If we define

$$IN^* = \min(IN_1, \ldots, IN_L)$$

we may define

$$d_i = 1 \quad \text{if} \quad IN^* > 0$$

$$d_i = 0 \quad \text{otherwise}$$

Replacing IN with IN^*, all of the preceding analyses go through as before so that with a suitable change in notation our analysis can be readily generalized to a multiple selection rules case.[10] However, for large L, explicit formulas for the components of IN^* are not available except in special cases. For simplicity we assume that $L = 1$.[11]

3 Cross-section methods

3.1 *Introduction*

In this section we present cross-section methods for consistently estimating α in (1.1) when (A-1) characterizes the data so that the assignment of persons to training is nonrandom. Our discussion proceeds in the following way.

We initially assume access to one postprogram cross section for a random sample (or exogenously stratified sample) of the population some fraction of which has participated in training. Six different consistent estimators of α are presented corresponding to six different types of assumptions about the earnings function (1.1) and the enrollment rule (1.2). The assumption sets are presented in decreasing order of the generality of their content as far as this is possible. However, all of the estimators cannot be ranked in this fashion because they rely on nonoverlapping assumption sets.

We then consider consistent estimation of a random coefficients model. We next examine the robustness of the proposed estimators to choice-based sampling schemes and errors in measuring d_i. The section concludes with a summary and discussion of the results.

Except in our discussion of identification through assumptions about the distribution of U_{it}, throughout most of this section we make the following assumption:

(A-5) There is at least one nondegenerate regressor in $\mathbf{Z}_i$ in decision rule (1.2) with a nonzero coefficient.

As discussed in Section 1, without this assumption α cannot be identified from a cross section without invoking a distributional assumption.

We also make the following additional technical assumptions about the data available in cross section t:

(A-6) (a) The earnings function is (1.1).
(b) The enrollment decision is governed by (1.2).
(c) $\{\mathbf{X}_{it}, \mathbf{Z}_i, V_i, U_{it}\}$ is an independent sequence with respect to i.
(d) $E(\mathbf{X}'_{it}U_{it}) = 0$ for all i.
(e) $E|X_{ijt}U_{it}|^{1+\delta} < \Delta < \infty$ for some $\delta > 0$, where $j = 1, \ldots, M$ denotes an element of the M vector, $\mathbf{X}_{it}$, for all i.
(f) $E|X^2_{ijt}|^{1+\delta} < \Delta < \infty$ for some $\delta > 0, j = 1, \ldots, M$ for all i.
(g) $E|d_i U_{it}|^{1+\delta} < \Delta < \infty$ for some $\delta > 0$ for all i.
(h) Array $\mathbf{X}_{it}$, d_i into vector $\mathbf{J}_i = (\mathbf{X}_{it}, d_i)$. In this notation,

$$\bar{J}_{I_t} \equiv E\left(\sum_{i=1}^{I_t} \frac{\mathbf{J}'_i\mathbf{J}_i}{I_t}\right)$$

has determinant det $\bar{J}_{I_t} > \delta > 0$ for all I_t sufficiently large.

Assumption (A-6) coupled with the assumption $E(d_i U_{it}) = 0$ ensures that ordinary least squares is (strongly) consistent for α in (1.1) (see *White*, 1980). Assumption (d) rules out lagged values of the dependent variable in $\mathbf{X}_{it}$ if the U_{it} are serially correlated. If (1.1) includes lagged values, we write out the reduced form expression for (1.1) and require that it satisfy (A-6). The reduced form is used in the ensuing analysis. The underlying samples are not restricted to be simple random samples – samples stratified on the basis of exogenous variables may also satisfy (A-6).

If the analyst has access to simple random samples, assumptions (A-6e) and (A-6f) may be eliminated and δ can be set to 0 in (A-6g). The stronger conditions (A-6) produce sufficient conditions for strong consistency for models estimated on samples in which the observations are independently but not identically distributed. Such samples are in wide use (e.g., exogenously stratified samples). Note further that conditions (A-6), although conventional and familiar (see, e.g., White, 1984), are overly strong. Weak consistency is all that is required in econometric analysis. For the sample sizes likely to be encountered in practice (500 or more independent observations), asymptotic theory should produce a reliable guide to the performance of estimators.

3.2 *The instrumental variables estimator*

The instrumental variables estimator is the least demanding in the a priori conditions that must be satisfied for its use. It requires in addition to (A-5) and (A-6) the following assumptions:

(A-7) (a) There is at least one variable in $\mathbf{Z}_i$, Z_i^e, with a nonzero γ coefficient in (1.2), such that for some known transformation of Z_i^e, $g(Z_i^e)$, $E[U_{it}g(Z_i^e)] = 0$.
(b) Array $\mathbf{X}_{it}$, $g(Z_i^e)$ into a vector $\mathbf{J}_{it}^* = [\mathbf{X}_{it}, g(Z_i^e)]$. In this notation, $E[\sum_{i=1}^{I_t} (\mathbf{J}_{it}^{*\prime}\mathbf{J}_{it}/I_t)]$ has full rank uniformly in I_t for I_t sufficiently large.
(c) Replacing $\mathbf{X}_{it}$ by $\mathbf{J}_{it}^*$, (A-6) holds except for (A-6h).

With these assumptions, the instrumental variable estimator

$$\begin{pmatrix} \hat{\beta} \\ \hat{\alpha} \end{pmatrix}_{IV} = \left(\sum_{i=1}^{I_t} \frac{\mathbf{J}_{it}^{*\prime}\mathbf{J}_{it}}{I_t} \right)^{-1} \sum_{i=1}^{I_t} \frac{\mathbf{J}_{it}^{*\prime} Y_{it}}{I_t}$$

is consistent for $\begin{pmatrix} \beta \\ \alpha \end{pmatrix}$. Thus α is identified if there is a regressor in (1.2) that satisfies (A-7).

It is important to notice how weak these conditions are. The functional form of the distribution of V_i need not be known. $\mathbf{Z}_i$ need not be distributed independently of V_i. Only some function of one of the nondegenerate arguments of $\mathbf{Z}_i$ is required to satisfy (A-7a). Moreover, in principle, $g(Z_i^e)$ may be a nonlinear function of variables appearing in $\mathbf{X}_{it}$ as long as (A-7b) is satisfied. Except for the linear probability model, $E(d_i|\mathbf{Z}_i)$ is nonlinear in the arguments of $\mathbf{Z}_i$, and so rank condition (b) is likely to be satisfied. Assuming that (A-7) is satisfied, we can conduct a test for the endogeneity of d_i in (1.1) using the Durbin–Wu–Hausman test (Durbin, 1954; Wu, 1973, 1983; Hausman, 1978).

In certainty decision rule (2.4) the list of potential instruments includes (transformations of) the costs of participation ($\mathbf{W}_i$) and the regressors explaining earnings in the training period ($\mathbf{X}_{ik}$). Only one variable in this list is required to identify α in (1.1). If there are a variety of instruments so that α is overidentified, standard methods can be used to produce more efficient estimators (see, e.g., White, 1984).

3.3 *Procedures when the functional form of F is known or can be consistently estimated*

Procedures when the functional form of F is known or can be consistently estimated require that assumptions (A-5) and (A-6) be strengthened in the following way:

(A-8) (a) $\mathbf{Z}_i$ is distributed independently of V_i.

(d) $E(U_{it}|\mathbf{Z}_i, \mathbf{X}_{it}) = 0$.

(c) Array $\mathbf{X}_{it}$, $E(d_i|\mathbf{Z}_i)$ into vector $\mathbf{J}_i = [\mathbf{X}_{it}, E(d_i|\mathbf{Z}_i)]$. In this notation,

$$\tilde{\tilde{J}}_{I_t} \equiv E\left(\sum_{i=1}^{I_t} \frac{\mathbf{J}_i'\mathbf{J}_i}{I_t} \right)$$

has determinant $\det \tilde{\tilde{J}}_{I_t} > \delta > 0$, as $I_t \to \infty$.

(d) $E(U_{it}|\mathbf{Z}_i, \mathbf{X}_{it}) = 0$.

(e) Distribution function F is known (up to a finite number of parameters) or can be consistently estimated, and γ is identified.

Cosslett (1983) demonstrates that if (a) is satisfied and $\mathbf{Z}_i$ includes at least one "continuous valued regressor" that takes values in an interval and if the $\mathbf{Z}_i$ are i.i.d. nondegenerate random variables, F can be consistently nonparametrically estimated.

Note that assumption (A-8d) is not implied by (d) in (A-6). Assumption (b) in (A-8) is not implied by any set of conditions in (A-6).

From assumptions (A-8b) and (A-8d), the conditional expectation of Y_{it} given $\mathbf{X}_{it}$ and $\mathbf{Z}_i$ may be written as

$$E(Y_{it}|\mathbf{X}_{it}, \mathbf{Z}_i) = \mathbf{X}_{it}\boldsymbol{\beta} + E(d_i|\mathbf{Z}_i)\alpha \tag{3.1}$$

From assumption (A-8a), this expectation may be written as

$$E(\mathbf{Y}_{it}|\mathbf{X}_{it}, \mathbf{Z}_i) = \mathbf{X}_{it}\boldsymbol{\beta} + [1 - F(-\mathbf{Z}_i\gamma)]\alpha \tag{3.2}$$

Given (A-5), (A-6), and (A-8), α can be consistently estimated by the following two-stage procedure.

(A) Use discrete choice analysis to estimate γ from data on the training decision (see Amemiya, 1981). Form $F(-\mathbf{Z}_i\hat{\gamma})$ and run a linear regression of Y_{it} on $\mathbf{X}_{it}$ and $F(-\mathbf{Z}_i\hat{\gamma})$.

Standard errors must be adjusted to account for estimation error in $\hat{\gamma}$ (see Heckman, 1979, and Amemiya, 1983). If Cosslett's procedure can be applied, no parametric position need be taken with regard to F.

An alternative procedure that identifies α under the same assumptions is:

(B) Estimate (3.2) directly by nonlinear least squares.

Method (B) can be implemented without assuming a parametric form for F using, for example, Gallant's (1981) procedures expanding F in terms of a Fourier series in $\mathbf{Z}_i\gamma$.

Method (B) is more general than (A) in the following sense. It is possible to relax (A-8a, b, and e) and still recover α if (A-8c) is satisfied replacing $E(d_i|\mathbf{Z}_i)$ by $E(d_i|\mathbf{Z}_i, \mathbf{X}_{it})$ and if $\boldsymbol{\beta}$, α and the independent parameters of $E(d_i|\mathbf{X}_{it}, \mathbf{Z}_i)$ can be recovered from the regression function

$$E(Y_{it}|\mathbf{X}_{it}, \mathbf{Z}_i) = \mathbf{X}_{it}\boldsymbol{\beta} + E(d_i|\mathbf{Z}_i, \mathbf{X}_{it})\alpha \tag{3.3}$$

Note further that even if (A-8a) is violated so that γ cannot be consistently estimated, $F_i = F(-\mathbf{Z}_i\hat{\gamma})$ is a valid instrument for d_i in (1.1) provided that the conditions of (A-5)–(A-7) are satisfied. Even if γ can be consistently estimated, use of F_i as an instrument is an alternative to methods (A) and (B) of this section.

Because the assumptions embodied in (A-8) are more stringent than those presented in (A-7), they are less likely to be satisfied by models generated by the decision rules in Section 2.1. For example, (A-8a) requires that $\mathbf{W}_i$ and $\mathbf{X}_{ik}$ be jointly independent of $\tau_i - U_{ik}$ in perfect-foresight decision rule (2.4), whereas the instrumental variable estimator requires no such assumption. (A-8b) is stronger than anything required for the instrumental variable estimator to be consistent for α. Assumption (A-8b) will not be satisfied for decision rules (2.2) and (2.7) if data on $\mathbf{X}_{ik}$ are not available. Assumption (A-8d) is not satisfied by uncertainty decision rule (2.9) because unless $\rho = 1$ or $\theta_i = 0$, $Y_{i,k-1}$ is not distributed independently of θ_i. This assumption can be satisfied if $Y_{i,k-1}$ is replaced with a reduced expression in terms of lagged $\mathbf{X}_{ik}$.

3.4 *Cross-section control function estimators*

We now consider the cross-section version of the control function estimators introduced in definitions (D-1) and (D-2). Here we use the strong form of these conditions – (D-2). As noted in Section 1, the strong form is robust to choice-based sampling.

Using (1.1) we write

$$E(Y_{it}|\mathbf{X}_{it}, d_i, \mathbf{Z}_i) = \mathbf{X}_{it}\boldsymbol{\beta} + d_i\alpha + E(U_{it}|\mathbf{X}_{it}, d_i, \mathbf{Z}_i) \tag{3.4}$$

If $E(U_{it}|\mathbf{X}_{it}, \mathbf{Z}_i)$ is known or its parameters can be consistently estimated from regression (3.4) applied to the available cross-section sample, then

$$E(U_{it}|\mathbf{X}_{it}, d_i, \mathbf{Z}_i) = K_{it}$$

is a control function for (1.1).

In the literature (Heckman, 1976, 1979) the following *sufficient* conditions in addition to (A-5) and (A-6) are invoked to produce a control function:

(A-9) (a) (A-8a).
(b) $E(U_{it}|\mathbf{X}_{it}, d_i, \mathbf{Z}_i) = E(U_{it}|d_i, \mathbf{Z}_i)$.
(c) The joint density of (U_i, V_i) denoted $h_i(U_{it}, V_i|\boldsymbol{\chi})$ is known up to a finite set of parameters $\boldsymbol{\chi}$. Typically it is assumed to be bivariate normal.[12] Elements of $\boldsymbol{\chi}$ are not functionally dependent on $(\alpha, \boldsymbol{\beta}, \gamma)$.
(d) (A-8e).
(e) In the population $[\mathbf{X}_{it}, d_i, \partial \mathrm{E}(U_{it}|d_i, \mathbf{Z}_i)/\partial \boldsymbol{\chi}]$ is a vector of nondegenerate random variables; that is, the joint distribution is nonsingular for the true value $\boldsymbol{\chi}$ that generates $E(U_{it}|d_i, \mathbf{Z}_i)$.

As a consequence of the assumptions, it is possible to fit (3.4) by nonlinear least squares and secure identification of α.[13]

Note that the role of (A-9c) is to produce an explicit functional form for $E(U_{it}|d_i, \mathbf{Z}_i)$:

$$E(U_{it}|d_i = 0, \mathbf{Z}_i) = \frac{\int_{-\infty}^{\infty} t_1 \int_{-\infty}^{-\mathbf{Z}_i\gamma} h_i(t_1, t_2|\boldsymbol{\chi})\, dt_1\, dt_2}{\int_{-\infty}^{-\mathbf{Z}_i\gamma} h_i(t_2)\, dt_2} \tag{3.5}$$

In principle, one could dispense with (A-9c) and postulate a functional form for (3.5) directly. Any assumed functional form for $E(U_{it}|d_i = 0, \mathbf{Z}_i)$ should reflect the fact that the conditional mean of U_{it} is a function of $\Pr(d_i = 0|\mathbf{Z}_i)$ and $\boldsymbol{\chi}$.

Thus by virtue of (A-8a),

$$\Pr(d_i = 0|\mathbf{Z}_i) = F(-\mathbf{Z}_i\gamma)$$

and so

$$\mathbf{Z}_i\gamma = -F^{-1}(\Pr(d_i = 0|\mathbf{Z}_i))$$

Substituting in (3.5),

$$E(U_{it}|d_i = 0, \mathbf{Z}_i) = \frac{\int_{-\infty}^{\infty} t_1 \int_{-\infty}^{F^{-1}[\Pr(d_i=0|\mathbf{Z}_i)]} h_i(t_1, t_2|\boldsymbol{\chi})\, dt_1\, dt_2}{\Pr(d_i = 0|\mathbf{Z}_i)} \tag{3.6}$$

Assuming that h_i is differentiable to all orders, it is possible to express $E(U_{it}|d_i = 0, \mathbf{Z}_i)$ as a power series in $\Pr(d_i = 0|\mathbf{Z}_i)$ and the relevant components of $\boldsymbol{\chi}$. Given (A-9e), $\Pr(d_i = 0|\mathbf{Z}_i)$ can be estimated from a discrete choice analysis of the training decision.[14]

There are three distinct estimators that exploit the additional information assumed in (A-9).

3.4.1. The two-stage method. This is developed in Heckman (1976, 1978, 1979).

(i) Estimate $E(d_i|\mathbf{Z}_i)$ by discrete choice analysis.
(ii) Exploit (3.6) using estimated $\Pr(d_i = 0|\mathbf{Z}_i)$ in place of actual values. If $h_i(U_{it}, V_i)$ is bivariate normal, then the corresponding expression for $E(U_{it}|d_i = 1, \mathbf{Z}_i)$ from (3.6) is linear in certain ratios of elements of $\boldsymbol{\chi}$.
(iii) Regress Y_{it} on $\mathbf{X}_{it}$, d_i, and $E(U_{it}|d_i, \mathbf{Z}_i)$, where the final expression is known up to a finite set of parameters in $\boldsymbol{\chi}$.

The standard errors must be adjusted to account for the estimated regressor (see Heckman, 1979, Amemiya, 1983).

3.4.2. Direct nonlinear regression. This method is suggested in Barnow, Cain, and Goldberger (1980). Estimate (3.4) directly without estimating $E(U_{it}|d_i, \mathbf{Z}_i)$ in a first stage.

3.4.3 Maximum likelihood. Application of this method to models with dummy endogenous variables is discussed in Heckman (1976, 1978) for models with normal error terms. Provided that (A-9c) is true, this procedure produces more efficient estimators.

Note that 3.4.1 and 3.4.2 do not require (A-9c). All that need be known is $E(U_{it}|d_i, \mathbf{Z}_i)$ up to a finite set of parameters provided that the other conditions are satisfied. In this sense 3.4.1 and 3.4.2 are less demanding methods. Note further that assumptions (A-9a) and (A-9b) can be relaxed. If $E(U_{it}|d_i, \mathbf{X}_{it}, \mathbf{Z}_i)$ is known up to a finite set of parameters and it is the case that when $E(U_{it}|d_i, \mathbf{X}_{it}, \mathbf{Z}_i)$ replaces $E(U_{it}|d_i, \mathbf{Z}_i)$ (A-9e) is satisfied, α is still identified. Mincer and Jovanovic (1981) invoke such assumptions in their analysis of job turnover.

In principle, if $E(U_{it}|d_i, \mathbf{X}_{it}, \mathbf{Z}_i)$ is known up to a finite set of parameters and *only* (A-5), (A-6), and (A-9e) (suitably modified) are true, α can be identified without an instrument (in the sense of Section 3.2) and without knowledge of $E(d_i|\mathbf{Z}_i)$ as is assumed in Section 3.3. In such a case identification is secured solely by the assumed a priori functional form. However, given such assumptions, it is in principle possible to devise consistent control function estimators of α for all of the fixed coefficient enrollment models considered in Section 2.

The additional assumptions invoked in this section are purely statistical in nature. Accordingly appeal to the prototypical decision rules of Section 2 offers little guidance in the choice of estimator.

3.5 *Controlling for selection on observables*

The condition for selection bias

(A-1) $E(U_{it}d_i) \neq 0$

can arise for one of two distinct reasons: (a) dependence between V_i and U_{it} or (b) dependence between $\mathbf{Z}_i$ and U_{it}. Under assumptions stated in (3.2), the instrumental variables (IV) estimator is consistent for α in either case. The procedures suggested in Section 3.3 abstract from dependence (b) [see assumption (A-8d)] whereas in principle the control function estimators of Section 3.4 are consistent for α when (A-1) occurs for either reason. Many of the commonly used estimators implicitly assume that there is no stochastic dependence between $\mathbf{Z}_i$ and U_{it}.

In this subsection, we consider the case when (A-1) occurs solely because of (b). Barnow, Cain, and Goldberger (BCG) (1980) first analyzed this case. Ashenfelter (1978) presents empirical evidence that enrollment into training depends on earnings in period $k-1$. If $\rho = 1$ in uncertainty decision rule (2.9) (or if $\theta_i = 0$ for all i), if τ_i is distributed independently of U_{it}, and if ε_i is unknown with mean zero at the time of enrollment, then selection occurs because of reason (b) provided that $Y_{i,k-1}$ is observed.

The BCG procedure is based on the following assumptions: (A-5), (A-6), and

(A-10) (a) $E(U_{it}|\mathbf{Z}_i, \mathbf{X}_{it}, d_i) = E(U_{it}|\mathbf{Z}_i) \neq 0$ for some $\mathbf{Z}_i$.
(b) The functional form of $E(U_{it}|\mathbf{Z}_i)$ is known up to a finite vector of parameters ω. [Thus we write $E(U_{it}|\mathbf{Z}_i, \omega)$.]
(c) In the population $[\mathbf{X}_{it}, d_i, \partial \mathrm{E}(U_{it}|\mathbf{Z}_i, \omega)/\partial\omega]$ is a nondegenerate vector of random variables (i.e., the joint distribution is nonsingular for the true values of ω).

As a consequence of (A-10a) we may write

$$E(Y_{it}|\mathbf{X}_{it}, d_i, \mathbf{Z}_i) = \mathbf{X}_{it}\boldsymbol{\beta} + d_i\alpha + E(U_{it}|\mathbf{Z}_i, \omega)$$

As a consequence of the assumptions, α is consistently estimated by (possibly nonlinear) regression methods.[15] BCG assume the special functional form

$$E(U_{it}|\mathbf{Z}_i, \omega) = \mathbf{Z}_i\omega$$

although this particular specification is not essential to their approach. Assumption (A-10c) in this case rules out perfect collinearity among $\mathbf{X}_{it}$, d_i, and $\mathbf{Z}_i$ [and thus excludes a linear probability model for $E(d_i|\mathbf{Z}_i)$ if $\mathbf{Z}_i$ lies in the column space of $\mathbf{X}_{it}$].

This estimator is another example of a control function estimator:

$$K_{it} = E(U_{it}|\mathbf{Z}_i, \omega)$$

The natural generalization of this control function and the one presented in Section 3.4 is

$$K_{it} = E(U_{it} | d_i, \mathbf{Z}_i, \mathbf{X}_{it}, \omega)$$

Provided (A-5) and (A-6) are true and (A-10) is appropriately modified {in particular, (A-10a) is dropped, (A-10b) is modified to include $\mathbf{X}_{it}$ and d_i in the conditioning set, and (A-10c) is replaced with the requirement that $[\mathbf{X}_{it}, d_i, \partial \mathbf{E}(U_{it} | d_i, \mathbf{Z}_i, \mathbf{X}_{it}, \omega)/\partial \omega]$ is a vector of full column rank in the population}, α is identified.

Selection solely on the basis of observables is implausible in the light of the decision rules presented in Section 2. In both certainty and uncertainty settings, this occurs only if unmeasured cost component τ_i is distributed independently of U_{it} and U_{it} is independent of U_{ik} (the certainty case) or U_{it} is independent of $E_{k-1}(U_{ik})$ (the uncertainty case).

3.6 *Identification through distributional assumptions about U_{it}*

If no regressor appears in decision rule (1.2), the estimators presented in the preceding sections do not consistently estimate α unless additional restrictions are imposed. Heckman (1978) demonstrates that if (U_{it}, V_i) is normally distributed, α is identified even if there is no regressor in enrollment rule (1.2). His conditions are overly strong.

In this section we demonstrate that if U_{it} has zero third and fifth moments, α is identified even if no regressor appears in the enrollment rule. This assumption about U_{it} is implied by normality or symmetry of the density of U_{it} (assuming the first five moments exist) but it is weaker than either. The fact that α can be identified by invoking distributional assumptions about U_{it} is an instance of the more general point that there is a tradeoff between assumptions about regressors and assumptions about the distribution of U_{it} that must be invoked to identify α.

We establish that under the following assumptions, α in (1.3) is identified even if (A-5) is not satisfied:

(A-11) (a) $E(U_{it}^3) = 0$.
(b) $E(U_{it}^5) = 0$.
(c) The earnings function is (1.3), so there are no regressors.
(d) $\{U_{it}, V_i\}$ is i.i.d.

The assumption that no regressor appears in the enrollment rule or in the earnings function is made only to simplify the initial analysis. We relax this assumption below. The i.i.d. assumption is made only to simplify the proofs. Its relaxation involves only minor changes but adds to the notational complication and so is not done here.

A method-of-moments estimator exploits these assumptions. We find $\hat{\alpha}$ that equates the sample analogs of $E(U_{it}^3)$ and $E(U_{it}^5)$ to zero. The proposed estimator solves

$$\frac{1}{I_t}\sum_{i=1}^{I_t}[(Y_{it}-\bar{Y}_t)-\hat{\alpha}(d_i-\bar{d}_t)]^3=0$$

and

$$\frac{1}{I_t}\sum_{i=1}^{I_t}[(Y_{it}-\bar{Y}_t)-\hat{\alpha}(d_i-\bar{d}_t)]^5=0$$

where, as before, "$^-$" denotes sample mean. By virtue of Slutsky's theorem we may replace sample means with population means in these expressions for the purpose of establishing consistency. Thus we propose the criterion

$$\frac{1}{I_t}\sum_{i=1}^{I_t}[(Y_{it}-\mu_t)-\hat{\alpha}(d_i-p)]^3=0 \tag{3.7a}$$

and

$$\frac{1}{I_t}\sum_{i=1}^{I_t}[(Y_{it}-\mu_t)-\hat{\alpha}(d_i-p)]^3=0 \tag{3.7b}$$

where $E(Y_{it})=\mu_t$ and $E(d_i)=p$.

For fixed $\hat{\alpha}$, (3.7a) converges in probability to

$$\begin{aligned}
&\operatorname*{plim}_{I_t\to\infty}\frac{1}{I_t}\sum_{i=1}^{I_t}[(Y_{it}-\mu_t)-\hat{\alpha}(d_i-p)]^3\\
&=\{\alpha^3(p)(1-p)(1-2p)+3\alpha^2E(U_{it}|d_i=1)(1-2p)p+3\alpha[E(U_{it}^2|d_i=1)p-p\sigma_u^2]\}\\
&\quad-3\tilde{\alpha}[\alpha^2(p)(1-p)(1-2p)+2\alpha E(U_{it}|d_i=1)(1-2p)p+E(U_{it}^2|d_i=1)p-p\sigma_u^2]\\
&\quad+3\tilde{\alpha}^2[\alpha(p)(1-p)(1-2p)+E(U_{it}|d_i=1)(1-2p)p]\\
&\quad-\tilde{\alpha}^3[p(1-p)(1-2p)]
\end{aligned} \tag{3.7a$'$}$$

where $E(U_{it}^2)=\sigma_u^2$ and where $\tilde{\alpha}=\operatorname{plim}\hat{\alpha}$. Setting $\tilde{\alpha}=\alpha$ and adding up the elements in each column establishes that there exists one root of (3.7a) that is consistent for α.

The other two roots of equation (3.7a) converge to

$$\operatorname{plim}\hat{\alpha}=\alpha+\frac{3}{2}\frac{E(U_{it}|d_i=1)}{1-p}\pm\frac{1}{2}\sqrt{9\left[\frac{E(U_{it}|d_i=1)}{1-p}\right]^2+\frac{12[\sigma^2-E(U_{it}^2|d_i=1)]}{(1-p)(1-2p)}}$$

for $p \neq \frac{1}{2}$. When $p = \frac{1}{2}$, (3.7a) converges to a linear equation in $\tilde{\alpha}$ that is consistent for α provided that $E(U_{it}^2 | d_i = 1) \neq E(U_{it}^2)$.

The fact that a consistent root of (3.7a) exists is empirically useless. Except in the case when $p = \frac{1}{2}$, we do not know which of the three roots is the consistent root unless the argument inside the square root is negative so that the inconsistent roots are complex conjugates. Nothing in the problem restricts this expression to be negative. A sufficient condition for the existence of complex roots is that selection increases the variance of U_{it} [i.e., $\text{Var}(U_{it} | d_i = 1) > \text{Var}(U_{it})$].

In order to pick the consistent root in the general case it is necessary to use the higher moment restriction (A-11b). We now establish that (a) there is one consistent root of (3.7b) and (b) the inconsistent roots of (3.7b) do not converge to the inconsistent roots of (3.7a). Thus in large samples it is possible to detect the consistent root of these equations. A consistent estimator of α is the value of $\hat{\alpha}$ that sets (3.7a) and (3.7b) as close to 0 as possible in a suitably defined metric.

In order to establish this claim, it is helpful to simplify the notation by defining

$$
\begin{aligned}
c_1 &= E(d_i - p)^5 &&= p(1 - 5p + 10p^2 - 10p^3 + 4p^4) \\
c_2 &= E[(d_i - p)^4 U_{it}] &&= p(1 - (4p - 6p^2 + 4p^3)E(U_{it} | d_i = 1)) \\
c_3 &= E[(d_i - p)^3 U_{it}^2] &&= p(E(U_{it}^2 | d_i = 1)(1 - 3p + 3p^2) - p^2\sigma_u^2) \\
c_4 &= E[(d_i - p)^2 U_{it}^3] &&= p(E(U_{it}^3 | d_i = 1)(1 - 2p)) \\
c_5 &= E[(d_i - p) U_{it}^4] &&= p(E(U_{it}^4 | d_i = 1) - E(U_{it}^4))
\end{aligned}
$$

In this notation, it is straightforward but tedious to establish that

$$
\begin{aligned}
&\operatorname*{plim}_{I_t \to \infty} \frac{1}{I_t} \sum_{i=1}^{I_t} [(Y_{it} - \mu_t) - \tilde{\alpha}(d_i - p)]^5 \\
&= \quad \{\alpha^5 c_1 + 5\alpha^4 c_2 + 10\alpha^3 c_3 + 10\alpha^2 c_4 + 5\alpha c_5\} \\
&\quad - 5\tilde{\alpha}\{\alpha^4 c_1 + 4\alpha^3 c_2 + 6\alpha^2 c_3 + 4\alpha c_4 + c_5\} \\
&\quad + 10\tilde{\alpha}^2\{\alpha^3 c_1 + 3\alpha^2 c_2 + 3\alpha c_3 + c_4\} \\
&\quad - 10\tilde{\alpha}^3\{\alpha^2 c_1 + 2\alpha c_2 + c_3\} \\
&\quad + 5\tilde{\alpha}^4\{\alpha c_1 + c_2\} \\
&\quad - \tilde{\alpha}^5\{c_1\}
\end{aligned}
\qquad (3.7b')
$$

Setting $\tilde{\alpha} = \alpha$ and adding down each column demonstrates the existence of a consistent root (3.7b′). However, there are four other roots of this equation, all of which may be distinct and real. We now establish that the other four roots of (3.7b′) are distinct from the inconsistent roots of (3.7a′).

To demonstrate that this is so it is helpful to define some additional notation.

$$b_3 = \alpha - 5\left(\alpha + \frac{c_2}{c_1}\right)$$

$$b_2 = 10\left(\alpha^2 + 2\frac{\alpha c_2}{c_1} + \frac{c_3}{c_1}\right) + \alpha\left[\alpha - 5\left(\alpha + \frac{c_2}{c_1}\right)\right]$$

$$b_1 = \alpha\left\{10\left(\alpha^2 + 2\frac{\alpha c_2}{c_1} + \frac{c_3}{c_1}\right) + \alpha\left[\alpha - 5\left(\alpha + \frac{c_2}{c_1}\right)\right]\right\}$$
$$- 10\left(\alpha^3 + 3\frac{\alpha^2 c_2}{c_1} + 3\frac{\alpha c_3}{c_1} + \frac{c_4}{c_1}\right)$$

$$b_0 = \alpha^4 + 5\frac{\alpha^3 c_2}{c_1} + 10\frac{\alpha^2 c_3}{c_1} + 10\frac{\alpha c_4}{c_1} + 5\frac{c_5}{c_1}$$

With this notation in hand, factor the right-hand side of (3.7b′) into a lower-order quartic multiplied by the factor $\tilde{\alpha} - \alpha$:

$$(\tilde{\alpha} - \alpha)\{\tilde{\alpha}^4 + \tilde{\alpha}^3 b_3 + \tilde{\alpha}^2 b_2 + \tilde{\alpha} b_1 + b_0\}$$

Let r denote either of the roots of the quadratic equation given below (3.7a)′. Here r is a root of the quartic if and only if

$$r^4 + r^3 b_3 + r^2 b_2 + r b_1 + b_0 = 0$$

In general, this equation cannot be satisfied because r does not depend on $E(U_{it}^3 \mid d_i = 1)$, $E(U_{it}^4 \mid d_i = 1)$, or $E(U_{it}^4)$ whereas b_1 and b_0 do. The formal condition for distinct roots for the two equations is that the parameters of the model are such that for both possible values of r (given the parameters of the model)

$$r^4 + r^3 b_3 + r^2 b_2 + r b_1 + b_0 \neq 0$$

In general, this condition will be satisfied if the third and fourth moments of the U_{it} can be freely specified.

The operational version of the estimator selects a common α that makes (3.7a) and (3.7b) as close to zero in a suitable metric. One obvious choice of metric is a least squares criterion summing squared deviations of the left-hand sides of (3.7a) and (3.7b) from equality with zero.

If regressors appear in the earnings function, the method-of-moments procedure proposed above can be modified in the following way. In place of (A-11) we write

(A-11′) (a) $E(U_{it}^3) = 0$.
(b) $E(U_{it}^5) = 0$.
(c) Assumptions (A-6) are satisfied except (A-6c).
(d) Assumption (A-6c) is strengthened to read that the vectors of variables in that assumption are i.i.d.

For each value of $\hat{\alpha}$, compute $\boldsymbol{\beta}(\hat{\alpha})$ by regressing

$$(Y_{it} - \hat{\alpha} d_i) \quad \text{on} \quad \mathbf{X}_{it}$$

Define $\tilde{Y}_{it}$ as the value of Y_{it} with the value of $\mathbf{X}_{it}$ removed:

$$\tilde{Y}_{it} = (Y_{it} - \bar{Y}_t) - (\mathbf{X}_{it} - \bar{\mathbf{X}}_t)\boldsymbol{\beta}(\hat{\alpha})$$

Then, under the conditions of (A-11′), there is a unique consistent root that solves

$$\frac{1}{I_t} \sum_{i=1}^{I_t} [\tilde{Y}_{it} - \hat{\alpha}(d_i - p)]^3 = 0 \tag{3.7a''}$$

and

$$\frac{1}{I_t} \sum_{i=1}^{I_t} [\tilde{Y}_{it} - \hat{\alpha}(d_i - p)]^5 = 0 \tag{3.7b''}$$

The proof is straightforward and is omitted.

The moment estimation proposed in this section is just one example of an entire class of consistent estimators for α that do not require a regressor in enrollment rule (1.2). Other restrictions on moments (e.g., functional restrictions between the second and fourth moments of U_{it} that are implied by a normality assumption) can be exploited to devise consistent estimators for α.

3.7 *Estimation in the random coefficients model*

In place of random coefficients model (1.13) we write the more general model with regressors

$$Y_{it} = \mathbf{X}_{it}\boldsymbol{\beta} + d_i\alpha_i + U_{it} \tag{3.8}$$

where $E(\alpha_i) = \bar{\alpha} < \infty$, $\varepsilon_i = \alpha_i - \bar{\alpha}$ and $E(\varepsilon_i) = 0$. To focus on essential issues we continue to assume that $\boldsymbol{\beta}$ is a fixed parameter vector. We strengthen assumption (A-6c) to read

(A-6c′) $\{\mathbf{X}_{it}, \mathbf{Z}_i, V_i, U_{it}, \varepsilon_i\}$ is an independent sequence with respect to i

and (A-6a) is modified appropriately. In addition, $U_{it} + d_i\varepsilon_i$ replaces U_{it} in (A-6d)–(A-6g). If (A-5) does not hold and (A-6) (as augmented) holds and if the (V_i, ε_i) are i.i.d., then it is not possible to identify $\bar{\alpha}$ without further prior information. Instead, only

$$\alpha^* = \bar{\alpha} + E(\varepsilon_i | d_i = 1)$$

can be identified without invoking distributional assumptions or other prior information.

If there is a regressor in (1.2), it is in principle possible to identify $\bar{\alpha}$. We write

$$E(\varepsilon_i | d_i = 1, \mathbf{Z}_i) = \phi(\mathbf{Z}_i) \tag{3.9}$$

A new econometric problem arises that has not previously appeared. To state it most clearly, rewrite (3.8) as

$$Y_{it} = \mathbf{X}_{it}\boldsymbol{\beta} + d_i\bar{\alpha} + [U_{it} + d_i\varepsilon_i] \tag{3.10}$$

In view of (3.9), the error term in brackets in (3.10) does not have mean zero, and in fact has a mean that depends on $\mathbf{Z}_i$.

Accordingly, the IV method presented in Section 3.2 applied to (3.10) does not produce consistent estimators because (A-7a) fails with respect to the composite error term (i.e., the term in brackets has a nonzero mean). The methodology of Section 3.3 breaks down because

$$\begin{aligned} E(Y_{it} | \mathbf{X}_{it}, \mathbf{Z}_i) &= \mathbf{X}_{it}\boldsymbol{\beta} + [\bar{\alpha} + \phi(Z_i)] \Pr(d_i = 1 | \mathbf{Z}_i) \\ &\neq \mathbf{X}_{it}\boldsymbol{\beta} + \bar{\alpha} \Pr(d_i = 1 | \mathbf{Z}_i) \end{aligned}$$

The control function methodology of Sections 3.4 and 3.5 continues to apply in the random coefficient case except now

$$E(d_i\varepsilon_i + U_{it} | d_i, \mathbf{X}_{it}, \mathbf{Z}_i)$$

must be specified. Provided that certain conditions are satisfied, $\bar{\alpha}$ can be identified from a (possibly nonlinear) regression:

$$E(Y_{it} | \mathbf{X}_{it}, d_i, \mathbf{Z}_i) = \mathbf{X}_{it}\boldsymbol{\beta} + d_i\bar{\alpha} + E(d_i\varepsilon_i + U_{it} | d_i, \mathbf{X}_{it}, \mathbf{Z}_i) \tag{3.11}$$

The required conditions are (A-5), (A-6) (as strengthened above), and

(A-12) (a) The functional form of $E(U_{it} + d_i\varepsilon_i | d_i, \mathbf{X}_{it}, \mathbf{Z}_i)$ is known up to a finite vector $\boldsymbol{\omega}$.

(b) In the population $[\mathbf{X}_{it}, d_i, \partial \mathbf{E}(U_{it} + d_i\varepsilon_i | d_i, \mathbf{X}_{it}, \mathbf{Z}_i, \boldsymbol{\omega})/\partial\boldsymbol{\omega}]$ is a nondegenerate vector of random variables (i.e., for true $\boldsymbol{\omega}$, the joint distribution is nondegenerate).

This contrast between the consistency of the IV method and the consistency of the control function estimator for the random coefficient model suggests a formal statistical test between random and fixed coefficient models using a Durbin (1954)–Wu (1973, 1983)–Hausman (1978) statistic.

Lee's model of unionism, which is a random coefficient model, generates (A-12a) by assuming that

(a) $(U_{it}, V_i, \varepsilon_i)$ are joint normal random variables with zero mean and a finite nondegenerate covariance matrix functionally independent of $(\alpha, \boldsymbol{\beta}, \gamma)$.
(b) $E(\varepsilon_i d_i + U_{it} | d_i, \mathbf{X}_{it}, \mathbf{Z}_i, \omega) = E(d_i \varepsilon_i + \mathbf{U}_{it} | d_i, \mathbf{Z}_i, \omega)$.
(c) $E(U_{it} | \mathbf{X}_{it}, d_i, \mathbf{Z}_i) = E(U_{it} | d_i, \mathbf{Z}_i)$.
(d) $\mathbf{Z}_i$ is distributed independently of V_i.
(e) The distribution of $\mathbf{Z}_i$ is nondegenerate.[16]

3.8 *Accounting for choice-based sampling and contamination bias*

The preceding analysis assumes access to simple random samples or samples stratified on the basis of exogenous variables. As noted in Section 1.5, the available data on training programs often are not random samples. More frequently the following types of data are available:

(i) Earnings, earnings characteristics, and enrollment characteristics (Y_{it}, $\mathbf{X}_{it}$ and $\mathbf{Z}_i$, respectively) for a sample of trainees ($d_i = 1$).
(ii) Earnings, earnings characteristics, and enrollment characteristics for a sample of nontrainees ($d_i = 0$).
(iii) Earnings, earnings characteristics, and enrollment characteristics for a national "control" sample of the population (e.g., CPS or Social Security records), where the training status of persons is not known.

If types (i) and (ii) data are combined and the sample proportion of trainees does not converge to the population proportion of trainees, then the combined sample is a choice-based sample as defined in Section 1.5. If types (i) and (iii) data are combined with or without type (ii) data, there is contamination bias, because the training status of certain persons is not known. In this subsection we examine the robustness of the estimators presented in Sections 3.2–3.6 to choice-based and contaminated samples, and we discuss how certain nonrobust estimators can be modified to produce consistent estimators.

Throughout this subsection we assume

(A-13) (a) There is access to type (i) data;

and we frequently invoke

(A-13) (b) The population proportion of trainees p is known:

$$\Pr(d_i = 1) = p$$

Assumption (a) is essential to any evaluation using cross-section data. Assumption (b) is satisfied for data on most training programs (Barnow, 1983).

We discuss each estimator in turn starting with the instrumental variable estimator presented in Section 3.2. The format of each discussion is identical. We first assume access to samples (i) and (ii) (i.e., a choice-based sample). Then we assume access to samples (i) and (iii) (i.e., a contaminated sample). Finally we assume access to pooled choice-based contaminated samples.

3.8.1. The IV estimator (Section 3.2)

3.8.1.A. Choice-based sampling [samples (i) and (ii) pooled]. If conditions (A-6d) and (A-7a) are strengthened to read

(A-6d′) $E(\mathbf{X}'_{it}U_{it} | d_i) = 0$
(A-7a′) $E[g(Z^e_i)U_{it} | d_i] = 0$

and the other conditions of Section 3.2 are met, the IV estimator is consistent for α in choice-based samples.

To see why this is so, write the normal equations for the IV estimator in the following form:

$$\begin{bmatrix} \frac{\sum \mathbf{X}'_{it}\mathbf{X}_{it}}{I_t} & \frac{\sum \mathbf{X}'_{it}d_i}{I_t} \\ \frac{\sum g(Z^e_i)\mathbf{X}_{it}}{I_t} & \frac{\sum g(Z^e_i)d_i}{I_t} \end{bmatrix} \begin{pmatrix} \hat{\boldsymbol{\beta}} \\ \hat{\alpha} \end{pmatrix} = \begin{pmatrix} \frac{\sum \mathbf{X}'_{it}Y_{it}}{I_t} \\ \frac{\sum g(Z^e_i)Y_{it}}{I_t} \end{pmatrix} = \begin{bmatrix} \frac{\sum \mathbf{X}'_{it}\mathbf{X}_{it}}{I_t} & \frac{\sum \mathbf{X}'_{it}d_i}{I_t} \\ \frac{\sum g(Z^e_i)\mathbf{X}_{it}}{I_t} & \frac{\sum g(Z^e_i)d_i}{I_t} \end{bmatrix} \begin{pmatrix} \boldsymbol{\beta} \\ \alpha \end{pmatrix} + \begin{pmatrix} \frac{\sum \mathbf{X}'_{it}U_{it}}{I_t} \\ \frac{\sum g(Z^e_i)U_{it}}{I_t} \end{pmatrix} \tag{3.12}$$

Since (A-6d′) and (A-7a′) guarantee that

$$\operatorname*{plim}_{I_t \to \infty} \frac{\sum X'_{it}U_{it}}{I_t} = 0 \quad \text{and} \quad \operatorname*{plim}_{I_t \to \infty} \frac{\sum g(Z^e_i)U_{it}}{I_t} = 0 \tag{3.13}$$

and rank condition (A-7b) is satisfied, the IV estimator is consistent.

In a choice-based sample for period t, the probability that individual i is enrolled in training is p^* in the notation of Section 1.5 and is not the population proportion of trainees. Thus, even if (A-6d) and (A-7a) are satisfied along with the other conditions, there is no guarantee that the conditions (3.13) are met. This is so because[17]

$$\operatorname*{plim}_{I_t \to \infty} \frac{\sum \mathbf{X}'_{it}U_{it}}{I_t} = \lim_{I_t \to \infty} \frac{\sum \{E(\mathbf{X}'_{it}U_{it} | d_i = 1)p^* + E(\mathbf{X}'_{it}U_{it} | d_i = 0)(1 - p^*)\}}{I_t}$$

$$\operatorname*{plim}_{I_t \to \infty} \frac{\sum g(Z^e_i)U_{it}}{I_t} = \lim_{I_t \to \infty} \frac{\sum \{E(g(Z^e_i)U_{it} | d_i = 1)p^* + E(g(Z^e_i)U_{it} | d_i = 0)(1 - p^*)\}}{I_t}$$

In general, the terms inside the braces are not zero and so the IV estimator is inconsistent.[18]

In a random sampling environment, $p^* = \Pr(d_i = 1) = p$ and the terms inside the braces are identically zero. They are also zero if (A-6d′) and (A-7a′) are satisfied. However, it is not necessary to invoke conditions (A-6d′) and (A-7a′). Since p is known, it is possible to reweight the data to secure consistent estimators under the assumptions of Section 3.2. Multiplying equation (1.3) by weight

$$\omega_i = d_i \frac{p}{p^*} + (1 - d_i)\left(\frac{1 - p}{1 - p^*}\right)$$

and applying IV to the transformed equation produces an estimator that satisfies (3.13). The proof is straightforward and hence is omitted. The intuition underlying this procedure is clear. By weighting the sample at hand back to random sample proportions, the IV estimator of Section 3.2 produces a consistent estimator (see Manski and Lerman, 1977).

3.8.1.B. Contamination bias [samples (i) and (iii)]. By assumption, d_i is not observed for observations in random sample (iii). Applying the IV estimator to pooled samples (i) and (iii), assuming that observations in (iii) have $d_i = 0$, produces an inconsistent estimator.

In terms of the IV equations (3.13), from sample (iii) data it is possible to generate the cross-products from the $I_{(\text{iii})}$ observations

$$\frac{\sum \mathbf{X}'_{it}\mathbf{X}_{it}}{I_{(\text{iii})}}, \quad \frac{\sum g(Z_i^e)\mathbf{X}_{it}}{I_{(\text{iii})}}, \quad \frac{\sum \mathbf{X}'_{it}Y_{it}}{I_{(\text{iii})}}, \quad \frac{\sum g(Z_i^e)Y_{it}}{I_{(\text{iii})}} \tag{3.14}$$

which under the conditions stated in (A-6) converge to the desired population counterparts. Equations (3.13) are satisfied in this sample. Missing is information on the cross-products

$$\frac{\sum \mathbf{X}'_{it}d_i}{I_{(\text{iii})}}, \quad \frac{\sum g(Z_i^e)d_i}{I_{(\text{iii})}} \tag{3.15}$$

Notice that if d_i were accurately measured in sample (iii), then[19]

$$\operatorname*{plim}_{I_{(\text{iii})}\to\infty} \frac{\sum \mathbf{X}'_{it}d_i}{I_{(\text{iii})}} = p\,\frac{\sum E(\mathbf{X}'_{it}\,|\,d_i = 1)}{I_{(\text{iii})}}$$

$$\operatorname*{plim}_{I_{(\text{iii})}\to\infty} \frac{\sum g(Z_i^e)d_i}{I_{(\text{iii})}} = p\,\frac{\sum E[g(Z_i^e)\,|\,d_i = 1]}{I_{(\text{iii})}}$$

But the means of $\mathbf{X}_{it}$ and $g(Z_i^e)$ in sample (i) converge to

$$\frac{\sum E(\mathbf{X}_{it}\,|\,d_i = 1)}{I_{(\text{i})}} \quad \text{and} \quad \frac{\sum E[g(Z_i^e)\,|\,d_i = 1]}{I_{(\text{i})}}$$

respectively. Hence inserting the sample (i) means of $\mathbf{X}_{it}$ and $g(Z_i^e)$ multiplied by p in the second column of the matrix of IV equations (3.12) produces a consistent IV estimator, provided that in the limit the sizes of samples (i) and (iii) both approach infinity at the same rate.

3.8.1.C. Choice-based sampling plus contamination bias [samples (i), (ii), and (iii)]. Samples (i) and (ii) can be pooled using the weights ω_i defined above. Sample (iii) can be used to improve the efficiency of the procedure by combining the moments in (3.14) constructed from sample (ii) with the corresponding moments for the weighted observations to form the normal questions for the IV estimator. In combining moments formed from different samples, weight the moments for each sample by the relative sample size.

3.8.2. Procedures based on known or estimated *F* (Section 3.3)

3.8.2.A. Choice-based sampling [samples (i) and (ii)]. Procedures that exploit knowledge of F and the other conditions listed in Section 3.3 are of three types: (1) nonlinear regression estimators of equation (3.2); (2) two-stage estimators that estimate F_i in stage 1 and use $\hat{F}_i$ as a regressor in the second stage; (3) a procedure that uses $\hat{F}_i$ as an instrument for d_i. In this subsection we consider how the estimators proposed for random samples can be adapted to yield consistent estimators for choice-based samples.

Manski and McFadden (1981) demonstrate that if (A-13b) is true, it is possible to consistently estimate γ and hence F_i from choice-based samples provided that standard regularity conditions are met. [In fact, they demonstrate that in certain cases (A-13b) is stronger than is required.] If their conditions are met, they propose several consistent estimators for F_i.

Provided that the data are appropriately reweighted, it is possible to apply estimators (1)–(3) listed above to data generated from choice-based samples. The appropriate weight for observation i in cross section t is

$$\phi_{it} = \frac{\Pr(d_i = 1 | \mathbf{Z}_i)}{p^*(d_i = 1, \mathbf{Z}_i)} d_i + \frac{\Pr(d_i = 0 | \mathbf{Z}_i)}{p^*(d_i = 0 | \mathbf{Z}_i)} (1 - d_i)$$

where $\Pr(d_i = 1 | \mathbf{Z}_i)$ is the probability that $d_i = 1$ in the population and $p^*(d = 1 | \mathbf{Z}_i)$ is the probability that $d_i = 1$ in the population generated by a choice-based sample. The terms $\Pr(d_i = 0 | \mathbf{Z}_i)$ and $p^*(d_i = 0 | \mathbf{Z}_i)$ are the corresponding conditional probabilities for the event $d_i = 0$. Consistent empirically feasible values of these weights are produced from the Manski–McFadden procedure (for the numerator expressions) and by direct estimation from the choice-based sample (for the denominator expressions).

Direct calculation using the law of iterated expectation reveals (for known ϕ_{it}) that in a reweighted choice-based sample[20]

$$E(\phi_{it} Y_{it} | \phi_{it}\mathbf{X}_{it}, \mathbf{Z}_i) = \phi_{it}\mathbf{X}_{it}\boldsymbol{\beta} + [1 - F(-\mathbf{Z}_i\gamma)]\alpha$$

Methods (1) and (2) listed above apply without modification to the reweighted data. Method (3) uses the $\hat{F}_i$ obtained from the Manski–McFadden procedure in the IV equations described in the preceding subsection. Conditional weights are not required in method 3 because unconditional moments are used in the IV method.

3.8.2.B. Contamination bias [samples (i) and (iii)]. By construction, estimation of equation (3.2) does not require knowledge of d_i, so that under the assumptions of Section 3.3 direct nonlinear estimation of (3.2) on sample (iii) produces consistent estimators of the parameters of that equation. Note that sample (i) is nowhere needed, nor is the population proportion of trainees [so assumption (A-13) is not required].

The two-stage estimator is not directly feasible. Assuming that it is possible to consistently estimate $p = \Pr(d_i = 1)$, it may be possible to consistently estimate γ and hence $F(-\mathbf{Z}_i\gamma)$. The proposed procedure posits the existence of two vector-valued functions $\mathbf{g}^*(\mathbf{Z}_i | \gamma)$ and $\mathbf{g}(\mathbf{Z}_i | \gamma)$, which have the property that

$$\int \mathbf{g}^*(\mathbf{Z}_i | \gamma) f(\mathbf{Z}_i | d = 1, \gamma_0)\, d\mathbf{Z}_i = \int \mathbf{g}(\mathbf{Z}_i | \gamma) f(\mathbf{Z}_i)\, d\mathbf{Z}_i \tag{3.16}$$

when

$$\gamma = \gamma_0$$

where γ_0 is the true value of the parameter and where for notational convenience we suppress the dependence of $f(\mathbf{Z}_i | d = 1, \gamma_0)$ and $f(\mathbf{Z}_i)$ on other parameters of the model.

The postulated functions are also assumed to possess the property that for all values of ρ sufficiently small

$$\{\gamma \,|\, |\gamma - \gamma_0| < \rho, \qquad \gamma \neq \gamma_0\}$$

implies

$$\int \mathbf{g}^*(\mathbf{Z}_i | \gamma) f(\mathbf{Z}_i | d = 1, \gamma_0)\, dZ_i \neq \int \mathbf{g}(\mathbf{Z}_i | \gamma) f(\mathbf{Z}_i)\, d\mathbf{Z}_i$$

so that γ is at least locally identified. If this condition is satisfied for all $\gamma \neq \gamma_0$, γ is globally identified. Given this identifiability condition, it is possible to consistently estimate γ from the means of $\mathbf{g}$ and $\mathbf{g}^*$ formed in samples (iii) and (i), respectively. The proposed estimator $\hat{\gamma}$ solves for the γ that equates the means of $\mathbf{g}^*(\mathbf{Z}_i | \gamma)$ and $\mathbf{g}(\mathbf{Z}_i | \gamma)$ in the two samples:

$$\frac{1}{I_{(\mathrm{i})}} \sum_{i=1}^{I_{(\mathrm{i})}} \mathbf{g}^*(\mathbf{Z}_i | \hat{\gamma}) = \frac{1}{I_{(\mathrm{iii})}} \sum_{i=1}^{I_{(\mathrm{iii})}} \mathbf{g}(\mathbf{Z}_i | \hat{\gamma}) \tag{3.17}$$

where $I_{(i)}$ and $I_{(iii)}$ are, respectively, the sample sizes in samples (i) and (iii). As $I_{(i)}$ and $I_{(iii)} \to \infty$, $\hat{\gamma}$ is consistent for γ_0 given standard assumptions that justify the uniform strong law of large numbers for stratified samples. For any value of γ that satisfies these conditions, the left-hand side of (3.17) converges to the left-hand side of (3.16) and the right-hand side of (3.17) converges to the right-hand side of (3.16).

One set of **g** and **g*** functions is produced from the following intuitive argument. In sample (i) choose γ to maximize the average of the logs of the probability of enrollment

$$\text{Max} \frac{1}{I_{(i)}} \sum_{i=1}^{I_{(i)}} \ln[1 - F(-\mathbf{Z}_i\gamma)] \tag{3.18}$$

subject to the constraint that in sample (iii)

$$\frac{1}{I_{(iii)}} \sum_{i=1}^{I_{(iii)}} [1 - F(-\mathbf{Z}_i\gamma)] = p \tag{3.19}$$

where p is known. A routine calculation reveals that, in large samples at $\hat{\gamma} = \gamma_0$, the Lagrange multiplier associated with the constraint has value $\lambda = -1/p$.

The first-order conditions for this problem are (asymptotically)

$$0 = \frac{1}{I_{(i)}} \sum_{i=1}^{I_{(i)}} \left(-\frac{F'(-\mathbf{Z}_i\hat{\gamma})\mathbf{Z}_i}{1 - F(\mathbf{Z}_i\hat{\gamma})} \right) + \frac{1}{I_{(iii)}} \sum_{i=1}^{I_{(iii)}} \left(\frac{1}{p}\right) F'(-\mathbf{Z}_i\hat{\gamma})\mathbf{Z}_i$$

It is easily verified that by defining

$$\mathbf{g}^*(\mathbf{Z}_i|\gamma) = \frac{F'(-\mathbf{Z}_i\gamma)\mathbf{Z}_i}{1 - F(\mathbf{Z}_i\gamma)}$$

and

$$\mathbf{g}(\mathbf{Z}_i|\gamma) = \frac{F'(-\mathbf{Z}_i\gamma)\mathbf{Z}_i}{p}$$

we produce **g***, **g** functions that satisfy the definition. Thus, solving the synthetic optimization problem produces one pair of appropriate **g**, **g*** functions. With consistent estimators for γ it is possible to estimate $F(-\mathbf{Z}_i\gamma)$ and hence perform the two-stage procedure.

3.8.2.C. Choice-based sampling plus contamination bias [samples (i), (ii), and (iii)]. Data from the contaminated sample can be pooled with data from the ω_i weighted choice-based sample to create a pooled sample on which nonlinear regression (3.2) – method 1 – consistently estimates α. Data from samples (i) and (ii) can be pooled to consistently estimate F_i. Now $\hat{F}_i$ can be constructed for each observation in sample (iii). Reweighting samples (i) and (ii) and pooling with sample (iii) produces a sample in which the two-stage estimator (method 2) consistently estimates α. Alternatively, $\hat{F}_i$ can be used as an instrument in the manner already described in the preceding subsection.

3.8.3. Control function estimators (Section 3.4)

3.8.3.A. Choice-based sampling [samples (i) and (ii) pooled]. If $E(U_{it}|\mathbf{X}_{it}, d_i, \mathbf{Z}_i)$ is known or can be consistently estimated (up to a finite set of parameters) and any one of the sets of conditions stated in Section 3.4 is satisfied, the conditional mean can be used as a control function. As already noted in Section 1.5, control function estimators are robust to choice-based sampling.

Method 3.4.2 of Section 3.4 (direct nonlinear regression) can be applied without modification to produce consistent estimators. The two-stage estimator (method 3.4.1) is also consistent if the Manski–McFadden procedures are used to estimate $\Pr(d_i = 0|\mathbf{Z}_i)$ and equation (3.6) is used to generate an estimate of $E(U_{it}|d_i = 0, \mathbf{Z}_i)$ up to a finite set of parameters. Maximum likelihood (method C) is consistent using the Manski–McFadden reweighted estimator for the joint frequency of (d_i, Y_{it}).

3.8.3.B. Contamination bias [samples (i) and (iii) pooled]. Using sample (i) it is possible to consistently estimate $f(\mathbf{Z}_i, Y_{it}, \mathbf{X}_{it}|d_i = 1)$ (see, e.g., Cosslett, 1981, for a discussion of nonparametric frequency estimation).[21] From sample (iii) it is possible to consistently estimate $f(\mathbf{Z}_i, Y_{it}, \mathbf{X}_{it})$. With these two frequencies and assumption A-13(b) [which gives $\Pr(d_i = 1) = p$] it is possible to solve for $f(\mathbf{Z}_i, Y_{it}, \mathbf{X}_{it}|d_i = 0)$ from the equation

$$f(\mathbf{Z}_i, Y_{it}, \mathbf{X}_{it}) = f(\mathbf{Z}_i, Y_{it}, \mathbf{X}_{it}|d_i = 1)\Pr(d_i = 1) + f(\mathbf{Z}_i, Y_{it}, \mathbf{X}_{it}|d_i = 0)\Pr(d_i = 0)$$

so that it is possible to consistently estimate

$$f(\mathbf{Z}_i, Y_{it}, \mathbf{Z}_{it}, d_i) = [f(\mathbf{Z}_i, Y_{it}, \mathbf{X}_{it}|d_i = 1)\Pr(d_i = 1)]^{d_i}[f(\mathbf{Z}_i, Y_{it}, \mathbf{X}_{it}|d_i = 0)\Pr(d_i = 0)]^{1-d_i}$$

and hence

$$\Pr(d_i = 0|\mathbf{Z}_i) \quad \text{and} \quad f(Y_{it}, d_i|\mathbf{Z}_i, \mathbf{X}_{it})$$

Adopting parametric functional forms for the conditional frequency functions, $\Pr(d_i = 0|\mathbf{Z}_i)$ and $f(Y_{it}, d_i|\mathbf{Z}_i, \mathbf{X}_{it})$, standard maximum likelihood procedures can be used to estimate α consistently. Sample (i) provides information on $f(Y_{it}|\mathbf{X}_{it}, d_i = 1, \mathbf{Z}_i)$ whereas sample (iii) provides information on $f(Y_{it}|\mathbf{X}_{it}, \mathbf{Z}_i)$. The samples can be pooled to form a likelihood function which, when maximized with respect to $\boldsymbol{\beta}$, α, ψ, produces a consistent estimator (method 3.4.3) under the assumptions of Section 3.3.

Although d_i is not known for any observation in sample (iii), the normal equations associated with nonlinear regression (3.4) can be formed by pooling moments from samples (i) and (iii) in a manner to be described next. To understand how the proposed method works, it is helpful to write out the appropriate normal equations for a case in which d_i is observed and the analyst has access to a random sample.

The required equations are obtained by minimizing

$$\frac{1}{I_t}\sum_{i=1}^{I_t}[Y_{it} - \mathbf{X}_{it}\boldsymbol{\beta} - d_i\alpha - E(U_{it}|d_i = 1, \mathbf{Z}_i, \psi)d_i - E(U_{it}|d_i = 0, \mathbf{Z}_i, \psi)(1 - d_i)]^2$$

with respect to $\boldsymbol{\beta}$, α, ψ. Note that we have made explicit the dependence of the conditional mean of the U_{it} on ψ. Let

$$K_i(d_i, \mathbf{Z}_i, \psi) = E(U_{it}|d_i = 1, \mathbf{Z}_i, \psi)d_i + E(U_{it}|d_i = 0, \mathbf{Z}_i, \psi)(1 - d_i)$$

to simplify notation. The first-order conditions for the minimization problem (suppressing the arguments of K_i) are

$$\begin{aligned}
\frac{1}{I_t}\sum \mathbf{X}'_{it} Y_{it} &= \left(\frac{1}{I_t}\sum \mathbf{X}'_{it}\mathbf{X}_{it}\right)\boldsymbol{\beta} + \left(\frac{1}{I_t}\sum \mathbf{X}'_{it} d_i\right)\alpha + \frac{1}{I_t}\sum \mathbf{X}'_{it} K_i \\
\frac{1}{I_t}\sum d_i Y_{it} &= \left(\frac{1}{I_t}\sum d_i \mathbf{X}_{it}\right)\boldsymbol{\beta} + \left(\frac{1}{I_t}\sum d_i\right)\alpha + \frac{1}{I_t}\sum d_i K_i \qquad (3.20)\\
\frac{1}{I_t}\sum\left(\frac{\partial K'_i}{\partial \psi} Y_{it}\right) &= \left(\frac{1}{I_t}\sum \frac{\partial K'_i}{\partial \psi}\mathbf{X}_{it}\right)\boldsymbol{\beta} + \left(\frac{1}{I_t}\sum \frac{\partial K'_i}{\partial \psi} d_i\right)\alpha + \frac{1}{I_t}\sum \frac{\partial K'_i}{\partial \psi} K_i
\end{aligned}$$

Under the assumptions of Section 3.4, there exists a consistent root of these equations.

All of the moments needed to form equation system (3.20) are not directly available from sample (iii). But the required moments can be formed by pooling sample (i) and sample (iii) information in the following way.

When we discussed the IV estimator, we showed how to use sample (i) and (iii) data to estimate the following moments consistently:

$$\operatorname{plim}\frac{1}{I_t}\sum \mathbf{X}'_{it} Y_{it}, \quad \operatorname{plim}\frac{1}{I_t}\sum \mathbf{X}'_{it}\mathbf{X}_{it}, \quad \operatorname{plim}\frac{1}{I_t}\sum \mathbf{X}'_{it} d_i,$$

$$\operatorname{plim}\frac{1}{I_t} Y_{it} d_i, \quad \operatorname{plim}\frac{1}{I_t}\sum d_i = p$$

The term

$$\text{plim}\,\frac{1}{I_t}\sum \frac{\partial K_i'}{\partial \psi} Y_{it}$$

can be estimated in a simple way. In sample (iii), form

$$\frac{1}{I_{(\text{iii})}}\sum Y_{it}\frac{\partial E}{\partial \psi}[U_{it}|d_i = 0, \mathbf{Z}_i, \psi]$$

In sample (i), form

$$\frac{p}{I_{(\text{i})}}\sum Y_{it}\left[\frac{\partial E}{\partial \psi}(U_{it}|d = 1, \psi, \mathbf{Z}_i) - \frac{\partial E}{\partial \psi}(U_{it}|d = 0, \psi, \mathbf{Z}_i)\right]$$

The sum of the preceding two quantities converges in probability to

$$\begin{aligned}(1-p)E&\left[Y_{it}\frac{\partial E}{\partial \psi}(U_{it}|d_i = 0, \psi, \mathbf{Z}_i)|d_i = 0\right]\\ &+ pE\left[Y_{it}\frac{\partial E}{\partial \psi}(U_{it}|d_i = 1, \psi, \mathbf{Z}_i)d_i = 1\right]\\ &= E\left[Y_{it}\frac{\partial K_i}{\partial \psi}\right] = \text{plim}\,\frac{1}{I_t}\sum Y_{it}\frac{\partial K_i}{\partial \psi}\end{aligned}$$

A parallel argument produces consistent estimators of

$$\text{plim}\,\frac{1}{I_t}\sum \mathbf{X}_{it}'K_i, \qquad \text{plim}\,\frac{1}{I_t}\sum d_iK_i, \qquad \text{plim}\,\frac{1}{I_t}\sum \frac{\partial K_i'}{\partial \psi}\mathbf{X}_{it}, \qquad \text{and}$$

$$\text{plim}\,\frac{1}{I_t}\sum \frac{\partial K_i'}{\partial \psi} d_i$$

Finally, we need to estimate

$$\text{plim}\,\frac{1}{I_t}\sum \frac{\partial K_i'}{\partial \psi} K_i$$

To this end it is helpful to notice that

$$\begin{aligned}\frac{1}{I_t}\sum \frac{\partial K_i}{\partial \psi}K_i &= \sum \frac{d_i}{I_t}\frac{\partial E(U_{it}|d_i = 1, \mathbf{Z}_i, \psi)}{\partial \psi}E(U_{it}|d_i = 1, \mathbf{Z}_i, \psi)\\ &+ \sum \frac{(1-d_i)}{I_t}\frac{\partial E(U_{it}|d_i = 0, \mathbf{Z}_i, \psi)}{\partial \psi}E(U_{it}|d_i = 0, \mathbf{Z}_i, \psi)\end{aligned}$$

so

$$\text{plim}\,\frac{1}{I_t}\sum \frac{\partial K_i}{\partial \psi} K_i = pE\left[\frac{\partial E(U_{it}|d_i = 1, \mathbf{Z}_i, \psi)}{\partial \psi} E[U_{it}|d_i = 1, \mathbf{Z}_i, \psi]\,|\,d_i = 1\right]$$
$$+ (1-p)E\left[\frac{\partial E(U_{it}|d_i = 0, \mathbf{Z}_i, \psi)}{\partial \psi} E(U_{it}|d_i = 0, \mathbf{Z}_i, \psi)\,|\,d_i = 0\right]$$

From samples (i) and (iii), we can construct the following two moments:

$$\frac{p}{I_{(\text{i})}}\sum\left[\frac{\partial E(U_{it}|d_i = 1, \mathbf{Z}_i, \psi)}{\partial \psi} E(U_{it}|d_i = 1, \mathbf{Z}_i, \psi) - \frac{\partial E(U_{it}|d_i = 0, \mathbf{Z}_i, \psi)}{\partial \psi} E(U_{it}|d_i = 0, \mathbf{Z}_i, \psi)\right] \tag{3.21}$$

and

$$\frac{1}{I_{(\text{iii})}}\sum \frac{\partial E(U_{it}|d = 0, \mathbf{Z}_i, \psi)}{\partial \psi} E(U_{it}|d = 0, \mathbf{Z}_i, \psi) \tag{3.22}$$

Adding (3.21) and (3.22) together produces a consistent estimator of

$$\text{plim}\,\frac{1}{I_t}\sum \frac{\partial K_i}{\partial \psi} K_i$$

An alternative nonlinear regression estimator that is available when the functional form of $\Pr(d = 1|\mathbf{Z})$ is known up to a finite number of parameters pools samples (i) and (iii). Let $\tilde{d}_i = 1$ if a person is drawn from sample (i). Otherwise the observation is from sample (iii) ($\tilde{d}_i = 0$). In place of equation (3.4) we write

$$Y_{it} = \mathbf{X}_{it}\boldsymbol{\beta} + [\tilde{d}_i + (1-\tilde{d}_i)\Pr(d_i = 1|\mathbf{Z}_i, \mathbf{X}_{it})]\alpha + E(U_{it}|\mathbf{Z}_i, d_i = 1, \psi)\tilde{d}_i + \chi_{it} \tag{3.4$'$}$$

where

$$\chi_{it} = U_{it} + (d_i - \tilde{d}_i)\alpha - (1-\tilde{d}_i)\Pr(d_i = 1|\mathbf{Z}_i, \mathbf{X}_{it})\alpha - \tilde{d}_i E(U_{it}|\mathbf{Z}_i, \tilde{d}_i = 1, \psi)$$

Under the assumptions of Section 3.4, and assuming that U_{it} is mean independent of $\mathbf{Z}_i$, $E(\chi_{it}|\mathbf{X}_{it}, \mathbf{Z}_i, d_i) = 0$. To show this, note that

$$E(\chi_{it}|\tilde{d}_i = 1, \mathbf{X}_{it}, \mathbf{Z}_i) = E(U_{it}|\mathbf{Z}_i, \tilde{d}_i = 1, \psi) - E(U_{it}|\mathbf{Z}_i, d_i = 1, \psi) = 0$$

(Note that we use the fact that $\tilde{d}_i = 1 \Rightarrow d_i = 1$.) Note further that

$$\begin{aligned} E(\chi_{it}|\tilde{d}_i = 0, \mathbf{X}_{it}, \mathbf{Z}_i) &= E(U_{it}|\mathbf{Z}_i, \psi) + \Pr(d_i = 1|\mathbf{Z}_i, \mathbf{X}_{it})\alpha \\ &\quad - \Pr(d_i = 1|\mathbf{Z}_i, \mathbf{X}_{it})\alpha \\ &= E(U_{it}|\mathbf{Z}_i, \psi) = 0 \end{aligned}$$

Under the assumptions of Section 3.4 nonlinear regression estimators of the parameters of (3.4′) are consistent for $(\alpha, \boldsymbol{\beta}, \psi)$ provided that the number of observations in both samples (i) and (iii) becomes large.

3.8.3.C. Choice-based sampling plus contamination bias [samples (i), (ii), and (iii)]. Data from the three samples may be pooled directly and the parameters consistently estimated by maximum likelihood. The choice-based sample data should be appropriately weighted as described above. The data from the three samples can be combined to form the elements of the normal equations (3.20).

3.8.4. Selection on observables and random coefficient models (Sections 3.5 and 3.7). Since the estimators proposed in Sections 3.5 and 3.7 are control function estimators, the preceding discussion applies to those estimators with obvious modifications for the change in the nature of the control functions.

3.8.5. Distributional assumptions invoked about U_{it} (Section 3.6)

3.8.5.A. Choice-based sampling [samples (i) and (ii) pooled]. The method-of-moments estimator of Section 3.6 consistently estimates α in choice-based samples provided that the data are appropriately reweighted. The appropriate weights are identical to the weights proposed in our discussion of the instrumental variables estimator. The moments formed in sample (i) should be weighted by p/p^*. The moments formed in sample (ii) should be weighted by $(1 - p)/(1 - p^*)$. The weighted sum of the moments converges to the desired random sample moments.

3.8.5.B. Contamination bias [samples (i) and (iii)]. Provided that the population proportion of trainees is known or can be consistently estimated, a consistent method-of-moments estimator can be devised for contaminated samples. We demonstrate the modifications required in (3.7a). The required modification for (3.7b) is a straightforward application of the principles used to modify (3.7a).

We write out (3.7a) in full:

$$\frac{1}{I_t}\sum(Y_{it} - \mu_t)^3 - 3\hat{\alpha}\frac{1}{I_t}\sum(Y_{it} - \mu_t)^2(d_i - p)$$
$$+ 3\hat{\alpha}^2\frac{1}{I_t}\sum(Y_{it} - \mu_t)(d_i - p)^2 - \frac{1}{I_t}\sum(d_i - p)^3 \qquad (3.23)$$

The probability limit of the first term can be consistently estimated from sample (iii) data. The probability limit of the final term can be consistently estimated since p is known or is assumed to be consistently estimable.

The normalized sum in the second term consists of two components:

$$\frac{1}{I_t}\sum_{i=1}^{I_t}(Y_{it}-\mu_t)^2 d_i \quad \text{and} \quad \frac{p}{I_t}\sum_{i=1}^{I_t}(Y_{it}-\mu_t)^2$$

The probability limit of the second component can be consistently estimated from sample (iii) (given p). The probability limit of the first component can be estimated from sample (i) data using the estimate of μ_t obtained from sample (iii) data.

The sample (i) moment converges to

$$\operatorname*{plim}_{I_{(i)}\to\infty}\frac{1}{I_{(i)}}\sum_{i=1}^{I_{(i)}}(Y_{it}-\mu_t)^2 = E[(Y_{it}-\mu_t)^2 \mid d_i = 1]$$

Weighting the sample (iii) moment by p and combining with the second component produces an expression that converges to the probability limit of the normalized sum in the second term in (3.23). Thus the probability limit of the normalized sum in the second term can be consistently estimated. A parallel procedure can be used to consistently estimate the probability limit of the normalized sum in the third term of (3.23). By combining sample moments in this fashion we produce an estimating equation that converges to the same limit as the estimating equation formed in a random sample. A parallel procedure can be used for equation (3.7b). Thus it is possible to solve the problems raised by contamination bias.

If there are regressors in the earnings equations, a small modification in the procedure of Section 3.6 is required. Using an obvious and conventional matrix notation, we get

$$\hat{\beta}(\hat{\alpha}) = (\mathbf{X}'\mathbf{X})^{-1}\mathbf{X}'(\mathbf{Y}-\hat{\alpha}\mathbf{d}) = (\mathbf{X}'\mathbf{X})^{-1}\mathbf{X}'\mathbf{Y} - (\mathbf{X}'\mathbf{X})^{-1}(\mathbf{X}'\mathbf{d})\hat{\alpha} \qquad (3.24)$$

where $\mathbf{X}$ is the sample $\mathbf{X}_{it}$ vectors arrayed in a matrix, and $\mathbf{Y}$ and $\mathbf{d}$ are defined in a similar fashion. In a random sample

$$\operatorname{plim}\hat{\beta}(\hat{\alpha}) = \operatorname*{plim}_{I_t-\infty}\left(\frac{\mathbf{X}'\mathbf{X}}{I_t}\right)^{-1}\operatorname*{plim}_{I_t\to\infty}\left(\frac{\mathbf{X}'\mathbf{Y}}{I_t}\right) - \operatorname*{plim}_{I_t\to\infty}\left(\frac{\mathbf{X}'\mathbf{X}}{I_t}\right)^{-1}\left(\operatorname*{plim}_{I_t\to\infty}\frac{\mathbf{X}'\mathbf{d}}{I_t}\right)\hat{\alpha} \qquad (3.25)$$

The first term on the right-hand side of (3.24) can be formed in sample (iii) and converges to the first term on the right-hand side of (3.25). Clearly $(\mathbf{X}'\mathbf{X}/I_t)^{-1}$ formed in sample (iii) converges to $\operatorname{plim}(\mathbf{X}'\mathbf{X}/I_t)^{-1}$.

The mean of the $\mathbf{X}_{it}$ in sample (i), $\bar{\mathbf{X}}^{(i)}$, converges to

$$E(\mathbf{X}_{it}|d_i = 1)$$

Multiplying $\bar{\mathbf{X}}^{(i)}$ by p produces an expression that converges to plim $(\mathbf{X}'\mathbf{d}/I_t)$. Then

$$\hat{\hat{\beta}}(\hat{\alpha}) = [(\mathbf{X}'\mathbf{X})^{-1}\mathbf{X}'\mathbf{Y}]_{(\text{iii})} - [(\mathbf{X}'\mathbf{X})^{-1}]_{(\text{iii})}\hat{\alpha}\bar{\mathbf{X}}^{(\text{i})}p$$

where $[\quad]_{\text{iii}}$ denotes that the term inside the brackets is formed in sample (iii), converges to the probability limit of $\hat{\beta}(\hat{\alpha})$. Inserting $\hat{\hat{\beta}}(\hat{\alpha})$ in place of $\hat{\boldsymbol{\beta}}(\hat{\alpha})$ in the estimator proposed in Section 3.5 produces an estimator that is consistent for α.

3.8.5.C. Choice-based sampling plus contamination bias [samples (i), (ii), and (iii)]. Data from the three samples may be pooled directly. The choice-based sample data should be appropriately weighted as described above. The data from sample (iii) may be used to form moments which when pooled with their weighted sample (i) and (ii) data will improve the efficiency of the estimator.

3.9 *Summary of cross-section procedures*

A variety of cross-sectional estimators have been presented. All of these estimators with the exception of the estimator presented in Section 3.6 share the common feature that in order for α in (1.1) to be identified, a regressor must appear in decision rule (1.2). However, little more than this is required if the regressor is exogenous with respect to U_{it} (in the sense of Section 3.2). For the fixed coefficient model, the regressor can be used as a valid instrument for d_i provided that the technical conditions specified in Section 3.2 are satisfied. No specific distributional assumptions with respect to (U_{it}, V_i) are required, nor is it necessary to specify the functional form of the conditional mean of U_{it} given d_i and $\mathbf{Z}_i$.

The same cannot be said about the random coefficients model (Section 3.7). Unless $E(\varepsilon_i|d_i, \mathbf{Z}_i) = 0$ or some other known constant, it is necessary to specify the functional form of $E(\varepsilon_i d_i + U_{it}|d_i, \mathbf{Z}_i)$ up to a finite number of unknown parameters in order to identify $\bar{\alpha}$. One way to do this is to assume that the joint distribution of (U_{it}, V_i) is known up to a finite set of parameters. This observation reiterates a main point of this section – that the random coefficient model requires much stronger identifying assumptions than the fixed coefficient model.

A variety of alternative cross-section estimators for the fixed coefficient model are presented in Sections 3.3–3.6. These estimators differ in the amount of prior information assumed to be available to the analyst. The regression estimators of Section 3.3 require information on the functional form of the distribution of V_i. The control function estimators of Sections 3.4 and 3.5 require that the functional form of the conditional expectation of U_{it} and d_i, $\mathbf{Z}_i$, and $\mathbf{X}_{it}$ be known up to a finite number of parameters. In principle, no regressor variable in the decision rule needs to be exogenous with respect to V_i or U_{it} to identify α. However, in this case, identification of α is secured strictly as a consequence of assumed functional forms. Provided that one is willing to accept identification via functional form, all of the fixed coefficient training models of Section 3.2 can be consistently estimated irrespective of the exogeneity of regressors.

Our discussion in Section 3.6 demonstrates that if certain restrictions are imposed on the density of U_{it}, no regressor need appear in the enrollment rule in order to consistently estimate α.

The control function estimators are robust to choice-based sampling. Provided that the population proportion of trainees is known, the remaining estimators can be modified to produce consistent estimators of α in the presence of contamination bias and choice-based sampling.

If there is access to multiple cross sections, a separate α can be fit for each sample. It is not necessary to assume that α is constant over the trainee's life cycle. The cross-sectional estimator is thus seen to be robust to aging and decay effects in training.

4 Repeated cross-section methods for the case when the training identity of individuals is unknown

4.1 *Time homogeneity*

As already noted in Section 1, there are two types of repeated cross-section estimators: (1) those that do not require that the training status of individuals be known and (2) those that do. This section considers the first type of estimator. The second type is discussed in Section 5 along with the longitudinal estimators. That section demonstrates a major conclusion of this chapter: Virtually all longitudinal estimators can be implemented using repeated cross-section data provided that the training status is known for each person in each cross section.

We first present an explicit statement of the conditions required to consistently estimate α that are implicitly presented in Section 1. Assumption (A-1) is assumed to characterize the data in each cross section. In addition it is further assumed that:

(A-14) (a) The earnings function is (1.3) (so there are no $\mathbf{X}_{it}$ variables in the earnings function and the model is of the fixed coefficient type).
(b) The environment is time-homogeneous (so $\beta_t = \beta_{t'}$ for all t, t').

(c) Condition (A-2) is satisfied.
(d) There is at least one preprogram cross section t' and one postprogram cross section t, $t > k > t'$.[22]
(e) The population proportion of trainees is known or can be consistently estimated in each cross section, and for each $t, p_t > 0$.

Conspicuously absent from this list is any statement about the enrollment rule. No regressor is required in enrollment rule (1.2), and any of the fixed coefficient enrollment rules of Section 2 can generate program participation. The repeated cross-section estimator is thus very robust to alternative specifications of the enrollment rule. In addition, it is robust to mean zero measurement error in the variables.

4.2 *Relaxing the time homogeneity assumption*

As already noted in Section 1, it is possible to relax assumption (A-14b) and still preserve consistency of the repeated cross-section estimator $\hat{\alpha}_{RC}$. It is useful to distinguish two cases. The first case assumes access to a cohort of persons all of whom have one opportunity to train in period k. The second case assumes access to multiple-cohort data in which individuals of different cohorts have identical period effects.

4.2.1 Single-cohort data. Provided that the available repeated cross-section data satisfy (A-14) except for (A-14b), α is identified provided that the environment is sufficiently regular. A more precise definition of sufficient regularity is as follows:

(D-3) Assume access to L temporally distinct cross sections of earnings data on a cohort of persons all of whom have access to training in period k. None of the cross sections is for period k. Now β_t in (1.3) is generated by a sufficiently regular environment if

$$\beta_t = g(t, \gamma)$$

where $g(t, \gamma)$ is a function of at most $L - 1$ independent parameters, arrayed in vector γ, and unique solutions for α and $g(t, \gamma)$ can be obtained from the probability limits of the L cross-section mean earnings.

More formally, if we array the L values of mean earnings in a $L \times 1$ vector $\bar{\mathbf{Y}}$, the environment is sufficiently regular if the equation system

$$\operatorname*{plim}_{I \to \infty} \bar{\mathbf{Y}} = [g(\gamma)] + (\mathbf{p})\alpha$$

has a unique solution, where γ is a vector of parameters in the g function, and where the tth element of $[g(\gamma)]$ is the value of $g(t, \gamma)$ for the appropriate year and the tth element of $\mathbf{p}$ is p_t for the appropriate year where $p_t = 0$, $t < k$. Here I denotes sample size.

From the L means it is possible to estimate consistently the $\beta_t + p_t\alpha$ for $t > k$ and β_t for $t < k$, where by virtue of assumption (A-14e) the p_t are assumed known. From the definition of sufficient regularity, it is possible to solve for $\mathbf{g}(t, \gamma)$ and hence α from the L means. A specimen $\mathbf{g}(t, \gamma)$ function is

$$\mathbf{g}(t, \gamma) = \gamma_0 + \gamma_1 t + \cdots + \gamma_{L-2} t^{L-2} \tag{4.1}$$

From L temporally distinct cross sections from a sufficiently regular environment it is possible to consistently estimate the $L - 1$ γ parameters and α provided that the number of observations in each cross section becomes large and there is at least one preprogram cross section.

If the effect of training differs across periods, it is still possible to identify α_t provided that the environment is more regular than is implied in (D-3). Define

$$\alpha_t = h(t), \qquad t > k$$

Then it is sometimes possible to identify $h(t)$ and $\mathbf{g}(t, \gamma)$ from L temporally distinct cross sections. For example, suppose

$$h(t) = \phi_0(\phi_1)^{t-k} \quad \text{for} \quad t > k \quad \text{and} \quad \mathbf{g}(t, \gamma) = \gamma_0 + \gamma_1 t$$

and $L = 4$. Then $h(t)$ and $\mathbf{g}(t, \gamma)$ are both identified, so long as there is at least one preprogram cross section or else $p_{t'} \neq p_t$. On the other hand, if $p_t = p_{t'}$, for all t, $t' > k$ and

$$h(t) = \phi_0 + \phi_1 t \quad \text{and} \quad \mathbf{g}(t, \gamma) = \gamma_0 + \gamma_1 t$$

it is not possible to identify $h(t)$ unless the analyst has two or more years of preprogram data.

4.2.2. Multiple-cohort data. We next assume access to samples of two or more cohorts satisfying (A-14) [except for (b)] that are spaced at least two periods apart. In place of (A-14b) we assume the following:

(A-14b′) All cohorts experience a common period effect.

With this assumption, it is possible to dispense with sufficient regularity assumption (D-3) altogether and still secure consistent estimators of α from repeated cross-section data. If each cohort experiences a unique period effect, there is no gain in identifying α from having access to multiple-cohort data.

To show how (A-14b′) aids in securing identification, it is instructive to consider Table 1. There we display the population mean earnings histories of three adjacent cohorts. To simplify the argument we assume that $p_t = p_{t'}$ for all t, t' for each cohort and that α_t is identical in all

Table 1. *Mean earnings history of three adjacent cohorts assuming that the training effect is common across time periods*

	Earnings in year before training	Earnings in first year after training	Earnings in second year after training
Cohort 1	β_{t^*-1}	$p^{(1)}\alpha + \beta_{t^*+1}$	$p^{(1)}\alpha + \beta_{t^*+2}$
Cohort 2	β_{t^*}	$p^{(2)}\alpha + \beta_{t^*+2}$	$p^{(2)}\alpha + \beta_{t^*+3}$
Cohort 3	β_{t^*+1}	$p^{(3)}\alpha + \beta_{t^*+3}$	$p^{(3)}\alpha + \beta_{t^*+4}$

Table 2. *Mean earnings history of three adjacent cohorts assuming that the training effect differs across time periods*

	Earnings in year before training	Earnings in first year after training	Earnings in second year after training
Cohort 1	β_{t^*-1}	$\beta_{t^*+1} + p^{(1)}\alpha_1$	$\beta_{t^*+2} + p^{(1)}\alpha_2$
Cohort 2	β_{t^*}	$\beta_{t^*+2} + p^{(2)}\alpha_1$	$\beta_{t^*+3} + p^{(2)}\alpha_2$
Cohort 3	β_{t^*+1}	$\beta_{t^*+3} + p^{(3)}\alpha_1$	$\beta_{t^*+4} + p^{(3)}\alpha_2$

periods. Now $p^{(i)}$ is the proportion of cohort i that takes training. We establish the convention that the first cohort takes its training in period t^*.

From the population mean earnings of cohort 3 in the last preprogram year (β_{t^*+1}) and the population mean of the first postprogram year earnings of cohort 1 [$p^{(1)}\alpha + \beta_{t^*+1}$], it is possible to solve for α since $p^{(1)}$ (>0) is assumed to be known. This estimator is consistent for α if the number of observations in each cross section goes to infinity.

Access to multiple-cohort data allows the analyst to estimate separate training effects for each year of posttraining earnings. Assume that each cohort experiences the same earnings impact α_j when it is j periods removed from training. Then population mean earnings streams of cohorts before and after training are as displayed in Table 2. From the mean preprogram earnings of cohort 3 and the mean first year postprogram earnings of cohort 1 it is possible to consistently estimate α_1. [Recall $p^{(1)}$ is known.] Given α_1, use the first year postprogram earnings of cohort 2 to consistently estimate β_{t^*+2} and use the second year postprogram earnings of cohort 1 to consistently estimate α_2. A second consistent estimator of α_2 uses α_1 in the first year postprogram earnings of cohort 3 to estimate

β_{t^*+3} and then uses this information coupled with the second year post-program earnings of cohort 2 to estimate α_2. The fact that α_1 and α_2 are overidentified suggests that it is possible to permit limited interactions among the α_j and the period effects.

4.3 *Allowing for regressors*

The methods described above can be modified to apply to data in which (1.1) rather than (1.3) characterizes the earnings function so that $\mathbf{X}_{it}$ appears in the earnings function. To see how this can be done, we rewrite equation (1.1) to isolate β_t from the other components of $\boldsymbol{\beta}$:

$$\begin{aligned} Y_{it} &= \beta_t + \mathbf{X}_{it}\boldsymbol{\pi} + d_i\alpha + U_{it}, & t > k \\ Y_{it} &= \beta_t + \mathbf{X}_{it}\boldsymbol{\pi} + U_{it}, & t \leq k \end{aligned} \tag{4.2}$$

Two methods can be used to extend the preceding analysis to account for regressors.

4.3.1. Method I: regression on preprogram earnings. Provide that (A-6) is satisfied [replacing $\boldsymbol{\beta}$ with $(\beta_t, \boldsymbol{\pi})$ in those conditions] for one year of preprogram data, it is possible to consistently estimate $\boldsymbol{\pi}$ and adjust the means of postprogram earnings appropriately (i.e., transform Y_{it} to $Y_{it} - \mathbf{X}_{it}\boldsymbol{\pi}$). The adjusted means can be used to consistently estimate the population means used above. This strategy fails if there are elements of $\mathbf{X}_{it}$ that become nonconstant only after period k.

4.3.2. Method II: use of sufficiently long postprogram repeated cross sections. In place of method I or as a supplement, from the means of earnings of successive cross sections it is possible to solve out for $\boldsymbol{\pi}$ using standard method-of-moments procedures. (If the mean of the $\mathbf{X}_{it}$, $\bar{\mathbf{X}}_t$ does not change over time, then $\bar{\mathbf{X}}_t\boldsymbol{\pi}$ is absorbed into β_t.) This method is just a variant of the procedure already proposed for sufficiently regular environments. Given $\hat{\boldsymbol{\pi}}$ so obtained it is possible to adjust the population mean earnings in the manner described in method I. Note that method II is robust to mean zero measurement error in $\mathbf{X}_{it}$ but that method I is not.

4.4 *Robustness to contamination bias and other measurement error*

Suppose the analyst has access to sample (iii) data as described in Section 3.8–random samples of the population in which the training status of persons is not known. Given (A-13b) so that the population proportion of trainees in each cohort is known, such contaminated samples can be used in all of the procedures proposed in Section 4. In none of these procedures is it necessary to know the training status of individuals. In addition, all of the repeated cross-section estimators based on sample means are robust to mean zero measurement error in *all* of the variables of the model.

4.5 *Robustness to choice-based sampling*

As noted in Section 1, unless (A-2) is satisfied, the repeated cross-section estimator that does not exploit knowledge of the training status of individuals is not robust to choice-based sampling. However, it is sometimes possible to satisfy (A-2) even in the presence of choice-based sampling.

Suppose, for example, that (A-3) strengthened to include the appropriate $\mathbf{X}_{it}$ in the conditioning set characterizes the earnings equation and that $p_t^* = p_{t'}^*$ in the notation of condition (A-2) (also strengthened to include the exogenous variables). Then the strengthened form of (A-2) is satisfied and $\hat{\alpha}_{RC}$ can be used to produce a consistent estimator of α provided one of the sets of conditions about the environment that have been stated above is satisfied for a model written in differences. For example, a permanent–transitory error structure for the unobservable in earnings equation (1.9) coupled with an independence assumption between S_i in decision rule (2.4) and ε_{it} in (1.9) produces a model that satisfies the strengthened form of (A-3). Assuming the sampling rule is such that trainees have the same chance of being observed in t and t', strengthened condition (A-2) is satisfied, and it is possible to consistently estimate α from differences in means between preprogram and postprogram earnings data even if the available samples are choice-based samples provided that the sample proportion of trainees is known for each sample.

This example is special. In general, repeated cross-section estimators do not consistently estimate α in choice-based samples even if $\beta_t = \beta_{t'}$. If the training status of persons were known, it would be possible to reweight the data in the manner described in Section 3.8.

5 Longitudinal and repeated cross-section estimators – methods that exploit information about the training status of individuals

5.1 *Introduction*

In this section of the chapter we present longitudinal methods for consistently estimating α. A major conclusion established here is that many longitudinal estimators have repeated cross-section counterparts provided that the training status of individuals is known.

All of the estimators presented in this section share the following features: (1) They are robust to general forms of time inhomogeneity of the environment provided that there are data on the earnings of both trainees and nontrainees. (2) They require an explicit characterization of the time series process of the unobservables in the earnings equation. (3) Except for one estimator, the proposed estimators require specification of an enrollment rule and the stochastic relationship of the observables and unobservables in the enrollment rule with the observables and unobservables in the earnings equation. (4) No regressor need appear in the enrollment rule (1.2). (5) Many of the estimators are control function estimators in the sense of (D-2). All of these estimators are robust to choice-based sampling. All of the estimators proposed here can be modified, when necessary, to control for choice-based sampling and contamination bias. In addition to these features, some of the estimators do not require data on preprogram earnings.

The plan of this section is as follows. Starting with the conventional fixed effect estimator, we present a variety of assumptions about the relationship between the unobservables in the earnings equation and the enrollment dummy d_i. These assumption sets are presented in increasing level of generality as far as this is possible (some sets of assumptions do not properly contain nor are contained in other sets). We present the estimators in this fashion because the "fixed effect" or "first-difference" estimator is also the most widely used estimator. For each assumption set we first assume access to simple random or stratified samples and give the longitudinal estimator. The plausibility of the identifying assumptions is evaluated in the light of the decision rules given in Section 2. We then present the repeated cross-section estimator where possible. Finally we discuss robustness to choice-based sampling and contamination bias.

5.2 *First-difference or fixed effect methods*

The first-difference (or fixed effect) method was developed by Mundlak (1961, 1978) and refined by Chamberlain (1982). It is based on the following assumptions:

(A-15) (a) (A-6) holds, stated in terms of differences in variables rather than levels.
(b) $E(U_{it} - U_{it'} | d, \mathbf{X}_{it} - \mathbf{X}_{it'}) = 0$ for all $t, t', t > k > t'$.
(c) There is access to at least one year of preprogram and postprogram earnings.

Notice that regressors are not required to appear in the enrollment equation (1.2). As a consequence of (A-15) we may write the difference regression as

$$E(Y_{it} - Y_{it'} | \mathbf{X}_{it} - \mathbf{X}_{it'}, d_i) = (\mathbf{X}_{it} - \mathbf{X}_{it'})\boldsymbol{\beta} + d_i\alpha, \qquad t > k > t'$$

Here $\boldsymbol{\beta}$ is defined to include the coefficients of year dummies. Regressing the difference between postprogram earnings in any year and earnings in any preprogram year on the change in regressors between those years and a dummy variable for training status produces a consistent estimator for α.

5.2.1. Economic models producing (A-15b). The statistical logic justifying this procedure is impeccable. We question the plausibility of (A-15) in the light of the prototypical enrollment rules presented in Section 2.

Some decision rules and error processes for earnings justify (A-15). For example, consider a certainty environment in which α is a fixed coefficient and error structure (1.9) characterizes the earnings residual so that

$$U_{it} = \phi_i + \varepsilon_{it} \tag{5.1}$$

where ε_{it} is a mean zero finite variance random variable independent of all other values of $\varepsilon_{it'}$, for all i, t, and t', and is distributed independently of ϕ_i, a mean zero finite variance person-specific time-invariant random variable. Assuming that S_i in decision rule (2.4) and $\mathbf{X}_{ij}$ are distributed independently of all ε_{it} for all i and j except possibly for ε_{ik}, (A-15b) is satisfied.

Assumption (A-15b) may also be satisfied in an environment of uncertainty. Suppose in error structure (5.1) that

$$E_{k-1}(\varepsilon_{ik}) = 0$$

but

$$E_{k-1}(\phi_i) = \phi_i$$

so that agents cannot forecast innovations in their earnings but they know their own permanent component. Provided that S_i and $\mathbf{X}_{it}$ are distributed independently of all ε_{it} except possibly for ε_{ik}, this model also produces (A-15b).

Another example of a model that satisfies (A-15b) is a random coefficient model (1.14) in an environment of perfect certainty in which no regressor appears in decision rule (1.2) so that only α^* is estimable. Provided that the error structure for U_{it} is given by (5.1) and S_i in (2.6) and ε_i are distributed independently of ε_{it} (except possibly for ε_{ik}) and the $\mathbf{X}_{ij}$ are distributed independently of ε_{it} for all j and t, (A-15b) is satisfied.[23]

A final example of a model that satisfies (A-15b) is a random coefficient model in which ε_i is unknown at the time enrollment decisions are made with mean zero, (5.1) characterizes the error process for earnings, and S_i in (2.6) and $\mathbf{X}_{ij}$ are distributed independently of ε_{it} for all t and j (except for ε_{ik}). In this case $\bar{\alpha}$ is identifiable from the first-difference estimator.

However, these examples are rather special. It is very easy to produce plausible models that do not satisfy (A-15b). For example, even if (5.1) characterizes U_{it}, if S_i in (2.4) or (2.6) does not have the same joint (bivariate) distribution with respect to all ε_{it}, except for ε_{ik}, (A-15b) is violated.

Even if S_i in (2.2) is distributed independently of U_{it} for all t, it is still not the case that (A-15b) is satisfied in a general model. For example, assume $\mathbf{X}_{ij}$ is distributed independently of all U_{it} for all t and j and let

$$U_{it} = \rho U_{i,t-1} + \varepsilon_{it} \tag{5.2}$$

where ε_{it} is a mean zero, i.i.d. random variable and $|\rho| < 1$.[24] If $\rho \neq 0$ and perfect-foresight decision rule (2.4) characterizes enrollment, (A-15b) is not satisfied because, for $t > k > t'$,

$$\begin{aligned} E(U_{it} | d_i = 1) &= E\left(U_{it} \middle| U_{ik} + \mathbf{X}_{ik}\boldsymbol{\beta} - \frac{\alpha}{r} < S_i \right) \\ &= \rho^{t-k} E(U_{ik} | d_i = 1) \\ &\neq E(U_{it'} | d_i = 1) = E\left(U_{it'} \middle| U_{ik} + \mathbf{X}_{ik}\boldsymbol{\beta} - \frac{\alpha}{r} < S_i \right) \end{aligned}$$

unless the conditional expectations are linear (in U_{it}) for all t and $k - t' = t - k$. In that case,

$$E(U_{it'} | d_i = 1) = \rho^{k-t'} E(U_{ik} | d_i = 1)$$

and so $E(U_{it} - U_{it'} | d_i = 1) = 0$ only for t', t such that $k - t' = t - k$. Thus (A-15b) is not satisfied for all $t > k > t'$.

With more general specifications of U_{it} and the stochastic dependence between S_i and U_{it}, (A-15b) will not be satisfied.[25]

5.2.2. The repeated cross-section version. Longitudinal data are not required to implement the fixed effect estimator. However, as noted in Section 1, the training status of individuals sampled in a preprogram year is more likely to be known in longitudinal data than in repeated cross-section data. The repeated cross-section version of the estimator was discussed in Section 1.3. Required modifications when regressors appear in earnings function (1.1) are presented in Section 4.3. If the random sampling assumption of that section is dropped and there is a choice-based sample, the regression required to implement the required modifications must be weighted as discussed in Section 3.8. Note that the repeated cross-section estimator based on means is robust to mean zero measurement error in all of the variables.

5.2.3. Robustness to choice-based sampling and contamination bias. Since (A-15b) is satisfied, the fixed effect estimator is robust to choice-based sampling when the data are transformed to differences. Samples (i) and (ii) defined in Section 3.8 may be combined freely without affecting the consistency of the estimator.

Note further that if conditions (A-15) are satisfied, it is possible to consistently estimate α using only trainee data [sample (i)] provided that (a) the environment is time-homogeneous or (b) there is sufficient regularity in the environment (in the sense of Section 4.2) or (c) there is access to multiple-cohort data. Either longitudinal or repeated cross-section methods can be used. The benefit of having data on nontrainees is that they allow the analyst to control for more general forms of time inhomogeneity if (b) is not satisfied and multiple-cohort data are not available. If, in addition to the sample (i) data on trainee earnings, the analyst has access to a contaminated control sample (iii), it is unnecessary to use these data if the sample (i) data satisfy one of the three conditions listed above.

If the sample (i) data do not satisfy these conditions and the model contains no regressor, it is still possible to consistently estimate $\beta_t - \beta_{t'} + \alpha$, $t > k > t'$ by fitting a difference regression on sample (i). The probability limit of the mean of sample (iii) differences converges to

$$\text{plim}(\bar{Y}_t^{(\text{iii})} - \bar{Y}_{t'}^{(\text{iii})}) = \beta_t - \beta_{t'} + p\alpha.$$

Given knowledge of p, it is thus possible to combine these two pieces of information to consistently estimate α using single-cohort data without invoking any assumption about time homogeneity of the environment. These procedures can be modified in a straightforward way if there are regressors in equation (1.1).[26]

5.2.4. An unconditional version. In place of (A-15b) it is possible to state weaker conditions and still secure a consistent first-difference estimator for α:

(A-15b′) (i) $E[(\mathbf{X}_{it} - \mathbf{X}_{it'})'(U_{it} - U_{it'})] = 0, \quad t > k > t'.$
(ii) $E[d_i(U_{it} - U_{it'})] = 0, \quad t > k > t'.$

In stating these conditions, it is to be understood that time-invariant variables are deleted from the model. Under these conditions, the first-difference estimator consistently estimates α. All of the models that rationalize (A-15b) also rationalize (A-15b′).

5.3 *More general first-difference methods*

In place of (A-15) we assume the following:

(A-16) (a) (A-6) holds, modified to allow $\mathbf{Z}_i$, the regressor in the enrollment rule, to be a constant, and written in terms of differences of variables rather than levels.
(b) $E(U_{it} - U_{it'} | d_i, \mathbf{X}_{it} - \mathbf{X}_{it'}) = 0$ for *some* t and t' such that $t > k > t'$.
(c) There is access to at least one year of preprogram and postprogram earnings.

The only new idea embodied in this assumption is that in place of (A-15b), in which $E(U_{it} - U_{it'} | d_i, \mathbf{X}_{it} - \mathbf{X}_{it'}) = 0$ for all $t > k > t'$, the conditional expectation need be zero only for some $t > k > t'$. For the appropriate values of t and t',

$$E(Y_{it} - Y_{it'} | \mathbf{X}_{it} - \mathbf{X}_{it'}, d_i) = (\mathbf{X}_{it} - \mathbf{X}_{it'})\boldsymbol{\beta} + d_i \alpha$$

so that least squares applied to the differenced data consistently estimates α.

An alternative unconditional version of these conditions, analogous to (A-15b′), writes

(A-16b′) (i) $E[(\mathbf{X}_{it} - \mathbf{X}_{it'})'(U_{it} - U_{it'})] = 0$ for some $t > k > t'$.
(ii) $E[d_i(U_{it} - U_{it'})] = 0$ for some $t > k > t'$.

Under these conditions, the generalized first-difference regression estimator consistently estimates α.

5.3.1. Examples of economic models producing (A-16b). We present three examples of models that satisfy (A-16b) but not (A-15b).

5.3.1.A. A multiple-selection-rules model. Suppose that the error structure of the earnings equation is given by (5.1) and that S_i and $\mathbf{X}_{ij}$ are distributed independently of U_{it} for all t and j. Assume an environment of perfect certainty and a fixed coefficient model so that α is common to all individuals.

Individuals use enrollment rule (2.2) to determine whether they would like to enroll in training. Administrators let a person enroll only if his income in period $k - 1$ is less than Y_c. Using the index function notation of Section 2.5,

$$I_{1i} = \frac{\alpha}{r} + S_i - Y_{ik}$$

$$I_{2i} = Y_c \qquad - Y_{i,k-1}$$

so that

$$d_i = 1 \quad \text{if and only if} \quad I_{1i} > 0 \quad \text{and} \quad I_{2i} > 0$$
$$E(U_{it} - U_{it'} | d_i, \mathbf{X}_{it} - \mathbf{X}_{it'}) = 0$$

for $t > k$ and $t' < k - 1$. Thus (A-16b) is satisfied if $t > k$ and $t' < k - 1$ but (A-15b) is not satisfied for $t > k$ and $t' = k - 1$. Clearly (A-16b′) is also satisfied.

5.3.1.B. Linearity of the regression. Suppose that

(i) U_{it} is covariance stationary [so $E(U_{it}U_{i,t-j}) = E(U_{it'}U_{i,t'-j})$ for all t, t', $j \geq 0$].
(ii) U_{it} has a linear regression on U_{ik} for all t [$E(U_{it}|U_{ik}) = \beta_{tk}U_{ik}$].[27]
(iii) The U_{it} are mutually independent of $(\mathbf{X}_{it}, S_i)$ for all t.
(iv) α is common to all individuals (so the model is of a fixed coefficient form).
(v) The environment is one of perfect foresight, so decision rule (2.2) determines participation.

Under these conditions assumption (A-16b′) characterizes the data.

To see this note that (i) and (ii) imply that there exists δ such that

$$U_{it} = U_{i,k+j} = \delta U_{ik} + \omega_{it}, \qquad j > 0$$

$$U_{it'} = U_{i,k-j} = \delta U_{ik} + \omega_{it'}, \qquad j > 0$$

and

$$E(\omega_{it} | U_{ik}) = E(\omega_{it'} | U_{ik}) = 0$$

Note that

$$E(U_{it} | d_i = 1) = \delta E(U_{ik} | d_i = 1) + E(\omega_{it} | d_i = 1)$$

But

$$E(\omega_{it} | d_i = 1) = 0$$

since $E(\omega_{it}) = 0$ and because (iii) ensures that the mean of ω_{it} does not depend on $\mathbf{X}_{ik}$ and S_i.[28]

Similarly,

$$E(\omega_{it'} | d_i = 1) = 0$$

and thus (A-16b′) holds.

It is straightforward to show that if, in addition, the $\mathbf{X}_{it}$ are mutually independent of all t and for each i and are independent of S_i for all t, (A-16b) holds.

5.3.1.C. Pivotal symmetry. Conditions (i)–(ii) in the previous section are not required to justify (A-16b) or (A-16b′). Pivotal symmetry also implies these conditions.

(D-4) A collection of continuous random variables $\{U_{it}\}_{t=-\infty}^{\infty}$ is pivotally symmetric with respect to U_{ik} if for all values of $(U_{i,k+j}, U_{ik}, U_{i,k-j})$, $f_j(U_{i,k+j}, U_{ik}) = f_j(U_{i,k-j}, U_{ik})$ for all j.

Replacing (i) and (ii) of the previous subsection with a pivotal symmetry assumption and retaining the rest of the assumptions produces a model that satisfies (A-16b′). If, in addition, it is assumed that the $\mathbf{X}_{it}$ are i.i.d. for all t and for each i, (A-16b) is satisfied. Condition (iii) is stronger than is required to generate (A-16b′). Provided that $(\mathbf{X}_{ik}, S_i)$ have the same joint distribution with respect to $U_{i,k+j}$ as with respect to $U_{i,k-j}$, (A-16b) and (A-16b′) are satisfied. Independence is not required.

Because the more general first-difference method is merely a variant of the first-difference method, the discussion of repeated cross-section versions and robustness to contamination bias and choice-based sampling presented in Section 5.2 applies to the methods discussed in Section 5.3. For the sake of brevity we do not repeat it here.

5.4 *Control function estimators*

In this subsection we propose three longitudinal control function estimators. The first two estimators satisfy the following conditions:

(A-17) (a) There exists a control function K_{it} that satisfies definition (D-2).
(b) Including the control function among the regressors $(\mathbf{X}_{it})$ in (1.1), (A-6) is satisfied.

Under these conditions the control function estimator is consistent for α.

The third estimator replaces (A-17a) with the following:

(A-17a′) There exists a control function that satisfies definition (D-1).

5.4.1. U_{it} follows a generalized first-order autoregressive process.

We suppose that

(i) U_{it} is a first-order autoregression $U_{it} = \rho U_{i,t-1} + v_{it}$, where $E(v_{it}) = 0$, $\operatorname{Var}(v_{it}) < \infty$ and the v_{it} are mutually independently (not necessarily identically) distributed random variables with $\rho \neq 1$.

(ii) Enrollment is determined by perfect-foresight rule (2.4), and α is common to all individuals.

(iii) The v_{ij}, $t' < j \leq t$, are distributed independently of S_i and $\mathbf{X}_{ik}$ in (2.4).

Heckman and Wolpin (1976) invoke these assumptions in their analysis of affirmative action programs.

Then

$$K_{it} = \rho^{t-t'} U_{it'}, \qquad t > t' > k, \qquad \rho \neq 1$$

is a valid control function which satisfies (A-17). The proof is by direct substitution using (1.1) to solve for $U_{it'}$ to obtain

$$Y_{it} = [\mathbf{X}_{it} - (\mathbf{X}_{it'}\rho^{t-t'})]\boldsymbol{\beta} + (1 - \rho^{t-t'})d_i\alpha + \rho^{t-t'}Y_{it'} + \left\{ \sum_{j=0}^{t-(t'+1)} \rho^j v_{i,t-j} \right\} \tag{5.3}$$

As a consequence of conditions (i)–(iii),

$$E(Y_{it}|\mathbf{X}_{it}, \mathbf{X}_{it'}, d_i, Y_{it'}) = [\mathbf{X}_{it} - (\mathbf{X}'_{it}\rho^{t-t'})]\boldsymbol{\beta} + (1 - \rho^{t-t'})d_i\alpha + \rho^{t-t'}Y_{it'} \tag{5.4}$$

so that (nonlinear) least squares applied to (5.3) consistently estimates α as the number of observations becomes large. (The appropriate nonlinear regression imposes the implied cross-coefficient restrictions.)

Notice that (iii) is overly strong. The v_{ij}, $t' < j < t$, need not be distributed independently of S_i and $\mathbf{X}_{ik}$ in (2.4). They need only satisfy the condition that (5.4) is the conditional expectation of (5.3) [so that $E(\sum_{j=0}^{t-(t'+1)} \rho^j v_{i,t-j}|\mathbf{X}_{it}, \mathbf{X}_{it'}, d_i, Y_{it'}) = 0$]. Note further that (ii) is not required either. If agents are uncertain about future v_{it} at the time they make their enrollment decision, (ii) may be replaced with decision rule (2.7). In this case $K_{it} = \rho^{t-t'}U_{it'}$ is a valid control function for $t > t' > k$ or $t > k$, $t' = k - 1$.

5.4.2. U_{it} follows a higher-order autoregression. The estimator considered in Section 5.4.1 may be extended to the case where U_{it} follows a higher-order autoregression. Assume in addition to (A-17) that

(i) $U_{it} = \sum_{j=1}^{N} \rho_j U_{i,t-j} + v_{it}$, where $E(v_{it}) = 0$, $\mathrm{Var}(v_{it}) < \infty$, and the v_{it} are mutually independently (not necessarily identically) distributed and $\sum_{j=1}^{N} \rho_j \neq 1$.

(ii) Enrollment is determined by perfect-foresight rule (2.4) and α is common to all individuals.

(iii) v_{it} is distributed independently of S_i and $\mathbf{X}_{ik}$ in (2.4), for $t > k$.

(iv) $t \geq k + N + 1$.

Then

$$K_{it} = \rho_1(Y_{i,t-1} - \mathbf{X}_{i,t-1}\boldsymbol{\beta} - d_i\alpha) + \cdots + \rho_N(Y_{i,t-N} - \mathbf{X}_{i,t-N}\boldsymbol{\beta} - d_i\alpha)$$

is a control function in the sense of (D-2) because

$$E(v_{it}d_i) = 0$$

The appropriate estimating equation is

$$Y_{it} = \left(\mathbf{X}_{it} - \sum_{j=1}^{N} \rho_j \mathbf{X}_{i,t-j}\right)\boldsymbol{\beta} + \sum_{j=1}^{N} \rho_j Y_{i,t-j} + \left(1 - \sum_{j=1}^{N} \rho_j\right) d_i\alpha + v_{it} \tag{5.5}$$

Nonlinear least squares applied to (5.5) consistently estimates $\rho_1, \ldots, \rho_N$, $\boldsymbol{\beta}$, and α as the number of persons in the longitudinal sample becomes large.

Assumption (iii) is overly strong. All that is required is that $E(v_{it} | \mathbf{X}_{it}, \mathbf{X}_{i,t-1}, \ldots, d_i, Y_{it-1}, \ldots, Y_{i,t-N}) = 0$. The estimator can be adapted to an uncertain environment using an argument directly analogous to that presented for the first-order autogressive model.

5.4.3. An unrestricted process for U_{it} when agents do not know future innovations in their earnings. The estimator proposed in this subsection assumes that agents cannot perfectly predict future earnings. More specifically, for an agent whose relevant earnings history begins N periods before period k, we assume that

(i) $E_{k-1}(U_{ik}) = E(U_{ik} | U_{i,k-1}, \ldots, U_{i,k-N})$

that is, that predictions of future U_{it} are made solely on the basis of previous values of U_{it}. Past values of the exogenous variables are assumed to have no predictive value for U_{ik}.

In addition, we assume that:

(ii) The relevant earnings history goes back N periods before period k.
(iii) The enrollment decision is characterized by rule (2.7).
(iv) S_i and $\mathbf{X}_{ik}$ are known as of period $k-1$ when the enrollment decision is being made.
(v) $\mathbf{X}_{it}$ is distributed independently of U_{ij} for all t and j.
(vi) S_i is distributed independently of U_{ij} for all j.

Defining

$$\boldsymbol{\psi}_i = (Y_{i,k-1} - \mathbf{X}_{i,k-1}\boldsymbol{\beta}, \ldots, Y_{i,k-N} - \mathbf{X}_{i,k-N}\boldsymbol{\beta})$$

and

$$G(\boldsymbol{\psi}_i) = E(d_i | \boldsymbol{\psi}_i)$$

then assuming conditions (i)–(v) above,

$$K_{it} = c(G(\boldsymbol{\psi}_i) - p)$$

is a valid control function in the sense of definition (D-1), where

$$p = E(d_i)$$

and

$$c = \frac{E[U_{it}(G(\boldsymbol{\psi}_i) - p)]}{E[G(\boldsymbol{\psi}_i) - p]^2} \tag{5.6}$$

To establish that $c(G(\psi_i) - p)$ is a valid control function, it is helpful to write (1.1) in the following way:

$$Y_{it} = \mathbf{X}_{it}\boldsymbol{\beta} + d_i\alpha + c(G(\psi_i) - p) + [U_{it} - c(G(\psi_i) - p)] \tag{5.7}$$

In the transformed equation

$$E[\mathbf{X}'_{it}(U_{it} - c(G(\psi_i) - p))] = 0$$

by assumption (v). The transformed residual is uncorrelated with $c(G(\psi_i) - p)$ from the definition of c.

Thus it remains to show that

$$E[d_i(U_{it} - c(G(\psi_i) - p))] = 0 \tag{5.8}$$

Before proving this it is helpful to notice that as a consequence of (i), (v), and (vi),[29]

$$\begin{aligned} &E(d_i | U_{it}, U_{i,t-1}, \ldots, U_{i,k-1}, \ldots, U_{i,k-N}) \\ &\quad = E(d_i | U_{i,k-1}, \ldots, U_{i,k-N}), \qquad t > k \end{aligned} \tag{5.9}$$

Since only preprogram innovations determine participation, and because U_{it} is distributed independently of $\mathbf{X}_{ik}$ and S_i in decision rule (2.7), the conditional mean of d_i does not depend on postprogram values of U_{it} given all preprogram values.

Intuitively, (5.8) follows from (5.9): The term $U_{it} - c(G(\psi_i) - p)$ is orthogonal to $G(\psi_i)$, the best predictor of d_i based on ψ_i; if $U_{it} - c(G(\psi_i) - p)$ were correlated with d_i, it would mean that U_{it} helped to predict d_i, contradicting (5.9).

The proof of the proposition uses the fact from equation (5.9) that $E(d_i | \psi_i, U_{it}) = G(\psi_i)$ in computing the expectation

$$\begin{aligned} E[d_i(U_{it} - c(G(\psi_i) - p))] &= E[E(d_i(U_{it} - c(G(\psi_i) - p)) | \psi_i, U_{it})] \\ &= E[(U_{it} - c(G(\psi_i) - p))E(d_i | \psi_i, U_{it})] \\ &= E[(U_{it} - c(G(\psi_i) - p))G(\psi_i)] \\ &= E[(U_{it} - c(G(\psi_i) - p))(G(\psi_i) - p)] \\ &= 0 \end{aligned} \tag{5.10}$$

as a consequence of the definition of c in (5.6).

The elements of ψ_i can be consistently estimated by fitting a preprogram earnings equation and forming the residuals from preprogram earnings data to estimate $U_{i,k-1}, \ldots, U_{i,k-N}$. One can assume a functional form for G and estimate the parameters of G using standard methods in discrete choice applied to enrollment data. The estimated residuals from preprogram earnings equations can be used to consistently estimate ψ_i.

5.4.4. Repeated cross-section versions. The repeated cross-section version of method I has already been discussed in Section 1.3. Preprogram earnings data can be used to consistently estimate $\boldsymbol{\beta}$ to adjust the means. The repeated cross-section version of method II is defined in an analogous fashion. We have been unable to produce a repeated cross-section version of method III. Note that the repeated cross-section estimators, when defined, are robust to mean zero measurement error.

5.4.5. Robustness to choice-based sampling and contamination bias. Methods I and II are control function estimators in the sense of definition D-2. Accordingly, they are robust to choice-based sampling. Methods for applying control function estimators to contaminated data are described in Section 3.8 (see the subsection on contamination bias for control function estimators).

Method III is not robust to choice-based sampling. This is so because

$$E[X'_{it}(U_{it} - c(G(\psi_i) - p)) | \psi_i, d_i, \mathbf{X}_{it}] \neq 0 \tag{5.11}$$

and

$$E[(G(\psi_i) - p)(U_{it} - c(G(\psi_i) - p)) | \psi_i, d_i, \mathbf{X}_{it}] \neq 0$$

Reweighting the data by weight ω_i introduced in the discussion of the IV method in Section 3.8 and fitting (5.7) using weighted variables produces a consistent estimator as the number of observations becomes large. Method III is also not robust to contamination bias. The moments of samples (i) and (iii) may be combined in a fashion analogous to that described in the discussion of the IV estimator in Section 3.8. The appropriate procedure for combining choice-based and contaminated samples closely parallels the method presented for the IV estimator in Section 3.8, so that a repetition of that discussion is not necessary.

5.5 *Partial K functions*

A partial K function $\tilde{K}_{it}$ satisfies (a) and (b) of definition (D-1) but fails condition (c) and as a consequence fails (d) unless additional prior restrictions are available.

An example of a partial K function can be constructed for the permanent–transitory model satisfying (A-3). In that case, assuming no regressors appear in the earnings function,

$$\tilde{K}_{it} = Y_{it'} - \beta_{t'} = U_{it'}, \qquad t' < k \tag{5.12}$$

and $\psi = \beta_{t'}$. For i.i.d. U_{it} with finite second moments

$$E(U_{it} - U_{it'})U_{it'} \neq 0$$

Least squares applied to

$$Y_{it} = \beta_t + d_i\alpha + \tilde{K}_{it} + (U_{it} - \tilde{K}_{it}) \quad (5.13)$$

is inconsistent. However, utilizing the prior information that the coefficient on $\tilde{K}_{it}$ is unity, we may rewrite (5.13) as a first-difference equation

$$Y_{it} - Y_{it'} = \beta_t - \beta_{t'} + d_i\alpha + U_{it} - U_{it'}$$

As a consequence of (A-3) least squares consistently estimates α. In this example, condition (c) of definition (D-1) is not required to identify α and so its failure is of no consequence.

In general this is not so and a condition like (c) is required to secure identification of α. The partial K function estimator replaces condition (c) of definition (D-1) with the requirement that there exists a vector of valid instrumental variables, $\mathbf{Z}_i^e$. (See, e.g., White, 1984, for one statement of such conditions.)

5.5.1. An example of a $\tilde{K}$ function. We depart from the format of previous sections and merely sketch an example of a $\tilde{K}$ function drawing freely from the work of Madansky (1964), Chamberlain (1977), and Pudney (1982). The reader is referred to those papers for a precise statement of conditions under which the estimator is consistent. Here we simply state the intuitive idea underlying one $\tilde{K}$ function.

The estimator assumes a factor structure for U_{it} so that

$$U_{it} = \pi_{1t}\phi_{1i} + \pi_{2t}\phi_{2i} + \cdots + \pi_{Nt}\phi_{Ni} + v_{it} \quad \text{for all} \quad t \quad (5.14)$$

where

(i) The v_{it} are mean zero mutually independent random variables with $\text{Var}(v_{it}) < \infty$ and they are distributed independently of the ϕ_{ij} for all i and j. $\text{Var}(\phi_{ij}) < \infty$ for all i and j, but the ϕ_{ij} may be freely correlated. The π_{jt} are nonzero bounded constants.

(ii) v_{it} is distributed independently of S_i in perfect-foresight decision rule (2.2) or in imperfect-foresight decision rule (2.7).

(iii) There are at least $2N$ years of earnings data in periods before t and at least one year in a period after t.

Note that if $N = 1$ and $\pi_{1t} = \pi$, the permanent–transitory model (5.1) is produced. If $\pi_{1t} = \pi_1$ and $\pi_{2t} = \pi_2 t$, (5.14) produces a special case of the Lillard–Weiss (1979) permanent component random growth model.

Array any N distinct observations on individual i for periods other than t into a matrix equation system

$$\begin{pmatrix} Y_{ij} \\ \cdots \\ Y_{ij'} \end{pmatrix} = \begin{pmatrix} \mathbf{X}_{ij} & d_i l_j \\ \cdots & \cdots \\ \mathbf{X}_{ij'} & d_i l_{j'} \end{pmatrix} \begin{pmatrix} \boldsymbol{\beta} \\ \cdots \\ \alpha \end{pmatrix} + \begin{pmatrix} \pi_{1j} \cdots \pi_{Nj} \\ \cdots \quad\quad \cdots \\ \pi_{1j'} \quad\quad \pi_{Nj'} \end{pmatrix} \begin{pmatrix} \phi_{1i} \\ \cdots \\ \phi_{Ni} \end{pmatrix} + \begin{pmatrix} v_{ij} \\ \cdots \\ v_{ij'} \end{pmatrix}$$

where $l_j = 1$ if $j > k$, $l_j = 0$ otherwise. Define

$$\mathbf{Y}_1 = \begin{pmatrix} Y_{ij} \\ \cdots \\ Y_{ij'} \end{pmatrix}, \quad \mathbf{X}_1 = \begin{pmatrix} \mathbf{X}_{ij} \\ \cdots \\ \mathbf{X}_{ij'} \end{pmatrix}, \quad d_i \mathbf{l}_1 = \begin{pmatrix} d_i l_j \\ \cdots \\ d_i l_{j'} \end{pmatrix}, \quad \mathbf{l}_1 = \begin{pmatrix} l_j \\ \cdots \\ l_{j'} \end{pmatrix}$$

$$\boldsymbol{\pi}_1 = \begin{pmatrix} \pi_{1j} & \pi_{Nj} \\ \cdots & \cdots \\ \pi_{1j'} & \pi_{Nj'} \end{pmatrix}, \quad \mathbf{v}_{i1} = \begin{pmatrix} v_{ij} \\ \cdots \\ v_{ij'} \end{pmatrix}, \quad \boldsymbol{\phi}_i = \begin{pmatrix} \phi_{1i} \\ \cdots \\ \phi_{Ni} \end{pmatrix}$$

In more compact notation, the equation system is

$$\mathbf{Y}_1 = [\mathbf{X}_1, d_i \mathbf{l}_1] \begin{bmatrix} \boldsymbol{\beta} \\ \alpha \end{bmatrix} + \boldsymbol{\pi}_1 \boldsymbol{\phi}_i + \mathbf{v}_{i1} \tag{5.15}$$

Assume that

(iv) $\boldsymbol{\pi}_i$ is of full rank.

Then (5.15) may be solved for $\boldsymbol{\phi}_i$ to obtain

$$\boldsymbol{\phi}_i = \boldsymbol{\pi}_1^{-1} \mathbf{Y}_1 - \boldsymbol{\pi}_1^{-1} [\mathbf{X}_1, d_i \mathbf{l}_1] \begin{bmatrix} \boldsymbol{\beta} \\ \alpha \end{bmatrix} - \boldsymbol{\pi}_1^{-1} \mathbf{v}_{i1}$$

Then this expression for $\boldsymbol{\phi}_i$ can be substituted for $\boldsymbol{\phi}_i$ in equation (1.1) with error structure (5.14) in the following way:

$$Y_{it} = \mathbf{X}_{it} \boldsymbol{\beta} + d_i \alpha + (\pi_{1t}, \ldots, \pi_{Nt}) \boldsymbol{\phi}_i + v_{it}$$

$$Y_{it} = \mathbf{X}_{it} \boldsymbol{\beta} + d_i \alpha + (\pi_{1t}, \ldots, \pi_{Nt}) \times \left[\boldsymbol{\pi}_1^{-1} \mathbf{Y}_1 - \boldsymbol{\pi}_1^{-1} (\mathbf{X}_1, d_i \mathbf{l}_1) \begin{pmatrix} \boldsymbol{\beta} \\ \alpha \end{pmatrix} - \boldsymbol{\pi}_1^{-1} \mathbf{v}_{i1} \right] + v_{it}$$

Collecting terms, we get

$$\begin{aligned} Y_{it} = {} & [\mathbf{X}_{it} - (\pi_{1t}, \ldots, \pi_{Nt}) \boldsymbol{\pi}_1^{-1} \mathbf{X}_1] \boldsymbol{\beta} + d_i \alpha (1 - (\pi_{1t}, \ldots, \pi_{Nt}) \boldsymbol{\pi}_1^{-1} \mathbf{l}_1) \\ & + (\pi_{1t}, \ldots, \pi_{Nt}) \boldsymbol{\pi}_1^{-1} \mathbf{Y}_1 + [v_{it} - (\pi_{1t}, \ldots, \pi_{Nt}) \boldsymbol{\pi}_1^{-1} \mathbf{v}_{i1}] \end{aligned} \tag{5.16}$$

By virtue of (5.15), $\mathbf{Y}_1$ and the composite error in (5.16) are correlated so that least squares applied to (5.16) is an inconsistent estimator [condition (D-1c) is violated].

Use the remaining N values of the Y_{im}, where $m \neq t$ and the Y_{im} are not elements of $\mathbf{Y}_1$, as instrumental variables for $\mathbf{Y}_1$ in (5.16). They are valid instruments because v_{im} is uncorrelated with the composite error in (5.16) but each Y_{im} is correlated with elements of $\mathbf{Y}_1$ through their common dependence on ϕ_i.

Provided that standard rank conditions for IV estimators hold, it is possible to consistently estimate $(\pi_{1t}, \ldots, \pi_{Nt})\boldsymbol{\pi}_1^{-1}$, and hence $\boldsymbol{\beta}$ and α, provided that the coefficient on α in (5.16) does not vanish $[1 - (\pi_{1t}, \ldots, \pi_{Nt})\boldsymbol{\pi}_1^{-1}\mathbf{l}_1 \neq 0]$. Chamberlain (1977) presents interesting examples of such $\tilde{K}$ functions where the IV rank conditions fail for subtle reasons.

5.5.2. The repeated cross-section version. The methods of Section 4.1 can be used to consistently estimate α from repeated cross-section data when (5.14) characterizes the earnings disturbance. We have not produced a repeated cross-section version of the $\tilde{K}$ estimator that exploits knowledge of the training status of persons and that does not require extra assumptions beyond those given above.

5.5.3. Robustness to choice-based sampling and contamination bias. After transformation, the $\tilde{K}$ function estimator is an IV estimator. Accordingly, our discussion of the modifications required in the cross-section IV estimator to account for choice-based sampling and contamination bias applies to the $\tilde{K}$ function.

5.6 U_{it} *is covariance-stationary*

The final procedure considered in this section invokes an assumption implicitly used in many papers on training (e.g., Ashenfelter, 1978; Bassi, 1983; and others) but exploits the assumption in a novel way. We assume the following:

(i) U_{it} is covariance-stationary and so

$$E(U_{it}U_{it-j}) = E(U_{it'}U_{it'-j}) = \sigma_j \quad \text{for} \quad j \geq 0$$

and all t, t'.

(ii) Access to at least two observations on preprogram earnings t', $t' - j$, and one on postprogram earnings t so that $t - t' = j$.

(iii) (A-6) describes the process generating the earnings data for each cross section.

(iv) $pE(U_{it'} \mid d_i = 1) \neq 0$.

Notably absent from the assumptions is any statement about the appropriate enrollment rule or about the stochastic relationship between U_{it} and the cost of enrollment S_i.

From the preprogram earnings data, it is possible to estimate $\boldsymbol{\beta}$ under the conditions given in Section 4 and adjust the Y_{it} back to the expression

$$\tilde{Y}_{it} = \beta_t + d_i\alpha + U_{it}, \qquad t > k$$
$$\tilde{Y}_{it'} = \beta_{t'} \qquad\quad + U_{it'}, \qquad t' < k \tag{5.17}$$

where β_t and $\beta_{t'}$ are period-specific shifters and $\tilde{Y}_{it}$ is Y_{it} with the effect of the regressors removed.

From a random sample of preprogram earnings from periods t' and $t' - j$, σ_j can be consistently estimated from the sample covariance between $\tilde{Y}_{it'}$ and $\tilde{Y}_{i,t'-j}$:

$$m_1 = \frac{\sum(\tilde{Y}_{it'} - \bar{\tilde{Y}}_{t'})(\tilde{Y}_{i,t'-j} - \bar{\tilde{Y}}_{t'-j})}{I}$$

$$\operatorname{plim} m_1 = \sigma_j$$

If $t > k$ and $t - t' = j$ so that the postprogram earnings data are as far removed in time from t' as t' is removed from $t' - j$, form the sample covariance between $\tilde{Y}_{it}$ and $\tilde{Y}_{it'}$:

$$m_2 = \frac{\sum(\tilde{Y}_{it} - \bar{\tilde{Y}}_t)(\tilde{Y}_{it'} - \bar{\tilde{Y}}_{t'})}{I}$$

which has the probability limit

$$\operatorname{plim} m_2 = \sigma_j + \alpha p E(U_{it'} \mid d_i = 1), \qquad t > k > t'$$

From the sample covariance between d_i and $\tilde{Y}_{it'}$

$$m_3 = \frac{\sum(\tilde{Y}_{it'} - \bar{\tilde{Y}}_{t'})d_i}{I}$$

$$\operatorname{plim} m_3 = pE(U_{it'} \mid d_i = 1), \qquad t' < k$$

Combining this information, and assuming $pE(U_{it'} \mid d_i = 1) \neq 0$ for $t' < k$,

$$\operatorname{plim} \hat{\alpha} = \operatorname{plim} \frac{m_2 - m_1}{m_3} = \alpha$$

This estimator is not to be confused with another apparently similar one. The alternative estimator notes that least squares applied to estimate α in

$$\tilde{Y}_{it} = \beta_t + d_i\alpha + U_{it}$$

from a random sample of postprogram year t earnings has the property that

$$\operatorname{plim} \hat{\alpha} = \alpha + \frac{1}{1-p} E(U_{it} \mid d_i = 1)$$

where $\hat{\alpha}$ is the least squares estimator. If a dummy is entered in a random sample of preprogram earnings, the least squares estimator of γ in

$$\tilde{Y}_{it'} = \beta_{t'} + \gamma d_i + U_{it'}, \qquad t' < k$$

converges to

$$\operatorname{plim} \tilde{\gamma} = \frac{1}{1-p} E(U_{it'} | d_i = 1)$$

If U_{it} is, for example, pivotally symmetric with respect to U_{ik}, $t - k = k - t'$, and the joint density of (S_i, U_{it}) is the same as the joint density of $(S_i, U_{it'})$, then

$$\operatorname{plim} (\hat{\alpha} - \tilde{\gamma}) = \alpha$$

The estimator proposed in this section requires only that U_{it} be covariance-stationary (something not required for the alternative estimator) and does not require that any position be taken with regard to the stochastic dependence between the U_{it} and S_i. Note that the variance of U_{it} is *not* required to be identical in all periods.

5.6.1. Repeated cross-section version. For simplicity of exposition we assume that there are no regressors in the earnings function. If regressors are present, we assume that the analyst can adjust Y_{it} to $\tilde{Y}_{it}$ in equation (5.17).

Before presenting the estimator, it is helpful to record the following facts:

$$\operatorname{Var}(Y_{it}) = \alpha^2(1-p)p + 2\alpha E(U_{it} | d_i = 1)p + \sigma_u^2, \qquad t > k \quad (5.18a)$$

$$\operatorname{Var}(Y_{it'}) = \sigma_u^2 \qquad t' < k \quad (5.18b)$$

$$\operatorname{Cov}(Y_{it}, d_i) = \alpha p(1-p) + pE(U_{it} | d_i = 1) \quad (5.18c)$$

Note that $E(U_{it}^2) = E(U_{it'}^2)$ by virtue of assumption (i) given in Section 5.6. Then

$$\hat{\alpha} = [(p(1-p)]^{-1} \left\{ \frac{\sum (Y_{it} - \bar{Y}_t) d_i}{I_t} - \sqrt{\left(\frac{\sum (Y_{it} - \bar{Y}_t) d_i}{I_t} \right)^2 - p(1-p) \left(\frac{\sum (Y_{it} - \bar{Y}_t)^2}{I_t} - \frac{\sum (Y_{it'} - \bar{Y}_{t'})^2}{I_{t'}} \right)} \right\} \quad (5.19)$$

is consistent for α.

This expression arises by substracting (5.18b) from (5.18a). Then use (5.18c) to get an expression for $E(U_{it} | d_i = 1)$, which can be substituted into the expression for the difference between (5.18a) and (5.18b). Replacing population moments by sample counterparts produces a quadratic equation in α, with the negative root given by (5.19). The positive root is inconsistent for α.

5.6.2. Robustness to choice-based sampling and contamination bias. If the available data are a choice-based sample and the population p is known or can be consistently estimated, the data can be reweighted to form a consistent estimator.

Letting d_i be the value of the variable indicating training status

$$\bar{\tilde{Y}}_l^* = p \frac{\sum d_i \tilde{Y}_{il}}{\sum d_i} + (1-p) \frac{\sum (1-d_i) \tilde{Y}_{il}}{\sum (1-d_i)}$$

and the reweighted moments are

$$m_1^* = p \frac{\sum d_i (\tilde{Y}_{it'} - \bar{\tilde{Y}}_{t'}^*)(\tilde{Y}_{i,t-j} - \bar{\tilde{Y}}_{t-j}^*)}{\sum d_i} + (1-p) \frac{\sum (1-d_i)(\tilde{Y}_{it} - \bar{\tilde{Y}}_{t'}^*)(\bar{\tilde{Y}}_{i,t-j} - \bar{\tilde{Y}}_{t-j}^*)}{\sum (1-d_i)}$$

$$m_2^* = p \frac{\sum d_i (\tilde{Y}_{it'} - \bar{\tilde{Y}}_{t'}^*)(\tilde{Y}_{it} - \bar{\tilde{Y}}_t^*)}{\sum d_i} + (1-p) \frac{\sum (1-d_i)(\tilde{Y}_{it'} - \bar{\tilde{Y}}_{t'}^*)(\tilde{Y}_{it} - \bar{\tilde{Y}}_t^*)}{\sum (1-d_i)}$$

$$m_3^* = p \frac{\sum d_i (\tilde{Y}_{it'} - \bar{\tilde{Y}}_{t'}^*)}{\sum d_i}$$

and so

$$\text{plim} \frac{(m_2^* - m_1^*)}{m_3^*} = \alpha \qquad \text{if } pE(U_{it'} \mid d_i = 1) \neq 0$$

If regressors appear in the equations, $\boldsymbol{\beta}$ can be consistently estimated from a regression on preprogram earnings using data weighted by ω_i introduced in Section 3.8, and the $\tilde{Y}_{it}$, $\tilde{Y}_{it'}$ and $\tilde{Y}_{i,t'-j}$ can be formed from Y_{it}, $Y_{it'}$, and $Y_{i,t'-j}$, respectively, using the procedure described in Section 4.

The covariance-stationary procedure can also be modified to solve the problems raised by contamination in the control group. Sample (iii) data can be used to consistently estimate m_1 and m_2.

Let $\bar{\tilde{Y}}_{t'}^{(i)}$ be the sample mean of $\tilde{Y}_{it'}$ in sample (i) data and let $\bar{\tilde{Y}}_{t'}^{(iii)}$ be the sample mean of $\tilde{Y}_{it'}$ in sample (iii) data. Then

$$\text{plim} \left[p \left(\bar{\tilde{Y}}_{t'}^{(i)} - \bar{\tilde{Y}}_{t'}^{(iii)} \right) \right] = pE(U_{it'} \mid d_i = 1)$$

and

$$\operatorname{plim}\left[\frac{m_2 - m_1}{p\left(\bar{\bar{Y}}_{t'}^{(i)} - \bar{\bar{Y}}_{t'}^{(iii)}\right)}\right] = \alpha$$

No postprogram data from sample (i) are required.

6 Summary and conclusions

This chapter has presented alternative methods for estimating the impact of training on earnings when nonrandom selection characterizes the enrollment of persons into training. The analysis of this problem serves as a prototype for the analysis of such closely related problems as estimating the impact of schooling, unionism, migration, and job turnover on earnings in the presence of a selection rule determining participation in those activities.

One contribution of this chapter has been to identify two different definitions associated with the notion of a selection-bias-free estimate of the impact of training on earnings. The first notion defines the structural parameter of interest as the impact of training on earnings if people are randomly assigned to training programs. The second notion defines the structural parameter of interest as the impact of training on the earnings of the trained, that is, the component of the increment in posttraining earnings attributable to training including the effect of enrollment rules on selecting people into training who have a more or less typical response to training. The two notions come to the same thing only when training has the same impact on everyone – that is, when a fixed (and not a random) coefficient earnings model describes the data, or when assignment to training is random. The second notion is frequently the most useful one for forecasting future program impacts when the same enrollment rules that have been used in available samples characterize future enrollment.

The first notion accords with the more commonly utilized definition of a "structural" impact of training on earnings and is a special case of a more general notion that defines the parameter of interest to be the impact of training on the earnings of the trained in the future if the future selection rule for trainees differs from previous selection rules.

This chapter presents a variety of new estimators for both versions of the parameter of interest. By considering the assumptions required to use the new estimators and more conventional ones to address the same problem using longitudinal, repeated cross-section, and cross-section data, we have explored the benefits of panel data and repeated cross-section data. We have also investigated the plausibility of assumptions required to justify various econometric procedures when viewed in the light of prototypical decision rules determining enrollment into training. Because many of the available samples are choice-based samples and because the problem of measurement error in training status (i.e., contamination bias) is pervasive in many available control samples, we have examined the robustness of all of the estimators discussed in this chapter to choice-based sampling and contamination bias.

We have reached the following main conclusions:

1. Unless distributional assumptions are invoked, methods based solely on cross-section data require at least one regressor in the decision rule analogous to the shifter variables required to secure identification of demand and supply functions from market data. Longitudinal and repeated cross-section methods do not require a regressor. This is a major benefit of access to multiple cross-section or longitudinal data.

2. However, given a regressor in the decision rule, if some function of it satisfies the exogeneity condition presented in Section 3.2 and if additional mild rank conditions are satisfied, the regressor can be used as an instrumental variable for the training status dummy in a fixed coefficient cross-section earnings equation. No further distributional or functional form assumptions are required in order to identify the structural impact of training on earnings, although such assumptions have frequently been invoked in the recent literature. Such assumptions *are* required for consistent estimation of random coefficient earnings functions produced from Roy (1951) choice models. The instrumental variable estimator does not consistently estimate the random coefficient earnings function in the presence of selection bias.

Because the IV estimator requires such weak assumptions, it produces consistent estimators of program impact for a wide variety of models of the enrollment decision provided that the earnings equation is of the fixed coefficient type. Virtually all of the other cross-section estimators require prior knowledge of the distribution of unobservables or of the functional form of the conditional mean of the unobservable in the earnings equation. The only exception to this rule is the two-stage method of Section 3.3 in which the choice probability can sometimes be estimated nonparametrically. The analysis of the decision rules of Section 2 provides little guidance on the choice of such distributions and functional forms. (However, the Barnow–Cain–Goldberger procedure that assumes selection on the basis of observables makes assumptions that appear to be implausible in the light of the prototypical enrollment rules of Section 2.)

3. Without invoking distributional assumptions, it is not possible to identify the population mean response to training in a random coefficient model of earnings unless a regressor appears in the enrollment rule or unless an individual does not know his own response to training at the time

enrollment decisions are made and the population mean forecast error is known to the econometrician. Accordingly, one benefit of longitudinal and repeated cross-section estimators that accrues in fixed coefficient earnings models vanishes in a random coefficient earnings model.

4. Provided that the population proportion of trainees is known or can be consistently estimated, all of the estimators presented in this chapter can be adapted to consistently estimate the structural parameters of interest from contaminated samples. Some require no modification at all (e.g., the direct nonlinear regression estimator of Section 3.3 or the repeated cross-section estimator of Section 4).

5. Provided that the training status of individuals is known, all of the estimators can be adapted to produce consistent estimators of program impact from choice-based samples. The control function estimators [in the sense of definition (D-2) in Section 1.5] require no modification at all. We have presented examples of cross-section, repeated cross-section, and longitudinal control function estimators.

6. Provided that the environment is time-homogeneous or sufficiently regular in the sense of definition (D-3) in Section 4, and provided that simple random samples are available, the repeated cross-section estimator which does not require that the training status of persons be known (but does require that the population proportion of trainees be known or consistently estimable) is robust to completely general specifications of the enrollment rule. In particular, no regressor need appear in the enrollment rule. No special assumptions need be invoked with respect to the stochastic dependence relationships among variables in the earnings and enrollment equations in order for this estimator to produce consistent estimators of program impact. Multiple-decision rules may characterize enrollment. The estimator is robust to contamination bias provided that the population proportion of trainees is known. For these reasons, this repeated cross-section estimator is quite attractive.

However, the estimator is inconsistent when applied to choice-based samples and to environments characterized by general forms of time inhomogeneity. To account for the problems induced by choice-based sampling and general forms of time inhomogeneity it is necessary to know the training status of persons.

7. The benefits from longitudinal data have been overstated in the recent literature. Many consistent estimators thought to be uniquely longitudinal in nature can in fact be implemented using repeated cross-section data on unrelated persons. In particular, the widely used fixed effect estimator can be employed to secure consistent estimators from repeated cross-section data. However, to use repeated cross-section data to implement the fixed effect estimator requires that the training status of persons be

known in preprogram cross sections. Longitudinal data with preprogram earnings observations will have this information while repeated cross-section data may not.

8. The longitudinal estimators secure identification of the impact of training on earnings by making assumptions about the time series processes of the unobservables and observables in the enrollment and earnings equations. The only exception to this rule is the covariance-stationary estimator of Section 5.6, which requires covariance stationarity for the unobservable in the earnings equation but requires no explicit specification of the enrollment rule. While some of these assumptions may be tested (e.g., assumptions about the time series process of the unobservables in the earnings equation), others cannot, in general, be tested (e.g., assumptions about independence between the unobservables in the enrollment and earnings equations).

Longitudinal estimators require different assumptions than cross-sectional estimators, and it is not obvious which sets of assumptions are more plausible. As noted by Chamberlain (1984), longitudinal data can sometimes be used to test cross-sectional identifying assumptions. But this is not always so. The sets of identifying assumptions for the two types of estimators are not necessarily nested (e.g., the existence of an IV estimator for the cross-section estimator and covariance stationarity of the earnings equation for the longitudinal estimator).

9. The specification of the earnings equation and the enrollment rule that justify the widely used fixed effect or first-difference estimator are very special and are not of general interest. Contrary to recent claims, fixed effect methods offer no panacea for selection and simultaneity problems that arise in estimating the impacts on earnings of training, unionism, job turnover, and migration.

10. The cross-section estimators do not require preprogram earnings data, nor do most of the longitudinal estimators. Two exceptions are the fixed effect longitudinal estimator and the covariance-stationary estimator of Section 5.6.

11. Virtually all of the estimators require a control group (i.e., a sample of nontrainees). The only exception is the fixed effect estimator in a time-homogeneous environment. The frequently stated claim that "if the environment is stationary, you don't need a control group" (see, e.g., Bassi, 1983) is false except for the special conditions that justify use of the fixed effect estimator.

12. The estimators differ in their robustness to aging and decay effects (i.e., time subscripted α). The cross-section estimators are robust in the sense that they identify the value of α_t appropriate to a particular cross section. The repeated cross-section estimator with the training status of persons unknown requires a strengthened definition of a sufficiently regular

environment if the α values change over time [see definition (D-3) in Section 4]. The longitudinal estimators require straightforward modifications to account for aging and decay effects.

13. The covariance-stationary estimator of Section 5.6 and the repeated cross-section estimator of Section 4 can be applied without modification to models with multiple enrollment rules. The IV estimator of Section 3.2 does not require an explicit statement of the enrollment rule – just a list of valid instruments. All of the other estimators must be modified if there are multiple selection rules.

Throughout this chapter we have deliberately avoided discussing the efficiency of alternative estimators. Many of the estimators presented here invoke different assumptions about the true model generating the data. An efficiency comparison for such estimators is meaningless because the assumptions required to justify one estimator do not justify another. Only by postulating a common assumption set bigger than what is required to justify any single estimator is it possible to compare such estimators. The required common set depends on the pair of estimators being considered. The outcome of such efficiency comparisons will hinge on specific values assumed by parameters and the value of making such comparisons is not obvious.

Even if a common set of assumptions about the underlying model were invoked to justify efficiency comparisons for a class of estimators, conventional efficiency comparisons are often meaningless – for two reasons. First, the frequently stated claim that longitudinal estimators are more efficient than cross-section estimators is superficial. It ignores the relative sizes of the *available* cross-section and longitudinal samples. Because of the substantially greater cost of collecting longitudinal data free of attrition bias, the number of persons followed in longitudinal studies rarely exceeds 500 in most economic analyses.[30] In contrast, the *available* cross-section samples often have hundreds of thousands of observations. Given the relative sizes of the *available* cross-section and longitudinal samples, "inefficient" cross-section and repeated cross-section estimators may have a much smaller sampling variance than "efficient" longitudinal estimators fit on much smaller samples. In this sense, our proposed cross-section and repeated cross-section estimators may be *feasibly efficient* given the relative sizes of the samples for the two types of data sources.

Second, many of the cross-section and repeated cross-section estimators proposed in this chapter require only sample means of variables. They are thus very simple to compute and are also robust to mean zero measurement error in all of the variables.

Nonlinear (longitudinal and cross-section) estimators that are computationally more demanding are often implemented on only a small fraction of the available data in order to economize on computer costs. The relevant comparison of the efficiency of apparently inefficient mean estimators recognizes that in most applications mean estimators use all the available data, whereas more sophisticated estimators use only a fraction of the data.

When we began writing this chapter we intended it to be a paean to longitudinal data; that it is not so is because the analysis presented here does not warrant such a conclusion. More data are preferred to less given zero cost, and different types of data are always useful. In certain cases, longitudinal data can be used to test assumptions maintained in cross-section work.

But a key conclusion of our analysis is that the benefits of longitudinal data have been overstated in the recent econometric literature because a false comparison has been made. A cross-section selection bias estimator does not require the elaborate and unjustified assumptions about functional forms often invoked in cross-sectional studies. Repeated cross-section data often can be used to identify the same parameters as longitudinal data. The uniquely longitudinal estimators require assumptions that are different from and often no more plausible than the assumptions required for the robust cross-section estimators.

ACKNOWLEDGMENTS

This research was supported by grants from the Department of Labor (DOL 20-17 82-20), National Science Foundation Grants SOC77-27136 and SES-8107963 and NIH-1-R01-HD16846-01 to the Economics Research Center/NORC at the University of Chicago. The first draft was written while Heckman was a fellow at the Center for Advanced Studies in the Behavioral Sciences in the year 1978 while supported, in part, by a fellowship from the J. S. Guggenheim Foundation. The first draft was read at a Social Science Research Council conference at Mt. Kisco, New York, October 1978. The second draft was read at a conference on Panel Data at London School of Economics in London, June, 1982. We are grateful for comments received at seminars at North Carolina State, M.I.T., Yale, Penn, Texas, and Michigan. We have benefited from comments received from John Abowd, Burt Barnow, Joe Hotz, William Kruskal, Robert Michael, Tom Stoker, Robert Tamura, Grace Tsiang, Jim Walker, and Adonis Yatchew. Ricardo Barros made especially helpful comments.

NOTES

1 Duncan, Juster, and Morgan (1982) claim that panel data are cheaper to collect per observation than cross-section data, but they do not present detailed evidence of their claim. They also do not consider the problem of nonrandom attrition that plagues panel data but not cross-section data.

2 Data on residual variances do not aid in securing identification unless the variance is known a priori. The sum of the squared normalized residuals converges to an expression that combines $\mathrm{Var}(U_{it})$ with $\mathrm{Cov}(U_{it}, d_i)$. Without prior information there is no information on α from higher moments.

3 Thus we assume that in large samples the sample frequency of $(\mathbf{X}, \mathbf{Z}, U)$ given d converges to the population density $f(\mathbf{X}, \mathbf{Z}, U \mid d)$.

4 Because in that case $E(\hat{\alpha}_{RC}) = \beta_t - \beta_{t'} + (p_t^* - p_{t'}^*)\alpha$. If $\beta_t = \beta_{t'}$ and the proportion of trainees is known for t' and t, then α is identified from $\bar{Y}_t$ and $\bar{Y}_{t'}$ by dividing $\bar{Y}_t - \bar{Y}_{t'}$ by $p_t^* - p_{t'}^*$ assuming $p_t^* \neq p_{t'}^*$.

5 If the α differ among time periods, the longitudinal estimator requires only that the values of α be identical in two successive time periods, whereas the repeated cross-section estimators require that it be identical in three successive time periods.

6 Longitudinal data aid in identifying $\text{Var}(\varepsilon_i \mid d_i = 1, \mathbf{Z}_i)$. With sufficient time series structure on U_{it} or the pre- and posttraining data on earnings, it is possible to use the squared least squares residuals to identify this parameter if, e.g., U_{it} and ε_i are independent, using standard components of variance models. See, e.g., Judge et al. (1980) for a description of such models.

7 In this case, the variance in ε_i can be estimated by standard variance components methods. See, e.g., Judge et al. (1980, chap. 8). Assuming normally distributed ε_i, τ_i, and U_{it}, this model is identical to that presented in Heckman's (1978) dummy endogenous variable model.

8 In a more general model agents might forecast ε_i using a richer information set. Denote the information set by $\mathscr{I}_i$ which may include lagged values of Y

$$E(\varepsilon_i \mid \mathscr{I}_i) = \Lambda(\mathscr{I}_i)$$

and the forecast error is

$$\rho_i = \varepsilon_i - \Lambda(\mathscr{I}_i)$$

where $\bar{\alpha} + \Lambda(\mathscr{I}_i)$ replaces $\bar{\alpha}$ everywhere in the text equations. This model does not have the same statistical structure as a random coefficients model under perfect certainty.

Earnings equation (1.14) becomes

$$Y_{it} = \beta_t + d_i\alpha + d_i\Lambda(\mathscr{I}_i) + (d_i\rho_i + U_{it}), \qquad t > k \tag{*}$$

where

$$E(\rho_i \mid d_i = 1, \mathscr{I}_i) = 0$$

Assuming ε_i is independent of U_{it}, and the functional form of $\Lambda(\mathscr{I}_i)$ is known equation (*) can be consistently estimated using, e.g., the methods in Heckman (1978).

9 This is the basis for a test between the two specifications of the assignment process conditional on error structure (2.8), which is itself testable using longitudinal data. However, the test is critically dependent on the assumption that the prospective trainee knows $\mathbf{X}_{ik}$ in period $k - 1$ and that $\mathbf{X}_{ik}$ is not contained in the space spanned by $\mathbf{X}_{i,k-1}$ (so $\mathbf{X}_{i,k-1}$ cannot consist entirely of time-invariant variables that also appear in $\mathbf{X}_{ik}$).

10 For an analysis of normal multiple-selection rules see Catsiapsis and Robinson (1982) and Abowd and Farber (1982).

11 One example with multiple-selection rules involves no new analysis whatsoever. Suppose that IN_1 is $PV(1) - PV(0)$. Suppose also that administrators fill available openings by choosing at random among willing prospective participants. Now IN_2 is independent of X, V, and S. There is no loss of generality in assuming that IN_2 exists for individuals who do not present themselves for

training and that IN_2 is independent of IN_1. Then we can define

$$S_i^* = S_i \quad \text{if} \quad IN_{2i} > 0$$

$$S_i^* = -\infty \quad \text{if} \quad IN_{2i} < 0$$

Replacing S_i with S_i^* in equation (2.2), the previous analyses go through.

12 See Lee (1982) for some nonnormal models.

13 Note that χ need not necessarily be identified to identify α as long as (A-9e) is satisfied.

14 This is the basis for a test of the null hypothesis of no selection bias in the absence of knowledge of the functional form of the density function h. Provided (A-9e) is satisfied, it is possible to expand $E(U_{it}|d_i = 0, \mathbf{Z}_i)$ and $E(U_{it}|d_i = 1, \mathbf{Z}_i)$ in terms of polynomials in $\Pr(d_i = 0|\mathbf{Z}_i)$, exploiting the fact that $E(U_{it}|\mathbf{Z}_i = 0) = 0$. Under the null hypothesis of no selection bias, polynomials in $\Pr(d_i = 0|\mathbf{Z}_i)$ should not appear as statistically significant in a regression of Y_{it} on d_i, $\mathbf{X}_{it}$, and the polynomials. For details on this test see Heckman (1980).

Note further that if the null is rejected, it appears possible to use the results of Gallant (1981) to expand $E(U_{it}|d_i, \mathbf{Z}_i)$ in a Fourier expansion in terms of estimated $\Pr(d_i = 0|\mathbf{Z}_i)$ and to estimate the parameters of (3.4) nonparametrically.

15 Note that even though α is identified, $\boldsymbol{\omega}$ need not be uniquely identified.

16 In independent work, Heckman and Neumann (1977) estimate a more general random coefficients model of this type with $\boldsymbol{\beta}$ random in addition to α_i. The only essential difference between the Lee (1978) model and the Heckman dummy endogenous variable model is that Heckman requires that $E(\varepsilon_i|d_i = 1) = 0$, whereas Lee does not. As noted in Section 2.3, in some environments of decision making under uncertainty it is plausible that $E(\varepsilon_i|d_i = 1) = 0$.

17 Note that in a simple random sample $E(\mathbf{X}'_{it}U_{it}|d_i)$ and the other conditional expectations are common for all i and the expressions in the text simplify to

$$\operatorname*{plim}_{I_t \to \infty} \frac{\sum \mathbf{X}'_{it} U_{it}}{I_t} = E(\mathbf{X}'_{it}U_{it}|d_i = 1)p^* + E(\mathbf{X}'_{it}U_{it}|d_i = 0)(1 - p^*)$$

$$\operatorname*{plim}_{I_t \to \infty} \frac{\sum g(Z_i^e) U_{it}}{I_t} = E[g(Z_i^e)U_{it}|d_i = 1]p^* + E[g(Z_i^e)U_{it}|d_i = 0](1 - p^*)$$

18 If $g(Z_i^e)$ and $\mathbf{X}_{it}$ are not independent of $\mathbf{X}_{ik}$ and U_{it} is serially dependent, the terms inside the braces are not zero when perfect-foresight rule (2.4) characterizes the enrollment decision.

19 In a random sample these expressions simplify to

$$\operatorname*{plim}_{I_t \to \infty} \frac{\sum \mathbf{X}'_{it} d_i}{I_t} = pE(\mathbf{X}_{it}|d_i = 1)$$

$$\operatorname*{plim}_{I_t \to \infty} \frac{\sum g(Z_i^e) d_i}{I_t} = pE[g(Z_i^e)|d_i = 1]$$

20 *Proof:* In the reweighted choice-based sample,

$$E(d_i \phi_{it}|\mathbf{X}_{it}, \mathbf{Z}_i) = 1 - F(-\mathbf{Z}_i\gamma)$$

and

$$E(\phi_{it}U_{it}|\mathbf{X}_{it},\mathbf{Z}_i) = E(U_{it}|d_i = 1,\mathbf{X}_{it},\mathbf{Z}_i)\left(\frac{\Pr(d_i = 1|\mathbf{Z}_i)}{p^*(d_i = 0|\mathbf{Z}_i)}\right)p^*(d_i = 1|\mathbf{Z}_i)$$
$$+ E(U_{it}|d_i = 0,\mathbf{X}_{it},\mathbf{Z}_i)\left(\frac{\Pr(d_i = 0|\mathbf{Z}_i)}{p^*(d_i = 0|\mathbf{Z}_i)}\right)p^*(d_i = 0|\mathbf{Z}_i)$$
$$= 0$$

by virtue of (A-8d).

21 The asymptotic theory is considerably simplified if the frequency is a member of a finite parameter family.

22 This assumption is not needed if p_t varies with t. See the discussion in Section 1.3.2.

23 We note parenthetically that in a random coefficient earnings model with regressors in the enrollment rule and with (5.1) as the error term in the earnings equation, the first-difference method does not consistently estimate $\bar{\alpha}$. Thus the Lee (1978) model of unionism is fundamentally different from the model implicit in Chamberlain's work (1982), although this difference has not been noticed by labor economists (see, e.g., Lewis, 1982). Heckman and Neumann (1977) and Lee (1978) estimate a different coefficient than does Chamberlain. Hence, comparisons of the impacts of union status from the two procedures are meaningless.

24 The requirement that $|\rho| < 1$ is needed only to guarantee the validity of the forecasting rules used in Section 2 for infinite horizon problems.

25 Notice that even if S_i and $\mathbf{X}_{it}$ are distributed independently of U_{it} for all t, (A-15b) does not imply error structure (5.1). (A-15b) only implies that

$$E(U_{it}|d_i) = E(U_{it'}|d_i) = l(d_i)$$

so we may uniquely write $U_{it} = \psi_i + \varepsilon_{it}$, where $E(\psi_i|d_i) = l(d_i)$ and $E(\varepsilon_{it}|d_i) = 0$. Here ψ_i need not be independent of ε_{it}.

26 Thus writing (1.1) as $Y_{it} = \beta_t + \mathbf{X}_{it}\pi + d_i\alpha + U_{it}$, it is possible to estimate π from sample (iii) preprogram data. (This assumes there are no time-invariant variables in $\mathbf{X}_{it}$. If there are such variables, they may be deleted from the regressor vector and π appropriately redefined without affecting the analysis.) Then from the mean of sample (i) it is possible to consistently estimate $\beta_t - \beta_{t'} + (\bar{\mathbf{X}}_t^{(i)} - \bar{\mathbf{X}}_{t'}^{(i)})\pi + \alpha$, where $\bar{\mathbf{X}}_t^{(i)}$ is the population mean of $\mathbf{X}_{it}$ in period t for sample (i), and from the mean of sample (iii) differences it is possible to consistently estimate $\beta_t - \beta_{t'} + (\bar{\mathbf{X}}_{it} - \bar{\mathbf{X}}_{it'})\pi + \alpha p$. Since π is known, the means can be adjusted for the effect of $\mathbf{X}$. The adjusted means can then be used in the procedure described in the text. Note that we are assuming that no $\mathbf{X}_{it}$ variables become nonconstant after period k.

27 Linearity of the regression does not imply that the U_{it} are normally distributed (although if the U_{it} are joint normal the regression is linear). Kagan, Linnik, and Rao (1973, p. 10) give necessary and sufficient conditions for linearity of the regression. The multivariate t density is just one example of a family of densities with linear regressions. There are many more.

28 From (iii), the joint density of U_{it}, U_{ik}, $\mathbf{X}_{ik}$, S_i may be written as $f(U_{it}, U_{ik})f(\mathbf{X}_{ik}, S_i)$. Substitute for U_{it} using $U_{it} = \delta U_{ik} + \omega_{it}$. Then $E(\omega_{it}|U_{ik}) =$

0 means that

$$\int \omega_{it} f(\delta U_{ik} + \omega_{it}, U_{ik})\, d\omega_{it} = 0. \qquad (*)$$

Thus $E(\omega_{it} | d_i = 1) = 0$ since

$$E(\omega_{it} | d_i = 1) = \frac{\int_{-\infty}^{\infty} \int_{-\infty}^{\infty} \int_{-\infty}^{-\mathbf{X}_{ik}\boldsymbol{\beta} + S_i + (\alpha/r)} \int_{-\infty}^{\infty} \omega_{it} f(\delta U_{ik} + \omega_{it}, U_{ik}) f(\mathbf{X}_{ik}, S_i)\, d\omega_{it}\, dU_{ik}\, d\mathbf{X}_{ik}\, dS_i}{\Pr(d_i = 1)}$$

and the firstfold integral (from within) is identically zero because of (*).

29 *Proof:* Using (2.7) and (i) above, define $R(\mathbf{X}_{ik}, U_{i,k-1}, \ldots, U_{i,k-N}, S_i)$ so that

$$\begin{aligned} R(\mathbf{X}_{ik}, U_{i,k-1}, \ldots, U_{i,k-N}, S_i) &= 1 \quad \text{if} \quad \mathbf{X}_{ik}\boldsymbol{\beta} + E(U_{ik} | U_{i,k-1}, \ldots, U_{i,k-N}) > S_i + \frac{\alpha}{r} \\ &= 0 \qquad \text{otherwise} \end{aligned}$$

From (i), $R(\mathbf{X}_{ik}, U_{i,k-1}, \ldots, U_{i,k-N}, S_i) = d_i$. Thus

$$\begin{aligned} &E(d_i | U_{it}, \ldots, U_{i,k-N}) \\ &= \underset{(S_i, \mathbf{X}_{ik})}{E} [R(\mathbf{X}_{ik}, U_{i,k-1}, \ldots, U_{i,k-N}, S_i) | U_{it}, \ldots, U_{i,k-1}, \ldots, U_{i,k-N}] \\ &= \underset{(S_i, \mathbf{X}_{ik})}{E} [R(\mathbf{X}_{ik}, U_{i,k-1}, \ldots, U_{i,k-N}, S_i) | U_{i,k-1}, \ldots, U_{i,k-N}] \end{aligned}$$

as a consequence of assumptions (v) and (vi). Similarly,

$$\begin{aligned} &E(d_i | U_{i,k-1}, \ldots, U_{i,k-N}) \\ &\quad = \underset{(S_i, \mathbf{X}_{ik})}{E} [R(\mathbf{X}_{ik}, U_{i,k-1}, \ldots, U_{i,k-N}, S_i) | U_{i,k-1}, \ldots, U_{i,k-N}] \end{aligned}$$

30 This is true for most analyses based on the Panel Survey of Income Dynamics, which began with observations on 5000 families. A typical empirical project based on this data set is for a single demographic group.

REFERENCES

Abowd, J., and Farber, H. (1982). "Jobs Queues and the Union Status of Workers." *Industrial and Labor Relations Review* 35, 354–67.

Aigner, D. (1973). "Regression with a Binary Independent Variable Subject to Errors of Observation." *Journal of Econometrics* 1, 49–60.

Amemiya, T. (1981). "Qualitative Response Models: A Survey." *Journal of Economic Literature* 19, 1483–1536.

(1983). "A Comparison of the Amemiya GLS and the Lee–Maddala–Trost G2SLS in a Simultaneous Equations Tobit Model." *Journal of Econometrics* 23, 295–300.

Ashenfelter, O. (1978). "Estimating the Effect of Training Programs on Earnings." *Review of Economics and Statistics* 60, 47–57.

Barnow, B. (1983). Personal discussions.
Barnow, B., Cain, G., and Goldberger, A. (1980). "Issues in the Analysis of Selectivity Bias." In *Evaluation Studies*, vol. 5, edited by E. Stromsdorfer and G. Farkas. San Franciso: Sage.
Bassi, L. (1983). "Estimating the Effect of Training Programs with Nonrandom Selection." Ph.D. dissertation, Princeton University.
Björklund, A., and Moffitt, R. (1983) "Estimation of Wage Gains and Welfare Gains from Self-Selection Models." Institute for Research on Poverty, University of Wisconsin.
Catsiapsis, B., and Robinson, C. (1982). "Sample Selection Bias with Multiple Selection Rules: An Application to Student Aid Grants." *Journal of Econometrics* 18, 351–68.
Chamberlain, G. (1977). "An Instrumental Variables Interpretation of Identification in Variance Components and MIMIC Models." In *Kinometrics: The Determinants of Socio-Economic Success within and between Families*, edited by P. Taubman. Amsterdam: North-Holland.
(1982). "Multivariate Regression Models for Panel Data." *Journal of Econometrics* 18, 1–46.
(1984). "The Analysis of Panel Data." In *Handbook of Econometrics*, vol. II, edited by Z. Griliches and M. Intriligator. Amsterdam: North-Holland.
Cochran, W. (1968). "Errors in Measurement in Statistics." *Technometrics* 10, 637–66.
Cosslett, S. (1981). "Maximum Likelihood Estimation for Choice-Based Samples." *Econometrica* 49, 1289–316.
(1983). "Distribution-Free Maximum Likelihood Estimators of the Binary Choice Model." *Econometrica* 51, 765–872.
Duncan, G. J., Juster, T., and Morgan, J. (1982). "The Role of Panel Studies in a World of Scarce Research Resources." Paper presented at SSRC Conference on Designing Research with Scarce Resources, Washington, D.C.
Durbin, J. (1954). "Errors in Variables." *Review of International Statistics Institute* 22, 23–32.
Gallant, A. R. (1981). "On the Bias in Flexible Functional Forms and an Essentially Unbiased Form: The Fourier Flexible Form." *Journal of Econometrics* 15, 211–45.
Hausman, J. (1978). "Specification Tests in Econometrics." *Econometrica* 46, 1251–71.
Heckman, J. (1976). "Simultaneous Equations Models with Continuous and Discrete Endogenous Variables and Structural Shifts." In *Studies in Nonlinear Estimation*, edited by S. Goldfeld and R. Quandt. Cambridge, Mass.: Ballinger.
(1978). "Dummy Endogenous Variables in a Simultaneous Equations Systems." *Econometrica* 46, 931–61.
(1979). "Sample Selection Bias as a Specification Error." *Econometrica* 47, 153–61.
(1980). "Addendum to Sample Selection Bias as a Specification Error." In *Evaluation Studies*, vol. 5, edited by E. Stromsdorfer and G. Farkas. San Francisco: Sage.
Heckman, J., and Neumann, G. (1977). "Union Wage Differentials and the Decision to Join Unions." Typescript, University of Chicago.

Heckman, J., and Wolpin, K. (1976). "Does the Contract Compliance Program Work? An Analysis of Chicago Data." *Industrial and Labor Relations Review* 29(4), 554–64.

Judge, G., Griffiths, W., Hill, R., and Lee, T. (1980). *The Theory and Practice of Econometrics*. New York: Wiley.

Kagan, A., Linnik, T., and Rao, C. (1973). *Some Characterization Theorems in Mathematical Statistics*. New York: Wiley.

Lee, L. F. (1978). "Unionism and Wage Rates: A Simultaneous Equations Model with Qualitative and Limited Dependent Variables." *International Economic Review* 19, 415–33.

(1982). "Some Approaches to the Correction of Selectivity Bias." *Review of Economic Studies* 49, 355–72.

Lewis, H. G. (1982). "Union Relative Wage Effects: A Survey." Typescript, Duke University.

Lillard, L., and Weiss, Y. (1979). "Components of Variation in Panel Earnings Data: American Scientists, 1960–70." *Econometrica* 47, 437–54.

MaCurdy, T. (1982). "The Use of Time Series Processes to Model the Error Structure of Earnings in a Longitudinal Data Analysis." *Journal of Econometrics* 18(1), 83–114.

Madansky, A. (1964). "Instrumental Variables in Factor Analysis." *Psychometrika* 29, 105–18.

Manski, C., and Lerman, S. (1977). "The Estimation of Choice Probabilities from Choice-Based Samples." *Econometrica* 45, 1977–88.

Manski, C., and McFadden, D. (1981). "Alternative Estimators and Sample Designs for Discrete Choice Analysis." In *Structural Analysis of Discrete Data with Econometric Applications*, edited by C. Manski and D. McFadden. Cambridge: MIT Press.

Mincer, J., and Jovanovic, B. (1981). "Labor Mobility and Wages." In *Studies in the Labor Market*, edited by S. Rosen. Chicago: University of Chicago Press.

Mundlak, Y. (1961). "Empirical Production Function Free of Management Bias." *Journal of Farm Economics* 43, 45–56.

(1978). "On the Pooling of Time Series and Cross Section Data." *Econometrica* 46, 69–85.

Pudney, S. E. (1982). "Estimating Latent Variable Systems When Specification Is Uncertain: Generalized Component Analysis and the Eliminant Method." *Journal of the American Statistical Association* 77, 883–9.

Roy, A. (1951). "Some Thoughts on the Distribution of Earnings." *Oxford Economic Papers* 3, 135–46.

Sargent, T. (1979). *Macroeconomic Theory*. New York: Academic Press.

Sisam, C. (1940). *College Algebra*. New York: Holt and Day.

White, H. (1980). "Nonlinear Regression on Cross Section Data." *Econometrica* 48, 721–46.

(1982). "Instrumental Variables Regressions with Independent Observations." *Econometrica* 50, 483–99.

(1984). *Asymptotic Theory for Econometricians*. Orlando, Fla.: Academic Press.

Willis, R., and Rosen, S. (1979). "Education and Self Selection." *Journal of Political Economy*, 87, S7–S36.

Wu, D. M. (1973). "Alternative Tests of Independence between Stochastic Regressors and Disturbances." *Econometrica* 41, 733–50.

(1983). "Tests of Causality, Predeterminedness, and Exogeneity." *International Economic Review* 24, 547–58.

Zellner, A., Kmenta, J., and Dreze, J. (1966). "Specification and Estimation of Cobb–Douglas Production Function Models." *Econometrica* 34, 784–95.

PART II

Statistical studies

CHAPTER 5

Weighting, misclassification, and other issues in the analysis of survey samples of life histories

Jan M. Hoem

1 Introduction

1.1 *Background and summary*

Despite the recent flowering of the literature concerned with methods to analyze human life history segments, comparatively little attention has been given to the particular problems of survey samples of such data. This chapter addresses selected issues of their analysis and provides solutions in a natural manner by combining elements of the relevant individual-based theory of stochastic processes with suitable parts of superpopulationist survey methodology. There are considerable divergences about some of these issues among current analysts, in particular about whether or when one should weight individual responses by means of reciprocal inclusion probabilities. There seems to be a standing dispute between those who would really like to see conventional weights applied in "most" circumstances and others who feel that the case for weighting is much weaker if the analyst wishes to use the data to estimate a properly specified model, since the model presumably "controls for" the effects of the factors which lead to the need for weights in the first place, except perhaps for particular dependent variables in the model. (Formulation essentially taken from PSID, 1983, p. A-13.) Still others may feel that weights are no advantage in model-based analyses.

In a particularly lucid passage, Schirm, Trussell, Menken, and Grady (1982, p. 71), who study contraceptive failure, correctly argue that the standard statistical theory on which significance tests are based collapses if a weighted sample is used in a model-based investigation of life histories. They check to find that "fortunately, our early analysis of these data revealed that the estimates of effects derived using an unweighted sample are approximately equal to those obtained using a weighted one; therefore, in the subsequent analyses, the . . . weights are ignored." They seem apologetic about it, however, and feel that "in the strictest sense, weighted arrays of [events] and of [exposures] should be employed if the results are to be representative of all married contraceptive users." Many analysts seem to have attitudes of this nature, or behave as if they do.

We contend that within a framework such as that of Schirm et al. (1982), there is no need to be apologetic about ignoring weights. The notion that weights are necessary as well as the appeal to representativeness probably are inherited from conventional sampling theory. It is important to realize that this theory must be modified for the analysis of samples of life histories as it must for any other model-based inference. To the extent that one can generalize the finding that weighting is empirically unimportant, it is an argument against the harmfulness of weighting rather than for the harmlessness of ignoring weights in settings like that of the quotation above. A move toward such generalization has been made by Särndal (1980), who has found that it essentially does not matter what weights are attached to the observations in the estimation of regression coefficients used in a procedure to finally estimate a finite population mean.

As we show below in great generality, it turns out that for the issue of weighting, the crucial question is whether the survey sampling mechanism is stochastically independent of the outcome of the life histories, in which case the sampling mechanism is called *noninformative*. If it is noninformative, then one may disregard the sampling plan and treat the sample of life histories as so many independent sample paths of stochastic processes with the probabilistic properties they would have had without the interference of survey sampling. Poststratification into behaviorally distinct groups is recommended, across prior stratum boundaries if this is suitable. Concomitant information should be exploited as usual. Conventional weighting is a needless complication.

By contrast, if the sample depends on the life histories, then weighting may be a useful tool to achieve consistency, though the weights need not be those conventionally recommended.

The question of dependence between the life histories and the sampling mechanism must be decided on the basis of the analyst's conception of reality as formulated in a model of human behavior. This model describes individual behavior in employment dynamics, child-bearing patterns, consumer behavior, migration, trends in party preferences, or whatever the subject of investigation is. It also includes the response behavior of individuals in the target sample. Unless the analyst "only" wants to generalize from the sample to values of statistics defined for the finite target population, a rational solution to the issue of weighting depends on the formulation of such a model. So long as the model determines the informatory status of the survey sampling mechanism correctly, the possibility of misspecification of other parts of the model is not involved in the issue of weighting.

A different issue which we address is the possibility that the observational design may give an outcome-based ("choice-based," endogenously selected) set of life history segments, as when female labor force participation at younger ages is investigated separately for women who remain unmarried until age 50, say. Outcome-based sampling has pitfalls lying in wait for the unwary. We give particular attention to selection by virtue of survival, which makes the sampling design informative in spite of the best efforts of the sampling practitioner. Ventures like enlarging the sample or reducing nonresponse are desirable on many counts, but they cannot eliminate the consequences of endogenously selective observations, which are problematic whether the data are available for a survey sample or for the whole target population.

Our final section is concerned with misclassification errors, another feature which plagues exhaustive censuses as well as survey samples but which seems particularly relevant to the latter. Again, a rational solution depends on the specification of a behavioral model, in this case a model for misclassification behavior in addition to the substantive transition structure.

Our presentation concerns the analysis of life history segments in many fields, such as criminology, demography, employment dynamics, epidemiology, and microsociology. In fact, the general theory of Section 2 is relevant for any study of model-generated survey sample data. We will allude freely to standard methods for the analysis of life history data and to superpopulationist theory. Overviews of the former have been given by Kalbfleisch and Prentice (1980), Coleman (1981), Gill (1979, 1982), Miller, Gong, and Muñoz (1981), Jacobsen (1982), Tuma and Hannan (1984), and Andersen (Chapter 6 in this volume). Reviews of the superpopulationist approach have been given by Cassel, Särndal, and Wretman (1977), and by Särndal (1978). Kalton (1981) has recently argued the sampling practitioner's position on the use of models in survey sampling again. He also has a good reference list. Kish, Groves, and Krotki (1976) and Verma, Scott, and O'Muircheartaigh (1980) give firmly design-based analyses and recommendations concerning survey samples of life histories.

Many of the points made in this chapter have been made before, at least in particular connections. [Compare, for instance, the overview by Little, 1982, and the nonmathematical formulations by Klevmarken, 1982, sec. 4.2, who is concerned with microeconomics. Neat formulations of the same main standpoint as in our Section 2 have been given by Fienberg (1980, pp. 335–338) and Smith (1982). The notions of our Section 2 were described at a slower pace by Hoem and Funck Jensen, 1982, sec. 6.] One seems to be approaching some kind of consensus on many issues. Since the dispute on a range of matters continues, and because of the uncertainty about the role of models which is apparent in some of the literature, it seems worthwhile to make the points again, however, especially because their relevance to life history analysis needs to be clarified. In addition, the central role which the informatory status of the sampling mechanism plays for the general theory needs to be made more explicit than it is in the current literature.

The application of these notions to life history analysis is more than merely a presentation of old ideas in new dress. The time parameter plays a quite different role in life history analysis than it does in fields where these issues have been raised before. The time sequence of life events is fundamental to the description of causality, and temporal aspects produce new problems in terms of the observational plan in general and for the sampling procedure, problems which may have been less important and certainly have received less attention previously. In life history analysis, the basic parameters automatically become time-dependent functions. Time-dependent exogenous variables are a natural feature, and the possibility of time censoring is ever-present. New conceptual distinctions need to be made. Informativity and ignorability of a sampling plan are different concepts; a plan may be informative but ignorable. Differentiality of a factor is something else than its selectivity; nonresponse is differential if it depends on exogenous, nonstochastic variables; it is selective if it depends on endogenous, stochastic variables. The methods of analysis may be different for the two cases. One needs to beware of outcome-dependent (endogenously based, "choice-based") observational plans, but such a plan disturbs the analysis only if the plan is anticipatory with respect to it. These concepts are interwoven: Survival as a condition for observation makes a plan informative and anticipatory but ignorable if separation is nonselective. Relations between these concepts are investigated in this chapter.

1.2 *Introductory example: labor force participation*

Before we embark on our general discussion, it is convenient to present an example for concreteness and easy reference. Consider, therefore, the (unrealistically) simple three-state model of labor force participation which is used for working life tables. It is a time-continuous Markov chain with age as its "time" parameter. The three states are "out of the labor force" (state 0), "in the labor force" (state 1), and "dead" (state 2). The probability of being in state j at age y when you are in state i at age x is $P_{ij}(x, y)$. The transition intensity from state i to state $j \neq i$ at age x is

$$\mu_{ij}(x) = \lim_{y \downarrow x} \frac{P_{ij}(x, y)}{y - x}$$

This means that there is a probability of $\mu_{ij}(x)\,dx$ of moving to state j by age $x + dx$ if you are in state i at age x. Then $\mu_{01}(\cdot)$ is called the intensity of accession to the labor force, $\mu_{10}(\cdot)$ is the intensity of separation from the labor force, while $\mu_{02}(\cdot)$ and $\mu_{12}(\cdot)$ are intensities of mortality. In the simplest version of this model, mortality is nonselective, that is, $\mu_{02}(\cdot) = \mu_{12}(\cdot)\,[=\mu(\cdot)$, say], and one may write

$$P_{01}(x, y) = \exp\left\{-\int_x^y \mu(t)\,dt\right\} \int_x^y \mu_{01}(t) \exp\left\{-\int_t^y \gamma(s)\,ds\right\} dt$$

with $\gamma(s) = \mu_{01}(s) + \mu_{10}(s)$. Similar explicit formulas hold for the other transition probabilities in this case.

Individuals are assumed to move independently between the states of this model. A complete life history is a table listing an individual's age at all entries into and exits from the labor force, as well as the age at death. From a collection of such tables, one may estimate the transition intensities, transition probabilities, mean sojourn times in the states, and so on. If the intensities are the same for all individuals and if they are constant in each single year age group, say, then the maximum likelihood estimator for the constant intensity μ_x^{ij} for age group x is the occurrence/exposure rate $\tilde{\mu}_x^{ij} = D_x^{ij}/L_x^i$, where D_x^{ij} is the recorded number of transitions $i \to j$ in age group x in the population, and L_x^i is the number of person-years recorded in state i for this age group. The estimators $\{\tilde{\mu}_x^{ij}\}$ will be asymptotically independent and normally distributed and have other nice, optimal properties. See Hoem and Funck Jensen (1982) for details and for a discussion of the assumption of piecewise constancy of the intensities. The statistical literature offers many other possibilities.

Complete life histories of labor force participation are rarely available. In the usual labor force surveys, which provide the major standard source of data on this topic, the status of an individual is observed at given time points only. The individual level data are aggregated into gross flows, which for each (x, i, j) give the number N_x^{ij} of individuals in age group x recorded in state i at some time t' and recorded again in state j at some later time $t'' = t' + h$. With constant intensities between ages x and $x + h$, it is possible to convert these data into intensity estimates in the simple working life table model above. Let

$$\hat{p}_x^{ij} = \frac{N_x^{ij}}{N_x^{i0} + N_x^{i1}} \quad \text{and} \quad \hat{b}_x = -\frac{1}{h}\frac{\ln(1 - \hat{p}_x^{10} - \hat{p}_x^{01})}{\hat{p}_x^{10} + \hat{p}_x^{01}}$$

Then

$$\hat{\mu}_x^{01} = \hat{b}_x \hat{p}_x^{01} \quad \text{and} \quad \hat{\mu}_x^{10} = \hat{b}_x \hat{p}_x^{10}$$

are suitable estimators for μ_x^{01} and μ_x^{10} with respectable statistical properties (asymptotic binormality, consistency, and so on; see Hoem and Funck Jensen, 1982, sec. 5.1).

To get a more realistic model, the state "in the labor force" needs to be split into two states, "employed" and "unemployed." At least some of the transition intensities would depend on duration in the current state (in addition to the age dependence). For instance, the intensity of accession into employment depends on how long an individual has been unemployed in the current unemployment spell. The intensities may also depend on the number of previous unemployments (occurrence dependence) and perhaps on statistics like time spent out of the labor force since maturity. In addition, mortality is likely to be selective, that is, to depend on current status. Such features require the use of increasingly complex models. At any state, comparison between cohorts and between population groups are made conveniently in terms of the transition intensities and their influence on other model quantities. Substantive interests lead us to concentrate on such comparisons; on modeling the intensities as functions of known, exogenous background variables (concomitant information) and of unknown, estimable parameters; and on exposing and explaining time trends in parameter values and in their differences between subgroups. It may also lead to comparisons between effects of endogenous factors, such as studies of how mortality depends on labor force status. The methods of statistical inference will depend on the observational plan and on the kind of data which it makes available to the analyst. Sometimes this plan will provide survey sample data of segments of life histories – for instance, the information obtained for individuals who participate in a number of subsequent rounds of a labor force survey with a rotating panel. The analysis of survey sample data of such a nature is the topic of this chapter.

The simple model on which working life tables are based was introduced for this purpose by Hoem and Fong (Hoem and Fong, 1976; Hoem, 1977). Its history goes back to DuPasquier (1912/13). Models incorporating duration dependence and occurrence dependence were studied by Schoenbaum (1924/5) and Simonsen (1936). Some mathematics of general models of this type (time-inhomogeneous semi-Markov models) was given by Hoem (1972). Methods of statistical inference for models of employment dynamics have been discussed recently by Heckman and Borjas (1980) and by Flinn and Heckman (1982), who provide some evidence in favor of a four-state rather than a three-state model (if you count "dead" as a state).

2 The observation of life histories

2.1 *The observational plan*

If a life history is regarded as the outcome of a stochastic process, then everybody's ideal data set would contain complete information on all relevant events and event dates for all individuals in the target population. Unfortunately, reality is usually less than ideal, and the analyst must be content with data which may be fragmentary, where events may be missing and event dates may be wrong or unrecorded, where individuals may be classified into incorrect statuses and where whole records may be missing due to nonresponse or nonrecording, or by design as in survey data. Matters like these are described in the observational plan, which converts what is potentially observable (by a Laplacian demon, say) into what is actually recorded. It specifies whether data are available for individuals or aggregates, whether only segments of each life history are observed and by which principles any segments are chosen, whether observation is complete or only fragmentary within each segment, whether the life histories observed are selected and by what mechanism, and whether in principle all paths in the target population are included or whether "only" a sample has been surveyed.

Assume that the target population consists of N stochastically independent individuals, numbered from 1 to N. Individual number i has a (complete) life history Y_i, from which the possibly fragmentary information $Z_i = h_i(Y_i)$ can be made available for analysis. Suppose that Z_i depends on Y_i alone, and not on the life histories of other individuals, as it would if, say, observation were kept going until the time when total exposure to a particular risk (say total unemployment time) reaches a predescribed level. If Z_i is a function of Y_i alone, we say that *observation of life histories is independent across individuals.* Then the transformation h_i is the *individual level observational plan.* We permit it to vary between individuals, as it will to some extent if observation is made over a fixed time interval, since then the corresponding age interval of observation may vary somewhat even between individuals in the same cohort. A sampling plan is a specification of a random mechanism which selects a target sample $\mathbf{S} = (I_1, I_2, \ldots, I_{n(\mathbf{S})})$ of distinct numbers from $\{1, 2, \ldots, N\}$, and we define

$$P(\mathbf{s}|\mathbf{y}) = P\{\mathbf{S} = \mathbf{s}|\mathbf{Y} = \mathbf{y}\}$$

where $\mathbf{s} = (i_1, i_2, \ldots, i_{n(\mathbf{s})})$, $\mathbf{Y} = (Y_1, \ldots, Y_N)$, and so on. We call the sampling plan *noninformative* if this function is independent of $\mathbf{Y}$. In this case, $\mathbf{S}$ and $\mathbf{Y}$ are stochastically independent. We disregard nonresponse for the moment. Then the data available for analysis are

$$\mathbf{D} = \{(i, Z_i): i \in \mathbf{S}\} = \{(I_i, Z'_j): j = 1, 2, \ldots, n(\mathbf{S})\}$$

for $Z'_j = Z_{I_j}$. Assume that the sample paths $Y_1, Y_2, \ldots, Y_N$ are stochastically independent and let Y_i have the probability distribution $\xi_i(\cdot)$. These distributions need not be equal to each other. Indeed, behaviorally distinct groups of individuals are permitted and (exogenous) concomitant information on the individual level is possible. So are unobservable heterogeneity parameters in the spirit of Heckman and Singer (1982a,b), Vaupel and Yashin (1982), and Hougaard (1982); compare also Hoem and Funck Jensen (1982, sec. 6.2). Then the distribution $\eta_i(\cdot)$ of Z_i is given as

$$P\{Z_i \in B_i\} = \xi_i\{Y_i: h_i(Y_i) \in B_i\} = \xi_i\{h_i^{-1}(B_i)\} = \eta_i(B_i)$$

for any measurable event B_i for Z_i. The probability distribution of the data is given by

$$P\left\{\mathbf{S} = \mathbf{s}, \bigcap_{j=1}^{n(\mathbf{s})} (Z_{i_j} \in B_j)\right\} = \int_A p(\mathbf{s}|\mathbf{y}) \prod_{i=1}^{N} d\xi_i(y_i) \tag{2.1}$$

where $\mathbf{s} = (i_1, i_2, \ldots, i_{n(\mathbf{s})})$ as before, while

$$A = \left\{\mathbf{y}: \bigcap_{j=1}^{n(\mathbf{s})} [h_{i_j}(y_{i_j}) \in B_j]\right\}$$

If p is noninformative, this reduces to

$$P\left\{\mathbf{S} = \mathbf{s}, \bigcap_{j=1}^{n(\mathbf{s})} (Z_{i_j} \in B_j)\right\} = p(\mathbf{s}) \prod_{j=1}^{n(\mathbf{s})} \xi_{i_j}\{h_{i_j}^{-1}(B_j)\}$$

or

$$P\left\{\bigcap_{j=1}^{n(\mathbf{s})} (Z_{i_j} \in B_j)|\mathbf{S} = \mathbf{s}\right\} = \prod_{j=1}^{n(\mathbf{s})} \eta_{i_j}(B_j) \tag{2.2}$$

Given the target sample $\mathbf{s}$ actually drawn, therefore, $Z'_1, Z'_2, \ldots, Z'_{n(\mathbf{s})}$ may be treated as $n(\mathbf{s})$ independent recorded life histories with the distributions they would have had in an imagined exhaustive census whose individual data had the same properties as those of the sample survey.

So long as the sampling plan is noninformative and observation is independent across individuals, *we need not worry about it in the analysis of the life histories. It has no independent effect on the outcome of the analysis* beyond being the channel which determines which histories to include in the target sample. Following Rubin's (1976, 1978, 1980) terminology, we call the sampling plan *ignorable.* In particular, the inclusion weights of conventional survey theory are not needed and finite population corrections or cluster intraclass correlations are not relevant.

Note that this main result is independent of the interpretation of Y_i as a life history. It is relevant to any set of independent random outcomes. Compare a similar formulation by Little (1982, sec. 2.2). Also note that the result is independent of the specification of the $\{\xi_i\}$, that is, of the model for individual behavior. In this respect, *model misspecification is not at issue.*

Some recent examples of life history analyses from various areas where the sampling design has been ignored in this manner are Flinn and Heckman (1982) in employment dynamics; Thomsen (1981) for use in party preference polls and elsewhere; as well as Menken et al. (1981), Schirm et al. (1982), and Finnäs and Hoem (1979) in demography.

Even though the analyst is advised to disregard the sampling *mechanism* if it is noninformative, he should not close his eyes to the peculiarities of the *sample* and follow what Royall (1976) amusingly has called the closurization principle. The sampled life histories should be treated as outcomes of a stochastic behavioral model and should be treated on their own merits, rather than, say, as representatives of a target population.

The standard sampler practice to weight the response records has rubbed off on some analyses of event history sample data. Weighting procedures are sometimes used to compute national averages for behavioral model parameters, even in the face of significant behavioral differences between subgroups – for instance, between racial or ethnic groups. The purpose may have been to achieve "representativity" on the national level, in the same spirit as in our quotation from Schirm et al. (1982). It is hard to see what such representativity would mean or what the national parameters would represent in a case of this sort. It would seem more sensible to analyze each behavioral group separately. If there is differential behavior, then surely group-specific parameter estimates must be more adequate and more interesting. It would also remove some needless practical problems, particularly some computational intricacies.

To illustrate simply, consider stratified random sampling where the linear model $Y = \beta_j x + U$ holds for individuals in stratum j. Here, x is a nonrandom and Y a random scalar for each individual, and the individual

U are independent and normal $(0, \sigma^2)$, all with same σ^2. This is an elementary version of the mixture model discussed by DuMouchel and Duncan (1981). In practice, interest would usually concentrate on each stratum-specific β_j rather than on some average $\bar{\beta} = \sum \pi_j \beta_j$ for suitable weights $\{\pi_j\}$. Presumably, DuMouchel and Duncan (1981) and their predecessors discuss the estimation of $\bar{\beta}$ for its theoretical interest and not for its practical meaningfulness. However this may be, they demonstrate that conventional weighting is no particular safeguard against biased estimation of $\bar{\beta}$.

Conventional weighting is often claimed to be a general buffer against model misspecification. Perhaps this argument is meant to hold for an inadequate group specification. If so, the adequacy of the argument remains to be demonstrated.

The recommendation to ignore inclusion weights when the sampling plan is noninformative is not a suggestion that weighting should be thrown out indiscriminately. Even if individual life histories are regarded as outcomes of stochastic processes, the analyst may decide to generalize to the level of the finite population "only." Let Z_i still be the information obtainable on individual i if this individual becomes a respondent, and let $\mathbf{Z} = (Z_1, \ldots, Z_N)$. As is generally recognized, it is perfectly legitimate to want to draw conclusions only about a function $f(\mathbf{Z})$ that depends on the (potential) outcomes $\mathbf{Z}$ alone, such as a mean number of unemployment periods by a given age in a cohort (or realized female labor force participation at a given age in a certain year) in the actual target population in question. Though superpopulationist survey theory offers other possibilities (see, e.g., Cassel, Särndal, and Wretman, 1977, and Särndal, 1980), it is also legitimate (though perhaps suboptimal) to condition on the values $z_1, z_2, \ldots, z_N$ of $Z_1, Z_2, \ldots, Z_N$ in the target population and to use conventional (design-based, nonsuperpopulationist) survey theory to make statements about the statistic $f(\mathbf{z})$. If individuals have different probabilities of being included in the sample, then reciprocal selection probabilities should be used as weights in the usual manner. This approach is what data-producing agencies invite when they attach a weight to each respondent's record indicating the number of individuals in the target population he or she is supposed to represent, and it surely is what Kish, Groves, and Krotki (1976) and Verma et al. (1980) had in mind. It may be the position taken by many investigators, among them Millman and Hendershot (1980).

Much of the analysis of life histories is based on an underlying model, however, either explicitly or tacitly because the procedures actually used can have little meaning otherwise. It is hard to see what meaningful finite population statistics are estimated by occurrence/exposure rates, Kaplan–Meier estimators, Nelson–Aalen plots, logistic regression coefficients, or the estimated coefficients of Cox-type life table regression analysis, all of which are used with samples as well as with complete sets of life history segments.

Under the superpopulationist approach, the informatory status of the sampling plan becomes important, for data from informative sampling designs may have quite different properties *and weighting may be appropriate* to achieve consistent estimators in individual cases, as we will show below. [Holt et al. (1980) and Nathan and Holt (1980) demonstrate that weighting may produce a robust though inefficient estimator for an informative sampling plan in a regression situation.] The informatory status again depends on the model, for the model defines which variables are seen as stochastic. Suppose, for instance, that one intends to analyze how a wife's labor force participation in a particular year depends on her husband's income in the same year. Suppose that a target sample of couples has been selected by nonproportional stratified random sampling with strata formed according to the husband's income in the previous year. Then the sampling plan is noninformative if the previous year's incomes are taken as exogenous (nonstochastic).

For another example, consider the sampling design of the 1979 U.S. National Longitudinal Study of Youth (Michael and Tuma, 1982, appendix). This study had five groups of strata, namely a large national stratified sample and four separate targeted smaller strata of military employees and of (apparently economically disadvantaged) Hispanics, non-Hispanic blacks, and non-Hispanic nonblacks, respectively. The four "special" strata of this study were oversampled. Since race or ethnic group is not part of the stochastic outcome of a life history, this element cannot have made the sampling design informative. For the sake of argument, it is possible that being an economically disadvantaged youth or a young military employee at the time of the survey can be incorporated as a random outcome of a model of educational and labor force behavior. Being a resident of a designated economically deprived survey area can conceivably be given similar status. Either of these would make the sampling plan informative and might legitimize the use of inclusion weights. To a distant observer, such ideas seem farfetched and the cause of needless complication, however. It seems equally legitimate to regard economic disadvantage and residence in early youth as part of the inheritance from the parental home along with race or ethnicity, that is, as exogenously determined and nonstochastic. The reader may figure out for himself how he wants to regard military employment.

Since the informatory status of the sampling mechanism depends on the model, one should recognize that model misspecification at this level may result in an unrealistic declaration that the sampling is noninformative. It is not clear what consequences this would have for statistical inference.

The claim of greater robustness against model misspecification often made for design-based procedures may not extend to and to the best of my knowledge has not been proved for this situation. For instance, the examples offered by Hansen, Madow, and Tepping (1978, sec. 2), Duncan (1982, appendix 2) and PSID (1983, pp. D-18–D-20) in support of the supremacy of the design-based approach have sampling mechanisms which are manifestly informative and therefore are not relevant for the issue of robustness against informatory status. Särndal (1980) proves a robustness result, but it is connected with the estimation of a finite population mean in a superpopulation setting and is not relevant here either.

We now turn to informative sampling plans. For them, general results on the level of our equation (2.2) do not seem to be available. Their theory largely becomes a series of case studies.

2.2 *Selection by virtue of survival*

Consider data gathered through retrospective interviews. Usually, samples for such surveys are drawn from a sampling frame which in principle consists of a representation (say an I.D. number) for each member of the target population on the date of sample selection. If an individual is dead or has otherwise left the target population and is unavailable when the sample is drawn, he or she is not regarded as a member of the sampling frame in the conventional sense, and such an individual has zero probability of inclusion in the sample, *even though the corresponding life history may belong among those potentially subject to analysis.* In the parlance of Hoem (1969), the sampling frame has been purged of such individuals.

To fix ideas, suppose that we want to investigate labor force participation in the cohort of women born in Sweden in 1936–40 by means of a (semi-)Markov model which recognizes the three statuses "employed," "unemployed," and "out of the labor force" for residents and the absorbing states "dead" and "out-migrated." The life histories we really want to analyze may be all who belong to this cohort (and to neighboring cohorts), but we must be content with a sample drawn from the central register of the resident population on some given date in 1982. Members of the cohort who are not included in the register do not belong to the sampling frame.

A move out of the resident Swedish population, through death or out-migration, is represented in the stochastic process model as a transition from one part of the state space to another part, possibly into an absorbing state, as in the case of death. If the intensity of such a transition depends on the state of an individual in the resident population, as when mortality is status-dependent, we say that there is *selective separation* (from the resident population). If separation is selective, then the data for the members who remain in the sampling frame on the date of sample selection suffer from a particular form of selection bias which Ryder (1965, p. 298) has called *selection by virtue of survival.* Conversely, if separation from the resident population is nonselective, then the selection bias due to the purging procedure vanishes as if by a magic wand. Note that this means that the informative sampling plan is ignorable (Rubin, 1976, 1978, 1980). This shows that ignorability and informatory status are separate concepts.

For concreteness we now state and prove these results for the case of a time-continuous Markov chain with a finite state space, although they can be proved for more general processes. (For some extensions, see Hoem, 1969, theorem 2; 1972, theorem 6.4.) Consider a Markov chain with a finite state space $\mathscr{I}$, transition probabilities $P_{ij}(x, y)$, and transition intensities $\mu_{ij}(x)$ defined as in Section 1.2. (We omit natural regularity conditions which simply make things work mathematically.) Let $P_{i\mathscr{B}} = \sum_{j \in \mathscr{B}} P_{ij}$, let $\mu_{i\mathscr{B}} = \sum_{j \in \mathscr{B} - i} \mu_{ij}$ for any $\mathscr{B} \subseteq \mathscr{I}$, and in particular let $\mu_i = \mu_{i\mathscr{I}}$. In applications to human populations, "time" may really be age-attained, as we noted before.

Suppose that $\mathscr{I}$ can be partitioned into an absorbing subset $\mathscr{D}$ and its complement $\mathscr{L} = \mathscr{I} - \mathscr{D}$. In our real-life example, $\mathscr{L}$ is the set of states for individuals in the resident population and transition into $\mathscr{D}$ corresponds to death or emigration. Separation is nonselective if $\mu_{i\mathscr{D}}(\cdot)$ is independent of $i \in \mathscr{L}$.

Collecting retrospective information on individuals of a given age who are members of the target population as of a particular date corresponds to conditioning on the event that $S(z) \in \mathscr{L}$ for a suitable age z and observing transitions prior to age z only for sample paths who satisfy this condition. The corresponding transition probabilities are

$$\begin{aligned} Q_{ij}(x, y, z) &= P\{S(y) = j \,|\, S(x) = i, S(z) \in \mathscr{L}\} \\ &= \frac{P_{ij}(x, y) P_{j\mathscr{L}}(y, z)}{P_{i\mathscr{L}}(x, z)} \end{aligned}$$

for $0 \leq x \leq y \leq z$ and $i, j \in \mathscr{L}$. The intensities which would be estimated by applying standard methods to the purged life history data are

$$\lambda_{ij}(x, z) = \lim_{y \downarrow x} \frac{Q_{ij}(x, y, z)}{(y - x)} = \mu_{ij}(x) \frac{P_{j\mathscr{L}}(x, z)}{P_{i\mathscr{L}}(x, z)} \tag{2.3}$$

for $i, j \in \mathscr{L}, i \neq j$. The distortion factor $P_{j\mathscr{L}}(x, z)/P_{i\mathscr{L}}(x, z)$ contains the bias due to selection by virtue of survival, that is, survival in the target population up to the date of sample selection. A factor of 1 corresponds to no bias, of course. *The distortion factor is identically equal to 1 if and only if separation from $\mathscr{L}$ is nonselective.* Our Appendix A1 contains a simple proof.

The purging bias distorts the transition intensities and makes it necessary to use some care in the interpretation of vital rates computed from the sample data. Other model quantities are functions of the transition intensities and should be approached with similar care. Selection biases have been discussed by Hoem (1969), Hoem and Funck Jensen (1982, secs. 5.2, 5.3) and their references, Borgan and Gill (1982), and others. Selection by virtue of survival persists in the face of any attempt at drawing a fair (noninformative) sample from the target population as of the sampling date or of increasing the sample size, even to an exhaustive enumeration, and no vigor in the fight against nonresponse can drive it out of existence. It is present from the outset, built into the whole procedure, simply because it is impossible to interview the dead and possibly those who have out-migrated.

The *extent* of the bias depends on the circumstances. The fact that it disappears when separation is nonselective gives some hope that it may often be small even when present. As yet, we seem to have few hard facts on which to base this judgment, but an epidemiological study by Andersen and Green (1982) as well as an investigation of the 1981 Swedish fertility survey by Lyberg (1983b) lend it strong support.

Even if separation is selective and its effects substantial, this need not be the end of the world if one is willing to work with an informative sampling plan. In this case, conventional weighting of individual responses can be used to counteract the selection biases, provided all relevant life histories have a positive and known probability of inclusion in the target sample. *In this connection, weighting has a legitimate role.* For retrospective interviews, one can imagine that efforts may be spent to interview a subsample of out-migrants and that mortality is nonselective. Alternatively, the data may be available in a population register rather than obtainable by retrospective interviews. Sampling may then be applied to reduce the cost and burden of data processing or to match data gathered from other sources for the same sample, as is done in connection with the Swedish level-of-living surveys.

Suppose that the records in the register are organized into separate files according to the outcome of the life histories, perhaps with one or more files for the resident population, one for the dead, and one for the out-migrated. It may be practical, then, to draw a sample from each file and to analyze the data by the notions of stratified samples. Note, however, that stratum membership is defined according to a (random) outcome which may be connected with the properties one wants to analyze, namely aspects of the life histories. This is not something which sampling theorists are too enthusiastic about, and it does make the sampling plan informative. If sample sizes are related to stratum sizes, then the selection probability of a member of a particular stratum even depends on the outcome of *other* life histories, for these outcomes determine stratum sizes. So long as the probabilities are positive and are known at the time of sample selection, however, an ordinary Horvitz–Thompson construction may be used to correct for selection biases and provide a consistent intensity estimator. We illustrate it for the simple estimation of a (piecewise) constant intensity as follows.

Assume that the estimand is an intensity λ defined for a particular kind of transition in a given age-and-duration interval, perhaps the intensity of accession into employment of middle-aged males after six months of unemployment. Individual number i in the target population experienced D_i such transitions (from unemployment to employment) in his or her life history, which for the sake of this argument we assume to be recorded without error. This individual was exposed to the risk of transition for a total time R_i and had a probability $\alpha_i(\mathbf{Y}) > 0$ of being included in the sample. For the reasons just noted, this probability may depend on life histories Y_j for $j \neq i$ as well as on Y_i. A natural estimator is

$$\hat{\lambda} = \frac{\sum_{i \in \mathbf{S}} D_i/\alpha_i(\mathbf{Y})}{\sum_{i \in \mathbf{S}} R_i/\alpha_i(\mathbf{Y})} \tag{2.4}$$

which can be shown to be consistent for λ (Hoem, 1983a) as $N \to \infty$ and $n \to \infty$.

As we prove in Appendix A3, $\hat{\lambda}$ need be a maximum likelihood estimator. When the model has more structure, the "choice-based" sampling literature may produce efficient competitors to $\hat{\lambda}$. Selection by virtue of survival is produced by an outcome-based (endogenously selective) observational plan. So are other selection biases, some of which will be discussed in our next section. Manski and McFadden (1981), Cosslett (1981), and their references have proved general results concerning statistical inference in parametric models for observational plans of this nature.

To the best of our knowledge, other properties of the estimator in (2.4) have not yet been investigated.

2.3 *Some other endogenously based observational plans*

2.3.1. Introduction. Selection by virtue of survival is perhaps the most insidious cause of selection bias, but a whole range of other biases are also relevant for life history analysis, both with sample data and with data for a whole population or a whole population segment. Some biases are inherent in the method of data collection, as in the previous section, and others are produced by the manner in which the data are organized after collection. For example, it is always dangerous to group life histories according to their final outcome, such as according to the level of education reached at interview (Hoem and Funck Jensen, 1982, sec. 5.3), or according to the number of unemployment periods recorded, or children ever born (Hobcraft and Rodríguez, 1980). The following examples extend the review by Hoem and Funck Jensen (1982, sec. 5).

In a check for the presence of selection bias, it is again convenient to work with the transition intensities. Other model elements (interval distributions and means, transition probabilities, and so on) are functions of the intensities, and consideration of any selection bias in the estimation of such a derived function can often be based on prior consideration of bias in the intensity estimates.

A useful instrument like Cox's life table regression model is defined directly in terms of transition intensities (Cox, 1972; Gill, 1982). The intensities are also a natural vehicle for extension to more general stochastic process models of human behavior.

2.3.2. Grouping by sibship size. Our first example is a particularly transparent illustration of the danger of grouping life histories by their final outcome. Bakketeig and Hoffman (1979) studied perinatal mortality by birth order in Norway in 1967–73 and organized female childbearing histories by sibship size. Their data show that the number of perinatal deaths among first births increased from 16.6 (per 1000 first births) for sibships of size 1 or 2, via 55.3 for sibships of size 3, to 61.9 for sibships of size 4. This was for women of parity 0 in 1967. They had similar findings for other groups and for other parities. In an interpretive discussion they noted correctly that results of this nature "are consistent with the known tendency to become pregnant again after a pregnancy with an early adverse outcome and the higher probability of stopping childbearing after a successful outcome of pregnancy." A prospective organization of the data obtained for the individual woman and analysis of events in temporal sequence would have *demonstrated* this causal connection. It would also have avoided the impression that having younger siblings can somehow be dangerous for the first-born *at birth*, an interpretation which is inherent in their analysis even though everyone realizes that it is impossible. Less transparent causal reversals might go undetected or unexplained. Roman et al. (1978) may have caused such reversal when they found that the overall risk of fetal loss appears to decrease with increasing pregnancy order and when they found no evidence of an increase in risk with age. They organized the data in the same manner as Bakketeig and Hoffman (1979).

2.3.3. Using last previous change of status. For our second example, let us consider the recommendation apparently sometimes made to data collection agencies to concentrate on obtaining date and type of last previous change of status in addition to status at interview. The residence history study by Taeuber et al. (1968) collected information on current residence and last previous residence (as well as second last previous residence and birthplace). The U.S. Census Bureau is said to receive similar recommendations for its census schedule. In labor force surveys, unemployed respondents are asked regularly about the length of their current unemployment. (Last previous employment status will usually be missing.) A similar restriction to the ascertainment of the most recent event(s) has been used for maternity histories in national contributions to the World Fertility Survey. Such restriction is often combined with an additional restriction to a recent period. The motivation is reduction in cost and improvement of response reliability.

Data of this nature are well known to be subject to *length bias*, whose importance depends on what model quantity one aims at estimating. Suppose that one is working with a Markov chain model as in Section 2.2, and suppose that someone suggests estimating the relative transition risk $\mu_{jk}(x)/\mu_j(x)$ by counting the recorded proportion of transitions leading to state k at age x among respondents aged $z > x$ at the time of data collection whose last previous reported transition was out of state j at age x. (The relative transition risk may for instance be the chance that an x-year-old woman leaves the labor force when she stops being unemployed.) To find what this recorded proportion actually estimates, define $S^-(z)$ to be the last previous state visited by an individual aged z and let $V(z)$ be the corresponding age at the last previous transition [with $V(z) = 0$ and $S^-(z) = S(z)$ if there is no previous transition after "age 0"]. If

$$P_j(x) = P\{S(x) = j\} = \sum_{i \in \mathscr{I}} P\{S(0) = i\} P_{ij}(0, x)$$

then

$$P\{x < V(z) < x + dx, S^-(z) = j, S(z) = k\}$$

$$= P_j(x)\mu_{jk}(x) \exp\left\{-\int_x^z \mu_k(u)\,du\right\} dx \qquad (2.5)$$

The quantity actually estimated is therefore

$$P\{S(z) = k \mid S^-(z) = j, V(z) = x\}$$

$$= \frac{\mu_{jk}(x) \exp\left\{-\int_x^z \mu_k(u)\,du\right\}}{\sum_{l \neq j} \mu_{jl}(x) \exp\left\{-\int_x^z \mu_l(u)\,du\right\}} \tag{2.6}$$

instead of $\mu_{jk}(x)/\sum_{l \neq j} \mu_{jl}(x)$, as desired. The amount of distortion involved depends on the relative sizes of the "survival factors" $\exp\{-\int_x^z \mu_l(u)\,du\}$. What counts is mainly the integrals $\int_x^z [\mu_l(u) - \mu_k(u)]\,du$ for all $l \in \mathscr{I} - j$. If they are all small in absolute value, the distortion may be quite tolerable.

Analyzing interval lengths will be more dangerous. Let $W^-(z) = z - V(z)$ be the the current duration of the sojourn interval at age z. This is the observed duration of the current spell of unemployment, or time since last previous migration, or present length of currently open birth interval, as the case may be. Let $W^+(z)$ be the waiting time up to the first subsequent transition, and let $W(z) = W^-(z) + W^+(z)$ be the total length of the current spell at age z. Then observation of $W(z)$ is heavily biased towards long intervals. Out of these, only the *backward recurrence time* $W^-(z)$ is known at age z. Its theoretical distribution follows from (2.5) and is given by

$$P\{w < W^-(z) < w + dw \mid S(z) = k\}$$

$$= \frac{1}{P_k(z)} \sum_{j \neq k} P_j(z - w)\mu_{jk}(z - w) \exp\left\{-\int_{z-w}^z \mu_k(u)\,du\right\} dw \tag{2.7}$$

The corresponding intensity is

$$\alpha_k(w) = \frac{\lim_{\Delta w \downarrow 0} P\{w < W^-(z) w + \Delta w \mid W^-(z) > w, S(z) = k\}/\Delta w}{\sum_{j \neq k} P_j(z - w)\mu_{jk}(z - w)}$$

$$= \frac{\sum_{j \neq k} P_j(z - w)\mu_{jk}(z - w)}{\sum_{j \neq k} \int_0^{z-w} P_j(s)\mu_k(s) \exp\left\{-\int_s^{z-w} \mu_k(u)\,du\right\} ds + P_k(0) \exp\left\{-\int_0^z \mu_k(u)\,du\right\}}$$

If we do not take $S(z)$ into account, $W^-(z)$ gets the "unconditional" intensity

$$\alpha(w) = \frac{\lim_{\Delta w \downarrow 0} P\{w < W^-(z) < w + \Delta w \,|\, W^-(z) > w\}}{\Delta w}$$

$$= \frac{\sum_j P_j(z-w)\mu_j(z-w)}{\sum_j \int_0^{z-w} P_j(s) \sum_{\neq} \mu_{jk}(s) \exp\left\{-\int_s^{z-w} \mu_k(u)\,du\right\} ds + \sum_k P_k(0) \exp\left\{-\int_0^z \mu_k(u)\,du\right\}}$$

This distribution is a complicated function of all $\{\mu_{ij}\}$, and so are its mean and variance. Changes in basic model parameters and in exogenous variables work their way through to the distribution and its moments via their influence on the intensities. Attempts to unravel these connections need to account for the functional dependences evident above. Simple analysis is not recommended except in simple cases. For example, regression analyses of the mean of (2.7) with respect to background variables run up against problems of a nature discussed recently by Flinn and Heckman (1982, sec. 3).

Some simplification does result if $S(\cdot)$ is a Poisson process, say, with intensity function $\phi(\cdot)$. Then we get

$$\alpha_k(w) = \frac{k\phi(z-w)}{\int_0^{z-w} \phi(s)\,ds}$$

and $\alpha(w) = \phi(z-w)$.

Data on last previous change need some prospective element if you want good estimators of basic intensities and probabilities. Björklund (1978) has recently exploited data from periodic labor force surveys to estimate holding probabilities of the form

$$P\{W^+(x) > t \,|\, S(x) = \text{"unemployed,"}\ W^-(x) = s\}$$

that is, probabilities of remaining unemployed for at least t more months if you have already been unemployed for s months.

Matters of this nature have been discussed by many others, among them Feller (1971), Henry (1972), and Sheps and Menken (1973). Backwards recurrence times were also discussed recently by Allison (1983).

2.3.4. Concentrating on the two most recent events. For our third and final example of selection bias, we take the analysis of the two most recent births in maternity histories, for which massive biases have been demonstrated by Page et al. (1980) and by Hobcraft and Rodríguez (1980). Similar problems would arise if one were to analyze the most recent completed unemployment period or the two most recent starts of unemployment. To begin a discussion of such problems softly, we first consider a common Poisson process with an age-dependent intensity $\phi(\cdot)$. Suppose that someone suggests estimating $\phi(\cdot)$ only from the dates of the two latest incidences of the Poisson event in question before age z. The purpose is to study event intervals by means of the hazard function. In imitation of natural procedures in the study of birth intervals, assume that one collects sample paths with a recorded event at some age x and subsequently at most one more before age z, and that $\phi(\cdot)$ is estimated between ages x and z from this data subset by means of occurrence/exposure rates or some more sophisticated procedure such as a Nelson–Aalen plot. This corresponds to estimating the function

$$\bar{\phi}(x, y, z) = \lim_{\Delta y \downarrow 0} \frac{1}{\Delta y} P\left\{\text{event in } \langle y, y+\Delta y] \,\middle|\, \begin{matrix}\text{event at age } x \text{ and} \\ \text{at most one more} \\ \text{event before age } z\end{matrix}\right\}$$

$$= \lim_{\Delta y \downarrow 0} \frac{\dfrac{1}{\Delta y} P\left\{\text{event in } \langle y, y+\Delta y] \begin{matrix}\text{and no other event} \\ \text{between ages } x \text{ and } z\end{matrix} \,\middle|\, \begin{matrix}\text{event at} \\ \text{age } x\end{matrix}\right\}}{P\{\text{no event or one event in } \langle x, z] \,|\, \text{event at age } x\}}$$

$$= \frac{\exp\left\{-\int_x^y \phi(s)\,ds\right\} \phi(y) \exp\left\{-\int_y^z \phi(s)\,ds\right\}}{\exp\left\{-\int_x^z \phi(s)\,ds\right\} + \int_x^z \exp\left\{-\int_x^t \phi(s)\,ds\right\} \phi(t) \times \exp\left\{-\int_t^z \phi(s)\,ds\right\} dt}$$

$$= \frac{\phi(y)}{\left\{1 + \int_x^z \phi(s)\,ds\right\}} \tag{2.8}$$

and we see that the suggested procedure leads to an underestimate of $\phi(\cdot)$. In the analysis of birth intervals, this corresponds to recording the two latest births for women in a given cohort, collecting histories with a birth recorded at age x, and computing age-specific birth rates for subsequent open as well as closed birth intervals, taken together. If attention is restricted to *closed* intervals (following the second latest recorded Poisson event), the function estimated is

$$\bar{\bar{\phi}}(x, y, z) = \frac{\phi(y)}{\int_x^z \phi(s)\,ds} \tag{2.9}$$

instead.

Note that both $\bar{\phi}$ and $\bar{\bar{\phi}}$ depend on x and z even though ϕ does not. The estimation procedure both distorts the level of the intensity and introduces a false dependence. The empirical birth interval distribution will be distorted correspondingly.

It is straightforward to translate these ideas into models for childbearing behavior which are more realistic than the Poisson process, but it causes some notational complication because of the need to keep track of parity and of the effect of duration since last previous birth, at a minimum. A similar translation into a model for unemployment behavior will also need to keep track of movements in and out of the labor force as well as in and out of employment. To simplify matters but still capture the main points of the case, we disregard mortality and let the probability that a woman of age y and parity $n \geq 1$ gives birth before age $y + dw$ be $\phi_n(w)\,dw$ when her last previous birth was at age $y - w$. The intensity $\phi_n(\cdot)$ is taken to be independent of y, of marital status, and of any other background variable. Such independence may be achieved reasonably well in practice by grouping according to background variables and by age at some previous event, much as above (2.4), and by concentrating on a single group. Let the ages at which a woman gives birth be $T_1, T_2, \ldots$, with $T_n = \infty$ if she stops at less than n births, and let $P\{t < T_n < t + dt\} = \lambda_n(t)\,dt$. Assume that attention is restricted to births between two selected ages x and z, which is a natural consequence of the current practice of analyzing cohort data from the most recent calendar period only. Then z is the age of the cohort at interview. Analysis of open as well as closed intervals between the two latest births from such data corresponds to working with birth intensities of the following form:

$$\begin{aligned}
&\bar{\phi}_n(w; x, z)\\
&\quad = \lim_{\Delta w \downarrow 0} \frac{1}{\Delta w} P\{w < T_{n+1} - T_n < w + \Delta w \mid x \leq T_n < z - w,\\
&\qquad\quad T_{n+1} - T_n > w, T_{n+2} > z\}\\
&\quad = \lim_{\Delta w \downarrow 0} \frac{\dfrac{1}{\Delta w} P\{x \leq T_n < z + w, w < T_{n+1} - T_n < w + \Delta w, T_{n+2} > z\}}{\begin{aligned}&P\{x \leq T_n < z - w, T_{n+1} > z\}\\ &\quad + P\{x \leq T_n < z - w, T_n + w < T_{n+1} < z < T_{n+2}\}\end{aligned}} = \frac{A}{B}
\end{aligned}$$

with

$$A = \int_x^{z-w} \lambda_n(t) \exp\left[-\int_0^w \phi_n(s)\, ds \right] \phi_n(w) \exp\left[-\int_0^{z-t-w} \phi_{n+1}(s)\, ds \right] dt$$

and

$$B = \int_x^{z-w} \lambda_n(t) \exp\left[-\int_0^w \phi_n(s)\, ds \right] \left\{ \exp\left[-\int_w^{z-t} \phi_n(s)\, ds \right] \right.$$
$$\left. + \int_w^{z-t} \exp\left[-\int_w^u \phi_n(s)\, ds \right] \phi_n(u) \exp\left[-\int_0^{z-t-u} \phi_{n+1}(s)\, ds \right] du \right\} dt$$

If we let

$$A' = \int_x^{z-w} \lambda_n(t) \exp\left[-\int_0^{z-t-w} \phi_{n+1}(s)\, ds \right] dt$$

and

$$B' = \int_x^{z-w} \lambda_n(t) \left\{ \exp\left[-\int_w^{z-1} \phi_n(s)\, ds \right] \right.$$
$$\left. + \int_w^{z-t} \exp\left[-\int_w^u \phi_n(s)\, ds \right] \phi_n(u) \exp\left[-\int_0^{z-t-u} \phi_{n+1}(s)\, ds \right] du \right\} dt$$

we therefore get

$$\bar{\phi}_n(w; x, z) = \phi_n(w) \frac{A'}{B'} \tag{2.10}$$

One may prove that $A'/B' < 1$. (See Appendix A4.) This means that *the statistical analysis described corresponds to working with birth intensities which are too small.* Thus, the procedure is biased toward long intervals. This mathematical result explains corresponding empirical findings by Hobcraft and Rodríguez (1980).

2.3.5. Anticipatory observational plans. The problems encountered in the analysis of the data organized by the observational plans discussed above are caused by the anticipatory nature of the designs. Selectivity by virtue of survival arises because behavior during a certain life phase is analyzed under the condition of survival to some later date, usually until closure of data collection. Grouping by sibship size causes problems because one analyzes perinatal mortality for births which appear before the date which defines the grouping criterion, in this case the date on which observation was terminated. Even the problems of using previous change of status or the two most recent events are due to the anticipatory status of the plans. If you know when the most recent event occurred before the terminal date, then you also know that no further event can appear in the interim, that is, you anticipate realized behavior between the recorded event date and the terminal date. Similar reasoning applies to the two most recent events.

In general, assume that the purpose of an investigation is to analyze human behavior between two values T and T' of the time parameter, say between ages T and T', where $T < T'$. (This may be part of a larger study.) These variables may be nonrandom, as when T is age 15 and T' is age at interview in a birth cohort. Alternatively, one or both may be random, as when T is age at first marriage and T' is age at first marriage dissolution or age at interview if smaller. If either variable is random, then let it be a *stopping time*. This means that when all observable events for the individual are known up to age x, then we know whether $T \leq x$ and whether $T' \leq x$, for any fixed x. Age at last birth before age 30 is not a stopping time; for a woman of age 25 we do not normally know whether she will have a birth between age 25 and 30.

Assume that the data have been organized in such a manner that in a certain portion of the analysis, all individuals have experienced a specified set of events which are determined by behavior up to some age T''. The behavior may be survival until the end of observation (actual survival until interview, survival in an intact first marriage until age 50, or whatever the case may be), or it may be a more complex pattern such as a specification of the ages at the two last births before age T''. Assume that T'' is also a stopping time. (Technically speaking, the behavioral process on the individual level is adapted to an increasing family of σ algebras $\{\mathscr{F}_t\}$, and we are conditioning on some sub-σ algebras $\mathscr{A} \subseteq \mathscr{F}_{T''}$, where $\mathscr{A} \nsubseteq \mathscr{F}_t$ for any $t < T''$.)

For simplicity, suppose that either $T'' \geq T'$ or $T'' \leq T$ by definition. If $T'' \geq T'$, then the observational plan (or the organization of the data) is *anticipatory with respect to* (*the analysis of behavior in*) $[T, T']$. If $T'' \leq T$, then the plan is not anticipatory with respect to $[T, T']$.

If $T'' \leq T$, then analysis in $[T, T']$ can be carried out without the risk of selection biases. For instance, female employment patterns after first marriage formation can be studied, conditional, say, on ages at first marriage and at first entry into the labor force, as well as conditional on educational level at entry. No selection bias results. But such biases may appear if the analysis is for behavior *before* first marriage or conditional on educational level at age T' (which may be the age at interview), for then the observational plan is anticipatory.

Whether an anticipatory plan causes selection bias depends on the circumstances. In historical demography, there is a tendency to concentrate on marital childbearing histories for women whose marriages remain intact until menopause and to disregard those who die or become widowed (or divorced, if applicable) at an earlier age. This will cause selection biases in the analysis of fertility if female marital mortality depends on parity. If mortality is nonselective, the biases disappear. (See Hoem, 1970.) We encounter the same phenomenon as we did with survival-dependent retrospective observation in Section 2.2. Similar problems arise if employment behavior during the year(s) of observation is studied after grouping according to status at the *end* as well as at the beginning of a period of participation in an ordinary labor force survey with a rotating panel or if migration histories are analyzed separately for each region of residence at the time of data collection.

Note that the observational plans discussed here are all outcome-dependent (with trivial exceptions such as when $T'' \equiv 0$). Collecting marital, childbearing, and employment histories for ever-married women alone gives an outcome-based plan, for individuals are eligible for inclusion only after first marriage. Thus an outcome-based plan need not induce selection biases in an analysis. As we have shown, whether it does depends on whether the plan is anticipatory, and even then the biases depend on the selectivity of endogenous factors.

As we noted above (2.1), unobservable heterogeneity parameters are covered by our theory for noninformative sampling. No account has been taken of such heterogeneity in our account of informative plans. The effects of outcome-based observation on the analysis of heterogeneous populations is an important topic of future research.

2.4 *Nonresponse errors*

As is well known, sample nonresponse may be strongly related to the purpose of the survey investigation. As a step toward modeling nonresponse, we introduce the response probability $\beta_i(Y_i)$ that individual i in the target population will become a member of the achieved sample if he is selected as a member of the target sample. It may depend on his values on exogenous variables and on the outcome of his own individual life history Y_i. In the Swedish fertility survey of 1981, for instance, women of age 36–40 who had children born in 1962 or later living with them at the time of sample selection had a response rate of 89 percent, while women in the same cohort without such children only had a response rate of 72 percent (Arvidsson et al., 1982, p. 98; Lyberg, 1983b). (The overall rate was 87 percent.) The corresponding rates for women of age 35–39 with and without registered lifetime live births in the corresponding Norwegian survey of 1977 were 85 and 64 percent, respectively, with an overall rate of 82 percent (Østby and Noack, 1981, sec. 3.2).

Let us say that the nonresponse is *differential* if the function $\beta_i(\cdot)$ is not the same for all i. Let us call it *selective* if $\beta_i(Y_i)$ depends on Y_i. Särndal and Hui (1981) discuss models of nonresponse which is differential but not selective. Anderson (1979) and others have discussed methods of adjusting for selective nonresponse. Little (1982) has reviewed both possibilities. See also Williams and Mallows (1970) and Williams (1975).

In the general framework at the beginning of Section 2.1, call the achieved sample $\mathbf{S}'$. When information is missing on some item k for some respondents, one may go further and introduce a subsample $\mathbf{S}_k'' \subseteq \mathbf{S}'$ for which information is obtained for this item and use values of other items to impute the missing values for item k among respondents in $\mathbf{S}' - \mathbf{S}_k''$. Greenlees, Reece, and Zieschang (1982), Anderson (1979), and Little (1982) have discussed imputation for selective unit nonresponse and have provided references to the previous literature. See also Marini, Olsen, and Rubin (1980). Valuable as they are, imputation techniques will introduce dependence relations between the values $\{Z_i: i \in \mathbf{S}_k''\}$ and those used instead of $\{Z_i: i \in \mathbf{S}' - \mathbf{S}_k''\}$, akin to similar dependences which occur in sampling with replacement (Hoem and Funck Jensen, 1982, sec. 6.1). To pursue these notions would detract from our main line of argument, so we will disregard item nonresponse and concentrate on unit nonresponse in this chapter. The data to be used for statistical analysis, then, are

$$\mathbf{D}' = \{(i, Z_i): i \in \mathbf{S}'\}$$

The complete (achieved) sampling mechanism consists of the survey sampling plan and the nonresponse mechanism. Let us call it informative (noninformative) if it is stochastically dependent on (independent of) the life histories $\mathbf{Y}$. If the sampling plan is noninformative and nonresponse is nonselective, the achieved sampling mechanism is noninformative. In this case, a result for the achieved sample can be proved in the same manner as (2.2) was proved for the target sample: *So long as the achieved sampling mechanism is noninformative, the achieved data* $\mathbf{D}'$ *can be treated as so many observations on the* Z_i *as if sampling and nonresponse had not interfered* beyond making the data available for analysis. The sampling mechanism is ignorable.

Now suppose that the sampling plan is noninformative and has inclusion probability α_i for individual i, but that nonresponse is selective with response probability $\beta_i(Y_i)$. Then the probability is $\alpha_i\beta_i(Y_i)$ that individual i will be a respondent, and the achieved sampling mechanism is informative. In the case where the $\beta_i(Y_i)$ are known, conventional weighting would lead to an estimate

$$\hat{\hat{\lambda}} = \frac{\sum_{i \in \mathbf{S}'} D_i/[\alpha_i\beta_i(Y_i)]}{\sum_{i \in \mathbf{S}'} R_i/[\alpha_i\beta_i(Y_i)]} \tag{2.11}$$

to replace $\hat{\lambda}$ in (2.4). While $\hat{\hat{\lambda}}$ is certainly consistent as $N \to \infty$ and $n \to \infty$, the use of the $\{\alpha_i\}$ represents a needless complication. One may as well use

$$\Lambda = \frac{\sum_{i \in \mathbf{S}'} D_i/\beta_i(Y_i)}{\sum_{i \in \mathbf{S}'} R_i/\beta_i(Y_i)}$$

instead. This estimator is also consistent, and it will have properties similar to $\hat{\lambda}$. We see that weights could be used, but they would not involve the inclusion probabilities of the sampling plan.

In practice, it is important to know the properties of a naive estimate

$$\tilde{\lambda} = \frac{D'}{R'}$$

with $D' = \sum_{i \in \mathbf{S}'} D_i$ and $R' = \sum_{i \in \mathbf{S}'} R_i$. This $\tilde{\lambda}$ will converge in probability to the ratio $E\{D_i\beta_i(Y_i)\}/E\{R_i\beta_i(Y_i)\}$, which can often be expressed sensibly as λ times an understandable distortion factor. Appendix A2 contains an account of the particularly simple example of a pure death process. In a more realistic setting, Lyberg (1983a) has studied the effects of selective nonresponse for the 1981 Swedish fertility survey. For that survey, one is in the unique situation of being able to find out what respondents and nonrespondents alike should have reported on items contained in the reliable data of the national vital statistics system. Lyberg (1983a) demonstrates that while nonresponse effects are present, they are often negligible, and they are never able to distort or even mask substantive trends in the aspects she has investigated. In her case, adjustment for such effects may not be helpful and is not needed. How general the application of such a result is is unknown at present. Lyberg (personal communication) speculates that it may be due to the particularly energetic follow-up of initial nonrespondents in this survey. In addition, it may be due in part to the fact that achieved childbearing is a relatively innocuous topic by comparison to induced abortion, own crime, venereal disease, and other hot potatoes. Own childbearing is also more easily "diagnosed" and remembered than (say) health survey topics like backaches or allergies. These features may work in the direction of smaller selectivity of childbearing nonresponse.

2.5 *Other nonsampling errors*

Data collection has been described as a minefield of errors in which the data collector tries to avoid causing detonation and the analyst attempts to assess the damage produced by explosions. Among errors which may cause particular problems for life history analysis, we may list unreported events, misreporting of event dates, and misclassification in the state space beside nonresponse. The underreporting of events which may be conceived

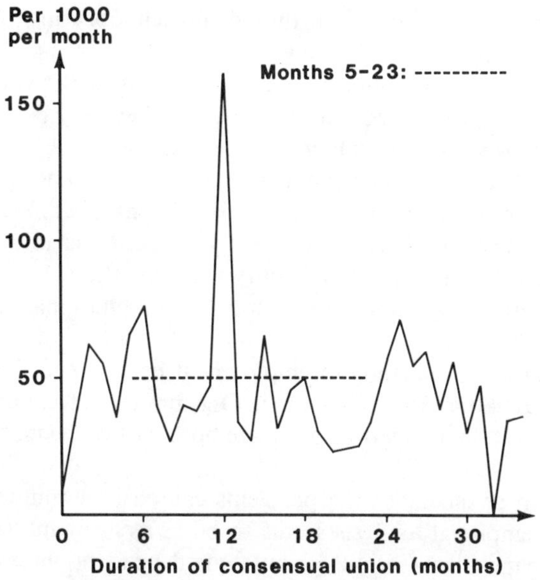

Figure 1. Marriage rates by reported duration of consensual union starting at ages 15–24. Cohort born 1946–50.

as stigmatizing (such as unemployment periods or abortions) or which are largely devoid of social ceremony (such as the start of a consensual union) is a perennial headache, and even when reported, the reliability of dates given may be questionable. For instance, the 1975 Danish fertility survey had 5240 respondents, for whom 1571 cases of nonmarital cohabitation were reported, but in 246 of these no starting date was given, and for many of the rest the woman must have estimated a starting date by counting a full year or half a year backward from the subsequent marriage date. This became evident when Hoem and Selmer (1982) computed marriage rates by duration of cohabitation, as in Figure 1. Inflated rates at durations of 6 and particularly 12 months reveal digital preference reminiscent of the age heaping which census takers often find in their reported age pyramids, though the latter actually are misclassification errors, not time-misreporting errors.

The importance of such misreporting again depends on the circumstances. Hoem and Selmer (1982) countered revealed digital preference simply by computing marriage rates for longer duration intervals, and we were much more worried about the selection bias produced by the observational plan on the individual level, for the respondents were largely asked for information only concerning their latest cohabitation and any latest marriage before the interview, though full childbearing histories were collected. (See also Hoem, 1983b.)

Of course, problems of unreported events are not restricted to interview data or to survey samples. In fact, in some aspects they may be worse in "complete" population registers, which only record events subject to official registration, while unrecorded events may be as significant for demographic behavior. For instance, the prevalence of consensual unions among the never-married in Scandinavia has greatly reduced the information value of published (say age-specific) fertility rates for the never-married as a group, because subgrouping according to cohabitational status is impossible.

This is important for the study of employment behavior to the extent that cohabitational patterns are related to it. One may expect a connection, for starting cohabitation and getting a job are both part of the maturation process.

The application of theory to the problems caused by event and time misreporting for empirical analysis seems to be in its early infancy. The problems will be particularly serious for outcome-dependent observational plans, since for them, misclassification can be an additional cause of selection bias.

Of course, misclassification is a problem even if the observational plan is not outcome-based. We now turn to that case.

3 Misclassification errors in panel data

3.1 *The structure of misclassifications*

So far, all of our examples and most of our discussion have been connected to data recorded in continuous time. For our present purposes, we turn to data on gross flows (panel data) recorded over periods between fixed, equidistant calendar dates, such as the data from labor force surveys or from periodic censuses, say the quinquennial Swedish censuses of population and housing. Such data may be of interest in their own right, or they may be converted into estimates of transition intensities, as indicated in Section 1.2 and described in the literature reviewed by Hoem and Funck Jensen (1982, sec. 5.1).

On each recording date, the individuals of the panel are classified into the statuses of the underlying state space, perhaps with error. Let α_{ij} be the probability that a panel member is classified into state j when the individual really belongs to state i. For most of our presentation, we will assume that these classification probabilities depend on i and j alone, and not on other factors, like the calendar time and the previous life history of the panel member, including the previous history of status classification.

We will indicate a model where the latter factor is taken into account at the end of Section 3.2.

In most reasonable investigations, the matrix $\mathbf{A} = (\alpha_{ij})$ of classification probabilities will be nonsingular, as we will assume, for presumably the probability α_{ii} of correct classification of an individual of any status i will dominate the misclassification probabilities α_{ij}, $j \neq i$. For the moment, we will reason as if $\mathbf{A}$ is known while the probabilities of the underlying population process are unknown and should be estimated from the data. This may sound farfetched, because in practice the structure of misclassification may be as badly charted as the real process. We proceed as noted anyway, for two reasons.

First, it turns out that we are able to give qualitative statements about the effects of misclassification, and the literature contains several numerical illustrations of the extent of these effects.

Secondly, one may demonstrate gains which can be achieved from better information about misclassifications, and this may help inspire further investigation of their structure and better use of existing knowledge. The U.S. National Commission on Employment and Unemployment Statistics (1979, sec. 13, p. 217) recently recommended that such research be undertaken. Information of this kind may perhaps be gleaned from reinterview programs and other control measures connected with periodic surveys. Sutcliffe (1965) has particularly relevant methodology. The double sampling schemes of Tenenbein (1970, 1972), Hochberg (1977), and others may also be useful. Progress on this front may make bureaus of statistics less reluctant to release data on gross flows. The U.S. Bureau of Labor Statistics (1982) just published theirs on labor force changes in 1970–80, apparently washing their hands of the consequences.

In any case, we note other possibilities of identifying the structure of misclassification in Section 3.4.

To proceed, consider panel member number k and let X_{kt} denote the state to which this individual belongs at time t, while he or she is classified as belonging to state Y_{kt}, for $t = 0, 1, \ldots$. For any t, then,

$$\alpha_{ij} = P\{Y_{kt} = j \mid X_{kt} = i\} \qquad \text{for all } k$$

We let $p_i = P\{X_{kt} = i\}$, which means that

$$v_j = P\{Y_{kt} = j\} = \sum_i p_i \alpha_{ij}$$

or

$$\mathbf{v} = \mathbf{A}'\mathbf{p} \tag{3.1}$$

where $\mathbf{v} = \{v_j : j \in \mathscr{I}\}$ and $\mathbf{p} = \{p_i : i \in \mathscr{I}\}$ are column vectors; $\mathscr{I}$ is the state space. The prime denotes a transpose.

Relation (3.1) has been used extensively in the literature to investigate the effects of misclassification in the multinomial situation and similar settings. Ideas of this nature have been reviewed by Cochran (1968). For further material, see Schwartz (1982) and his annotated bibliography and Fleiss (1981). Dalenius and Frank (1968) recognize the situation where classification may be impossible for some individuals. Aigner (1973) has studied regression analysis with a binary independent variable subject to misclassification.

If **A** is known, (3.1) may also be used to estimate **p**. For nonsingular **A**,

$$\mathbf{p} = (\mathbf{A}')^{-1}\mathbf{v} \tag{3.2}$$

Let $N_j = \#\{k: Y_{k0} = j\}$ be the recorded number of members in state j at time 0, some of which may really belong in different states. Let $n = \sum N_j$ be the (fixed) panel size, and let $\mathbf{N} = \{N_j: j \in \mathscr{I}\}$ be the column vector of class size counts. Then the maximum likelihood estimator of **p** is

$$\hat{\mathbf{p}} = (\mathbf{A}')^{-1}\hat{\mathbf{v}} \quad \text{with} \quad \hat{\mathbf{v}} = \frac{\mathbf{N}}{n} \tag{3.3}$$

when we assume that $X_{10}, X_{20}, \ldots, X_{n0}$ are stochastically independent.

We have concentrated on the multinomial setting, but very similar notions pertain to the multihypergeometric situation, where the members of a population are grouped into prespecified classes and the problem is to determine the (nonstochastic) number of individuals in each class in the face of misclassification. Census age misreporting is a case in point. Some information about the error structure is required, though outside knowledge of the real population structure, perhaps at a previous count, may be helpful.

3.2 *The transition structure*

Assume now that $\{X_{kt}: t = 0, 1, \ldots\}$ is a sample path of a time-homogeneous Markov chain, and suppose that different sample paths are stochastically independent. Let

$$p_{ij} = P\{X_{k,t+1} = j \mid X_{kt} = i\} \quad \text{for all} \quad k, t$$

and define

$$q_{ij} = P\{Y_{k1} = j \mid Y_{k0} = i\}$$

Then

$$q_{ab} = \sum_i \sum_j \frac{p_i \alpha_{ia} p_{ij} \alpha_{jb}}{v_a} \quad \text{for} \quad a, b \in \mathscr{I} \tag{3.4}$$

This setup is closely related to the theory of misclassification in a two-way contingency table; see Cochran (1968, sec. 7). Coleman's (1964) models of change and response uncertainty look very similar. Kristiansson (1979) has used (3.4) to demonstrate that the effects of reasonable misclassification may be startling in Swedish labor force surveys, using a classification with only two states, namely "employed" and "unemployed." We will give the two-state case particular attention in Section 3.3.

For any column vector $\mathbf{v} = \{v_i: i \in \mathscr{I}\}$, let us define $\check{\mathbf{v}} = \operatorname{diag}\{v_i: i \in \mathscr{I}\}$. Then (3.4) may be written in matrix form as

$$Q = \check{\mathbf{v}}^{-1}\mathbf{A}'\check{\mathbf{p}}\mathbf{P}\mathbf{A} \tag{3.5}$$

where $\mathbf{Q} = \{q_{ij}\}$ and $\mathbf{P} = \{p_{ij}\}$. Solving (3.5) for $\mathbf{P}$, we get

$$\mathbf{P} = \check{\mathbf{p}}^{-1}(\mathbf{A}')^{-1}\check{\mathbf{v}}\mathbf{Q}\mathbf{A}^{-1} \tag{3.6}$$

which may be used to estimate $\mathbf{P}$ when $\mathbf{A}$ is known, as follows.

Let $M_{ij} = \#\{k: Y_{k0} = i, Y_{k1} = j\}$ be the recorded number of transitions from state i to state j between times 0 and 1, and let $\mathbf{M} = \{M_{ij}\}$. Then q_{ij} may be estimated by

$$\hat{q}_{ij} = \frac{M_{ij}}{N_i}$$

which means that

$$\hat{\mathbf{Q}} = \check{\mathbf{N}}^{-1}\mathbf{M} \tag{3.7}$$

Combining (3.7) with (3.3) and (3.6), we get the following estimator for $\mathbf{P}$:

$$\hat{\mathbf{P}} = (\check{\hat{\mathbf{p}}})^{-1}(\mathbf{A}')^{-1}\mathbf{M}\mathbf{A}^{-1} \tag{3.8}$$

where $\check{\hat{\mathbf{p}}} = \operatorname{diag}\{\hat{p}_i: i \in \mathscr{I}\}$.

So far, we have assumed the misclassifications at time 1 to be unrelated to those at time 0, except through the effects of real state membership. This is reflected in the appearance of the matrix $\mathbf{A}$ twice in (3.5). Kristiansson (1979, 1983) has suggested, however, that one ought to expect some carry-over effect from a classification at time 0, since the classifications of a respondent in two subsequent rounds of a labor force survey are likely to be made by the same interviewer. This should make the classification at time 1 directly dependent on the classification at time 0, and he has shown (Kristiansson, 1982, 1983) that this idea seems empirically sound. To see how this can appear within our theory, define

$$\beta_{ijkl} = P\{Y_0 = k, Y_1 = l \mid X_0 = i, X_1 = j\}$$

as the probability of observing a classification into k followed by one into l when the real sequence is (i, j). We keep $\alpha_{ik} = P\{Y_0 = k \mid X_0 = i\}$. In these latter definitions, X_t and Y_t are the real and recorded classifications of an individual, respectively, but we have dropped the individual number in the subscript to save notation. In our previous model, $\beta_{ijkl} = \alpha_{ik}\alpha_{jl}$. Kristiansson (1979, 1983) has essentially proposed to replace this relation with one of the following form:

$$\beta_{ijkl} = \alpha_{ik}\alpha_{jl} \quad \text{when} \quad i \neq j$$

$$\beta_{iikl} = \alpha_{ik}\phi_{ikl}$$

where

$$\phi_{iii} > \alpha_{ii} > \phi_{iki} \quad \text{for} \quad k \neq i$$

The idea is that

1. a change in real status should make the classifications recorded at times 0 and 1 independent when the real statuses are given; and
2. the classifications recorded at the two dates should be conditionally dependent, given the real statuses, when no real change has happened, and in such a manner that a correct classification is reinforced ($\phi_{iii} > \alpha_{ii}$) and a misclassification also stands an improved chance of being maintained ($\phi_{iki} < \alpha_{ii}$ for $k \neq i$).

Whichever specification β_{ijkl} is given it turns out that the theory at the end of Section 3.1 can be used to provide relations between the various quantities involved. Let $a = (i, j)$, $b = (k, l)$, and define $\pi_a = \pi_{ij} = p_i p_{ij} = P\{X_0 = i, X_1 = j\}$ and $\gamma_b = \gamma_{kl} = v_k q_{kl} = P\{Y_0 = k, Y_1 = l\}$. Then

$$v_k q_k = \sum_i \sum_j \pi_{ij}\beta_{ijkl}$$

or

$$\gamma_b = \sum_a \pi_a \beta_{ab}$$

which has the same form as (3.1). If we form a two-dimensional matrix $\mathbf{B} = \{\beta_{ab}\}$ and column vectors $\boldsymbol{\pi}$ and $\boldsymbol{\gamma}$ by organizing the pairs (i, j) lexicographically, say, then

$$\gamma = \mathbf{B}'\pi \tag{3.9}$$

and we can use the same formalism as before, assuming that $\mathbf{B}$ is nonsingular. It will be if $\beta_{ijkl} = \alpha_{ik}\alpha_{jl}$ and $\mathbf{A}$ is nonsingular, for then $\mathbf{B} = \mathbf{A} \otimes \mathbf{A}$ is the direct product of $\mathbf{A}$ with itself. See, for instance, Andersson (1958, pp. 347–8). In what follows, we assume that $\mathbf{B} = \mathbf{A} \otimes \mathbf{A}$.

Notions similar to those which led up to (3.9) appeared in a discussion of selective nonresponse in two-wave, two-state panel surveys by Williams and Mallows (1970).

3.3 *The two-state model*

If $\mathscr{I}$ only has two states, say 0 and 1, then things simplify considerably, and one gets further insight by studying particular formulas. If $\mathbf{B} = \mathbf{A} \otimes \mathbf{A}$, as usual, we let $\alpha_{01} = \varepsilon$, $\alpha_{00} = 1 - \varepsilon$, $\alpha_{10} = \delta$, and $\alpha_{11} = 1 - \delta$, so that our entire set of *mis*classification probabilities is (ε, δ).

In this case,

$$p_{00} = \frac{1}{1 - \varepsilon - \delta}\left[q_{00} - \delta + \delta(q_{00} - q_{10})\frac{\varepsilon\pi + (1 - \pi)(1 - \delta)}{\pi(1 - \varepsilon - \delta)}\right] \tag{3.10}$$

and

$$q_{00} = \frac{p_{00} + (\delta - \delta_0)(1 - \pi)(1 - \varepsilon p_{00})p_{11}\delta}{[\pi(1 - \varepsilon) + (1 - \pi)\delta]} \tag{3.11}$$

where $\pi = p_0$ is the prevalence of state 0 at time 0, and where

$$\delta_0 = \frac{1 - \varepsilon}{1 - \pi} \cdot \frac{\pi_0 - \pi(1 - \varepsilon p_{00})}{1 - \varepsilon p_{00}} \quad \text{for} \quad \pi_0 = \frac{p_{00} + p_{11} - 1}{p_{11}} \tag{3.12}$$

We assume that $p_{00} + p_{11} > 1$, which is equivalent to assuming that the matrix $\mathbf{P}$ is embeddable in a time-continuous Markov chain (Goodman, 1970). Then $\pi_0 \in \langle 0, 1 \rangle$.

We may get $\delta_0 \notin [0, 1]$; in fact both $\delta_0 < 0$ and $\delta_0 > 1$ are possible in general. If $\delta_0 \leq 0$, then by (3.11), $q_{00} > p_{00}$, which means that recorded stability in state 0 exceeds real stability. If $\delta_0 \geq 1$, then $q_{00} < p_{00}$, and recorded flows out of state 0 exceed real flows (except for random variation). If $0 < \delta_0 < 1$, then $q_{00} \gtreqless p_{00}$ as $\delta \gtreqless \delta_0$; that is, whether recorded flows out of state 0 are inflated or deflated in comparison to real flows depends on the misclassification probability for state 1. As is seen in (3.12), the turning point δ_0 depends on the prevalence π of state 0 at time 0 as well as on the other model parameters. In any case *recorded flows are not necessarily inflated by misclassification.* (A statement to the contrary by Singer and Cohen, 1980, p. 298, has been corrected in their later erratum.) This has also been recognized empirically by Kristiansson (1982, 1983) and by Smith and Vanski (1979, p. 144) who found, however, that misclassification errors in U.S. data mostly tended to inflate gross changes in labor force status. Some of the largest overvaluations occurred in the flows (from employment or from unemployment) out of the labor force. Of all age groups, teenagers demonstrated the greatest tendency to have their reported statistics inflated. Presumably, individuals with a tenuous connection to the labor force will be hardest to classify, as documented by Kristiansson (1982, 1983), and such tenuity is likely to be differentiated by age and gender.

For the Swedish population, for all ages and both genders combined, Bergman and Thorslund (1980, table 5) have estimated $\varepsilon = .008$ and $\delta = .036$ when state 0 corresponds to the employed and state 1 corresponds to the nonemployed. For the dichotomy in/out of the labor force, they found $\varepsilon = .012$ and $\delta = .045$.

If ε and δ are known (or can be estimated from other sources) for a population group, then the corresponding p_{00} and p_{10} can be estimated by

$$\hat{p}_{00} = \frac{1}{1-\varepsilon-\delta}\left(\frac{M_{00}-\delta N'_0}{N_0-\delta n} - \delta\right) \tag{3.13}$$

and

$$\hat{p}_{10} = \frac{1}{1-\varepsilon-\delta}\left(\frac{M_{10}-\varepsilon N'_0}{N_1-\varepsilon n} - \delta\right) \tag{3.14}$$

As before, N_j is the number of individuals recorded in state j at time 0, while $N'_0 = M_{00} + M_{10}$ is the corresponding number recorded in state 0 at time 1. Note how (3.13) and (3.14) have the nature of elaborate adjustments of $\hat{q}_{00} = M_{00}/N_0$ and $\hat{q}_{10} = M_{10}/N_1$, respectively.

Of course, one prefers estimates which satisfy $0 \leq \hat{p}_{ij} \leq 1$. For the two estimators above, these conditions lead to the following relations:

$$1-\varepsilon-\frac{N_1}{N_0}\frac{1-\varepsilon}{\varepsilon}(1-\varepsilon-\hat{q}_{10}) < \hat{q}_{00} < 1-\varepsilon-\frac{\delta}{1-\delta}\frac{N_1}{N_0}(1-\varepsilon-\hat{q}_{10})$$
$$\delta+\frac{\delta}{1-\delta}\frac{N_1}{N_0}(\hat{q}_{10}-\delta) < \hat{q}_{00} < \frac{1-\varepsilon}{\varepsilon}\frac{N_1}{N_0}(\hat{q}_{10}-\delta) \tag{3.15}$$

Failure to satisfy these conditions, or similar conditions for $\hat{q}_{11}$, is an indication that something is wrong with the application of the model. It is immediately apparent that a successful application requires that $\hat{q}_{00} < 1-\varepsilon$ and $\hat{q}_{10} > \delta$, which requirements are necessary but not sufficient. If ε and δ are not really known but are given guessed values, say in sensitivity analyses, then failure to satisfy (3.15) may be an indication of unrealistic guesses for the misclassification errors.

Similarly, the requirement that $p_{00} \leq 1$ implies that

$$q_{00} \leq 1-\varepsilon-\delta(q_{00}-q_{10})\frac{\varepsilon\pi+(1-\pi)(1-\delta)}{\pi(1-\varepsilon-\delta)}$$

We expect that $q_{00} > q_{10}$ and see that $q_{00} < 1-\varepsilon$ is a necessary condition for a tenable model.

The two extreme cases where $\delta = 0$ or, alternatively, $\varepsilon = 0$, deserve special attention. If $\delta = 0$, (3.10) reduces to $q_{00} = p_{00}(1-\varepsilon)$, which can be seen by direct reasoning, as follows. If an individual is classified in state 0 at time 0, then that is his true state also, for no members of state 1 are classified in state 0 when $\delta = 0$. A recorded classification of this individual in state 0 at time 1 as well can then only appear if the individual stays in state 0 and is correctly classified at time 1.

The case where $\varepsilon = 0$ has been given some attention by Singer and Cohen (1980, p. 298). In this case, $\delta_0 = (\pi_0 - \pi)/(1 - \pi) < 1$, but $\delta_0 \leq 0$ if $\pi \geq \pi_0$. In the latter case, $q_{00} > p_{00}$ when $\delta > 0$. If $\pi < \pi_0$, then $q_{00} \gtreqless p_{00}$ as $\delta \gtreqless \delta_0$, as in the general case. From (3.11), we also get that $q_{00} \gtreqless p_{00}$ as $q_{00} \gtreqless (1 - \pi)q_{10}$. Furthermore, (3.15) reduces to $\hat{p}_{10} = (\hat{q}_{10} - \delta)/(1 - \delta)$, but the formula for $\hat{p}_{00}$ does not seem to simplify appreciably.

Devore (1973a,b) and Rudemo (1974) have studied the reconstruction of real sample path $\{X_0, X_1, \ldots\}$ from a recorded path $\{Y_0, Y_1, \ldots\}$ in the symmetric case where $p_{00} = p_{11}$, $p_0 = p_1 = \frac{1}{2}$, and $\varepsilon = \delta$. They show that under certain general conditions, $\{Y_0, Y_1, \ldots\}$ itself is the best reconstruction of $\{X_0, X_1, \ldots\}$, as follows.

1. Let

$$p_t = p_t(y_0, y_1, \ldots, y_t) = P\left\{X_t = 1 \,\middle|\, \bigcap_{s=0}^{t} (Y_s = y_s)\right\}$$

and assume that $p_{00} + \varepsilon(1 - \varepsilon) \leq 1$. Then $p_t \geq \frac{1}{2}$ if $y_t = 1$ and $p_t \leq \frac{1}{2}$ if $y_0 = 0$ (Devore, 1973a; Rudemo, 1974, sec. 7.6).

2. If $(1 - p_{00})^2(1 - \varepsilon) \geq \varepsilon p_{00}^2$, then

$$P\left\{\bigcap_{s=0}^{t} (X_s = y_s) \,\middle|\, \bigcap_{s=0}^{t} (Y_s = y_s)\right\} \geq P\left\{\bigcap_{s=0}^{t} (X_s = x_s) \,\middle|\, \bigcap_{s=0}^{t} (Y_s = y_s)\right\}$$

for any possible sequence $(x_0, x_1, \ldots, x_t)$ (Devore, 1973b).

3.4 *Identification and estimation*

We have argued as if the matrix **A** of classification probabilities is known or can be estimated from outside sources, but most often it is not available in this manner, and it is not identifiable from the parameters **v** and **Q** of the distribution of the gross flows observed. Following Reiersøl (1963), we will call **p**, **P**, and **A** *genoparameters*, and the characteristics of the distribution of the actual observations will be called *phenoparameters*.

If the model had more structure, there might be fewer genoparameters, and they might be identifiable. For instance, Ekholm and Palmgren (1982) study a sequence of sets of binomial trials where the binomial success probability is given by a linear logit model,

$$p(k) = \frac{\exp(\alpha + \beta k)}{1 + \exp(\alpha + \beta k)}$$

in the kth set of trials, and where the misclassification probabilities ε (of classifying a success as a failure) and δ (of classifying a failure falsely as a success) are common to all sets of trials. Under certain restrictions, the genoparameters α, β, ε, and δ all turn out to be identifiable and are estimated from the available data.

It is an exciting challenge to develop models for the misclassification structure, to see the $\{\alpha_{ij}\}$ as (say multinomial logistic) functions of exogenous variables, and to exploit any age dependences in them beyond Eklund and Palmgren's (1982) simple assumption of age constancy. One needs to unravel the influence of such factors from that of alternative subdivisions into population subgroups according to the various specifications of states $i \in \mathscr{I}$. The usefulness of the classification probabilities for the estimation of transition probabilities from recorded gross flows also depends on the greater stability of the former over time, for in practice the estimation of the $\{p_{ij}\}$ for a certain month must be based on estimates of the $\{\alpha_{ij}\}$ computed over an extended earlier period. There seems to be little empirical basis for such modeling at present. Hopefully, this will change in the future.

For the moment, assume that there are no nontrivial connections between the genoparameters of the panel study, however, but that gross flows are available between times 1 and 2 as well as between times 0 and 1. Let

$$q_{klm} = P\{Y_1 = l, Y_2 = m \mid Y_0 = k\} = \frac{\sum_h p_h \alpha_{hk} \sum_i p_{hi} \alpha_{il} \sum_j p_{ij} \alpha_{jm}}{v_k} \tag{3.16}$$

If the state space $\mathscr{I}$ has $s \geq 2$ states, then the panel model has $(2s+1)(s-1)$ "free" genoparameters, given that $\sum_j p_{ij} \equiv \sum_j \alpha_{ij} \equiv \sum_j p_j = 1$, while there are now $s^3 - 1$ "free" phenoparameters, since $\sum_l \sum_m q_{klm} \equiv \sum_k v_k = 1$ provide $s + 1$ restrictions. Because $s^3 - 1 > (2s+1)(s-1)$ for all $s \geq 2$, there should be enough phenoparameters to solve (3.16) and (3.1) with respect to the genoparameters, at least in most cases.

This utilizes the fact that $\{Y_t\}$ is not normally a Markov chain and that q_{klm} does not equal $q_{kl} q_{lm}$, except possibly in special cases. For whatever it may be worth, we note that (3.16) can be written in matrix form as follows.

Let $\mathbf{Q}_l = \{q_{klm}: k, m \in \mathscr{I}\}$ for fixed $l \in \mathscr{I}$, and let $\breve{\mathbf{A}}_l = \operatorname{diag}\{\alpha_{il}: i \in \mathscr{I}\}$. Then

$$\mathbf{Q}_l = \breve{v}^{-1} \mathbf{A}' \breve{\mathbf{p}} \mathbf{P} \breve{\mathbf{A}}_l \mathbf{P} \mathbf{A} \tag{3.17}$$

The practical usefulness of these latter results are limited by the fact that seasonal variations on the labor market may make the transition probabilities $\{p_{ij}\}$ less than stable from one quarter or month to the next.

Indeed, one central purpose of labor force surveys is to detect instabilities of this nature. Again, models with more structure may be easier to handle. We close with an appeal for further research.

Mathematical appendix

A1. *The distortion factor* $P_{j\mathscr{L}}(x,z)/P_{i\mathscr{L}}(x,z)$ *in* (2.3) *equals* 1 *for all* $i, j \in \mathscr{L}$ *and all* x, z *where* $0 \leq x \leq z$, *if and only if* $\mu_{i\mathscr{D}}(\cdot)$ *is independent of* $i \in \mathscr{L}$.

Proof: 1. To make the distortion factor identically equal to 1, $P_{i\mathscr{L}}(\cdot,\cdot)$ must be independent of $i \in \mathscr{L}$. If this is the case, then $P_{i\mathscr{D}} = 1 - P_{i\mathscr{L}}$ is also independent of i. Since $\mu_{i\mathscr{D}}(x) = \lim P_{i\mathscr{D}}(x, y)/(y - x)$ as $y \downarrow x$, then $\mu_{i\mathscr{D}}(\cdot)$ is also the same for all $i \in \mathscr{L}$.

2. To prove the converse, we rely on Kolmogorov's forward differential equation for $P_{ij}(x, y)$, which can be written as follows for $i, j \in \mathscr{L}$:

$$\frac{\partial}{\partial y} P_{ij}(x, y) = -P_{ij}(x, y)\mu_{j\mathscr{L}}(y) - P_{ij}(x, y)\mu_{j\mathscr{D}}(y) + \sum_{k \in \mathscr{L} - j} P_{ik}(x, y)\mu_{kj}(y)$$

Assume that $\mu_{j\mathscr{D}}(\cdot) = \gamma(\cdot)$ for all $j \in \mathscr{L}$, add over $j \in \mathscr{L}$ above, and reorganize to get

$$\frac{\partial}{\partial y} P_{i\mathscr{L}}(x, y) = -P_{i\mathscr{L}}(x, y)\gamma(y)$$

Since $P_{i\mathscr{L}}(x, x) = 1$ for $i \in \mathscr{L}$, we get

$$P_{i\mathscr{L}}(x, y) = \exp\left\{-\int_x^y \gamma(u)\, du\right\} \tag{A.1}$$

a result of some independent interest. For our purposes, what is important, however, is that $P_{i\mathscr{L}}$ is independent of $i \in \mathscr{L}$, which makes the distortion factor identically equal to 1 in (2.3). □

Note that lack of selection bias in (2.3) is not entirely equivalent to the identity to 1 of the distortion factor, for whatever the latter is, λ_{ij} equals μ_{ij} if μ_{ij} is 0. Nevertheless, our result is what has most practical interest.

Cohen (1972) has proved a closely related result.

A2. *Inference in a pure death process with selective nonresponse.*

For its theoretical interest, we study the following situation. Suppose that the members of a homogeneous population of N individuals are subject to a pure death process with constant force of mortality λ. Then each member starts in a state 0 at time 0 and stays there until transition into an absorbing state 1, with a constant transition intensity λ. Suppose that a simple random sample of n individuals is drawn at time 0 and that at time 1 an attempt is made to assess transitions made by individuals in the sample during the time interval $[0, 1]$. There is a response probability $\gamma_k = \gamma(k)$ of an individual in state k at time 1. For respondents, the existence and timing of any transition is obtained without inaccuracy; for nonrespondents, no such information is obtained. For individual i in the target population, D_i is the actual number of transitions in $[0, 1]$. If $D_i = 1$, then R_i is the time of the transition. If $D_i = 0$, then $R_i = 1$. The target sample is $\mathbf{S} = (I_1, I_2, \ldots, I_n)$. If individual I_j responds, then $A'_j = 1$. Otherwise, $A'_j = 0$. (We use A for "answer.") Let $D'_j = D_{I_j}$ and $R'_j = R_{I_j}$. If no account were taken of the nonresponse, then

$$\tilde{\lambda} = \frac{\sum_{j=1}^{n} A'_j D'_j}{\sum_{j=1}^{n} A'_j R'_j} = \frac{D'}{R'}$$

would be the natural occurrence/exposure estimator for λ, since using $\tilde{\lambda}$ would amount to counting occurrences D' and exposures R' for respondents only. By the main result (2.2) for noninformative sampling plans, (D'_j, R'_j) is distributed like (D_i, R_i). Since

$$E(A'_j \mid D'_j, R'_j) = \gamma(D'_j) \tag{A.2}$$

we get

$$E(A'_j D'_j) = E\{D'_j E(A'_j \mid D'_j, R'_j)\} = E\{D'_j \gamma(D'_j)\} = q\gamma_1$$

where $q = P\{D_i = 1\} = 1 - e^{-\lambda}$. By the same token,

$$E(A'_j R'_j) = E\{R'_j \gamma(D'_j)\} = p\Delta + \frac{q\gamma_1}{\lambda}$$

with $p = 1 - q = e^{-\lambda}$ and $\Delta = \gamma_0 - \gamma_1$. Therefore, $\tilde{\lambda}$ is strongly consistent (as $N \to \infty, n \to \infty$) for

$$g(\lambda, \gamma_0, \gamma_1) = \frac{q\gamma_1}{q\gamma_1 + p\Delta}\,\lambda \tag{A.3}$$

If $\gamma_0 \neq \gamma_1$, so that nonresponse is selective, $\tilde{\lambda}$ is "consistency biased."

If γ_0 and γ_1 are known, other estimators of λ can be found. By the kind of reasoning which led up to (A.3),

$$\hat{\lambda} = \frac{\sum_{j=1}^{n} A'_j D'_j / \gamma(D'_j)}{\sum_{j=1}^{n} A'_j R'_j / \gamma(D'_j)} \tag{A.4}$$

will then be consistent for λ. One can exploit (A.3) to get a moment estimator λ^* as the solution of

$$\tilde{\lambda} = g(\lambda^*, \gamma_0, \gamma_1)$$

This estimator λ^* can be found by a few steps of simple Newton iteration. Lyberg (1983a) has demonstrated that $\hat{\lambda}$ and λ^* largely have the same properties under normal circumstances. They are both approximately unbiased and each represents an improvement on the naive estimator $\tilde{\lambda}$ when γ_0 and γ_1 are much different. If the values of the response probabilities must be guessed, one is playing a more chancy game. If the guessed ratio between them deviates considerably from the true ratio, then the analyst may actually end up by making things worse if he uses $\hat{\lambda}$ or λ^*, for they may then be more strongly biased than $\hat{\lambda}$. A standard result in sample survey practice has reappeared here in a possibly nonstandard situation.

If the response probabilities are known, maximum likelihood provides an alternative estimator. Let $\theta(\lambda) = P\{A'_j = 0\} = p(1 - \gamma_0) + q(1 - \gamma_1)$. Then the likelihood of what is observed for individual number I_j is

$$(p\gamma_0)^{(1-D'_j)A'_j}[(\exp(-\lambda R'_j))\lambda\gamma_1]^{D'_jA'_j}[\theta(\lambda)]^{1-A'_j}$$

and the complete log-likelihood is

$$D' \ln \lambda - \lambda R' + (n - A') \ln \theta(\lambda) \tag{A.5}$$

plus terms independent of λ. Here, $A' = \sum A'_j$ is the number of respondents in the target sample. Maximization in (A.5) will not lead to $\tilde{\lambda}$, $\hat{\lambda}$, or λ^*. As usual, the maximum likelihood estimator will be consistent and asymptotically normal. To find its asymptotic variance is an elementary exercise.

A3. *In Section 2.2, (2.4) need not give an MLE.*

In the situation of Appendix A2, let $\alpha(D_i, R_i) = (n/N)\gamma(D_i)$ and let $\mathbf{S}'$ be the *achieved* sample, as in the general theory. Then (A.4) can be rewritten as

$$\hat{\lambda} = \frac{\sum_{i \in \mathbf{S}'} D_i/\alpha(D_i, R_i)}{\sum_{i \in \mathbf{S}'} D_i/\alpha(D_i, R_i)}$$

which we recognize as a special case of (2.4). The reasoning around (A.5) shows that $\hat{\lambda}$ is not a maximum likelihood estimator for the relevant situation.

The theoretical interest of this result is greater than its practical relevance. One would not *sample* from state 0 of a pure death process if the size of this stratum is known at time 1. Sparre Andersen (1951) has discussed sampling from state 1.

A4. *In* (2.10) *of Section* 2.3.4, $A'/B' < 1$.

Sketch of proof: Let B'' result from substituting $\int_0^{z-t-w} \phi_{n+1}(s)\,ds$ for $\int_0^{z-t-u} \phi_{n+1}(s)\,ds$ in the final member of B'. Then $B'' < B'$. Let A_0 and B_0 result from substituting 0 for $\phi_{n+1}(s)$ for all $s \in \langle 0, z-t-w \rangle$ in A' and B'', respectively. Since

$$\exp\left[-\int_w^{z-t} \phi_n(s)\,ds\right] + \int_w^{z-t} \exp\left[-\int_w^u \phi_n(s)\,ds\right] \phi_n(u)\,du \equiv 1$$

we get $B_0 = \int_x^{z-w} \lambda_n(t) = A_0$. Therefore, $A'/B' < A'/B'' < A_0/B_0 = 1$. □

ACKNOWLEDGMENTS

I am grateful for conversations and correspondence with James Heckman, Anders Klevmarken, Karl-Erik Kristiansson, Burton Singer, and Carl-Erik Särndal, and for many references which they provided.

Discussions in the Stockholm Joint Seminar in Sociology and Demography, in the November 1982 Task Force Meeting on Multistate Life History Analysis at the International Institute of Applied Systems Analysis, Laxenburg, Austria, and in seminars with colleagues in Statistics Sweden were also helpful in my work with this chapter.

REFERENCES

Aigner, Dennis J. 1973. Regression with a binary independent variable subject to errors of observation. *Journal of Econometrics* 1, 49–60.

Allison, Paul D. 1983. Survival analysis of backward recurrence times. Mimeo. University of Pennsylvania, Department of Sociology.

Andersen, P. Kragh, and A. Green. 1982. Robustness to differential mortality of incidence estimation in an illness–death–emigration model, illustrated by early onset diabetes mellitus. Copenhagen: Statistical Research Unit, Research Report 82/3.

Anderson, Harald. 1979. On nonresponse bias and response probabilities. *Scandinavian Journal of Statistics* 6(3), 107–112.

Anderson, T. W. 1958. *An Introduction to Multivariate Statistical Analysis*. New York: Wiley.

Arvidsson, Arne, Eva M. Bernhardt, Cecilia Etzler, Hans Lundström, Ingrid Lyberg, and Ulla Nordenstam. 1982. *Kvinnor och barn: Intervjuer med kvinnor om familj och arbete*. Stockholm: National Central Bureau of Statistics, Information i prognosfrågor.

Bakketeig, Leiv S., and Howard J. Hoffman. 1979. Perinatal mortality by birth order within cohorts based on sibship size. *British Medical Journal* 2, 693–696.

Bergman, Lars R., and Mats Thorslund. 1980. *Response Quality in the Swedish Labor Force Surveys: Findings of Two Reinterview Studies*. Stockholm: Statistics Sweden, Methodological Studies from the Research Institute for Statistics on Living Conditions, No. 13E.

Björklund, Anders. 1978. On the duration of unemployment in Sweden, 1965–1976. *Scandinavian Journal of Economics* 4, 421–439.

Borgan, Ørnulf, and Richard D. Gill. 1982. *Case-control Studies in a Markov Chain Setting*. Amsterdam: Mathematisch Centrum. (Preprint.)

Cassel, C.-M., C.-E. Särndal, and J. H. Wretman. 1977. *Foundations of Inference in Survey Sampling*. New York: Wiley.

Cochran, W. G. 1968. Errors of measurement in statistics. *Technometrics* 10(4), 637–666.

Cohen, J. E. 1972. When does a leaky compartment model appear to have no leaks? *Theoretical Population Biology* 3, 404–405.

Coleman, James S. 1964. *Models of Change and Response Uncertainty*. Englewood Cliffs, N.J.: Prentice-Hall.

1981. *Longitudinal Data Analysis*. New York: Basic Books.

Cosslett, Stephen R. 1981. Maximum likelihood estimator for choice-based samples. *Econometrica* 49(5), 1289–1316.

Cox, D. R. 1972. Regression models and life tables (with discussion). *Journal of the Royal Statistical Society*, Series B 34(2), 187–220.

Dalenius, T. E., and O. Frank. 1968. Control of classification. *Review of the International Statistical Institute* 36(3), 279–295.

Devore, J. 1973a. The naive rule for reconstructing a noisy Markov chain. *Biometrika* 60, 227–233.

1973b. Reconstructing a noisy Markov chain. *Journal of the American Statistical Association* 68, 394–398.

DuMouchel, William H., and Greg J. Duncan (1981). Using sample survey weights in multiple regression analyses of stratified samples. *Proceedings of the Section on Survey Research Methods of the American Statistical Association*, pp. 629–637.

Duncan, Greg J. 1982. The implications of changing family composition for the dynamic analysis of family economic well-being. Paper prepared for Conference on Analysis of Panel Data on Incomes, June 1982.

DuPasquier, L. G. 1912/13. Mathematisch Theorie der Invaliditätsversicherung. *Mitteilungen der Vereinigung schweizerischer Versicherungsmathematiker* 7, 1–7, and 8, 1–153.

Ekholm, Anders, and Juni Palmgren. 1982. A model for a binary response with misclassifications. In R. Gilchrist (ed.), *GLIM 82: Proceedings of the International Conference on Generalized Linear Models*. Springer Lecture Notes in Statistics, Vol. 14.

Feller, William. 1971. *An Introduction to Probability Theory and Its Applications*, Vol. 2. New York: Wiley.

Fienberg, Stephen E. 1980. The measurement of crime victimization: Prospects of a panel study. *The Statistician* 29(4), 313–350.

Finnäs, Fjalar, and Jan M. Hoem. 1979. Starting age and subsequent birth intervals in cohabiting unions in current Danish cohorts, 1975. *Demography* 17(3), 275–295.

Fleiss, Joseph L. 1981. *Statistical Methods for Rates and Proportions*. New York: Wiley.

Flinn, C. J., and J. J. Heckman. 1982. Models for the analysis of labor force dynamics. *Advances in Econometrics* 1, 35–95.

Gill, Richard D. 1979. *Censoring and Stochastic Integrals*. Amsterdam: Mathematisch Centrum. (Ph.D. dissertation.)

1982. Understanding Cox's regression model: A martingale approach. Amsterdam: Mathematisch Centrum. (Preprint.)

Goodman, G. S. 1970. An intrinsic time for non-stationary finite Markov chains. *Zeitschrift für Wahrscheinlichkeitstheorie und verwandte Gebiete* 16, 165–180.

Greenlees, John S., William S. Reece, and Kimberly D. Zieschang. 1982. Imputation of missing values when the probability of response depends on the variable being imputed. *Journal of the American Statistical Association* 77, 251–261.

Hansen, Morris H., William G. Madow, and Benjamin J. Tepping. 1978. On inference and estimation from sample surveys (with discussion). *Proceedings of the Section on Survey Research Methods of the American Statistical Association*, pp. 82–107.

Heckman, James J., and George J. Borjas. 1980. Does unemployment cause future unemployment? Definitions, questions, and answers from a continuous time model of heterogeneity and state dependence. *Economica* 47, 247–283.

Heckman, James J., and Burton Singer. 1982a. The identification problem in econometric models for duration data. In Werner Hildenbrand (ed.), *Advances in Econometrics*. Cambridge: Cambridge University Press.

1982b. Population heterogeneity in demographic models. In Kenneth C. Land and Andrei Rogers (eds.), *Multidimensional Mathematical Demography*. New York: Academic Press.

Henry, Louis. 1972. *On the Measurement of Human Fertility: Selected Writings*. Amsterdam: Elsevier, for the Population Council.

Hobcraft, John, and Germán Rodríguez. 1980. Methodological issues in life table analysis of birth histories. Typescript.

Hochberg, Y. 1977. On the use of double sampling schemes in analyzing categorical data with misclassification errors. *Journal of the American Statistical Association* 72, 914–921.

Hoem, Jan M. 1969. Purged and partial Markov chains. *Skandinavisk Aktuarietidskrift* 52, 147–155.

1970. Probabilistic fertility models of the life table type. *Theoretical Population Biology* 1(1), 11–38.

1972. Inhomogeneous semi-Markov processes, select actuarial tables, and duration-dependence in demography. In T. N. E. Greville (ed.), *Population Dynamics*. New York: Academic Press.

1977. A Markov chain model working life tables. *Scandinavian Actuarial Journal* 1, 1–20.

1983a. Balancing bias in vital rates due to an informative sampling plan. In Lars Lyberg (ed.), *Essays in Honour of Tore E. Dalenius*. Stockholm: Statistics Sweden, *Statistical Review*, 3rd Series, 21(5), 81–88.

1983b. Distortion caused by nonobservation of periods of cohabitation before the latest. *Demography*, 20(4), 491–506.

Hoem, Jan M., and Monica S. Fong. 1976. A Markov chain model of working life tables. Report No. 1. A new method for the construction of tables of working life. Copenhagen University, Laboratory of Actuarial Mathematics, Working Paper No. 2, with supplementary tables separately issued, and with a Correction Note of 9 August 1978.

Hoem, Jan M., and Ulla Funck Jensen, 1982. Multistate life table methodology: A probabilist critique. In Kenneth C. Land and Andrei Rogers (eds.), *Multidimensional Mathematical Demography*. New York: Academic Press.

Hoem, Jan M., and Randi Selmer. 1982. The interaction between premarital cohabitation, marriage, and the first two births in current Danish cohorts, 1975. University of Stockholm, Department of Statistics, Stockholm Research Reports in Demography, No. 1.

Holt, D., T. M. F. Smith, and P. D. Winter. 1980. Regression analysis of data from complex surveys. *Journal of the Royal Statistical Society*, Series A, 143(4), 474–487.

Hougaard, Philip. 1982. Life table methods for heterogeneous populations: Distributions describing heterogeneity. Copenhagen: Statistical Research Unit, Research Report 82/5.

Jacobsen, Martin. 1982. *Statistical Analysis of Counting Processes*. Lecture Notes in Statistics, Vol. 12. Heidelberg: Springer-Verlag.

Kalbfleisch, J. D., and R. L. Prentice. 1980. *The Statistical Analysis of Failure Time Data*. New York: Wiley.

Kalton, Graham. 1981. Models in the practice of survey sampling. Paper presented to the 43rd Session of the International Statistical Institute, Buenos Aires.

Kish, L., R. M. Groves, and K. P. Krotki. 1976. Sampling errors for fertility surveys. World Fertility Survey, Occasional Paper No. 17.

Klevmarken, Anders. 1982. There is a need for applied micro economics. University of Gothenburgh, Department of Statistics.

Kristiansson, Karl-Erik. 1979. Försök till bedömning av tillförlitligheten i flödesdata ur AKU. PM 1979-09-10 Stockholm: National Central Bureau of Statistics.

1982. Resultat från några studier av kvaliteten i flödesdata från AKU, 1982-02-01. Stockholm: National Central Bureau of Statistics.

1983. Gross-flow estimates in the Swedish labour force surveys. Paper prepared for the Meeting on Manpower Statistics, organized by the Conference of European Statisticians jointly with the International Labor Organization, Geneva, May 1983.

Little, Roderick J. A. 1982. Models for nonresponse in sample surveys. *Journal of the American Statistical Association* 77, 237–250.

Lyberg, Ingrid. 1983a. Nonresponse effects on survey estimates in the analysis of competing exponential risks. Stockholm Research Reports in Demography, No. 12. University of Stockholm, Section of Demography.

1983b. The effects of sampling and nonresponse on estimates of transition intensities: Some empirical results from the 1981 Swedish fertility survey. Stockholm Research Reports in Demography, No. 14. University of Stockholm, Section of Demography.

Manski, Charles F., and Daniel McFadden. 1981. Alternative estimators and sample designs for discrete choice analysis. In C. F. Manski and D. McFadden (eds.), *Structural Analysis of Discrete Data*. Cambridge, Mass.: MIT Press.

Marini, Margaret Mooney, Anthony R. Olsen, and Donald B. Rubin. 1980. Maximum-likelihood estimation in panel studies with missing data. In Karl F. Schuessler (ed.), *Sociological Methodology 1980*. San Francisco: Jossey-Bass.

Menken, Jane, James Trussell, Debra Stempel, and Ozer Babakol. 1981. Proportional hazards life table models: An illustrative analysis of socio-demographic influences on marriage dissolution in the United States. *Demography* 18(2), 181–200.

Michael, Robert T., and Nancy Brandon Tuma, 1982. Employment, unemployment, schooling, marriage, and fertility patterns of American youths. University of Chicago, Economics Research Center/NORC, Discussion Paper No. 82-5.

Miller, Rupert G., Jr., Gail Gong, and Alvaro Muñoz. 1981. *Survival Analysis.* New York: Wiley.

Millman, S. R., and G. E. Hendershot. 1980. Early fertility and lifetime fertility. *Family Planning Perspectives* 12(3), 139–149.

Nathan, G., and D. Holt. 1980. The effect of survey design on regression analysis. *Journal of the Royal Statistical Society*, Series B, 42(3), 377–386.

Østby, Lars, and Turid Noack. 1981. *Fruktbarhetsundersøkelse 1977.* Oslo: Central Bureau of Statistics of Norway, Norges Offisielle Statistikk B197.

Page, H. J., B. Ferry, I. H. Shah, and R. J. Lesthaeghe. 1980. The most recent births: Some analytical possibilities and underlying problems. To appear in W. Brass (ed.), *The Analysis of Maternity Histories.* Liege: International Union for the Scientific Study of Population.

PSID. 1983. User Guide for the Panel Study of Income Dynamics. Preliminary Draft. Ann Arbor, Mich.: University of Michigan Survey Research Center.

Reiersøl, Olav. 1963. Identifiability, estimability, pheno-restricting specifications, and zero Lagrange multipliers in the analysis of variance. *Skandinavisk Aktuarietidskrift* 46, 131–142.

Roman, Eve, Pat Doyle, Valerie Beral, Eva Alberman, and Peter Pharoah. 1978. Fetal loss, gravidity, and pregnancy order. *Early Human Development* 2(2), 131–138.

Royall, Richard. 1976. Current advances in sampling theory: Implications for human observational studies. *American Journal of Epidemiology* 104(4), 463–474.

Rubin, D. B. 1976. Inference and missing data. *Biometrika* 63, 581–692.

1978. Multiple imputations in sample surveys–A phenomenological Bayesian approach to nonresponse (with discussion). In *Imputation and Editing of Faulty or Missing Survey Data.* Washington, D.C.: U.S. Social Security Administration and Census Bureau.

1980. Conceptual issues in the presence of nonresponse. In *Nonresponse in Sample Surveys: The Theory of Current Practice*, Part III. Washington D.C.: Panel on Incomplete Data, National Academy of Sciences.

Rudemo, Mats. 1974. *Prediction and Filtering for Markov Processes: Lecture Notes.* TRITA-MAT-1974-6. Stockholm: Royal Institute of Technology, Department of Mathematical Statistics.

Ryder, N. B. 1965. The measurement of fertility patterns, In M. S. Sheps and J. C. Ridley (eds.), *Public Health and Population Change.* Pittsburgh: University of Pittsburgh Press.

Särndal, Carl-Erik. 1978. Design-based and model-based inference in survey sampling. *Scandinavian Journal of Statistics* 5, 27–52.

1980. On π-inverse weighting versus best linear unbiased weighting in probability sampling. *Biometrika* 67(3), 639–650.

Särndal, Carl-Erik, and Tak-Kee Hui. 1981. Estimation of nonresponse situations: To what extent must we rely on models? In D. Krewski, R. Platek, and J. N. K. Rao (eds.), *Current Topics in Survey Sampling.* New York: Academic Press.

Schirm, Allen L., James Trussell, Jane Menken, and William R. Grady. 1982. Contraceptive failure in the United States: The impact of social, economic, and demographic factors. *Family Planning Perspectives* 14(2), 68–75.

Schoenbaum, Emil. 1924/5. Anwendung der Volterra'schen Integralgleichungen in der mathematischen Statistik. *Skandinavisk Aktuarietidskrift* 7(4), 241–265; 8(1), 1–22.

Schwartz, Joseph E. 1982. The neglected problem of measurement error in categorical data. University of Stockholm, Institute of Social Research, Meddelande 6/1982.

Sheps, Mindel C., and Jane A. Menken. 1973. *Mathematical Models of Conception and Birth.* Chicago: University of Chicago Press.

Simonsen, W. 1936. Veber die Grundformeln der Invaliditätsversicherung. *Skandinavisk Aktuarietidskrift* 19, 27–41.

Singer, Burton, and Joel E. Cohen. 1980. Estimating malaria incidence and recovery rates from panel surveys. *Mathematical Biosciences* 49, 273–305. Erratum (1982): 62, 151–152.

Smith, Ralph E., and Jean I. Vanski. 1979. Gross change data: The neglected data base (with discussion). In *Counting the Labor Force*, Appendix 2. Washington, D.C.: U.S. National Commission on Employment and Unemployment Statistics.

Smith, T. M. F. 1982. On the validity of inferences from non-random samples. Typescript.

Sparre Andersen, E. 1951. The influence on the observed death rate of measuring the exposure by a sample. *Transactions of the 13th International Congress of Actuaries* 1, 593–606.

Sutcliffe, J. P. 1965. A probability model for errors of classification. *Psychometrica* 30, 73–96, 129–155.

Taeuber, Karl E., J. Chiazze, Jr., and W. Haenszel. 1968. *Migration in the United States.* Washington, D.C.: U.S. Government Printing Office.

Tenenbein, Aaron. 1970. A double sampling scheme for estimating from binomial data with misclassification. *Journal of the American Statistical Association* 65, 1350–1361.

1972. A double sampling scheme for estimating from misclassified multinomial data with applications to sampling inspection. *Technometrics* 14, 187–202.

Thomsen, Ib. 1981. The use of Markov chain models in sampling from finite populations. *Scandinavian Journal of Statistics* 8(1), 1–9.

Tuma, Nancy, and Michael Hannan. 1984. *Social Dynamics: Models and Methods.* New York: Academic Press.

U.S. Bureau of Labor Statistics. 1982. *Gross Flow Data from the Current Population Survey, 1970–80.* PB 82-174327. Washington, D.C.: U.S. Department of Labor.

U.S. National Commission on Employment and Unemployment Statistics. 1979. *Counting the Labor Force.* Stock No. 052-003-00695-2. Washington. D.C.: U.S. Government Printing Office.

Vaupel, J. W., and A. I. Yashin. 1982. The deviant dynamics of death in heterogeneous populations. International Institute of Applied Systems Analysis Working Paper 82–47.

Verma, Vijay, Christopher Scott, and Colm O'Muircheartaigh. 1980. Sample designs and sampling errors for the World Fertility Survey (with discussion). *Journal of the Royal Statistical Society*, Series A 143(4), 431–473.

Williams, W. H. 1975. The seriousness of selection biases including nonresponse. *Proceedings of the Social Statistical Section of the American Statistical Association*, p. 11–15.

Williams, W. H., and C. L. Mallows. 1970. Systematic biases in panel surveys due to differential nonresponse. *Journal of the American Statistical Association* 65, 1338–1349.

CHAPTER 6

Statistical models for longitudinal labor market data based on counting processes

Per Kragh Andersen

1 Introduction

The aim of this chapter is to present a survey of how the statistical theory of *multivariate counting processes* can be useful when studying labor market dynamics. Throughout it will be assumed that *longitudinal data* are available on some sample S of individuals during a *fixed calendar time interval* $I = [t_0, t_1]$.

We shall be working with the basic three-state model illustrated in Figure 1. The state "unemployed" will be denoted 0, the state "employed" will be denoted 1, and the state "out of labor force" will be denoted 2. The number of individuals in state i ($i = 0, 1, 2$) at time $t-$ ($t \in I$) is denoted $Y_i(t)$. The requirement of having longitudinal data implies that for each individual $v \in S$ and for each time $t \in I$ the state to which v belongs at t is known and thus that $Y_0(t)$, $Y_1(t)$, and $Y_2(t)$ are known and that the numbers $N_{ij}(t)$ of direct transitions from i to j before t are known. These *stochastic processes* $N_{ij}(t)$ counting the transitions between the states are the basic observations, and in the rest of this chapter statistical models for these counting processes will be discussed. In the presentation, only references to the statistical literature where these methods have been developed will be given. The methods will, however, be related to the specific problem of studying unemployment, and as far as possible terminology from econometrics will be used. Also, in the final section of the chapter the models will be related to various models suggested previously in the econometric literature.

2 Counting processes

A *univariate* counting process $N^v(t)$ is a stochastic process counting the number of times some specific event has occurred in the time interval $[t_0, t]$. Thus the sample function of N^v is a right-continuous step function

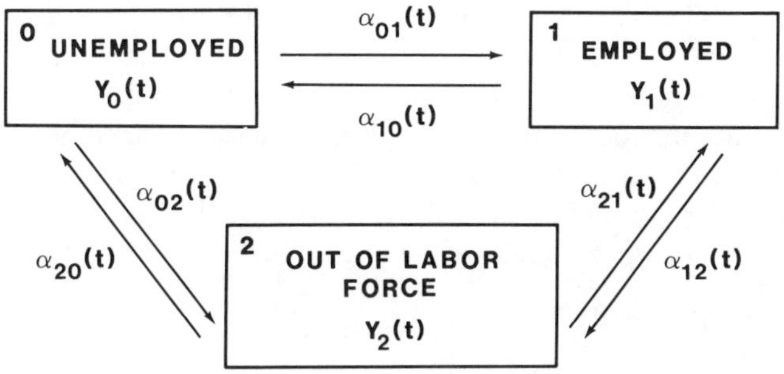

Figure 1. The basic three-state model for unemployment.

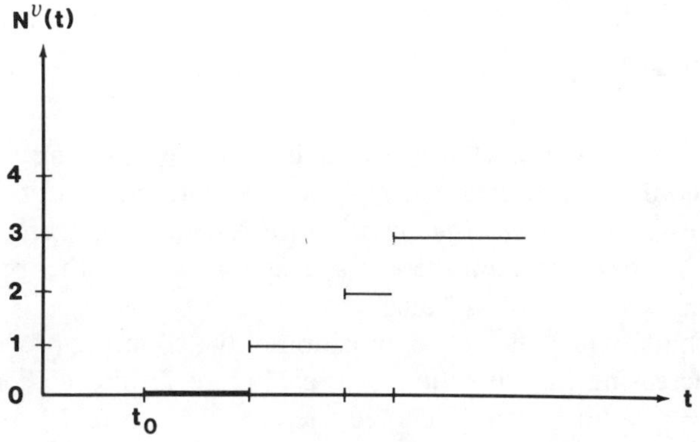

Figure 2. A counting process $N^{\nu}(t)$.

zero at time t_0 with jumps of size $+1$ only. A realization of N^{ν} is shown in Figure 2.

A *multivariate* counting process is a, say, n-component stochastic process $\mathbf{N}(t) = [N^1(t), \ldots, N^n(t)]$, the νth component $N^{\nu}(t)$ being a univariate counting process. It is assumed that no two components can jump at the same time.

In the unemployment model n could be the number of individuals in the sample S and $N^{\nu}(t)$ could be the number of times the νth individual got unemployed before t. Then in the notation of Section 1 we would have $N_{10}(t) = \sum_{\nu=1}^{n} N^{\nu}(t)$. In this model it is desirable to include information on individual characteristics such as age, sex, and income as well as on previous unemployment statuses when assessing the probability for the future development of the process $\mathbf{N}$. This is possible because the distribution of $\mathbf{N}$ is governed by the (random) intensity process $\boldsymbol{\lambda}(t) = [\lambda_1(t), \ldots, \lambda_n(t)]$ defined by

$$\lambda_{\nu}(t)\,dt = P(N^{\nu}(t + dt) - N^{\nu}(t-) = 1 \,|\, \mathscr{F}_{t-}), \qquad t \in I \tag{2.1}$$

Here (the σ algebra) $\mathscr{F}_{t-}$ records the complete *history* of N up to (but not including) t as well as other events to be included in the model which have occurred before t. Thus in the unemployment model it can be specified how the previous employment statuses, age, sex, income, and so on influence the intensity process.

Since in the small interval dt the process N^{ν} either jumps once or does not jump at all, we have (at least intuitively) by (2.1) that

$$\lambda_{\nu}(t)\,dt = E(dN^{\nu}(t)\,|\,\mathscr{F}_{t-}), \qquad t \in I \tag{2.2}$$

where $dN^{\nu}(t) = N^{\nu}(t + dt) - N^{\nu}(t-)$, and hence defining $dM_{\nu}(t) = dN^{\nu}(t) - \lambda_{\nu}(t)\,dt$, it follows that $E(dM_{\nu}(t)\,|\,\mathscr{F}_{t-}) = 0$, showing that the stochastic process M_{ν} defined by

$$M_{\nu}(t) = N^{\nu}(t) - \int_{t_0}^{t} \lambda_{\nu}(u)\,du \tag{2.3}$$

is a *martingale*. This fact is used throughout when studying statistical models for counting processes, since many estimators and test statistics can be expressed as *stochastic integrals* with respect to martingales and since furthermore central limit theorems, inequalities, and other properties of martingales are very well studied.

We can think of (2.3) as a decomposition of the counting process $N^{\nu}(t)$ (which is increasing as a function of t; cf. Figure 2) into an increasing *trend* $\Lambda_{\nu}(t) = \int_{t_0}^{t} \lambda_{\nu}(u)\,du$ often denoted the *compensator* of N^{ν} and some random *noise* represented by the zero-mean martingale $M_{\nu}(t)$.

3 The multiplicative intensity model

A particularly simple statistical model for a counting process is obtained by specifying the intensity process $\boldsymbol{\lambda}$ to have the form

$$\lambda_{\nu}(t) = \alpha(t) Y^{\nu}(t), \qquad t \in I, \qquad \nu = 1, \ldots, n \tag{3.1}$$

That is, $\lambda_{\nu}(t)$ is a product of an *observable* stochastic process $Y^{\nu}(t)$ and an *unknown* (hazard) function $\alpha(t)$. In the unemployment model with $N^{\nu}(t)$ counting the number of times, the individual $\nu \in S$ got unemployed before t, $Y^{\nu}(t)$ would be the indicator of being in the state 1 ("employed") at $t-$, and $\alpha(t) = \alpha_{10}(t)$ would be the intensity or hazard for an individual of getting unemployed at calendar time t. Thus we would have $Y_1(t) = \sum_{\nu=1}^{n} Y^{\nu}(t)$. In this very simple model it is assumed that for every $\nu \in S$ the calendar time specific unemployment intensities are the same; in particular, it is assumed that we have a *Markov process model*. These assumptions will be relaxed in the following sections. Here it will also be studied how models where t represents the duration in a given state rather than the calendar time can be discussed.

Estimation of the unknown hazard function $\alpha(t)$ in the model (3.1) when $\mathbf{N}$ and $\mathbf{Y} = (Y^1, \ldots, Y^n)$ are observed continuously over I can be based on the likelihood function

$$L = \prod_{\nu=1}^{n} \left(\prod_{t \in I} [\alpha(t) Y^\nu(t)]^{dN^\nu(t)} \right) \exp\left[- \int_I \alpha(u) Y^\nu(u)\, du \right] \tag{3.2}$$

It is not possible to maximize L under the assumption of the compensators $\Lambda_\nu = \int \lambda_\nu$ being absolutely continuous, but in an extended model allowing discontinuities in Λ_ν the maximum likelihood estimator $\hat{A}$ for the integrated hazard function $A = \int \alpha$ becomes

$$\hat{A}(t) = \int_{t_0}^{t} \frac{d\bar{N}(u)}{\bar{Y}(u)}, \qquad t \in I \tag{3.3}$$

where $\bar{N} = N^1 + \cdots + N^n$ and $\bar{Y} = Y^1 + \cdots + Y^n$. Thus we estimate $A(t)$ by a step function jumping each time a jump in one of the component processes is observed, the jump size of $\hat{A}$ at t being the ratio between the number of jumps observed at t and the number $\bar{Y}(t)$ "at risk" for making a jump at t. Thus in the case where all $d\bar{N}(u)$ are 0 or 1 this step function is given by

$$\hat{A}(t) = \sum_{\substack{\text{jump times} \\ u \leq t}} \frac{1}{\bar{Y}(u)}, \qquad t \in I$$

A typical estimator is displayed in Figure 3.

The estimated hazard $\hat{\alpha}(t)$ can be approximately read from a plot of $\hat{A}(t)$ as the *slope* at t. Sometimes it can be difficult to get a feeling for the slope of a step function, and thus it may be useful to estimate $\alpha(t)$ by smoothing the curve $\hat{A}$. A *kernel function estimate* $\hat{\alpha}(t)$ of $\alpha(t)$ is

$$\hat{\alpha}(t) = \frac{1}{b} \int_I K\left(\frac{t-u}{b}\right) d\hat{A}(t), \qquad t \in I \tag{3.4}$$

where the *kernel function* K is nonnegative with integral 1 and the *window* b is a positive parameter determining in how broad a neighborhood around t jumps in A are used when estimating $\alpha(t)$. Smoothing the curve in Figure 3 would yield an increasing estimate of α as displayed in Figure 4.

In the unemployment model such estimates could be used, for example, for studying secular trends or seasonal variations in the unemployment rate $\alpha_{10}(t)$.

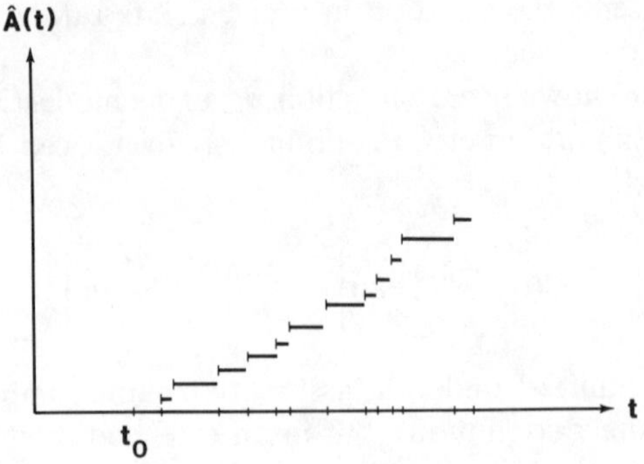

Figure 3. An estimator for the integrated hazard $A(t)$.

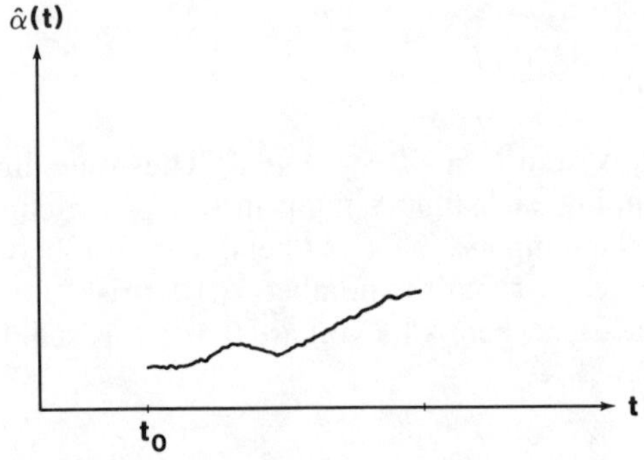

Figure 4. An estimator for the hazard $\alpha(t)$.

In studies of unemployment the object will not always be the variation with calendar time but rather the distribution of individual spells of unemployment or employment. Also in this case the counting process approach is applicable; however, a redefinition of the basic processes N^ν is needed. For simplicity we shall consider the situation where at most one completed spell of unemployment is available for each individual, or equivalently it can be assumed that successive spells are independent and have the same distribution. (Again the assumption will be relaxed in the following sections.) Thus we define T_ν to be the (possibly incomplete) length of the unemployment spell for individual ν and we define δ_ν as the indicator of the spell being completed.

Then the basic counting processes are given by

$$N^\nu(t) = I(T_\nu \leq t, \delta_\nu = 1), \quad \nu = 1, \ldots, n, \qquad t > 0$$

and if F is the distribution function for the spell length and $\alpha = F'/(1 - F)$ is the corresponding hazard function, then $(N^1, \ldots, N^n)$ is a multivariate counting process with intensity process $\boldsymbol{\lambda} = (\lambda_1, \ldots, \lambda_n)$, where $\lambda_v(t) = \alpha(t)Y^v(t)$, and $Y^v(t) = I(T_v \geq t)$. Thus the multiplicative intensity model is satisfied and we can go on as described above and estimate the integrated hazard function $A(t)$ specifying the spell length distribution. From plots of $\hat{A}(t)$ one may decide on a given parametric form of the distribution, such as a Weibull or lognormal distribution.

Note how easily right censoring was introduced when studying the distribution of the spell length. In fact, analysis of censored survival data has so far been the main example of a multiplicative intensity model for a multivariate counting process.

4 Inclusion of a single exogenous variable

Often the description of the unemployment rate as being the same for all individuals in the sample will be unrealistic, since various exogenous variables such as age, sex, education, or geographical region are known to cause differences. Thus in the statistical analysis it must be possible to include such observed heterogeneities. The simplest way of doing this is to group the individuals in S according to their value of the variable of interest and in each group to estimate the intensity by (3.3) or (3.4). These estimates can be plotted, and thus a visual comparison can be made. Also, a statistical test for the comparison can be constructed as follows.

Denote by $\hat{A}_f(t)$ the estimated integrated hazard function in group f, $f = 1, \ldots, k$, where k is the number of levels of the variable of interest. Under the hypothesis H_0 of no influence of the variable the common estimate for all groups is $\hat{A}(t)$ given by (3.4). A general test statistic for H_0 can now be defined as

$$Z_f = \int_{t_0}^{t_1} L_f(u)[d\hat{A}_f(u) - d\hat{A}(u)], \qquad f = 1, \ldots, k \tag{4.1}$$

where $L_f(u)$ is a "weighting process" that can be specified according to which alternative hypotheses one is interested in. Thus $L_f(u) = Y_{(f)}(u) =$ the number "at risk" in group f at time $u-$ yields a test (the so-called logrank test) with good power against proportional hazards alternatives. The asymptotic distribution of the statistic $Z'V^-Z$, where $Z = (Z_1, \ldots, Z_k)$ can be shown (using the martingale convergence results) to be chi-square with $k - 1$ degrees of freedom. Here V^- is a (generalized) inverse of the estimated covariance matrix with elements

$$V_{f_1 f_2} = \int_{t_0}^{t_1} L_{f_1}(u) L_{f_2}(u) \left[\frac{\delta_{f_1 f_2}}{Y_{(f)}(u)} - \frac{1}{\bar{Y}(u)} \right] \frac{d\bar{N}(u)}{\bar{Y}(u)}$$

where δ is the Kronecker delta; that is, $\delta_{ij} = 1$ if $i = j$ and 0 otherwise.

In the case $k = 2$ a simpler equivalent test statistic for H_0 is given by

$$Z = \int_{t_0}^{t_1} L(u)[d\bar{A}_2(u) - d\hat{A}_1(u)] \tag{4.2}$$

and the distribution of $Z/\sqrt{V}$, where

$$V = \int_{t_0}^{t_1} \left[\frac{L^2(u)\, d\bar{N}(u)}{Y_{(1)}(u) Y_{(2)}(u)} \right]$$

is asymptotically standard normal.

5 Inclusion of several exogenous variables: regression models

When correcting the intensities for several variables simultaneously the methods described in Section 4 can be applied, but often the groups thus obtained will become too small to get a powerful between-group comparison. The usual approach in such a situation is to consider instead some sort of regression model, thus putting more structure into the statistical model. It then becomes an important part of the analyses to check whether the extra assumptions are fulfilled.

Frequently a *proportional hazards model* is considered. Let the exogenous variables be represented by the vector $\mathbf{z} = (z_1, \ldots, z_p)$; here z_1 could be 1 for males and 0 for females, z_2 could be the individual's age at t_0 [or some function of the age such as log(age)], z_3 could be an indicator of the geographical region to which the individual belongs (thus if r regions are considered, z_3 would consist of $r - 1$ indicators), and so on. The proportional hazards model for the individual intensities $\alpha^\nu(t)$, $\nu \in S$ in the multiplicative intensity model (4) is now specified by

$$\alpha^\nu(t) = \alpha_0(t) \exp(\beta_1 z_1^\nu + \cdots + \beta_p z_p^\nu) \tag{5.1}$$

where $(\beta_1, \ldots, \beta_p)$ are unknown regression coefficients specifying how the variables $\mathbf{z}^\nu$ for individual $\nu \in S$ influence the *underlying* hazard function $\alpha_0(t)$ common for all individuals. In addition to the assumption of proportional hazards, $\alpha^{\nu_1}(t)/\alpha^{\nu_2}(t) = \exp[\beta_1(z_1^{\nu_1} - z_1^{\nu_2}) + \cdots + \beta_p(z_p^{\nu_1} - z_p^{\nu_2})]$, it is assumed in the model specified by (5.1) that the variables enter log-linearly in the intensity.

Estimation of the parameters $\boldsymbol{\beta} = (\beta_1, \ldots, \beta_p)$ and $\alpha_0(t)$ can be based on the likelihood function (3.2), which in the model (5.1) amounts to estimating $\boldsymbol{\beta}$ by the value $\hat{\boldsymbol{\beta}}$ that maximizes the function

$$L_C = \prod_{\nu=1}^{n} \prod_{t} \left[\frac{Y^\nu(t) \exp(\boldsymbol{\beta}'\mathbf{z}^\nu)}{\sum_{\mu=1}^{n} Y^\mu(t) \exp(\boldsymbol{\beta}'\mathbf{z}^\mu)} \right]^{dN^\nu(t)} \tag{5.2}$$

and the integrated underlying hazard $A_0(t) = \int_{t_0}^{t} \alpha_0(u)\,du$ by

$$\hat{A}_0(t) = \int_{t_0}^{t} \frac{d\bar{N}(u)}{\sum_{v=1}^{n} Y^v(u)\exp(\hat{\boldsymbol{\beta}}'\mathbf{z}^v)} \tag{5.3}$$

This estimate can, similar to (3.3), be smoothed using a kernel function K, and thus an estimate of $\alpha_0(t)$ can be obtained.

Hypotheses about $\boldsymbol{\beta}$ can be tested using the asymptotic distribution of $\sqrt{n}(\hat{\boldsymbol{\beta}} - \boldsymbol{\beta})$ which (using martingale techniques) can be shown to be multivariate normal with mean zero and a covariance matrix $\boldsymbol{\Sigma}$, where $\boldsymbol{\Sigma}^{-1}$ can be estimated consistently by

$$\hat{\boldsymbol{\Sigma}}^{-1} = -\frac{1}{n}\frac{\partial^2}{\partial\beta^2}\log L_C(\hat{\boldsymbol{\beta}}).$$

In the unemployment model with t denoting the spell duration (see Section 3) the probability for individual v of being unemployed for a period longer than τ can be estimated by

$$\hat{S}_v(\tau) = \exp\{-\hat{A}_0(\tau)\exp(\hat{\boldsymbol{\beta}}'\mathbf{z}^v)\} \tag{5.4}$$

The approximate standard deviation of (5.4) can be estimated combining the asymptotic distribution of $\hat{\boldsymbol{\beta}}$ with a central limit theorem for $\hat{A}_0(\cdot)$ given by (5.3).

6 Inclusion of endogenous and other time-dependent variables

In the regression model (5.1) only information available at time t_0 was included in the hazard. The definition (2.1) of the intensity, however, leaves open the possibility of considering more general models that include observable endogenous variables such as income history or employment history. These can, for example, be incorporated in the exponent part of a model like (5.1); that is,

$$\lambda_v(t) = Y^v(t)\alpha_0(t)\exp[\boldsymbol{\beta}'\mathbf{z}^v(t)] \tag{6.1}$$

where $\mathbf{z}^v(t)$ now represents the total set of exogenous and endogenous variables available at time t. Thus in the unemployment model $\mathbf{z}^v(t)$ could include quantities such as the income during the latest spell of employment and number of previous periods of unemployment. The parameters can be estimated from (5.2) and (5.3), replacing $\mathbf{z}^v$ by $\mathbf{z}^v(t)$.

In the case where t represents calendar time, $\alpha_0(t)$ gives the general calendar time variation, which is modified for each individual by the factor

$\exp[\boldsymbol{\beta}'\mathbf{z}^v(t)]$. In this model, also, duration dependence can be introduced by appropriately chosen time-dependent variables. Thus, for example, Weibull-distributed unemployment spell lengths correspond to specifying a time-dependent variable for individual v equal to $\log(t - t_v)$, where t_v is the time when v became unemployed. Specifically, it is seen that in the case where $\alpha_0(t) = \alpha_0$ (independent of calendar time t) and no other variables included, we would have the Weibull intensity $\alpha(t) = (t - t_v)^\beta \cdot \alpha_0$ only depending on the unemployment duration $t - t_v$ at time t. Thus the model defined by (6.1) includes as special cases the Markov regression model (5.1) and the model with Weibull-distributed spell lengths. Furthermore, it gives a method for combining these models, allowing a general calendar time variation "superimposed" by Weibull-distributed spells of unemployment and regression of exogenous as well as endogenous observable variables.

As noted in Section 3, *right* censoring is easily incorporated in these analyses. In the model with duration dependence, *left* censoring will, however, cause problems in that the duration of the spell including t_0 will generally not be known. If *negative* duration dependence is expected, then one way of approaching this problem would be to neglect dependence of durations longer than some τ and restrict attention to the interval $[t_0 + \tau, t_1]$.

7 Inclusion of unobserved heterogeneities

In the models discussed so far it has been assumed that all heterogeneities in the sample S can be explained by the observable variables $\mathbf{z}^v(t)$. Often this assumption is not realistic and it is desirable to include in the model also unobserved heterogeneities. This can be done in the present framework by specifying the intensity process of the counting process $N^v(t)$ as

$$\lambda_v(t) = Y^v(t)\alpha_0(t)\exp[\boldsymbol{\beta}'\mathbf{z}^v(t)]X_v \tag{7.1}$$

where as in (6.1) the observable variables are represented by $\mathbf{z}^v(t)$, whereas the X_v are individual unobservable variables. In the survival data literature the X_v are sometimes denoted *frailties* but in the present section we shall use the term *unobservables.*

For given X_v the parameters $\boldsymbol{\beta}$ and $\alpha_0(t)$ can be estimated as described in Section 5; that is, $\boldsymbol{\beta}$ is estimated by the value $\hat{\boldsymbol{\beta}}_X$ maximizing

$$L_{CX} = \prod_v \prod_t \left(\frac{Y^v(t)X_v \exp[\boldsymbol{\beta}'\mathbf{z}^v(t)]}{\sum_{\mu=1}^{n} Y^\mu(t)X_\mu \exp[\boldsymbol{\beta}'\mathbf{z}^\mu(t)]} \right)^{dN^v(t)} \tag{7.2}$$

and $A_0(t)$ is estimated by the step function

$$\hat{A}_{OX}(t) = \int_{t_0}^{t} \frac{d\bar{N}(u)}{\sum_{\nu=1}^{n} Y^{\nu}(u)X_{\nu} \exp[\hat{\boldsymbol{\beta}}'_X \mathbf{z}^{\nu}(t)]} \tag{7.3}$$

Now the X_ν are not observed, but assuming that the $X_1, \ldots, X_n$ are independent identically Γ-distributed with mean 1 and shape parameter γ, the joint likelihood for X and $(N, Y, \mathbf{Z})$ and hence the conditional likelihood for X given $(N, Y, \mathbf{Z})$ can be found. Thus for fixed value of the shape parameter γ the unobservables X_ν can be predicted by the conditional expectation given $(N, T, \mathbf{Z})$, that is, by

$$\hat{X}_\nu = \frac{\gamma + N^{\nu}(t_1)}{\gamma + \int_{t_0}^{t_1} Y^{\nu}(u) \exp[\hat{\boldsymbol{\beta}}'_X \mathbf{z}^{\nu}(u)]\, d\hat{A}_{OX}(u)} \tag{7.4}$$

With these new values $\hat{X}_\nu$ new estimates $\hat{\boldsymbol{\beta}}_X$ and $\hat{A}_{OX}(t)$ can be calculated by (7.2) and (7.3) and so on. After convergence the procedure can be repeated for new values of γ and finally the parameter values giving the maximal marginal likelihood of $(N, Y, \mathbf{Z})$ can be chosen.

This use of the EM-algorithm gives a way of technically handling the models with unobserved heterogeneities, whereas the derivation says nothing about qualitative differences between including unobservables or not. It is to be expected, however, that the exclusion of important unobservable heterogeneities will lead to an underestimation of the variance of the regression parameters $\boldsymbol{\beta}$.

8 Relations to econometric literature

This chapter has surveyed models discussed in the statistical literature adequate when analyzing continuously observed discrete state stochastic processes such as the usual unemployment model. The requirement of having longitudinal data at hand is crucial (Aalen, 1982a,b) since the basic likelihood function (3.2) will be different when, for example, cross-sectional samples of data are available.

In this final section the counting process models will be related to some of the models discussed in the econometric literature. A two-state Markov process model (sometimes extended by a third state of attrition) was discussed by Tuma, Hannan, and Groeneveld (1979) and by Tuma and Robins (1980). In this model the transition rates are usually assumed to be time-independent but possibly depending on exogenous variables, thus being an example of the regression model (5.1) with $\alpha_0(t) = \alpha_0$. Extensions of the model to one with piecewise constant $\alpha_0(t)$ were also introduced.

Heckman and Borjas (1980) also start by considering a two-state Markov process model but turn to a specification of the spell length distribution as being of the Weibull family and consider in this model regression on prior spell lengths. Also, regression on exogenous variables and inclusion of unobserved heterogeneity are introduced.

Burdett et al. (1982) and Flinn and Heckman (1982) derived Markov process models for unemployment via economic search theory and used the models for analyzing real data.

Parametric proportional hazards models for the duration of spells were considered by Lancaster (1979); see also Lancaster and Nickell (1980). Here special attention was paid the exponential and Weibull families of distributions and the impact of including an unobservable unit mean Γ-distributed component was discussed.

Finally, Elbers and Ridder (1982) and Heckman and Singer (1982) discussed the problem of identifiability of the distribution of the unobservables in a proportional hazards model.

ACKNOWLEDGMENT

An early version of this paper was presented at the workshop on Labor Market Dynamics held at Sandjerg, Denmark, August 24–28, 1982, the proceedings of which have been published in Springer-Verlag's series: Studies in Contemporary Economics.

BIBLIOGRAPHIC NOTES

Section 1. Surveys of how the counting process framework can be used when studying censored survival data are found in Aalen (1982) and Andersen (1982). An example of how the methods can be used in a particular case study is given by Andersen and Rasmussen (1982).

Section 2. A survey of the "martingale approach" to the theory of counting processes is found in Brémaud and Jacod (1977). Central limit theorems for martingales are found, e.g., in Rebolledo (1978, 1980). An introduction to the theory aimed at its applications to survival data was given by Gill (1982).

Section 3. The multiplicative intensity model for counting processes was introduced by Aalen (1975, 1978), who also demonstrated that censored survival data and (possibly censored) finite-state Markov processes are special cases. The estimator (3.3) for the integrated intensity was also introduced by Aalen in this framework generalizing the estimators discussed by Altshuler (1970) in a biomedical context and by Nelson (1969, 1972) in reliability theory. The possibility of choosing a particular parametric family of distributions from a plot of $\hat{A}$ was discussed by Nelson (1972). The smoothed version $\hat{\alpha}$ of the Aalen estimator was introduced by Ramlau–Hansen (1983), and both Aalen and Ramlau–Hansen used martingale theory to find asymptotic properties of the estimators. The derivation of $\hat{A}$ as a maximum likelihood estimator is due to Johansen (1983), who extended the Aalen model allowing for discontinuous compensators Λ_v. Another extension of the model giving rise to slightly different but asymptotically equivalent maximum likelihood estimators was introduced by Jacobsen (1982). A review of the model in the case of censored survival data with particular emphasis on a discussion of various censoring mechanisms is found in Gill (1980).

Section 4. The two-sample test statistic (4.2) was introduced by Aalen (1975, 1978), who also demonstrated the optimality properties of the logrank test against proportional hazards alternatives. The general k-sample test statistic (4.1) was introduced by Andersen, Borgan, Gill, and Keiding (1982). In both of these papers it was demonstrated that in the special case of censored survival data, specific choices of the process $L_f(u)(L(u))$ correspond to test statistics previously suggested in the survival data literature. Efficiency properties of two-sample tests were discussed by Gill (1980) in the censored survival data case.

Section 5. The proportional hazards model (5.1) for censored survival data is known as the Cox model, having been suggested by Cox (1972); see also Cox (1975). The formulation of (5.1) as a model for the deterministic part of the intensity process of a multivariate counting process is due to Andersen and Gill (1982), who also proved the asymptotic results for the estimators. In the survival data model these results were proved previously by Tsiatis (1981). The derivation of $\hat{\beta}$ and $\hat{A}_0(t)$ as maximum likelihood estimators was carried out by Johansen (1983). Methods for checking the proportional hazards assumption in the case of censored survival data were reviewed by Kalbfleisch and Prentice (1980) and Andersen (1982). These methods also apply to more general Markov process models such as the unemployment model.

Section 6. The inclusion of time-dependent variables in the regression model was introduced by Cox (1972). The asymptotic properties of the estimators in the model (6.1) were derived by Andersen and Gill (1982). An example of analyzing a model with negative duration dependence was given by Andersen and Rasmussen (1982).

Section 7. A discussion of the impact of unobserved heterogeneity in survival models is found in Vaupel, Manton, and Stallard (1979) who also used the Γ-distribution with mean 1 as the general "frailty" distribution. The inclusion of unobservables in counting process models is due to Gill (1983), who suggested using the EM-algorithm of Dempster, Laird, and Rubin (1977) in the estimation procedure.

REFERENCES

Aalen, O. O. (1975). Statistical inference for a family of counting processes. Ph.D. dissertation. Department of Statistics, University of California, Berkeley.

(1978). Nonparametric inference for a family of counting processes. *Ann. Statist.* 6, 701–26.

(1982a). Contribution to the discussion of P. K. Andersen, Ø. Borgan, R. D. Gill, and N. Keiding, linear nonparametric tests for comparison of counting processes, with applications to censored survival data (with discussion), *Int. Statist. Rev.* 50, 219–58.

(1982b). Practical applications of the nonparametric statistical theory for counting processes. Statistical Research Report No. 2. Institute of Mathematics, University of Oslo.

Altshuler, B. (1970). Theory for the measurement of competing risks in animal experiment. *Math. Biosci.* 6, 1–11.

Andersen, P. K. (1982a). On the application of the theory of counting processes in the statistical analysis of censored survival data. In *Survival Analysis: Proceedings of the 178th IMS Conference* (ed. J. J. Crowley and R. A. Johnson). IMS Lecture Notes–Monographs, 2.

(1982b). Testing goodness of fit of Cox's regression and life model. *Biometrics* 38, 67–77.

Andersen, P. K., Borgan, Ø., Gill, R. D., and Keiding, N. (1982). Linear nonparametric tests for comparison of counting processes, with applications to censored survival data (with discussion). *Int. Statist. Rev.* 50, 219–58.

Andersen, P. K., and Gill, R. D. (1982). Cox's regression model for counting processes: a large sample study. *Ann. Statist.* 10, 1100–20.

Andersen, P. K., and Rasmussen, N. K. (1982). Admissions to psychiatric hospitals among women giving birth and women having induced abortion: a statistical analysis of a counting process model. Research Report 82/6, Statistical Research Unit, Danish Medical and Social Science Research Councils, Copenhagen.

Brémaud, P., and Jacod, J. (1977). Processus ponctuels et martingales: Résultats récents sur la modélisation et filtrage. *Adv. Appl. Prob.* 9, 362–416.

Burdett, K., Kiefer, N. M., Mortensen, D. T., and Neumann, G. R. (1982). Earnings, unemployment, and allocation of time over time. Mimeo, Northwestern University.

Cox, D. R. (1972). Regression models and life-tables (with discussion). *J. Roy. Statist. Soc. B.* 34, 187–220.

(1975). Partial likelihood. *Biometrika* 62, 269–76.

Dempster, A. P., Laird, N. M., and Rubin, D. B. (1977). Maximum likelihood from incomplete data via the EM algorithm (with discussion). *J. Roy. Statist. Soc. B* 39, 1–38.

Elbers, C., and Ridder, G. (1982). True and spurious duration dependence: the identifiability of the proportional hazard model. *Rev. Econ. Stud.* XLIX, 403–9.

Flinn, C., and Heckman, J. (1982). New methods for analyzing structural models for labor force dynamics. *J. Econometrics* 18, 155–68.

Gill, R. D. (1980). Censoring and stochastic integrals. Mathematical Centre Tracts 124. Mathematisch Centrum, Amsterdam.

(1982). Understanding Cox's regression model: a martingale approach. Preprint 81/82, Mathematisch Centrum, Amsterdam.

(1983). Models for censored matched pairs. Preprint 83. Mathematisch Centrum, Amsterdam.

Heckman, J. J., and Borjas, G. J. (1980). Does unemployment cause future unemployment? Definitions, questions, and answers from a continuous time model of heterogeneity and state dependence. *Economica* 47, 247–83.

Heckman, J. J., and Singer, B. (1982). The identification problem in econometric models for duration data. In *Advances in Econometrics* (W. Hildenbrand, ed.). New York: Cambridge University Press.

Jacobsen, M. (1982). Statistical analysis of counting processes. *Lecture Notes in Statistics* 12. Springer, New York.

Johansen, S. (1983). An extension of Cox's regression model. *Int. Statist. Rev.* 51, 258–62.

Kalbfleisch, J. D., and Prentice, R. L. (1980). The statistical analysis of failure time data. Wiley, New York.

Lancaster, A. (1979). Econometric methods for the duration of unemployment. *Econometrica* 47, 939–56.

Lancaster, A., and Nickell, S. J. (1980). The analysis of re-employment probabilities for the unemployed. *J. Roy. Statist. Soc. A.* 143, 141–65.

Nelson, W. (1969). Hazard plotting for incomplete failure data. *J. Qual. Teach.* 1, 27–52.

(1972). Theory and application of hazard plotting for censored failure data. *Technometrics* 14, 945–66.

Ramlau-Hansen, H. (1983). Smoothing counting process intensities by means of kernel functions. *Ann. Statist.* 11, 453–66.

Rebolledo, R. (1978). Sur les applications de la théorie des martingales à l'étude statistique d'une famille de processus ponctuels. *Springer Lecture Notes in Mathematics* 636, 27–70.

(1980). Central limit theorems for local martingales. *Zeitschrift für Wahrschemlichkeits theorie verw, Gebiete* 51, 269–86.

Tsiatis, A. A. (1981). A large sample study of Cox's regression model. *Ann. Statist.* 9, 93–108.

Tuma, N. B., Hannan, M. T., and Groeneveld, L. P. (1979). Dynamic analysis of event histories. *Amer. J. Sociol.* 84, 820–54.

Tuma, N. B., and Robins, P. K. (1980). A dynamic model of employment behaviour: an application to the Seattle and Denver income maintenance experiments. *Econometrica* 48, 1031–52.

Vaupel, J. W., Manton, K. G., and Stallard, E. (1979). The impact of heterogeneity in individual frailty on the dynamics of mortality. *Demography* 16, 439–54.

CHAPTER 7

Assessing qualitative features of longitudinal data

Halina Frydman and Burton Singer

1 Introduction

Most empirical analyses of discrete choice processes in economics utilize classes of models which are partially based on economic theory but which also contain disturbance terms and unobserved individual-specific sources of heterogeneity that are described by ad hoc parametric families of distributions. The primary focus of interest in such studies is usually the estimation and interpretation of structural parameters, some of which may be associated with unobserved variables. The fine-grained characteristics of error terms are not generally of central importance, and their principal role is to facilitate estimation of what are interpreted as structural parameters. Unobserved variables are incorporated in models of choice processes for at least two reasons: (1) to reduce bias in estimates of parameters associated with observed variables and (2) because some characteristic, such as the variance, of an unobserved variable plays a critical role in behavioral interpretations of a system of equations.

Strong a priori parametric assumptions about error distributions or the distributions of unobserved variables which are not grounded in economic theory or previous empirical studies can lead to a variety of incorrect conclusions. Among the more prominent negative consequences of this form of model misspecification are the following:

1. Estimates of structural parameters in a heterogeneous population model can be very sensitive to the choice of a distribution of unobserved variables (Heckman and Singer, 1982a,b). In particular, even the signs of key parameters can be a consequence of these choices.

2. Rejection of a class of heterogeneous population models based on a test where a "flexible" parametric family of distributions of an unobserved variable are imposed in the models can be an unnecessary erroneous conclusion. For example, mixtures of Bernoulli trials in which beta distributions represent the distribution of binary choices may fail to describe observed data on actual choices. Nevertheless, this data may be represented

by some mixture of Bernoulli trials. This possibility is a consequence of the fact that beta mixtures of Bernoulli trials are not dense in the set of all such mixtures.

3. Estimators of structural parameters in choice probability models may be inconsistent simply as a result of misspecification of an error term in a random utility decomposition (see e.g., Cosslett, 1983). In such models there is virtually no economic theory to guide the error specifications, and the error terms may really be viewed as nuisance parameters. The primary objects of interest are usually structural parameters governing choice probabilities. However, if prediction of choice probabilities is of interest, then what is really needed is a nonparametric estimate of the disturbance distribution together with an estimate of what are interpreted as structural parameters.

Assuming that the functional form of the structural part of a discrete choice model is defensible via an economic theory, a natural first step in an empirical analysis is to ask whether any member of a broad class of models is compatible with observed data on choice behavior. This kind of question can only be addressed using statistical tests in which rejection of a class of models implies that restrictive structural specifications coupled to very general distributions of error terms and unobserved variables are all ruled out at once. Implementation of such tests requires that we can delineate qualitative features of any observed data which arise from all models in a very broad class. The fundamental purpose of tests for compatibility of data with broad classes of models is to provide a clear signal of when a given family of structural models must be modified in order to possibly account for observed choice behavior over time. It is also important that such tests do not depend on any fine-grained details of distributions of error terms or unobserved variables. In essence, they must be insensitive to misspecification of such terms and only depend on the behaviorally interpretable part of a model specification.

The purpose of this chapter is to present examples of tests which can be utilized to reject broad classes of models and which are insensitive to functional forms of the distributions of error terms and unobserved variables. Section 2 contains new specifications of some discrete choice models which have previously been discussed in the economics literature (e.g., McFadden, 1976; Heckman, 1981) but with strong parametric assumptions on the distributions of errors and unobserved variables. The common feature of these models which allows us to assess them with distribution-free tests is that they are reducible to either mixtures of Bernoulli trials or mixtures of Markov chains. This in turn means that DeFinetti's characterization of these mixtures (DeFinetti, 1972, 1975; see also Diaconis, 1977, and Diaconis and Freedman, 1980) in terms of exchangeable and partially exchangeable distributions, respectively, can form the basis of a test. We also present a continuous time specification of unobserved utility dynamics via stochastic differential equations with unobserved person-specific initial conditions. Observed data consist of first-passage times for the diffusion process governed by the stochastic differential equations above a threshold. The basis of a distribution-free test for compatibility of first-passage time data with the general class of stochastic differential equations with positive drift is the fact that the density $g(t)$ of observed first-passage times must be sign-regular (see, e.g., Karlin, 1964, 1968) in t and s when $g(t)$ is replaced by $g(t+s)$.

Section 3 contains a detailed discussion of DeFinetti's results on exchangeability and partial exchangeability and indicates the specific manner in which they can be used for model rejection. A difficulty with exchangeability and partial exchangeability criteria on longitudinal data with long observed sequences of choices is that sampling zeros appear for many of the possible choice sequences. In order to alleviate this potential source of bias in a formal test, we recommend using smoothed sequence frequencies produced via algorithms discussed in Section 4.

Exchangeability and partial exchangeability assessments reduce to simple chi-square tests based on multinomial sampling. Details of this reduction, as they pertain to the discrete choice models in Section 2, are presented in Section 5. Finally the first-passage time model assessment using the sign regularity property of the density of observed waiting times reduces to a simple consideration of simultaneous confidence intervals for odds ratios in 2×2 contingency tables. This reduction is described in Section 6. The chapter concludes with a brief summary and statement of open research problems.

2 Statistical models of discrete choices

2.1 *Binary sequences in discrete time*

Consider an observable binary valued stochastic process $\{X(t),\ t = 0, 1, 2, \ldots\}$ governed by a continuous state latent stochastic process $\{Y(t),\ t = 0, 1, \ldots\}$ according to the rule

$$X(t) = \begin{cases} 1 & \text{if} \quad Y(t) \geq 0 \\ 0 & \text{if} \quad Y(t) < 0 \end{cases}$$

This basic structure arises in studies of labor force participation of women, where $Y(t)$ is identified with the difference between the lifetime utility of an individual if she is in the labor force at time t and her lifetime utility if she does not participate. A similar interpretation appears in studies of the purchase of consumer durable goods. In the analysis of job search $Y(t)$ is interpreted as a difference between offered market wages and reservation wages. When this difference is positive an individual will terminate the search process by accepting an offered job. For a detailed discussion of such interpretations see Heckman (1981) and McFadden (1976).

In each of the above contexts we would, ideally, like the full specification of $Y(t)$ to be a consequence of a formal microeconomic theory. Then all empirical tests of the model would automatically be tests of a specific economic theory. This level of rigorous specification, if it is achievable, lies in the future. In current empirical analysis, specification of $Y(t)$ tends to be loosely grounded in economic theory with parametric forms of disturbance terms frequently defended only on the basis of analytical and computational simplicity. For purposes of assessing whether any member of a broad class of models could have generated given data on $X(t)$ it is unnecessary and frequently misleading to bring in strong assumptions on disturbance terms. In this regard the models presented below will differ from much of the empirical literature.

2.1.1. Random effect Bernoulli models. Let $Y(t, w) = \boldsymbol{\beta} \cdot \mathbf{Z}(w) + \tau(w) + U(t, w)$, where $\mathbf{Z}(w)$ is a time-invariant vector of observed covariates, $\tau(w)$ is an individual-specific fixed component assumed to be distributed independently of $\{U(t, w), t = 0, 1, \ldots\}$. The disturbance terms $\{U(t, w)\}_{t=0,1,\ldots}$ are assumed to be independent, identically distributed (i.i.d.) symmetric (about 0) random variables with cumulative distribution function (c.d.f.) $F_U(u)$. Let $F_{\tau,\mathbf{Z}}(\tau, \mathbf{z})$ denote the joint distribution of τ and $\mathbf{Z}$. With these ingredients at hand the joint distributions of the choice process $X(t)$ are given by

$$\begin{aligned} P(X(0) &= i_0, X(1) = i_1, \ldots, X(n) = i_n) \\ &= \int_{\tau \times \mathbf{Z}} [F_U(\boldsymbol{\beta} \cdot \mathbf{z} + \tau)]^{(\Sigma_{k=0}^{n} i_k)} \\ &\quad \times [1 - F_U(\boldsymbol{\beta} \cdot \mathbf{z} + \tau)]^{(n+1-\Sigma_{k=0}^{n} i_k)}\, dF_{\tau \times \mathbf{Z}}(\tau, \mathbf{z}) \end{aligned} \tag{2.1}$$

with $i_k = 0$ or 1 for $0 \leq k \leq n$ and $n = 0, 1, 2, \ldots$.

2.1.2. Current utilities dependent on past choices. Consider $Y(t, w) = \boldsymbol{\beta} \cdot \mathbf{Z}(w) + \gamma X(t-1, w) + \varepsilon(t, w)$ where $\varepsilon(t, w) = \tau(w) + U(t, w)$. As before, $\{U(t), t = 0, 1, \ldots\}$ are i.i.d. symmetric about 0 random variables which are also independent of $\tau(w)$. Now $\mathbf{Z}(w)$ is a vector of observed time-invariant covariates and $X(t-1, w)$ is the lagged choice variable defined via the criterion

$$X(t-1, w) = \begin{cases} 1 & \text{if} \quad Y(t-1, w) \geq 0 \\ 0 & \text{if} \quad Y(t-1, w) < 0 \end{cases}$$

With this structure each individual's choice process is first-order Markovian; however, the observed process $X(t)$ is a mixture of Markov chains with joint distributions given by

$$P(X(0) = i_0, \ldots, X(n) = i_n)$$

$$= \int_{\tau \times \mathbf{Z}} \rho_{i_0}^{(\mathbf{z},\tau)} \prod_{k=1}^{n} F_U((2i_k - 1)(\boldsymbol{\beta} \cdot \mathbf{z} + \gamma i_{k-1} + \tau)) \, dF_{\tau,\mathbf{Z}}(\tau, \mathbf{z}) \tag{2.2}$$

where $i_k = 0$ or 1 for $0 \leq k \leq n$, $n = 1, 2, \ldots$ and

$$\rho_{i_0}^{(\mathbf{z},\tau)} = [F_U(\boldsymbol{\beta} \cdot \mathbf{z} + \tau)]^{i_0}[1 - F_U(\boldsymbol{\beta} \cdot \mathbf{z} + \tau)]^{1-i_0}$$

is the initial-period choice probability for the initial period utility $Y(0, w) = \boldsymbol{\beta} \cdot \mathbf{Z}(w) + \tau(w) + U(0, w)$.

2.1.3. Higher-order dependence. Again consider current utilities based on lagged choices but now allow dependence two periods back. In particular, set

$$Y(t, w) = \boldsymbol{\beta} \cdot \mathbf{Z}(w) + \gamma_1 X(t-1, w) + \gamma_2 X(t-2, w) + \tau(w) + U(t, w)$$

subject to the same assumptions employed in 2.1.2. Now define the four-state process $[X(t, w), X(t-1, w)]$ for $t = 1, 3, 5, \ldots$ with states identified by the binary vectors $(0, 0)$, $(0, 1)$, $(1, 0)$, and $(1, 1)$. Denote the vector $[X(2t-1, w), X(2t-2, w)]$ by $\mathbf{X}(2t-1)$. Then the joint distributions of $\mathbf{X}(2t-1)$, $t = 1, 2, \ldots,$ are given by

$$P(\mathbf{X}(1) = \mathbf{i}_1, \mathbf{X}(3) = \mathbf{i}_3, \ldots, \mathbf{X}(2n-1) = \mathbf{i}_{2n-1})$$

$$= \int_{\tau \times \mathbf{Z}} \rho_{\mathbf{i}_1}^{(\tau,\mathbf{z})} \prod_{k=2}^{n} F_U((2i_{2k-1} - 1)(\boldsymbol{\beta} \cdot \mathbf{z} + \tau + \gamma_1 i_{2k-2} + \gamma_2 i_{2k-3}))$$

$$\times F_U((2i_{2k-2} - 1)(\boldsymbol{\beta} \cdot \mathbf{z} + \tau + \gamma_1 i_{2k-3} + \gamma_2 i_{2k-4})) \, dF_{\tau,\mathbf{Z}}(\tau, \mathbf{z}) \tag{2.3}$$

where $\mathbf{i}_{2k-1} = (i_{2k-1}, i_{2k-2})$ with $i_j = 0$ or 1 for $j \geq 0$, $1 \leq k \leq n$, $n = 0, 1, 2, \ldots.$

An analogous expansion of the state space can accommodate arbitrary lagged choices governing current utilities and thereby lead to a representation of joint distributions as a mixture of first-order Markov chains. In (2.3), the product of the c.d.f. F_U with itself but evaluated at two possibly different levels is just the one-step transition probability from $\mathbf{i}_{2k-3}$ to $\mathbf{i}_{2k-1}$ for an individual with covariates $\mathbf{z}$ and person effect τ.

2.2 *Inhomogeneous Poisson subordination*

In assessing the impact of advertising campaigns on probabilities of individuals' adopting new products or switching among existing alternatives, it is frequently found that switching occurs rapidly near the initiation of the campaign and then slows down to a new stationary regime. If the nonstationary switching rate is common to all individuals but transition probabilities between alternative products vary across individuals, we can consider modeling the switching process by a special mixture of Markov chains.

In particular, let $N(t)$ be an inhomogeneous Poisson process with intensity function $\phi(t)$. For a declining transition rate over time, we must constrain $\phi(t)$ to be decreasing over time–for example, $\phi(t) = c/(1+t)^{\alpha}$, $0 < \alpha \leq 1$, $c > 0$. Then let $Y_{\mathbf{B}}(k)$, $k = 0, 1, 2, \ldots$, be a time-homogeneous Markov chain with one-step transition matrix $\mathbf{B}$. The states occupied by $Y_{\mathbf{B}}(\cdot)$ are identified with possible products that an individual may purchase, and $t = 0$ is identified with the time of initiation of the advertising campaign. Now $\mathbf{B}$ is presumed to vary across individuals and is distributed according to some a priori unknown probability on $r \times r$ stochastic matrices, where r = number of states. Then $X(t) = Y_{\mathbf{B}}(N(t))$ is the switching process for the full population, and its joint distributions are governed by

$$P(X(0) = i_0, X(t_1) = i_1, \ldots, X(t_n) = i_n)$$
$$= \int_{\mathscr{B}} \rho_{i_0}^{(\mathbf{B})} \{\exp[\Phi(t_1)](\mathbf{B} - \mathbf{I})\}_{i_0,i_1} \{\exp[\Phi(t_2) - \Phi(t_1)](\mathbf{B} - \mathbf{I})\}_{i_1,i_2}$$
$$\cdots \{\exp[\Phi(t_n) - \Phi(t_{n-1})](\mathbf{B} - \mathbf{I})\}_{i_{n-1},i_n} \, d\mu(\mathbf{B}) \tag{2.4}$$

where $\Phi(t) = \int_0^t \phi(u)\,du = EN(t)$, $i_k \in [1, 2, \ldots, r]$, $\mu(\cdot)$ is a probability distribution on the space $\mathscr{B}$ of $r \times r$ stochastic matrices, and $0 = t_0 < t_1 < \cdots < t_n$, $\rho_{i_0}^{(\mathbf{B})} = P(X(0) = i_0 | \mathbf{B})$ = initial probability for type-$\mathbf{B}$ individual.

The specification (2.4) can be detrended to facilitate tests of whether observed data are compatible with this special heterogeneous population model according to the following rule. Introduce the sequence of ordered time points

$$s_0 = 0 < s_1 < \cdots < s_n,$$

where $s_k = \Phi^{-1}(t_k)$. Then

$$P(X(0) = i_0, X(s_1) = i_1, \ldots, X(s_n) = i_n)$$
$$= \int_{\mathscr{B}} \rho_{i_0}^{(\mathbf{B})} [\exp t_1(\mathbf{B} - \mathbf{I})]_{i_0,i_1} \cdots [\exp(t_n - t_{n-1})(\mathbf{B} - \mathbf{I})]_{i_{n-1},i_n} \, d\mu(\mathbf{B}) \tag{2.5}$$

Then selecting $\{t_i\}$ such that $t_k - t_{k-1} \equiv$ constant, the expression (2.5) describes sequence frequencies for a mixture of discrete-time-homogeneous Markov chains analogous to (2.2) and (2.3).

It is important to observe that the above reduction of a mixture of inhomogeneous Markov chains to a mixture of time-homogeneous chains cannot be carried out if the intensity function $\phi(t)$ varies across individuals. For this and most other forms of nonstationarity in heterogeneous populations, deterministic detrending is impossible, and new forms of random time substitutions remain to be developed for such models. In particular, some nontrivial extensions of the methods of Aalen and Hoem (1978) will be required to detrend broad classes of heterogeneous population models.

2.3 *First-passage times*

Suppose that current utility depends on past utility according to a stochastic differential equation

$$dY(t) = a(Y(t))\,dW(t) + b(Y(t))\,dt \tag{2.6}$$

where $W(t)$ is standard Brownian motion, $b(y) > 0$ is a positive continuously differentiable local drift, and $a^2(y)$ is a continuously differentiable local variance defined, respectively, by

$$b(y) = \lim_{h \to 0} \frac{1}{h} E[Y(t+h) - Y(t) \mid Y(t) = y]$$

$$a^2(y) = \lim_{h \to 0} \frac{1}{h} E\{[Y(t+h) - Y(t)]^2 \mid Y(t) = y\}$$

Assume that unobserved initial utilities θ vary across persons. Then in the context of labor force participation with $\theta < 0$, $Y(t, w) < 0$ iff $X(t, w) = 0$ corresponds to not participating, and a change in state to $X(t, w) = 1$ occurs at the first-passage time $T_\theta = \min(t\colon Y(t, w) \geq 0 \mid Y(0, w) = \theta)$. The observed first-passage time density $g(t)$ is then represented as

$$g(t) = \int_{-\infty}^{0} f(t \mid \theta)\, d\mu(\theta) \tag{2.7}$$

where $f(t \mid \theta)$ is the density associated with T_θ and $\mu(\theta)$ is a distribution of initial utilities.

An important feature of this class of models which facilitates tests of whether observed duration data – that is, estimates of $g(t)$ – can be generated by this class of models is that if $\mu(\theta)$ has a density $m(\theta)$ for which $m(\theta + \phi)$ is sign-regular in $\theta > 0$ and $\phi > 0$, then $g(t + s)$ is sign-regular in $t > 0$ and $s > 0$ (see, e.g., Karlin, 1964). Recall that a function $h(x + y)$

for $x > 0$ and $y > 0$ is called sign-regular of all orders in x and y with sign sequence $\varepsilon_m = (-1)^{m(m-1)/2}$ provided that for $0 < x_1 < \cdots < x_m$ and $0 < y_1 < \cdots < y_m$,

$$\varepsilon_m \det \begin{bmatrix} h(x_1 + y_1) & \cdots & h(x_1 + y_m) \\ \vdots & & \vdots \\ h(x_m + y_1) & \cdots & h(x_m + y_m) \end{bmatrix} \geq 0$$

Furthermore, a broad class of densities $m(\theta)$ for which $m(\theta + \phi)$ is sign-regular are generated according to

$$m(\theta) = \int_{-\infty}^{+\infty} \exp(\theta z) w(z)\, dz$$

where $w(z)$ is a probability density on an interval in $(-\infty, +\infty)$ (see Karlin, 1968, p. 70, for details). If the support of $w(z)$ is contained in $(-\infty, 0]$, then $m(\theta)$ is itself a mixture of exponentials.

The central role of the sign regularity property of g, for our purposes, is that a violation of this condition implies that *all* diffusion processes with positive drift and continuously differentiable coefficients are ruled out as candidates to describe individual-level dynamics. It is unnecessary to restrict tests to special parameterizations of $a(y)$ and $b(y)$.

3 Exchangeability and partial exchangeability

The general tests for model rejection in Section 5 are based on two fundamental theorems of B. DeFinetti (1972, 1975). These are listed below.

Theorem 1. *Let $\{X_i\}_{i=0}^{\infty}$ be an infinite sequence of binary-valued random variables with $\{X_i\}_{i=0}^{n-1}$ exchangeable for each n. Recall that by an exchangeable sequence we mean that for every fixed sequence of zeroes and ones $\{i_k\}_{k=0}^{n-1}$ and for all permutations π of the set $\{0, 1, \ldots, n-1\}$ we have*

$$P(X_0 = i_0, \ldots, X_{n-1} = i_{n-1}) = P(X_0 = i_{\pi(0)}, \ldots, X_{n-1} = i_{\pi(n-1)})$$

Then $\exists$ a unique probability measure μ on $[0,1]$ such that for each fixed sequence $\{i_j\}_{j=0}^{n-1}$ we have

$$P(X_0 = i_0, \ldots, X_{n-1} = i_{n-1}) = \int_0^1 a^k(1-a)^{n-k}\, d\mu(a) \qquad (3.1)$$

where $k = \sum_{j=0}^{n-1} i_j$ and $i_j = 0$ or 1, $0 \leq j \leq n-1$.

Thus infinite exchangeable binary-valued sequences are mixtures of Bernoulli trials.

Before stating the second of DeFinetti's theorems we require the following definition.

Definition: *Let C denote a collection of states labeled $\{0, 1, 2, \ldots, c-1\}$. For an initial state i_0 and subsequent states $\{i_k\}_{k=1}^{n}$ define $t_{l,m}^{(n)}(\mathbf{i}) = \sum_{k=0}^{n-1} I(X_k = l, X_{k+1} = m) =$ (number of $l \to m$ transitions for the sequence of random variables $\{X_k\}_{k=0}^{n}$ when it assumes the values $\mathbf{i} = (i_0, i_1, \ldots, i_n)$ with each $i_k \in C$). Denote the collection of sequences which have the same transition count as $\mathbf{i}$ for all pairs $(l, m) \in C \times C$ by $[\mathbf{i}]_n$. Formally we have $[\mathbf{i}]_n = \{\mathbf{i}': i_0 = i'_0$ and $\forall l, m, t_{l,m}^{(n)}(\mathbf{i}) = t_{l,m}^{(n)}(\mathbf{i}')\}$; and all members of $[\mathbf{i}]_n$ are said to belong to the same equivalence class. We call a probability measure P partially exchangeable if for each $\mathbf{i}$, it satisfies*

$$P(X_0 = i_0, \ldots, X_n = i_n) = P(X_0 = i'_0, \ldots, X_n = i'_n) \;\forall \mathbf{i}' \in [\mathbf{i}]_n$$

In other words, sequences in the same equivalence class occur with the same frequency.

Now we have the following theorem.

Theorem 2. *Let $X_0, X_1, \ldots$ be a finite state (c = number of states) partially exchangeable stationary sequence. Then $\exists$ a unique probability measure μ on the $C \times C$ stochastic matrices M_c such that*

$$P(X_0 = i_0, \ldots, X_n = i_n) = \int_{M_c} a_{i_0}^{(M)} m_{i_0,i_1} \cdots m_{i_{n-1},i_n} \, d\mu(M) \tag{3.2}$$

for $n = 0, 1, 2, \ldots$. Here $a_{i_0}^{(M)} = P(X_0 = i_0 \mid \mathbf{M} = M)$, $m_{i_k,i_{k+1}} = P(X_{k+1} = i_{k+1} \mid X_k = i_k, \mathbf{M} = M)$, and $\mathbf{M}$ is a random stochastic matrix in M_c. Thus finite state partially exchangeable stationary sequences are mixtures of Markov chains.

The essential idea in utilizing Theorems 1 and 2 to assess whether observed sequence frequencies arise from a mixture of Bernoulli trials or, more generally, from a mixture of Markov chains is to observe that

$\boldsymbol{\mu}_{n+1}$ = sequence frequencies for mixtures of Markov chains for times $0 \le k \le n$

$\subset \prod_{n+1}$ = sequence frequencies for partially exchangeable distributions on sequences of length $n + 1$

with proper inclusion. In terms of these sets, the content of Theorem 2 is $\boldsymbol{\mu}_\infty = \bigcap_{n=1}^{\infty} \boldsymbol{\mu}_n = \bigcap_{n=1}^{\infty} \prod_n = \prod_\infty$. However, for any given n, if the observed sequence frequencies are not members for $\prod_n$, then they clearly cannot be in μ_n. Thus partial exchangeability for sequences of length n provides a simple criterion on which to base a test for possible compatibility of data with mixtures of Markov chains. Exchangeability is the analogous criterion for possible compatibility of observed sequence frequencies with mixtures of Bernoulli trials.

In terms of the models in Section 2, observe, for example, that the random effect Bernoulli model (2.1) simply treats the probabilities a in (3.1) as parameterized by $\mathbf{z}$ and τ. Especially, $a = F_U(\boldsymbol{\beta} \cdot \mathbf{z} + \tau)$ and the mixing measure μ in (3.1) is, for this particular model, the bivariate distribution $F_{\tau \times \mathbf{Z}}(\tau, \mathbf{z})$. Similarly, the specifications (2.2) and (2.3) are simply mixtures of Markov chains. Thus a violation of exchangeability in the former case or of partial exchangeability in the latter case implies that no specification of the form (2.1), respectively (2.2), (2.3), or (2.5), could have generated observed sequence frequencies. This conclusion is valid over the class of *all* symmetric distributions F_U and bivariate distributions $F_{\tau \times \mathbf{Z}}$. The importance of this general rejection criterion stems from the fact that tests of compatibility of observed sequence frequencies with parametric families of mixtures of Bernoulli trials or mixtures of Markov chains can lead to rejection of the parametric family but not necessarily rejection of the general heterogeneous population models defined by (2.1)–(2.3). This is a consequence of the fact that simple families of mixing distributions – for example, beta distributions in (3.1) – do not generate sequence frequencies which are dense in the family of sequence frequencies for arbitrary mixtures of Bernoulli trials. The same remark holds for many parametric families of mixtures of Markov chains.

Thus in the early stages of empirical analyses where we simply want an indication of whether any model with the qualitative characteristics of (2.1)–(2.3) or (2.5) can account for observed sequence frequencies, the exchangeability and partial exchangeability criteria are a natural basis for such assessments.

4 Sparse multinomials

For binary sequences of length n, the natural data structure to consider is the 1×2^n contingency table where each cell is identified with a particular binary sequence. Quite modest values of n (e.g., $n = 5$ or 6) tend to represent situations where numerous empty cells – interpreted as sampling zeroes – occur among the set of 2^n, in principle, possible binary sequences. Thus it seems imperative to smooth contingency tables based on sequence frequencies prior to testing for compatibility with models such as those in Sections 2.1 and 2.2.

To this end bring in the pseudo-Bayes estimators (see, e.g., Bishop, Fienberg, and Holland, 1975, p. 401) based on multinomial cell frequencies in the 1×2^n table and a Dirichlet prior distribution on the cell frequencies $p_{\mathbf{i}} = P(X_0 = i_0, \ldots, X_{n-1} = i_{n-1})$, where $\mathbf{i} = (i_0, \ldots, i_{n-1})$ and $i_k = 0$ or 1 for $0 \le k \le n-1$. With this structure the Bayesian point estimates for the cell frequencies $p_{\mathbf{i}}$ are given by

$$\hat{p}_{\mathbf{i}} = \frac{N}{N + \hat{K}} (N_{\mathbf{i}} - \hat{K}\lambda_i) \tag{4.1}$$

where $N_{\mathbf{i}}$ = number of observations of the sequence $\mathbf{i}$, N = total number of observed sequences, $\lambda_{\mathbf{i}}$ = prior probability of observing sequence $\mathbf{i}$, and

$$\hat{K} = \frac{N^2 - \sum_{\mathbf{i}} N_{\mathbf{i}}^2}{\sum_{\mathbf{i}} (N_{\mathbf{i}} - N\lambda_{\mathbf{i}})^2}$$

Estimated sequence frequencies based on (4.1) should be viewed as a smoothed adjustment of the raw sequence frequencies $N_{\mathbf{i}}/N$. The essential difficulty with this or any other smoothing procedure is the necessity of specifying a priori constraints on sequence frequencies in an exploratory setting where there is little previous empirical experience or strong economic theory on which to base restrictions. Thus *general* guidance on reasonable choices of $\lambda_{\mathbf{i}}$ cannot be delineated. It is, however, useful to illustrate what is at issue with a simple example.

Consider binary sequences of length 4 where the observed frequencies are to be compared with those generated by (2.2). This requires a test of partial exchangeability and hence designation of equivalence classes $[\mathbf{i}]_4$ among the 16 possible sequences. There are only two nontrivial equivalence classes for binary sequences of length 4. These are $\{0010, 0100\}$ and $\{1011, 1101\}$. Thus a minimal condition for (2.2) to account for observed sequence frequencies is that $P_{0010} = P_{0100}$ and $P_{1011} = P_{1101}$. Now suppose that $N_{0010}/N = \frac{1}{8}$, $N_{1101}/N = \frac{1}{4}$, and $N_{1011}/N = N_{0100}/N = 0$. In addition, we interpret the raw frequencies of 0100 and 1011 to be sampling zeroes.

Then if, for example, based on evidence external to a data set at hand we can assert that $P_{0010} + P_{0100} \approx \frac{3}{16}$ and $P_{1101} + P_{1011} \approx \frac{5}{16}$, it is reasonable to bring in the prior probabilities $\lambda_{0010} = \lambda_{0100} = \frac{3}{32}$ and $\lambda_{1011} = \lambda_{1101} = \frac{5}{32}$. Setting $\lambda_{\mathbf{i}} = N_{\mathbf{i}}/N$ for all other sequences – assumed to occur at least once – and substituting the full set of prior probabilities in (4.1) yields a new set of smoothed sequence frequencies $\hat{p}_{\mathbf{i}}$ which we now view as appropriate for a formal test of partial exchangeability.

As a final point, observe that for processes with c states, $c \ge 3$, the adjustment formula (4.1) is still appropriate. The number of, in principle, possible sequences now becomes c^n, and the necessity of specifying prior probabilities on large numbers of cells containing sampling zeroes becomes more demanding than for the case $c = 2$. A collection of detailed empirical studies documenting the *substantive* judgments supporting one or more smoothing algorithms for sparse contingency tables would be very useful, but this regrettably still lies in the future.

5 Chi-square tests

In order to formally specify a test of exchangeability for binary sequences of length n we require some additional notation for equivalence classes of sequences. To this end, let $F_{k,n} = (\{i_j\}_{j=0}^{n-1}: \sum_{j=0}^{n-1} i_j = k)$ and observe that $|F_{k,n}| = \binom{n}{k}$, where $|\cdot|$ = cardinality of $\cdot$. Label the sequences $\{i_j\}_{j=0}^{n-1} \in F_{k,n}$ in lexicographic order as $l = 1, 2, \ldots, \binom{n}{k}$. Then for N observed sequences let $N_{l,k}$ = number of observed sequences of type l in $F_{k,n}$. In the test statistic described below, $N_{l,k}$ should be a smoothed – as in (4.1) – rather than raw frequency. If $(i_0, \ldots, i_{n-1}) = l$th sequence in $F_{k,n}$, then define $\rho_{l,k} = p_{i_0, \ldots, i_{n-1}} = \text{Prob}[X(0) = i_0, \ldots, X_{n-1} = i_{n-1}]$.

Now we assume that the sampling distribution of the N observed realizations of binary sequences of length n is multinomial with parameters $\rho_{l,k}$, $1 \le l \le \binom{n}{k}$, $0 \le k \le n$. In terms of these parameters the exchangeability hypothesis is $\rho_{l,k} \equiv \rho_k$ for $1 \le l \le \binom{n}{k}$ and $0 \le k \le n$. Then the chi-square statistic for testing this null hypothesis against all alternatives is

$$X_N^2 = \sum_{k=0}^{n} \sum_{l=1}^{\binom{n}{k}} \frac{[N_{l,k} - N_{+,k}/\binom{n}{k}]^2}{[N_{+,k}/\binom{n}{k}]}$$

where

$$N_{+,k} = \sum_{l=1}^{\binom{n}{k}} N_{l,k}$$

Standard asymptotics (see, e.g., Bishop, Fienberg, and Holland, 1975, chap. 14) yield that as $N \to \infty$, $X_N^2 \xrightarrow{\mathscr{L}} \chi^2_{2^n-n-1}$ = chi-square distributed random variable with $2^n - n - 1$ degrees of freedom.

The analogous test for partial exchangeability – also based on smoothed frequencies – is formalized as follows. For sequences of length $n + 1$, let $F_{1,n}, \ldots, F_{\mathscr{C}_n,n}$ denote the *nondegenerate* equivalence classes $[\mathbf{i}]_n$, where $\mathscr{C}_n$ = number of such classes. Then define $|F_{k,n}|$ = number of sequences in equivalence class $F_{k,n}$, and lexicographically order the sequences in each equivalence class. Let $\mathbf{i}_{l,k}^{(n)}$ be the lth sequences in equivalence class $F_{k,n}$, and define $\rho_{l,k} = P(\mathbf{X} = \mathbf{i}_{l,k}^{(n)})$, where $\mathbf{X} = [X(0), X(1), \ldots, X(n)]$. With these ingredients at hand, the partial exchangeability hypothesis is $\rho_{l,k} = \rho_k$ for $1 \leq l \leq |F_{k,n}|$ and $1 \leq k \leq \mathscr{C}_n$. The chi-square statistic for assessing this null hypothesis is

$$X_N^2 = \sum_{k=1}^{\mathscr{C}_n} \sum_{l=1}^{|F_{k,n}|} \frac{[N_{l,k} - N_{+,k}/|F_{k,n}|]^2}{[N_{+,k}/|F_{k,n}|]}$$

and for $N \to \infty$ we have $X_N^2 \xrightarrow{\mathscr{L}} \chi^2_{c^{n+1} - \mathscr{C}_n - (\text{number of degenerate classes})}$. Here c = number of states, and c^{n+1} = number of sequences of length $n + 1$ of the form $(i_0, \ldots, i_n)$, where each $i_k \in (0, 1, \ldots, c - 1)$.

It is important to observe that for given n, all equivalence classes are not necessarily of the same cardinality. To illustrate the diversity of equivalence classes consider the binary sequences with $c = 2$, $n = 4$. Then $c^{n+1} = 2^5 = 32$ and $\mathscr{C}_4 = 8$. The equivalence classes are

$$F_{1,4} = \begin{bmatrix} 0 & 0 & 0 & 1 & 0 \\ 0 & 0 & 1 & 0 & 0 \\ 0 & 1 & 0 & 0 & 0 \end{bmatrix}, \qquad F_{5,4} = \begin{bmatrix} 1 & 0 & 0 & 1 & 0 \\ 1 & 0 & 1 & 0 & 0 \end{bmatrix}$$

$$F_{2,4} = \begin{bmatrix} 0 & 0 & 1 & 0 & 1 \\ 0 & 1 & 0 & 0 & 1 \end{bmatrix}, \qquad F_{6,4} = \begin{bmatrix} 1 & 0 & 0 & 1 & 1 \\ 1 & 1 & 0 & 0 & 1 \end{bmatrix}$$

$$F_{3,4} = \begin{bmatrix} 0 & 0 & 1 & 1 & 0 \\ 0 & 1 & 1 & 0 & 0 \end{bmatrix}, \qquad F_{7,4} = \begin{bmatrix} 1 & 0 & 1 & 1 & 0 \\ 1 & 1 & 0 & 1 & 0 \end{bmatrix}$$

$$F_{4,4} = \begin{bmatrix} 0 & 1 & 0 & 1 & 1 \\ 0 & 1 & 1 & 0 & 1 \end{bmatrix}, \qquad F_{8,4} = \begin{bmatrix} 1 & 0 & 1 & 1 & 1 \\ 1 & 1 & 0 & 1 & 1 \\ 1 & 1 & 1 & 0 & 1 \end{bmatrix}$$

and $|F_{1,4}| = |F_{8,4}| = 3$, $|F_{j,4}| = 2$ for $2 \leq j \leq 7$.

6 Sign regularity and odds ratios

We require a test to assess compatibility of the diffusion specification (2.6) with observed data on first-passage times of a continuous time utility process above the level 0. The basis of such a test is the sign regularity property of the first-passage time density $g(t)$ in the equation

$$g(t) = \int_{-\infty}^{0} f(t \mid \theta) \, d\mu(\theta) \tag{6.1}$$

where $f(t \mid \theta)$ is the density of the random variable $T_\theta = \min[t\colon Y(t, w) \geq 0 \mid Y(0, w) = \theta]$, $\mu(\theta)$ is the distribution of unobserved initial utilities θ, and

$Y(t, w)$ is the solution of the stochastic integral equation

$$Y(t,w) = \theta + \int_0^t a(Y(s,w))\,dW(s,w) + \int_0^t b(Y(s,w))\,ds \tag{6.2}$$

as delineated in (2.6).

Although $g(t+s)$, as defined in Section 2.3, is sign-regular of all orders in $s > 0$ and $t > 0$, most data on labor force dynamics and consumer buying behavior is not sufficiently rich to allow for sign regularity testing beyond order 3. However, even sign regularity of order 2 imposes severe constraints on $g(t)$. In particular, a violation of this condition implies that no specification of the form (6.1)–(6.2) with $b(y) > 0$ and μ having a density m which is sign-regular in $m(\theta + \phi)$ can generate observed first-passage times. Thus the most widely applicable type of test for compatibility of given duration data with the entire broad class of models (6.1)–(6.2) is an assessment of sign regularity of order 2 for $g(t+s)$.

A formal test first requires an estimator for the density of observed durations (or first-passage times), $g(t)$. To this end consider a histogram estimator based on a sequence of class intervals $t_{i-1} \leq t < t_i$, $1 \leq i \leq m$ with

$$\hat{g}(t) = \hat{p}_i \quad \text{for} \quad t_{i-1} \leq t < t_i \tag{6.3}$$

and

$$\hat{p}_i = \frac{1}{N}\sum_{j=1}^{N} I_{(j:T_j \in [t_{i-1},t_i))} = \begin{array}{l}\text{proportion of observed durations}\\ \text{in the interval } [t_{i-1}, t_i)\end{array}$$

where T_j = observed duration (first-passage time) for the jth individual, N = number of individuals in the sample, and

$$I_{(j:T_j \in [t_{i-1},t_i))} = \begin{cases} 1 & \text{if} \quad T_j \in [t_{i-1}, t_i) \\ 0 & \text{otherwise} \end{cases}$$

The class intervals $[t_{i-1}, t_i)$ should be chosen according to the guidelines in Freedman and Diaconis (1981) in order to obtain a reasonable approximation of $\hat{g}(t)$ to the actual underlying density $g(t)$. A useful rule of thumb is to choose the interval widths as twice the interquartile range of the data divided by the cube root of the sample size.

Now choose ordered time points $s_1 < s_2$ and $t_1 < t_2$ such that $s_1 + t_1$, $s_1 + t_2$, $s_2 + t_1$, and $s_2 + t_2$ are each in a different class interval. Labeling the respective class intervals as $\mathscr{I}_1$, $\mathscr{I}_3$, $\mathscr{I}_2$, and $\mathscr{I}_4$, respectively, with $\mathscr{I}_1 < \mathscr{I}_2 < \mathscr{I}_3 < \mathscr{I}_4$, we form the 2×2 matrix

$$\begin{bmatrix} \hat{g}(\mathscr{I}_1) & \hat{g}(\mathscr{I}_3) \\ \hat{g}(\mathscr{I}_2) & \hat{g}(\mathscr{I}_4) \end{bmatrix} \equiv \begin{bmatrix} \hat{g}(s_1 + t_1) & \hat{g}(s_1 + t_2) \\ \hat{g}(s_2 + t_1) & \hat{g}(s_2 + t_2) \end{bmatrix}$$

Sign regularity of order 2 means that

$$(-1)\det\begin{bmatrix}\hat{g}(s_1+t_1) & \hat{g}(s_1+t_2)\\ \hat{g}(s_2+t_1) & \hat{g}(s_2+t_2)\end{bmatrix} \geq 0 \tag{6.4}$$

The minimum number of class intervals for a nontrivial test of sign regularity of order 2 is 5 intervals. If we order them as $\mathscr{I}_1 < \mathscr{I}_2 < \mathscr{I}_3 < \mathscr{I}_4 < \mathscr{I}_5$, then sign regularity of order 2 implies that the following five inequalities hold:

$$(-1)\det\begin{bmatrix}\hat{g}(\mathscr{I}_1) & \hat{g}(\mathscr{I}_3)\\ \hat{g}(\mathscr{I}_2) & \hat{g}(\mathscr{I}_4)\end{bmatrix} \geq 0, \qquad (-1)\det\begin{bmatrix}\hat{g}(\mathscr{I}_1) & \hat{g}(\mathscr{I}_4)\\ \hat{g}(\mathscr{I}_3) & \hat{g}(\mathscr{I}_5)\end{bmatrix} \geq 0$$

$$(-1)\det\begin{bmatrix}\hat{g}(\mathscr{I}_2) & \hat{g}(\mathscr{I}_4)\\ \hat{g}(\mathscr{I}_3) & \hat{g}(\mathscr{I}_5)\end{bmatrix} \geq 0, \qquad (-1)\det\begin{bmatrix}\hat{g}(\mathscr{I}_1) & \hat{g}(\mathscr{I}_4)\\ \hat{g}(\mathscr{I}_2) & \hat{g}(\mathscr{I}_5)\end{bmatrix} \geq 0$$

$$(-1)\det\begin{bmatrix}\hat{g}(\mathscr{I}_1) & \hat{g}(\mathscr{I}_3)\\ \hat{g}(\mathscr{I}_2) & \hat{g}(\mathscr{I}_5)\end{bmatrix} \geq 0,$$

Interpreting the estimated proportions $\hat{g}(\mathscr{I}_j)$ as estimates of cell probabilities for a multinomial distribution, observe that the above inequalities for determinants will hold if and only if the odds ratio for *each* corresponding 2×2 matrix is less than 1. This, in turn, is equivalent to 2×2 tables where the logarithm of the odds ratio is negative. Setting simultaneous confidence limits on log odds ratios for all five 2×2 tables (see, e.g., Goodman, 1964, 1969) and finding that the intervals are to the left of 0 implies that the observed durations are compatible with the null hypothesis of sign regularity of order 2. If any one of the confidence intervals extends to the right of 0, then we reject sign regularity and conclude that no member of the class of models (6.1)–(6.2) could have generated the observed first-passage times. Thus a simple test based on the log odds ratio for 2×2 contingency tables suffices to rule out an analytically complicated class of models.

7 Conclusions

We have presented two testing strategies which can be used to assess possible compatibility of broad classes of discrete choice models with longitudinal data on observed choices. The minimal a priori distributional assumptions required for these tests represent a sharp departure from much current practice where model testing is combined with estimation within narrowly defined parametric families of models which are not supported by economic theory. We have shown that exchangeability, partial exchangeability, and sign regularity are characteristic properties of broad classes of discrete choice models and that they may be assessed with very conventional contingency table procedures.

A limitation of exchangeability and partial exchangeability is that they are properties of models evolving in time-homogeneous environments. Thus their applicability is restricted to inherently stationary processes or, as in specification (2.4), to nonstationary processes which can be detrended, leaving only a stationary component for testing. Methods for detrending broad classes of nonstationary heterogeneous population models are currently lacking, and this is an important topic for future research. Without such a technology it would be necessary to develop new test criteria for each form of nonstationarity which is to be incorporated in a model. This is a highly undesirable state of affairs. However, it suggests the importance of extending the random time substitution methods of Aalen and Hoem (1978) to heterogeneous population models.

Although the details are outside the scope of this chapter, the next step in modeling of choice processes which should follow a failure to reject one of the tests described herein is consistent and minimally biased estimation of structural parameters in the presence of infinitely many incidental parameters. Thus procedures which yield good estimates of $\boldsymbol{\beta}$ in (2.1)–(2.3) without invoking parametric assumptions on F_U and $F_{\tau,\mathbf{Z}}$ are in need of development. Some first steps in this direction but in simpler classes of models appear in Cosslett (1983) and Heckman and Singer (1982b). This topic, however, is of major importance if the knowledge boundaries of economic theory are to have a smooth interface with econometric methods. This is our basic goal.

ACKNOWLEDGMENTS

The work reported here was supported by NIH grant NIH-1-R01-HD16846-01 and by a John Simon Guggenheim Memorial Foundation fellowship to Singer. Stimulating discussions with James J. Heckman are gratefully acknowledged.

REFERENCES

Aalen, Odd, and Jan M. Hoem (1978). "Random Time Changes for Multivariate Counting Processes." *Scandinavian Actuarial Journal*: 81–101.

Bishop, Y. M. M., S. E. Fienberg, and P. W. Holland (1975). *Discrete Multivariate Analysis: Theory and Practice*. Cambridge: MIT Press.

Cosslett, Stephen R. (1983). "Distribution-Free Maximum Likelihood Estimator of the Binary Choice Model." *Econometrica*, 51(3):765–82.

DeFinetti, B. (1972). *Probability, Induction, and Statistics*. New York: Wiley.

(1975). *Theory of Probability*. New York: Wiley.

Diaconis, P. (1977). "Finite Forms of DeFinetti's Theorem on Exchangeability." *Syntheses*, 36:271–81.

Diaconis, P., and D. Freedman (1980). "DeFinetti's Theorem for Markov Chains." *Annals of Probability*, 8:115–30.

Freedman, D., and P. Diaconis (1981). "On a Histogram as a Density Estimator: L_2 Theory." *Zeitschrift Wahrscheinlichkeitstheorie verw. Gebiete*, 57: 453–76.

Goodman, L. (1964). "Simultaneous Confidence Limits for Cross-Product Ratios in Contingency Tables." *Journal of Royal Statistical Society*, ser. B, 26: 86–102.

(1969). "How to Ransack Social Mobility Tables and Other Kinds of Cross-Classification Tables." *American Journal of Sociology*, 75:1–40.

Heckman, J. (1981). "Statistical Models for Discrete Panel Data." In C. Manski and D. McFadden (eds.), *Structural Analysis of Discrete Data with Econometric Applications*. Cambridge: MIT Press.

Heckman, J., and B. Singer (1982a). "Population Heterogeneity in Demographic Models." In K. C. Land and A. Rogers (eds.), *Multidimensional Mathematical Demography*. New York: Academic Press.

(1982b). "The Identification Problem in Econometric Models for Duration Data." In W. Hildenbrand (ed.), *Advances in Econometrics*. Cambridge: Cambridge University Press.

Karlin, S. (1964). "Total Positivity, Absorption Probabilities, and Applications." *Transactions of the American Mathematical Society*, 111:33–107.

(1968). *Total Positivity*. Stanford, Calif.: Stanford University Press.

McFadden, D. (1976). "Quantal Choice Analysis: A Survey." *Annals of Economic and Social Measurement*, 5:363–90.

PART III

Sociometric studies

CHAPTER 8

Effects of labor market structure on job shift patterns

Nancy Brandon Tuma

A recurring theme in the literature on labor market structure is that different labor markets are characterized by different patterns of job mobility. For example, Doeringer and Piore (1971, p. 40) regard stability of employment as "the most salient feature of the internal labor market." Kerr (1954, pp. 95–6) contrasts "structureless" markets that lack "barriers to the mobility of workers" with institutional markets in which entrance, movement, and exit are constrained by rules. Spilerman (1977) emphasizes career lines, noting how these may depend not only on personal characteristics but also on the occupation, industry, and firm of a person's port of entry.

Not everyone agrees that job shift patterns reflect differences in labor market structure. Some attribute these differences to various labor market imperfections: search costs (Oi, 1962), specific investments (Becker, 1964), uncertainty (Becker et al., 1977), and so forth. Others (e.g., Heckman and Willis, 1977; Doeringer and Piore, 1971, pp. 175–6) associate differences in job shift patterns with differences in workers: in nonmarket productivity, in preferences for leisure versus money and prestige, and so forth. Even those who attribute differences in job shift patterns to labor market structure do not agree on the boundaries of labor markets or on the reasons why occupants of certain kinds of jobs have similar job shift patterns.

Resolution of these disagreements requires an explanation of the forms of labor market structure and of the consequences of these forms for job shift patterns. It also requires translation of verbal explanations into testable models, data that allow competing explanations to be tested, and a method for organizing the data so that consequences of competing arguments can confront one another. This chapter reports research that attempts to begin resolving these disagreements. It is organized as follows. Section 1 contains definitions of basic terms. Section 2 reviews several theories of labor market structure and suggests hypotheses about job shifts congruent with these explanations. Section 3 describes the models, methods, and data used in testing these hypotheses. Section 4 reports the results.

1 Basic terms

1.1 *Labor market*

Consider a system with uncoerced exchanges among three kinds of parties: employees (A), employers (B), and consumers (C). Suppose A performs tasks for B in return for money, B exchanges the products of A's labor with C for money, and A and C do not exchange directly with one another. "Labor market" refers to the first set of exchanges; "product market" refers to the second set of exchanges. According to this definition, the labor market does not include those who consume what they produce (for example, peasants), those who are not paid for their labor (for example, slaves, prisoners, volunteers), and those who exchange their labor directly with the consumer (for example, those who are self-employed).

1.2 *Labor market structure*

Variability in usage makes it somewhat difficult to define labor market structure.[1] This variability, more than disagreements about actual empirical relationships, seems to be a major source of arguments about whether the United States has a single labor market, dual markets, or multiple (segmented) markets. An accurate tally is probably unimportant. What matters is the answer to the questions underlying these debates. In particular, is there a single process by which people are allocated to jobs and rewards are distributed among them? Or are there several different processes? If several, what are they, and how and why do they arise? In this chapter the term *labor market structure* refers to the basic features and patterns of the processes that allocate people to differentially rewarded positions in the labor market.

2 Alternative explanations

A fundamental – but usually implicit – premise of traditional microeconomic theory of the labor market is that the main conditions surrounding a particular job–person match are *flexible*. That is, if desired, an employer can readily raise or lower an employee's wage rate, and either the employer or the employee can terminate the match at any time.

In recent years some economists and sociologists (e.g., Thurow, 1975; Sørensen, 1977a; Sørensen and Kalleberg, 1981) have claimed that in many sectors of the U.S. economy the conditions of employment are *inflexible*. In particular, they assert that employers cannot readily adjust an employee's wage rate (especially down) and that the right to terminate job–person matches has been relinquished by employers, though not by employees.[2]

For these notions to have general theoretical value, proponents of each view must explain why employment is flexible or inflexible. They must also explain how each type of employment condition accounts for three well-documented empirical generalizations: (1) a positive cross-sectional correlation between job rewards (for example, occupational prestige, the wage rate) and personal resources (for example, education, genetic endowments); (2) an increase in job rewards over a person's life cycle; (3) greater employment stability of persons holding jobs with greater rewards.[3]

In this chapter I make only passing remarks about the implications of each type of employment for the first and second generalizations, and I attend only briefly to arguments about why employment is flexible or inflexible. Instead, I concentrate on comparing implications of flexible and inflexible employment for job shift patterns.

2.1 *Flexible employment*

2.1.1. Perfect competition. Because of its simplicity and theoretical centrality, I begin with the explanation that assumes a single, perfectly competitive market for labor. A number of premises, in addition to flexible employment, underlie this explanation. One is that goods exchanged in the market are homogeneous: People are equally productive, and jobs are equally attractive as long as they pay the same wage. A second is that buyers and sellers have perfect information about the goods and prices offered in the market: No one is uncertain about the outcome of any possible exchange. A third is that the market contains many buyers and sellers: Alone no one can determine prices.[4]

When employment is flexible, these postulates imply that there is a single price for labor (that is, a single wage rate) in a short-run equilibrium. The first empirical generalization mentioned earlier contradicts this, as Adam Smith and other early economists recognized. Microeconomists commonly alter the first premise to assume that workers vary in productivity (according to their education, strength, and so forth) and that jobs vary in nonpecuniary ways (in prestige, working conditions, and so forth). The modified set of assumptions predicts a positive covariation between job rewards and personal resources in equilibrium; it is usually termed *marginal productivity theory* because it predicts that each laborer's marginal utility (his reward) equals his marginal product (a function of his resources) in equilibrium. But this set of assumptions still cannot explain the second generalization mentioned above: the typical rise in job rewards over a person's life cycle.

Both the first and second generalizations are explained by human capital theory, which extends marginal productivity theory. Human capital theory postulates that workers invest in their resources (productive capacity) as long as their expected return on these investments exceeds their expected direct and indirect costs. Human capital theory predicts that workers invest heavily in training (some formal and some on-the-job) when they are young and reap the benefits in the form of increased wages as they become older. Furthermore, those who invest heavily in their resources during youth have age–earnings curves that rise more steeply than the curves of those whose investments are smaller.

But what are the implications of marginal productivity theory and human capital theory for job shifts? In equilibrium, job shifts do not occur because no one can improve upon his present situation. Thus, the occurrence of a job shift implies that either the employer or the employee is not in equilibrium. Marginal productivity theory suggests a list of exogenous changes causing disequilibrium, but it does not explain *why* or *how frequently* disequilibrating changes occur. Out of ignorance one might hypothesize that these disequilibrating events and the job shifts generated by them occur at a random rate α that does not depend on characteristics of jobs or jobholders (see Sørensen and Tuma, 1981).[5]

2.1.2. Imperfect competition. Various imperfections have been postulated so that human capital theory will predict differential stability that accords with the third empirical generalization mentioned earlier. A good example is the explanation of marital stability offered by Becker, Landes, and Michael (1977), hereafter referred to as BLM. Because BLM make only tangential remarks about job stability, I translate their arguments about marital stability into arguments about the stability of job–person matches.

BLM's key assumptions are the absence of perfect information and the costliness of searching, which suggests the name *imperfect competition* for their modification of human capital theory. Employers must use observable indicators of a person's resources to select employees (see also Spence, 1974); similarly, laborers must use observable indicators of a job's rewards to select jobs. Some mismatches occur, even in equilibrium, partly because indicators are not perfectly reliable and partly because search is costly. A shift occurs when a mismatch is discovered and both partners gain from the shift. This conclusion is important because exogenous changes in the social system need not be invoked to explain the existence of mobility.

BLM also consider the determinants of stability. Their argument has several components; I concentrate on those aspects suggesting effects of rewards and resources on job shifts.[6] They reason that stability increases with the expected gains from a match and decreases with unexpected gains (the discrepancy between actual and expected gains), assuming expected and unexpected gains do not have a strong negative correlation.[7] Expected gains rise with increases in traits positively associated in an optimal sorting of all potential exchange partners in the system (Becker, 1974). Since the skill level of a job and a person's education are complementary traits, they are positively associated in an optimal sorting. Therefore, employment stability is hypothesized to increase with personal resources and job rewards, assuming job rewards partly reflect a job's skill level. Another way of stating this hypothesis is

> Under imperfect competition, the rate of leaving a job falls as job rewards and personal resources rise.

In sum, imperfect competition predicts the third empirical generalization, as well as the first two.

Although BLM explain differential stability of matches, they have little to say about the level of rewards in successive matches, perhaps because they are discussing marriages. But flexible employment has clear implications for the difference between rewards of the jobs entered and left (hereafter called the *change in rewards*): It is zero on the average. Rewards rise (decline) if a person's resources rise (decline), but this occurs within a job because employment is flexible. According to this theoretical perspective, job shifts are not necessary to obtain rewards commensurate with one's resources. Shifts occur because mismatches are discovered and can be resolved. On average gains balance losses, as long as each partner is equally likely to benefit from newly acquired information and from unexpected gains.

To be concrete, suppose that the change in rewards is divided into three categories: a gain, a loss, and no change. The above discussion suggests the following hypothesis:

> Under imperfect competition, the rate of a job shift leading to a gain (an upward shift) equals the rate of a job shift leading to a loss (a downward shift).

The rate of a shift with no change in rewards (a lateral shift) may occur at a different rate than upward and downward shifts because of special conditions of a job.[8]

It is also possible to tease out hypotheses about the effects of rewards and resources on rates of upward, downward, and lateral shifts. Let D represent the difference between the rewards obtained in a job and those expected on the basis of a person's resources. As argued above, adding the assumption of imperfect information to human capital theory implies that D has a random (symmetric) distribution with a mean of zero. For positive D, the employee is overrewarded; for negative D, underrewarded. Because of regression toward the mean, shifts are more likely to be downward when D is positive and upward when D is negative. But, other things being equal, D is an increasing function of observable job rewards and a decreasing function of an employee's observable resources. These ideas lead to the following hypotheses:

> Under imperfect competition, the rate of a downward shift increases with job rewards and decreases with personal resources. In contrast, the rate of an upward shift decreases with job rewards and increases with personal resources.

A hint of this argument, similar to one sketched by Tuma (1976), appears in BLM's paper (1977, p. 1145).

Although imperfect competition does predict the third generalization and does generate hypotheses about effects of rewards and resources on the rate of upward and downward shifts, it is important to stress that *mobility plays no major role in the process by which rewards are differentially distributed among people.* In contrast, mobility is central if employment is inflexible, as outlined below.

2.2 *Inflexible employment*

Under conditions of inflexible employment, employers terminate employees only rarely and do not adjust wages to the productivity of jobholders in the short run. Because of this, employers have a strong incentive to hire the "best" people – those with the most personal resources. Similarly, employees have a strong incentive to accept the "best" jobs – those with the greatest rewards. Thus, the assumption of inflexible employment also predicts the first empirical generalization: a positive correlation between rewards and resources in a cross section.

When employment is inflexible, an employee leaves a job only because of access to a better job; hence the gain from a job shift is positive on the average. Rewards rise over the life cycle for people who shift jobs, but not for those who remain in the same job. Thus, the assumption of inflexible employment predicts the second empirical generalization, too. More importantly, *when employment is inflexible, job shifts are the fundamental means by which people increase job rewards.*

2.2.1. Job competition. Thurow (1975) assumes that jobs with the highest rewards require the most skills and the longest training period. He argues that people are allocated to jobs with different training requirements on the basis of their personal resources, which serve primarily as indicators of their trainability, and not of their existing productivity. Training occurs mainly on the job, or, as Thurow puts it, jobs are training slots. Implicitly Thurow assumes that employment conditions are inflexible.

Thurow mainly wishes to show that job competition predicts a positive correlation between rewards and resources and a rise in rewards over the life cycle. He gives little attention to its implications for job shift patterns. Nevertheless, his remarks clearly imply that the change in rewards from shifting jobs, D, is positive on the average. This implies the following:

> Under job competition, the rate of an upward shift is much larger than the rate of a downward shift.

Given Thurow's lack of interest in job shifts, it is not surprising that the implications of his arguments for the effects of rewards and resources on rates of job shifts are ambiguous. According to one possible interpretation, personal resources both increase with work experience and depend on the kinds of jobs held in the past. This suggests that the increase in resources from on-the-job training rises with the skill level of the job, as indicated by its rewards. Therefore, as a person's resources and training increase, a shift to a job with more rewards (that is, one providing more training) becomes more likely. This interpretation leads to the following hypothesis:

> Under job competition, the rate of an upward shift increases with resources at the start of the job, such as education and length of work experience, and with job rewards, which indicate the level of skills that can be acquired in on-the-job training.

Note that according to this hypothesis, the effects of rewards on the rate of an upward shift are exactly opposite those predicted by imperfect competition. The "rich" (those in highly rewarded jobs) are those most likely to become "richer" (promoted to more highly rewarded jobs).

2.2.2. Vacancy competition. As mentioned above, it is not completely clear from Thurow's remarks whether he claims that acquired resources (as indicated by job rewards and work experience) influence employers' selection of persons to fill jobs. Sørensen (1977a) assumes explicitly that they do not; that is, that resources are fixed over a person's career. He contends that people compete for vacancies in jobs with the highest rewards, a process that he calls *vacancy competition.*

In Sørensen's model people entering the labor market are distributed randomly among jobs according to their level of resources. He assumes that rewards of the first job are positively correlated with a person's resources, but lower than expected.[9] Over time opportunities to change jobs occur. Since employment is inflexible, workers wait for an opportunity to move to a better job. This means the following:

> Under vacancy competition, the rate of a downward shift is virtually zero.

How rapidly individuals move to better jobs depends on the rate at which vacancies in better jobs occur, which in turn depends on the rewards of their current jobs, their fixed resources, and the overall rate at which vacancies in the system are generated. Sørensen shows that his assumptions imply that as work experience increases,[10] job rewards rise on average and the rate of mobility falls. The decline in the rate of mobility with increasing work experience reflects a decreasing gap between actual and expected rewards, and *not* an increase in personal resources, as posited by human capital theory. In short, it is a spurious effect. This implication can be summarized as follows:

> Under vacancy competition, work experience has no effect on the rate of a job shift when fixed resources and current job rewards are controlled.

In contrast, personal resources and current job rewards have genuine (nonspurious) influences on the rate of shifts to better jobs:

> Under vacancy competition, the rate of an upward shift rises with fixed resources and declines with current job rewards.

Note that the pattern of effects of rewards and resources on the rate of an upward shift is the same under vacancy competition as under imperfect competition, except for the effect of work experience. The two theories differ primarily in their implications for the rate of a downward shift. According to imperfect competition, this rate equals (at least roughly) the rate of an upward shift; according to vacancy competition, it is negligible.

The assumptions of job and vacancy competition have only indirect implications for the rate of leaving a job. Since both arguments imply that the rate of a downward shift is much smaller than the rate of an upward shift, both imply that the rate of leaving a job is primarily determined by the rate of an upward shift. This suggests the following hypothesis:

> Under job and vacancy competition, effects of rewards, resources, and experience on the rate of leaving a job are the same as their effects on the rate of an upward shift.

2.3 *When is employment flexible/inflexible?*

Most proponents of either marginal productivity theory or human capital theory assume that the theory applies equally well to all people and all jobs in the United States. On the other hand, the literature on dual and segmented labor markets claims that the process of labor allocation and reward distribution varies within the United States. A full explanation of why one set of assumptions applies to some jobs but not others is beyond the scope of this chapter. It could also not be tested with the available data (described in Section 3), which provide fairly extensive information on attributes of persons but only rudimentary information on their jobs. Consequently, I concentrate on those situations identifiable with available data for which one set of assumptions rather than the other seems likely to apply.

I contend that conditions of employment tend to be flexible in small firms and inflexible in large firms, and consequently that patterns of job shifts in small firms resemble those predicted by imperfect competition, while patterns of job shifts in large firms resemble those predicted by job or vacancy competition.

The reasons given by Thurow (1975) and by Sørensen and Kalleberg (1981) for the development of inflexible employment suggest that it occurs primarily in large firms with a complex division of labor. In such firms, production often depends on the smooth and synchronous meshing of many people's skills, personalities, and actions. These interdependencies make it costly to supervise and difficult to evaluate any one person's contribution to the firm's product. They also increase the chance that successful work performance requires knowledge specific to the work setting.

When supervision and evaluation of an individual's work are difficult, employers often find it useful to develop job ladders – jobs with increasing rewards linked by a promotion schedule – to motivate workers to perform at their capacity. When a firm has job ladders, adjusting one person's wages within a job because of exceptional performance (assuming exceptional performance can be identified) undermines the system of incentives provided by these job ladders. In contrast, promoting a high performer not only rewards the person but also helps to institutionalize and legitimate a system of incentives founded on job ladders. In this fashion wages become linked to jobs rather than to individual productivity.

Wage rigidity is only one aspect of employment inflexibility. The other is control over the termination of a job. Thurow (1975, pp. 81–4) argues that employers relinquish control over the termination of employment so that co-workers will assent to training and sharing specific knowledge with one another. Firm-specific knowledge seems likely to increase with a firm's size, other things being equal. In addition, medium and large firms are much more likely than small ones to be the target of unionization, which has traditionally limited the employer's ability to terminate any *particular* job–person match, except during a brief probationary period or for carefully circumscribed causes.[11]

An employer's ability to retain control over the conditions of employment for a single job–person match seems much greater in small firms than in large ones. First, with few employees to train and supervise, an owner/manager may not need to delegate these tasks to an employee's co-workers. Furthermore, both successes and mistakes may be more visible and more easily tagged to one person in a small firm than in a large one.[12] In addition, a small firm may simply not have enough jobs to create job ladders to motivate employees' performances, even if the employer should want to use this system of incentives. Consequently, an employer in a small firm seems more likely to rely on immediate rewards like raises and bonuses. Finally, in a small firm very few people are likely to have similar job titles, in which case one person's wages may be adjusted to match productivity without other employees feeling that their opportunities or worth have been downgraded.

Unfortunately, the available data lack information on firm size. They do record, however, whether a job shift involves a change of employer. Because a small firm has few jobs that can become vacant, most intrafirm shifts are likely to occur in large firms and not in small ones. Shifts originating in small firms are likely to be shifts to another firm. Of course, some interfirm shifts originate in large firms; nevertheless, firm size and type of shift are probably associated.[13] This supplementary assumption leads to the following hypothesis:

> Patterns of intrafirm job shifts resemble those predicted by job or vacancy competition, while patterns of interfirm shifts resemble those predicted by imperfect competition.

2.4 *Other issues*

Reflection on labor allocation by employers hiring from within and without the firm suggests several subsidiary hypotheses worth examining. When a firm hires an outsider, it must rely heavily on a few easily observed indicators of trainability and productivity – in particular, level and kind of schooling. Such indicators may be screening devices (Spence, 1974), but poor ones. When a firm promotes an insider, it can not only use easily observed indicators but also assess the person's performance in a similar (though perhaps less skilled) job.[14] In an analogous fashion, a person evaluating job opportunities must rely on easily observed indicators of job rewards, such as prestige and the wage rate, when jobs are in different firms more than when they are in the same firm as his current job. This reasoning suggests the following hypotheses:

1. The effects of easily observed indicators of job rewards and personal resources on the rate of an upward shift are smaller for intrafirm shifts than for interfirm shifts.
2. The effect of ability (a less easily measured characteristic) on the rate of an upward shift is larger for intrafirm shifts than for interfirm shifts.
3. Easily observed characteristics of persons and jobs (for example, education, the wage rate, and so forth) explain variation in the rate of upward shifts out of a firm better than variation in the rate within a firm.

Parental advantages are often regarded as additional personal resources. As is well known (see, for example, Blau and Duncan, 1967), parental advantages are important determinants of an individual's educational level and measured mental ability as an adult. Net of their effect on such indicators of labor productivity as schooling and mental ability, however, parental advantages seem to increase an individual's opportunities in the labor market mainly through their impact on information about "good" jobs (Granovetter, 1974). Since such information is not usually relevant for intrafirm job shifts, this suggests the following hypothesis:

> When rewards and other personal resources are controlled, parental advantages increase the rate of upward interfirm job shifts, decrease the rate of downward interfirm job shifts, and have no effect on the rate of intrafirm job shifts.

3 Research methods

3.1 *Data*

The hypotheses in Section 2 are tested using life histories collected by James S. Coleman and Peter H. Rossi to study the educational, familial, residential, and work experiences of U.S. men (see Blum et al., 1969). The universe is the total population of 30- to 39-year-old males residing in the United States in 1968. There were two samples: a national probability sample and a supplementary sample of blacks. Interviews were conducted in January of 1969 and completed for a total of 1589 men (822 whites, 738 blacks, and 29 others). The rate of interview completion was 76.1 percent for the national sample and 78.2 percent for the supplementary sample. Results reported below are based on analyses of the data on white men only.

Because the arguments discussed earlier pertain to shifts from jobs in which a person works as an uncoerced wage laborer, I excluded data on periods of self-employment and military service.[15] I also eliminated data on jobs in agriculture because the wage rate and prestige of agricultural and nonagricultural jobs are probably incommensurate. Thus, I analyzed only data on shifts from full-time jobs in the civilian nonagricultural labor force (CNALF). I did not include jobs entered prior to school completion because such jobs may be left for reasons quite unrelated to the issues considered in this chapter.

Data problems necessitated exclusion of data on some of respondents' full-time jobs in the CNALF. I dropped data when information was missing on variables (see Table 1) needed to estimate the models considered in this chapter. In addition, I omitted 192 jobs "nested" within another job, that is, ones that begin after, but end before, some other job. Using these selection criteria, I retained for analysis data on 3484 jobs of 713 white men.

The basic explanatory variables discussed in Section 2 are job rewards and personal resources. Table 1 gives definitions and simple descriptive statistics for the measures of rewards and resources used in the analyses.

One measure of job rewards is the wage rate (in dollars per hour). This is, of course, the indicator preferred by economists. Another aspect of a job's rewards is its occupational prestige, which is measured here by Siegel's (1970) score. Prestige reflects many nonpecuniary values associated with an occupation, as well as its monetary value (Goldthorpe and Hope, 1972). Not surprisingly, the wage rate and prestige of respondents' jobs are moderately correlated (.395).

The primary measures of personal resources are education (years of completed schooling), a score on a 10-item test of verbal ability, and father's education (years of completed schooling). The correlation between (own) education and verbal ability is .634. The correlation between father's education and these other measures of personal resources are considerably smaller, though still substantial. Father's education and the respondent's education are correlated .388, while father's education and the respondent's verbal ability are correlated .324.

Time (in years) since school completion is also included in Table 1 and in some unreported analyses. Economists often call this variable *labor force experience* under the assumption that it measures general skills acquired through working (see, for example, Mincer, 1974). But this variable measures acquired work experience imperfectly because it includes time out of work since school completion. Time in jobs (since school completion), which seems to be a better measure of a person's acquired resources than total time since school completion (or total time since labor force

Table 1. *Variables used in the analysis: definitions, means, and standard deviations*[a]

Variable	Definition	White men Mean	White men S.D.
Father's eduation	Father's years of completed schooling	8.34	3.53
Verbal ability	Number of correct numbers on a 10-item word recognition test, adjusted for missing values on single items	5.99	1.87
Education	Years of completed schooling at start of job	11.82	2.81
Prestige	Siegel (1970) prestige score for job	36.47	13.88
Wage rate	Estimated wage in dollars per hour at start of job – calculated as $\frac{12\text{ (monthly earnings in \$)}}{52\text{ (av. weekly hours worked)}}$	2.18	1.11
Years in jobs	Total years in previous jobs since schooling completed	6.35	5.32
Years since school	Total years since school completed	7.02	5.59
Duration in job (years)	Last date in job – first date (based on reported year and month for each date)	2.17	2.65
Job left (dummy variable)	1 if job exist observed 0 otherwise	.83	
Employer change (nominal variable)	2 if employers for j and k differ 1 if employers for j and k are the same 0 otherwise		
Wage change (nominal variable)	3 if wage rate of $k \geq 1.05$(wage rate of j) 2 if wage rate of $k \leq .95$(wage rate of j) 1 otherwise		
Prestige change (nominal variable)	2 if prestige of $k \geq 1.05$(prestige of j) 1 if prestige of $k \leq .95$(prestige of j) 0 otherwise		
Kind of job shift (nominal variable)	(Employer change) · [wage change + 3(prestige change)]		
Number of individuals		713	713
Number of matches		3484	3484

[a] Reported means and standard deviations are for matches, not individuals; they are not computed for nominal variables.

entry), is also included in Table 1 and in some of the analyses I performed. Below I report results solely for this measure of experience; however, findings are quite comparable when (total) time since school completion is used instead.

One unresolved complication arises because age and time in jobs have a very high positive correlation (.822).[16] Still another arises because the sample design forces a high positive correlation between the historical period and time in jobs (.713).[17] Because of this high collinearity, age and historical period are not included in the analyses reported below. As a result, the effect of time in jobs on job shift rates undoubtedly reflects the effects of age and historical period in part, and therefore must be interpreted with caution.

As indicated in the discussion of estimation below, the main "dependent" variables are the time of job exit and the kind of job shift that occurs. The time of job exit is not known for jobs held by respondents at the interview (16.7 percent of all job–person matches analyzed), but the method of estimation still allows information on these matches to be used in the analysis; see Section 3.2 below.

Some hypotheses mentioned in Section 2 pertain to the kind of job shift that occurs, in particular, whether the rewards in the job entered are greater, the same, or less than the rewards in the job left. Table 1 also defines the variable used to describe the change in rewards. Note that changes in both occupational prestige and the wage rate are distinguished and that the "same" reward is treated as a change less than 5 percent. Reporting error makes it difficult to be confident that a very small change is really a gain or a loss. The choice of 5 percent is arbitrary; naturally results would be somewhat different for another choice.[18]

As I mentioned earlier, the data lack information on firm size, but do indicate whether a job shift involves a change of employers. In some empirical analyses, I distinguish between intra- and interfirm shifts, assuming that the former originate in large firms and that most of the latter originate in small firms. It should be kept in mind, however, that some interfirm shifts originate in large firms, which weakens testing of the hypotheses. This means that a comparison of patterns of intra- and interfirm shifts provides a conservative test of the hypotheses discussed in Section 2.

3.2 *Modeling job shift patterns*

As mentioned in the introduction, Doeringer and Piore (1971) focus on "stability of employment." Kerr (1954) is concerned with "barriers to mobility." Spilerman (1977) emphasizes "career lines" – the relative frequency of holding different kinds of jobs in a certain order. All of these are important aspects of job shift patterns, and models of job shifts should have implications for each aspect.

Continuous time stochastic models of change in categorical variables have implications for all of the above aspects of job shift patterns. Such models can be defined in terms of assumptions about three random variables relevant to job shift patterns:[19] $N(t)$, the number of jobs ever held at time t; Y_n, a categorical variable denoting characteristics of the nth job; and T_n, the time of entering the nth job.

One relevant concept is the survivor function for the $(n-1)$th job, $j = y_{n-1}$, which gives the probability that a person still "survives" in this job at some time t:

$$G_j(t|t_{n-1}) = \Pr[T_n > t | T_{n-1} = t_{n-1}, Y_{n-1} = y_{n-1} = j] \tag{3.1}$$

for any positive n, where t_0 and y_0 are the starting time and state of the process, respectively. The survivor function equals 1 when $t = t_{n-1}$ and tends to fall towards zero as $t - t_{n-1}$ increases. (It is zero for $t < t_{n-1}$.)

The above definition of a survivor function implicitly assumes that the time of leaving the $(n-1)$th job depends only on attributes of this job, y_{n-1}, and the time it was entered, t_{n-1}. The assumption, which is a form of Markov assumption, is not intrinsically necessary. However, it simplifies analyses and serves as a useful baseline.

The exit rate, the instantaneous rate of leaving the $(n-1)$th job, which has characteristic $j = y_{n-1}$, is defined as

$$h_j(t|t_{n-1}) = \lim_{\Delta t \downarrow 0} \frac{G_j(t|t_{n-1}) - G_j(t + \Delta t|t_{n-1})}{G_j(t|t_{n-1})\,\Delta t} \tag{3.2}$$

The numerator in (3.2) cannot be negative because $G_j(t|t_{n-1})$ cannot increase as t increases. Both terms of the denominator are also nonnegative; consequently, an exit rate must be nonnegative. In theory it can take any positive value, but I assume that it is always finite. A large exit rate in a job j means that people leave this kind of job rapidly.

The conditional probability of moving from job $j = y_{n-1}$ to job $k = y_n$ at time t, given $T_{n-1} = t_{n-1}$ and $T_n = t$, is denoted by $m_{jk}(t|t_{n-1})$ and is defined as

$$m_{jk}(t|t_{n-1}) = \Pr[Y_n = k | T_n = t, T_{n-1} = t_{n-1}, Y_{n-1} = j] \tag{3.3}$$

One can put the exit rate and the conditional transition probability together to define the rate of shifting from one job j to another k:

$$r_{jk}(t|t_{n-1}) = h_j(t|t_{n-1}) m_{jk}(t|t_{n-1}) \tag{3.4}$$

These mathematical concepts parallel substantive notions mentioned earlier. "Stability of employment" in a job of type j implies that the exit rate, $h_j(t|t_{n-1})$, is small. "Barriers to mobility" between two kinds of jobs j and k connotes that $m_{jk}(t|t_{n-1})$ is very low, which implies that the rate of a shift from j to k, $r_{jk}(t|t_{n-1})$, is comparatively small. "Career lines" can also be described in terms of transition rates; however, describing them may require that these rates depend on characteristics of previous jobs. This substantive issue calls for attention to the definition of the categories that Y_n can take (its so-called state space), but the modeling strategy remains the same. Finally, the rate of upward (downward) mobility refers to the rate of moving from a job with some level of rewards to another whose rewards are higher (lower), that is, $r_{jk}(t|t_{n-1})$, where the rewards of a job in category k are higher (lower) than those of a job in category j.

3.3 *Forms of models estimated*

The arguments in Section 2 suggest that the rate of shifting from a job of type j to a job of type k for some individual i may depend on attributes of i (at the start of the job), j, and k, but does not depend on time:[20]

$$r_{ijk}(t|t_{n-1}) = r_{ijk} \tag{3.5}$$

The various explanations considered in Section 2 generate different hypotheses about the direction of effects of variables on job shift rates, but not the specific form of the relationship. I consider two forms. In form A (discussed at some length in Tuma et al., 1979), I assume that job shift rates are log-linear functions of observed i, j, and k. In form B, I assume that a job shift rate is the product of two terms, one identical to that in form A and the other a gamma-distributed random disturbance, ε_{ijk}, whose mean is 1 and whose variance is σ_{jk}^2.[21] Each form has four versions, which express the various hypotheses discussed in Section 2. Table 2 lists the four versions of each form and gives each one a *model number* that provides a short-hand designation for the particular assumptions specified in Table 2. Below I comment briefly on each form.

3.3.1. Form A. Models with form A imply that the completed duration in a job has an exponential distribution and that the mean completed duration in a job is the inverse of the rate of leaving the job. They also imply that the distribution of the number of job shifts in a given time interval has a compound Poisson distribution; however, in general its exact form cannot be written explicitly without knowing the joint distribution of the explanatory variables. Model IVA, which distinguishes among the kinds of jobs entered, implies that the conditional probability of a transition from one kind of job to another has a logistic distribution (that is, is a log-linear function of the explanatory variables). Thus, it allows the probabilities of various job sequences to be calculated.

3.3.2. Form B. Most previously proposed models of transition rates have depended *either* on observable characteristics of persons and jobs (see,

Table 2. *Models for the rate of a job shift*

Model number	Assumption
IA	The rate of leaving each job j is the same for each individual i. $\log_e h_{ij} = \alpha$
IB	The mean rate of leaving a job does not depend on characteristics of individual i or of job j. However, the rate varies due to random error ("luck," etc.), which has variance σ^2. $\log_e h_{ij} = \alpha + \log_e \varepsilon_{ij}, \quad E(\varepsilon_{ij}) = 1, \quad \mathrm{Var}(\varepsilon_{ij}) = \sigma^2$
IIA	The rate of leaving a job is a log-linear function of $\mathbf{x}_{ij}$ – characteristics of individual i and job j. $\log_e h_{ij} = \boldsymbol{\alpha}'\mathbf{x}_{ij}$
IIB	The mean of the rate of leaving a job is a log-linear function of $\mathbf{x}_{ij}$ – characteristics of individual i and job j. The rate varies due to random error, which has variance σ^2. $\log_e h_{ij} = \boldsymbol{\alpha}'\mathbf{x}_{ij} + \log_e \varepsilon_{ij}, \quad E(\varepsilon_{ij}) = 1, \quad \mathrm{Var}(\varepsilon_{ij}) = \sigma^2$
IIIA	The rate of moving from one job j to another job k is a constant for particular kinds of jobs j and k, but does not depend on characteristics of an individual i. $\log_e r_{ijk} = \alpha_{jk}$
IIIB	The mean rate of moving from one job j to another job k depends on the particular j and k, but does not depend on characteristics of individual i. The rate varies due to random error, which has variance σ^2_{jk}. (In general σ^2_{jk} depends on j and k.) $\log_e r_{ijk} = \alpha_{jk} + \log_e \varepsilon_{ijk}, \quad E(\varepsilon_{ijk}) = 1, \quad \mathrm{Var}(\varepsilon_{ijk}) = \sigma^2_{jk}$
IVA	The rate of moving from one job j to another job k is a log-linear function of characteristics of individual i and job j; this function may depend on k – the kind of job entered next. $\log_e r_{ijk} = \boldsymbol{\alpha}'_{jk}\mathbf{x}_{ij}$
IVB	The mean rate of moving from one job j to another job k is a log-linear function of characteristics of individual i and job j; this function may depend on k – the kind of job entered next. The rate varies due to random error, which has variance σ^2_{jk}. (In general, σ^2_{jk} depends on j and k.) $\log_e r_{ijk} = \boldsymbol{\alpha}'_{jk}\mathbf{x}_{ij} + \log_e \varepsilon_{ijk}, \quad E(\varepsilon_{ijk}) = 1, \quad \mathrm{Var}(\varepsilon_{ijk}) = \sigma^2_{jk}$

e.g., Coleman, 1964; Spilerman, 1972a; Tuma, 1976) *or* on unobservable characteristics (see, e.g., Silcock, 1954; Blumen et al., 1955; Spilerman, 1972b). Models with form B combine these features.[22] Such models let one examine the effects of observed characteristics on transition rates without making the unrealistic assumption that one has specified *all* determinants of each rate. Furthermore, the proportional reduction in the variance σ^2_{jk} that results from adding explanatory variables to a model provides an indicator of the fit of a model to the data. (If the fit is perfect, σ_{jk}^2 is zero.)

The assumption that the random disturbance is gamma-distributed follows the suggestions of Silcock (1954) and Spilerman (1972b), neither of whom included observable variables in their models.[23] A gamma distribution has the advantage that it can range over all positive values (as can transition rates) and can assume a variety of shapes, from highly skewed to nearly normal. One can derive implications for the same kinds of quantities that I discussed above for form A, but the results are more complicated. Selected implications are derived in this chapter's Appendix.

One well-known implication of allowing unobservable heterogeneity in transition rates is that every transition rate declines with duration (the length of time since the last shift), even in a population with identical observable characteristics (see, e.g., McFarland, 1970). A less-well-known implication is that the population-level odds of entering one state (for example, kind of job) rather than another depend on duration.

One would like to distinguish the effects of unobserved heterogeneity in a population from the true duration dependence of transition rates. In principle, unobserved heterogeneity can be distinguished from genuine duration dependence *if* one has a priori knowledge of the functional form of either the duration dependence or the unobserved heterogeneity. For example, unobserved characteristics of persons or jobs that have the same effect on every transition rate can be detected by allowing the random disturbances (the ε_{ijk} terms) to covary for the successive jobs of person i and for successive occupants of job j. This strategy, which has been used very successfully in linear variance–components models, is difficult to implement in the case of models of transition rates and has not been attempted in this chapter. Consequently, interpreting estimates of σ_{jk}^2 for various models is ambiguous: it may reflect unobserved heterogeneity, as assumed in form B, or it may reflect time dependence in each individual's transition rates. The discussion and presentation of results in Section 4 largely ignore this ambiguity, but readers should keep it in mind.

3.4 *Estimation*

Coefficients of variables are estimated by the method of maximum likelihood, which gives asymptotically unbiased, minimum variance estimators under very weak regularity conditions on a probability distribution function (Dhrymes, 1970). The general form of the likelihood when event history data are available for an independent random sample of I individuals is (see Tuma et al., 1979):

$$\mathscr{L} = \prod_{i=1}^{I} \prod_{n=1}^{\infty} \prod_{j=1}^{\Psi} G_j(u_{in} | t_{i,n-1}, \mathbf{x}_{ijk}) \prod_{k=1}^{\psi} r_{ijk}(u_{in} | t_{i,n-1}\ \mathbf{x}_{ijk})^{w_{in} v_{i,n-1,j} v_{ink}} \qquad (3.6)$$

where i denotes an individual; n the number of an event; $j = y_{i,n-1}$ the kind of job individual i entered at the $(n-1)$th event; Ψ the total number of kinds of jobs distinguished; $t_{i,n-1}$ the time individual i enters the nth job; u_{in} the observed duration in the nth job; $\mathbf{x}_{ijk}$ a vector of observed explanatory variables describing i, j, and k; w_{in} a dummy variable that equals 1 if individual i's nth event is observed; v_{ink} a dummy variable that equals 1 if individual i's nth event consists of a shift to k. The forms of $r_{ijk}(\cdot)$ and of the survivor function $G_j(\cdot)$ are determined by the model assumed to describe the process of shifting jobs.

The variables $\mathbf{x}_{ijk}$, w_{in}, v_{ink}, and t_{in} are obtained from the data as described in Table 1. In this empirical application $\mathbf{x}_{ijk}$ stands for the various indicators of rewards and resources of individual i in a job of type j. The variable w_{in} is labeled "job left" in Table 1, while v_{ink} comes from the variable labeled "kind of job shift." The variables "date job entered" and "last date in job" give the information on, respectively, $t_{i,n-1}$ and t_{in} for person i's nth job. The observed duration in the nth job, u_{in}, is calculated as the difference between "last date in job" and "date job entered." The likelihood equation in (3.6), which is general, allows transition rates and survivor functions to depend on n. Table 1 does not mention n, the number of the event (that is, the number of jobs held) because the explanations discussed in Section 2 assume n is irrelevant to the job-shifting process.

Maximum likelihood (ML) estimation has several advantages. In particular, it lets one use censored observations on respondents' jobs, that is, their jobs at the time of the interview, which have not yet ended. Deleting observations on such jobs can bias estimates of transition rates seriously (Sørensen, 1977b; Tuma and Hannan, 1978) because the average completed length is longer for censored jobs than for jobs with an observed termination date (Feller, 1968). By including a probabilistic statement for censored observations, ML estimation usually provides estimators with desirable properties, even when samples are only medium in size and the proportion of censored observations is high. In the analyses reported below, the number of job–person matches is large (3484) and the proportion of censored matches is small (.167). Consequently, censoring probably makes a negligible contribution to bias in findings reported below.

ML estimation also has advantages in terms of the kinds of hypothesis tests that it allows. First, one can test the relative fit of nested models. Suppose we have a model Ω_1, such as one of those in Table 2, and constrain q parameters in it to take certain values (perhaps that some members of the vector $\boldsymbol{\alpha}_{jk}$ are zero or that $\boldsymbol{\alpha}_{jk}$ does not depend on j or k). Call the constrained model Ω_0 (the null hypothesis). The likelihood ratio λ is defined as $\max(\mathscr{L}_1)/\max(\mathscr{L}_0)$ and has the property that $-2 \log_e \lambda$ is asymptotically distributed as χ^2 with q degrees of freedom under the null hypothesis. The hypothesis expressed by the constrained model Ω_0 is rejected if the observed value of $-2 \log_e \lambda$ exceeds the critical value of χ^2 with q degrees of freedom for the selected significance level.

One can also test whether a single variable affects a transition rate. The inverse of the Fisher information matrix – the matrix of second partial derivatives of $\log_e \mathscr{L}$ with respect to the parameters in a model – provides an estimate of the variance–covariance matrix of parameters. A parameter's standard error is estimated by the square root of a parameter's estimated variance. Since ML estimators are asymptotically normal, one can then perform either F- or t-tests for a significant difference between estimated and hypothesized values of a parameter.

An iterative procedure must be used to find the values of parameters that maximize $\mathscr{L}$ in equation (3.6) for all models in Table 2 except IA and IIIA. ML estimates can be written explicitly for these. For model IA,

$$\alpha = \frac{\text{mean of "job left"}}{\text{mean observed duration in a job}} \tag{3.7}$$

and for model IIIA,

$$\alpha_{jk} = \frac{\text{fraction of moves from a job of type } j \text{ to a job of type } k}{\text{mean observed duration in a job of type } j} \tag{3.8}$$

Suppose that job shifts are patternless, implying that α_{jk} does not depend on j or k, that is,

$$\alpha_{jk} = \frac{\alpha}{\Psi} \tag{3.9}$$

It is important to note that the maximum of $\mathscr{L}$ depends on Ψ even if (3.9) is true and the type of job entered is totally due to "luck." The maximum of $\mathscr{L}$ for model IA equals the maximum of $\mathscr{L}$ for model IIIA multiplied by Ψ. A likelihood ratio test of model IIIA against IA must allow for this fact.

4 Results

In spite of ample previous evidence that employment stability depends on characteristics of jobs and persons (see note 3), it is useful to begin by demonstrating this. This procedure lets one begin with a simple model and introduce complexity gradually.

Table 3 reports estimates for several models of the rate of leaving a job, hereafter called the exit rate. The models referenced in Table 3 are alike in ignoring the outcome of a job shift, but differ in other respects.

Table 3. *Leaving a job: estimates of models IA, IB, IIA, and IIB*

	White men	
	A	B
Model I		
Mean rate	.385	.595
Variance σ^2	0	.507
Chi-square for		
IB vs. IA		386.2**
(df)		1
Model II		
Constant	−.231	.510
Father's education	.016**	.017*
Verbal ability	.043**	.052**
Education	−.002	−.017
Prestige	−.022**	−.025**
Wages in $/hr	−.070**	−.101**
Years in jobs	−.025**	−.034**
Variance σ^2	0	.453
% decrease in σ^2 (IIB vs. IB)	—	7.1
Chi-square for model:		
vs. model IA	311.0**	706.9**
(df)	6	7
vs. model IB		320.7**
(df)		6
vs. model IIA		395.9**
(df)		1
Number of job–person matches	3484	3484

* Statistically significant at the .05 level.
** Statistically significant at the .01 level.

Model IA assumes that the exit rate is a constant α that applies to all jobs shifts. (Recall that this model is suggested by human capital theory under the assumptions of perfect information, costless search, and random exogenous disequilibrating events.) From (3.7) the ML estimate of α is .385 per year. Under the assumption that the exit rate is a constant, the average completed duration in a job is the inverse of the exit rate, or 2.60 years.

Model IB assumes that the exit rate has a gamma distribution within the population from which the sample was drawn but is a constant for any given job–person match. This is exactly the model proposed by Silcock (1954). Table 3 says that the estimated average exit rate is .595 per year and that the estimated variance in the exit rate is .570. Silcock's formula (1954, p. 435) implies that the average completed duration in a job is $[.595 - .595(.570)]^{-1} = 3.41$ years. Thus, the average duration in a job is higher in model IB than in IA, even though the mean exit rate is higher in model IB than in IA. This occurs because model IB predicts that some job–person matches are extremely stable. These very stable matches raise the average completed duration more than enough to compensate for the increase in the average exit rate.

Model IA can be viewed as having the same form as model IB except that a constraint has been imposed, namely, that the variance in the exit rate is identically zero. Thus, a likelihood ratio test comparing models IA and IB indicates whether the exit rate varies significantly within the population sampled. The value of χ^2 for this test, which has one degree of freedom, is 386.2, implying that model IA can be rejected at any reasonable level of significance. (The probability that χ^2 with 1 degree of freedom exceeds 10.8 is .001.)

The heterogeneity in exit rates that leads model IA to be rejected may arise from effects of attributes of jobs or persons. Model IIA permits the exit rate to depend on personal resources, job rewards, and time in jobs. The likelihood ratio test of model IIA versus model IA is significant at the .001 level, and most variables included in model IIA affect the exit rate significantly (.05 level).

Model IIB has the same form as model IIA but does not constrain the variance in the exit rate to be zero, as IIA does. The likelihood ratio test of model IIB versus any other model referenced in Table 3 (each of which is nested within IIB) is statistically significant at the .001 level. But in spite of these impressively small significance levels, the addition of the six variables has reduced the variance in the exit rate by only 7.1 percent. Thus, the improvement in fit obtained by allowing the exit rate to depend on rewards, resources, and time in jobs is modest by customary standards. Not surprisingly, the overall pattern of effects of the explanatory variables is extremely similar to that found for model IIA.

The estimates for both models IIA and IIB indicate that the exit rate is smaller for jobs with greater prestige and higher wages. This finding agrees with the implications of imperfect and vacancy competition, but not job competition. Assuming time in jobs measures acquired resources (recall its correlation with age and historical period, however), its effect implies that the exit rate falls as resources rise. This result supports the hypothesis predicted by imperfect competition, but not those predicted by job and vacancy competition. In contrast, the effects of fixed resources – father's education and ability – have the opposite sign: The exit rate increases significantly as these resources increase. These findings fit the predictions of job and vacancy competition, but not imperfect competition. In sum, the pattern of effects of rewards, fixed resources, and time in jobs on the exit rate does not entirely support any of the three arguments outlined in Section 2.

These mixed results are not surprising if, as I argued in Section 2.2, employment is flexible in some jobs and inflexible in others. A better test of these arguments is obtained by distinguishing between jobs governed by flexible and inflexible employment. Recall that I argued that, in the United States, intrafirm job shifts are mainly shifts from jobs governed by inflexible employment, whereas interfirm shifts are a mixture of shifts from jobs governed by flexible and inflexible employment. I also pointed out the importance of considering whether the change in rewards accompanying a job shift is positive, negative, or zero; these distinctions are helpful in testing the theories of imperfect, job, and vacancy competition.

For these reasons, the rest of the analysis concentrates on interfirm and intrafirm job shifts. In these analyses I ignore the roughly 9–10 percent of shifts from a job within the CNALF to a job outside the CNALF (for example, to military service or to agricultural jobs) because the prestige and wages of jobs outside the CNALF are measured very poorly. I also focus only on shifts to jobs entered within six months after exit from the previous job.[24] Of all shifts from a job within the CNALF to another job in the CNALF, 3.2 percent did not occur within this time interval.

To study effects of labor market structure on job shifts with different reward changes, one must first select a measure of the change in rewards. Simplicity makes it appealing to focus on changes in either prestige or wages. Given the moderately high correlation between a job's wage rate and its prestige in these data (.395), this strategy might sound satisfactory because it suggests that prestige and wage changes are *also* moderately correlated. But this is not the case. Based on an absolute scale, changes in prestige and the wage rate are correlated .087; based on a percentage scale, they are correlated .035.

Table 4 reports the joint relative frequency distribution of prestige and wage changes, where a "gain" means that the job entered has a prestige (wage) more than 5 percent higher than the job left and a "loss" means that the job entered has a prestige (wage) more than 5 percent lower than the job left. ("Same" is a residual category.)

Look first at the rows and columns labeled "out." Each entry with this heading gives the fraction of shifts within the CNALF but *out* of the firm that are of the type indicated. For example, of the shifts to another firm within the CNALF, 18.7 percent led to both prestige and wage gains,

Table 4. *Joint relative frequency distribution of changes in occupational prestige and the wage rate for shifts among jobs in the CNALF (civilian nonagricultural labor force) by type of move (within and out of a firm)*

		White men (1819 out, 640 in)						
		Prestige gain		Prestige same		Prestige loss		
		Out	In	Out	In	Out	In	Marginals
Wage gain	Out	.187		.161		.122		.470
	In		.211		.302		.080	.593
Wage same	Out	.052		.081		.043		.176
	In		.070		.209		.056	.335
Wage loss	Out	.141		.091		.122		.354
	In		.022		.031		.019	.072
Marginals		.380	.303	.333	.542	.287	.155	1.000

Definitions: A "gain" occurs when the job entered has a wage rate (prestige) more than 5% higher than that of the job left. A "loss" occurs when the job entered has a wage rate (prestige) more than 5% lower than that of the job left.

while only 12.2 percent led to both prestige and wage losses. Table 4 also gives the joint distribution of reward changes for shifts *within* a firm, which have the heading "in." If each type of change in rewards was equally likely, every entry would be $\frac{1}{9} = .111$. One would not expect this value, given the marginal distributions for prestige and wage changes, which favor a gain, especially in the wage rate.[25]

In terms of testing my arguments, the more important issue is the degree of similarity between the distribution of changes in rewards for shifts within and out of a firm. The hypothesis that the distribution of changes in rewards is the same for interfirm and intrafirm shifts can be rejected at the .01 level (χ^2 with 9 degrees of freedom = 265.6).[26] This hypothesis can also be rejected at the same level even when lateral job shifts are excluded and when only job shifts involving gains and losses are included. Thus, it seems clear that the pattern of gains and losses in job rewards differs for interfirm and intrafirm job shifts.

How these patterns differ is of considerable interest for the issues discussed in Section 2. The fraction of certain shifts is very similar both within and out of a firm: shifts with both a prestige and a wage gain and shifts with the same wage and either a prestige gain or loss. But there are also some very marked differences. There is a much *smaller* proportion of shifts within than out of a firm that involve a wage loss, a prestige loss, both a wage and prestige loss, or a gain in one and a loss in the other. On the other hand, there is a much *larger* proportion of shifts within than out of a firm that involve no change in either prestige or the wage and that involve a wage gain but no change in prestige.

The nature of the differences found in Table 4 is consistent with the hypothesis that the conditions of employment within large firms are more inflexible than those in small firms. (As discussed earlier, this assumes that shifts within small firms are a very small proportion of intrafirm shifts.) The joint distribution of prestige and wage changes is much more nearly balanced for interfirm shifts than for intrafirm shifts. Nevertheless, the fraction of gains outweighs the fraction of losses even for shifts out of a firm. One would not expect this imbalance if employment conditions were flexible. This finding may arise because some interfirm shifts are from jobs in large firms, in which employment is inflexible.

Even though the distributions of reward changes for intra- and interfirm shifts are strikingly different, the effects of rewards and resources on the rate of a job shift could be the same. To examine this issue, I estimated models IVA and IVB for the rate of a job shift for all 18 types of shifts. Space limitations prevent me from reporting these results in their entirety.[27] I focus on two main types of reward changes for shifts within and out of a firm: those with a gain in both prestige and the wage rate (upward shifts), and those with a loss in both (downward shifts). I also make occasional remarks about those with no change in both (lateral shifts). Results for model IVB for the four main types of shifts are given in Table 5.

Consider the results for shifts out of a firm. First, the percentage reduction in the variance in the rate that results from including the six observed explanatory variables is quite high for upward interfirm shifts (69 percent), much smaller for downward interfirm shifts (22 percent), and still smaller for lateral interfirm shifts (5 percent). The substantial reduction in the variance for upward interfirm shifts suggests that, to a considerable extent, workers leaving a firm for a better job judge their new job and are judged by their new employers in terms of these observed variables. These variables may explain upward interfirm shifts better than downward interfirm shifts because many downward shifts result from layoffs due to exogenous changes in demand for the product of the firm left, rather than from firings due to the characteristics of a particular job–person match. Lateral interfirm shifts may occur for various reasons quite unrelated to rewards and resources, so I did not expect the rate of such shifts to depend much on these six variables.

Turn next to the pattern of effects of the six variables on the rate of an upward interfirm shift. As predicted by imperfect competition, this rate rises with personal resources and falls with current job rewards. All effects

Table 5. *Upward and downward job shifts within and out of a firm: estimates of models IIIA, IIIB, and IVB for white men*

	Upward		Downward	
Estimates for:	Out	In	Out	In
Model IIIA				
Mean rate	.045	.018	.029	.002
Variance σ^2_{jk}	0	0	0	0
Model IIIB				
Mean rate	.083	.025	.045	.002
Variance σ^2_{jk}	6.330	8.129	6.293	5.630
Chi-square for IIIB vs. IIIA:	70.5**	12.4**	29.7**	.01
(df)	1	1	1	
Estimates for model IVB				
Constant	−.840	−3.428	−1.408	Not est'd.
Father's education	.048*	.018	.005	
Verbal ability	.106*	.149*	−.115*	
Education	.142**	.116*	−2.10**	
Prestige	−.100**	−.075**	.035**	
Wages in $/hr	−.838**	−.166	.133	
Years in jobs	.030*	.025	−.058**	
Variance σ^2_{jk}	1.936	4.681	4.906	
% decrease in σ^2_{jk} (IVB vs. IIIB)	69.4	42.4	22.0	Not calc'd.
Chi-square for model:				
vs. model IIIA	438.5**	78.5**	75.9**	Not est'd.
(df)	7	7	7	7
vs. model IIIB	368.0**	66.1**	46.2**	Not calc'd.
(df)	6	6	6	6
vs. model IVA	42.2**	9.4**	31.7	0
(df)	1	1	1	1
Number of shifts	340	135	222	12
Number of job–person matches = 3484				

* Statistically significant at the .05 level.
** Statistically significant at the .01 level.

are significant at the .05 level. Now look at the rate of a downward inter-firm shift. As predicted by imperfect competition, this rate tends to decline with resources and rise with rewards.

Thus far we have seen that the results for upward and downward shifts out of a firm agree well with the hypotheses predicted by imperfect competition. This fits my claim that interfirm shifts originate in jobs governed by flexible employment, as well as in some governed by inflexible employment. In contrast, I argued that virtually all intrafirm shifts originate in jobs governed by inflexible employment. The main implication of my argument is that the rate of downward intrafirm shifts is very small. This hypothesis is strongly supported by the results in Table 4, which show that less than 2 percent of all intrafirm shifts lead to losses in both prestige and wages. In fact, the number of downward intrafirm shifts is so small (12) that the eight parameters of model IVB cannot be estimated from these data. The rarity of downward intrafirm shifts is clear evidence that intrafirm job shifts are almost always from jobs governed by inflexible employment.

Now consider the effects of the six explanatory variables on the rate of an upward intrafirm shift (the promotion rate, for short): Does the observed pattern fit the predictions of job competition, vacancy competition, or neither of these?

Both job and vacancy competition predict that the promotion rate increases with fixed resources. The results support this hypothesis in the case of education, which is usually regarded as a person's primary fixed resource, and verbal ability. Father's education is insignificant, as hypothesized. This is plausible if this variable is a proxy for information about better jobs. (Such information is rarely relevant insofar as intrafirm shifts are concerned.)

Job and vacancy competition differ in their predictions about the effects of job rewards on the promotion rate: The effect is positive according to job competition, but negative according to vacancy competition. Table 5 shows that the promotion rate decreases as prestige and wages rise, although the estimated effect is statistically significant only in the case of prestige. Thus, these results support the prediction of vacancy competition – not job competition.

A final prediction of vacancy competition is that time in jobs has a negligible effect on the promotion rate when rewards and fixed resources are controlled. The coefficient of this variable does not differ significantly from zero (as predicted by vacancy competition). But it is positive, and it is not appreciably smaller in magnitude than in the case of upward interfirm shifts. Hence it is unclear whether time in jobs measures the gap between actual and expected rewards (as Sørensen claims) or is an indicator of acquired resources (as human capital theorists assert). Further research is necessary to clarify this particular issue.

Next notice the reduction in the variance in the promotion rate that results from inclusion of the six explanatory variables. It is 42.4 percent, which is considerably lower than the 69.4 percent reduction in the rate of upward interfirm shifts. These relative values agree with my hypothesis that unobserved attributes of jobs and workers affect the rate of an upward *intra*firm shift more than the rate of an upward *inter*firm shift.

Finally, some hypotheses mentioned in Section 2.4 concern the effects of easily observed rewards and resources on the promotion rate relative to their effect on the rate of an upward interfirm shift. I argued that easily observed indicators of rewards and resources influence the promotion rate less than the rate of an upward interfirm shift. The findings uniformly support the hypotheses: The magnitude of each easily observed indicator of rewards and resources is greater in the case of the rate of an upward interfirm shift than in the case of the promotion rate. Moreover, ability has a much larger effect on the promotion rate than on the rate of an upward interfirm shift.

5 Conclusions

In this research I have undertaken three main tasks: (1) I have examined the implications for job shift patterns of several arguments (imperfect competition, job competition, and vacancy competition) about the way people with varying resources (for example, education, ability) are allocated to jobs with different rewards (for example, prestige, wages). (2) I have proposed an extension of existing methods of analyzing job shifts. (3) I have used the proposed method on data on job shifts of white males ages 30–39 in 1968 to test hypotheses arising from various arguments. In discussing each of the three tasks, I reached a number of different conclusions – far too many to summarize all of them here. I shall mention only the most important points.

1. Employment conditions surrounding a job may be flexible or inflexible. Flexible employment means that an employer can freely adjust a worker's wage and terminate his job; inflexible employment means that an employer is constrained (if not completely prevented) in taking either course of action. When employment is flexible, a person's gain from a job shift is zero on the average, and mobility, though an interesting phenomenon, is not terribly important for understanding the distribution of rewards among persons or over one person's career. When employment is inflexible, a person's gain from a job shift is positive on the average, and mobility is of fundamental importance for understanding the distribution of rewards. Whether employment is flexible or inflexible, hypotheses can be derived concerning the effects of rewards, resources, and work experience on employment stability and the relative frequency of different kinds of job shifts.

2. These hypotheses can be translated into models of the instantaneous rate of a shift from one kind of job to another. Previous models have assumed that the rate of a job shift depends either on observable variables or on unobservable variables. I propose combining these assumptions. In this way one avoids the unrealistic assumption that the model of the rate of a job shift has been specified perfectly. It also lets one estimate the proportion of variance in the rates within some population that is explained by some set of observed explanatory variables.

3. For young white men in the United States, the proportion of job shifts accompanied by gains (in either prestige or wages) exceeds that of those accompanied by losses. This tendency is especially marked for intrafirm shifts but also noticeable for interfirm shifts. This finding is consistent with the argument that employment tends to be inflexible in large firms and flexible in small ones, assuming that intrafirm shifts originate mainly in large firms and that interfirm shifts originate partly in small firms and partly in large ones.

I examined the effects of several fixed resources (verbal ability, own education, father's education), two job rewards (prestige and wages), and time in jobs (an acquired resource according to human capital theory) on rates of upward and downward shifts within and between firms. The findings for interfirm shifts agree well with hypotheses predicted by imperfect competition, which assumes employment is flexible. In addition, the results for intrafirm shifts support all but one hypothesis predicted by vacancy competition, which assumes employment is inflexible.

Overall these findings imply that mobility is *not* just an interesting side issue in understanding the distribution of rewards in the United States. Shifting jobs may not be the only mechanism by which people increase their job rewards, but it is certainly one such mechanism, apparently an important one.

Appendix

This appendix outlines implications of the assumption that the instantaneous rate of a transition from state j to state k for some individual i, r_{ijk}, is the product of two terms: A_{ijk}, a function of observable variables describing i, j, and k; and ε_{ijk}, a gamma-distributed random disturbance representing pure noise (including unobservable characteristics of i, j, and k that are uncorrelated with the observable variables in A_{ijk}). Thus, I assume that

$$r_{ijk} = A_{ijk}\varepsilon_{ijk} \tag{A.1}$$

where

$$E[\varepsilon_{ijk}] = 1 \tag{A.2}$$

$$\mathrm{Var}(\varepsilon_{ijk}) = \sigma^2_{ijk} = \frac{1}{B_{ijk}} \tag{A.3}$$

$$\mathrm{Cov}(A_{ijk}, \varepsilon_{ijk}) = 0 \tag{A.4}$$

$$f(\varepsilon_{ijk}) = \frac{B_{ijk}^{B_{ijk}}}{\Gamma(B_{ijk})} \varepsilon_{ijk}^{B_{ijk}-1} \exp(-B_{ijk}\varepsilon_{ijk}) \tag{A.5}$$

for all i, j, and k.

In this chapter I also assume that $B_{ijk} = B_{jk}$ for any particular j and k and for all i, and that $\log_e A_{ijk} = \log_e r_{ijk}$ as specified for one of the models with form A in Table 2 (that is, IA, IIA, IIIA, or IVA). The steps that follow do not depend on the functional form relating A_{ijk} to observed explanatory variables. Moreover, it could be assumed, for example, that

$$\log_e B_{ijk} = \boldsymbol{\beta}'_{jk}\mathbf{x}_{ijk} \tag{A.6}$$

which would imply that the variance in the transition rate from j to k depends on the vector of observed variables $\mathbf{x}_{ijk}$. The ensuing derivations are expressed in terms of A_{ijk} and B_{ijk} to retain generality.

Together (A.1) and (A.5) imply that each transition rate r_{ijk} is gamma-distributed with probability density

$$f(r_{ijk}) = f(\varepsilon_{ijk}) \frac{d\varepsilon_{ijk}}{dr_{ijk}} \tag{A.7}$$

$$f(r_{ijk}) = \frac{(B_{ijk}/A_{ijk})^{B_{ijk}}}{\Gamma(B_{ijk})} r_{ijk}^{B_{ijk}-1} \exp\left(\frac{-B_{ijk}r_{ijk}}{A_{ijk}}\right) \tag{A.8}$$

The above expression implies that the rate r_{ijk} has the following mean and variance:

$$E[r_{ijk}] = A_{ijk} \tag{A.9}$$

$$\mathrm{Var}(r_{ijk}) = \frac{A^2_{ijk}}{B_{ijk}} \tag{A.10}$$

Since transition rates are unobservable variables, (A.8) cannot be used to estimate A_{ijk} and B_{ijk} directly. However, (A.8) can be used to deduce the probability density of various observable variables. Given data on one of these observable variables, the method of maximum likelihood can then be used to estimate A_{ijk} and B_{ijk}.

I assume that event history data are available so that one knows the number, timing, and sequence of events. More concretely, I assume that the values of t_n, the time of the nth event, and y_n, the state entered at the nth event, are observed for $n = 0$ to some number that varies from case to case. The observations on the times of successive events provide information on the duration in a state $j = y_{n-1}$ because $u_n = t_n - t_{n-1}$. Below I sketch the derivation of the probability density of t_n and the expected value of r_{ijk} in the population.

Because r_{ijk} is a constant for any i, j, and k by the assumption in (A.1), the time of leaving the $(n-1)$th job, t_{n-1}, conditional on the type of job $j = y_{n-1}$ and the time of entry t_{n-1}, has an exponential distribution with probability density

$$\begin{aligned} f_j(t_n \mid t_{n-1}, h_{ij}) &= h_{ij} \exp[-h_{ij}(t_n - t_{n-1})] \\ &= h_{ij} \exp[-h_{ij} u_n] \end{aligned} \qquad \text{(A.11)}$$

where

$$h_{ij} = \sum_{k=1}^{\Psi} r_{ijk} \qquad \text{(A.12)}$$

Note that (A.11) is a *conditional* density: the distribution of t_n depends on the unobservable hazard function h_{ij} as given by (A.12), as well as on t_{n-1}. But to estimate parameters from data, one needs a density of t_n that depends only on observables. This can be obtained by multiplying the conditional density in (A.11) times the probability density of the hazard function and then integrating over all possible values of each h_{ij} (that is, from 0 to ∞):

$$f_j(t_n \mid t_{n-1}) = \int f_j(t_n \mid t_{n-1}, h_{ij}) f(h_{ij})\, dh_{ij} \qquad \text{(A.13)}$$

Equation (A.11) provides the first term within the integral. The second term is the probability density of the hazard function for individual i in state j, which has not yet been specified. [Equation (A.8) gives only the probability density for a *particular* transition rate.]

Though it is reasonable to assume that in general transition rates to different states are *not* statistically independent, that is, that the disturbances for different transition rates are correlated, the succeeding steps in the derivation are enormously simplified by assuming statistical independence. Then the probability density of the hazard function is just the product of the probability densities for transition rates from the state j to all possible states:

$$f(h_{ij}) = \prod_{k=1}^{\Psi} f(r_{ijk}) \qquad \text{(A.14)}$$

where (A.8) gives $f(r_{ijk})$. Similarly,

$$dh_{ij} = \prod_{k=1}^{\Psi} dr_{ijk} \tag{A.15}$$

Thus, the single integration in (A.13) becomes a multiple, Ψ-fold integration.

One need only substitute (A.11), (A.14), and (A.15) into (A.13) and integrate to obtain a probability density for t_n that does not depend on any unobservables. Numerous tedious but straightforward steps yield

$$f_j(t_n | t_{n-1}) = \left(\sum_{k=1}^{\Psi} \frac{A_{ijk} B_{ijk}}{A_{ijk} u_n + B_{ijk}} \right) \prod_{k=1}^{\Psi} \left(\frac{B_{ijk}}{A_{ijk} u_n + B_{ijk}} \right)^{B_{ijk}} \tag{A.16}$$

Equation (A.16) implies that the survivor function for a case i selected at random is

$$G_j(t_n | t_{n-1}) = \prod_{k=1}^{\Psi} \left(\frac{B_{ijk}}{A_{ijk} u_n + B_{ijk}} \right)^{B_{ijk}} \tag{A.17}$$

Moreover, the unconditional rate of leaving j at time t_n is related to the probability density function for t_n and the survivor function at t_n as follows:

$$\frac{f_j(t_n | t_{n-1})}{G_j(t_n | t_{n-1})} = h_{ij}(t_n | t_{n-1}) \tag{A.18}$$

$$= \sum_{k=1}^{\Psi} t_{ijk}(t_n | t_{n-1}) \tag{A.19}$$

So (A.16) through (A.19) imply that the rate of leaving j (the hazard function) for a randomly selected case i is

$$h_{ij}(t_n | t_{n-1}) = \sum_{k=1}^{\Psi} \frac{A_{ijk} B_{ijk}}{A_{ijk} u_n + B_{ijk}} \tag{A.20}$$

It can be shown in an analogous fashion that for a randomly selected case i

$$r_{ijk}(t_n | t_{n-1}) = \frac{A_{ijk} B_{ijk}}{A_{ijk} u_n + B_{ijk}} \tag{A.21}$$

ACKNOWLEDGMENTS

The first version of this chapter was presented at the annual meetings of the American Sociological Association, San Francisco, September 4–8, 1978. A revised version was presented at the Conference on Life Cycle Aspects of Employment, Mt. Kisco, N.Y., October 18–20, 1978, sponsored by the Social Science Research Council. The present version differs from the earlier versions primarily in the numerical results, which correct errors in the data analyzed in the earlier versions. The present version benefits from the helpful comments on earlier versions made by Michael T. Hannan, Joanne Julius, Camille Marder, John W. Meyer, Burton Singer, Louise Smith-Donals, and Arthur Stinchombe.

The research reported in this paper was supported by the National Institute of Education Grant NIE-G-76-0082, the Social Science Research Council, and National Science Foundation Grant SES-80-23542. I wish to thank Glenn Carroll, Camille Marder, Gary Sandefur, and Barbara Warsavage for valuable research assistance and Roy Sutton for programming assistance. The International Institute for Applied Systems Analysis provided a supportive atmosphere for completion of the final revisions to this chapter.

NOTES

1 For a useful discussion of definitions of labor market structure, see Althauser and Kalleberg (1981).

2 Sørensen and Kalleberg (1981) and Sørensen and Tuma (1981) distinguish between "open" and "closed" employment. An employer is free to terminate an employee's job in the former, but not in the latter. These authors implicitly assume that wage rigidity accompanies closed employment and that wage flexibility is present when employment is open. But this need not be the case. I use a different terminology to emphasize that *both* rigid wages *and* closed employment are necessary for the conclusions reached about inflexible employment below.

3 For evidence of the first, see Blau and Duncan (1967). For evidence of the second, see Mincer (1974). Byrne (1975) and Hayghe (1975) give evidence of the third. Numerous other sources could be cited.

4 An additional assumption is that buyers and sellers maximize utility: Employers maximize profits, and workers maximize utility that depends on leisure, money, and occasionally other, nonpecuniary values.

5 The rate of a job shift is analogous to the probability of the shift per unit of time among those at risk of the shift. A formal definition is given in equation (3.4).

6 Another aspect deals with investments specific to the match, for example, job-specific training. BLM argue that stability of the match increases with specific investments. See also Becker (1964), Tuma (1976). This argument also suggests that the rate of a shift declines as the duration of the match increases. Tuma (1976) and Sørensen and Tuma (1981) have estimated models in which the rate of a job shift declines as duration increases. Technical difficulties precluded studying these issues in this chapter (see note 20).

7 Perhaps surprisingly, BLM argue that even positive unexpected gains (that is, "windfalls") decrease stability. They argue that the match is no longer optimal after a windfall, which makes the match unstable.

8 For example, the organization of the construction industry leads to a much higher rate of lateral shifts in that industry than in most others.

9 Sørensen (1977a) does not explain why initial job rewards are lower than expected for a given level of resources. If labor market entrants are dependent upon vacancies in jobs whose rewards are commensurate with their resources, their alternatives may be to wait until a suitable job becomes available or to

accept a job whose rewards are less than they expect. Given these two alternatives, most individuals will choose the latter – as long as this choice does not prevent them from obtaining a better job later.

10 Sørensen (1977a) refers to *time in the labor force* rather than *work experience*. The two concepts are equivalent when employment is continuous once the labor force is entered, which Sørensen assumes. In reality and in the data analyzed, employment is not continuous. In my opinion the notion of *work experience*, by which I mean *time in jobs*, fits Sørensen's arguments better than *total time in the labor force* when employment is discontinuous. Consequently, I have substituted *work experience* for *time in the labor force* in my discussion of vacancy competition. Further pertinent discussion appears in the description of the data in Section 3.

11 The layoff rate may be high in certain industries, and layoffs probably lead to a high proportion of downward shifts. However, layoffs are not triggered by characteristics of a *particular* job–person match but by a slackened demand for a firm's product.

12 Jobs at the highest rungs of a large firm bear many similarities to jobs in small firms insofar as flexibility of employment is concerned. For example, top executives appear much more likely than those in middle management to be demoted or fired if their job performance does not meet expectations.

13 Leigh (1976) has compared gains of blacks and whites who shift industries and who remain in the same industry. For both races he finds that movers tend to gain more than stayers. Unfortunately, he does not report effects of variables indicating the resources of workers, although they were included in his analysis.

14 March and March (1978) have developed a model of intrafirm shifts based on the assumption that performance records on the job are the sole criterion used by employers in allocating employees to different jobs.

15 Although in principle military service can be uncoerced, many respondents may have been drafted because their military service occurred in the era of the Korean War.

16 Age and time since school completion are correlated .832.

17 Historical period and time since school completion are correlated .720.

18 Another approach that I have not yet explored is to assume that the change in rewards is a metric variable with some postulated distribution.

19 I use capital letters to denote random variables and lowercase letters to indicate their realizations.

20 Time independence is an admittedly unrealistic assumption. It is easy to formulate arguments why job shift rates depend on age, duration, and historical period. (For such arguments, see Tuma, 1976.) But it is beyond the scope of this chapter to encompass these arguments or to include these variables.

21 This assumption implies that the coefficient of variation in the rate is σ_{jk}.

22 Michael C. Keeley first suggested this to me. Since I wrote the first version of this chapter in 1978, Heckman and his associates (Heckman and Borjas, 1980; Flinn and Heckman, 1982) have also proposed models that combine these features.

23 Both Silcock and Spilerman assume that only the rate of leaving a job has a random disturbance.

24 I imposed a maximum length on the interval between successive jobs because I think that the kind of job held previously has a declining impact on changes in rewards as this interval lengthens. Clearly the choice of a six-month maximum is arbitrary.

25 Given the small correlation between prestige and wage changes (whether measured on absolute or percentage scales), one might expect cell entries for intra- and interfirm shifts to be close to the product of the marginals in Table 4, indicating that prestige and wage changes are statistically independent. This null hypothesis can be rejected at the .05 level (χ^2 with 4 degrees of freedom = 46.58 for interfirm shifts and 18.68 for intrafirm shifts). The main deviations from statistical independence seem to occur because the same changes in prestige and wages occur much more often than independence predicts. This finding does not, of course, contradict the finding of a small correlation between the two kinds of changes.

26 I also tested the hypothesis that the *rates* of these nine types of changes in rewards are the same for interfirm and intrafirm job shifts. This hypothesis can also be rejected at well below the .01 level (χ^2 with 9 degrees of freedom = 2522.0).

27 There are other reasons for not reporting these. In particular, it is difficult to know whether a move involving a gain in one reward and a loss in the other should be considered a net gain, a net loss, or no change. Consequently, it is difficult to know whether the results for these shifts support a hypothesis or not.

REFERENCES

Althauser, Robert P., and Arne L. Kalleberg. 1981. "Firms, occupations, and the structure of labor markets: a conceptual analysis." Pp. 119–49 in Ivar Berg (ed.), *Sociological Perspectives on Labor Markets*. New York: Academic Press.

Becker, Gary S. 1964. *Human Capital*. New York: National Bureau of Economic Research.

1974. "A theory of marriage." In T. W. Schultz (ed.), *Economics of the Family*. Chicago: University of Chicago Press.

Becker, Gary S., Elisabeth Landes, and Robert T. Michael. 1977. "An economic analysis of marital instability." *Journal of Political Economy* 85:1141–87.

Blau, Peter M., and Otis Dudley Duncan. 1967. *The American Occupational Structure*. New York: Wiley.

Blum, Zahava D., Nancy L. Karweit, and Aage B. Sørensen. 1969. "A method for the collection and analysis of retrospective life histories." Johns Hopkins University Center for the Study of Social Organization of Schools, Report No. 48.

Blumen, I., M. Kogan, and P. J. McCarthy. 1955. "The industrial mobility of labor as a probability process." *Cornell Studies in Industrial and Labor Relations* 6. Ithaca: Cornell University Press.

Byrne, James J. 1975. "Occupational mobility of workers." Special Labor Force Report 176. U.S. Department of Labor, Bureau of Labor Statistics.

Coleman, James S. 1964. *Introduction to Mathematical Sociology*. New York: Free Press.

Dhrymes, Phoebus J. 1970. *Econometrics: Statistical Foundations and Applications*. New York: Harper & Row.

Doeringer, P. B., and M. J. Piore. 1971. *Internal Labor Markets and Manpower Analysis*. Lexington, Mass.: Heath Lexington Books.

Feller, William. 1968. *An Introduction to Probability Theory and Its Applications*, vol. I, 3rd ed. New York: Wiley.

Flinn, Christopher, and James J. Heckman. 1982. "New methods for analyzing individual event histories." Pp. 99–140 in S. Leinhardt (ed.), *Sociological Methodology 1982*. San Francisco: Jossey-Bass.

Goldthorpe, J. H., and Keith Hope. 1972. "Occupational grading and ocupational prestige." Pp. 19–80 in K. Hope (ed.), *The Analysis of Social Mobility: Methods and Approaches*. Oxford: Clarendon Press.

Granovetter, Mark. 1974. *Getting a Job*. Cambridge: Harvard University Press.

Hayghe, Howard. 1975. "Job tenure of workers, January 1973." Special Labor Force Report 172. U.S. Department of Labor, Bureau of Labor Statistics.

Heckman, James J., and George Borjas. 1980. "Does unemployment cause future unemployment? Definitions, questions, and answers from a continuous-time model of heterogeneity and state dependence." *Economica* 47:247–83.

Heckman, James J., and Robert J. Willis. 1977. "A beta-logistic model of the analysis of sequential labor force participation by married women." *Journal of Political Economy* 85:27–58.

Kerr, Clark. 1954. "The Balkanization of labor markets." Pp. 92–110 in E. W. Bakke et al. (eds.), *Labor Mobility and Economic Opportunity*. New York: Wiley.

Leigh, Duane E. 1976. "Occupational advancement in the 1960's: an indirect test of the dual labor market hypotheses." *Journal of Human Resources* 11:155–71.

McFarland, David D. 1970. "Intergenerational social mobility as a Markov process: including a time-stationary Markovian model that explains observed declines in mobility rates." *American Sociological Review* 35:463–76.

March, James C., and James G. March. 1978. "Performance sampling in social matches." *Administrative Science Quarterly* 23:434–53.

Mincer, Jacob. 1974. *Schooling, Experience, and Earnings*. New York: National Bureau of Economic Research.

Oi, Walter Y. 1962. "Labor as a quasi-fixed factor." *Journal of Political Economy* 70 (December): 538–55.

Siegel, Paul M. 1970. "Prestige in the American occupational structure." Ph.D. dissertation, University of Chicago.

Silcock, H. 1954. "The phenomenon of labour turnover." *Journal of the Royal Statistical Society* 117A:429–40.

Sørensen, Aage B. 1977a. "The structure of inequality and the process of attainment." *American Sociological Review* 42:965–78.

1977b. "Estimating rates from retrospective questions." Pp. 209–23 in D. Heise (ed.), *Sociological Methodology 1977*. San Francisco: Jossey-Bass.

Sørensen, Aage B., and Arne L. Kalleberg. 1981. "An outline of a theory for the matching of persons to jobs." Pp. 47–74 in Ivar Berg (ed.), *Sociological Perspectives on Labor Markets*. New York: Academic Press.

Sørensen, Aage B., and Nancy Brandon Tuma. 1981. "Labor market structures and job mobility." *Research in Social Stratification and Mobility* 1:67–94.

Spence, A. M. 1974. *Market Signalling*. Cambridge: Harvard University Press.

Spilerman, Seymour. 1972a. "The analysis of mobility processes by the introduction of independent variables into a Markov chain." *American Sociological Review* 37:277–94.

1972b. "Extension of the mover-stayer model." *American Journal of Sociology* 78:599–626.

1977. "Careers, labor market structure, and socioeconomic achievement." *American Journal of Sociology* 83:551–93.

Thurow, Lester C. 1975. *Generating Inequality*. New York: Basic Books.

Tuma, Nancy Brandon. 1976. "Rewards, resources, and the rate of mobility." *American Sociological Review* 41:338–60.

Tuma, Nancy Brandon, and Michael T. Hannan. 1978. "Approaches to the censoring problem in analysis of event histories." Pp. 209–40 in K. Schuessler (ed.), *Sociological Methodology 1979*. San Francisco: Jossey-Bass.

Tuma, Nancy Brandon, Michael T. Hannan, and Lyle P. Groeneveld. 1979. "Dynamic analysis of event histories." *American Journal of Sociology* 84:820–54.

CHAPTER 9

School enrollment, military enlistment, and the transition to work: implications for the age pattern of employment

Robert D. Mare and Christopher Winship

1 Introduction

An empirical regularity in most societies is that a young man's likelihood of holding a job increases with age. In 1980, for example, the U.S. Department of Labor classified as "employed" 39.7, 55.9, 70.0, 83.5, and 88.3 percent of men aged 16–17, 18–19, 20–24, 25–29, and 30–34, respectively (U.S. Department of Labor, 1981). Employment remains stable at between 85 and 90 percent for men through midlife and declines after 50 as retirements become prevalent. Although the level of employment varies with its precise definition and among demographic groups, rapidly rising employment with age among men under age 30 is a fundamental pattern.

The age pattern of employment among young men is important for understanding the transition from youth to adult. For men, employment is generally a prerequisite for moving from family of origin to establishment of a family of procreation. The age pattern of employment reflects this transition and concomitant age-related changes in school enrollment, living arrangements, financial dependence, and marital and fertility status.

Employment is also an important source of age variation in the distribution of social and economic welfare. It is a precondition of access to occupational status, earnings, and, for most men, general economic security, as well as a determinant of perceived self-worth (Cohn, 1978). Differential rates of employment, therefore, are one cause of economic inequality between the old and the young (Coleman et al., 1974; Winsborough, 1978).

Youth employment has recently been a key social policy concern in many Western nations (for example, National Commission for Employment Policy, 1979; Organisation for Economic Co-Operation and Development, 1980). An appraisal of the causes and the seriousness of youth joblessness should rest in part on an understanding of the social and economic forces giving rise to the "natural" age gradient of employment.

This chapter describes and partly explains age variation in employment among men under age 30 in the United States in the mid-1970s. Employment generally and variation over the life cycle in particular have been neglected topics in sociology. Section 2 of this chapter reviews typical approaches to analysis of intracohort change in other aspects of socioeconomic welfare and achievement and finds them inadequate to explain the transition into employment. It proposes that the link between employment and other statuses and transitions accounts for a substantial portion of the increase in employment between ages 16 and 29. Section 3 outlines mechanisms through which young men's involvement in two activities, enrollment in school and enlistment in the armed forces, affects their employment probabilities. The mechanisms include the constraining effects of each activity on the other, the disruptive effects of leaving school or the armed forces, and the differential retention of schools and the military of men of varying employment prospects. Sections 4, 5, and 6 describe respectively the data employed in the analysis, the statistical methods used, and the empirical specification of the arguments. Section 7 presents empirical findings, and Section 8 summarizes and discusses the implications of the arguments and findings.

2 Sociological approaches to intracohort variation in socioeconomic achievement

Although few sociologists have systematically examined the determinants of individual employment probabilities or their life cycle variation (however, see DiPrete, 1981), many have studied intracohort change in other aspects of socioeconomic achievement. Research on socioeconomic status, rooted in the concept of the "socioeconomic life cycle" (Duncan, Featherman, and Duncan, 1972, p. 5), explores the associations among family background, schooling, and occupational and earnings achievement by viewing these statuses as sequential and causally dependent (Duncan and Hodge, 1963; Blau and Duncan, 1967; Duncan, Featherman, and Duncan, 1972; Jencks et al., 1972; Sewell and Hauser, 1975; Featherman and Hauser, 1978). In describing the associations of achievements within a cohort, this research tradition typically views the temporal and causal ordering of achievements as unproblematical (Alexander and Pallas, 1981) and is seldom explicit about either the social positions associated with particular statuses (White, 1970) or the mechanisms that generate the observed relations among variables (Mare, 1980a; Bielby, 1981). Instead, models of socioeconomic achievement are descriptive and recognize a variety of possible mechanisms governing intragenerational mobility (Featherman and Hauser, 1978; Hauser, 1980).

Other approaches to the study of intracohort variation in achievement explicitly assume that occupational and earnings mobility result from "careers" of job shifts (e.g., Spilerman, 1977; Tuma, 1976; Sørensen, 1975; Stinchcombe, 1979). These approaches view socioeconomic achievement as a sequence of positions (rather than statuses) through which individuals move according to specific mechanisms and view as problematic both the empirical identification of careers (Spilerman, 1977; Kaufman and Spilerman, 1982) and the mechanisms that govern movement between jobs. One such mechanism is the accumulation of "resources," including work experience, savvy about job hunting, and formal training. Through life, as individuals accumulate these resources, they receive greater economic rewards, including high-status jobs, higher earnings, and lower probabilities of unemployment (Tuma, 1976; DiPrete, 1981). An alternative mechanism is that the creation of job vacancies governs opportunities for worker movement among jobs (White, 1970; Sørensen, 1975, 1977; Stewman, 1975). Obviously, changes in the resources individuals bring to the labor market and in the opportunity structure both determine lifetime patterns of job mobility.

Both of these research traditions largely ignore the employment status of individuals. Work on job shifts and careers focuses on occupational careers, leaving undiscussed other elements of individuals' lives; and research on the "socioeconomic life cycle" treats employment status as inconsequential for the relationships among family background, schooling, occupational status, and earnings.

Neither of these approaches is easily extended to take account of the complexities of the employment experiences of young persons. Unlike occupational and earnings attainment of mature workers, which can be fruitfully abstracted from individuals' involvement in other institutions, employment is but one activity among others that are important in early life. Youth is a time of transition among a number of market and nonmarket activities, including work, schooling, military service, marriage, family formation, and experimentation with unconventional styles of life. Which of these activities dominates the lives of young persons is obviously variable both across and within the lives of individuals (Winsborough, 1978; Sweet, 1979a, 1979b). Young persons also differ in how they order these activities in time. Although cohorts of young men clearly move from school to work during this period, the nature and ordering of this transition is conceptually and empirically problematical (Coleman, 1976; Hogan, 1978, 1981). The transition is not a single change of status because persons typically enter and leave schooling and employment a number of times. Moreover, as young persons become adults they need not pursue each of their principal activities serially. Rather, they may engage in several activities at once and in varying quantities subject to the constraints of time. Finally, the timing of individuals' status changes varies with their social characteristics. As argued below, for example, men who leave school when they are in their twenties differ systematically from men who leave in their teens, not only in the amount of schooling they have received, but also in other characteristics that affect their labor market success.

These complexities suggest that intracohort changes in employment are closely linked to other activities and events both in and out of the labor market. School attendance, employment, service in the armed forces, marriage, establishment of a separate place of residence, and the onset of childbearing are closely linked for young persons. The research reported in this chapter examines a subset of these linkages, namely those among employment status, school enrollment, and participation in the armed forces. In particular, it explores the connection and timing of school, military, and work activities in the lives of young men and attempts to "explain" age variation in employment by age variation in school attendance and military service.[1]

In describing the linkage among work and nonwork roles that young men pass through as they age, this chapter parallels previous research on the "age-gradedness" of occupations in the adult labor force (Kaufman and Spilerman, 1982) and on occupational careers (Spilerman, 1977). We attempt to provide a partial structural description of the temporal and cross-sectional connections among major statuses and roles in the early life cycle and to extend prior work on the age pattern of statuses and transitions in the socioeconomic career to an earlier phase of the life cycle. At the same time, however, the approach taken here differs from this research in its emphasis on the overlapping, interrupted, irregular, and varied character of roles and role transitions in a population that is not yet fully integrated into the adult labor force.

3 Enrollment, enlistment, and employment

This section discusses mechanisms linking school enrollment, military enlistment, and employment, first discussing the conceptualization of the transition into employment and then turning to specific explanations of increasing employment with age.

3.1 *The transition to employment*

This chapter focuses on the linkages among the roles and statuses of young men and on how the movement of a cohort through these roles and statuses affects intracohort growth in the probability of employment. Much previous research has viewed transitions between social statuses and roles as single, irreversible events. Transitions that have been viewed in this way include entry into first marriage, departure from school, entry into first job, and onset of first birth (e.g., Marini, 1978, 1982; Alexander and Reilly, 1981; Rindfuss et al., 1981; Ornstein, 1976). In the case of employment, the point at which young persons first work is conceptually ambiguous (Coleman, 1976). Many definitions, implying varying degrees of commitment to work, can be used: first work for pay, first regular job in a work organization, first full-time job, or first job after school completion. In the arguments and analyses presented below, we avoid making an arbitrary definition of entry into employment. We view the transition simply as the increase in individuals' probabilities of employment. The "transition," therefore, is the continuous increase in employment probabilities and reflects, albeit abstractly, the various definitions of first entrance into employment mentioned above. An important consequence of this view is that the data required for analysis of intracohort change in employment for young persons are much simpler than for analysis of specific events.[2]

The following discussion considers three mechanisms through which involvement in school and the armed forces affects the intracohort pattern of employment among young persons. These include (1) the competition among schooling, the armed forces, and employment for young men's time; (2) the disruptive effects on employment of leaving school and the armed forces; and (3) the differential timing of movement into employment by men of varying social characteristics.

3.2 *Competition between work and nonwork roles*

Young men enhance their employment chances by accumulating formal schooling and thereby obtaining credentials or knowledge and training useful in the labor market (Becker, 1975; Mincer, 1974). In the short run, however, school enrollment obviously delays their entrance into employment or reduces the hours they can work. Students work substantially less than nonstudents, whether measured by the proportions of each group employed or the quantity of time spent working in each group (Fearn, 1968; Bowen and Finegan, 1969; Lerman, 1970; Parsons, 1974; Gustman and Steinmeier, 1979). Many students do not need to work because they receive economic support from parents or other sources. Others rely on part-time or intermittent employment to cover expenses. Students are also handicapped in competing with nonstudents for jobs inasmuch as they have fewer and less flexible hours for work (Lazear, 1977).

As is well known, however, the proportion of a cohort that remains in school declines precipitously with age. Approximately half of each cohort has left school by the late teenage years, the bulk of persons leaving school after high school graduation. For the half that remains in school, attrition is substantial in each of the college years, with the result that by the mid-twenties, most of a cohort has left school (Duncan, 1968; Mare, 1980b). Thus, a significant part of the increase in employment with age results from departures from school. In addition, the rate of increase in employment with age should vary directly with the rate of attrition from school; that is, the largest increases in proportions employed should occur during the ages when high school graduations and departures from college are most prevalent.[3]

A smaller but still substantial proportion of young men enlist in the armed forces. Typically, men enlist in their late teens, usually following high school graduation, and are discharged in their early twenties. The "effect" of military enlistment on employment is in large part definitional. If, as some analysts have recommended (National Commission on Employment and Unemployment Statistics, 1979), the armed forces are counted as employed, then the age pattern of civilian employment is an overstatement of the degree to which proportions employed increase with age inasmuch as the proportion of persons in their late teens and early twenties counted as employed would be higher. If, on the other hand, the armed forces are counted as not employed, then the civilian age pattern is enhanced when the age pattern of the percentage employed in the civilian work force is calculated. In the latter case, military enlistment, like school enrollment, competes with civilian employment. Were the armed forces not an activity for young men, then proportions employed as civilians would be significantly higher.

3.3 *Gaps between work and nonwork roles*

Some young men may already hold jobs when they leave school or the armed forces and others may have a job already "lined up." For many, however, initial withdrawal from school or the military is accompanied by unemployment, job search, and job experimentation (Folk, 1969; Feldstein, 1973; Gover and McCeady, 1974). During this period, men try various jobs and possibly experience high layoff rates resulting from their low seniority and potential employer dissatisfaction with their performance. For others, work is difficult to obtain at first because of their lack of work experience and on-the-job training. Still others may be reluctant to work at prevailing wage rates and may engage in a "moratorium" from all legitimate activities (Osterman, 1980). Work may also be relatively unattractive to school leavers who have not yet taken on the financial obligations of raising a family and paying for major purchases. Taken together, these styles of movement between schooling and armed forces on the one hand and employment on the other suggest that rising employment with age may reflect, in part, the differences among age groups in the amount of time young persons have been out of school or the armed forces. The decline with age in the proportion of a cohort that is made up of recent school leavers and veterans may partly explain the increase with age in the proportion of a cohort that is employed.

3.4 *Employability and the timing of transitions*

The arguments presented above attempt to account for intracohort increases in employment probabilities for young men as a whole. If we focus, however, on the age pattern of employment for young men who are not enrolled in school, then a third major mechanism may explain rising employment as a cohort ages, namely the tendency for men of varying degrees of "employability" to seek work at varying ages. In particular, men who have the best prospects for success in the labor market typically enter the labor force at older ages than men with poorer prospects.

Prolonged schooling and service in the armed forces are two principal sources of delayed labor force entry for young men. Delayed entry into the labor force of men pursuing higher education and serving in the armed forces affects the intracohort pattern of employment in two ways. First, persons who leave school later have, on average, more schooling than persons who leave earlier. As a cohort leaves school, therefore, the average level of formal schooling of persons out of school increases. Because the credentials and skills associated with formal schooling are attractive to employers, probabilities of employment vary directly with their educational attainment (Katz, 1974; Conley, 1974; Feldstein and Ellwood, 1979; Nickell, 1979). As the average education of the out-of-school population increases, therefore, its average probability of employment also increases.[4]

Second, in addition to having superior levels of education, persons entering the labor force later are more attractive to employers than early entrants in other respects. That is, schools retain and the armed forces recruit persons with personal characteristics that lead to relatively good employment prospects. The following discussion focuses first on the effect of enrollment selection and then on differential selection into the armed forces.

Persons with higher ability, motivation, and other learning skills stay in school longer than their less capable counterparts because of their more favorable family circumstances (Sewell and Hauser, 1975) and the greater anticipated economic reward to their schooling (Willis and Rosen, 1979).

These persons may also obtain employment more easily, especially when they finally leave school, than persons who leave school earlier.[5] If they were not enrolled in school, they would be more likely to be employed than persons who actually are out of school.[6] Thus, at younger ages the youth labor force consists largely of persons of lower employability[7] (Bowen and Finegan, 1969; Kalachek, 1969; Feldstein and Ellwood, 1979). As a cohort ages, persons with not only more formal qualifications, but also greater employability, leave school. The flow of more and more persons of higher employability out of school as a cohort ages affects the composition of the out-of-school population. To the extent that timing of leaving school varies directly with employability, the average employability of persons out of school increases with age, thereby raising the average probability of employment as a cohort ages.[8]

Although the armed forces do not necessarily retain their most capable recruits, recruitment and withdrawal from the military may affect civilian employment in a manner that parallels the effects of school enrollment. Some individuals may enter the armed forces to avoid bleak civilian job market prospects. On balance, however, the armed forces recruit from among men who are of approximately average ability because higher-ability persons either remain in school or find civilian jobs, and persons of lowest ability fail to qualify (Cooper, 1978). Because the effect of ability on employment is most likely to be strongest in the below-average segment of the ability distribution, the armed forces may retain a population with better civilian employment prospects than the actual civilian population.[9] This suggests that discharges from the military may raise the average employability of the civilian population and contribute to the positive relationship between age and employment for civilians in the 21–29 age range.

At this point, this effect of the armed forces must remain a conjecture, since adequate data for its examination are lacking. Moreover, the proportion of the 16- to 29-year-old population enlisted in the armed forces during the post-Vietnam era is small. The quantitative importance of the effect discussed here, therefore, is likely to be small relative to the effect of selective retention by schools.

4 Data

The analyses reported below use the October Current Population Surveys (CPS) of 1973–8. From the October CPS microdata files, civilian noninstitutional males aged 16–29 were selected, a total of 95,698 observations.[10] The number of independent observations, however, is approximately 50 percent of this because the rotation group structure of the CPS dictates that one-half of the housing units in a given month of the survey are interviewed in the same month one year later (U.S. Bureau of the Census, 1978). The CPS, moreover, is based on a multistage stratified cluster sample. Thus the assumption of simple random sampling, made in the multivariate analyses reported below, is not met. Because neither data nor test statistics have been adjusted for the nonrandomness of the CPS samples, the statistical significance of estimated parameters is likely to be overstated.

To reduce computation time, the CPS data were grouped into a table of the following dimensions: (1) employment status (employed, not employed); (2) schooling (less than 12 grades, 12 grades, greater than 12 grades); (3) age (seven 2-year categories over the 14-year span 16–29); (4) race (nonblack, black); (5) veteran status (nonveteran, veteran); (6) enrollment status (enrolled, first year out of school, second or third year out of school, fourth or more year out of school). Years out of school was estimated from survey questions on dates of last attendance for high school dropouts and of graduation for graduates, on grades of schooling completed, and on age.[11] In most models, age is parameterized as a third-order polynomial, the terms of which are calculated by raising the midpoints of the two-year age categories to their appropriate powers. School enrollment is defined as either full-time enrollment only or as full or part-time enrollment, depending upon the analytic context. For examining the effect of enrollment status on employment for the population as a whole, enrollment is defined as full-time only because the part-time enrolled tend to be mainly full-time workers taking a limited amount of schooling rather than persons dividing their time equally between schooling and work. In the analysis of employment for the not-enrolled population alone, however, part-time students are excluded because no information on their "time since leaving school" is available. For the not-enrolled, however, estimates of the effects of other variables are unaffected by the enrollment definition.

5 Statistical methods

The dependent variable in the analyses reported below is a dichotomy, d_y, taking the value one if an individual is employed and zero otherwise. The multivariate analyses include single-equation probit models predicting employment and a two-equation probit model that jointly predicts employment for out-of-school men and a second dichotomy, d_z, indicating whether or not an individual is enrolled in school. Thus the two-equation model consists of a "sample selection" equation (for enrollment) and a structural equation (for employment).[12]

Under the single-equation probit model, the probability that an individual is employed is a nonlinear function of a linear combination of independent variables. That is, for the ith individual ($i = 1, \ldots, N$),

$$p(d_{y_i} = 1) = \int_{-\infty}^{c_{y_i}} \frac{1}{\sqrt{2\pi}} \exp\left(\frac{-t_{y_i}^2}{2}\right) dt_y \tag{5.1}$$

where $c_{y_i} = \sum \beta_k X_{ik}$, X_{ik} denotes the value on the kth independent variable ($k = 1, \ldots, K$), and the β_k are parameters to be estimated. This model is applied to the young male population as a whole to summarize the age pattern of employment and assess the effect of school enrollment status on employment and to out-of-school young men to examine the effects of several independent variables.

Under the two-equation model, the probabilities of both employment for out-of-school young men and school enrollment are nonlinear functions of the independent variables. This model allows for common unmeasured variables to affect the probabilities of school enrollment and employment. The model can be written in terms of the probabilities of enrollment, of nonenrollment and employment, and of nonenrollment and nonemployment:

$$p(d_{z_i} = 1) = \int_{-\infty}^{c_{z_i}} \frac{1}{\sqrt{2\pi}} \exp\left(\frac{-t_{z_i}^2}{2}\right) dt_z \tag{5.2}$$

$$p(d_{y_i} = 1, d_{z_i} = 0) = \int_{-\infty}^{c_{y_i}} \int_{c_{z^i}}^{\infty} h(t_{y_i}, t_{z_i})\, dt_z\, dt_y \tag{5.3}$$

$$p(d_{y_i} = 0, d_{z_i} = 0) = \int_{c_{yi}}^{\infty} \int_{c_{z^i}}^{\infty} h(t_{y_i}, t_{z_i})\, dt_z\, dt_y \tag{5.4}$$

where $c_{z_i} = \sum \gamma_k W_{ik}$, $c_{y_i} = \sum \beta_k X_{ik}$, W_k and X_k denote the kth independent variables in the enrollment and employment equations respectively, and $h(t_{y_i}, t_{z_i})$ denotes the standard bivariate normal density function, that is

$$h(t_y, t_z) = \frac{1}{2\pi\sqrt{1-\rho^2}} \exp\left[\frac{1}{1-\rho^2}(t_y^2 - 2\rho t_y t_z + t_z^2)\right]$$

From (5.2) and (5.3) the employment equation under this model can be rewritten as the probability that a young man is employed conditional on his being out of school. That is,

$$p(d_{y_i} = 1 | d_{z_i} = 0) = \int_{-\infty}^{c_{y_i}} \frac{1}{\sqrt{2\pi}\sqrt{1-\rho^2}} \exp\left[-\frac{(t_y - \rho t_z)^2}{2(1-\rho)^2}\right] dt_y$$

$$= \int_{-\infty}^{c_{y_i}} \frac{1}{\sqrt{2\pi}} \exp\left(\frac{-t_y^{*2}}{2}\right) dt_y^* \tag{5.5}$$

where $t_y^* = (t_y - \rho t_z)/\sqrt{(1-\rho)^2}$ and

$$c_y^* = \frac{c_{y_i}}{\sqrt{1-\rho^2}} + \frac{\rho t_z}{\sqrt{1-\rho^2}} = \sum_{k=1}^{K} \frac{\beta_k}{\sqrt{1-\rho^2}} X_{ik} + \frac{\rho t_z}{\sqrt{1-\rho^2}} \qquad (5.6)$$

Under this model, the correlation coefficient ρ denotes the degree to which the (z-transformed) probabilities of enrollment and employment are correlated once the measured independent variables are taken into account. If $\rho = 0$, enrollment and employment share no common unmeasured determinants and the employment equation in the two-equation model reduces to the single-equation model (5.1). If, however, $\rho > 0$, then common factors such as ability affect the probabilities of both enrollment and employment. As (5.5) and (5.6) show, this specification is tantamount to adding to the employment equation the unmeasured determinant t_z of the (z-transformed) probability of enrollment, a method that could be applied directly if the dependent variables in the two equations were continuous (Heckman, 1978). To the extent that such determinants include a common employability component, t_z enters the employment equation with a positive coefficient proportional to ρ. Moreover, to the extent that t_z is correlated with measured independent variables, the coefficients for the latter will differ between the single- and two-equation models. Specifically, if t_z is positively correlated with age for not-enrolled men, then this indicator of unmeasured ability will explain part of the age effect on employment observed in the single-equation model.

The two-equation model is estimated by maximum likelihood. The likelihood is

$$L = \prod_{i=1}^{N} [p(d_{z_i} = 1)]^{d_{y_i}} [p(d_{y_i} = 1, d_{z_i} = 0)]^{d_{y_i}(1-d_{z_i})} \times [p(d_{y_i} = 0, d_{z_i} = 0)]^{(1-d_{y_i})(1-d_{z_i})}$$

The parameters β_k and γ_k and the correlation ρ are obtained using the Berndt–Hall–Hall–Hausman modified scoring algorithm applied to this likelihood function (Berndt et al., 1974).

6 Empirical specification

This section describes the empirical models used to examine the arguments discussed above. As noted, our investigation concerns the rise in the probability of employment throughout the life cycle of a birth cohort, but we lack longitudinal data for a single cohort that are well suited to this investigation. Thus we adopt a synthetic cohort approach (Shryock and Siegel, 1976) and infer intracohort processes from cross-sectional age variation. Although this is an obvious shortcoming of the analysis, it is unlikely to distort the findings inasmuch as a relatively small number of cohorts are represented in the October CPS data for 16- to 29-year-olds in the 1973–8 period.

The analysis consists of two parts: (1) description of the age pattern of employment for all young men and the contribution of age variation in school enrollment rates to the age effect on employment, and (2) analysis of the determinants of employment status for out-of-school young men.

6.1 *Age and enrollment effects on employment*

To describe the age pattern of employment we first summarize employment differences among two-year age groups within the 16–29 age range with the following single-equation model:

$$\Phi^{-1}[p(d_{y_i} = 1)] = \beta_0 + \sum_{k=18\text{-}19}^{28\text{-}29} \beta_k d_{ki}$$

where Φ is the standard normal distribution function, d_{ki} is a dummy variable that equals one if the ith individual is in the kth two-year age group ($k = 18\text{–}19, \ldots, 28\text{–}29$) and zero otherwise, and β_0 and the β_k are probit coefficients to be estimated. If age differences in school enrollment rates strongly affect age differences in employment, then age variation in employment may approximately follow the age pattern of rates of school withdrawal. Since school attrition is relatively slight during the mid-teens when youths are completing high school, large in the late teens and early twenties when they finish high school and attend college, and more gradual in the mid-twenties when most have already left school, a simple curve, such as a third-degree polynomial, may describe the age pattern. Thus we consider a model

$$\Phi^{-1}[p(d_{y_i} = 1)] = \beta_0 + \beta_1 A_i + \beta_2 A_i^2 + \beta_3 A_i^3 \qquad (6.1)$$

where A_i denotes the midpoint of the two-year age interval for the ith individual. Because the third-degree polynomial model implies employment rates that are close to the observed rates, we adopt this parameterization for the balance of the analysis.

To assess the effect of enrollment status on employment and its age pattern, we augment (6.1) as follows:

$$\Phi^{-1}[p(d_{y_i} = 1)] = \beta_0 + \beta_1 A_i + \beta_2 A_i^2 + \beta_3 A_i^3 + \beta_4 d_{z_i} \qquad (6.2)$$

where $d_{z_i} = 1$ if the individual is enrolled in school full-time and $d_{z_i} = 0$ otherwise. By comparing age-specific employment probabilities under the simple age model (6.1), that is, for the kth two-year age group

$$p_k = \int_{-\infty}^{\beta_0+\beta_1 A_k+\beta_2 A_k^2+\beta_3 A_k^3} \frac{1}{\sqrt{2\pi}} \exp\left(\frac{-t_y^2}{2}\right) dt_y$$

to the employment probabilities adjusted to a common level of school enrollment for all ages, that is

$$p_k^a = \int_{-\infty}^{\beta_0+\beta_1 A_k+\beta_2 A_k^2+\beta_3 A_k^3+\beta_4 p_z} \frac{1}{\sqrt{2\pi}} \exp\left(\frac{-t_y^2}{2}\right) dt_y$$

where p_z denotes the proportion of young men enrolled in school for the 16- to 19-year-old age group as a whole and A_k denotes the midpoint of the age interval for the kth-year age group ($k = 16\text{–}17, 18\text{–}19, \ldots, 28\text{–}29$), we can show how much of the increase in employment with age results from age variation in school enrollment rates. This method of computing net age-specific employment probabilities is also used for the models of effects of independent variables on employment of out-of-school men discussed below. That is, we estimate age-specific probabilities of employment adjusted to the means for the entire 16–29 group of the other independent variables included in the models.

Finally, we investigate whether employment is more strongly age-graded among out-of-school young men than among students by modifying (6.2) to allow age effects to vary with enrollment status.

6.2. *Determinants of employment for out-of-school young men*

6.2.1. The effects of measured variables. To investigate determinants of employment for out-of-school men we examine first the effects of several measured independent variables on employment and then the effects of common unmeasured factors ("employability") on enrollment and employment. After examining the basic age pattern of employment for out-of-school men using a model of the same form as (6.1), but restricted to the out-of-school population, we consider additional independent variables to obtain models of the form

$$\Phi^{-1}[p(d_y = 1)] = \beta_0 + \beta_1 A_i + \beta_2 A_i^2 + \beta_3 A_i^3 + \sum_{k=4}^{K} \beta_k X_{ik}$$

where X_{ik} denotes the value of the kth independent variable for the ith individual. The independent variables considered in the analysis are as follows:[13]

6.2.1.A. Race. Young blacks have lower probabilities of employment than whites. Since blacks leave school at an earlier average age than whites, the rise in employment with age may be partly explained by the rising proportion of the out-of-school population that is white as a cohort ages. Thus we include a variable indicating race (black versus white and other) in the model and examine its impact on the estimated net effects of age.

6.2.1.B. Grades of schooling. Men with more formal schooling are more attractive to employers and thus should have higher employment probabilities. As a cohort ages, the average level of education of men newly leaving school increases and thus the average education level of the out-of-school population as a whole also increases. To see if the increasing education level of the out-of-school population with age may partly explain the positive effect of age on employment for out-of-school men, we include measures of educational attainment in the employment model and observe the reduction in net age effects.

6.2.1.C. Years out of school. By the arguments presented above, men who have been out of school longer have higher probabilities of employment. Additionally, as a cohort ages, the proportion of out-of-school men who are recent school leavers declines, suggesting that a further component of the increase in employment with age increases with age in average length of time since leaving school. Thus, we augment the employment equation with measures of time since leaving school and examine the reduction in net age effects on employment.

6.2.1.D. Veteran status and veteran status–age interaction. As discussed above, the armed forces recruit men with good long-run employment prospects and possibly provide skills and training useful in civilian life (see note 4). Recent veterans, however, may be handicapped in obtaining employment until they are more fully integrated into the workforce. To observe directly whether movement from military or civilian life lowers employment probabilities requires a measure of how long veterans have been out of the armed forces. Because this measure is not available in the October CPS, we use an indirect approach. If veterans are potentially an advantaged group in the labor market and are handicapped in obtaining employment only temporarily, then the negative effect of veteran status should decline with age, reflecting that older veterans have typically been out of the armed forces for longer periods than younger veterans. Employment probabilities for veterans and nonveterans should converge and may eventually be to the net advantage of veterans. Thus we augment the employment equation with an indicator of whether or not a young man is a veteran and variables that measure the interaction of veteran status with age, thereby allowing the negative effect of veteran status to diminish as individuals age.

6.2.2. Unmeasured determinants of employability. The final stage of the analysis of employment for out-of-school men attempts to assess whether schools retain the most employable young men for the longest period and whether increases in employment with age for out-of-school men result in part from the influx of more employable men to the labor force at advanced ages. To investigate this directly requires measures of ability, motivation, and other personal attributes affecting employment that are not obtained in the October CPS. Thus we adopt the indirect approach described in the previous section, that is, to model the probabilities of school enrollment and employment as joint outcomes affected by common unmeasured variables. The employment equation includes the measured variables discussed above. The enrollment equation includes the effects of age, formal schooling, race, veteran status, and the interactions of age with the latter three variables on the probability of being enrolled in school. The latter equation reflects the notion that enrollment rates differ among the sociodemographic groups defined by the independent variables, although additional variables might also be determinants of enrollment.

We estimate these two equations using the bivariate probit model discussed above [equations (5.1)–(5.5)] and thus estimate the correlation ρ between the (z-transformed) probabilities of enrollment and employment controlling for the effects of the measured independent variables. A positive correlation indicates that similar unmeasured factors affect remaining in school and, if one is not in school, obtaining employment and suggests that schools retain the most employable young men. As noted, this model is tantamount to augmenting the single-equation model for the effects of measured independent variables with a latent variable representing common influences on enrollment and employment. Declining enrollment with age implies that these influences are positively correlated with age in the out-of-school population and thus reduce the net effect of age on employment when they are included in the model.

7 Empirical results

This section reports the empirical findings. It first discusses the single-equation probit results for all civilian men aged 16–29. Then it presents the single- and two-equation results for out-of-school men. It concludes

Table 1. *Single-equation probit estimates for selected models of determinants of "employment": civilian noninstitutional males 16–29*

	Model			
Variable	1	2	3	4
Constant	−.27	−9.74	8.38	−18.46
18–19 (vs. 16–17)	.51			
20–21 (vs. 16–17)	.79			
22–23 (vs .16–17)	1.12			
24–25 (vs. 16–17)	1.36			
26–27 (vs. 16–17)	1.55			
28–29 (vs. 16–17)	1.67			
Age*		9.46	−11.27	22.35
Age²**		−2.78	5.27	−8.59
Age³***		2.89	−7.60	11.23
Enrolled full-time (vs. not enrolled full-time)			−1.10	25.19
Enrolled × age*				−31.84
Enrolled × age²**				12.63
Enrolled × age³***				−16.54
Employed at 16–17[a]	39.4	39.3	64.2	52.2
Employed at 28–29[a]	91.9	91.4	87.1	86.8
−2 Log likelihood	97,474	97,506	88,799	88,325
Degrees of freedom	621	624	623	620

Note: All coefficients are greater than twice their estimated standard errors.
[a] Percent employed for persons aged 16–17 and 28–29 adjusted to mean levels of independent variables.
* Age/10.
** $Age^2/100$.
*** $Age^3/10,000$.

with a summary of the contributions of measured and unmeasured variables to explaining the age pattern of employment for out-of-school men.

7.1 *Age and enrollment effects for all young men*

Table 1 reports probit coefficient estimates for models predicting whether or not a young man is employed. The coefficients for age in the models reported in Table 1 should be examined in conjunction with Figure 1, which reports the age-specific employment probabilities under the models. The first column of estimates in Table 1 corresponds to a classification of

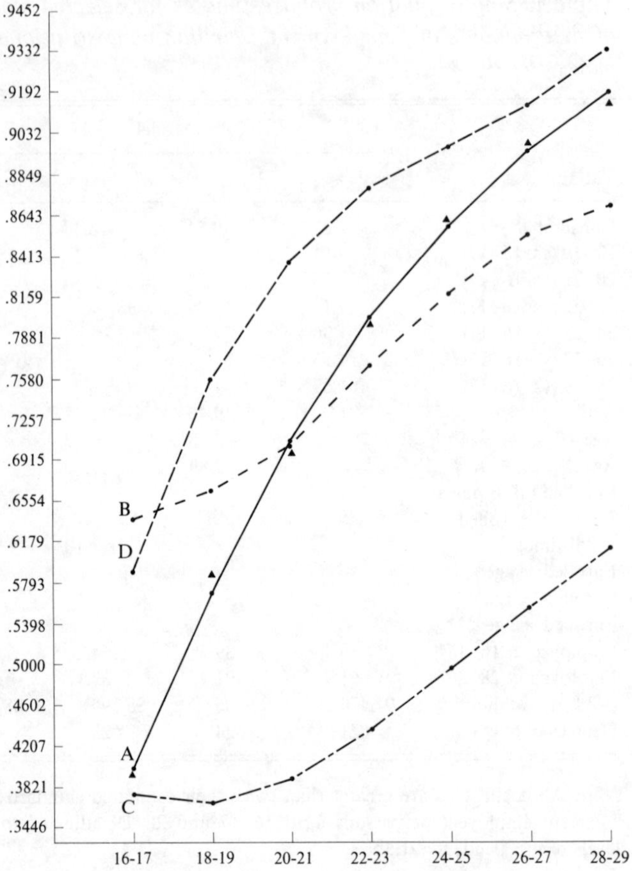

Figure 1. Proportion employed (probit scale) by age for selected models. Models are: A, third-order age polynomial (model 2, Table 1); B, third-order age polynomial, controlling enrollment status (model 3, Table 1); C, third-order age polynomial, full-time enrolled (model 4, Table 1); D, third-order age polynomial, not full-time enrolled (model 4, Table 1); ▲, observed age-specific employment probabilities (model 1, Table 1).

the seven two-year age groups in the 16- to 29-year-old group. The second column parameterizes this age pattern as a third-degree polynomial. The likelihood statistics reported at the bottom of these two columns suggest that the data reject the polynomial constraint inasmuch as their difference of 32 (distributed chi-square with 3 degrees of freedom under the assumption of random sampling) is statistically significant. Here and throughout this section, however, differences in the log likelihoods of nested models are merely descriptive measures of relative fit because the number of individual observations is so large and the random sampling assumption is clearly violated in the CPS data. In proportionate terms the change in chi-square when the polynomial restriction is applied is trivial. As Figure 1 shows, moreover, the polynomial accurately charts the observed employment probabilities. Under both the observed and predicted patterns, employment rises with age, first gradually in the teenage years, then more dramatically during the years of high school graduation and college attendance, and then gradually again in the late twenties.

Consider next the age pattern of employment adjusted for age variation in the proportion of young men enrolled in school full time. By entering an additive term for enrollment status we can show whether or not the increase in employment between ages 16 and 29 is a result of age differentials in the degree to which schooling substitutes for work. This model is reported in the third column of Table 1. As the log-likelihood statistic indicates, the enrollment term substantially improves the fit of the model over the age polynomial alone. The effect on the age pattern of employment is also considerable. When enrollment is not controlled, employment varies from approximately 40 percent for 16- and 17-year-olds to approximately 90 percent for 28- and 29-year-olds. If proportions enrolled is held constant at its level for 16- to 29-year-olds as a whole, however, employment varies only from 64 to 87 percent, suggesting that at least one-half of the age variation is accounted for by the tendency for young men to leave school as they grow older.

The last column of Table 1 reports coefficients for a model in which the age pattern of employment differs for in-school and out-of-school young men. The likelihood statistics imply a considerable improvement in fit of the model when age–enrollment status interactions are included. As Figure 1 shows, employment increases much more steeply with age for out-of-school young men than for students, although the age gradient of employment for both groups is flatter than for the two groups combined.

That employment rises more steeply for out-of-school young men than for students suggests that at least some of the mechanisms discussed above, including the accumulation of experience and credentials, the experience of difficulties in making the transition to work, and the entry into the workforce of more employable young men, are more important for out-of-school persons than for students. For students, other factors, including availability of family financial support, the differential necessity of taking jobs related to formal training, and compatibility between academic demands and the availability of part-time employment, may be more salient. As noted above, the empirical analyses reported below focus on the former set of mechanisms as they apply to the out-of-school population.

Table 2. *Single-equation probit estimates for selected models of the determinants of "employment": out-of-school civilian noninstitutional males 16–29*

	Model				
Variable	1	2	3	4	5
Constant	−19.20	−19.72	−12.50	−12.51	−12.01
Black (vs. nonblack)		−.58	−.52	−.52	−.52
<12 Grades (vs. 12 grades)			−.40	−.43	−.45
>12 Grades (vs. 12 grades)			.07	.10	.09
Out 1 year (vs. out 4+ years)				−.13	−.14
Out 2–3 years (vs. out 4+ years)				−.03[a]	−.05
Veteran (vs. nonveteran)					−.11
Age*	23.49	24.33	15.83	16.25	15.64
Age^2**	−9.12	−9.49	−6.14	−6.44	−6.18
Age^3***	12.02	12.54	8.16	8.67	8.35
Employed at 16–17[b]	61.1	61.8	71.1	73.2	73.8
Employed at 28–29[b]	93.8	93.6	94.0	92.7	94.0
−2 Log Likelihood[c]	121,851	120,975	120,252	120,226	120,190
Degrees of freedom	604	603	601	599	598

[a] Coefficient less than twice its estimated standard error.

[b] Implied percentage employed for persons aged 16–17 and 28–29 at mean value of the independent variables.

[c] Log likelihoods and degrees of freedom adjusted to be comparable to two-equation estimates in Table 3 on assumption of an auxiliary enrollment equation (see Table 4) and correlation of zero between disturbances of employment and enrollment equations.

7.2 *Employment of out-of-school young men: effects of observed variables*

Table 2 reports single-equation probit coefficient estimates for the effects on employment status of the independent variables discussed above. The various models confirm a number of well-established relationships between social factors and the chances of employment. Blacks are less likely to be employed than whites, the probability of employment varies directly with level of formal schooling, and veterans in this age group experience lower employment than nonveterans. The coefficients in Table 2 also suggest that the critical educational distinction for employment is whether or not young men have a high school diploma rather than whether or not they have postsecondary schooling. Equations in columns 4 and 5 also show that persons newly out of school experience substantially lower probability of employment than persons who have left school a number of years prior to the survey date.

Below the estimated age coefficients for each model are the employment probabilities for 16- to 17- and 28- to 29-year-olds adjusted to mean levels on the included independent variables. When no independent variables are controlled, the employment probabilities of the two age groups differ by approximately 30 percentage points. As the probabilities in the second column show, age differences in racial composition account for a negligible fraction of the age difference in employment. Age differences in levels of formal schooling, however, explain a substantial portion of the employment disadvantage of the youngest group, as is indicated by the reduction of the difference in employment by approximately 10 percentage points when grades of schooling is controlled. Column 4 shows that age differences in the distribution of time out of school account for some of the age difference in employment (approximately 5 percent), although by no means the fraction due to grades of schooling. Finally, the distribution of veterans across age groups explains none of the age difference in employment. This latter result is to be expected inasmuch as veterans, who experience relatively low employment, are a negligible fraction of the 16–17 group.

To examine the arguments that members of the armed forces experience a transitional period between discharge and integration into the workforce, we augment the final equation in Table 2 with terms measuring the interaction of age and veteran status. Under this model, the handicap of veteran status is confined to the youngest veterans who are experiencing the transition into civilian life, and gradually disappears with age, reflecting that as the veteran population ages it includes a growing number of persons many years out of the armed forces. The first column of Table 3 reports coefficients for the variables included in the models already discussed as well as for terms measuring the varying effect of veteran status with age. The interaction terms are highly significant, as is indicated in the second column of Table 3 and by comparison of the log-likelihood statistic with the additive model presented in the final column of Table 2. Figure 2a plots the age pattern of employment for veterans and nonveterans, using the coefficients of the model presented in the first column of Table 3. The

Table 3. *Probit estimates for determinants of "employment" under alternative estimation methods: out-of-school civilian noninstitutional males 16–29*

	Single-equation estimates		Two-equation estimates	
Variable	$\hat{\beta}$	$\hat{\beta}$/S.E. ($\hat{\beta}$)	$\hat{\beta}$	$\hat{\beta}$/S.E. ($\hat{\beta}$)
Constant	−15.65	−6.8	−2.71	−.9
Black (vs. nonblack)	−.52	−26.5	−.49	−25.6
<12 Grades (vs. 12 grades)	−.44	−24.0	−.41	−23.0
>12 Grades (vs. 12 grades)	.09	4.7	.21	8.1
Out 1 year (vs. out 4+ years)	−.15	−5.6	−.14	−5.5
Out 2–3 years (vs. out 4+ years)	−.04	−1.9	−.04	−1.8
Veteran (vs. nonveteran)	24.44	2.6	10.20	1.1
Age*	20.39	6.7	4.93	1.2
Age^2**	−8.21	−6.1	−2.07	−1.3
Age^3***	11.15	5.8	3.04	1.3
Veteran × age*	−33.28	11.7	−16.11	−1.4
Veteran × age^2**	14.57	4.8	7.73	1.6
Veteran × age^3***	−20.71	6.6	−11.70	−1.8
Employed at 16–17[a]	71.4	—	90.7	—
Employed at 28–29[a]	92.8	—	96.6	—
ρ[b]	0	—	.28	5.8
−2 Log likelihood	120,133[c]		120,104	
Degrees of freedom	595		594	

[a] Implied percentage employed for persons aged 16–17 and 28–29 at mean values of the independent variables.
[b] Disturbance correlation for equations predicting "employment" and "enrollment."
[c] Log likelihood and degrees of freedom for single-equation estimation assume enrollment equation in Table 4 with correlation of zero between disturbances of enrollment and employment equations.
* Age/10.
** Age^2/100.
*** Age^3/10,000.

figure shows that the disadvantage of participation in the military for employment is indeed concentrated among the youngest veterans. As veterans approach age 30, their employment probabilities converge to those of nonveterans. This result illustrates the disruptive impact of the transition from the armed forces to employment and parallels the observation that employment chances vary directly with time out of school.

The results presented thus far for out-of-school young men are summarized in lines A and B in Figure 3, which plot expected age-specific

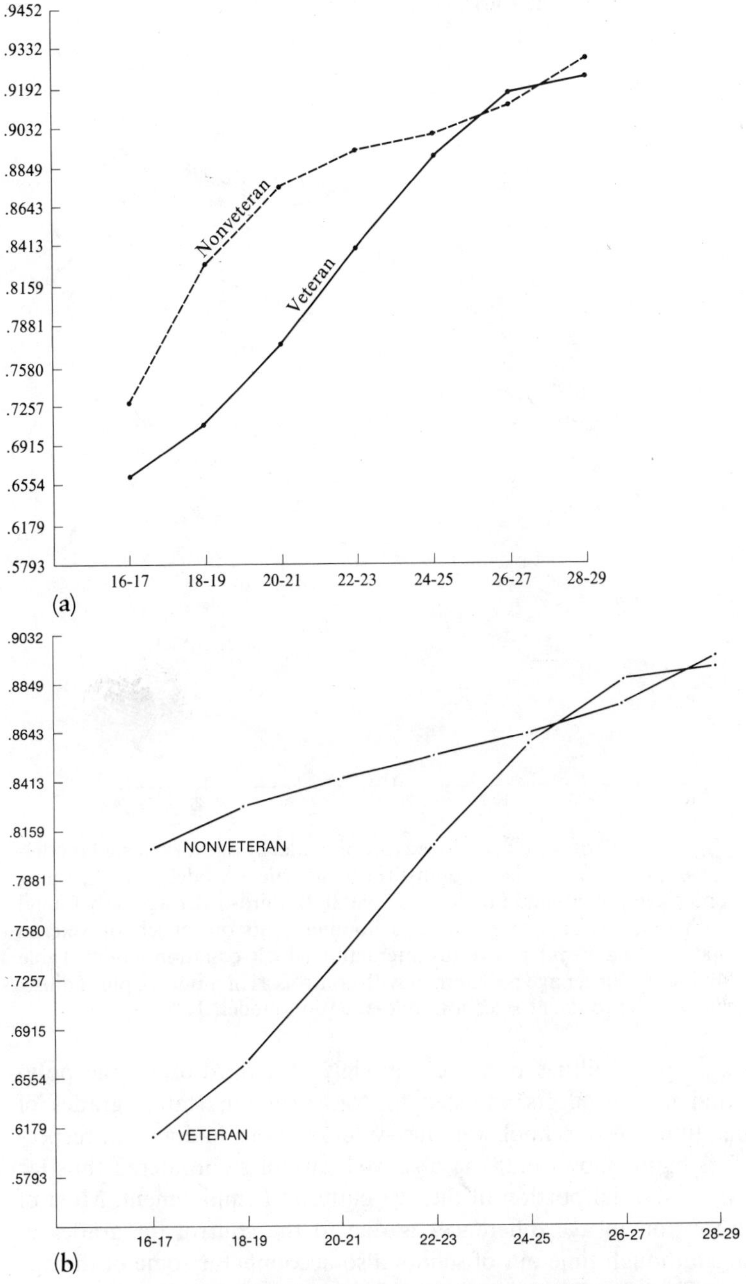

Figure 2. Proportion employed (probit scale) by age and veteran status for *out-of-school* civilian noninstitutional males. Estimates are adjusted for age and veteran status differences in race, grades of schooling, and time out of school. Estimates are based on models reported in Table 3. Figure 2a shows single-equation results. Figure 2b shows two-equation results.

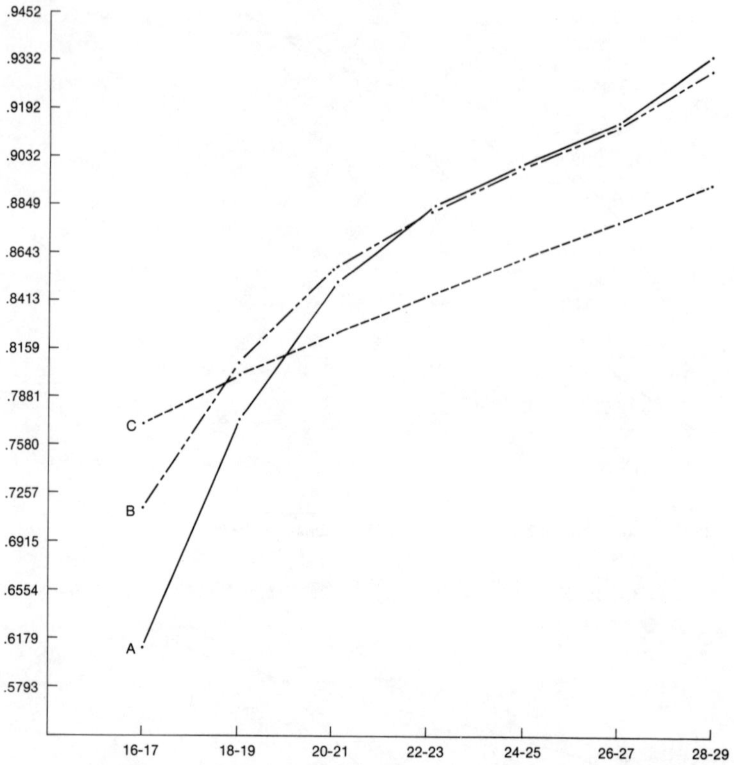

Figure 3. Proportion employed (probit scale) by age for selected models for *out-of-school* civilian noninstitutional males. Models are: A, third-order age polynomial (model 1, Table 2); B, third-order age polynomial with controls for race, grades of schooling, years out of school, veteran status, and age–veteran status interaction (single-equation model, Table 4); C, third-order age polynomial with controls as in model B, plus adjustment for enrollment selection (two-equation model, Table 3).

employment probabilities under the models of a third-order age polynomial and of age effects adjusted for race, veteran status, grades of schooling, time out of school, and age–veteran status interaction, respectively. This figure shows that the observed variables considered thus far explain a substantial portion of the age pattern of employment. Most of the compression in age differences is due to the control for grades of schooling, although time out of school also accounts for some of the age difference. The effects of schooling and time out of school are greatest where the increases in age-specific employment are largest, namely between the 16–17 and 18–19 and between the 18–19 and 20–21 age groups. This pattern suggests that age differences in the proportion of persons with a high school diploma are a key component of age differences in employment.

7.3 *Employment of out-of-school young men: effects of unmeasured factors*

As discussed in the previous sections, a potentially important cause of rising employment with age is the influx of more able or employable young persons into the labor force. This argument suggests that the equations presented thus far are misspecified inasmuch as they fail to recognize that the out-of-school population differs systematically on unmeasured factors from the student population. In particular, one might regard the single-equation estimates presented here as subject to the "selection bias" of excluding enrolled persons. If persons who remain in school for lengthy periods have above average chances of securing employment when they do leave school, then unmeasured determinants of whether or not an individual is enrolled and of whether or not he is employed should have a positive correlation. Since, moreover, the degree of selection into enrollment varies inversely with age, a control for systematic selection may also account for part of the positive association of age and the probability of employment.

To examine these conjectures, we estimated a two-equation model with equations for enrollment and employment. The third column of Table 3 reports the coefficient estimates for the employment equation and for the correlation between unmeasured determinants of employment and enrollment. Table 4 reports the estimates for the enrollment equation, which will not be discussed here.

These results strongly suggest that schools systematically retain the most employable young men. The bottom of the third column of Table 3 reports a significant positive correlation of .28, which indicates that the enrolled more closely resemble the employed than the not-employed on unmeasured factors. Note also that although coefficients in the single- and two-equation models are similar, there are several important differences. The effect of receiving some college (relative to a high school diploma) on employment increases markedly when selection is taken into account. This suggests that schooling effects are underestimated in the single-equation model because those individuals who are most able to benefit from their investment in formal schooling are excluded from the analysis. When selection is taken into account, the schooling effect increases.

Table 4. *Probit estimates for determinants of "enrollment": civilian noninstitutional males 16–29*

Variable	$\hat{\beta}$	$\hat{\beta}$/S.E. ($\hat{\beta}$)
Constant	26.12	8.0
Veteran (vs. nonveteran)	−37.79	−4.3
Black (vs. nonblack)	−12.57	−2.9
<12 Grades (vs. 12 grades)	28.71	6.4
>12 Grades (vs. 12 grades)	−36.72	−7.1
Age*	−26.19	−6.1
Age²**	7.86	4.2
Age³***	−7.36	−2.7
Veteran × age*	38.47	3.6
Veteran × age²**	−12.46	−2.8
Veteran × age³***	12.82	2.2
Black × age*	17.26	2.9
Black × age²**	−7.74	−2.9
Black × age³***	11.42	2.9
<12 × age*	−34.49	−5.7
<12 × age²**	13.66	5.0
<12 × age³***	−18.03	−4.5
>12 × age*	49.12	7.4
>12 × age²**	−20.52	−7.3
>12 × age³***	27.70	7.0

* Age/10.
** Age²/100.
*** Age³/10,000.

The effects of age are substantially attenuated once selection on unmeasured factors is taken into account. As the last lines of Table 3 show, the residual difference in employment probabilities between 16–17- and 28–29-year-olds is approximately 20 percentage points. This difference is cut by more than half when enrollment selection is taken into account. Figure 2 shows the effects of selection on unmeasured factors on the complete age pattern of employment. Taking account of selection compresses the employment difference over the 16–29 age span by at least as much as taking account of age variation on measured variables. As for the effects of measured variables, the greatest reduction in age variation occurs for the youngest men. (Compare line C with lines A and B.)

Finally, Figure 2b plots the age pattern of employment for veterans and nonveterans using the age coefficients in the two-equation model. As in the single-equation model, the employment chances of the two groups converge over the 16–29 age range. Enrollment selection, however, ex-

Table 5. *Components of change in employment (probit) between ages 16–17 and 28–29: out-of-school civilian noninstitutional males*

Component[a]	Change	Proportion of total change
Race (means)	.023	.018
Grades of schooling (means)	.372	.291
Years out of school (means)	.074	.058
Veteran status (means)	−.235 (−.009)[b]	−.184 (−.007)[b]
Veteran status (coefficients)	.003 (.231)[b]	.002 (.181)[b]
Veteran status (interaction)	−.226 (−.226)[b]	.177 (−.177)[b]
Selection on employability (means)	.431	.337
Residual	.384	.300
Total:	1.278[c]	1.000[c]

[a] Decomposition based on coefficients in Table 3 for employment equation estimated by two-equation method.
[b] Components in parentheses assume 28- to 29-year-olds are base group; other components assume 16- to 17-year-olds are base group.
[c] Components may not sum to reported totals because of rounding.

plains a much greater part of the age difference in employment for non-veterans than for veterans. This results from the relatively low proportions of veterans enrolled in school.

7.4 *Accounting for age variation in employment: summary*

The sources of rising employment with age for out-of-school young men can be summarized with a decomposition based on age differences in average values on unmeasured variables and the coefficients of the two-equation model reported in Table 3.[14] Table 5 presents the decomposition of change in the *z*-transformed employment probabilities between ages 16–17 and 28–29. The decomposition shows clearly that two components account for most of the rise in employment between ages 16 and 30, namely the changing educational composition of the out-of-school population and the changing composition on unmeasured factors, including ability, motivation, and other common determinants of employment and school enrollment. The former component accounts for slightly less than 30 percent of the rise in employment, whereas the latter, denoted "selection on employability" in Table 5, accounts for one-third of the change. A minor portion of the change is due to an increase in the proportion of young persons who have been out of school for several years. The various effects of veteran status are largely offsetting. When veteran status has a very large negative effect on employment, few young men are veterans (at the youngest ages); but when a significant fraction of young men are veterans, the effect of veteran status is negligible (at the oldest ages). Taken together, the mechanisms that are considered in this analysis account for approximately two-thirds of the rise in employment between ages 16–17 and 28–29.

8 Conclusion

This chapter has sought to explain intracohort change in employment by showing how employment is linked to other social statuses and how, as a result of these linkages, age variation in these other statuses determines age variation in employment. The chapter has explored the relationships among three important activities in the lives of young men – school enrollment, service in the armed forces, and employment – and has attempted to account for rising employment between ages 16 and 29. For all civilian young men, school enrollment competes with employment for young men's time. Differential enrollment rates account for a substantial fraction of the differences in proportions employed between men in their mid-teens and men in their late twenties. Among men who are out of school, more than one-half of the difference in proportions employed between men in their teens and men turning 30 is attributable to the late departure from school of men with the best employment prospects. Within a cohort, persons with the most formal schooling and who are the most employable on the basis of their other social characteristics typically are the last to leave school and do not contribute to proportions employed until they are well into their twenties. Recent departures from school and from the armed forces are handicaps in obtaining employment for young men, although age variation in proportions of young men who have newly left school or the armed forces accounts for only a small part of the growth in employment with age among out-of-school men. It remains a plausible – though far from fully examined – conjecture that employment rises with age when a cohort is in its twenties in part because of discharges from the armed forces of men with above average employability.

This research has several important limitations. We have emphasized the connections among schooling, the armed forces, and employment and ignored their relationship to living circumstances, marriage, childbearing, and other statuses and events that make up the lives of young persons. Further elaboration of the mechanisms considered here to take account of these other aspects of the early life cycle is clearly in order.

In addition, we have relied on synthetic cohort analysis to infer intracohort processes and on unobserved normally distributed variables to infer the selective retention by schools of the most employable young men.

Analyses similar to those reported here but based on panel data would remedy many of the problems created by these assumptions. The Department of Labor National Longitudinal Study of Labor Force Behavior (DOL NLS) cohorts, aged 16–21 in 1979, will in a few years provide appropriate data. Analyses of panel data such as these would ensure that inter- and intracohort processes were not confounded. Such data would also afford repeated observations on individuals, permitting rigorous statistical separation of the effects of invariant characteristics of individuals from those of changing characteristics such as formal school credentials. Moreover, repeated observations on individuals permit relaxation of the assumption made here that unmeasured variables affecting employment and enrollment follow a normal distribution inasmuch as distribution-free, person-specific fixed effects can be specified (e.g., Chamberlain, 1980). In addition, because the DOL NLS data include explicit measures of ability, motivation, and family background, they will allow direct measurement of at least some of the unobservable variables postulated here. Finally, the DOL NLS data represent both civilian and armed forces populations. This will permit direct assessment of the selective effects of armed forces, paralleling the analysis of enrollment selection presented here.

Taken at face value, however, the findings of this chapter do suggest that a substantial part of measured youth joblessness results from the absence from the labor force of young persons most likely to obtain employment. Although much commentary has stressed that many young persons do not participate in the labor force because they are discouraged by their employment prospects (e.g., Congressional Budget Office, 1982), our results indicate that the potential employability of those withholding their labor during their teens and early twenties is high. Without denying the seriousness of youth joblessness for disadvantaged subgroups of the population, our results suggest that substantial joblessness for young persons is in part the result of young persons' pursuit of other socially sanctioned and economically rewarding activities.

Although the arguments and findings of this chapter pertain to the process of integration into the workforce of a single birth cohort, they suggest that changes over cohorts in both level and timing of youth employment may arise from changes across cohorts in participation in other activities (Mare and Winship, 1980). They suggest that rising school enrollment for all youths over the twentieth century and for minority youths in recent decades may have reduced youth employment levels and shifted the timing of labor force entry. In particular, rising enrollment has not only led to increasing substitution of schooling for work among young persons generally and blacks in particular, but also, schools may be keeping from the workforce until a relatively advanced age young persons who are most likely to have the best prospects for employment, giving rise to increasing joblessness among the reduced fraction of the youths who leave school early.

ACKNOWLEDGMENTS

This research was supported by National Science Foundation Grants SOC 7912648 to Mare and Winship and DAR 7917585 to Winship. Computations were performed on the VAX 11/780 at the University of Wisconsin Center for Demography and Ecology, supported by National Institute of Child Health and Human Development Grant HD 05876-11.

NOTES

1 This research explains age variation in employment only in the sense that it shows how employment is linked to other roles and activities over the life cycle. It does not explain the existence of commonly observed linkages nor the decision-making patterns of individuals. We account for age variation in employment in the same sense that one might "explain" the distribution of a cohort in a given occupation over the life cycle by showing that that occupation typically fits between two other occupations in careers and that, as a result, the temporal distribution of persons in these two occupations "determines" the distribution of persons in the occupation of concern.

2 An alternative solution to the problem of defining entry into employment is to model the complex interactions in time between schooling and work by focusing on transitions by individuals among the various states defined by the first employment definitions considered above. The potential richness of this approach must be traded off against its much more severe data requirements and the possibility that the simpler approach adopted in this chapter may reveal important processes more clearly.

3 Of course, young persons may also time their school departure in accordance with the availability of employment (e.g., Duncan, 1965; Edwards, 1976; Mare, 1981). Thus, the intracohort age pattern of school enrollment may also reflect the age pattern of available job opportunities. This possibility is not taken into account in the empirical analyses reported below.

4 Service in the armed forces may also raise men's skill levels and thus their employment prospects. Thus, as a cohort ages, the out-of-school population includes larger fractions of men with training obtained in the armed forces, a factor that may also partly explain rising employment with age. The effects of service in the military on economic success, however, are not well-established (see, e.g., Mason, 1970; Cutright, 1973; Smith and Welch, 1974; De Tray, 1980, 1982).

5 On the other hand, persons with more education, skills, and ability might be no more likely to be employed than those with less if their greater desirability to employers is offset by their higher reservation wages.

6 There are two independent sources of evidence on this. First, students seem to have a much easier time finding employment than nonstudents during the summer months (Mare and Winship, 1980; Clark and Summers, 1979), suggesting

that students are more desirable employees than nonstudents. Second, Meyer and Wise (1979) show that unmeasured determinants of school enrollment and of employment for out-of-school youths are strongly correlated, suggesting that if students were not in school, they would be more likely to be employed than those who are actually out of school.

7 The term *employability* is used throughout this chapter to summarize factors that affect success, including mental ability, interpersonal skills, motivation, willingness to take orders, and personal contacts.

8 School attrition affects the composition of the student populations as well. Since, on average, the least capable students leave school, the average ability of persons remaining in school also increases. By itself, however, this change may not raise the probability of employment of the enrolled group. Much more than for out-of-school persons, for students employment depends on factors other than motivation, qualifications, or ability. Students most likely to work may be those living away from home, those whose parents are unable to fully support them, or those who are least committed to school. Much student employment is linked to programs of study and is unaffected by market mechanisms. In addition, student employment often depends on the availability of part-time jobs that are compatible with student schedules. Thus, not only may employment rise less steeply with age for students, but also it may respond largely to factors independent of the mechanisms affecting the employment prospects of out-of-school persons. The former expectation is borne out in the analyses presented below. Further empirical examination of the market for student employment is beyond the scope of this chapter.

9 The armed forces retain persons with above average civilian employment prospects for two reasons. First, many of the highest-ability persons are not in the labor force because they are in school. By recruiting from the middle-ability group, the armed forces leave a disproportionate number of lower-ability individuals in the not-enrolled, not-enlisted population. Together, the military and the schools lower the average ability of persons in the civilian labor force. Second, although persons in the armed forces may typically be of average ability, they may have higher than average probabilities of being employed. To see this, assume that the probability of employment is a nonlinear function of ability: Prob(emp) = f(ability). If f is concave downward (high-ability persons have only slightly higher probabilities of employment than middle-ability persons), then by recruiting middle-ability persons the armed forces recruit persons with higher than average probabilities of employment. Although the mean ability for the military approximates the mean in the population, the mean of f(ability) is higher in the military since low-ability persons have been excluded.

10 Ideally, the arguments developed above should be assessed by examining intracohort variation in employment, preferably with panel data. Existing panel data, however, suffer other serious disadvantages. The Panel Study of Income Dynamics omits much of the employment experience of young persons because detailed labor force information is confined to household heads. The Department of Labor National Longitudinal Study of Young Men is plagued with complex problems of sample attrition and reentry owing to the exclusion of the armed forces from the survey (Social Science Research Council, 1977). And the "new" National Longitudinal Survey of Labor Force Behavior cohorts are as yet too young to provide information about entry into employment of young persons in their twenties. Another potentially useful data source is the March

CPS, for which a longer time series of microdata is available, permitting examination of intracohort variation, albeit through a replicated cross-sectional design. The March surveys, however, lack information on school enrollment and on the timing of leaving school. By contrast, the October CPS provides a large sample of the civilian population for which adequate enrollment, employment, and school-leaving information is obtained for young men of all ages.

11 In the October CPS high school dropouts are asked when they last attended school. Persons obtaining 12 or more grades of schooling were asked when they graduated from high school but not when they last attended. For persons with 12 or fewer grades, therefore, a direct estimate of years spent out of school is available. For persons with more than 12 grades, no information on interruptions and delays in postsecondary schooling is available, and thus a crude estimate that assumes no delays after high school graduation must be used. Thus years out of school is defined as follows:

Survey year − year last attended + 1 (<12 Grades)
Survey year − year of graduation + 1 (12 Grades)
Survey year − year of graduation + (highest grade attended − 12) + 1 (>12 Grades)

For persons with at least some college education this measure will somewhat overestimate the time since leaving school.

12 We adopt the normality assumption of the probit model primarily for analytic convenience. Our results may depend on this assumption, and other univariate and bivariate distributional assumptions might be equally well suited to our arguments. Exploration of the robustness of our conclusions under alternative distributional assumptions is a topic for further work.

13 In addition to the variables discussed here and in the next section, we considered other factors such as two-way interactions between race, age, grades of schooling, and time out of school. Some of these interactions are statistically insignificant (race–age) and others, while significant, do not alter our interpretation of the lower-order effects considered here. We also examined alternative classifications of the independent variables (grades of schooling and years out of school), but these did not affect our conclusions.

14 The components in Table 5 for "Race," "grades of schooling," and "years out of school" are the differences in proportions of men in the categories listed in Table 3 between men aged 28–29 and those aged 16–17 weighted by their respective parameters for the two-equation model reported in Table 3. The veteran status components for "means," "coefficients," and "interaction" are respectively the three terms in the following expression:

$$\left[(p_{29}^v - p_{16}^v)\beta^v + \sum_{r=1}^{3}(p_{29}^v - p_{16}^v)(17^r\gamma^r)\right] + \sum_{r=1}^{3}\gamma_r(29^r - 17^r)p_{16}^v + \sum_{r=1}^{3}\gamma_r(29^r - 17^r)(p_{29}^v - p_{16}^v)$$

where p_{29}^v and p_{16}^v denote the proportions of out-of-school young men who are veterans at ages 28–29 and 16–17, respectively; the γ_r are the coefficients for the age polynomial–veteran status interaction in the two-equation model reported in Table 3; β^v is the coefficient for veteran status in the two-equation model; and 29 and 17 are the midpoints of the 28–29 and 16–17 age intervals, respectively. The component for "selection on employability" is

$$\frac{\rho}{\sqrt{1-\rho^2}}\,\frac{\phi(c)}{1-\Phi(c)_{29}} - \frac{\phi(c)}{1-\Phi(c)_{17}}$$

where ρ is the correlation between unmeasured determinants of enrollment and employment; c denotes predicted values in the enrollment equations reported in Table 4; ϕ and Φ are the standard normal density and distribution functions, respectively; and the subscripts 29 and 17 denote that the ratios are evaluated at their means for the 28–29 and 16–17 age groups. The component for "residual" is

$$\sum_{r=1}^{3} \beta_r^a(29^r - 17^r) + \sum_{r=1}^{3} \gamma_r(29^r - 17^r)p_{16}^v$$

where the β_r^a are the coefficients for the third-degree age polynomial in the two-equation model.

REFERENCES

Alexander, K. L., and A. M. Pallas. 1981. "Bringing the Arrow Back In: On the Recursivity Assumptions in School Process Models." Typescript, Johns Hopkins University.

Alexander, K. L., and T. W. Reilly. 1981. "Estimating the Effects of Marriage Timing on Educational Attainment: Some Procedural Issues and Substantive Clarifications." *American Journal of Sociology* 87:143–56.

Becker, Gary S. 1975. *Human Capital*, 2nd ed. Chicago: University of Chicago Press.

Berndt, E. K., B. Hall, R. E. Hall, and J. A. Hausman. 1974. "Estimation and Inference in Nonlinear Structural Models." *Annals of Economic and Social Measurement* 2:653–66.

Bielby, William T. 1981. "Models of Status Attainment." Pp. 3–26 in *Research in Social Stratification and Mobility*, vol. 1, edited by Donald J. Treiman and Robert V. Robinson. Greenwich, Conn.: JAI Press.

Blau, Peter M., and O. D. Duncan. 1967. *The American Occupational Structure*. New York: Wiley.

Bowen, W. G., and T. A. Finegan. 1969. *The Economics of Labor Force Participation*. Princeton, N.J.: Princeton University Press.

Chamberlain, Gary. 1980. "Analysis of Covariance with Qualitative Data." *Review of Economic Studies* 47:225–38.

Clark, Kim, and Lawrence Summers. 1979. "The Dynamics of Youth Unemployment." Typescript, Harvard University.

Cohn, Richard M. 1978. "The Effect of Employment Status Change on Self-Attitudes." *Social Psychology* 41:81–93.

Coleman, James S. 1976. "The School to Work Transition." Pp. 35–40 in *The Teenage Unemployment Problem: What Are the Options*? Washington, D. C.: Congressional Budget Office.

Coleman, James S., Robert H. Bremner, Burton R. Clark, John B. Davis, Dorothy H. Eichorn, Zvi Griliches, Joseph F. Kett, Norman B. Ryder, Zahava Blum Doering, and John M. Mays. 1974. *Youth: Transition to Adulthood*. Chicago: University of Chicago Press.

Congressional Budget Office. 1982. *Improving Youth Employment Prospects: Issues and Options.* Washington, D.C.: U.S. Congress.

Conley, S. 1974. "Education and Labor Market Tightness." *Monthly Labor Review* 97:51–3.

Cooper, R. V. 1978. "Youth Labor Markets and the Military." In *Conference Report on Youth Unemployment: Its Measurement and Meaning.* Washington, D.C.: U.S. Government Printing Office.

Cutright, P. 1973. "Achievement, Mobility, and the Draft: The Impact on the Earnings of Men." Staff Paper No. 73–11854, Office of Research and Statistics, U.S. Department of Health, Education, and Welfare. Washington, D.C.: U.S. Government Printing Office.

De Tray, Dennis. 1980. "Veteran Status and Civilian Earnings." Paper No. R-1929-ARPA, Rand Corporation.

1982. "Veteran Status as a Screening Device." *American Economic Review* 72:133–42.

DiPrete, T. A. 1981. "Unemployment over the Life Cycle: Racial Differences and the Effect of Changing Economic Conditions." *American Journal of Sociology* 87: 286–307.

Duncan, Beverly. 1965. "Dropouts and the Unemployed." *Journal of Political Economy* 73:121–34.

1968. "Trends in Output and Distribution of Schooling." Pp. 601–72 in *Indicators of Social Change*, edited by E. B. Sheldon and W. E. Moore. New York: Russell Sage Foundation.

Duncan, O. D., D. L. Featherman, and B. Duncan. 1972. *Socioeconomic Background and Achievement.* New York: Seminar Press.

Duncan, O. D., and R. W. Hodge. 1963. "Education and Occupational Mobility." *American Journal of Sociology* 68:629–44.

Edwards, Linda M. 1976. "School Retention of Teenagers over the Business Cycles." *Journal of Human Resources* 11:200–8.

Fearn, R. 1968. "Labor Force and School Participation of Teenagers." Ph.D. dissertation, University of Chicago.

Featherman, D. L., and R. M. Hauser. 1978. *Opportunity and Change.* New York: Academic Press.

Feldstein, M. 1973. "The Economics of the New Unemployment." *The Public Interest* 33:3–42.

Feldstein, M., and D. Ellwood. 1979. "Teenage Unemployment: What Is the Problem?" Typescript, National Bureau of Economic Research.

Folk, H. 1969. "The Problem of Youth Unemployment." Pp. 76–107 in *The Transition from School to Work: A Report Based on the Princeton Manpower Symposium.* Princeton, N.J.: Princeton University Press.

Gover, K. R., and B. J. McCeady. 1974. "Job Situation of Vietnam-Era Veterans." *Monthly Labor Review* 97:17–26.

Gustman, A. L., and T. L. Steinmeier. 1979. "The Impact of the Market and the Family on Youth Enrollment and Labor Supply." Typescript, Dartmouth College.

Hauser, R. M. 1980. "Comment on Beck et al., 'Stratification in a Dual Economy.'" *American Sociological Review* 45:702–12.

Heckman, James J. 1978. "Dummy Endogenous Variables in a Simultaneous Equation System." *Econometrica* 46:931–59.

Hogan, Dennis P. 1978. "The Variable Order of Events in the Life Course." *American Sociological Review* 43:573–86.
1981. *Transitions and Social Change: The Early Lives of American Men.* New York: Academic Press.
Jencks, Christopher S., Marshall Smith, Henry Acland, Mary Jo Bane, David Cohen, Herbert Gintis, Barbara Heyns, and Stephen Michelson. 1972. *Inequality: A Reassessment of the Effect of Family and Schooling in America.* New York: Harper & Row.
Kalachek, E. D. 1969. "The Youth Labor Market." Policy Papers in Human Resources and Industrial Relations No. 12, Institute of Labor and Industrial Relations, University of Michigan and Wayne State University.
Katz, A. 1974. "Schooling, Age, and Length of Employment." *Industrial and Labor Relations Review* 27:125–32.
Kaufman, Robert L., and Seymour Spilerman. 1982. "The Age Structures of Occupations and Jobs." *American Journal of Sociology* 87:827–51.
Lazear, E. 1977. "Schooling as a Wage Depressant." *Journal of Human Resources* 12:164–76.
Lerman, R. I. 1970. "An Analysis of Youth Labor Force Participation, School Activity, and Employment Rates." Ph.D. dissertation, Massachusetts Institute of Technology.
Mare, Robert D. 1980a. "Correlates of Achievement." *Science* 208:707–9.
1980b. "Social Background and School Continuation Decisions." *Journal of the American Statistical Association* 75:295–305.
1981. "Market and Institutional Sources of Educational Growth." Pp. 205–45 in *Research in Social Stratification and Mobility*, edited by Donald J. Treiman and Robert V. Robinson. Greenwich, Conn.: JAI Press.
Mare, Robert D., and Christopher Winship. 1980. "Changes in Race Differentials in Youth Labor Force Status: A Review of the Literature." Pp. 1–29 in Fifth Annual Report to the President and the Congress of the National Commission for Employment Policy, *Expanding Employment Opportunities for Disadvantaged Youth: Sponsored Research.* Washington, D.C.: National Commission for Employment Policy.
Marini, M. M. 1978. "The Transition to Adulthood: Sex Differences in Educational Attainment and Age at Marriage." *American Sociological Review* 43:483–507.
1982. "Determinants of the Timing of Adult Role Entry." Typescript, Battelle Human Affairs Research Centers.
Mason, W. M. 1970. "On the Socioeconomic Effects of Military Service." Ph.D. dissertation, University of Chicago.
Meyer, R. H., and D. A. Wise. 1979. "High School Preparation and Early Labor Force Experience." Typescript, Harvard University.
Mincer, Jacob. 1974. *Schooling, Experience, and Earnings.* New York: Columbia University Press.
National Commission for Employment Policy. 1979. *Expanding Employment Opportunities for Disadvantaged Youth.* Fifth Annual Report to the President and the Congress. Washington, D.C.: U.S. Government Printing Office.
National Commission on Employment and Unemployment Statistics. 1979. *Counting the Labor Force.* Washington, D.C.: U.S. Government Printing Office.

Nickell, Stephen. 1979. "Education and Lifetime Patterns of Unemployment." *Journal of Political Economy* 87:S117–31.

Organisation for Economic Co-Operation and Development. 1980. *Youth Unemployment: The Causes and Consequences.* Paris: Organisation for Economic Co-Operation and Development.

Ornstein, Michael D. 1976. *Entry into the American Labor Force.* New York: Academic Press.

Osterman, Paul. 1980. *Getting Started: The Youth Labor Market.* Cambridge: MIT Press.

Parsons, Donald O. 1974. "The Cost of School Time, Forgone Earnings, and Human Capital Formation." *Journal of Political Economy* (March/April): 251–66.

Rindfuss, R. R., L. Bumpass, and C. St. John. 1981. "Education and Fertility: Implications for the Roles Women Occupy." *American Sociological Review* 45:431–47.

Sewell, William H., and Robert M. Hauser. 1975. *Education, Occupation, and Earnings.* New York: Academic Press.

Shryock, H. S., and J. S. Siegel. 1976. *The Methods and Materials of Demography.* New York: Academic Press.

Smith, James P., and Finis Welch. 1974. "Black–White Earnings and Employment: 1960–1970." Paper No. R-1666-DOL, Rand Corporation.

Social Science Research Council. 1977. *A Research Agenda for the National Longitudinal Surveys of Labor Market Experience.* Washington, D.C.: Social Science Research Council.

Sørensen, Aage B. 1975. "The Structure of Intragenerational Mobility." *American Sociological Review* 40:456–71.

1977. "The Structure of Inequality and the Process of Attainment." *American Sociological Review* 42:965–78.

Spilerman, Seymour. 1977. "Careers, Labor Market Structure, and Socioeconomic Achievement." *American Journal of Sociology* 83:551–93.

Stewman, Shelby. 1975. "Two Markov Models of Open System Occupational Mobility Underlying Conceptualizations and Empirical Tests." *American Sociological Review* 40:298–321.

Stinchcombe, Arthur L. 1979. "Social Mobility in Industrial Labor Markets." *Acta Sociologica* 22:217–45.

Sweet, James A. 1979a. "Changes in the Allocation of Time of Young Men among Schooling, Marriage, Work, and Childrearing: 1960–1976." Working Paper 79–28, Center for Demography and Ecology, University of Wisconsin, Madison.

1979b. "Changes in the Allocation of Time of Young Women among Schooling, Marriage, Work, and Childrearing: 1960–1976." Working Paper 79–15, Center for Demography and Ecology, University of Wisconsin, Madison.

Tuma, Nancy B. 1976. "Rewards, Resources, and the Rate of Mobility: A Nonstationary Multivariate Stochastic Model." *American Sociological Review* 41:338–60.

U.S. Bureau of the Census. 1978. *The Current Population Survey: Design and Methodology.* Washington, D.C.: U.S. Bureau of the Census.

U.S. Department of Labor. 1981. "Employment and Unemployment: A Report on 1980." Special Labor Force Report 244. Washington, D.C.: U.S. Department of Labor.

White, Harrison C. 1970. *Chains of Opportunity: System Models of Mobility in Organizations*. Cambridge: Harvard University Press.
Willis, R. J., and S. Rosen. 1979. "Education and Self-Selection." *Journal of Political Economy* 87:S7–36.
Winsborough, H. H. 1978. "Statistical Histories of the Life Cycle of Birth Cohorts: The Transition from School Boy to Adult Male." Pp. 231–59 in *Social Demography*, edited by K. E. Taeuber, L. L. Bumpass, and J. A. Sweet. New York: Academic Press.

Name index

Subject index